Get a Jump!

What's Next After High School?

THOMSON

PETERSON'S

Australia • Canada • Mexico • Singapore • Spain • United Kingdom • United States

About The Thomson Corporation and Peterson's

With revenues of US$7.2 billion, The Thomson Corporation (www.thomson.com) is a leading global provider of integrated information solutions for business, education, and professional customers. Its Learning businesses and brands (www.thomsonlearning.com) serve the needs of individuals, learning institutions, and corporations with products and services for both traditional and distributed learning.

Peterson's, part of The Thomson Corporation, is one of the nation's most respected providers of lifelong learning online resources, software, reference guides, and books. The Education Supersite℠ at www.petersons.com—the Internet's most heavily traveled education resource—has searchable databases and interactive tools for contacting U.S.-accredited institutions and programs. In addition, Peterson's serves more than 105 million education consumers annually.

For more information, contact Peterson's, 2000 Lenox Drive, Lawrenceville, NJ 08648; 800-338-3282; or find us on the World Wide Web at www.petersons.com/about.

ACKNOWLEDGEMENTS: Peterson's would like to acknowledge the following authors for their contribution to this publication: Kenneth Edwards, Michele Kornegay, Emily Law, Brenna McBride, Charlotte Thomas, and Amy Tomcavage.

For permission to use material from this text or product, contact us by

Phone: 800-730-2214

Fax: 800-730-2215

Web: www.thomsonrights.com

ISBN: 0-7689-1301-2

Printed in the United States of America

10 9 8 7 6 5 4 3 2 1   04 03 02

Dear Student:

Whether graduation seems light-years away or alarmingly close, it's never too early—or too late—to think about what comes after high school. Do you know what your next step will be?

Get a Jump can help you figure that out. This book is designed to help you launch your career, whether this means going on for more education or directly entering the workforce. You have a multitude of options and some crucial choices to make. In the pages that follow, we have tried to give you a jumpstart on planning the future that's right for you.

The book is arranged in four parts. Part One provides general introductory information about your options after high school and how to use your high school education to plan for the next phase of your life. Part Two offers more detailed information about postsecondary education, whether you choose a two-year, four-year, career, or technical college or the military. Part Three provides useful information about the world of work and how to handle stress, peer pressure, conflict, and other obstacles you may encounter in the real world. Finally, Part Four contains appendices for each state in your part of the United States, including valuable information on two- and four-year colleges and universities in your area and your state's high school graduation requirements, internships, scholarship and financial aid programs, summer opportunities, and vocational schools.

We hope you find this publication helpful as you begin thinking about the rest of your life. If you have questions or feedback on *Get a Jump*, please e-mail us at getajump@petersons.com.

Sincerely,

Peterson's Editorial Staff

Contents

Contents

PART THREE: YOU AND THE WORKPLACE

PART FOUR: APPENDICES

Part 1

JUMPSTART YOUR FUTURE

Come on, admit it. You know that big question—what will I do when I graduate from high school?—is right around the corner. Some of your classmates know what they want to do, but you're freaking out about all of the decisions you have to make.

You've got a lot of possibilities from which to choose. Maybe you'll attend a two-year or four-year college or vocational or technical school. Or you'll join the armed forces. Or perhaps you'll go right into the workplace with a full-time job. But before you march across that stage to get your diploma, *Get a Jump* will help you to begin thinking about your options and to open up doors you never knew existed.

FIRST, A LOOK AT YOURSELF

Deciding what to do with your life is a lot like flying. Just look at the many ways you can fly and the many directions your life can take.

A TEACHER ONCE asked her students to bring something to class that flies. Students brought kites, balloons, and models of airplanes, blimps, hot-air balloons, helicopters, spaceships, gliders, and seaplanes. But when class began, the teacher explained that the lesson was about career planning, not flying.

She was making the point that your plans for life after high school can take many forms. Some people take direct flights via jets. Others are carried along by circumstances. How you will make the journey is an individual matter. That's why it's important to know who you are and what you want before taking off.

You may not choose your life's career by reading Get a Jump (GAJ), but you'll learn how to become part of the decision-making process and find resources that can help you plan your future.

Ready to Fly?

Just having a high school diploma is not enough for many occupations. But, surprise, surprise, neither is a college degree. Different kinds of work require different kinds of training. Knowing how to operate a particular type of equipment, for instance, takes special skills and work experience that you might not learn in college. Employers always want to hire the best-qualified people available, but this does not mean that they always choose those applicants who have the most education. The type of education and training you have is just as important as how much. Right now, you're at the point in your life where you can choose how much and what kind of education and training you want to get.

If you have a definite career goal in mind, like being a doctor, you probably already know what it will take in terms of education. You're looking at about four years of college, then four years of medical school, and, in most states, one year of residency. Cosmetologists, on the other hand, complete a state-approved training program that ranges from eight to eighteen months.

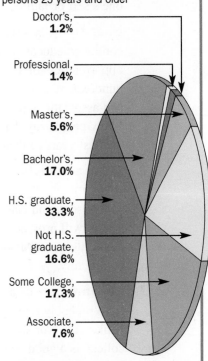

EDUCATIONAL ATTAINMENT
Highest level of education attained by persons 25 years and older

- Doctor's, **1.2%**
- Professional, **1.4%**
- Master's, **5.6%**
- Bachelor's, **17.0%**
- H.S. graduate, **33.3%**
- Not H.S. graduate, **16.6%**
- Some College, **17.3%**
- Associate, **7.6%**

Source: Digest of Educational Statistics, U.S. Department of Commerce, Bureau of the Census, Current Population Survey

But for most of you, deciding what to do after high school is not so easy. Perhaps you haven't chosen a field of work yet. You might just know for certain that you want a job that will give you status and a big paycheck. Or maybe you know what you want to do, but you're not sure what kind of education you'll need. For instance, you may love fixing cars, and the idea of being an auto mechanic sounds great. But you need to decide whether to learn on the job, attend a vocational school, seek an apprenticeship, or pursue a combination of these options.

THE TOP 10 REASONS TO CONTINUE YOUR EDUCATION

Continuing your education after high school is one choice that can give you a good start no matter what your final career decision is. There are many good reasons to do so. If you think college is not for you at all, take a look at this list. It might change your mind.

10. **Fulfill a dream—or begin one.** Some people hope to become teachers or scientists. For many, continuing their education provides the opportunity to make that wish a reality for one's self or family.

9. **Have fun.** Classes are an important part of continued education, but there are plenty of opportunities for some great times. There are hundreds of sports, clubs, groups, activities, and associations just waiting for you to join. Many people say that their college years were the best years of their lives.

8. **Make connections that can link you to future jobs.** The friends, professors, supervisors, and classmates you meet after high school will provide valuable ties for future jobs, committees, and associations within the community.

7. **Become part of a cultural stew.** As you have probably already figured out, not everyone is like you. Nor should they be. Being in college is a good way to expose yourself to many types of people from various backgrounds and geographic locations, with different viewpoints and opinions. You may discover that you like people and things you never knew existed.

6. **Meet new people.** By furthering your education, you will widen your circle of friends and, chances are, form meaningful lifelong relationships.

5. **Do what you love doing and get paid for it.** Have you ever taken a test during which everything clicked or played a video game and caught on immediately? This is what happens when you combine education and training with the right job. Work becomes more like play, which is far more satisfying and rewarding than just going through the motions.

4. **Exercise your mind.** Just as physical exercise keeps your body in shape, mental exercise keeps your mind free of cobwebs. No matter what your area of interest, education holds the key to the most interesting and challenging information you can imagine. Explore your outer limits and become a lifelong learner.

3. **Earn a higher income.** Although money isn't everything, it is necessary for survival. A good education prepares you to become a solid member of society. (See the chart "Increase Your Earning Power.")

2. **Learn critical-thinking and analytical skills.** More than any other skill, education teaches you to think. Furthering your learning will help you to think critically, organize and analyze information, and write clearly.

1. **You won't get left behind.** In the twenty-first century, you will need to be prepared to change jobs and continually learn new skills in order to keep up with changes in industry, communications, and technology. Education and training will give you a solid background.

INCREASE YOUR EARNING POWER

People with more education tend to earn more money. Look at the average yearly earnings of workers over the age of 25 by education level.

Professional Degree	$80,230
Doctoral Degree	$70,476
Master's Degree	$55,302
Bachelor's Degree	$46,276
Associate Degree	$35,389
Some College	$32,400
High School Diploma	$28,807
Less Than High School Diploma	$21,391

Source: Bureau of the Census; Bureau of Labor Statistics

Breaking Down the Barriers to Continuing Your Education

Some of you may say, "Forget the reasons why I should continue my education. I can't because (fill in the blank)." Let's see if your objections stand up to this list.

You say:

Nobody in my family has ever gone to college.

GAJ says:

You can be the first! It's a little scary and not always easy, but just think how great you'll feel being the first person in your family to receive a degree, diploma, or certificate.

You say:

My grades are not good enough.

GAJ says:

Don't let less-than-perfect grades stand in your way. Different institutions have different requirements, including what grades they accept. Schools also evaluate you for admission as a whole person, such as participation in extracurricular activities; your talents, such as academics and athletics; and your employment and volunteer history. There are also classes that you can take to improve your skills in various subject areas. Get a tutor now or form a study group in high school to improve your grades as much as possible. Talk to your guidance counselor about what the appropriate high school curriculum for you is so you'll have more options when making decisions about continuing your education.

You say:

I can't afford it.

GAJ says:

Many families cannot afford to pay education costs completely out of pocket. That's why there are so many opportunities for financial aid, scholarships, grants, and work-study programs. Federal, state, school-sponsored, private, and career-specific financial aid resources are available to students who take the time to look. Talk to a guidance counselor, go to the library, and look on the Internet. Read the "Financial Aid Dollars and Sense" section of GAJ for more information about how to finance your continued education. Be creative and persistent. It can happen for you.

You say:

I don't know how to apply or where I want to go.

GAJ says:

Fortunately, there are resources to help you decide which institution to select. Talk to friends, family members, neighbors, your guidance counselor, pastor, coach, or librarian. Take a look at the appendix at the back of GAJ for a guide to two-year and four-year colleges as well as vocational and technical schools in your state.

You say:

I think it may be too difficult for me.

GAJ says:

Think back to something you have done in your life that seemed too difficult in the beginning. Didn't you find that once you began, put your mind to it, and stuck with it that you succeeded? You can do almost anything if you set your mind to it and are willing to work for it.

You say:

I'm not sure I'll fit in.

GAJ says:

One of the best things about furthering your education is the chance to meet new people and be part of new experiences in new surroundings. Colleges and other continuing education options attract a wide variety of students from many different backgrounds. Chances are you won't have any problem finding someone else with interests that are similar to yours. Because schools differ in size, location, student body, and lifestyle, you'll surely find one that meets your needs. Advance visits and interviews can help you determine which school is right for you.

FASTEST-GROWING OCCUPATIONS

Want to have a career that's going places? Check out this chart to see which occupations are expected to grow the fastest by the year 2010 and what type of training you'll need to get the job.

Occupation	Expected Openings	Required Education
Computer Software Engineers, applications	760,000	Bachelor's degree
Computer Support Specialists	996,000	Associate degree
Computer Software Engineers, systems software	601,000	Bachelor's degree
Network and Computer Systems Administrators	416,000	Bachelor's degree
Network Systems and Data Communications Analysts	211,000	Bachelor's degree
Desktop Publishers	63,000	Postsecondary Vocational Training
Database Administrators	176,000	Bachelor's degree
Personal and Home Care Aides	672,000	On-the-job training
Computer Systems Analysts	689,000	Bachelor's degree
Medical Assistants	516,000	On-the-job-training
Social and Human Service Assistants	418,000	On-the-job training
Physician Assistants	89,000	Bachelor's degree
Medical Records and Health Information Technicians	202,000	Associate degree
Computer and Information Systems Managers	463,000	Master's degree
Home Health Aides	907,000	On-the-job training
Physical Therapist Aides	53,000	On-the-job training
Occupational Therapist Aides	12,000	On-the-job training
Physical Therapist Assistants	64,000	Associate degree
Audiologists	19,000	Master's degree
Fitness Trainers and Aerobics Instructors	222,000	Postsecondary Vocational Training
Computer and Information Scientists	39,000	Doctoral degree
Veterinary Assistants and Lab Animal Caretakers	77,000	On-the-job training
Occupational Therapist Assistants	23,000	Associate degree
Veterinary Technologists and Technicians	69,000	Associate degree
Speech-language Pathologists	122,000	Master's degree
Mental Health and Substance Abuse Social Workers	116,000	Master's degree
Dental Assistants	339,000	On-the-job training
Dental Hygienists	201,000	Associate degree
Special Education Teachers, grades Pre-K to 6	320,000	Bachelor's degree
Pharmacy Technicians	259,000	On-the-job training

Source: Bureau of Labor Statistics, Occupational Outlook Handbook

You say:

I don't even know what I want to do with my life.

GAJ says:

Many students don't know this about themselves until they get to experience some of the possibilities. Take the self-assessment on page 8 to help you determine what your interests and talents are. Read "How to Choose a Major" on page 101 for a listing of the most popular college majors and their related careers.

You say:

There is no way I can pursue my education full-time.

GAJ says:

Part-time students are becoming the norm. In fact, a recent study determined that 43 percent of undergraduate students attend school part-time. Most schools offer evening and weekend classes, and many offer work-study opportunities to help students pay for their education. Also, some employers will pay or reimburse you if you are working and want to further your education. If you are enrolled part-time, it takes longer to graduate. But if full-time enrollment is not an option for you, don't give up the opportunity to continue your education. There are many nontraditional ways to achieve your goals.

CHOOSING A CAREER YOU'LL BE HAPPY WITH

Did you know that of the estimated 15 million people searching for employment in the American job market, approximately 12 million are looking for a new occupation or a different employer? That's an awful lot of people who aren't happy with their jobs. Hopefully, you won't be one of them if you take some time to consider what it is you really want to do now, while you're still in school. Is there a particular type of job you've always dreamed of doing? Or perhaps you're one of the many high school students who say:

"I Kind of Know What I Want, But I'm Not Really Sure."

A good way to gather information about potential occupations is by talking with people who have achieved goals that are similar to yours. Talk to teachers, neighbors, and adult friends about their work experiences. The formal name for that activity is an "informational interview." You're interviewing them about the work they do—not to get a job from them but to gather information about their jobs.

If you don't have any contacts in a field that sparks your interest, do some poking around in the workplace. For instance, if you're interested in a career in nursing, you could visit a hospital, doctor's office, or nursing home. Most people love to talk about themselves, so don't be afraid to ask if they'll chat with you about their profession. Offering to volunteer your services can be the best way to know whether you'll be happy doing that type of work.

"I Haven't a Clue about What I Want to Do."

If you're completely unsure about what kind of work you'd like to do, contact a career counselor who can help you explore your options and possibly administer some interest and aptitude tests. You also might think about contacting a college career planning and placement office, a vocational school placement office, the counseling services of community agencies, or a private counseling service, which may charge you a fee. Many high schools offer job-shadowing programs, where students actually shadow someone in a particular occupation for an entire day or more. Don't forget that as a high school student, your best resource is your high school guidance counselor. Take a look at the list of the fastest-growing occupations on page 6 to get a sampling of the careers with the largest projected job growth in the coming years.

ON THE HUNT FOR INFORMATION

Regardless of how unsure you may be about what you want to do after high school, here's a list of things you can do to get the information you need to head in the right direction. Many people start off thinking they want one career and end up doing something completely different. But this is a good place to begin:

- Investigate careers both in and out of school. Participate in mentoring, job shadowing, and career day opportunities whenever possible.

- Get some on-the-job experience in a field that interests you.

- Research two-year and four-year colleges, vocational and technical schools, and apprenticeship programs.

- Participate in school and state career development activities.

- Prepare for and take aptitude and college entrance tests.

Here are a few Web sites where you can receive valuable direction by completing a career interest questionnaire or by reading about various occupations:

Peterson's

www.petersons.com

On Peterson's Web site, you can read helpful articles about the world of work and search for undergraduate academic and career-oriented degree and certificate programs.

Occupational Outlook Handbook

www.bls.gov/oco

The Bureau of Labor Statistics, an agency within the U.S. Department of Labor, produces this Web site, which offers more information than you'll ever need about a specific career.

SELF-ASSESSMENT INVENTORY

In addition to looking to outside sources for information, there's another rich source of data: yourself. Knowing what you want to do begins with knowing yourself—the real you. That's because the better you understand your own wants and needs, the better you will be able to make decisions about your career goals and dreams. This self-assessment inventory can help.

Who do you admire most, and why?

_____

What is your greatest strength?

_____

What is your greatest talent?

_____

What skills do you already have?

_____

DESCRIBE HOW YOU CURRENTLY USE THESE SKILLS IN YOUR LIFE:

Athletic ability_____

Mechanical ability_____

Ability to work with numbers_____

Leadership skills_____

Teaching skills_____

Artistic skills_____

Analytical skills_____

CHECK THE AREAS THAT MOST INTEREST YOU.

❑ Providing a practical service for people

❑ Self-expression in music, art, literature, or nature

❑ Organizing and record keeping

❑ Meeting people and supervising others

❑ Helping others in need, either mentally, spiritually, or physically

❑ Solving practical problems

❑ Working in forestry, farming, or fishing

❑ Working with machines and tools

❑ Taking care of animals

❑ Physical work out of doors

❑ Protecting the public via law enforcement or fire fighting

❑ Medical, scientific, or mathematical work

❑ Selling, advertising, or promoting

WHAT GIVES YOU SATISFACTION?

Answer the following questions True (T) or False (F).

T F I get satisfaction not from personal accomplishment, but from helping others.

T F I'd like to have a job in which I can use my imagination and be inventive.

T F In my life, money will be placed ahead of job security and personal interests.

T F It is my ambition to have a direct impact on other people's lives.

T F I am not a risk-taker and would prefer a career that offers little risk.

T F I enjoy working with people rather than by myself.

T F I would not be happy doing the same thing all the time.

WHAT MATTERS THE MOST TO YOU?

Rate the items on the list below from 1 to 10, with 10 being extremely important and 1 being not at all important.

___ Good health

___ Justice

___ Marriage/family

___ Faith

___ Fame

___ Beauty

___ Safety

___ Friendship

___ Respect

___ Accomplishment

___ Seeing the world

___ Love

___ Fun

___ Power

___ Individualism

___ Charity

___ Honor

___ Intelligence

___ Wealth

Mapping Your Future

www.mapping-your-future.org

On this site, you can find out how to choose a career and how to reach your career goals. You can also pick up useful tips on job hunting, resume writing, and job interviewing techniques. This site also provides a ten-step plan for determining and achieving your career goals.

University of Waterloo Career Development Manual

www.cdm.uwaterloo.ca/

This site provides a thorough online career interest survey, and you can use strategies to get the job that's right for you.

Motivational Appraisal of Personal Potential

www.assessment.com

Features a free 71-question career assessment that analyzes your motivation and points you to the ten best careers for you.

Monster.com

www.monster.com

Includes information about thousands of job and career fairs, advice on resumes, and much more.

WHAT WOULD YOU DO IF YOU WERE IN A BLIZZARD SURVIVAL SITUATION?

Check the one that would be your most likely role.

- ❏ The leader
- ❏ The one who explains the situation to the others
- ❏ The one who keeps morale up
- ❏ The one who invents a way to keep warm and melt snow for water
- ❏ The one who listens to instructions and keeps the supplies organized
- ❏ The one who positions sticks and rocks to signal SOS

LOOKING AHEAD AND LOOKING BACK

What are your goals for the next five years?

Where would you like to be in ten years?

What has been your favorite course, and why?

What was your least favorite course, and why?

Who was your favorite teacher, and why?

What are your hobbies?

What are your extracurricular activities?

What jobs have you held?

What volunteer work, if any, have you performed?

Have you ever shadowed a professional for a day? If so, what did you learn?

Do you have a mentor? If so, who? What have you learned from this person?

Do you want to stay close to home, or would you prefer to travel to another city after high school?

WHAT ARE YOUR CAREER GOALS?

My interests, skills, and knowledge supporting my career goals:

To fulfill my career goals, I will need additional skills and knowledge in:

I will obtain the additional skills and knowledge by taking part in the following educational activities:

I will need a degree, certification, and/or specialized training in:

When I look in the classified ads of the newspaper, the following job descriptions sound attractive to me:

WHAT WILL YOU NEED TO GET WHERE YOU'RE GOING?

The information I have given indicates that I will be selecting courses that are primarily:

- ❏ College path (Four-year or two-year education that offers liberal arts courses combined with courses in your area of interest.)
- ❏ Vocational path (One or more years of education that includes hands-on training for a specific job.)
- ❏ Combination of the two

WHAT ARE YOUR IMMEDIATE PLANS AFTER HIGH SCHOOL?

After high school, I plan to:

- ❏ work full-time
- ❏ work part-time and attend school
- ❏ attend college full-time
- ❏ attend technical college
- ❏ enter the military

MY PERFECT JOB WOULD BE …

Let your imagination run wild. You can have any job you want. What's it like? Start by describing to yourself the following job conditions:

Work conditions: What hours are you willing to work? Do you feel most satisfied in an environment that is indoors/outdoors, varied/regular, noisy/quiet, or casual/traditional?

Duties: What duties do you feel comfortable carrying out? Do you want to be a leader, or do you perform best as a team player?

People: Do you want to work with other people or more independently? How much people contact do you want/need?

Education: How much special training or education is required? How much education are you willing to seek? Can you build upon the education or experience you have to date? Will you need to gain new education or experience?

Benefits: What salary and benefits do you expect? Are you willing to travel?

Disadvantages: There are disadvantages with almost any job. Can you imagine what the disadvantages may be? Can you confirm or disprove these beliefs by talking to someone or researching the industry or job further? If these disadvantages really exist, can you live with them?

Personal qualities: What qualities do you want in the employer you ultimately choose? What are the most important qualities that you want in a supervisor? In your coworkers?

Look over your responses to this assessment. Do you see recurring themes in your answers that start to show you what kind of career you might like? If not, there are many more places to get information to decide where your interests lie. You can go to your guidance counselor for advice. You can take the Campbell (TM) Interest and Skills Inventory, the Strong Interest Inventory, the Self-Directed Search, or other assessment tests that your guidance counselor recommends.

THE FIRST STEPS TO A CAREER

Don't be too surprised when your summer job turns into your career.

THE WORD "CAREER" has a scary sound to it when you're still in high school. Careers are for college graduates or those who have been in the workplace for years. But unless you grew up knowing for sure that you wanted to fly airplanes or be a marine biologist, what will you do? You'll be happy to know that interests you have now can very possibly lead to a college major or into a career. A job at a clothing store, for instance, could lead to a career designing clothes. Perhaps those hours you spend chasing Laura Croft, Tomb Raider, will lead to a career creating video games! Maybe you baby-sit and love being around kids, so teaching becomes an obvious choice. Perhaps cars fascinate you, and you find out you want to fix them for a living.

This section will show you how you can begin exploring your interests—sort of like getting into a swimming pool starting with your big toe, rather than plunging in. Vocational/career and tech-prep programs, summer jobs, and volunteering are all ways you can test various career paths to decide if you like them.

THE VOCATIONAL/CAREER EDUCATION PATH

If you're looking for a more real-world education, add yourself to the nearly 11 million youths and adults who are getting a taste of the workplace through vocational and career education programs offered in high schools across the nation. These programs are designed to help you develop competency in the skills you'll need in the workplace as well as in school.

What makes this kind of program different is that you learn in the classroom and in the "real world" of the workplace. Not only do you learn the academics in school, but you also get hands-on training by job shadowing, working under a mentor, and actually performing a job outside of school. Your interests and talents are usually taken into consideration, and you can choose from a variety of traditional, high-tech, and service industry training programs. Take a look at the following categories and see what piques your interest.

STUDENT COUNSEL

Q: What do you like about vocational training?

A: I jumped into the tech center my first year when I was a junior because I thought it was a good way to get out of school. But as the year went on, I said, "Hey, this is a good place to be because it's giving me job experience, and I'm learning how to dress and present myself like I was at a real job." I go during the first 3 or last 3 hours out of the school day. When we're in class, we get to do real jobs for people who ask our instructor for help. Then our teacher lets our creative minds go. We just designed a CD cover. One guy here designed a motorcycle and built it, and now he has three people asking him to come and work for them.

Trisha Younk
Tuscola County Tech Center
Reese High School
Reese, Michigan

Agricultural education. These programs prepare students for careers in agricultural production, animal production and care, agribusiness, agricultural and industrial mechanics, environmental management, farming, horticulture and landscaping, food processing, and natural resource management.

Business education. Students prepare for careers in accounting and finance and computer and data processing as well as administrative/secretarial and management/supervisory positions in professional environments (banking, insurance, law, public service).

Family and consumer sciences. These programs prepare students for careers in child care, food management and production, clothing and interiors, and hospitality and facility care. Core elements include personal development, family life and planning, resource management, and nutrition and wellness.

Trade and industrial and health occupations. Students prepare for careers in such fields as auto mechanics, the construction trades, cosmetology, electronics, graphics, public safety, and welding. Health occupation programs offer vocational training for careers in dental and medical assisting, practical nursing, home health care, and medical office assisting.

Marketing education. These programs prepare individuals for careers in sales, retail, advertising, food and restaurant marketing, and hotel management.

There are many vocational/career education programs available; the kinds listed above represent only a few of the possibilities. To find a program that suits your interests and that is located near you, refer to the listing of schools in the appendix of this book. Or, you can get more information about vocational education programs by calling 202-205-5451 or e-mailing the U.S. Department of Education, Office of Vocational and Adult Education via its Web site, www.ed.gov/offices/OVAE.

FROM THE GUIDANCE OFFICE

Q: **What if going to college is not for me?**

A: **When adults ask kids what they want to do as a career, kids feel pressured. They think adults want them to identify with one single career. But there are more than 40,000 job titles a person can hold. We tell kids to pick a path first. When you exit high school, there are three paths you can take. One is to the workplace. One leads to the military as a career or as a stepping stone. The third leads to more education—a professional degree, a four-year degree, or a two-year degree. They have to determine which path they'll take.**

One of the main selling points about getting career education in high school is that nearly every employer wants you to have some experience before you are hired. In career tech, students are in a workplace environment and can list their time as work experience, and they'll have previous employers who can vouch for them.

Lenore Lemanski
Counselor, Technology Center
Tuscola ISD
Caro, Michigan

THE TECH-PREP PATH

An even more advanced preparation for the workplace and/or an associate degree from a college is called tech prep. It's an educational path that combines college-prep and vocational/technical courses of study.

During the two-year course, the focus is on blending academic and vocational/technical competencies. When you graduate from high school, you'll be able to jump right into the workforce or get an associate degree. But if you want to follow this path, you've got to plan for it starting in the ninth grade. Ask your guidance counselor for more information.

USING THE SUMMER TO YOUR ADVANTAGE

When you're sitting in class, a summer with nothing to do might seem appealing. But after you've listened to all of your CDs, aced all of your video games, hung out at the same old mall, and talked to your friends on the phone about being bored, what's left? How about windsurfing on a cool, clear New England lake? Horseback riding along breathtaking mountain trails? Parlez en français in Paris? Trekking through spectacular canyon lands or living with a family in Costa Rica, Spain, Switzerland, or Japan? Exploring college majors or possible careers? Helping out on an archeological dig or community-service project? Along the way, you'll meet some wonderful people and maybe even make a couple of lifelong friends.

Interested? Get ready to pack your bags and join the 1 million kids and teens who will be having the summer of a lifetime at thousands of terrific camps, academic programs, sports clinics, arts workshops, internships, volunteer opportunities, and travel adventures throughout North America and abroad.

Oh, you don't have the money, you say? Not to worry. There are programs to meet every budget, from $50 workshops to $4,500 world treks and sessions that vary in length from just a couple of hours to a couple of months.

For a list of summer opportunities, take a look at the appendix in this book. You can also find out about summer opportunities by visiting www.petersons.com.

FROM THE GUIDANCE OFFICE

Q: What options are open to students who take high school career and technology classes and who feel they can't go to college?

A: Students have the opportunity to develop many skills through classes, student organizations, and career/technology classes during high school. These skills form an essential core that they can use to continue on to college, enter the job market, or participate in additional training after graduation. When students can identify those skills and make the connection by applying and expanding their skills as lifelong learners, then the possibilities are endless.

Linda S. Sanchez
Career and Technology Counselor
South San Antonio I.S.D.
Career Education Center
San Antonio, Texas

FLIP BURGERS AND LEARN ABOUT LIFE

A lot of teenagers who are anxious to earn extra cash spend their summers in retail or food service since those jobs are plentiful. If you're flipping burgers or helping customers find a special outfit, you might think the only thing you're getting out of the job is a paycheck. Think again. You will be amazed to discover that you have gained far more.

Being employed in these fields will teach you how to get along with demanding (and sometimes downright unpleasant) customers, how to work on a team, and how to handle money and order supplies. Not only do summer jobs teach you life skills, but they also offer ways to explore potential careers. What's more, when you apply to college or for a full-time job after high school graduation, the experience will look good on your application.

Sometimes, summer jobs become the very thing you want to do later in life. Before committing to a college major, summer jobs give you the opportunity to try out many directions. Students who think they want to be engineers, lawyers, or doctors might spend the summer shadowing an engineer, being a gofer in a legal firm, or volunteering in a hospital.

However, rather than grab the first job that comes along, find out where your interests are and build on what is natural for you. Activities you take for granted provide clues to what you are good at. What about that bookcase you built? Or those kids you love to baby-sit? Same thing with that big party you arranged. The environments you prefer provide other hints, too. Perhaps you feel best in the middle of a cluttered garage or surrounded by people. That suggests certain types of jobs.

Getting a summer job while in high school is the first step in a long line of work experiences to come. And the more experience you have, the better you'll be at getting jobs all your life. To search for summer jobs on the Internet, visit www.petersons.com, and click on the Summer Opportunities button.

TRY YOUR HAND AT AN INTERNSHIP

Each year, thousands of interns work in a wide variety of places, including corporations, law firms, government agencies, media organizations, interest groups, clinics, labs, museums, and historical sites. How popular are internships? Consider the recent trends. In the early 1980s, only 1 in 36 students completed an internship or other experiential learning program. Compare this to 2000, where one study found that 86 percent of college students had completed internships, with 69 percent reporting having had two or more. And an increasing number of high school students are signing up for internships now, too.

The Employer's Perspective

Employers consider internships a good option in both healthy and ailing economies. In healthy economies, managers often struggle to fill their positions with eager workers who can adapt to changing technologies. Internships offer a low-cost way to get good workers into "the pipeline" without offering them a full-time position up front. In struggling economies, on the other hand, downsizing often requires employers to lay off workers without thinking about who will cover their responsibilities. Internships offer an inexpensive way to offset position losses resulting from these disruptive layoffs.

The Intern's Perspective

If you are looking to begin a career or supplement your education with practical training, internships are a good bet for several reasons.

1. **Internships offer a relatively quick way to gain work experience and develop job skills.** Try this exercise. Scan the Sunday want ads of your newspaper. Choose a range of interesting advertisements for professional positions that you would consider taking. List the desired or required job skills and work experiences specified in the ads. How many of these skills and experiences do you have?

Chances are, if you are still in school or a recent graduate, you don't have most of the skills and experience that employers require of their new hires. What do you do?

The growing reality is that many entry-level positions require skills and experiences that schools and part-time jobs don't provide. Sure, you know your way around a computer. You have some customer service experience. You may even have edited your school's newspaper or organized your senior prom. But you still lack the relevant skills and on-the-job experiences that many hiring managers require. A well-chosen internship can offer a way out of this common dilemma by providing you job training in an actual career field. Internships help you take your existing knowledge and skills and apply them in ways that will help you compete for good jobs.

2. **Internships offer a relatively risk-free way to explore a possible career path.** Believe it or not, the best internship may tell you what you *don't* want to do for the next ten or twenty years. Think about it. If you put all your eggs in one basket, what happens if your dream job turns out to be the exact opposite of what you want or who you are? Internships offer a relatively low-cost opportunity to "try out" a career field to see if it's right for *you*.

3. **Internships offer real opportunities to do career networking and can significantly increase your chances of landing a good full-time position.** Have you heard the saying: "It's not what you know, but who you know"? For good or ill, the reality is that who you know (or who knows you) can make a big difference in your job search. Studies show fewer than 20 percent of job placements occur through traditional application methods, including newspaper and trade journal advertisements, employment agencies, and career fairs. Instead, 60 to 90 percent of jobs are found through personal contacts and direct application.

Career "networking" is the exchange of information with others for mutual benefit. Your career network can tell you where the jobs are and help you compete for them. Isn't it better to develop your networking skills now, when the stakes aren't as high, than later when you are competing with everyone else for full-time jobs? The internship hiring process and the weeks you actually spend on the job provide excellent opportunities to talk with various people about careers, your skills, and ways to succeed.

VOLUNTEERING IN YOUR COMMUNITY

You've probably heard the saying that money isn't everything. Well, it's true, especially when it comes to volunteering and community service. There are a number of benefits you'll get that don't add up in dollars and cents but do add up to open doors in your future.

Community service looks good on a college application. Admissions staff members look for applicants who have volunteered and done community service in addition to grades. You could have gotten top grades, but if that's all that's on your application, you won't come across as a well-rounded person.

Community service lets you try out careers. How will you know you'll like a certain type of work if you haven't seen it done? For instance, you might think you want to work in the health-care field. Volunteering in a hospital will let you know if this is really what you want to do.

Community service is an American tradition. You'll be able to meet some of your own community's needs and join with all of the people who have contributed their talents to our country. No matter what your talents, there are unlimited ways for you to serve your community. Take a look at your interests, and then see how they can be applied to help others.

Here are some ideas to get you started:

- ❑ **Do you like kids?** Volunteer at your local parks and recreation department, for a Little League team, or as a big brother or sister.

- ❑ **Planning a career in health care?** Volunteer at a blood bank, clinic, hospital, retirement home, or hospice. There are also several organizations that raise money for disease research.

- ❑ **Interested in the environment?** Volunteer to assist in a recycling program. Create a beautification program for your school or community. Plant trees and flowers or design a community garden.

- ❑ **Just say no.** Help others stay off drugs and alcohol by volunteering at a crisis center, hotline, or prevention program. Help educate younger kids about the dangers of drug abuse.

- ❑ **Lend a hand.** Collect money, food, or clothing for the homeless. Food banks, homeless shelters, and charitable organizations need your help.

- ❑ **Is art your talent?** Share your knowledge and skills with youngsters, the elderly, or local arts organizations that depend on volunteers to help present their plays, recitals, and exhibitions.

- ❑ **Help fight crime.** Form a neighborhood watch or organize a group to clean up graffiti.

- ❑ **Your church or synagogue may have projects that need youth volunteers.** The United Way, your local politician's office, civic groups, and special interest organizations also provide exceptional opportunities to serve your community. Ask your principal, teachers, or counselors for additional ideas.

For more information on joining in the spirit of youth volunteerism, write to the Consumer Information Center, CIC-00A, P.O. Box 100, Pueblo, Colorado 81002, and request the *Catch the Spirit* booklet, or call 719-948-3334. Also check out the CIC's Web site at www.pueblo.gsa.gov.

Part 2

THE ROAD TO MORE EDUCATION

SOME PEOPLE WAKE up at age three and announce that they want to be doctors, teachers, or marine biologists—and they do it.

They're the exceptions. Many high school students don't have a clue about what they want to be. They dread the question, "So, what are you doing after graduating from high school?" Unfortunately, some of those same people also end up in careers that don't satisfy them.

You don't have to plan the rest of your life down to the last detail, but you can start to take some general steps toward your future and lay the groundwork. Then, when you do decide what you want to do, you'll be able to seize hold of your dream and go with it.

Chapter 3

PLANNING YOUR EDUCATION IN HIGH SCHOOL

Some people are planners. They make a plan, and they follow it. Then there are the non-planners.

Non-planners see the words "plan" and "future" and say, "Yeah, yeah, I know." Meanwhile, they're running out the door for an appointment they were supposed to be at 5 minutes ago.

Unfortunately, when it comes time to really do something about those goals and future hopes, the non-planners often discover that much of what should have been done wasn't done—which is not good when they're planning their future after high school. What about those classes they should have taken? What about those jobs they should have volunteered for? What about that scholarship they could have had if only they'd found out about it sooner?

But there is hope for poor planners. Now that you've thought about yourself and the direction you might want to go after graduating, you can use this section to help you plan what you should be doing while still in high school and when you should be doing it.

Regardless of what type of education you're planning on after high school, here's a plan to help you get there.

YOUR EDUCATION TIMELINE

Use this timeline to help you make sure you're accomplishing everything you need to accomplish on time.

Ninth Grade

- As soon as you can, meet with your counselor to begin talking about colleges and careers.

- Make sure you are enrolled in the appropriate college-preparatory or tech-prep courses.

- Get off to a good start with your grades. The grades you earn in ninth grade will be included in your final high school GPA and class rank.

- College might seem a long way off now, but grades really do count toward college admission and scholarships.

- Explore your interests and possible careers. Take advantage of Career Day opportunities.

- Get involved in extracurricular activities (both school and non-school-sponsored).

- Talk to your parents about planning for college expenses. Continue or begin a savings plan for college.

- Look at the college information available in your counselor's office and library. Use the Internet to check out college Web sites. Visit Peterson's at www.petersons.com to start a list of colleges that might interest you.

- Tour a nearby college, if possible. Visit relatives or friends who live on or near a college campus. Check out the dorms, go to the library or student center, and get a feel for college life.

- Investigate summer enrichment programs. Visit www.petersons.com for some neat ideas about summer opportunities.

Tenth Grade

Fall

- In October, take the Preliminary SAT/National Merit Scholarship Qualifying Test (PSAT/NMSQT) for practice. When you fill out your test sheet, check the box that releases your name to colleges so you can start receiving brochures from them.

- Ask your guidance counselor about the American College Testing program's PLAN (Pre-ACT) assessment program, which helps determine your study habits and academic progress and interests. This test will prepare you for the ACT Assessment next year.

- Take geometry if you have not already done so. Take biology and a second year of a foreign language.

- Become familiar with general college entrance requirements.

- Participate in your school's or state's career development activities.

PARENT PERSPECTIVE

Q: **When should parents and their children start thinking about preparing for college?**

A: **The discussion needs to start in middle school. If parents don't expose their children to these concepts at that time, then it can be too late in the game. Children need to take the right courses in high school. Many kids here end up going to junior colleges because they don't meet the minimum requirements when they graduate. Many universities and private colleges don't count some of the classes kids take in high school. You can't wait until the child is 18 and then say, "Maybe we should do something about getting into college."**

Kevin Carr
Parent
Oak Park, California

- Visit Petersons.com for advice on test taking and general college entrance requirements.

Winter

- Discuss your PSAT score with your counselor.

- The people who read college applications aren't looking just for grades. Get involved in activities outside the classroom. Work toward leadership positions in the activities that you like best. Become involved in community service and other volunteer activities.

- Read, read, read. Read as many books as possible from a comprehensive reading list, like the one on pages 24 and 25.

- Read the newspaper every day to learn about current affairs.

- Work on your writing skills—you'll need them no matter what you do.

- Find a teacher or another adult who will advise and encourage you to write well.

Spring

- Keep your grades up so you can have the highest GPA and class rank possible.

- Ask your counselor about postsecondary enrollment options and Advanced Placement (AP) courses.

- Continue to explore your interests and careers that you think you might like.

- Begin zeroing in on the type of college you would prefer (two-year or four-year, small or large, rural or urban). To get an idea of what's available, take a look at college profiles on Petersons.com or read books about college.

- If you are interested in attending a military academy such as West Point or Annapolis, now is the time to start planning and getting information.

- Write to colleges and ask for their academic requirements for admission.

- Visit a few more college campuses. Read all of the mail you receive from colleges. You may see something you like.

- Attend college fairs.

- Keep putting money away for college. Get a summer job.

- Consider taking SAT II Subject Tests in the courses you took this year while the material is still fresh in your mind. These tests are offered in May and June.

Eleventh Grade

Fall

- Meet with your counselor to review the courses you've taken, and see what you still need to take.

- Check your class rank. Even if your grades haven't been that good so far, it's never too late to improve. Colleges like to see an upward trend.

- If you didn't do so in tenth grade, sign up for and take the PSAT/NMSQT. In addition to National Merit Scholarships, this is the qualifying test for the National Scholarship Service and Fund for Negro Students and the National Hispanic Scholar Recognition Program.

- Make sure that you have a social security number.

- Take a long, hard look at why you want to continue your education after high school so you will be able to choose the best college or university for your needs.

- Make a list of colleges that meet your most important criteria (size, location, distance from home, majors, academic rigor, housing, and cost). Weigh each of the factors according to their importance to you.

- Continue visiting college fairs. You may be able to narrow your choices or add a college to your list.

PARENT PERSPECTIVE

Q: How involved should parents get in the selection of a college for their children?

A: Parents are getting more involved than ever before in supporting their children in the college process. This phenomenon is due to two factors:

This generation of parents has been much more involved with their children in dealing with the outside world than were their parents.

The investment made by today's parents is much more than that made by parents 20 or 30 years ago. As parents focus on the cost of this big-ticket item, there's interest to be more involved, to get the proper return.

Parents certainly should be involved in the college selection and application process. Studies clearly indicate that parental support in this process and throughout the college years can make a big difference in the success of a student. But this process also should be a learning opportunity in decision making for students. In that regard, parents shouldn't direct the student but provide input and the framework to assist their students.

Parents should not feel uncomfortable making suggestions to help their children through the thought and selection process—especially when it comes to identifying schools that their pocketbooks can accommodate. However, the child must be comfortable with the final decision and must have ultimate responsibility for the selection of the school. When students have made the final decision, it can help in their level of commitment because they've invested in it. They have a responsibility to do well and complete their academics at that location.

Richard Flaherty
President, College Parents of America

- Speak to college representatives who visit your high school.

- If you want to participate in Division I or Division II sports in college, start the certification process. Check with your counselor to make sure you are taking a core curriculum that meets NCAA requirements.

- If you are interested in one of the military academies, talk to your guidance counselor about starting the application process now.

SIX STUDY SKILLS THAT LEAD TO SUCCESS

1. **SET A REGULAR STUDY SCHEDULE.** No one at college is going to hound you to do your homework. Develop the study patterns in high school that will lead to success in college. Anyone who has ever pulled an all-nighter knows how much you remember when you are on the downside of your fifth cup of coffee and no sleep—not much! Nothing beats steady and consistent study habits.

2. **SAVE EVERYTHING.** To make sure your history notes don't end up in your math notebook and your English papers don't get thrown at the bottom of your friend's locker, develop an organized system for storing your papers. Stay on top of your materials, and be sure to save quizzes and tests. It is amazing how questions from a test you took in March can miraculously reappear on your final exam.

3. **LISTEN.** Teachers give away what will be on the test by repeating themselves. If you pay attention to what the teacher is saying, you will probably notice what is being emphasized. If what the teacher says in class repeats itself in your notes and in review sessions, chances are that material will be on the test. So really listen.

4. **TAKE NOTES.** If the teacher has taken the time to prepare a lecture, then what he or she says is important enough for you to write down. Develop a system for reviewing your notes. After each class, rewrite them, review them, or reread them. Try highlighting the important points or making notes in the margins to jar your memory.

5. **USE TEXTBOOKS WISELY.** What can you do with a textbook besides lose it? Use it to back up or clarify information that you don't understand from your class notes. Reading every word may be more effort than it is worth, so look at the book intelligently. What is in boxes or highlighted areas? What content is emphasized? What do the questions ask about in the review sections?

6. **FORM A STUDY GROUP.** Establish a group that will stay on task and ask one another the questions you think the teacher will ask. Compare notes to see if you have all the important facts. And discuss your thoughts. Talking ideas out can help when you have to respond to an essay question.

Winter

- Collect information about college application procedures, entrance requirements, tuition and fees, room and board costs, student activities, course offerings, faculty composition, accreditation, and financial aid. The Internet is a good way to visit colleges and obtain this information. Begin comparing the schools by the factors that you consider to be most important.

- Discuss your PSAT score with your counselor.

- Begin narrowing down your college choices. Find out if the colleges you are interested in require the SAT I, ACT Assessment, or SAT II Subject Tests for admission.

- Register for the SAT I and additional SAT II Subject Tests, which are offered several times during the winter and spring of your junior year (see the "Tackling the Tests" section for a schedule). You can take them again in the fall of your senior year if you are unhappy with your scores.

- Register for the ACT Assessment, which is usually taken in April or June. You can take it again late in your junior year or in the fall of your senior year, if necessary.

- Begin preparing for the tests you've decided to take.

- Have a discussion with your parents about the colleges in which you are interested. Examine financial resources, and gather information about financial aid. Check out the chapter on financial aid later in this book for a step-by-step explanation of the financial aid process.

- Set up a filing system with individual folders for each college's correspondence and printed materials.

Spring

- Meet with your counselor to review senior-year course selection and graduation requirements.

- Discuss ACT Assessment/SAT I scores with your counselor. Register to take the ACT Assessment and/or SAT I again if you'd like to try to increase your score.

- Discuss the college essay with your guidance counselor or English teacher.

- Stay involved with your extracurricular activities. Colleges look for consistency and depth in activities.

🕐 Consider whom you will ask to write your recommendations. Think about asking teachers who know you well and who will write positive letters about you. Letters from a coach, activity leader, or an adult who knows you well outside of school (e.g., volunteer work contact) are also valuable.

🕐 Inquire about personal interviews at your favorite colleges. Call or write for early summer appointments. Make necessary travel arrangements.

🕐 See your counselor to apply for on-campus summer programs for high school students. Apply for a summer job or internship. Be prepared to pay for college application, financial aid, and testing fees in the fall.

🕐 Request applications from schools you're interested in by mail or via the Internet.

Summer

🕐 Visit the campuses of your top-five college choices.

🕐 After each college interview, send a thank-you letter to the interviewer.

🕐 Talk to people you know who have attended the colleges in which you are interested.

🕐 Continue to read books, magazines, and newspapers.

🕐 Practice filling out college applications, and then type the final application forms or apply on line through the Web sites of the colleges in which you're interested.

🕐 Volunteer in your community.

🕐 Compose rough drafts of your college essays. Have a teacher read and discuss them with you. Polish them, and prepare final drafts. Proofread your final essays at least three times.

🕐 Develop a financial aid application plan, including a list of the aid sources, requirements for each application, and a timetable for meeting the filing deadlines.

ADMISSIONS ADVICE

Q: Other than grades and test scores, what are the most important qualities that you look for in students?

A: We consider the types of classes students have taken. A grade of a B in an honors class is competitive to an A in a regular course. We seek not only academically talented students but those who are well rounded. They need to submit their interests and activities, letters of recommendation, and writing samples in addition to their test scores. We look for someone that's involved in his or her community and high school, someone that holds leadership positions and has a balance of activities outside of academics. This gives us a look at that person as a whole.

Cheyenna Smith
Admission Counselor
University of Houston
Houston, Texas

Twelfth Grade

Fall

🕐 Continue to take a full course load of college-prep courses.

🕐 Keep working on your grades. Make sure you have taken the courses necessary to graduate in the spring.

🕐 Continue to participate in extracurricular and volunteer activities. Demonstrate initiative, creativity, commitment, and leadership in each.

🕐 To male students: you must register for selective service on your eighteenth birthday to be eligible for federal and state financial aid.

🕐 Talk to counselors, teachers, and parents about your final college choices.

🕐 Make a calendar showing application deadlines for admission, financial aid, and scholarships.

🕐 Check resource books, computer programs, and your guidance office for information on scholarships and grants. Ask colleges about scholarships for which you may qualify.

Check out Petersons.com for information on scholarships.

⏰ Give recommendation forms to the teachers you have chosen, along with stamped, self-addressed envelopes so your teachers can send them directly to the colleges. Be sure to fill out your name, address, and school name on the top of the form. Talk to your recommendation writers about your goals and ambitions.

⏰ Give School Report forms to your high school's guidance office. Fill in your name, address, and any other required information on top. Verify with your guidance counselor the schools to which transcripts, test scores, and letters are to be sent. Give your counselor any necessary forms at least two weeks before they are due or whenever your counselor's deadline is, whichever is earlier.

⏰ Register for and take the ACT Assessment, SAT I, or SAT II Subject Tests, as necessary.

⏰ Be sure you have requested (either by mail or on line) that your test scores be sent to the colleges of your choice.

⏰ Mail or send electronically any college applications for early decision admission by November 1.

⏰ If possible, visit colleges while classes are in session.

⏰ If you plan to apply for an ROTC scholarship, remember that your application is due by December 1.

⏰ Print extra copies or make photocopies of every application you send.

Winter

⏰ Attend whatever college-preparatory nights are held at your school or by local organizations.

⏰ Send midyear grade reports to colleges. Continue to focus on your schoolwork!

⏰ Fill out the Free Application for Federal Student Aid (FAFSA) and, if necessary, the Financial Aid Profile (FAP). These forms can be obtained from your guidance counselor or at www.ed.gov/offices/OPE/express.html to download the forms or to file electronically. These forms may not be processed before January 1, so don't send it before then.

⏰ Mail or send electronically any remaining applications and financial aid forms before winter break. Make sure you apply to at least one college that you know you can afford and where you know you will be accepted.

⏰ Follow up to make sure that the colleges have received all application information, including recommendations and test scores.

⏰ Meet with your counselor to verify that all applicable forms are in order and have been sent out to colleges.

Spring

⏰ Watch your mail between March 1 and April 1 for acceptance notifications from colleges.

⏰ Watch your mail for notification of financial aid awards between April 1 and May 1.

⏰ Compare the financial aid packages from the colleges and universities that have accepted you.

⏰ Make your final choice, and notify all schools of your intent by May 1. If possible, do not decide without making at least one campus visit. Send your nonrefundable deposit to your chosen school by May 1 as well. Request that your guidance counselor send a final transcript to the college in June.

⏰ Be sure that you have received a FAFSA acknowledgment.

⏰ If you applied for a Pell Grant (on the FAFSA), you will receive a Student Aid Report (SAR) statement. Review this Pell notice, and forward it to the college you plan to attend. Make a copy for your records.

🕐 Complete follow-up paperwork for the college of your choice (scheduling, orientation session, housing arrangements, and other necessary forms).

Summer

🕐 If applicable, apply for a Stafford Loan through a lender. Allow eight weeks for processing.

🕐 Receive the orientation schedule from your college.

🕐 Get residence hall assignment from your college.

🕐 Obtain course scheduling and cost information from your college.

🕐 Congratulations! You are about to begin the greatest adventure of your life. Good luck.

CLASSES TO TAKE IF YOU'RE GOING TO COLLEGE

Did you know that classes you take as early as the ninth grade will help you get into college? Make sure you take at least the minimum high school curriculum requirements necessary for college admission. Even if you don't plan to enter college immediately, take the most demanding courses you can handle.

Review the list of suggested courses on this page. Some courses, categories, and names might vary from state to state, but the following may be used as a guideline. Talk with your guidance counselor to select the curriculum that best meets your needs and skills.

Of course, learning also occurs outside of school. While outside activities will not make up for poor academic performance, skills learned from jobs, extracurricular activities, and volunteer opportunities will help you become a well-rounded student and will strengthen your college or job application.

Getting a Head Start on College Courses

You can take college courses while still in high school so that when you're in college, you'll be ahead of

---

SUGGESTED COURSES

College-Preparatory Curriculum

ENGLISH. Four units, with emphasis on composition (English 9, 10, 11, 12)

MATHEMATICS. Three units (algebra I, algebra II, geometry) are essential. Trigonometry, precalculus, calculus, and computer science are recommended for some fields of study.

SOCIAL SCIENCE. Three units (American history, world history, government/economics)

SCIENCE. Four units (earth science, biology, chemistry, physics)

FOREIGN LANGUAGE. Three units (at least 2 years in the same language)

FINE ARTS. One to 2 units

OTHER. Keyboarding, computer applications, computer science I, computer science II, physical education, health

College-Preparatory Curriculum Combined with a Career Education or Vocational Program

ENGLISH. Four units

MATHEMATICS. Three units (algebra I, algebra II, geometry)

SOCIAL SCIENCE. Three units (American history, world history, government/economics)

SCIENCE. Two units (earth science, biology)

FOREIGN LANGUAGE. Three units (at least 2 years in the same language)

FINE ARTS. One to 2 units

OTHER. Keyboarding, computer applications, physical education, and health and half-days at the Career Center during junior and senior year

---

everyone else. The formal name is postsecondary enrollment. What it means is that some students can take college courses and receive both high school and college credit for the courses taken. It's like a two-for-one deal!

Postsecondary enrollment is designed to provide an opportunity for qualified high school students to experience more advanced academic work. Participation in a postsecondary enrollment program is not intended to replace courses available in high school but rather to enhance the educational opportunities available to students while in high school. There are two options for postsecondary enrollment:

Option A: Qualified high school juniors and seniors take courses for college credit. Students enrolled under Option A must pay for all books, supplies, tuition, and associated fees.

Option B: Qualified high school juniors and seniors take courses for high school and college credit. For students enrolled under this option, the local school district covers the related costs, provided that the student completes the selected courses. Otherwise, the student and parent will be assessed the costs.

Certain preestablished conditions must be met for enrollment, so check with your high school counselor for more information.

SUGGESTED READING LIST FOR GRADES 9 THROUGH 12

Instead of flipping on the TV or putting on those headphones, how about picking up a book instead? Reading not only will take you to wonderful, unexplored worlds in your imagination, but there are practical reasons as well. Reading gives you a more well-rounded background. College admissions and future employers pick up on that. And you'll be able to answer the questions, "Did you read that book? What did you think of it?" How many of the books on this list have you read?

Adams, Richard
  Watership Down
Aesop
  Fables
Agee, James
  A Death in the Family
Anderson, Sherwood
  Winesburg, Ohio
Anonymous
  Go Ask Alice
Asimov, Isaac
  Short Stories
Austen, Jane
  Emma
  Northanger Abbey
  Pride and Prejudice
  Sense and Sensibility
Baldwin, James
  Go Tell It on the Mountain
Balzac, Honore de
  Pere Goriot
Beckett, Samuel
  Waiting for Godot
Bolt, Robert
  A Man for All Seasons
Brontë, Charlotte
  Jane Eyre
Brontë, Emily
  Wuthering Heights
Brooks, Gwendolyn
  In the Mecca
  Riot

Browning, Robert
  Poems
Buck, Pearl
  The Good Earth
Butler, Samuel
  The Way of All Flesh
Camus, Albert
  The Plague
  The Stranger
Cather, Willa
  Death Comes for the Archbishop
  My Antonia
Cervantes, Miguel
  Don Quixote
Chaucer, Geoffrey
  The Canterbury Tales
Chekhov, Anton
  The Cherry Orchard
Chopin, Kate
  The Awakening
Collins, Wilkie
  The Moonstone
Conrad, Joseph
  Heart of Darkness
  Lord Jim
  The Secret Sharer
  Victory
Crane, Stephen
  The Red Badge of Courage
Dante
  The Divine Comedy

Defoe, Daniel
  Moll Flanders
Dickens, Charles
  Bleak House
  David Copperfield
  Great Expectations
  Hard Times
  Oliver Twist
  A Tale of Two Cities
Dickinson, Emily
  Poems
Dinesen, Isak
  Out of Africa
Dostoevski, Fyodor
  The Brothers Karamazov
  Crime and Punishment
Douglas, Frederick
  The Life of Frederick Douglas
Dreiser, Theodore
  An American Tragedy
  Sister Carrie
Early, Gerald
  Tuxedo Junction
Eliot, George
  Adam Bede
  Middlemarch
  The Mill on the Floss
  Silas Marner

Eliot, T. S.
  Murder in the Cathedral
Ellison, Ralph
  Invisible Man
Emerson, Ralph Waldo
  Essays
Faulkner, William
  Absalom, Absalom!
  As I Lay Dying
  Intruder in the Dust
  Light in August
  The Sound and the Fury
Fielding, Henry
  Joseph Andrews
  Tom Jones
Fitzgerald, F. Scott
  The Great Gatsby
  Tender Is the Night
Flaubert, Gustave
  Madame Bovary
Forster, E. M.
  A Passage to India
  A Room with a View
Franklin, Benjamin
  The Autobiography of Benjamin Franklin
Galsworthy, John
  The Forsyte Saga

Golding, William
  Lord of the Flies
Goldsmith, Oliver
  She Stoops to Conquer
Graves, Robert
  I, Claudius
Greene, Graham
  The Heart of the Matter
  The Power and the Glory
Hamilton, Edith
  Mythology
Hardy, Thomas
  Far from the Madding Crowd
  Jude the Obscure
  The Mayor of Casterbridge
  The Return of the Native
  Tess of the D'Urbervilles
Hawthorne, Nathaniel
  The House of the Seven Gables
  The Scarlet Letter
Hemingway, Ernest
  A Farewell to Arms
  For Whom the Bell Tolls
  The Sun Also Rises
Henry, O.
  Stories

Hersey, John
  A Single Pebble
Hesse, Hermann
  Demian
  Siddhartha
  Steppenwolf
Homer
  The Iliad
  The Odyssey
Hughes, Langston
  Poems
  The Big Sea
Hugo, Victor
  Les Misérables
Huxley, Aldous
  Brave New World
Ibsen, Henrik
  A Doll's House
  An Enemy of the People
  Ghosts
  Hedda Gabler
  The Master Builder
  The Wild Duck
James, Henry
  The American
  Daisy Miller
  Portrait of a Lady
  The Turn of the Screw
Joyce, James
  Dubliners
  A Portrait of the Artist as a Young Man

Kafka, Franz
The Castle
The Metamorphosis
The Trial

Keats, John
Poems

Kerouac, Jack
On the Road

Koestler, Arthur
Darkness at Noon

Lawrence, Jerome, and Robert E. Lee
Inherit the Wind

Lewis, Sinclair
Arrowsmith
Babbitt
Main Street

Llewellyn, Richard
How Green Was My Valley

Machiavelli
The Prince

MacLeish, Archibald
J.B.

Mann, Thomas
Buddenbrooks
The Magic Mountain

Marlowe, Christopher
Dr. Faustus

Maugham, Somerset
Of Human Bondage

McCullers, Carson
The Heart Is a Lonely Hunter

Melville, Herman
Billy Budd
Moby-Dick
Typee

Miller, Arthur
The Crucible
Death of a Salesman

Monsarrat, Nicholas
The Cruel Sea

Naylor, Gloria
Bailey's Cafe
The Women of Brewster Place

O'Neill, Eugene
The Emperor Jones
Long Day's Journey Into Night
Mourning Becomes Electra

Orwell, George
Animal Farm
1984

Pasternak, Boris
Doctor Zhivago

Poe, Edgar Allan
Short Stories

Remarque, Erich
All Quiet on the Western Front

Rolvaag, O. E.
Giants in the Earth

Rostand, Edmond
Cyrano de Bergerac

Salinger, J. D.
The Catcher in the Rye

Sandburg, Carl
Abraham Lincoln: The Prairie Years
Abraham Lincoln: The War Years

Saroyan, William
The Human Comedy

Sayers, Dorothy
The Nine Tailors

Shakespeare, William
Plays and Sonnets

Shaw, George Bernard
Arms and the Man
Major Barbara
Pygmalion
Saint Joan

Sheridan, Richard B.
The School for Scandal

Shute, Nevil
On the Beach

Sinclair, Upton
The Jungle

Sophocles
Antigone
Oedipus Rex

Steinbeck, John
East of Eden
The Grapes of Wrath
Of Mice and Men

Stowe, Harriet Beecher
Uncle Tom's Cabin

Swift, Jonathan
Gulliver's Travels

Thackeray, William M.
Vanity Fair

Thoreau, Henry David
Walden

Tolstoy, Leo
Anna Karenina
War and Peace

Trollope, Anthony
Barchester Towers

Turgenev, Ivan
Fathers and Sons

Twain, Mark
Pudd'nhead Wilson

Updike, John
Rabbit, Run

Vergil
The Aeneid

Voltaire
Candide

Walker, Alice
The Color Purple
Meridian

Warren, Robert Penn
All the King's Men

Waugh, Evelyn
Brideshead Revisited
A Handful of Dust

Wharton, Edith
The Age of Innocence

White, T. H.
The Once and Future King
The Sword in the Stone

Wilde, Oscar
The Importance of Being Earnest
The Picture of Dorian Gray

Wilder, Thornton
Our Town

Williams, Tennessee
The Glass Menagerie
A Streetcar Named Desire

Wolfe, Thomas
Look Homeward, Angel

Woolf, Virginia
Mrs. Dalloway
To the Lighthouse

Wouk, Herman
The Caine Mutiny

Wright, Richard
Black Boy
Native Sun

Source: The National Endowment for the Humanities.

For more book recommendations, see what college professors suggest in **Arco's Reading Lists for College-Bound Students**, *available at your local bookstore.*

TACKLING THE TESTS

Unless you've been on another planet for the last two or three years, you've probably heard older high school students buzzing about the alphabet soup list of college entrance exams—SAT, ACT, and PSAT.

SOME OF THE STUDENTS who are getting ready to take one of these tests look like they're in various shades of hysteria. Others have been studying for months on end, so when they open their mouths, out pops the definition for "meretricious" or the answer to "What is the ratio of 3 pounds to 6 ounces?" Well, the talk that you've heard about the tests is partly true. They are a big deal and can be crucial to your academic plans. On the other hand, you don't have to walk in cold. Remember that word "planning"? It's a whole lot nicer than the word "panic." Preparing for the tests takes a lot of planning and time, but if you're reading this section, you're already ahead of the game.

A FEW FACTS ABOUT THE MAJOR TESTS

The major standardized tests students take in high school are the PSAT, SAT I, and ACT Assessment. Colleges across the country use them to get a sense of a student's readiness to enter their ivy-covered halls. These tests, or "boards" as they are sometimes called, have become notorious because of how important they can be. There is a mystique that surrounds them. People talk about the "magic number" that will get you into the school of your dreams.

Beware! There is a lot of misinformation out there. First and foremost, these are not intelligence tests; they are reasoning tests designed to evaluate the way you think. These tests assess the basic knowledge and skills you have gained through your classes in

school, and they also gauge the knowledge you have gained through outside experience. The material on these tests is not curriculum-based, but the tests do emphasize those academic experiences that educational institutions feel are good indicators of your probable success in college.

THE ACT ASSESSMENT

The ACT Assessment is a standardized college entrance examination that measures knowledge and skills in English, mathematics, reading, and science reasoning and the application of these skills to future academic tasks. The ACT Assessment consists of four multiple-choice tests.

Test 1: English

- 75 questions, 45 minutes
- Punctuation
- Grammar and usage
- Sentence structure
- Strategy
- Organization
- Style

Test 2: Mathematics

- 60 questions, 60 minutes
- Pre-algebra
- Elementary algebra
- Intermediate algebra

- Coordinate geometry
- Plane geometry
- Trigonometry

Test 3: Reading

- 40 questions, 35 minutes
- Prose fiction
- Humanities
- Social studies
- Natural sciences

Test 4: Science Reasoning

- 40 questions, 35 minutes
- Biology
- Physical science
- Chemistry
- Physics

Each section is scored from 1 to 36 and is scaled for slight variations in difficulty. Students are not penalized for incorrect responses. The composite score is the average of the four scaled scores.

To prepare for the ACT Assessment, ask your guidance counselor for a free guidebook called *Preparing for the ACT Assessment*. Besides providing general test-preparation information and additional test-taking strategies, this guidebook describes the content and format of the four ACT Assessment subject area tests, summarizes test administration procedures followed at ACT Assessment test centers, and includes a practice test.

THE SAT

The SAT I measures developed verbal and mathematical reasoning abilities as they relate to successful performance in college. It is intended to supplement the secondary school record and other information about the student in assessing readiness for college. There is one unscored, experimental section on the exam, which is used for equating and/or

STUDENT COUNSEL

Q: What kept you from stressing out about the tests?

A: The best way I found to prepare was to take practice tests to get to know the questions. At first, I'd set the kitchen timer and practice while ignoring the time, just to see what I could do. Practice is the best because they don't really change the type of questions. You read that in every review book, and it's true.

My advice for dealing with the stress on test day? The night before, I watched movies and had popcorn. When you take the test, definitely bring candy. A candy bar in between each section helps.

Theresa-Marie Russo
Edgemont High School
Scarsdale, New York

pretesting purposes and can cover either the mathematics or verbal subject area.

Verbal Reasoning

- 78 questions, 75 minutes
- Analogies
- Sentence completions
- Critical reading passages

Mathematical Reasoning

- 60 questions, 75 minutes
- Student-produced responses
- Quantitative comparisons
- Regular math

Experimental Section

- 30 minutes

Students receive one point for each correct response and lose a fraction of a point for each incorrect response (except for student-produced responses). These points are totaled to produce the raw scores, which are then scaled to equalize the scores for slight variations in difficulty for various editions of the test. Both the verbal scaled score range and the math scaled

THE NEW SAT I

You've probably heard a rumor that the SAT I is changing. The rumor's true, but don't worry: Nothing will happen until 2005. In case you're not planning on taking the exam until then, here's what you have to look forward to:

- The dreaded Analogy questions in the Verbal section will disappear. Taking their place will be more Reading Comprehension passages.

- The Verbal section will get a new name: "Critical Reading."

- A third section, Writing, will be added. It will be similar to the SAT II Writing Test, with multiple-choice grammar usage questions and a 25-minute essay. Your essay will be read and scored, and then it will be posted on a Web site for college admissions officials to read when they review your college application package.

- Quantitative Comparisons will disappear from the Math section, replaced by multiple-choice math questions from Algebra II.

- The current test takes 3 hours to complete; the new SAT I will take 3½ hours.

- Instead of a top score of 1600 points, the new SAT I will have a top score of 2400 points.

score range are from 200 to 800. The total scaled score range is from 400 to 1600.

To prepare for the SAT I, you should carefully review the pamphlet, Taking the SAT I: Reasoning Test, which you should be able to get from your guidance counselor. Also, most libraries and bookstores stock a large selection of material about the SAT I and other standardized tests.

RECOMMENDED TEST-TAKING DATES

Sophomore Year

| October | PSAT/NMSQT and PLAN For practice, planning, and preparation |
| May–June | SAT II Subject Tests (if necessary) |

Junior Year

| October | PSAT/NMSQT For the National Merit Scholarship Program and practice |
| January–June | ACT and/or SAT I, SAT II Subject Tests (if necessary) For college admission |

Senior Year

| October–December | ACT and/or SAT I, SAT II Subject Tests (if necessary) For college admission |

Which Should I Take? The ACT vs. the SAT

It's not a bad idea to take both. This assures that you will have the test scores required for admission to all schools, because some colleges accept the results of one test and not the other. Some institutions use test results for proper placement of students in English and math courses.

You should take the ACT Assessment and SAT I during the spring of your junior year, if not earlier. This enables you to retake the test in the fall of your senior year if you're not satisfied with your scores. Also, this makes it possible for institutions to receive all test scores before the end of January. Institutions generally consider the better score when determining admission and placement. Because most scholarship applications are processed between December and April of the senior year, your best score results can then be included in the application.

THE PSAT/NMSQT

The Preliminary SAT/National Merit Scholarship Qualifying Test, better known as the PSAT/NMSQT, is a practice test for the SAT I. Many students take the PSAT more than once because scores tend to increase with repetition and because it allows students to become more comfortable with taking standardized tests. During the junior year, the PSAT is also used as a qualifying test for the National Merit Scholarship Program and the National Scholarship Service and Fund for Negro Students. It is also used in designating students for the National Hispanic Scholar Recognition Program. The PSAT includes a writing skills section, which consists entirely of multiple-choice questions. This section does not appear on the SAT.

Verbal Reasoning

- Approximately 50 questions, two 25-minute sections

- Analogies

- Sentence completion

- Critical reading passages

Mathematical Reasoning

- 40 questions, two 25-minute sections
- Student-produced responses
- Quantitative comparisons
- Regular math

Writing Skills

- 39 questions, one 30-minute section
- Identifying sentence errors
- Improving sentences
- Improving paragraphs

Students receive a score in each content area (verbal, math, and writing). Each score ranges from 20 to 80 and is totaled with the others for the combined score.

WHAT DOES IT TAKE TO GET IN?

College Admission Policy	Class Rank	Average ACT Range (1–36)	Average SAT Range (400–1600)
Highly Selective	Top 10% of class very strong academic record	27–31	1220–1380
Selective	Top 25% of class, strong academic record	22–27	1150–1230
Traditional	Top 50% of class, good academic record	20–23	950–1070
Liberal	Many accepted from lower half of class	18–21	870–990
Open	All accepted to limit of capacity	17–20	830–950

The total score ranges from 60 to 240.

Selection Index (used for National Merit Scholarship purposes)

- Verbal + Math + Writing
- Score Range: 60 to 240
- Mean Junior Score: 147

National Merit Scholarship Program

- Semifinalist Status: Selection
- Index of 201 to 222
- Commended Student: Selection Index of 199

SAT II SUBJECT TESTS

Subject Tests are required by some institutions for admission and/or placement in freshman-level courses. Each Subject Test measures one's knowledge of a specific subject and the ability to apply that knowledge. Students should check with each institution for its specific requirements. In general, students are required to take three Subject Tests (one English, one mathematics, and one of their choice).

Subject Tests are given in the following areas:

ADMISSIONS ADVICE

Q: What can students who don't have the best grades do to improve their chances of getting into the college of their choice?

A: We encourage students to take the SAT or ACT more than once and see how they do. There are options for students who may not meet the academic requirements because they've had to work or are gifted in other areas, such as art or athletics, or who perhaps have been through something tragic. We ask them to submit letters or recommendations, a personal statement, and any other documentation that might help support their cases. What were the factors that affected their grades? What else can they offer the university?

We often encourage students who still may not meet the requirements to start at a community college and then transfer. We'll look at their college credit vs. their high school credit. They can prove to us that they can handle a college curriculum.

Cheyenna Smith
Admission Counselor
University of Houston
Houston, Texas

biology, chemistry, Chinese, English language proficiency, French, German, Italian, Japanese, Korean, Latin, literature, mathematics, modern Hebrew, physics, Spanish, U.S. history, world history, and writing. These tests are 1 hour long and are primarily multiple-choice tests. Three Subject Tests may be taken on one test date.

Scored like the SAT I, students gain a point for each correct answer and lose a fraction of a point for each incorrect answer. The raw scores are then converted to scaled scores that range from 200 to 800.

THE TOEFL TEST

The Test of English as a Foreign Language (TOEFL) is designed to help assess a student's grasp of English if it is not the student's first language. Performance on the TOEFL test may help interpret scores on the verbal section of the SAT I. The 3-hour test consists of four sections: listening comprehension, structure and written expression, reading comprehension, and a writing section. The test is given at more than 1,260 centers in 180 countries and is administered by Educational Testing Service (ETS). For further information, visit www.toefl.org.

WHAT OTHER TESTS SHOULD I KNOW ABOUT?

The AP Program

This program allows high school students to try college-level work and build valuable skills and study habits in the process. Subject matter is explored in more depth in AP courses than in other high school classes. A qualifying score on an AP test—which varies from school to school—can earn you college credit or advanced placement. Getting qualifying grades on enough exams can even earn you a full year's credit and sophomore standing at more than 1,400 higher-education institutions. There are currently thirty-two AP courses in eighteen different subject areas, including art, biology, and computer science. Speak to your guidance counselor for information about your school's offerings.

College-Level Examination Program (CLEP)

The CLEP enables students to earn college credit for what they already know, whether it was learned in school, through independent study, or through other experiences outside of the classroom. More than 2,800 colleges and universities now award credit for qualifying scores on one or more of the 34 CLEP exams. The exams, which are 90 minutes in length and are primarily multiple choice, are administered at participating colleges and universities. For more information, check out the Web site at www.collegeboard.com/clep.

Armed Services Vocational Aptitude Battery (ASVAB)

ASVAB is a career exploration program consisting of a multi-aptitude test battery that helps students explore their interests, abilities, and personal preferences. A career exploration workbook gives students information about the world of work, and a career information resource book helps students match their personal characteristics to the working world. Finally, an occupational outlook handbook describes in detail approximately 250 civilian and military occupations. Students can use ASVAB scores for military enlistment up to two years after they take the test. A student can take the ASVAB as a sophomore, junior, or senior, but students cannot use their sophomore scores to enter the armed forces. Ask your guidance counselor or your local recruiting office for more information. Also, see Chapter 10 of GAJ, "The Military Option."

General Educational Development (GED) Test

If you have not completed your high school education, you may earn an equivalence by taking the GED test, sponsored by your state Department of Education. However, taking the GED test is not a legitimate reason for dropping out of school. In fact, it is more difficult to get into the armed services with only a GED, and some employees have difficulty getting promoted without a high school diploma.

You're eligible to take the GED if you are not enrolled in high school, have not yet graduated from high school, are at least 16 years old, and meet your local requirements regarding age, residency, and length of time since leaving school.

There are five sections to the GED test, covering writing skills, social studies, science, interpreting literature and the arts, and mathematics. Part II of the Writing Skills Test requires writing an essay. The GED costs an average of $35 but can vary from state to state, and the application fee may be waived under certain circumstances. You should contact your local GED office to arrange to take the exam. Call 800-62-MYGED to find your local GED office and for more information.

WHAT CAN I DO TO PREPARE FOR THESE TESTS?

Know what to expect. Get familiar with how the tests are structured, how much time is allowed, and the directions for each type of question. Get plenty of rest the night before the test and eat breakfast that morning.

There are a variety of products, from books to software to videos, available to help you prepare for most standardized tests. Find the learning style that suits you best. As for which products to buy, there are two major categories—those created by the test makers and those created by private companies. The best approach is to talk to someone who has been through the process and find out which product or products he or she recommends.

Some students report significant increases in scores after participating in coaching programs.

Longer-term programs (40 hours) seem to raise scores more than short-term programs (20 hours), but beyond 40 hours, score gains are minor. Math scores appear to benefit more from coaching than verbal scores.

Preparation Resources

There are a variety of ways to prepare for standardized tests—find a method that fits your schedule and your budget. But you should definitely prepare. Far too many students walk into these tests cold, either because they find standardized tests frightening or annoying or they just haven't found the time to study. The key is that these exams are standardized. That means these tests are largely the same from administration to administration; they always test the same concepts. They have to, or else you couldn't compare the scores of people who took the tests on different dates. The numbers or words may change, but the underlying content doesn't.

So how do you prepare? At the very least, you should review relevant material, such as math formulas and commonly tested vocabulary words, and know the directions for each question type or test section. You should take at least one practice test and review your mistakes so you don't make them again on test day. Beyond that, you know best how much preparation you need. You'll also find lots of material in libraries or bookstores to help you: books and software from the test makers and from other publishers (including Peterson's) or live courses that range from national test-preparation companies to teachers at your high school who offer classes.

THE TOP 10 WAYS NOT TO TAKE THE TEST

10. Cramming the night before the test.
9. Not becoming familiar with the directions before you take the test.
8. Not becoming familiar with the format of the test before you take it.
7. Not knowing how the test is graded.
6. Spending too much time on any one question.
5. Not checking spelling, grammar, and sentence structure in essays.
4. Second-guessing yourself.
3. Forgetting to take a deep breath to keep from—
2. Losing It!
1. Writing a one-paragraph essay.

THE COLLEGE SEARCH

Now that you have examined your interests, talents, wants, and needs in great detail, it's time to start investigating colleges.

THE BEST RESOURCES

There are hundreds of colleges and universities in the United States, so before you can start filling out applications, you need to narrow down your search. There are a number of sources that will help you do this.

BESTCOLLEGEPICKS: AN EASY WAY TO PICK A COLLEGE

College guides, brochures, Web sites, and the lists that rank colleges are necessary sources of information for applicants, but they only provide part of the picture. They give data about incoming students such as GPAs and required test scores. This information is useful, but those facts are similar to finding out what materials go into the production of a car, not the results from driving it. BestCollegePicks looks at the driving record of a college by surveying college graduates about how well their colleges prepared them for the real world.

After filling out a comprehensive survey that pinpoints your skills, abilities, goals, and personal preferences, you'll get a list of colleges whose graduates most closely fit your goals, aspirations, and values and whose size, location, and kind of institution best match what you're interested in.

Then, BestCollegePicks matches what you say you want with what graduates say they've gotten from a wide range of colleges and universities. You can take the survey more than once, each time setting different goals. Say you are not sure if you want to go into law or business. You can take the survey twice—once for law and once for business—by signing in under a different name each time. When you get the list of schools, you can compare them to see which schools overlap. If you choose to attend one of those schools, you'll know that either way, a high percentage of graduates from that school have been successful in business or law.

The benefits of BestCollegePicks are enormous. You will be led to lesser-known schools you might never have thought of whose graduates match your future plans. And the vague ideas that you have about what you want out of college will take shape. You can get to BestCollegePicks by going to www.bestcollegepicks.com.

Your Guidance Counselor

Your guidance counselor is your greatest asset in the college search process. She has access to a vast repository of information, from college bulletins and catalogs to financial aid applications. She knows how well graduates from your high school have performed at colleges across the country, and she has probably even visited many of the colleges to get some first-hand knowledge about the places she has sent her students to. The more your guidance counselor sees you and learns about you, the easier it is for her to help you. So make sure you stop by her office often, whether it's to talk about your progress or just to say "hi."

Your Teachers

Use your teachers as resources, too. Many of them have had twenty to thirty years of experience in their field. They have taught thousands of students and watched them go off to college and careers. Teachers often stay in contact with graduates and know about their experiences in college and may be familiar with the schools you are interested in attending. Ask your teachers how they feel about the match between you and your choice schools and if they think you will be able to succeed in that environment.

Mom and Dad

Your parents or guardians need to be an integral part of the college selection process, whether they are financing your education or not. They have opinions and valuable advice. Listen to them carefully. Try to take in all their information and see if it applies to you. Does it fit with who you are and what you want?

What works and what doesn't work for you? Is some of what they say dated? How long ago were their experiences, and how relevant are they today? Take in the information, thank them for their concern, compare what they have said with the information you are gathering, and discard what doesn't fit.

Colleges and Universities

Don't forget to go to college fairs. Usually held in large cities in the evening, they are free and sponsored by your local guidance counselors' association and the National Association of College Admissions Counselors (NACAC). The admissions counselors of hundreds of colleges, vocational/technical schools, and universities attend college fairs each year. Whether your questions are as general as what the overall cost of education is at a particular institution or as specific as how many biology majors had works published last year, the admissions office works to assist you in locating the people who can answer your questions. Bring a shopping bag for all the information you will get.

Admissions officers also visit high schools. Don't forget to attend these meetings during your junior and senior years. Generally, college admissions counselors come to a school to get a general sense of the high school and the caliber and personality of the student body. Although it is difficult to make an individual impression at these group sessions, the college counselors do take names on cards for later contact, and you will occasionally see them making notes on the cards when they are struck by an astute questioner. It is helpful to attend these sessions because consistent contact between a student and a college is tracked by colleges and universities. An admissions decision may come down to examining the size of your admissions folder and the number of interactions you have had with the school over time.

College and university brochures and catalogs are a good place to look, too. After reading a few, you will discover that some offer more objective information than others. You will also start to learn what information colleges think is essential to present. That's important. If a college's brochure does not present the same information as most of the other college brochures, you have to ask yourself why.

PARENT PERSPECTIVE

Q: Now that you've been through the process of getting three of your children into college, what's your best advice for parents and teens?

A: Apply early and meet deadlines. Both of our older sons were sitting there after high school graduation wondering why they were on college waiting lists: "I have good grades. I can't figure it out." At eighteen, they don't see tomorrow, much less way down the line, but do you want to deal with their heartbreak at not getting into the college where they want to be? It's their future. It's hard because they're in their senior year and you want it to be fun for them. However, you see the reality out there that they will be facing for the rest of their lives. They don't want to look at it, but you have to keep bringing them back to it—not in a preachy way. If they start earlier than their senior year, it won't be as much of a shock when they become seniors.

Jeanette and Amedee Richard
San Antonio, Texas

What might this say about the college's academic offerings, athletic or extracurricular programs, or campus life? What does the campus look like? How is the campus environment presented in the brochure? The brochures should present clues to what schools feel are their important majors, what their mission is, and which departments they are spending their budgets on. Take the time to do these informational resources justice. They have a great deal to say to the careful reader.

A college's Web site can give you a glimpse of campus life that does not appear in the college's brochure and catalog. It is true that the virtual tour will show you the shots that the college marketing department wants you to see and that shows the campus in the best light, but you can use the home page to see other things, too. Read the student newspaper. Visit college-sponsored chat rooms. Go to the department in the major you are investigating. Look at the Course Bulletin to see what courses are required.

ONLINE HELP

To help you find two-year and four-year colleges or universities in your specific region, take a look at the

CRITERIA TO CONSIDER

Depending on your personal interests, the following characteristics should play a role in helping you narrow down the field of colleges.

AFFILIATION
- Public
- Private, independent
- Private, church affiliated
- Proprietary

SIZE
- Very small (fewer than 1,000 students)
- Small (1,000–3,999 students)
- Medium (4,000–8,999 students)
- Large (9,000–19,999 students)
- Very large (more than 20,000 students)

COMMUNITY
- Rural
- Small town
- Suburban
- Urban

LOCATION
- In your hometown
- Less than 3 hours from home
- More than 3 hours from home

HOUSING
- Dorm
- Off-campus apartment
- Home
- Facilities and services for students with disabilities

STUDENT BODY
- All male
- All female
- Coed
- Minority representation
- Primarily one religious denomination
- Primarily full-time students
- Primarily part-time students
- Primarily commuter students
- Primarily residential students

ACADEMIC ENVIRONMENT
- Majors offered
- Student-faculty ratio
- Faculty teaching reputation
- Instruction by professors versus teaching assistants
- Facilities (such as classrooms and labs)
- Libraries
- Independent study available
- International study available
- Internships available

FINANCIAL AID
- Scholarships
- Grants
- Loans
- Work-study program
- Part-time or full-time jobs

SUPPORT SERVICES
- Academic counseling
- Career/placement counseling
- Personal counseling
- Student health facilities

ACTIVITIES/SOCIAL CLUBS
- Clubs, organizations
- Greek life
- Athletics, intramurals
- Other

ATHLETICS
- Division I, II, or III
- Sports offered
- Scholarships available

SPECIALIZED PROGRAMS
- Gifted student services
- Services for students with disabilities or special needs

appendix in the back of this book for a table of schools in each state of your region. Then check out the following online resources for additional information on college selection, scholarships, student information, and much more.

Peterson's Undergraduate Channel. Petersons.com provides information and tools that will help you prepare, search, and pay for college. You can find the schools that BestCollegePicks matched you to in order to view in-depth profiles or do a side-by-side comparison of selected colleges. Or you can search for a school by name or location. In addition to college search and selection tools, the undergraduate channel on Petersons.com also offers tips on financial aid, test preparation, and online applications.

The National Association for College Admission Counseling. This home page offers information for professionals, students, and parents. The Internet address is www.nacac.com.

U.S. Department of Education. This federal agency's National Center for Education Statistics produces reports on every level of education, from elementary to postgraduate. Dozens are available for downloading. You can hook up with these and other links at www.ed.gov.

CAMPUS VISITS

You've heard the old saying, "A picture is worth a thousand words." Well, a campus visit is worth a thousand brochures. Nothing beats walking around a campus to get a feel for it. Some students report that all they needed to know that they loved or hated a campus was to drive through it. Then there is the true story of the guy who applied to a school because it had a prestigious name. Got accepted. Didn't visit, and when he arrived to move into the dorms, discovered to his horror it was an all-male school. A visit would have taken care of that problem.

The best time to experience the college environment is during the spring of your junior year or the fall of your senior year. Although you may have more time to make college visits during your summer off, your observations will be more accurate when you can see the campus in full swing. Open houses are a good idea and provide you with opportunities to talk to students, faculty members, and administrators. Write or call in advance to take student-conducted campus tours. If possible, stay overnight in a dorm to see what living at the college is really like.

Bring your transcript so that you are prepared to interview with admission officers. Take this opportunity to ask questions about financial aid and other services that are available to students. You can get a good snapshot of campus life by reading a copy of the student newspaper. The final goal of the campus visit is to study the school's personality and decide if it matches yours. Your parents should be involved with the campus visits so that you can share your impressions. Here are some additional campus visit tips:

- Read campus literature prior to the visit.
- Ask for directions, and allow ample travel time.
- Make a list of questions before the visit.
- Dress in neat, clean, casual clothes and shoes.
- Ask to meet one-on-one with a current student.
- Ask to meet personally with a professor in your area of interest.
- Ask to meet a coach or athlete in your area of interest.
- Offer a firm handshake.
- Use good posture.
- Listen, and take notes.
- Speak clearly, and maintain eye contact with people you meet.
- Don't interrupt.
- Be honest, direct, and polite.
- Be aware of factual information so that you can ask questions of comparison and evaluation.
- Be prepared to answer questions about yourself. Practice a mock interview with someone.
- Don't be shy about explaining your background and why you are interested in the school.
- Ask questions about the background and experiences of the people you meet.
- Convey your interest in getting involved in campus life.
- Be positive and energetic.
- Don't feel as though you have to talk the whole time or carry the conversation yourself.
- Relax, and enjoy yourself.
- Thank those you meet, and send thank-you notes when appropriate.

After you have made your college visits, use the "College Comparison Worksheet" on page 38 to rank the schools in which you're interested. This will help

WRITING TO A COLLEGE FOR INFORMATION

If neither you nor your guidance counselor has an application for a college that you are interested in, write a brief letter to the college admissions office to request an application.

Date

Your Name
Street Address
City, State, Zip

Office of Admission
Name of College
Street Address
City, State, Zip

To Whom It May Concern:

I am a (freshman, sophomore, junior, senior) at (name of your school) and plan to graduate in (month) (year).

Please send me the following information about your college: a general information brochure, program descriptions, an admission application, financial aid information, and any other information that might be helpful. I am considering _____ as my major field of study (optional, if you know your major).

I am interested in visiting your campus, taking a campus tour, and meeting with an admission counselor and a financial aid officer. I would also like to meet with an adviser or professor in the (your preferred field of study) department, if possible (optional, if you know your major). I will contact you in a week to set up a time that is convenient.

If you would like to contact me directly, I can be reached at (your phone number with area code). Thank you.

Sincerely,

(Signature)

Name

you decide not only which ones to apply to, but also which one to attend once you receive your acceptance letters.

THE COLLEGE INTERVIEW

Not all schools require or offer an interview. However, if you are offered an interview, use this one-on-one time to evaluate the college in detail and to sell

(Continued on page 38)

IT'S ALL ABOUT *YOU!* Read each question and respond by circling Y (Yes), N (No), or C (Combination). Complete all the questions and return to the top. Highlight each action that coordinates with your answer, and then read it. Where you chose C, read both actions. Is there a pattern? Do the questions seem to lead to a certain type of college or university? Certain size? Certain location? Read the suggestions at the end of "The Matching Game" for more ideas.

Question	Yes/No/ Combination	Action
1. Do I have a goal in life?	Y/N/C	Y: State it._____. N: Don't worry, many students start college without knowing what they want to do. Look into colleges that specialize in the arts and sciences.
2. Do I know what I want to achieve with a college diploma?	Y/N/C	Y: List specifically what those goals are. _____ N: Think about what college can offer you.
3. Do I want to broaden my knowledge?	Y/N/C	Y: Consider a liberal arts college. N: You might need to consider other options or educational opportunities.
4. Do I want specific training?	Y/N/C	Y: Investigate technical colleges or professional training programs in universities. N: You don't know what you want to study. Only 20 percent of seniors who apply to college are sure.
5. Am I willing to work hard?	Y/N/C	Y: When you are visiting colleges, ask students about handling the work load. N: Check the work load carefully. If no one is on campus on a sunny day, it may not be the school for you
6. Am I self-directed enough to finish a four-year college program?	Y/N/C	Y: Consider only four-year colleges and universities. N: Maybe a two-year junior or community college is a better way to begin your college experience. Also consider a tech/vocational school.
7. Do I know what I do well?	Y/N/C	Y: Consider how your abilites relate to majors. Identify some. _____ N: Spend a little more time asking yourself questions about your interests. Speak to your counselor and do an interest inventory.
8. Do I like to spend time learning any one subject more than others?	Y/N/C	Y: Check to see what some majors are in that area. _____ _____ N: Look at your high school courses. Do you like any of them better than others? Which ones? _____
9. Do I know what matters to me and what my values are?	Y/N/C	Y: Look for the schools that talk about the values on their campus. Do they have an honor code for students? Do the values confirm or conflict with your values? N: Values are less important to you, so places that really expound their values may seem confining to you.
10. Do I need to be in affluent surroundings?	Y/N/C	Y: Look at the schools that deliver that package. Check the small, private liberal arts colleges. N: How strong is your reaction against this setting? If it is strong, check larger, more diverse settings, like an urban school.
11. Am I going to college for the financial gains?	Y/N/C	Y: What majors are going to give you the payback you want? Look at business colleges and professional programs, like premed. N: If a big financial payback does not interest you, look at social service majors, like counseling, teaching, and social work.
12. Am I focused?	Y/N/C	Y: Search out the programs that will offer you the best options. N: Avoid those schools whose programs are not strong in your focused area.
13. Am I conservative in my views and behavior?	Y/N/C	Y: The political policies of schools are important. Look into them carefully. You might look at the schools in the Midwest or the South. N: If you're a liberal, look closely at the political climate. Check the schools in the Northeast and the West Coast.

14. Do I need to be around people who are similar to me?	Y/N/C	Y: If you are African American, check the historically black colleges. If socioeconomic level or a certain look is important to you, study the student populations carefully during campus visits. If it is religious orientation you are interested in, look into religiously sponsored colleges and universities.
		N: Look at large, midsize, and small universities in urban settings.
15. Are the name and prestige of the school important to me?	Y/N/C	Y: Look into the Ivies and the competitive schools to see if you are eligible and what they offer you. Broaden your search to include other colleges and compare their offerings for your specific needs and interests.
		N: Don't exclude the well-known institutions if they fit in every other way.
16. Do I like sports?	Y/N/C	Y: Large universities with Division I teams will give you all the sports you need—as a competitor or a fan. If you do not want to compete at that level, check schools in other divisions. Look at the liberal arts colleges for athletes.
		N: Look into smaller universities and liberal arts colleges with good teams.
17. Am I a techie?	Y/N/C	Y: Check for computer engineering courses at technical universities and large universities near research centers and major computer business areas. Ask about hardwiring, e-mail, and computer packages before you enroll.
		N: It still helps to know what computer services are available where you enroll.
18. Do I need to live in or be near a city?	Y/N/C	Y: How close to a city do you need to be? In the city or an hour away? Do you still want a campus feel? Consider these questions as you visit campuses.
		N: Do you need space, natural beauty, and peaceful surroundings to think? Look into small liberal arts schools in rural and suburban settings. Explore universities in the Midwest and South.
19. Will I need counseling for support?	Y/N/C	Y: Investigate the quality of student services and the mechanism for accessing them. Smaller schools often pride themselves on their services. Look at liberal arts colleges. Universities connected to medical centers often provide extensive services. N: It is still good to know what is offered.
20. Do I need an environment in which questioning is important?	Y/N/C	Y: Liberal arts colleges, honors colleges, and smaller universities place an emphasis on academic inquiry. N: You like to hear others discuss issues, gather as much information and opinions as you can, and think it over by yourself. Try the university setting.

Suggestions

Here are some ideas for you to consider based on the way you answered the questions.

1. If you answered *no* to numbers 2 and 3, why not investigate apprenticeships, vocational/technical schools, military enlistment options, and certification or two-year college programs?

2. If you answered *yes* to numbers 4, 11, and 17, technical or professional colleges and universities with hands-on training may give you the direction you are looking for.

3. If you answered *yes* to numbers 9, 10, and 20, you are leaning toward a liberal arts setting.

4. If you answered *yes* to numbers 5 and 6, examine the competitive and Ivy League colleges.

5. If you answered *no* to numbers 9, 10, 14, and 20 and yes to 16, 17, and 18, larger universities may offer you the best options.

Once you have completed your self-evaluation, made a decision whether college is for you, have some ideas about your personality and likes and dislikes, and can relate them to the different personalities of colleges, it is time to gather information. It needs to be quality information from the right sources. The quality of information you put into the search now will determine whether your list of colleges will represent a good or a bad match.

yourself to the admission officer. The following list of questions can help you collect the information you may need to know.

☐ How many students apply each year? How many are accepted?

☐ What are the average GPA and average ACT or SAT I score(s) for those accepted?

☐ How many students in last year's freshman class returned for their sophomore year?

☐ What is the school's procedure for credit for Advanced Placement high school courses?

☐ As a freshman, will I be taught by professors or teaching assistants?

☐ How many students are there per teacher?

☐ When is it necessary to declare a major?

☐ Is it possible to have a double major or to declare a major and a minor?

☐ What are the requirements?

☐ How does the advising system work?

☐ Does this college offer overseas study, cooperative programs, or academic honors programs?

☐ What is the likelihood, due to overcrowding, of getting closed out of the courses I need?

☐ What technology is available?

☐ How well equipped are the libraries and laboratories?

☐ Are internships available?

☐ How effective is the job placement service of the school?

☐ What is the average class size in my area of interest?

☐ Have any professors in my area of interest recently won any honors or awards?

☐ What teaching methods are used in my area of interest (lecture, group discussion, fieldwork)?

COLLEGE COMPARISON WORKSHEET

Fill in your top five selection criteria and any others that may be of importance to you. Once you narrow your search of colleges to five, fill in the colleges across the top row. Using a scale of 1 to 5, where 1 is poor and 5 is excellent, rate each college by your criteria. Total each column to see which college rates the highest based upon your criteria.

SELECTION CRITERIA	COLLEGE 1	COLLEGE 2	COLLEGE 3	COLLEGE 4	COLLEGE 5
1.					
2.					
3.					
4.					
5.					
OTHER CRITERIA					
6.					
7.					
8.					
9.					
10.					
TOTAL					

Sample criteria: (Use this list as a starting point—there may be other criteria important to you not listed here.) Arts facilities, athletic facilities, audiovisual center, campus setting, class size, classrooms/lecture halls, computer labs, dining hall, dorms, financial aid, fraternity/sorority houses, majors offered, religious facilities, professor profiles, student-professor ratio, student profile, student union, surrounding community.

- ☑ How many students graduate in four years in my area of interest?

- ☑ What are the special requirements for graduation in my area of interest?

- ☑ What is the student body like? Age? Sex? Race? Geographic origin?

- ☑ What percentage of students live in dormitories? Off-campus housing?

- ☑ What percentage of students go home for the weekend?

- ☑ What are some of the regulations that apply to living in a dormitory?

- ☑ What are the security precautions taken on campus and in the dorms?

- ☑ Is the surrounding community safe?

- ☑ Are there problems with drug and alcohol abuse on campus?

- ☑ Are there dorms available that are free of any use of drugs and alcohol?

- ☑ Do faculty members and students mix on an informal basis?

- ☑ How important are the arts to student life?

- ☑ What facilities are available for cultural events?

- ☑ How important are sports to student life?

- ☑ What facilities are available for sporting events?

- ☑ What percentage of the student body belongs to a sorority/fraternity?

- ☑ What is the relationship between those who belong to the Greek system and those who don't?

- ☑ Are students involved in the decision-making process at the college? Do they sit on major committees?

- ☑ What other activities can students get involved in?

- ☑ What percentage of students receive financial aid based on need?

- ☑ What percentage of students receive scholarships based on academic ability?

- ☑ What percentage of a typical financial aid offer is in the form of a loan?

- ☑ If my family demonstrates financial need on the FAFSA (and FAF, if applicable), what percentage of the established need is generally awarded?

- ☑ How much did the college increase the cost of room, board, tuition, and fees from last year?

- ☑ Do opportunities for financial aid, scholarships, or work-study increase each year?

- ☑ When is the application deadline?

- ☑ When does the school notify you of the admission decision?

- ☑ If there is a deposit required, is it refundable?

Keep in mind that you don't need to ask all these questions—in fact, some of them may have already been answered for you in the catalog, on the Web site, or in the interview. Ask only the questions for which you still need answers.

SHOULD YOU HEAD FOR THE IVY LEAGUES?

Determining whether to apply to one of the eight Ivy League schools is something you should think long and hard about. Sure, it can't hurt to toss your application into the ring if you can afford the application fee and the time you'll spend writing the essays. But if you want to figure out if you'd be a legitimate candidate for acceptance at one of these top-tier schools, you should understand the type of student that they look for and how you compare, says John Machulsky, a guidance counselor at Lawrence High School in New Jersey. Take a look at these statistics:

- Only 30 percent or fewer applicants are accepted at these highly competitive colleges each year.

- Most Ivy League students have placed in the top 10 percent of their class and have SAT I scores in the 700 levels for math and verbal each or ACT scores of 29 or higher.

- Because Ivy League schools are so selective, they want a diverse student population. That means they want students that represent not only the fifty states but also a wide selection of other countries.

Lirio Jimenez, a guidance counselor at New Brunswick High School in New Jersey, says that being accepted by an Ivy League school is a process that starts early in the ninth grade. You should select demanding courses and maintain good grades in those courses throughout all four years of high school. Get involved in extracurricular activities as well, and, of course, do well on your standardized tests. When it comes time to apply for college, select at least three schools: one ideal, one possible, and one shoe-in. Your ideal can be an Ivy League if you wish.

GAJ certainly doesn't want to discourage you from applying to one of these prestigious schools. We're in your corner and want to see you get the best education possible. However, students are sometimes more concerned about getting accepted than with taking a hard look at what a school has to offer them. Often, a university or college that is less competitive than an Ivy League may have exactly what you need to succeed in the future. Keep that in mind as you select the colleges that would offer you what you need.

MINORITY STUDENTS GO TO COLLEGE

African-American, Hispanic/Latino, and Native-American high school students have a lot of doors into higher education opening for them. In fact, most colleges want to respond to the social and economic disadvantages of certain groups of Americans. They want to reflect the globalization of our economy. They want their student populations to look like the rest of America, which means people from many different backgrounds and ethnic groups. This isn't just talk either. You'll find that most colleges have at least one member of the admissions staff who specializes in recruiting minorities.

One of the reasons college admissions staff are recruiting minorities and want to accommodate their needs is because there are more minorities thinking of attending college—and graduating. Let's put some numbers to these statements. According to the Department of Education, in 1976, 16 percent of college students were minorities, compared to 27 percent in 1997. Much of the change can be attributed to rising numbers of Hispanic and Asian students. The proportion of Asian and Pacific Islander students rose from 2 percent to 6 percent, and the Hispanic proportion rose from 4 percent to 9 percent during that same time period. The proportion of black students fluctuated during most of the early part of the period before rising slightly to 11 percent in 1997, the last year for which data was collected on this subject.

STUDENT COUNSEL

Q: What made you choose to apply to an Ivy League school?

A: My mother recommended that I apply to Princeton. She said, "Why not just try? What do you have to lose? All they can tell you is no." I was afraid of being rejected. I wasn't a straight-A student, and I thought they weren't going to want me—they get thousands of applications. Through the whole college process I had a whole lot of self-doubt. Looking back, I realize that you won't know if you don't try. Take the chance and fill out the application. If you don't get in, it doesn't mean you're less intelligent. It just wasn't the correct fit.

Zoelene Hill, College Freshman
Princeton University

SHOULD YOU ATTEND A HISTORICALLY BLACK COLLEGE OR UNIVERSITY?

Choosing which college to attend is usually a difficult decision for anyone to make, but when an African-American student is considering attending a historically black college or university (HBCU), a whole other set of family and cultural issues are raised.

There are many valid reasons that favor one or the other. Some are obvious differences. Parents and their children have to be honest with themselves and take a long, hard look at the needs of the student and how the campus environment can fulfill them. To help you decide, here are some questions to ask:

DO I KNOW WHAT'S REALLY IMPORTANT TO ME?

Look at the reasons why you want a degree and what you want to achieve with it. Is the choice to attend an HBCU yours or your family's? Do you have a particular field of study you want to pursue? Sometimes students can get so caught up in applying to a particular institution, they don't realize it doesn't even offer their major.

HOW WILL THIS CAMPUS FIT MY PLANS FOR THE FUTURE?

There's no substitute for doing your homework about the campuses you're seriously considering. Know the reputation of those campuses in the community and among employers and the general population. Find out about graduation, retention, and placement rates.

DOES THIS CAMPUS HAVE THE FACILITIES AND LIVING CONDITIONS THAT SUIT MY COMFORT LEVEL?

Finding a campus where you're comfortable is a big factor in choosing a college. What do you want in campus facilities and living conditions? For instance, if you currently attend a small private high school in a suburban setting, perhaps you wouldn't like living on a large urban campus with peers who don't mirror your kind of background.

WHAT LEVEL OF SUPPORT WILL I GET ON CAMPUS?

Students considering institutions where few people are like them should look at the available support systems and organizations that will be available to them. Parents need to feel comfortable with the contact person on campus.

When all the factors that determine the choice of a college are laid out, the bottom line is which institution best meets your needs. For some African-American students, an HBCU is the best choice. For others, it's not. African-American students reflect many backgrounds, and there is no single decision that will be right for everyone.

GAJ has a lot of information in this section to help you make decisions about college and paying for college. Perhaps the most important information we can give you is that if you want to go to college, you can. There are a lot of organizations ready to assist you. So go for it. See the list of organizations in this section and check with the colleges in which you're interested to connect with the minority affairs office.

Academic Resources for Minority Students

In addition to churches, sororities and fraternities, and college minority affairs offices, minority students can receive information and assistance from the following organizations:

ASPIRA

An association of community-based organizations that provide leadership, development, and educational services to Latino youths.

1444 Eye Street, NW, Suite 800
Washington, D.C. 20005
202-835-3600
www.aspira.org

INROADS

A national career-development organization that places and develops talented minority students (African American, Hispanic American, and Native American) in business and industry.

10 South Broadway, Suite 700
St. Louis, Missouri 63102
314-241-7488
www.inroadsinc.org

National Action Council for Minorities in Engineering (NACME)

An organization that aims to increase the number of minorities who earn bachelor's degrees in engineering by offering an Incentive Grants Program, Summer Engineering Employment Project, field services, and publications for parents and students.

The Empire State Building
350 Fifth Avenue, Suite 2212
New York, New York 10118-2299
212-279-2626
www.nacme.org

STUDENT COUNSEL

Q: How did you make the decision to attend a historically black college or university?

A: Selecting a college was one of the hardest decisions I've ever had to make. As a recipient of the National Achievement Scholarship and a National History Day winner, I was offered scholarships to a number of colleges across the country, including many HCBUs. I tried to figure out which institution would be able to give me the most help in achieving my goals. I finally decided on Florida A&M University (FAMU) in my hometown of Tallahassee.

There are many pluses to attending college in my hometown. By living on campus, I have the freedom to make my own decisions and live as a young adult while being close to the loving support of my parents. Also, FAMU will help me succeed in my objective of obtaining a bachelor's degree in broadcast journalism. As I look back, I am glad that I, unlike some of my other high school peers, did not rush to judgment during the process of choosing a college. I am very happy with my decision.

Larry Rivers
Florida A&M University

National Association for the Advancement of Colored People (NAACP)

The purpose of the NAACP is to improve the political, educational, social, and economic status of minority groups; to eliminate racial prejudice; to keep the public aware of the adverse effects of racial discrimination; and to take lawful action to secure its elimination, consistent with the efforts of the national organization.

> 4805 Mt. Hope Drive
> Baltimore, Maryland 21205
> 410-358-8900
> www.naacp.org

The National Urban League

The Education and Youth Services Department of the Urban League provides services for African Americans and economically disadvantaged people. These services include basic academic development, GED test preparation for youths and adults, after-school tutoring for children, parent training classes, scholarships, an annual tour of historically black colleges and universities, and summer employment for youths. Call individual Urban League offices in your state.

> 120 Wall Street
> 8th Floor
> New York, New York 10005
> 212-558-5300 (national office)
> www.nul.org

United Negro College Fund (UNCF)

The UNCF provides scholarships for undergraduates who attend one of forty private, historically black colleges. Students must be accepted first and then nominated by the college's financial aid director. Programs and services include summer learning programs, internships, precollege and mentoring programs, and international programs.

> 8260 Willow Oaks Corporate Drive
> Fairfax, Virginia 22031
> 800-331-2244 (toll-free)
> www.uncf.org

Online Resources

Hispanic Association of Colleges and Universities

> www.hacu.com

The American Indian Higher Education Consortium

> www.aihec.org

Minority On-Line Information Service (MOLIS)

> www.sciencewise.com/molis

STUDENTS WITH DISABILITIES GO TO COLLEGE

The Americans with Disabilities Act (ADA) requires educational institutions at all levels, public and private, to provide equal access to programs, services, and facilities. Schools must be accessible to students, as well as to employees and the public, regardless of any disability. To ensure such accessibility, they must follow specific requirements for new construction, alterations or renovations, academic programs, and institutional policies, practices, and procedures. Students with specific disabilities have the right to request and expect accommodations, including auxiliary aids and services that enable them to participate in and benefit from all programs and activities offered by or related to a school.

To comply with ADA requirements, many high schools and universities offer programs and information to answer questions for students with disabilities and to assist them both in selecting appropriate colleges and in attaining full inclusion once they enter college. And most colleges and universities have disabilities services offices to help students negotiate the system. When it comes time to apply to colleges, write to the ones that you're interested in to find out what kinds of programs they have in place. When it comes time to narrow down your choices, make a request for a visit.

What is Considered a Disability?

A person is considered to have a disability if he or she meets at least one of three conditions. The individual must:

1. have a documented physical or mental impairment that substantially limits one or more major life activities, such as personal self-care, walking, seeing, hearing, speaking, breathing, learning, working, or performing manual tasks;

2. have a record of such an impairment; or

3. be perceived as having such an impairment.

Physical disabilities include impairments of speech, vision, hearing, and mobility. Other disabilities, while less obvious, are similarly limiting; they include diabetes, asthma, multiple sclerosis, heart disease, cancer, mental illness, mental retardation, cerebral palsy, and learning disabilities.

Learning disabilities refer to an array of biological conditions that impede a person's ability to process and disseminate information. A learning disability is commonly recognized as a significant deficiency in

DIRECTORY FOR STUDENTS WITH DISABILITIES

The following resources can help students, families, and schools with the legal requirements for accommodating disabilities. They can also link you with other groups and individuals that are knowledgeable in students' rights and the process of transition into postsecondary education.

Also, there are special interest, education, support, and advocacy organizations for persons with particular disabilities. Check with your counselor or contact one of the following organizations for information:

ACTAssessment Administration

Special Testing
P.O. Box 4028
Iowa City, Iowa 52243
319-337-1332
www.act.org

Association on Higher Education and Disability (AHEAD)

University of Massachusetts Boston
100 Morrissey Boulevard
Boston, Massachusetts 02125-3393
617-287-3880
www.ahead.org

Attention Deficit Disorder Association (ADDA)

1788 Second Street, Suite 200
Highland Park, Illinois 60035
847-432-ADDA
www.add.org

Children and Adults with Attention Deficit Disorders (CHADD)

8181 Professional Place, Suite 201
Landover, Maryland 20785
800-233-4050 (toll-free)
www.chadd.org

ERIC Clearing House on Disabilities and Gifted Children

1110 North Glebe Road
Arlington, Virginia 22201-5704
800-328-0272 (toll-free)

Council for Learning Disabilities (CLD)

P.O. Box 40303
Overland Park, Kansas 66204
913-492-8755

HEATH Resource Center National Clearinghouse on Postsecondary Education for Individuals with Disabilities

American Council on Education
One Dupont Circle, NW, Suite 800
Washington, D.C. 20036
800-544-3284 (toll-free)
www.heath-resource-center.org

International Dyslexia Association The Chester Building

8600 LaSalle Road, Suite 382
Baltimore, Maryland 21286-2044
800-222-3123 (toll-free)
www.interdys.org

Learning Disabilities Association of America, Inc. (LDA)

4156 Library Road
Pittsburgh, Pennsylvania 15234-1349
412-341-1515
www.ldanatl.org

Learning Disabilities Association of Canada (LDAC)

323 Chapel Street, Suite 200
Ottawa, Ontario K1N 7Z2
613-238-5721
www.ldac-taac.ca

National Center for Law and Learning Disabilities (NCLLD)

P.O. Box 368
Cabin John, Maryland 20818
301-469-8308

National Center for Learning Disabilities (NCLD)

381 Park Avenue South, Suite 1401
New York, New York 10016
888-575-7373 (toll-free)
www.ncld.org

National Information Center for Children and Youth with Disabilities

P.O. Box 1492
Washington, D.C. 20013
800-695-0285 (toll-free)
www.nichcy.org

Recording for the Blind & Dyslexic

20 Roszel Road
Princeton, New Jersey 08540
609-452-0606
www.rfbd.org

SAT Services for Students with Disabilities

The College Board
P.O. Box 6226
Princeton, New Jersey 08541-6226
609-771-7137
www.collegeboard.com

TIPS FOR STUDENTS WITH DISABILITIES

- **Document your disability with letters from your physician(s), therapist, case manager, school psychologist, and other service providers.**

- **Get letters of support from teachers, family, friends, and service providers that detail how you have learned to work despite your disability.**

- **Learn the federal laws that apply to students with disabilities.**

- **Research support groups for peer information and advocacy.**

- **Visit several campuses.**

- **Determine the best point in the admissions process at which to identify yourself as having a disability.**

- **Look into the services available, the pace of campus life, and the college's expectations for students with disabilities.**

- **Ask about orientation programs, including specialized introductions for or about students with disabilities.**

- **Ask about flexible, individualized study plans.**

- **Ask if the school offers technology such as voice synthesizers, voice recognition, and/or visual learning equipment to its students.**

- **Ask about adapted intramural/social activities.**

- **Ask to talk with students who have similar disabilities to hear about their experiences on campus.**

- **Once you select a college, get a map of the campus and learn the entire layout.**

- **If you have a physical disability, make sure the buildings you need to be in are accessible to you. Some, even though they comply with the ADA, aren't as accessible as others.**

- **Be realistic. If you use a wheelchair, for example, a school with an exceptionally hilly campus may not be your best choice, no matter what other accommodations it has.**

one or more of the following areas: oral expression, listening comprehension, written expression, basic reading skills, reading comprehension, mathematical calculation, or problem solving. Individuals with learning disabilities also may have difficulty with sustained attention, time management, or social skills.

If you have a disability, you will take the same steps to choose and apply to a college as other students, but you should also evaluate each college based on your special need(s). Get organized, and meet with campus specialists to discuss your specific requirements. Then, explore whether the programs, policies, procedures, and facilities meet your specific situation.

It is usually best to describe your disability in a letter attached to the application so the proper fit can be made between you and the school. You may even want to have your psychoeducational evaluation and testing record sent to the school. Some colleges help with schedules and offer transition courses, reduced course loads, extra access to professors, and special study areas to help address your needs.

Remember, admission to college is a realistic goal for any motivated student. If you invest the time and effort, you can make it happen.

STUDENT COUNSEL

The following quotes are from students who attend a college that offers services for learning disabled students.

"I have delayed development. I need help getting things done, and I need extra time for tests. As long as I'm able to go up to teachers and ask questions, I do well on tests."

—**Anita**

"I have dyslexia. I thought the term 'disabilities services' was for people with visual and hearing impairments. But when I got here, I found it covered a variety of disabilities. It was like Christmas. You got everything you wanted and more."

—**Debra**

"I am hard of hearing. I was always afraid I wouldn't be able to hear what [teachers] said. It's hard to read lips and listen at the same time. With note takers, I still get what I need even if the teacher moves around. They want you to make it through."

—**Jeannette**

APPLYING TO COLLEGE

The big moment has arrived. It's time to make some decisions about where you want to apply.

ONCE THAT LIST IS FINALIZED, the worst part is filling out all the forms accurately and getting them in by the deadlines. Because requirements differ, you should check with all the colleges that you are interested in attending to find out what the specific requirements are at those schools.

WHAT SCHOOLS LOOK FOR IN PROSPECTIVE STUDENTS

As if you were sizing up the other team to plan your game strategy, understand what admissions committees want from you as you assemble all the pieces of your application.

Academic record: Admission representatives look at the breadth (how many), diversity (which ones), and difficulty (how challenging) of the courses on your transcript.

Grades: You should show consistency in your ability to work to your potential. If your grades are not initially good, colleges look to see that significant improvement has been made. Some colleges have minimum grade point averages that they are willing to accept.

Class rank: Colleges consider the academic standing of a student in relation to the other members of his or her class. Are you in the top 25 percent of your class? Top half? Ask your counselor for your class rank.

Standardized test scores: Colleges look at test scores in terms of ranges. If your scores aren't high but you did well academically in high school, you shouldn't be discouraged. There is no set formula for admission. Even at the most competitive schools, some students' test scores are lower than you would think.

Out-of-class activities: Colleges look for depth of involvement (variety and how long you participated), initiative (leadership), and creativity demonstrated in activities, service, or work.

Recommendations: Most colleges require a recommendation from your high school guidance counselor. Some ask for references from teachers or other adults. If your counselor or teachers don't know you well, you should put together a student resume, or

PARENT PERSPECTIVE

Q: How did you help your daughter get into college?

A: The key is to start early, like in the junior year. We didn't do that. At this point in the fall of our daughter's senior year, deadlines are coming up, and we haven't really looked at any colleges yet or gone on visits. It's kind of like choosing a house to buy without going to the house. The parent's role is to ask a lot of questions to get your child to figure out exactly what it is he or she wants to do. It's a big decision.

We hired a financial aid consultant who is helping us look at different colleges. The biggest worry is the FAFSA form. If you get it wrong, and they send it back to you—you have to start all over again. In the meantime, you're behind and others are getting grants. The whole process is very confusing, and there's no one to walk you through it. We've looked at different colleges on the Internet, and college fairs are a good resource. Plus, our daughter has done a lot on her own.

Doug and Judy Ames
Colorado Springs, Colorado

Q: What can parents do to help their children make decisions about colleges?

A: Parents and teens should visit college campuses early and trust their gut feelings about whether the campus feels right. Above all, don't be blinded by name-brand colleges and the strong peer pressure that seems to steer your teen in the direction of prestigious colleges. Just as in shopping for clothing: Would you rather have a name brand or something that fits you well and makes you feel comfortable?

Ask your teen some questions. Do you really want to live in a pressure-cooker for the next four years? Some students thrive in a highly competitive environment, but many do not—even if they are excellent students. Before making a final decision, a teen should spend three or four days at the two colleges that interest him or her the most.

Senior year in high school is a time when teens go through many changes and experiment with many different roles. This can be bewildering to parents. Be patient. Realize that the time is equally bewildering to your son or daughter. Parents can be supportive and understanding, even though their teen may seem to be pushing them away. Offer guidance about choosing the right college, even though your teen might seem to be rejecting it. Teens hear everything, though they might not show it.

Marilyn Wedge, Ph.D.

Parent, family therapist, and educational consultant

Agoura Hills, California

brag sheet, that outlines what you have done during your four years of high school. In this section, you'll find a worksheet that will help you put together your resume.

College interview: Required by most colleges with highly selective procedures. For further information, see "The College Interview" in the previous section.

ADMISSION PROCEDURES

Your first task in applying is to get application forms. That's easy. You can get them from your high school's guidance department, at college fairs, or by calling or writing to colleges and requesting applications. (See "Writing to a College for Information" in the previous section.) The trend, however, is leaning toward online applications, which you can do at the school's Web site. Admission information can also be gathered from college representatives, catalogs, Web sites, and directories; alumni or students attending the college; and campus visits. Take a look at "Do's and Don'ts for Filling out an Application" on page 51 for some guidelines.

Which Admissions Option Is Best for You?

One of the first questions you will be asked on applications for four-year colleges and universities is which admission option you want. What they're talking about is whether you want to apply early action, early decision, etc.

If you're going to a two-year college, this doesn't apply to you. Two-year colleges usually have an "open-door" admission policy, which means that high school graduates may enroll as long as space is available. Sometimes vo-tech schools are somewhat selective, and competition for admission may be fairly intense for programs that are highly specialized.

Four-year institutions generally offer the following admissions options:

Early admission: A student of superior ability is admitted into college courses and programs before completing high school.

Early decision: A student declares a first-choice college, requests that the college decide on acceptance early (between November and January), and agrees to enroll if accepted. Students with a strong high school record who are sure they want to attend a certain school should consider early decision admission. (See "More on Early Decision," on the next page.)

Early action: Similar to early decision, but if a student is accepted, he or she has until the regular admission deadline to decide whether or not to attend.

Early evaluation: A student can apply under early evaluation to find out if the chance of acceptance is good, fair, or poor. Applications are due before the regular admission deadline, and the student is given an opinion between January and March.

Regular admission: This is the most common option offered to students. A deadline is set when all applications must be received, and all notifications are sent out at the same time.

Rolling admission: The college accepts students who meet the academic requirements on a first-come, first-served basis until it fills its freshman class. No strict application deadline is specified. Applications are reviewed and decisions are made immediately (usually within two to three weeks). This method is commonly used at large state universities, so students should apply early for the best chance of acceptance.

Open admission: Virtually all high school graduates are admitted, regardless of academic qualifications.

Deferred admission: An accepted student is allowed to postpone enrollment for a year.

More on Early Decision

Early decision is a legally binding agreement between you and the college. If the college accepts you, you pay a deposit within a short period of time and sign an agreement stating that you will not apply to other colleges. To keep students from backing out, some colleges mandate that applicants' high school counselors cannot send transcripts to other institutions.

In many ways, early decision is a win-win for both students and colleges. Students can relax and enjoy their senior year of high school without waiting to see if other colleges have accepted them. And colleges know early in the year who is enrolled and can start planning the coming year.

When Is Early Decision the Right Decision?

For good and bad reasons, early decision is a growing trend, so why not just do it? Early decision is an excellent idea that comes with a warning. It's not a good idea unless you have done a thorough college search and know without a shred of doubt that this is the college for you. Don't go for early decision unless you've spent time on the campus, in classes and

dorms, and you have a true sense of the academic and social climate of that college.

Early decision can get sticky if you change your mind. Parents of students who have signed agreements and then want to apply elsewhere get angry at high school counselors, saying they've taken away their rights to choose among colleges. They try to force them to send out transcripts even though their children have committed to one college. To guard against this scenario, some colleges ask parents and students to sign a statement signifying their understanding that early decision is a binding plan. Even some high schools now have their own form for students and parents to sign acknowledging that they completely realize the nature of an early decision agreement.

The Financial Reason Against Early Decision

Another common argument against early decision is that if an institution has you locked in, there's no incentive to offer applicants the best financial packages. The consensus seems to be that if you're looking to play the financial game, don't apply for early decision.

STUDENT COUNSEL

Q: What made you want to apply to college early decision?

A: I visited lots of schools in Pennsylvania, but the minute I walked on the campus at Gettysburg, I knew I wanted to come here. I liked the way the campus was set up. It was small, and everything was together. The student-teacher ratio was low, and it had a good political science program. It had everything that I wanted.

But if you want to go early decision, you have to visit the schools to be able to compare and contrast the different campuses. Many of the schools will have the same things, like small class size, but the way you feel about the campus is the largest factor because that's where you will be living. I visited Gettysburg four times, so when I went early decision, I was confident about it. I realized it was a huge step and knew I had to be sure. But after visiting here so many times, I knew I'd be unhappy anywhere else.

Kelly Keegan
Gettysburg College

However, some folks argue that the best financial aid offers are usually made to attractive applicants. Generally, if a student receives an early decision offer, they fall into that category and so would get "the sweetest" financial aid anyway. That doesn't mean that there aren't colleges out there using financial incentives to get students to enroll. A strong candidate who applies to six or eight schools and gets admitted to them all will look at how much money the colleges throw his or her way before making a decision.

Before You Decide...

If you're thinking about applying for early decision at a college, ask yourself these questions first. You'll be glad you did.

- Why am I applying early decision?

- Have I thoroughly researched several colleges and know what my options are?

- Do I know why I'm going to college and what I want to accomplish there?

- Have I visited several schools, spent time in classes, stayed overnight, and talked to professors?

- Do the courses that the college offers match my goals?

- Am I absolutely convinced that one college clearly stands out above all others?

MORE MUMBO JUMBO

Besides confusing terms like deferred admission, early decision, and early evaluation discussed previously in this section, you'll most likely stumble upon some additional terms that might bamboozle you. Here, we explain a few more:

Academic Calendar

Traditional semesters: Two equal periods of time during a school year.

Early semester: Two equal periods of time during a school year. The first semester is completed before Christmas.

Trimester: Calendar year divided into three equal periods of time. The third trimester replaces summer school.

Quarter: Four equal periods of time during a school year.

4-1-4: Two equal terms of about four months separated by a one-month term.

Accreditation

Accreditation is recognition of a college or university by a regional or national organization, which indicates that the institution has met its objectives and is maintaining prescribed educational standards. Colleges may be accredited by one of six regional associations of schools and colleges and by any one of many national specialized accrediting bodies.

Specialized accreditation of individual programs is granted by national professional organizations. This is intended to ensure that specific programs meet or exceed minimum requirements established by the professional organization. States may require that students in some professions that grant licenses graduate from an accredited program as one qualification for licensure.

Accreditation is somewhat like receiving a pass/fail grade. It doesn't differentiate colleges and universities that excel from those that meet minimum requirements. Accreditation applies to all programs within an institution, but it does not mean that all programs are of equal quality within an institution. Accreditation does not guarantee transfer recognition by other colleges. Transfer decisions are made by individual institutions.

Affiliation

Not-for-profit colleges are classified into one of the following categories: state-assisted, private/independent, or private/church-supported. The institution's affiliation does not guarantee the quality or nature of the institution, and it may or may not have an effect on the religious life of students.

State-assisted colleges and universities and private/independent colleges do not have requirements related to the religious activity of their students.

The influence of religion varies among private/church-supported colleges. At some, religious services or study are encouraged or required; at others, religious affiliation is less apparent.

Articulation Agreement

Articulation agreements facilitate the transfer of students and credits among state-assisted institutions of higher education by establishing transfer procedures and equitable treatment of all students in the system.

One type of articulation agreement links two or more colleges so that students can continue to make progress toward their degree, even if they must attend different schools at different times. For example, some states' community colleges have agreements with their universities that permit graduates of college parallel programs to transfer with junior standing.

A second type of articulation agreement links secondary (high school) and postsecondary institutions to allow students to gain college credit for relevant vocational courses. This type of agreement saves students time and tuition in the pursuit of higher learning.

Because articulation agreements vary from school to school and from program to program, it is recommended that students check with their home institution and the institution they are interested in attending in order to fully understand the options available to them and each institution's specific requirements.

Cross-Registration

Cross-registration is a cooperative arrangement offered by many colleges and universities for the purpose of increasing the number and types of courses offered at any one institution. This arrangement allows students to cross-register for one or more courses at any participating host institution. While specific cross-registration program requirements may vary, typically a student can cross-register without having to pay the host institution additional tuition.

If your college participates in cross-registration, check with your home institution concerning any additional tuition costs and request a cross-registration form. Check with your adviser and registrar at your home institution to make sure that the course you plan to take is approved, and then contact the host institution for cross-registration instructions. Make sure that there is space available in the course you want to take at the host institution, as some host institutions give their own students registration priority.

To participate in cross-registration, you may need to be a full-time student (some programs allow part-time student participation) in good academic and financial standing at your home institution. Check with both colleges well in advance for all of the specific requirements.

THE COMPLETE APPLICATION PACKAGE

Freshman applications can be filed any time after you have completed your junior year of high school. Colleges strongly recommend that students apply by April (at the latest) of their senior year in order to be considered for acceptance, scholarships, financial aid, and housing. College requirements may vary, so always read and comply with specific requirements. In general, admission officers are interested in the following basic materials:

- A completed and signed application and any required application fee.

- An official copy of your high school transcript, including your class ranking and grade point average. The transcript must include all work completed as of the date the application is submitted. Check with your guidance counselor for questions about these items. If you apply on line, you must inform your guidance counselor and request that he or she send your transcript to the schools you're applying to. Your application will not be processed without a transcript.

- An official record of your ACT or SAT I scores.

COLLEGE APPLICATION CHECKLIST Keep track of your applications by inserting a check mark or the completion date in the appropriate column and row.

	College 1	College 2	College 3	College 4
Campus visit				
Campus interview				
Letters of recommendation				
NAME:				
Date requested				
Follow-up				
NAME:				
Date requested				
Follow-up				
NAME:				
Date requested				
Follow-up				
Counselor recommendation form to counselor				
Secondary school report form to counselor				
Test scores requested				
Transcripts sent				
Application completed				
Essay completed				
All signatures collected				
Financial aid forms enclosed				
Application fee enclosed				
Postage affixed/copies made/return address on envelope				
Letters of acceptance/denial/wait list received				
Colleges notified of intent				
Tuition deposit sent				
Housing and other forms submitted to chosen college				
Orientation scheduled				

- Other items that may be required include letters of recommendation, an essay, the secondary school report form and midyear school report (sent in by your guidance counselor after you fill out a portion of the form), and any financial aid forms required by the college.

Use the "College Application Checklist" on the previous page to make sure you have everything you need before you send off that application.

Filling out the Forms

Filling out college applications can seem like a daunting task, but there are six easy steps to follow for the successful completion of this part of your college selection process.

Step 1: Practice Copies

Make a photocopy of each college's application that you plan to apply to. Since the presentation of your application may be considered an important aspect in the weighting for admission, you don't want to erase, cross out, or use white-out on your final application. Make all your mistakes on your copies. When you think you have it right, then transfer the information to your final original copy or go on line to enter it on the college's electronic application. If you are mailing in your applications, try to use a word processor. But if you have to type your applications, make the effort to line up your responses in those tiny spaces. Remember, at the larger universities, the application packet may be the only part of you they see.

Step 2: Decide on Your Approach

What is it about your application that will grab the admission counselor's attention so that it will be pulled out of the sea of applications on his or her desk for consideration? Be animated and interesting in what you say. Be memorable in your approach to your application, but don't overdo it. You want the admissions counselor to remember you, not your Spanish castle made of popsicle sticks. Most

DO'S AND DON'TS FOR FILLING OUT YOUR APPLICATIONS

One of the most intimidating steps of applying for admission to college is filling out all the forms. This list of do's and don'ts will help you put your best foot forward on your college applications.

DO

- ☑ **Read applications and directions carefully.**

- ☑ **Make sure that everything that is supposed to be included is enclosed.**

- ☑ **Fill out your own applications. Type the information yourself to avoid crucial mistakes.**

- ☑ **Start with the simple applications and then progress to the more complex ones.**

- ☑ **Make copies of applications, and practice filling one out before you complete the original.**

- ☑ **Type or neatly print your answers, and then proofread the applications and essays several times for accuracy. Also ask someone else to proofread it for you.**

- ☑ **If asked, describe how you can make a contribution to the schools to which you apply.**

- ☑ **Be truthful, and do not exaggerate your accomplishments.**

- ☑ **Keep a copy of all forms you submit to colleges.**

- ☑ **Be thorough and on time.**

DON'T

- ☑ **Use correction fluid. If you type your application, use a correctable typewriter or the liftoff strips to correct mistakes. Better yet, fill out your application on line.**

- ☑ **Write in script. If you don't have access to a computer or typewriter, print neatly.**

- ☑ **Leave blank spaces. Missing information may cause your application to be sent back or delayed while admission officers wait for complete information.**

- ☑ **Be unclear. If the question calls for a specific answer, don't try to dodge it by being vague.**

- ☑ **Put it off! Do it early.**

importantly, be honest and don't exaggerate your academics and extracurricular activities. Approach this process with integrity every step of the way. First of all, it is the best way to end up in a college that is the right match for you. Second, if you are less than truthful, the college will eventually learn about it. How will they know? You have to request that support materials accompany your application, things like transcripts and recommendations. If you tell one story and they tell another, the admissions office will notice the disparity—another red flag!

Step 3: Check the Deadlines

In September of your senior year, organize your applications in chronological order. Place the due dates for your final list of schools next to their names on your stretch, target, and safety list and on your "College Application Checklist." Work on the earliest due date first.

Step 4: Check the Data on You

You need to make sure that the information you will be sending to support your applications is correct. The first thing to double-check is your transcript. This is an important piece because you must send a transcript with each application you send to colleges. Take a trip to the guidance office and ask for a "Transcript Request Form." Fill out the request for a formal transcript indicating that you are requesting a copy for yourself and that you will pick it up. Pay the fee if there is one.

When you get your transcript, look it over carefully. It will be several pages long and will include everything from the titles of all the courses that you have taken since the ninth grade along with the final grade for each course to the community service hours you have logged each year. Check the information carefully. It is understandable that with this much data, it is easy to make an input error. Because this information is vital to you and you are the best judge of accuracy, it is up to you to check it. Take any corrections or questions you have back to your guidance counselor to make the corrections. If it is a

questionable grade, your counselor will help you find out what grade should have been posted on your transcript. Do whatever needs to be done to make sure your transcript has been corrected no later than October 1 of your senior year.

Step 5: List Your Activities

When you flip through your applications, you will find a section on extracurricular activities. It is time to hit your word processor again to prioritize your list of extracurricular activities and determine the best approach for presenting it to your colleges. Some students will prepare a resume and include this in every application they send. Other students will choose to develop an "Extracurricular, Academic, and Work Experience Addendum" and mark those specific sections of their application, "See attached Addendum."

If you are a powerhouse student with a great deal to say in this area, it will take time to prioritize your involvement in activities and word it succinctly yet interestingly. Your "Brag Sheet" will help (see "The Brag Sheet" on page 53). Put those activities that will have the strongest impact, show the most consistent involvement, and demonstrate your leadership abilities at the top of the list. This will take time, so plan accordingly. If you feel you have left out important information because the form limits you, include either an addendum or your resume as a back-up.

Step 6: Organize Your Other Data

What other information can you organize in advance of sitting down to fill out your applications?

The Personal Data Section

Most of this section is standard personal information that you will not have any difficulty responding to, but some items you will need to think about. For example, you may find a question that asks, "What special college or division are you applying to?" Do you have a specific school in mind, like the College of Engineering? If you are not sure about your major, ask yourself what interests you the most and then enter

THE BRAG SHEET

At the beginning of this section, we described how a student resume can help your guidance counselors and teachers write their letters of recommendation for you. Putting together a list of your accomplishments will also help you organize all of the information you will need to include when you fill out your college applications.

ACADEMICS

GPA (Grade Point Average) _____

THE HONORS COURSES I HAVE TAKEN ARE:

English _____

History _____

Math _____

Science _____

Language _____

Electives _____

STANDARDIZED TEST SCORES

PSAT _____

1st SAT I _____

2nd SAT I _____

ACT _____

THE AP COURSES I HAVE TAKEN ARE:

English _____

History _____

Math _____

Science _____

Language _____

Electives _____

SAT II SUBJECT TESTS

Test 1 _____ **Score** _____

Test 2 _____ **Score** _____

Test 3 _____ **Score** _____

SPECIAL TALENTS

I have received the following academic awards:

_____

_____

_____

_____

I have performed in various theatrical productions: _____

I am lettered in the following sports: _____

I have played on the following traveling teams: _____

_____

_____

I am a member of the following musical groups: _____

_____

EXTRACURRICULAR ACTIVITIES

I participate on a regular basis in the following extracurricular activities: _____

I have held the following offices: _____

_____

_____

I have established the following extracurricular organizations:

_____

_____

I have held the following after-school and summer jobs: _____

_____

GOALS

I plan to major in the following area in college: _____

_____

that college. Once you are in college and have a better a sense of what you want to do, you can always change your major later.

The application will provide an optional space to declare ethnicity. If you feel you would like to declare an area and that it would work to your advantage for admission, consider completing this section of the application.

You are also going to need your high school's College Entrance Examination Board (CEEB) number. That is the number you needed when you filled out your test packets. It is stamped on the front of your SAT and ACT packets, or, if you go to the guidance department, they'll tell you what it is.

The Standardized Testing Section

Applications ask you for your test dates and scores. Get them together accurately. All your College Board scores should be recorded on the latest test results you received. Your latest ACT record will only have the current scores unless you asked for all your past test results. If you have lost this information, call these organizations or go to your guidance department. Your counselor should have copies. Be sure the testing organizations are sending your official score reports to the schools to which you're applying. If you are planning to take one of these tests in the future, the colleges will want those dates, too; they will wait for those scores before making a decision. If you change your plans, write the admissions office a note with the new dates or the reason for canceling.

The Senior Course Load Section

Colleges will request that you list your present senior schedule by semester. Set this information up in this order: List any AP or honors-level full-year courses first; these will have the most impact. Then list other required full-year courses and then required semester courses, followed by electives. Make sure you list first-semester and second-semester courses appropriately. Do not forget to include physical education if you are taking it this year.

Your Recommendation Writers

Most schools will require you to submit two or three letters of recommendation from adults who know you well.

Guidance Counselor Recommendations

Nearly all colleges require a letter of recommendation from the applicant's high school guidance counselor. Some counselors will give students an essay question that they feel will give them the background they need in order to structure a recommendation. Other counselors will canvass a wide array of individuals who know a student in order to gather a broader picture of the student in various settings. No one approach is better than the other. Find out which approach is used at your school. You will probably get this information as a handout at one of those evening guidance programs or in a classroom presentation by your school's guidance department. If you are still not sure you know what is expected of you or if the dog has eaten those papers, ask your guidance counselor what is due and by what date. Make sure that you complete the materials on time and that you set aside enough of your time to do them justice.

Teacher Recommendations

In addition to the recommendation from your counselor, colleges may request additional recommendations from your teachers. Known as formal recommendations, these are sent directly to the colleges by your subject teachers. Most colleges require at least one formal recommendation in addition to the counselor's recommendation. However, many competitive institutions require at least two, if not three, academic recommendations. Follow a school's directions regarding the exact number.

Approach your recommendation writers personally to request that they write for you. If they agree, provide them with a copy of your Brag Sheet. On the other hand, you may be met with a polite refusal on the order of "I'm sorry, but I'm unable to write for you. I've been approached by so many seniors already

Chapter 6: Applying to College

that it would be difficult for me to accomplish your recommendation by your due dates." This teacher may really be overburdened with requests for recommendations, especially if this is a senior English teacher, or the teacher may be giving you a signal that someone else may be able to write a stronger piece for you. Either way, accept the refusal politely, and seek another recommendation writer.

How do you decide whom to ask? Here are some questions to help you select your writers:

- How well does the teacher know you?

- Has the teacher taught you for more than one course? (A teacher who taught you over a two- to three-year period has seen your talents and skills develop.)

- Has the teacher sponsored an extracurricular activity in which you made a contribution?

- Do you get along with the teacher?

- Does the college/university indicate that a recommendation is required or recommended from a particular subject-area instructor?

- If you declare an intended major, can you obtain a recommendation from a teacher in that subject area?

TIP: Provide recommendations from two subject areas (e.g., English and math).

Other Recommendation Writers

Consider getting recommendations from your employer, your rabbi or pastor, the director of the summer camp where you worked for the last two summers, and so on—but only if these additional letters are going to reveal information about you that will have a profound impact on the way a college will view your candidacy. Otherwise, you run the risk of overloading your application with too much paper.

Writing the Application Essay

Application essays show how you think and how you write. They also reveal additional information about you that is not in your other application material. Not all colleges require essays, and those that do often have a preferred topic. Make sure you write about the topic that is specified and keep to the length of pages or words. If the essay asks for 300 words, don't submit 50 or 500. Some examples of essay topics include:

Tell us about yourself. Describe your personality and a special accomplishment. Illustrate the unique aspects of who you are, what you do, and what you want out of life. Share an experience that made an impact on you, or write about something you have learned from your parents.

Tell us about an academic or extracurricular interest or idea. Show how a book, experience, quotation, or idea reflects or shapes your outlook and aspirations.

Tell us why you want to come to our college. Explain why your goals and interests match the programs and offerings of that particular school. This question requires some research about the school. Be specific.

Show us an imaginative side of your personality. This question demands originality but is a great opportunity to show off your skills as a writer. Start writing down your thoughts and impressions well before the essay is due. Think about how you have

FROM THE GUIDANCE OFFICE

Q: Why are essays so important to the college application?

A: Students focus more on grades than anything else. They think grades are the be-all and end-all and that an SAT score will get them in. For most selective schools, that's just one piece of the pie. Many of the schools in the upper 20 percent of competitive schools consider the essay more heavily. Essays show whether the student is a thinker, creative, and analytical. They're looking for the type of personality that can shine rather than one that simply can spit out names and dates. When everyone has high SATs in a pool of applicants, the essay is what makes one student stand out over another.

Patsy Lovelady
Counselor
MacArthur High School
San Antonio, Texas

GET A JUMP

www.petersons.com   55

changed over the years so that if and when it comes time to write about yourself, you will have plenty of information. Write about something that means a lot to you, and support your thoughts with reasons and examples. Then explain why you care about your topic.

The essay should not be a summary of your high school career. Describe yourself as others see you, and use a natural, conversational style. Use an experience to set the scene in which you will illustrate something about yourself. For example, you might discuss how having a disabled relative helped you to appreciate life's simple pleasures. Or you may use your athletic experiences to tell how you learned the value of teamwork. The essay is your chance to tell something positive or enriching about yourself, so highlight an experience that will make the reader interested in you.

Outline in the essay what you have to offer the college. Explain why you want to attend the institution and how your abilities and goals match the strengths and offerings at the university. Write, rewrite, and edit. Do not try to dash off an essay in one sitting. The essay will improve with time and thought. Proofread and concentrate on spelling, punctuation, and content. Have someone else take a look at your essay. Make copies and save them after mailing the original.

Admission officers look for the person inside the essay. They seek students with a breadth of knowledge and experiences, someone with depth and perspective. Inner strength and commitment are admired, too. Not everyone is a winner all the time. The essay is a tool you can use to develop your competitive edge. Your essay should explain why you should be admitted over other applicants.

As a final word, write the essay from the heart. It should have life and not be contrived or one-dimensional. Avoid telling them what they want to hear; instead, be yourself.

SAMPLE APPLICATION ESSAY

Here is one student's college application essay. She answered the question, "Indicate a person who has had a significant influence on you, and describe that influence."

Mrs. Morrone did not become my guidance counselor until my sophomore year of high school. During my first meeting with her, I sat across from her in an uncomfortable vinyl chair and refused to meet her eyes as I told her about my long and painful shyness, how I detested oral reports, and how I feared raising my hand in class or being called on to answer a question—all because I didn't want to be the center of attention.

She did not offer me advice right away. Instead, she asked me more about myself—my family, my friends, what kinds of music, books, and movies I liked. We talked easily, like old friends, and it was not long before I began to look forward to our weekly meetings. Her office was one of the few places where I felt like I could be myself and let my personality shine through, where I knew that I was accepted and liked unconditionally.

In November of that year, the drama club announced auditions for the spring play, The Glass Menagerie. I had studied it in English class and it was one of my favorites; not surprisingly, I identified strongly with the timid Laura. I talked with Mrs. Morrone about the play and how much I liked theater. At one point I sighed, "I'd love to play Laura."

"Why don't you try out for the show?" Mrs. Morrone suggested.

The very idea of performing, onstage, in a spotlight, in front of dozens of people frightened me. She did not press the matter, but at the end of the session she encouraged me to bring a copy of the play to our next few meetings and read some of the character's lines, "just for fun." I did, and found myself gradually transforming into Laura as I recited her lines with increasing intensity.

After a couple of these amateur performances, she told me that I was genuinely good as Laura, and she would love to see me at least audition for the part. "I would never force you to do it," she said, "but I would hate to see you waste your potential." I insisted that I was too frightened, but she promised that she would come and watch my audition. She told me to pretend she was the only person in the audience.

A week later, I did read for the part of Laura. Mrs. Morrone beamed with pride in the back of the auditorium. I discovered that I truly enjoyed acting; slipping into another character cracked the shell that I had built around myself. I did not get the part, but I had found a passion that enriched my life in immeasurable ways. I owe Mrs. Morrone so much for putting me on the path to becoming a professional actress and for helping me to finally conquer my shyness. Without her quiet support and strength, none of this would have come to pass.

SPECIAL INFORMATION FOR ATHLETES

If you weren't a planner before, but you want to play sports while in college or go to college on an athletic scholarship, you'd better become a planner now. There are many regulations and conditions you need to know ahead of time so that you don't miss out on possible opportunities.

First, think about whether or not you have what it takes to play college sports. It's a tough question to ask, but it's a necessary one. In general, playing college sports requires the basic skills and natural ability, a solid knowledge of the sport, overall body strength, speed, and sound academics. Today's athletes are stronger and faster because of improved methods of training and conditioning. They are coached in skills and techniques, and they begin training in their sport at an early age. Remember, your talents will be compared with those from across the U.S. and around the world.

Second, know the background. Most college athletic programs are regulated by the National Collegiate Athletic Association (NCAA), an organization that has established rules on eligibility, recruiting, and financial aid. The NCAA has three membership divisions: Division I, Division II, and Division III. Institutions are members of one or another division according to the size and scope of their athletic programs and whether they provide athletic scholarships.

If you are planning to enroll in college as a freshman and you wish to participate in Division I or Division II athletics, you must be certified by the NCAA Initial-Eligibility Clearinghouse. The Clearinghouse was established as a separate organization by the NCAA member institutions to ensure consistent interpretation of NCAA initial-eligibility requirements for all prospective student athletes at all member institutions.

You should start the certification process when you are a junior in high school. Check with your counselor to make sure you are taking a core curriculum that meets NCAA requirements. Also, register to take the ACT or SAT I as a junior. Submit your Student Release Form (available in your

guidance counseling office) to the Clearinghouse by the beginning of your senior year.

Initial Eligibility of Freshman Athletes for Division I and II

Students who plan to participate in NCAA Division I or II college sports must obtain the Student Release Form from their high school, complete it, and send it to the NCAA Clearinghouse. This form authorizes high schools to release student transcripts, including test scores, proof of grades, and other academic information, to the Clearinghouse. It also authorizes the Clearinghouse to release this information to the colleges that request it. The form and corresponding fee must be received before any documents will be processed. (Fee waivers are available for economically disadvantaged students. Check with your counselor for fee waiver information.)

Students must also make sure that the Clearinghouse receives ACT and/or SAT I score reports. Students can have score reports sent directly to the Clearinghouse by entering a specific code (9999) printed in the ACT and SAT I registration packets.

Once a year, high schools will send an updated Form 48-H, which lists each course offering that meets NCAA core course requirements. The Clearinghouse personnel will validate the form.

ATHLETIC RESUME

Name _____

Address _____

_____

High school address and phone number

_____

_____

_____

Coach's name _____

Height/weight _____

Foot speed (by specific event) _____

Position played _____

Weight classification _____

GPA _____

Class rank _____

ACT or SAT I scores (or when you plan to take them)

_____

Athletic records _____

_____

All-state teams _____

Special awards _____

Off-season accomplishments _____

Weightlifting exercises _____

Vertical jumps _____

Push-ups _____

Bench jumps _____

Shuttle run _____

Leadership characteristics _____

Former successful athletes from your high school

_____

Outstanding capabilities _____

Citizenship _____

Alumni parents/relatives _____

Include the following with your resume:

- **Team schedule with dates and times**
- **Videotape with jersey number identified**
- **Newspaper clippings about you or your team**

Thereafter, the Clearinghouse will determine each student's initial eligibility. Collegiate institutions will request information from the Clearinghouse on the initial eligibility of prospective student-athletes. The Clearinghouse will make a certification decision and report it directly to the institution.

Three types of eligibility are possible

1. Certification of eligibility for expense-paid campus visits.

2. Preliminary certification of eligibility to participate in college sports (appears likely to meet all NCAA requirements but not yet graduated).

3. Final certification granted when proof of graduation is received.

Additional information about the Clearinghouse can be found in the *Guide for the College-Bound Student-Athlete*, published by the NCAA. To get a copy of this guide, call 800-638-3731 (toll-free).

You can also visit the NCAA Web site at www.ncaa.org.

National Association of Intercollegiate Athletics (NAIA) Regulations

The National Association of Intercollegiate Athletics (NAIA) has different eligibility requirements for student-athletes. To be eligible to participate in intercollegiate athletics as an incoming freshman, two of the following three requirements must be met:

1. Have a 2.0 (C) or higher cumulative final grade point average in high school.

2. Have a composite score of 18 or higher on the ACT or an 860 total score or higher on the SAT I on a single test administered on a national test date.

3. Have a top-half final class rank in his or her high school graduating class.

Student-athletes must also have on file at the college an official ACT or SAT I score report from the appropriate national testing center. Results reported on the student's high school transcript are not acceptable. Students must request that their test scores be forwarded to the college's admission office.

If you have additional questions about NAIA eligibility, write to:

NAIA
6120 South Yale Avenue
Suite 1450
Tulsa, Oklahoma 74136
Telephone: 918-494-8828
Or visit their Web site at *www.naia.org*

AUDITIONS AND PORTFOLIOS

If you decide to study the arts, such as theater, music, or fine arts, you may be required to audition or show your portfolio to admissions personnel. The following tips will help you showcase your talents and skills when preparing for an audition or portfolio review.

Music Auditions

High school students who wish to pursue a degree in music, whether it is vocal or instrumental, typically must audition. If you're a singer, prepare at least two pieces in contrasting styles. One should be in a foreign language, if possible. Choose from operatic, show music, or art song repertories, and make sure you memorize each piece. If you're an instrumentalist or pianist, be prepared to play scales and arpeggios, at least one etude or technical study, and a solo work. Instrumental audition pieces need not be memorized. In either field, you may be required to do sight-reading.

When performing music that is sight-read, you should take time to look over the piece and make certain of the key and time signatures before proceeding with the audition. If you're a singer, you should bring a familiar accompanist to the audition.

"My advice is to ask for help from teachers, try to acquire audition information up front, and know more than is required for the audition," says one student. "It is also a good idea to select your audition time and date early."

"Try to perform your solo in front of as many people as you can as many times as possible," says another student. "You may also want to try to get involved in a high school performance."

Programs differ, so students are encouraged to call the college and ask for audition information. In general, music departments seek students who demonstrate technical competence and performance achievement.

Admission to music programs varies in degree of competitiveness, so you should audition at a minimum of three colleges and a maximum of five to amplify your opportunity. The degree of competitiveness varies also by instrument, especially if a renowned musician teaches a certain instrument. Some colleges offer a second audition if you feel you did not audition to your potential. Ideally, you will be accepted into the music program of your choice, but keep in mind that it's possible to not be accepted. You must then make the decision to either pursue a music program at another college or consider another major at that college.

Dance Auditions

At many four-year colleges, an open class is held the day before auditions. A performance piece that combines improvisation, ballet, modern, and rhythm is taught and then students are expected to perform the piece at auditions. Professors look for coordination, technique, rhythm, degree of movement, and body structure. The dance faculty members also assess your ability to learn and your potential to complete the curriculum. Dance programs vary, so check with the college of your choice for specific information.

STUDENT COUNSEL

Q: What's it like going to an art school?

A: This is not your normal college experience. You totally immerse yourself in art and commit all your time to it. It's intense and can be stressful. The teachers are great. Most are working professionals. The student body is impressive. I have people in my class who are 35 and have gone to a regular college.

Coming from high school, it's hard to get into an art school. You're disadvantaged because you haven't worked. I suggest going to the portfolio days in high school where schools will evaluate your portfolio and you can get an idea of where you want to go. Since my sophomore year in high school, I kept in touch with the admissions person I talked to at portfolio day. She followed me along and saw my interest.

Eric Davidson
Art Center
Pasadena, California

Art Portfolios

A portfolio is simply a collection of your best pieces of artwork. The pieces you select to put in your portfolio should demonstrate your interest and aptitude for a serious education in the arts. A well-developed portfolio can help you gain acceptance into a prestigious art college and increase your chances of being awarded a scholarship in national portfolio competitions. The pieces you select should show diversity in technique and variety in subject matter. You may show work in any medium (oils, photography, watercolors, pastels, etc.) and in either black-and-white or color. Your portfolio can include classroom assignments as well as independent projects. You can also include your sketchbook.

Specialized art colleges request that you submit an average of ten pieces of art, but remember that quality is more important than quantity. The admission office staff will review your artwork and transcripts to assess your skill and potential for success. Usually, you will present your portfolio in person; however, some schools allow students to mail slides if distance is an issue. There is no simple formula for success other than hard work. In addition, there is no such thing as a "perfect portfolio," nor any specific style or direction to achieve one.

Tips to Pull Your Portfolio Together:

- Try to make your portfolio as clean and organized as possible.

- It is important to protect your work, but make sure the package you select is easy to handle and does not interfere with the viewing of the artwork.

- Drawings that have been rolled up are difficult for the jurors to handle and view. You may shrink-wrap the pieces, but it is not required.

- Avoid loose sheets of paper between pieces.

- If you choose to mount or mat your work (not required), use only neutral gray tones, black, or white.

- Never include framed pieces or three smudge.

- A slide portfolio should be presented in a standard 8 × 11 plastic slide sleeve, which can be purchased at any photo or camera supply store.

- Be sure paintings are completely dry before you place them in your portfolio.

- Label each piece with your name, address, and high school.

Theater Auditions

Most liberal arts colleges do not require that students who audition be accepted into the theater department unless the college offers a Bachelor of Fine Arts (B.F.A.) degree in theater. You should apply to the college of your choice prior to scheduling an audition. You should also consider spending a full day on campus so that you may talk with theater faculty members and students, attend classes, meet with your admission counselor, and tour the facilities.

Although each college and university has different requirements, you should prepare two contrasting monologues taken from plays of your choice if you're auditioning for a B.F.A. acting program. The total length of both pieces should not exceed 5 minutes, and you should take a theater resume and photo to the audition with you.

Musical theater requirements generally consist of one up-tempo musical selection and one ballad as well as one monologue from a play or musical of your choice. The total of all your pieces should not exceed 5 minutes. Music for the accompanist, a resume of your theater experience, and a photo are also required.

Tips to Get You Successfully through an Audition:

- Choose material suitable for your age.

- If you choose your monologue from a book of monologues, you should read the entire play and be familiar with the context of your selection.

- Select a monologue that allows you to speak directly to another person; you should play only one character.

- Memorize your selection.

- Avoid using characterization or style, as they tend to trap you rather than tapping deeper into inner resources.

Chapter 7

FINANCIAL AID DOLLARS AND SENSE

Getting financial aid can be intimidating—but don't let that stop you.

IT'S COMPLICATED, and there are a lot of pieces to this puzzle. Leave a few out or put too many in, and the puzzle doesn't come out right. However, if you look at each piece separately rather than trying to understand the whole process all at once, it will be much easier to absorb. The trick is to start early, be organized, and plan ahead.

Finding the money you need to attend a two- or four-year institution or vocational or trade school is a challenge, but you can do it if you devise a strategy well before you actually start applying to college. Financial aid comes from a lot of different sources. But this is where GAJ comes in. You'll find lots of help here to locate those sources and find out where to get advice. Financial aid is available to help meet both direct educational costs (tuition, fees, books) and personal living expenses (food, housing, transportation).

PROJECTED COLLEGE EXPENSES

The following chart estimates the cost of one year of college education, including tuition, room, and board. Estimates are based on a 6 percent annual increase.

School Year	Public 4-Year	Private 4-Year
2002–2003	$12,712	$27,289
2006–2007	15,452	33,291
2010–2011	18,782	40,466
2014–2015	22,829	49,186

Source: The College Entrance Examination Board

Times have changed to favor the student in the financial aid process. Because the pool of potential traditional college students has diminished, colleges and universities are competing among themselves to attract good students. In fact, some colleges and universities no longer use financial aid primarily as a method to help students fund their college education but rather as a marketing and recruitment tool. This puts students and families at an advantage, one that should be recognized and used for bargaining power.

It used to be that colleges and universities offered need-based and merit-based financial aid to only needy and/or academically exceptional students. Now some schools offer what might be called incentive or discount aid to encourage students to choose them over another college. This aid, which is not necessarily based on need or merit, is aimed at students who meet the standards of the college but who wouldn't necessarily qualify for traditional kinds of aid.

A BIRD'S-EYE VIEW OF FINANCIAL AID

You and your family should be assertive in negotiating financial aid packages. It used to be that there was no room for such negotiation, but in today's environment, it is wise to be a comparison shopper. Families should wait until they've received all of their financial offers and then talk to their first-choice college to see if the college can match the better offers from other colleges.

To be eligible to receive federal/state financial aid, you must maintain satisfactory academic progress

FINANCIAL AID GLOSSARY

ASSETS. The amount a family has in savings and investments. This includes savings and checking accounts, a business, a farm or other real estate, and stocks, bonds, and trust funds. Cars are not considered assets, nor are such possessions as stamp collections or jewelry. The net value of the principal home is counted as an asset by some colleges in determining their own awards but is not included in the calculation for eligibility for federal funds.

CITIZENSHIP/ELIGIBILITY FOR AID. To be eligible to receive federally funded college aid, a student must be one of the following:

1. A United States citizen

2. A non-citizen national

3. A permanent resident with an I-151 or I-551 without conditions

4. A participant in a suspension of deportation case pending before Congress

5. A holder of an I-94 showing one of the following designations: "Refugee," "Asylum Granted," "Indefinite Parole" and/or "Humanitarian Parole," "Cuban/Haitian Entrant, Status Pending," or "Conditional Entrant" (valid if issued before April 1, 1980).

Individuals in the U.S. on an F1 or F2 visa only or on a J1 or J2 exchange visa only cannot get federal aid.

COOPERATIVE EDUCATION. A program offered by many colleges in which students alternate periods of enrollment with periods of employment, usually paid, and that can lengthen the usual baccalaureate program to five years.

EXPECTED FAMILY CONTRIBUTION (EFC) OR PARENTAL CONTRIBUTION. A figure determined by a congressionally mandated formula that indicates how much of a family's resources should be considered "available" for college expenses. Factors such as taxable and nontaxable income and the value of family assets are taken into account to determine a family's financial strength. Allowances for maintaining a family and future financial needs are then taken into consideration before determining how much a family should be able to put toward the cost of college.

INDEPENDENT STUDENT. A student who reports only his or her own income (and that of a spouse, if relevant) when applying for federal financial aid. Students who will be 24 or older by December 31, 2002, will automatically be considered "independent" for 2002–2003. Students who are under 24 will be considered independent if they are:

- married and not claimed as a dependent on their parents' 2002 federal income tax return

- the supporter of a legal dependent other than a spouse

- a veteran of the U.S. Armed Forces

- an orphan or ward of the court

- classified as independent by a college's financial aid administrator because of other unusual circumstances

- a graduate or professional student

MERIT-BASED AID. Any form of financial aid awarded on the basis of personal achievement or individual characteristics without reference to financial need.

SUBSIDIZED LOAN. A loan for which the borrower is not responsible for all of the interest payments. For Subsidized Federal Stafford and/or Direct Loans, the government pays interest to the lender on behalf of the borrower while the student is in college and during approved grace periods.

toward a degree or certificate. This criterion is established by each college or university. You'll also need a valid social security number, and all male students must register for selective service on their eighteenth birthday.

Once you apply for federal aid, your application will be processed in approximately four weeks (one week if applying electronically). You'll then receive a Student Aid Report (SAR) in the mail, which will report the information from your application and your expected family contribution (EFC—the number used in determining your eligibility for federal student aid). Each school you listed on the application will also receive your application information.

You must reapply for federal aid every year. Also, if you change schools, your aid doesn't necessarily go with you. Check with your new school to find out what steps you must take to continue receiving aid.

Once you've decided to which schools you want to apply, talk to the financial aid officers of those schools. There is no substitute for getting information from the source when it comes to understanding your financial aid options. That personal contact can lead you to substantial amounts of financial aid.

If you qualify, don't let the sticker price of the college or program scare you away, because you may get enough outside money to pay for the education you want. Don't rule out a private institution until you have received the financial aid package from the school. Private colleges, in order to attract students from all income levels, offer significant amounts of financial aid. Public-supported institutions tend to offer less financial aid because the lower tuition acts as a form of assistance (see "Projected College Expenses"). In addition, students attending school in their home state often have more aid possibilities than if they attend an out-of-state college. Use the "College Funds Available" chart to determine how much you and your family can contribute to your education and the "College Cost Comparison" table to figure out which schools best suit you financially.

COLLEGE FUNDS AVAILABLE

Use this chart to estimate your family's resources that will be available for college expenses. Check your progress at the end of your sophomore and junior years to see if your plans for seeking financial aid need to be revised.

	Estimated amount available	Actual amount: 11 grade	Actual amount: 12th grade
YOUR RESOURCES			
Savings and other assets			
Summer earnings			
Part-time work during school year			
Miscellaneous			
PARENTS' RESOURCES			
From their current income			
From college savings			
Miscellaneous (insurance, annuities, stocks, trusts, home equity, property assets)			
TOTAL			

Source: American College Testing Program

TYPES OF FINANCIAL AID

Be sure that you understand the differences between the types of financial aid so you are fully prepared to apply for each. One or more of these financial resources may make it possible to pursue the education you want.

Grants: Grants are given for athletics (Division I only), academics, demographics, special talent potential, and/or need. Repayment is not required.

Scholarships: Scholarships, also called "merit aid," are awarded for academic excellence. Repayment is not required.

Loans: Student loans, which have lower interest rates, may be college sponsored or federally sponsored or may be available through commercial financial institutions. Loans must be repaid, generally after you have graduated or left school.

College work-study: College work-study is a federally sponsored program that enables colleges to hire students for employment. If eligible, students work a limited number of hours throughout the school year. Many private colleges offer forms of self-help employment aid as their own supplement to the diminishing supply of federally funded work-study.

FEDERAL FINANCIAL AID PROGRAMS

A number of sources of financial aid are available to students from the federal government, state governments, private lenders, foundations and private agencies, and the colleges and universities themselves. In addition, as discussed earlier, there are four different forms of aid: grants, scholarships, loans, and work-study.

COLLEGE COST COMPARISON WORKSHEET

Chart your course to see which college or university best fits your financial resources. Your totals in expenses and funds available should be the same amount. If not, you have a funding gap, meaning that you have more expenses than funds available and will need to take out a loan (most likely), or vice versa (less likely).

EXPENSES	College 1	College 2	College 3	College 4
Tuition and fees	$	$	$	$
Books and supplies	$	$	$	$
Room and board	$	$	$	$
Transportation	$	$	$	$
Miscellaneous	$	$	$	$
TOTAL	$	$	$	$
FUNDS AVAILABLE				
Student and parent contributions	$	$	$	$
Grants	$	$	$	$
Scholarships	$	$	$	$
Work-study	$	$	$	$
TOTAL	$	$	$	$
Funding gap	$	$	$	$

The federal government is the single largest source of financial aid for students, making more than an estimated $60 billion available in loans, grants, and other aid to millions of students. Following are listings of federal financial aid programs available to you.

FEDERAL GRANTS

The federal government offers a number of educational grants, which are outlined below:

Federal Pell Grant

The Federal Pell Grant is the largest grant program in the nation; about 4 million students receive awards annually. This grant is intended to be the base or starting point of assistance for lower-income families. Eligibility for a Federal Pell Grant depends on the EFC, or Expected Family Contribution. (See the "Financial Aid Glossary" for a description of commonly used terms.) The amount you receive will depend on your EFC, the cost of education at the college or university you attend, and whether you attend full-time or part-time. The highest award depends on how much the program is funded. The maximum for the 2002–2003 school year was $4,000. How much you get will depend not only on your financial need but also on your cost of attending school, whether you're a full-time or part-time student, and whether you attend school for a full academic year or less.

Note that the actual maximum for each of these academic years will be determined by the amount Congress appropriates for the program. Historically, the amount appropriated has resulted in maximum awards that are greater than the awards in previous years but less than the authorized award.

Federal Supplemental Educational Opportunity Grant

As its name implies, the Federal Supplemental Educational Opportunity Grant (FSEOG) provides additional need-based federal grant money to supplement the Federal Pell Grant. Each participating college is given funds to award to especially needy students. The maximum award is $4,000 per year, but the amount a student receives depends on the college's policy, the availability of FSEOG funds, the total cost of education, and the amount of other aid awarded.

Federal Scholarships

The following comprise the scholarships available through the federal government:

ROTC Scholarships

The Armed Forces (Army, Air Force, Navy, Marines) may offer up to a four-year scholarship that pays full college tuition plus a monthly allowance; however, these scholarships are very competitive and based upon GPA, class rank, ACT or SAT scores, and physical qualifications. Apply as soon as possible before December 1 of your senior year. Contact the headquarters of each of the armed forces for more information: Army, 800-USA-ROTC; Air Force, 800-423-USAF; Navy, 800-USA-NAVY; Marines, 800-MARINES (all numbers are toll-free).

Scholarships from Federal Agencies

Federal agencies, such as the CIA, NASA, Department of Agriculture, and Office of Naval Research, offer an annual stipend as well as a scholarship. In return, the student must work for the agency for a certain number of years or else repay all the financial support. See your counselor for more information.

Robert C. Byrd Honors Scholarship

To qualify for this scholarship, you must demonstrate outstanding academic achievement and excellence in high school as indicated by class rank, high school grades, test scores, and leadership activities. Award amounts of $1,500 are renewable for four years. Contact your high school counselor for application information. Deadlines may vary per state, so contact your state's Department of Education.

National Science Scholars Program (NSSP)

To qualify, you must be a graduating high school senior with a minimum 3.5 GPA and an ACT score of at least 25 or SAT I score of at least 1100 and demonstrate excellence and achievement in the physical, life, or computer sciences; mathematics; or engineering. Scholarships are as much as $5,000 per year or the student's cost of attendance, whichever is less, for up to five years of study. Awards are made to two students from each congressional district. Contact your high school counselor or NSSP coordinators at your state's Department of Education for application and deadline information.

Federal Loans

Following are methods through which you may borrow money from the federal government:

Federal Perkins Loan

This loan provides low-interest (5 percent) aid for students with exceptional financial need (students with the lowest expected family contribution). The Federal Perkins Loans are made through the college's financial aid office—that is, the college is the lender. For undergraduate study, you may borrow a maximum of $4,000 per year for up to five years of undergraduate study and may take up to ten years to repay the loan, beginning nine months after you graduate, leave school, or drop below half-time status. No interest accrues while you are in school and, under certain conditions (e.g., if you teach in a low-income area, work in law enforcement, are a full-time nurse or medical technician, or serve as a Peace Corps or VISTA volunteer), some or all of your loan can be canceled within fourteen days after the date that your school sends notice of crediting the transaction, or by the first day of the payment period, whichever is later. Payments also can be deferred under certain conditions, such as unemployment.

FINANCIAL AID ADVICE

Q: **What do you wish students and their parents knew about financial aid?**

A: **They don't know they should get their financial application filed early enough, so if we run into snags, it can be corrected. They make mistakes, such as not answering the question about the amount of taxes paid the previous year. A lot of parents think that if they didn't send in a check to the IRS, they didn't pay taxes. Something as simple as that causes a lot of problems. If their financial information is recorded incorrectly, it can really mess them up. They should read all the information on the financial aid form, and if they have questions, they should ask someone. Speaking from my experience, if you can't get in touch with the college you're child is thinking of attending, then call a local college. Any time an application doesn't go through the system smoothly, it can cause major problems.**

Now that you can apply over the Internet, the applications are much simpler and worded in layman's terms. If applicants miss filling in some information, that will trigger a warning that they omitted something. I realize that not all students have access to the Internet, but they can go to the public library and look into getting onto the Internet there.

Trudy Masters, Financial Aid Officer

Lee College

Baytown, Texas

FFEL Stafford Student Loan

An FFEL Stafford Student Loan may be borrowed from a participating commercial lender, such as a bank, credit union, or savings and loan association. The interest rate varies annually (it has gone up to a maximum of 8.25 percent). If you qualify for a need-based subsidized FFEL Stafford Student Loan, the interest is paid by the federal government while you are enrolled in school. There is also an unsubsidized FFEL Stafford Student Loan that is not based on need and for which you are eligible, regardless of your family income.

The maximum amount you may borrow as a dependent in any one year is $2,625 when you're a freshman, $3,500 when you're a sophomore, and $5,500 when you're a junior or senior, with a maximum of $23,000 for the total undergraduate program. The maximum amount you may borrow as an independent is $6,625 when you're a freshman (no more than $2,625 in subsidized Stafford Loans), $7,500 when you're a sophomore (no more than $3,500 in subsidized Stafford Loans), and $10,500 when you're a junior or senior (no more than $5,500 in subsidized Stafford Loans). You will be required to pay a 4 percent fee, which is deducted from the loan proceeds.

To apply for an FFEL Stafford Student Loan, you must first complete a FAFSA to determine eligibility for a subsidized loan and then complete a separate loan application that is submitted to a lender. The financial aid office can help you select a lender, or you can contact your state's Department of Higher Education to find a participating lender. The lender will send you or your parents a promissory note that you must sign indicating that you agree to repay the loan. The proceeds of the loan, less the origination fee, will be sent to your college to be either credited to your student account or paid to you directly.

If you qualify for a subsidized Stafford Loan, you don't have to pay interest while in school. For an unsubsidized FFEL Loan, you will be responsible for paying the interest from the time the loan is established. However, some FFEL lenders will permit you to delay making payments and will add the interest to your loan. Once the repayment period

THINKING AHEAD TO PAYING BACK YOUR STUDENT LOAN

More than ever before, loans have become an important part of financial assistance. The majority of students find that they must borrow money to finance their education. If you accept a loan, you are incurring a financial obligation. You will have to repay the loan in full, along with all of the interest and any additional fees (collection, legal, etc.). Since you will be making loan payments to satisfy the loan obligation, carefully consider the burden your loan amount will impose on you after you leave college. Defaulting on a student loan can jeopardize your financial future. Borrow intelligently.

SOME REPAYMENT OPTIONS

A number of repayment options are available to borrowers of federally guaranteed student loans.

The Standard Repayment Plan: requires fixed monthly payments (at least $50) over a fixed period of time (up to ten years). The length of the repayment period depends on the loan amount. This plan usually results in the lowest total interest paid because the repayment period is shorter than under the other plans.

The Extended Repayment Plan: allows loan repayment to be extended over a period from generally twelve to thirty years, depending on the total amount borrowed. Borrowers still pay a fixed amount each month (at least $50), but usually monthly payments will be less than under the Standard Repayment Plan. This plan may make repayment more manageable; however, borrowers usually will pay more interest because the repayment period is longer.

The Graduated Repayment Plan: allows payments to start out low and increase every two years. This plan may be helpful to borrowers whose incomes are low initially but will increase steadily. A borrower's monthly payments must be at least half but may not be more than one-and-a-half times what he or she would pay under Standard Repayment. As in the Extended Repayment Plan, the repayment period will usually vary from twelve to thirty years, depending on the total amount borrowed. Again, monthly payments may be more manageable at first because they are lower, but borrowers will pay more interest because the repayment period is longer.

The Income Contingent Repayment Plan: bases monthly payments on adjusted gross income (AGI) and the total amount borrowed. This is currently only available to students who participate in Direct Loans; however, some FFEL lenders and guaranty agencies provide income-sensitive repayment plans. As income rises or falls each year, monthly payments will be adjusted accordingly. The required monthly payment will not exceed 20 percent of the borrower's discretionary income as calculated under a published formula. Borrowers have up to twenty-five years to repay; after that time, any unpaid amount will be discharged, and borrowers must pay taxes on the amount discharged. In other words, if the federal government forgives the balance of a loan, the amount is considered to be part of the borrower's income for that year.

starts, whether you're a borrower of either subsidized or unsubsidized FFEL Loans, you will have to pay a combination of interest and principal monthly for up to a ten-year period.

William D. Ford Direct Stafford Loans

The Federal Direct Stafford Student Loan is basically the same as the Federal Stafford Student Loan Program. The difference is that the U.S. Department of Education, rather than a bank, is the lender. If your college does not participate in this program, you can still apply for an FFEL Stafford Student Loan.

Many of the terms of the Direct Stafford Loan are similar to those of the FFEL Stafford Loan. In particular, the interest rate, loan maximums, deferments, and cancellation benefits are the same. However, under the terms of the Direct Stafford Student Loan, you have a choice of repayment plans. You may choose:

- A standard fixed monthly repayment for up to ten years
- An extended repayment plan with lower fixed monthly payments for twelve to thirty years at a rate with a higher total amount of interest payment
- A graduated monthly repayment plan for twelve to thirty years in which payments grow from 50 percent to 150 percent of the standard plan
- Or an income contingent repayment plan with monthly payments based on your yearly income and family size
- You cannot receive both a Direct Stafford Loan and an FFEL Stafford Loan for the same period of time but may receive both in different enrollment periods.

PLUS Loans

The PLUS loans are for parents of dependent students and are designed to help families with cash-flow problems. There is no needs test to qualify, and the loans are made by FFEL lenders or directly by the Department of Education. The loan has a variable interest rate that cannot exceed 9 percent, and there is no specific yearly limit; your parents can borrow up to the cost of your education, less other financial aid received. Repayment begins sixty days after the money is advanced. A 4 percent fee is subtracted from the proceeds. Parent borrowers must generally have a good credit record to qualify for PLUS loans.

The PLUS loan will be processed under either the Direct or the FFEL system, depending on the type of loan program for which the college has contracted.

Federal Direct Lending

Provisions are identical to the Federal Stafford Student Loan programs. However, the primary lending institution is the college or university participating in the Federal Direct Lending Program, as opposed to a bank or other financial institution.

Lender of Last Resort

This program assists students who have tried to obtain a Federal Stafford Student Loan and have been denied by two lending institutions. Eligible students must be enrolled at an eligible postsecondary educational institution.

Nursing Student Loan Program

Awarded to nursing students with demonstrated financial need. This loan has a 5 percent interest rate, repayable after completion of studies. Repayment is to be completed within ten years. Contact your college's financial aid office for deadline and other information, including maximum borrowing amounts.

Other Federal Programs

The following programs offer alternative ways to earn money for college:

Federal Work-Study (FWS)

This program provides jobs for students who need

financial aid for their educational expenses. The salary is paid by funds from the federal government and the college (or the employer). You work on an hourly basis in jobs on or off campus and must be paid at least the federal minimum wage. You may earn only up to the amount awarded, which depends on the calculated financial need and the total amount of money available to the college.

AmeriCorps

AmeriCorps is a national service program for a limited number of students. Participants work in a public or private nonprofit agency that provides service to the community in one of four priority areas: education, human services, the environment, and public safety. In exchange, they earn a stipend for living expenses and up to $4,725 for up to two years to apply toward college expenses. Students can work either before, during, or after they go to college and can use the funds to either pay current educational expenses or repay federal student loans. If you successfully complete one full-time term of service (at least 1,700 hours over one year or less), you will be eligible for an award of $4,725. If you successfully complete one part-time term of service (at least 900 hours over two years or less), you will be eligible for an award of $2,362.50. You should speak to your

college's financial aid office for more details about this program and any other new initiatives available to students.

FAMILIES' GUIDE TO TAX CUTS FOR EDUCATION

Many new tax benefits for adults who want to return to school and for parents who are sending or planning to send their children to college will be available due to the balanced budget that was signed into law in 1997. These tax cuts effectively make the first two years of college universally available, and they give many more working Americans the financial means to go back to school if they want to choose a new career or upgrade their skills. About 12.9 million students benefit—5.8 million under the "HOPE Scholarship" tax credit and 7.1 million under the Lifetime Learning tax credit.

HOPE Scholarship Tax Credit

The HOPE Scholarship tax credit helps make the first two years of college or career school universally available. Students receive a 100 percent tax credit for the first $1,000 of tuition and required fees and a 50 percent credit on the second $1,000. This credit is available for tuition and required fees minus grants, scholarships, and other tax-free educational assistance and became available for payments made after December 31, 1997, for college enrollment after that date.

This credit is phased out for joint filers who have between $80,000 and $100,000 of adjusted gross income and for single filers who have between $40,000 and $50,000 of adjusted gross income. The credit can be claimed in two years for students who are in their first two years of college or career school and who are enrolled on at least a half-time basis in a degree or certificate program for any portion of the year. The taxpayer can claim a credit for his own tuition expense or for the expenses of his or her spouse or dependent children.

The Lifetime Learning Tax Credit

This tax credit is targeted at adults who want to go back to school, change careers, or take a course or two to upgrade their skills and to college juniors, seniors, graduate and professional degree students. A family will receive a 20 percent tax credit for the first $5,000 of tuition and required fees paid each year through 2002 and for the first $10,000 thereafter. Just like the HOPE Scholarship tax credit, the Lifetime Learning Tax Credit is available for tuition and required fees minus grants, scholarships, and other tax-free educational assistance; families may claim the credit for amounts paid on or after July 1, 1998, for college or career school enrollment beginning on or after July 1, 1998. The maximum credit is determined on a per-taxpayer (family) basis, regardless of the number of postsecondary students in the family, and is phased out at the same income levels as the HOPE Scholarship tax credit. Families will be able to claim the Lifetime Learning tax credit for some members of their family and the HOPE Scholarship tax credit for others who qualify in the same year.

NATIONAL, STATEWIDE, AND LOCAL SCHOLARSHIPS

Requirements for the financial resources listed below are approximate and may vary. Check with your guidance counselor for the most up-to-date information regarding the availability of these resources and the requirements to qualify.

National Scholarships

Following is an abridged list of national scholarship programs:

Coca-Cola Scholars Program

Awards to seniors planning to attend an accredited college or university. Based on academics, school and community activities, and motivation to serve and succeed in all endeavors. Call for deadline and application information at 800-306-2653 (toll-free) or check www.cocacola.com.

Duracell/National Science Teachers Association Scholarship Competition

Open to all students in grades 9 through 12. Student must design and build a device powered by Duracell batteries. Call 703-243-7100 for application and deadline information.

Elks National Scholarship

Awards more than $1 million to "most valuable students" nationwide. To qualify, you must be in the upper 5 percent of your class and have an A average. Awards are based upon scholarship, leadership, and financial need. Call 773-755-4732 for application and deadline information or visit their Web site at www.elks.org.

National Foundation for Advancement in the Arts/Arts Recognition and Talent Search (NFAA/ARTS)

Awards are based on talent in dance, music, theater, visual arts, writing, voice, jazz, or photography. Call 800-970-2787 (toll-free). Early application is June 1 of junior year, and the final application deadline is October 1 of senior year.

National Merit Scholarship Program

Based on the PSAT exam taken in the junior year. Also investigate the National Honor Society Scholarship.

National Society of Professional Engineers

Awarded to high school seniors who plan to study engineering in college. Applications are accepted from August 1 through December 1, and the scholarships are awarded in January. Must be a U.S. citizen planning to attend an engineering program in the United States approved by the Accreditation Board for Engineering and Technology. Visit the NSPE's Web site at www.nspe.org for more information.

National Association of Secondary School Principals

The NASSP sponsors scholarships that recognize

students who are involved in activities such as student council, the National Honor Society, community service, and athletics. Contact the National Association of Secondary School Principals at 703-860-0200 for application and deadline information, or visit their Web site at www.nassp.org.

Tylenol

This award is based 40 percent on leadership in school and community, 50 percent on grade point average, and 10 percent on clear statement of goals. Call 800-676-8437 (toll-free) for an application. Deadline: January.

State and Local Scholarships

It is not possible within the scope of this book to list all of the sources of state and local scholarship dollars. The following are excellent resources for seeking financial assistance:

- Your guidance counselor
- A high school teacher or coach
- Your high school and elementary school PTA (yes, many elementary school PTAs award scholarships to alumni)
- The local librarian
- College admissions office
- Your parents' alma mater
- Your employer
- Your parents' employer
- Professional and social organizations in your community

SCHOLARSHIPS FOR MINORITY STUDENTS

The following is just a sample of the many scholarships available to minority students.

Blackfeet Tribal Education Grants

Available to members of the Blackfeet Tribe. Up to $3,500 in awards.
P.O. Box 850
Browning, Montana 59417
406-338-7521

Bureau of Indian Affairs Office of Indian Education Programs

Available to undergraduates in a federally recognized tribe. Award amounts vary.
1849 C Street, NW, MS 3512-MIB
Washington, D.C. 20240
202-208-6123

Hispanic Scholarship Fund General Program

Limited to Hispanic students enrolled at a two- or four-year institution. Up to $2,000 in awards.
Scholarship Committee
Hispanic Scholarship Fund
One Sansome Street, Suite 1000
San Francisco, California 94104
415-445-9930

National Achievement Scholarship Corporation

Limited to African-American high school students who have taken the PSAT/NMSQT. Up to $2,000 in awards.
Achievement Program
1560 Sherman Avenue, Suite 200
Evanston, Illinois 60201
847-866-5100

National Association of Minority Engineering Program Administrators National Scholarship Fund

Limited to African-American, Hispanic, and Native-American/Eskimo students with interest and potential for an undergraduate degree in engineering. Up to $30,000.
National Scholarship Selection
Committee Chair
NAMEPA National Scholarship Foundation
1133 West Mores Boulevard
Suite 201
Winter Park, Florida 32789-3788
407-647-8839

Jackie Robinson Foundation Scholarship

For minority students accepted to a four-year college and with demonstrated academic achievement and financial need. Award up to $6,000. Visit the Web site at www.jackierobinson.org for more information.

APPLYING FOR SCHOLARSHIPS

Here are some tips to help make a success of your scholarship hunt.

1. **Start early.** Your freshman year is not too early to plan for scholarships academically, choose extracurricular activities that will highlight your strengths, and get involved in your church and community—all things that are important to those who make scholarship decisions.

2. **Search for scholarships.** A couple of hours a week in the public library will help you learn about hundreds of scholarships and assess those for which you might qualify.

3. **Apply, apply, apply.** One student applied for nearly sixty scholarships and was fortunate enough to win seven. "Imagine if I'd applied for five and only gotten one," she says.

4. **Plan ahead.** It takes time to get transcripts and letters of recommendation. Letters from people who know you well are more effective than letters from prestigious names who know you only vaguely.

5. **Be organized.** In the homes of scholarship winners, you can often find a file box where all relevant information is stored. This method allows you to review deadlines and requirements every so often. Computerizing the information, if possible, allows you to change and update information quickly.

6. **Follow directions.** Make sure that you don't disqualify yourself by filling the forms out incorrectly, missing the deadline, or failing to supply important information. Type your applications, if possible, and have someone proofread them.

WHAT YOU NEED TO KNOW ABOUT ATHLETIC SCHOLARSHIPS

Whether you're male or female or interested in baseball, basketball, crew, cross-country, fencing, field hockey, football, golf, gymnastics, lacrosse, sailing, skiing, soccer, softball, swimming and diving, tennis, track and field, volleyball, or wrestling, there may be scholarship dollars available for you. But, there's that word again—planning. You must plan ahead if you want to get your tuition paid for in return for your competitive abilities.

At the beginning of your junior year, ask your guidance counselor to help you make sure that you take the required number and mix of academic courses and to inform you of the SAT I and ACT score minimums that must be met to play college sports. Also ask your counselor about academic requirements, because you must be certified by the NCAA Initial-Eligibility Clearinghouse, and this process must be started by the end of your junior year.

But before you do all that, think. Do you want and need an athletic scholarship? Certainly, it is prestigious to receive an athletic scholarship, but some athletes compare having an athletic scholarship to having a job at which you are expected to perform. Meetings, training sessions, practices, games, and (don't forget) studying take away from social and leisure time. Also, with very few full-ride scholarships available, you will most likely receive a partial scholarship or a one-year renewable contract. If your scholarship is not renewed, you may be left scrambling for financial aid. So ask yourself if you are ready for the demands and roles associated with accepting an athletic scholarship.

If you decide that you want an athletic scholarship, you need to market yourself to beat the stiff competition. Think of yourself as a newly designed sports car, and you're selling the speed, look, and all those other goodies to a waiting public. The point is that you're going to have to sell, or market, your abilities to college recruiters. You're the product, and the college recruiter is the buyer. What makes you stand out from the rest?

College recruiters look for a combination of the following attributes when awarding athletic scholarships: academic excellence, a desire to win, self-motivation, ability to perform as a team player, willingness to help others, cooperation with coaching staff, attitude in practice, attitude in games/matches, toughness, strength, optimal height and weight, and excellence.

In order to successfully sell your skills to a college or university, you'll need to take three main

steps: 1) locate the colleges and universities that offer scholarships in your sport, 2) contact the institution in a formal manner, and 3) follow up each lead.

Finding and Getting Athletic Scholarships

Ask your coach or assistant coaches for recommendations; learn about the conference or institution from newspaper or television coverage; ask your guidance counselor; review guidebooks, reference books (check out Peterson's *Sports Scholarships and College Athletics Programs*), and the Internet; ask alumni; or attend a tryout or campus visit. You can also call the NCAA to request a recruiting guide for your sport. The following steps can help you snag that scholarship.

1. **Contact the school formally.** Once you make a list of schools in which you are interested, get the name of the head coach and write a letter to the top twenty schools on your list. Then compile a factual resume of your athletic and academic accomplishments. Put together 10 to 15 minutes of video highlights of your athletic performance (with your jersey number noted), get letters of recommendation from your high school coach and your off-season coach, and include a season schedule.

2. **Ace the interview.** When you meet a recruiter or coach, exhibit self-confidence with a firm handshake, by maintaining eye contact, and by making sure that you are well groomed. According to recruiters, the most effective attitude is quiet confidence, respect, sincerity, and enthusiasm.

3. **Ask good questions.** Don't be afraid to probe the recruiter by getting answers to the following questions: Do I qualify athletically and academically? If I am recruited, what would the parameters of the scholarship be? For what position am I being considered? It's okay to ask the recruiter to declare what level of interest he or she has in you.

TYPES OF ATHLETIC SCHOLARSHIPS

Colleges and universities offer two basic types of athletic scholarships: the institutional grant, which is an agreement between the athlete and the college, and the conference grant, which also binds the college to the athlete. The difference is that the athlete who signs an institutional grant can change his or her mind and sign with another team. The athlete who signs a conference contract cannot renegotiate another contract with a school that honors conference grants. Here are the various ways that a scholarship may be offered.

Full four-year. Also known as full ride, these scholarships pay for room, board, tuition, and books. Due to the high cost of awarding scholarships, this type of grant is being discouraged by conferences around the country in favor of the one-year renewable contract or the partial scholarship.

Full one-year renewable contract. This type of scholarship, which has basically replaced the four-year grant, is automatically renewed at the end of each school year for four years if the conditions of the contract are met. The recruiter will probably tell you in good faith that the intent is to offer a four-year scholarship, but he is legally only allowed to offer you a one-year grant. You must ask the recruiter as well as other players what the record has been of renewing scholarships for athletes who comply athletically, academically, and socially. Remember—no athlete can receive more than a full scholarship.

One-year trial grant (full or partial). A verbal agreement between you and the institution that at the end of the year, your renewal will be dependent upon your academic and athletic performance.

Partial scholarship. The partial grant is any part of the total cost of college. You may be offered room and board but not tuition and books, or you may be offered just tuition. The possibility exists for you to negotiate to a full scholarship after you complete your freshman year.

Waiver of out-of-state fees. This award is for out-of-state students to attend the college or university at the same fee as an in-state student.

4. **Follow up**. Persistence pays off when it comes to seeking an athletic scholarship, and timing can be everything. There are four good times when a follow-up letter from your coach or a personal letter from you is extremely effective: prior to your senior season, during or just after the senior season, just prior to or after announced conference-affiliated signing dates or national association signing dates, and late summer, in case scholarship offers have been withdrawn or declined.

To sum up, you know yourself better than anyone, so you must look at your skills—both athletic and academic—objectively. Evaluate the skills you need to improve, and keep the desire to improve alive in your heart. Develop your leadership skills, and keep striving for excellence with your individual achievements. Keep your mind open as to what school you want to attend, and keep plugging away, even when you are tired, sore, and unsure. After all, athletes are trained to be winners!

MYTHS AND MISCONCEPTIONS ABOUT SCHOLARSHIPS AND FINANCIAL AID

The scholarship and financial aid game is highly misunderstood by many high school students. And high school guidance counselors, overburdened with paperwork and complaints, often lack the time to fully investigate scholarship opportunities and to inform students about them. The myths and misconceptions persist while the truth about scholarships remains hidden, the glittering prizes and benefits unknown to many teenagers.

Myth 1: Scholarships are rare, elusive awards won only by valedictorians, geniuses, and whiz kids.

The truth is that with proper advice and strategies, private scholarships are very much within the grasp of high school students who possess talent and ability in almost any given field. Thousands of high school students like you compete and win.

Myth 2: My chances of being admitted to a college are reduced if I apply for financial aid.

The truth is that most colleges have a policy of "need-blind" admissions, which means that a student's financial need is not taken into account in the admission decision. However, there are a few colleges that do consider ability to pay before deciding whether or not to admit a student. There are a few more that look at ability to pay of those whom they placed on a waiting list to get in or those students who applied late. Some colleges will mention this in their literature, others may not. In making decisions about the college application and financing process, however, families should apply for financial aid if the student needs the aid to attend college.

Myth 3: All merit scholarships are based on a student's academic record.

The truth is that many of the best opportunities are in such areas as writing, public speaking, leadership, science, community service, music and the arts, foreign languages, and vocational-technical skills. So that means you don't always have to have a 3.99 GPA to win if you excel in a certain area.

Myth 4: You have to be a member of a minority group to get a scholarship.

The truth is that there are indeed some scholarships that are targeted toward women and minority students. There are also scholarships for which you must be a member of a specific national club or student organization (such as 4-H and the National Honor Society), which makes these scholarships just as exclusive. But most scholarship opportunities are not exclusive to any one segment of the population.

Myth 5: If you have need for and receive financial aid, it's useless to win a scholarship from some outside organization because the college will just take away the aid that the organization offered.

It's true that if you receive need-based aid, you can't receive more than the total cost of attendance (including room and board, books, and other expenses, not just tuition). If the financial aid that you've been awarded meets the total cost and you win an outside scholarship, colleges have to reduce something. But usually, they reduce the loan or work-study portion of your financial aid award before touching the grant portion that they've awarded you. This means that you won't have to borrow or earn as much. Also, most colleges don't meet your full financial need when you qualify for need-based financial aid. So, if you do win an outside scholarship, chances are that your other aid will not be taken away or reduced.

SCHOLARSHIP SCAMS

Unfortunately for prospective scholarship seekers, the private aid sector exists virtually without patterns or rules. Regrettably, the combination of the urgency to locate money, limited time, and a complex and bewildering system has created opportunities for fraud. Although most scholarship sponsors and most scholarship search services are legitimate, schemes that pose as either legitimate scholarship search services or scholarship sponsors have cheated thousands of families.

These fraudulent businesses advertise in campus newspapers, distribute flyers, mail letters and postcards, provide toll-free phone numbers, and even have sites on the Web. The most obvious frauds operate as scholarship search services or scholarship clearinghouses. Another quieter segment sets up as a scholarship sponsor, pockets the money from the fees and charges that are paid by thousands of hopeful scholarship seekers, and returns little, if anything, in proportion to the amount it collects. A few of these frauds inflict great harm by gaining access to individuals' credit or checking accounts with the intent to extort funds.

The Federal Trade Commission (FTC), in Washington, D.C., has a campaign called Project $cholar$cam to confront this type of fraudulent activity. There are legitimate services. However, a scholarship search service cannot truthfully guarantee that a student will receive a scholarship, and students almost always will fare as well or better by doing their own homework using a reliable scholarship information source, such as Peterson's *Scholarships, Grants & Prizes*, than by wasting money and time with a search service that promises a scholarship.

The FTC warns you to be alert for these six warning signs of a scam:

1. **"This scholarship is guaranteed or your money back."** No service can guarantee that it will get you a grant or scholarship. Refund guarantees often have impossible conditions attached. Review a service's refund policies in writing before you pay a fee.

2. **"The scholarship service will do all the work."** Unfortunately, nobody else can fill out the personal information forms, write the essays, and supply the references that many scholarships may require.

3. **"The scholarship will cost some money."** Be wary of any charges related to scholarship information services or individual scholarship applications, especially in significant amounts. Before you send money to apply for a scholarship, investigate the sponsor.

4. **"You can't get this information anywhere else."** In addition to Peterson's, scholarship directories from other publishers are available in any large bookstore, public library, or high school guidance office.

5. **"You are a finalist"** or **"You have been selected by a national foundation to receive a scholarship."** Most legitimate scholarship programs almost never seek out particular applicants. Most scholarship sponsors

will contact you only in response to an inquiry because they generally lack the budget to do anything more than this. Should you think that there is any real possibility that you may have been selected to receive a scholarship, before you send any money, investigate first to be sure that the sponsor or program is legitimate.

6. **"The scholarship service needs your credit card or checking account number in advance."** Never provide your credit card or bank account number on the telephone to the representative of an organization that you do not know. Get information in writing first. An unscrupulous operation does not need your signature on a check. It will scheme to set up situations that will allow it to drain a victim's account with unauthorized withdrawals.

In addition to the FTC's six signs, here are some other points to keep in mind when considering a scholarship program:

- Fraudulent scholarship operations often use official-sounding names, containing words such as *federal, national, administration, division, federation,* and *foundation.* Their names are often a slight variant of the name of a legitimate government or private organization. Do not be fooled by a name that seems reputable or official, an official-looking seal, or a Washington, D.C., address.

- If you win a scholarship, you will receive written official notification by mail, not by telephone. If the sponsor calls to inform you, it will follow up with a letter in the mail. If a request for money is made by phone, the operation is probably fraudulent.

- Be wary if an organization's address is a box number or a residential address. If a bona fide scholarship program uses a post office box number, it usually will include a street address and telephone number on its stationery.

- Beware of telephone numbers with a 900-area code. These may charge you a fee of several dollars a minute for a call that could be a long

recording that provides only a list of addresses or names.

- Watch for scholarships that ask you to "act now." A dishonest operation may put pressure on an applicant by saying that awards are on a "first-come, first-serve" basis. Some scholarship programs will give preference to the earlier qualified applications. However, if you are told, especially on the telephone, that you must respond quickly but that you will not hear about the results for several months, there may be a problem.

- Be wary of endorsements. Fraudulent operations will claim endorsements by groups with names similar to well-known private or government organizations. The Better Business Bureau (BBB) and government agencies do not endorse businesses.

- Don't pay money for a scholarship to an organization that you've never heard of before or whose legitimacy you can't verify. If you have already paid money to such an organization and find reason to doubt its authenticity, call your bank to stop payment on your check, if possible, or call your credit card company and tell it that you think you were the victim of consumer fraud.

To find out how to recognize, report, and stop a scholarship scam, you may write to the Federal Trade Commission's Consumer Response Center at 600 Pennsylvania Avenue NW, Washington, D.C. 20580. On the Web, go to www.ftc.gov, or call 877-FTC-HELP (toll-free). You can also check with the Better Business Bureau (BBB), which is an organization that maintains files of businesses about which it has received complaints. You should call both your local BBB office and the BBB office in the area of the organization in question; each local BBB has different records. Call 703-276-0100 to get the telephone number of your local BBB, or look at www.bbb.org for a directory of local BBBs and downloadable BBB complaint forms.

APPLYING FOR FINANCIAL AID

Applying for financial aid is a process that can be made easier when you take it step by step.

1. You must complete the Free Application for Federal Student Aid (FAFSA) to be considered for federal financial aid. Pick up the FAFSA from your high school guidance counselor or college financial aid office or download it from the Department of Education's Web site at www.fafsa.ed.gov. The FAFSA is due any time after January 1 of the year you will be attending school. Submit the form as soon as possible but never before the first of the year. If you need to estimate income tax information, it is easily amended later in the year.

2. Apply for any state grants.

3. Complete the PROFILE in addition to the FAFSA, because many four-year private colleges and some public universities require it. The PROFILE is a need analysis report, not an aid application. Some institutions have developed their own need analysis report. Check with your college or university to see what is required. The PROFILE registration is a one-page form available from your guidance counselor or through the College Board at www.collegeboard.com.

4. Complete individual colleges' required financial aid application forms on time. These deadlines are usually before March 15, but check with your institution to be sure.

5. Make sure your family completes the required forms during your senior year of high school.

6. Always apply for grants and scholarships before applying for student loans. Grants and scholarships are essentially free money. Loans must be repaid with interest.

Use the "Checklist for Seniors" to keep track of the financial aid application process.

FINANCIAL AID ON THE WEB

A number of good financial aid resources exist on the Web. It is quick and simple to access general financial aid information, links to relevant Web sites, loan information, employment and career information, advice, scholarship search services, interactive worksheets, forms, and free expected family contribution (EFC) calculators.

Also visit the Web sites of individual colleges to find more school-specific financial aid information.

FAFSA Online

The Free Application for Federal Student Aid can be downloaded from the U.S. Department of Education's World Wide Web page and filed electronically. The address is www.ed.gov/offices/OSFAP/Students/apply/express.html.

The Education Resource Institute (TERI)

TERI is a private, not-for-profit organization that was founded to help middle-income Americans afford a college education. This site contains a database describing more than 150 programs that aim to increase college attendance from underrepresented groups. (The target population includes students from low-income families and those who are the first in their family to pursue postsecondary education.) Visit TERI's Web site at www.teri.org.

FinAid

Sponsored by the National Association of Student Financial Aid Administrators, it includes a comprehensive alphabetical index of all financial aid resources on the Web. You can find the site at www.finaid.org.

Student Financial Assistance Information, Department of Education

This page takes you to some of the major publications

A CHECKLIST FOR SENIORS

Applying for financial aid can become confusing if you don't record what you've done and when. Use this chart to keep track of important information. Remember to keep copies of all applications and related information.

COLLEGE APPLICATIONS	COLLEGE 1	COLLEGE 2	COLLEGE 3	COLLEGE 4
Application deadline				
Date sent				
Official transcript sent				
Letters of recommendation sent				
SAT/ACT scores sent				
Acceptance received				
INDIVIDUAL COLLEGE FINANCIAL AID AND SCHOLARSHIP APPLICATIONS				
Application deadline				
Date sent				
Acceptance received				
FREE APPLICATION FOR FEDERAL STUDENT AID (FAFSA), FINANCIAL AID FORM (FAF), AND/OR PROFILE				
Form required				
Date sent				
School's priority deadline				
FAFSA ACKNOWLEDGMENT				
Date received				
Correct (Y/N)				
Date changes made, if needed				
Date changes were submitted				
STUDENT AID REPORT				
Date received				
Correct (Y/N)				
Date changes made, if needed				
Date changes were submitted				
Date sent to colleges				
FINANCIAL AWARD LETTERS				
Date received				
Accepted (Y/N)				

Source: The Dayton-Montgomery County Scholarship Program

on student aid, including the latest edition of the Student Guide. Visit www.ed.gov/finaid.html.

Petersons.com

Get advice on finding sources to pay for college and search for scholarships at www.petersons.com/resources/finance.html.

AESmentor.com

American Education Services works with nearly 4 million students through its guaranty, servicing, and financial aid processing system. Its Web site provides information on paying and saving for college as well as an application process for securing student loans.

FINANCIAL AID DIRECTORY

You can use these numbers for direct access to federal and state agencies and processing services. However, your guidance counselor may have the answers or information you need.

FEDERAL STUDENT AID INFORMATION CENTER

Provides duplicate student aid reports and aid applications to students. Also answers questions on student aid, mails Department of Education publications, makes corrections to applications, and verifies college federal aid participation. Write to the Federal Student Aid Information Center, P.O. Box 84, Washington, D.C. 20044-0084 or call 800-4-Fed-Aid (toll-free).

UNITED STUDENT AID FUNDS (USAF)

Provides aid application forms and information on loan amounts. Also provides information on guarantee dates and assists students in filling out application forms. Write to P.O. Box 6180, Indianapolis, Indiana 46206-6180, or call 877-USA-Group (toll-free).

VETERANS BENEFITS ADMINISTRATION

Provides dependent education assistance for children of disabled veterans. College-bound students should call the VBRO to determine whether or not they qualify for assistance, what the benefits are, and if a parent's disability qualifies them for benefits. Call 800-827-1000 (toll-free) or visit their Web site at www.gibill.va.gov.

ACT FINANCIAL AID NEED ESTIMATOR (FANE)

Mails financial tabloids to students, provides information on filling out financial aid forms, and estimates financial aid amounts. Also mails financial need estimator forms. Forms are also accessible on line. Go to www.ACT.org or write to P.O. Box 4029, Iowa City, Iowa 52243-4029, or call 319-337-1615.

COLLEGE SCHOLARSHIP SERVICE (PROFILE)

Provides free applications and registration forms for federal student aid. Helps students fill out applications. Write to P.O. Box 6350, Princeton, NJ 08541-6350 or call 800-239-5888 (toll-free).

Chapter 8

WHAT TO EXPECT IN COLLEGE

If you were going on a long trip, wouldn't you want to know what to expect once you reached your destination? The same should hold true for college.

GET A JUMP CAN'T FILL IN all the details of what you'll find once you begin college. However, we can give you information about some of the bigger questions you might have, such as how to choose your classes or major and how you can make the most of your life outside the classroom.

CHOOSING YOUR CLASSES

College is designed to give you freedom, but at the same time, it teaches you responsibility. You will probably have more free time than in high school, but you will also have more class material to master. Your parents may entrust you with more money, but it is up to you to make sure there's enough money in your bank account when school fees are due. The same principle applies to your class schedule: You will have more decision-making power than ever, but you also need to know and meet the requirements for graduation.

To guide you through the maze of requirements, all students are given an adviser. This person, typically a faculty member, will help you select classes that meet your interests and graduation requirements. During your first year or two at college, you and your adviser will focus on meeting general education requirements and selecting electives, or non-required classes, that meet your interests. Early on, it is a good idea to take a lot of general education classes. They are meant to expose you to new ideas and help you explore possible majors. Once you have selected a major, you will be given an adviser for that particular area of study. This person will help you understand and meet the requirements for that major.

In addition to talking to your adviser, talk to other students who have already taken a class you're interested in and who really enjoyed the professor. Then try to get into that professor's class when registering. Remember, a dynamic teacher can make a dry subject engaging. A boring teacher can make an engaging subject dry.

As you move through college, you will notice that focusing on the professor is more important than focusing on the course title. Class titles can be cleverly crafted. They can sound captivating. However, the advice above still holds true: "Pop Culture and Icons" could turn out to be awful when "Beowulf and Old English" could be a blast.

When you plan your schedule, watch out how many heavy reading classes you take in one semester. You don't want to live in the library or the dorm study lounge. In general, the humanities, such as history, English, philosophy, and theology, involve a lot of reading. Math and science classes involve less reading; they focus more on solving problems.

Finally, don't be afraid to schedule a fun class. Even the most intense program of study will let you take a few electives. So take a deep breath, dig in, and explore!

CHOOSING YOUR MAJOR

You can choose from hundreds of majors—from accounting to zoology—but which is right for you?

Should you choose something traditional or select a major from an emerging area? Perhaps you already know what career you want, so you can work backward to decide which major will best help you achieve your goals.

If you know what you want to do early in life, you will have more time to plan your high school curriculum, extracurricular activities, jobs, and community service to coincide with your college major. Your college selection process may also focus upon the schools that provide strong academic programs in a certain major.

Where Do I Begin?

Choosing a major usually starts with an assessment of your career interests. Once you have taken the self-assessment test in Section 1, you should have a clearer understanding of your interests, talents, values, and goals. Then review possible majors, and try several on for size. Picture yourself taking classes, writing papers, making presentations, conducting research, or working in a related field. Talk to people you know who work in your fields of interest and see if you like what you hear. Also, try reading the classified ads in your local newspaper. What jobs sound interesting to you? Which ones pay the salary that you'd like to make? What level of education is required in the ads you find interesting? Select a few jobs that you think you'd like and then consult the following list of majors to see which major(s) coincide. If your area of interest does not appear here, talk to your counselor or teacher about where to find information on that particular subject.

Majors and Related Careers

Agriculture

Many agriculture majors apply their knowledge directly on farms and ranches. Others work in industry (food, farm equipment, and agricultural supply companies), federal agencies (primarily in the Departments of Agriculture and the Interior), and state and local farm and agricultural agencies. Jobs might be in research and lab work, marketing and sales, advertising and public relations, or journalism and radio/TV (for farm communications media). Agriculture majors also pursue further training in biological sciences, animal health, veterinary medicine, agribusiness, management, vocational agriculture education, nutrition and dietetics, and rural sociology.

Architecture

Architecture and related design fields focus on the built environment as distinct from the natural environment of the agriculturist or the conservationist. Career possibilities include drafting, design, and project administration in architectural, engineering, landscape design, interior design, industrial design, planning, real estate, and construction firms; government agencies involved in construction, housing, highways, and parks and recreation; and government and nonprofit organizations interested in historic or architectural preservation.

Area/Ethnic Studies

The research, writing, analysis, critical thinking, and cultural awareness skills acquired by Area/Ethnic Studies majors, combined with the expertise gained in a particular area, make this group of majors valuable in a number of professions. Majors find positions in administration, education, public relations, and communications in such organizations as cultural, government, international, and (ethnic) community agencies; international trade (import-export); social service agencies; and the communications industry (journalism, radio, and TV). These studies also provide a good background for further training in law, business management, public administration, education, social work, museum and library work, and international relations.

Arts

Art majors most often use their training to become practicing artists, though the settings in which they work vary. Aside from the most obvious art-related career—that of the self-employed artist or craftsperson—many fields require the skills of a visual artist. These include advertising; public relations; publishing; journalism; museum work; television, movies, and theater; community and social service agencies concerned with education, recreation, and entertainment; and teaching. A background in art is also useful if a student wishes to pursue art therapy, arts or museum administration, or library work.

Biological Sciences

The biological sciences include the study of living organisms from the level of molecules to that of populations. Majors find jobs in industry; government agencies; technical writing, editing, or illustrating; science reporting; secondary school teaching (which usually requires education courses); and research and laboratory analysis and testing. Biological sciences are also a sound foundation for further study in medicine, psychology, health and hospital administration, and biologically oriented engineering.

Business

Business majors comprise all the basic business disciplines. At the undergraduate level, students can major in a general business administration program or specialize in a particular area, such as marketing or accounting. These studies lead not only to positions in business and industry but also to management positions in other sectors. Management-related studies include the general management areas (accounting, finance, marketing, and management) as well as special studies related to a particular type of organization or industry. Management-related majors may be offered in a business school or in a department dealing with the area in which the management skills are to be applied. Careers can be found throughout the business world.

Communication

Jobs in communication range from reporting (news and special features), copywriting, technical writing, copyediting, and programming to advertising, public relations, media sales, and market research. Such positions can be found at newspapers, radio and TV stations, publishing houses (book and magazine), advertising agencies, corporate communications departments, government agencies, universities, and firms that specialize in educational and training materials.

Computer, Information, and Library Sciences

Computer and information science and systems majors stress the theoretical aspects of the computer and emphasize mathematical and scientific disciplines. Data processing, programming, and computer technology programs tend to be more practical; they are more oriented toward business than to scientific applications and to working directly with the computer or with peripheral equipment. Career possibilities for computer and information sciences include data processing, programming, and systems development or maintenance in almost any setting: business and industry, banking and finance, government, colleges and universities, libraries, software firms, service bureaus, computer manufacturers, publishing, and communications.

STUDENT COUNSEL

Q: Why did you choose a seven-year premed program instead of a traditional four-year college program?

A: I'm one of those people who knew what I wanted to do since I was very little, so that made choosing easier. If I was not 100 percent sure that I wanted to go into medicine, I would not be in this seven-year program. For students who are interested but not really sure that they want to go into medicine, they should pick a school they will enjoy, get a good education, and then worry about medical school. That way, if they decide in their junior year that medicine is not for them, they have options.

Elliot Servais
Premed
Boston University

STUDENT COUNSEL

Q: What advice do you have for high school students who are considering going into engineering?

A: In high school, take AP courses in a lot of different areas. That gives you an idea of what those subjects will be like in college. I knew I was good at science and math but didn't know which direction would really interest me. I took an AP English course and didn't do so well. Then I took a chemistry course and knew I could see myself digging deeper. An AP course will give you an idea if this subject is something you want to pursue as a major.

Most engineering majors don't have to decide on what engineering discipline they want until their sophomore year. As a freshman, you can take courses and not really know what type of engineering you want. I took an introduction to engineering course and it convinced me that this is what I want to do. Your freshman year will give you a flavor for different engineering majors so you don't end up in your junior year and realize you don't like that major. The first semester here is totally an adjustment period.

Michael Romano
Chemical Engineering
Cornell University

Library science gives preprofessional background in library work and provides valuable knowledge of research sources, indexing, abstracting, computer technology, and media technology, which is useful for further study in any professional field. In most cases, a master's degree in library science is necessary to obtain a job as a librarian. Library science majors find positions in public, school, college, corporate, and government libraries and research centers; book publishing (especially reference books); database and information retrieval services; and communications (especially audiovisual media).

Education

Positions as teachers in public elementary and secondary schools, private day and boarding schools, religious and parochial schools, vocational schools, and proprietary schools are the jobs most often filled by education majors. However, teaching positions also exist in noneducational institutions, such as museums, historical societies, prisons, hospitals, and nursing homes as well as jobs as educators and

(Continued on page 86)

trainers in government and industry. Administrative (nonteaching) positions in employee relations and personnel, public relations, marketing and sales, educational publishing, TV and film media, test development firms, and government and community social service agencies also tap the skills and interests of education majors.

Engineering and Engineering Technologies

Engineering and science technology majors prepare students for practical design and production work rather than for jobs that require more theoretical, scientific, and mathematical knowledge. Engineers work in a variety of fields, including aeronautics, bioengineering, geology, nuclear engineering, and quality control and safety. Industry, research labs, and government agencies where technology plays a key role, such as in manufacturing, electronics, construction communications, transportation, and utilities, hire engineering as well as engineering technology and science technology graduates regularly. Work may be in technical activities (research, development, design, production, testing, scientific programming, or systems analysis) or in nontechnical areas where a technical degree is needed, such as marketing, sales, or administration.

Foreign Language and Literature

Knowledge of foreign languages and cultures is becoming increasingly recognized as important in today's international world. Language majors possess a skill that is used in organizations with international dealings as well as in career fields and geographical areas where languages other than English are prominent. Career possibilities include positions with business firms with international subsidiaries; import-export firms; international banking; travel agencies; airlines; tourist services; government and international agencies dealing with international affairs, foreign trade, diplomacy, customs, or immigration; secondary school foreign language teaching and bilingual education (which usually require education courses); freelance translating and

MAKING THAT MAJOR DECISION: REAL-LIFE ADVICE FROM COLLEGE SENIORS

Somewhere between her junior and senior year in high school, Karen Gliebe got the psychology bug. When choosing a major in college, she knew just what she wanted. Justin Bintrim, on the other hand, did a complete 180. He thought he'd study physics, then veered toward philosophy. It wasn't until he took survey courses in literature that he found where his heart really lay, and now he's graduating with a degree in English.

You might find yourself at either end of this spectrum when choosing a major. Either you'll know just what you want or you'll try on a number of different hats before finally settling on one. To give you a taste of what it could be like for you, meet four college seniors who have been through the trials and errors of choosing their majors. Hopefully you'll pick up some pointers from them or at least find out that you don't have to worry so much about what your major will be.

From Grove City College, a liberal arts school in Pennsylvania, meet Karen Gliebe, who will graduate with a degree in psychology, and English major Justin Bintrim. From Michigan State University, meet computer engineering major Seth Mosier and Kim Trouten, who is finishing up a zoology degree. Here's what they had to say:

HOW THEY CHOSE THEIR MAJORS

Karen: During high school, I volunteered at a retirement center, and my supervisor gave me a lot of exposure to applied psychology. After my freshman year in college, I talked to people who were using a psychology degree. You put in a lot of work for a degree and can wonder if it's worth all the work. It helps to talk to someone who has gone through it so you can see if that's what you want to be doing when you graduate.

Justin: I wasn't sure about what my major would be. One professor told me to take survey courses to see if I was interested in the subject. I took English literature, math, psychology, and philosophy. I liked English the best and did well in it. The next semester, I took two English courses and decided to switch my major. My professors told me not to worry about choosing a major. They said to get my feet wet and we'll talk about your major in two years. I decided that if they're not worried about a major, I wouldn't be either, but I still had it on my mind. I was around older students who were thinking about their careers, so I talked to them about the jobs they had lined up.

Seth: I liked computers in high school. In college, I started out in computer science but got sick of coding. My interest in computers made me pick computer science right off the bat. I didn't know about computer engineering until I got to college.

Kim: I wanted to be a veterinarian but after two years decided that I didn't want to go to school for that long. I was still interested in animals and had two options. One was in animal science, which is working more with farm animals, or going into zoology. I decided to concentrate on zoo and aquarium science. Besides being a vet, the closest interaction with animals would be being a zookeeper.

THE ELECTIVES THEY TOOK AND WHY

Karen: My adviser told me to take different classes, so I took philosophy, art, religion, and extra psychology classes that weren't required.

Justin: I was planning to do a double major, but my professors said to take what interested me. English majors have lots of freedom to take different courses, unlike science majors.

Seth: Because I'm in computer engineering, I don't get to take a lot of electives. I am taking a swimming class right now and took a critical incident analysis class where we look at major accidents. I wanted something that wasn't computer engineering-related but extremely technical.

Kim: I took some kinesiology classes, which was pretty much an aerobics class. I needed to work out and figured I could get credit for it. I also took sign language because I'm interested in it.

WHAT THEY'RE GOING TO DO WITH THEIR DEGREES

Karen: I want to go to graduate school and hopefully get some experience working with kids.

Justin: I'm applying to graduate

school in English literature and cultural studies. I want to do research and become a college professor.

Seth: I'm going to work for the defense department. It's not the highest offer I've gotten, but it will be the most fun, which is more important to me than the money.

Kim: My goals have changed again. I don't plan on using my degree. I just got married a year ago, and my husband and I want to go into full-time ministry. I'll use my degree to get a job and then we'll go overseas.

THE CHANGES THEY WOULD MAKE IN THE CLASSES THEY TOOK IF THEY COULD

Karen: There are classes I wouldn't necessarily take again. But even though I didn't learn as much as I wanted to, it was worth it. I learned how to work and how to organize my efforts.

Justin: I should have worried less about choosing a major when I first started college. I didn't have the perspective as to how much time I had to choose.

Seth: I have friends who would change the order in which they took their humanities classes. I was lucky enough to think ahead and spread those classes out over the entire time. Most [engineering] students take them their freshman year to get them all out of the way. Later on, they're locked in the

engineering building all day. Because I didn't, it was nice for me to get my mind off engineering.

Kim: Something I can't change are the labs. They require a lot of work, and you only get one credit for 3 hours. Some labs take a lot of work outside of class hours. I had a comparative anatomy lab, which kept me busy over entire weekends. I suggest you don't take a lot of classes that require labs all at once.

THEIR ADVICE FOR YOU

Karen: You don't have to know what you want to do with the rest of your life when you get to college. Most people don't even stay with the major they first choose. Colleges recognize that you will see things you may have not considered at first. Some high school students say they won't go to college unless they know what they want to do.

Justin: If it's possible, take a little of this and a little of that. If you're an engineering student, you'll have it all planned out [for you], but if you're a liberal arts major and are not sure, you probably can take something from each department.

Seth: If possible, take AP exams in high school. You'll be able to make a decision about a major. Freshmen who think they want to do engineering suffer through math and physics classes. Then by their sophomore or junior year, they realize they don't want to be

engineers. If they'd taken AP classes, they'd know by their freshman year.

Kim: When I changed my major, I was worried that I might have spent a year in classes that wouldn't count toward my new major. But you shouldn't be scared to change majors because if you stick with something you don't like, you'll have to go back and take other classes anyway.

Though these four seniors arrived at a decision about which major they wanted in different ways, they had similar things to say:

- **It's okay to change your mind about what you want out of college.**

- **To find out which major you might want, start with what you like to do.**

- **Talk to professionals who have jobs in the fields that interest you.**

- **Ask your professors about what kinds of jobs you could get with the degree you're considering.**

- **Talk to seniors who will be graduating with a degree in the major you're considering.**

- **Take electives in areas that interest you, even though they may have nothing to do with your major.**

- **College is a time to explore many different options, so take advantage of the opportunity.**

interpreting (high level of skill necessary); foreign language publishing; and computer programming (especially for linguistics majors).

Health Sciences

Health professions majors, while having a scientific core, are more focused on applying the results of scientific investigation than on the scientific disciplines themselves. Allied health majors prepare graduates to assist health professionals in providing diagnostics, therapeutics, and rehabilitation. Medical science majors, such as optometry, pharmacy, and the premedical profession sequences, are, for the most part, preprofessional studies that compose the scientific disciplines necessary for admission to graduate or professional school in the health or medical fields. Health service and technology majors prepare students for positions in the health fields that primarily involve services to patients or working with complex machinery and materials. Medical technologies cover a wide range of fields, such as cytotechnology, biomedical technologies, and operating room technology.

Administrative, professional, or research assistant positions in health agencies, hospitals, occupational health units in industry, community and school health departments, government agencies (public health, environmental protection), and international health organizations are available to majors in health fields, as are jobs in marketing and sales of health-related products and services, health education (with education courses), advertising and public relations, journalism and publishing, and technical writing.

Home Economics and Social Services

Home economics encompasses many different fields—basic studies in foods and textiles as well as consumer economics and leisure studies—that overlap with aspects of agriculture, social science, and education. Jobs can be found in government and community agencies (especially those concerned with education, health, housing, or human services), nursing homes, child-care centers, journalism,

radio/TV, educational media, and publishing. Types of work also include marketing, sales, and customer service in consumer-related industries, such as food processing and packaging, appliance manufacturing, utilities, textiles, and secondary school home economics teaching (which usually requires education courses).

Majors in social services find administrative aide or assistant positions in government and community health, welfare, and social service agencies, such as hospitals, clinics, YMCAs and YWCAs, recreation commissions, welfare agencies, and employment services. See the "Law and Legal Studies" section for information on more law-related social services.

Humanities (Miscellaneous)

The majors that constitute the humanities (sometimes called "letters") are the most general and widely applicable and the least vocationally oriented of the liberal arts. They are essentially studies of the ideas and concerns of human kind. These include classics, history of philosophy, history of science, linguistics, and medieval studies. Career possibilities for humanities majors can be found in business firms, government and community agencies, advertising and public relations, marketing and sales, publishing, journalism and radio/TV, secondary school teaching in English and literature (which usually requires education courses), freelance writing and editing, and computer programming (especially for those with a background in logic or linguistics).

Law and Legal Studies

Students of legal studies can use their knowledge of law and government in fields involving the making, breaking, and enforcement of laws; the crimes, trials, and punishment of law breakers; and the running of all branches of government at local, state, and federal levels. Graduates find positions in all types in law firms, legal departments of other organizations, the court or prison system, government agencies (such as law enforcement agencies or offices of state and federal attorneys general), and police departments.

Mathematics and Physical Sciences

Mathematics is the science of numbers and the abstract formulation of their operations. Physical sciences involve the study of the laws and structures of physical matter. The quantitative skills acquired through the study of science and mathematics are especially useful for computer-related careers. Career possibilities include positions in industry (manufacturing and processing companies, electronics firms, defense contractors, consulting firms); government agencies (defense, environmental protection, law enforcement); scientific/technical writing, editing, or illustrating; journalism (science reporting); secondary school teaching (usually requiring education courses); research and laboratory analysis and testing; statistical analysis; computer programming; systems analysis; surveying and mapping; weather forecasting; and technical sales.

Natural Resources

A major in the natural resources field prepares students for work in areas as generalized as environmental conservation and as specialized as groundwater contamination. Jobs are available in industry (food, energy, natural resources, and pulp and paper companies), consulting firms, state and federal government agencies (primarily the Departments of Agriculture and the Interior), and public and private conservation agencies. See also the "Agriculture" and "Biological Sciences" sections for more information on natural resources-related fields.

Psychology

Psychology majors involve the study of behavior and can range from the biological to the sociological. Students can study individual behavior, usually that of humans, or the behavior of crowds. Students of psychology do not always go into the more obvious clinical fields, the fields in which psychologists work with patients. Certain areas of psychology, such as industrial/organizational, experimental, and social, are not clinically oriented. Psychology and counseling careers can be in government (such as mental health agencies), schools, hospitals, clinics, private practice, industry, test development firms, social work, and personnel. The careers listed in the general "Social Sciences" section are also pursued by psychology and counseling majors.

Religion

Religion majors are usually seen as preprofessional studies for those who are interested in entering the ministry. Career possibilities for religion also include casework, youth counseling, administration in community and social service organizations, teaching in religious educational institutions, and writing for religious and lay publications. Religious studies also prepare students for the kinds of jobs other humanities majors often pursue.

Social Sciences

Social sciences majors study people in relation to their society. Thus, social science majors can apply their education to a wide range of occupations that deal with social issues and activities. Career opportunities are varied. People with degrees in the social sciences find careers in government, business, community agencies (serving children, youth, senior citizens), advertising and public relations, marketing and sales, secondary school social studies teaching (with education courses), casework, law enforcement, parks and recreation, museum work (especially for anthropology, archaeology, geography, and history majors), preservation (especially for anthropology, archaeology, geography, and history majors), banking and finance (especially for economics majors), market and survey research, statistical analysis, publishing, fundraising and development, and political campaigning.

Technologies

Technology majors, along with trade fields, are most often offered as two-year programs. Majors in technology fields prepare students directly for jobs; however, positions are in practical design and production work rather than in areas that require more theoretical, scientific, and mathematical knowledge. Engineering technologies prepare students with the basic training in specific fields (e.g., electronics, mechanics, or chemistry) that are necessary to become technicians on the support staffs of engineers. Other technology majors center more on maintenance and repair. Work may be in technical activities, such as production or testing, or in nontechnical areas where a technical degree is needed, such as marketing, sales, or administration. Industries, research labs, and government agencies in which technology plays a key role—such as in manufacturing, electronics, construction, communications, transportation, and utilities—hire technology graduates regularly.

Still Unsure?

Relax! You don't have to know your major before you enroll in college. More than half of all freshmen are undecided when they start school and prefer to get a feel for what's available at college before making a decision. Most four-year colleges don't require students to formally declare a major until the end of their sophomore year or beginning of their junior year. Part of the experience of college is being exposed to new subjects and new ideas. Chances are your high school never offered anthropology. Or marine biology. Or applied mathematics. So take these classes and follow your interests. While you're fulfilling your general course requirements, you might stumble upon a major that appeals to you, or maybe you'll discover a new interest while you're volunteering or involved with other extracurricular activities. Talking to other students might even lead you to a decision.

Can I Change My Major if I Change My Mind?

Choosing a major does not set your future in stone, nor does it necessarily disrupt your life if you need to change your major. However, there are advantages to choosing a major sooner rather than later. If you wait too long to choose, you may have to take additional classes to satisfy the requirements, which may cost you additional time and money.

THE OTHER SIDE OF COLLEGE: HAVING FUN!

There is more to college than writing papers, reading books, and sitting through lectures. Social life plays an integral part in forming your college experience.

Meeting New People

The easiest time to meet new people is at the beginning of something new. New situations shake people up and make them feel just uncomfortable enough to take the risk of extending their hand in friendship. Fortunately for you, college is filled with new experiences. There are the first weeks of being the newest students. This can be quickly followed by being a new member of a club or activity. And with each passing semester, you will be in new classes with new teachers and new faces. College should be a time of constantly challenging and expanding yourself, so never feel that it is too late to meet new people.

But just how do you take that first step in forming a relationship? It's surprisingly easy. The first few weeks of school will require you to stand in many lines. Some will be to buy books; others will be to get meals. One will be to get a student I.D. card. Another will be to register for classes. While standing in line, turn around and introduce yourself to the person behind you. Focus on what you have in common and try to downplay the differences. Soon you will find the two of you have plenty to talk about. When it is time to leave the line, arrange to have coffee later or to see a movie. This will help you form relationships with the people you meet.

Be open to the opportunities of meeting new people and having new experiences. Join clubs and activities that pique your interest. Investigate rock-climbing. Try ballet. Write for the school paper. But most of all, get involved.

Campus Activities

College life will place a lot of demands on you. Your classes will be challenging. Your professors will expect more responsibility from you. You will have to budget and manage your own money. But there is a plus side you probably haven't thought of yet: college students have a lot of free time.

The average student spends about three hours a day in class. Add to this the time you will need to spend studying, eating, and socializing, and you will still have time to spare. One of the best ways to use this time is to participate in campus activities.

Intramural Sports

Intramurals are sports played for competition between members of the same campus community. They provide competition and a sense of belonging without the same level of intensity in practice schedules. Anyone can join an intramural sport. Often there are teams formed by dormitories, sororities, or fraternities that play games such as soccer, volleyball, basketball, flag-football, baseball, and softball. There are also individual intramural sports such as swimming, golf, wrestling, and diving. If you want to get involved, just stop by the intramural office. Usually it is located near the student government office. If not, they should be able to tell you where to go.

Student Government

Student government will be set up in a way that is probably similar to your high school. Students form committees and run for office. However, student government in college has more power than in high school. The officers address all of their class's concerns directly to the President of the college or university and the Board of Trustees. Most student governments have a branch responsible for student activities that brings in big name entertainers and controversial speakers. You may want to get involved to see how such contacts are made and such appearances negotiated.

Community Service

Another aspect of student life is volunteering, commonly called community service. Many colleges offer a range of opportunities. Some allow you to simply commit an afternoon to a cause, such as passing out food at a food bank. Others require an ongoing commitment. For example, you might decide to help an adult learn to read every Thursday at 4 p.m. for three months. Some colleges will link a service commitment with class credit. This will enhance your learning, giving you some real-world experience. Be sure to stop by your community service office and see what is available.

Clubs

There are a variety of clubs on most college campuses spanning just about every topic you can imagine. Amnesty International regularly meets on most campuses to write letters to help free prisoners in foreign lands. Most college majors band together in a club to discuss their common interests and career potential. There are also clubs based on the use of certain computer software or that engage in outdoor activities like sailing or downhill skiing. The list is endless. If you cannot find a club for your interest, consider starting one of your own. Stop by the student government office to see what rules you will need to follow. You will also need to find a location to hold meetings and post signs to advertise your club. When you hold your first meeting, you will probably be surprised at how many people are willing to take a chance and try a new club.

Greek Life

A major misconception of Greek life is that it revolves around wild frat parties and alcohol. In fact, the vast majority of fraternities and sororities focus on instilling values of scholarship, friendship, leadership, and service in their members. From this point forward, we will refer to both fraternities and sororities as fraternities.

Scholarship

A fraternity experience helps you make the academic transition from high school to college. Although the classes taken in high school are challenging, they'll be even harder in college. Fraternities usually require members to meet certain academic standards. Many hold mandatory study times, old class notes and exams are usually kept on file for study purposes, and personal tutors are often available. Members of a fraternity have a natural vested interest in seeing that other members succeed academically, so older members often assist younger members with their studies.

Friendship

Social life is an important component of Greek life. Social functions offer an excellent opportunity for freshmen to become better acquainted with others in the chapter. Whether it is a Halloween party or a formal dance, there are numerous chances for members to develop poise and confidence. By participating in these functions, students enrich friendships and build memories that will last a lifetime. Remember, social functions aren't only parties; they can include such activities as intramural sports and Homecoming.

Leadership

Because fraternities are self-governing organizations, leadership opportunities abound. Students are given hands-on experience in leading committees, managing budgets, and interacting with faculty members and administrators. Most houses have as many as ten officers, along with an array of committee members. By becoming actively involved in leadership roles, students gain valuable experience that is essential for a successful career. Interestingly, although Greeks represent less than 10 percent of the undergraduate student population, they hold the majority of leadership positions on campus.

Service

According to the North-American Interfraternity Council, fraternities are increasingly becoming involved in philanthropies and hands-on service projects. Helping less fortunate people has become a major focus of Greek life. This can vary from work with Easter Seals, blood drives, and food pantry collections to community upkeep, such as picking up trash, painting houses, or cleaning up area parks.

Greeks also get involved in projects with organizations such as Habitat for Humanity, the American Heart Association, and Children's Miracle Network. By being involved in philanthropic projects, students not only raise money for worthwhile causes, but they also gain a deeper insight into themselves and their responsibility to the community.

Roommates

When you arrive on campus, you will face a daunting task: to live peacefully with a stranger for the rest of the academic year.

To make this task easier, most schools use some type of room assignment survey. This can make roommate matches more successful. For example, two people who prefer to stay up late and play guitar can be matched, while two people who prefer to rise at dawn and hit the track can be a pair. Such differences are easy to ask about on a survey and easy for students to report. However, surveys cannot ask everything, and chances are pretty good that

HOMESICKNESS

Homesickness in its most basic form is a longing for the stuff of home: your parents, friends, bedroom, school, and all of the other familiar people and objects that make you comfortable. But on another level, homesickness is a longing to go back in time. Moving away to college forces you to take on new responsibilities and begin to act like an adult. This can be scary.

While this condition is often described as a "sickness," no pill will provide a quick fix. Instead, you need to acknowledge that your feelings are a normal reaction to a significant change in your life. Allow yourself to feel the sadness of moving on in life and be open to conversations about it that may crop up in your dorm or among your new friends. After all, everyone is dealing with this issue. Then, make an effort to create a new home and a new life on campus. Create new habits and routines so that this once-strange place becomes familiar. Join activities and engage in campus life. This will help you to create a feeling of belonging that will ultimately be the key to overcoming homesickness.

something about your roommate is going to get on your nerves.

In order to avoid conflict, plan ahead. When you first meet, work out some ground rules. Most schools have roommates write a contract together and sign it during the first week of school. Ground rules help eliminate conflict from the start by allowing each person to know what is expected. You should consider the following areas: privacy, quiet time, chores, and borrowing.

When considering privacy, think about how much time alone you need each day and how you will arrange for each person to have private time. Class schedules usually give you some alone time. Be aware of this; if your class is cancelled, consider going for a cup of coffee or a browse in the bookstore instead of immediately rushing back to the room. Privacy also relates to giving your roommate space when he or she has had a bad day or just needs time to think. Set up clear hours for quiet time. Your dorm will already have some quiet hours established. You may choose to simply reiterate those or add additional time. Just be clear.

Two other potentially stormy issues are chores and borrowing. If there are cleaning chores that need to be shared, make a schedule and stick to it. No one appreciates a sink full of dirty dishes or a dingy shower. Remember the golden rule: do your chores as you wish your roommate would. When it comes to borrowing, set up clear rules. The safest bet is to not allow it; but if you do, limit when, for how long, and what will be done in case of damage.

Another issue many students confront is whether or not to live with a best friend from high school who is attending the same college. Generally, this is a bad idea for several reasons. First, you may think you know your best friend inside and out, but you may be surprised by her personal living habits. There is nothing like the closeness of a dorm room to reveal the annoying routines of your friend. Plus, personalities can change rapidly in college. Once you are away from home, you may be surprised at how you or your friend transforms from shy and introverted to late night partygoer. This can cause

conflict. A final downfall is that the two of you will stick together like glue in the first few weeks and miss out on opportunities to meet other people who are also new, vulnerable, and open to new friendships.

Armed with this information, you should have a smooth year with your new roommate. But just in case you are the exception, most colleges will allow students who absolutely cannot get along to move. Prior to moving, each student must usually go through a dispute resolution process. This typically involves your Resident Adviser, you, and your roommate trying to work through your problems in a structured way.

Living with a roommate can be challenging at times, but the ultimate rewards—meeting someone new, encountering new ideas, and learning how to compromise—will serve you well later in life. Enjoy your roommate and all the experiences you will have, both good and bad, for they are all part of the college experience.

Commuting from Home

For some students, home during the college years is the same house they grew up in. Whether you are in this situation because you can't afford to live on campus or because you'd just rather live at home with your family, some basic guidelines will keep you connected with campus life.

By all means, do not just go straight home after class. Spend some of your free time at school. Usually there is a student union or a coffee shop where students gather and socialize. Make it a point to go there and talk to people between classes. Also, get involved in extracurricular activities, and visit classmates in the dorms.

If you drive to school, find other students who want to carpool. Most schools have a Commuter's Office or Club that will give you a list of people who live near you. Sharing a car ride will give you time to talk and form a relationship with someone else who knows about the challenges of commuting.

Commuter's clubs also sponsor a variety of activities throughout the year. Try out these activities.

Be sure also to consider the variety of activities open to all members of the student body, ranging from student government to community service to intramural sports. You may find this takes a bit more effort on your part, but the payoff in the close friendships you'll form will more than make up for it.

WHAT IF YOU DON'T LIKE THE COLLEGE YOU PICK

In the best of all worlds, you compile a list of colleges, find the most compatible one, and are accepted. You have a great time, learn a lot, graduate, and head off to a budding career. However, you may find the college you chose isn't the best of all worlds. Imagine these scenarios:

1. Halfway through your first semester of college, you come to the distressing conclusion that you can't stand being there for whatever reason. The courses don't match your interests. The campus is out in the boonies, and you don't ever want to see another cow. The selection of extracurricular activities doesn't cut it.

2. You have methodically planned to go to a community college for two years and move to a four-year college to complete your degree. Transferring takes you nearer to your goal.

3. You thought you wanted to major in art, but by the end of the first semester, you find yourself more interested in English lit. Things get confusing, so you drop out of college to sort out your thoughts and now you want to drop back in, hoping to rescue some of those credits.

4. You didn't do that well in high school— socializing got in the way of studying. But you've wised up, have gotten serious about your future, and two years of community college have brightened your prospects of transferring to a four-year institution.

Circumstances shift, people change, and, realistically speaking, it's not all that uncommon to transfer. Many people do. The reasons why students transfer run the gamut, as do the institutional policies that govern them. The most common transfers are students who move from a two-year to a four-year university or the person who opts for a career change midstream.

Whatever reasons you might have for wanting to transfer, you will be doing more than just switching academic gears. Aside from losing credits, time, and money, transferring brings up the problem of adjusting to a new situation. This affects just about all transfer students, from those who made a mistake in choosing a college to those who planned to go to a two-year college and then transferred to a four-year campus. People can choose colleges for arbitrary reasons. That's why admissions departments try to ensure a good match between the student and campus before classes begin. Unfortunately, sometimes students don't realize they've made a mistake until it's too late.

The best way to avoid having to transfer is to extensively research a college or university before choosing it. Visit the campus and stay overnight, talk to admissions and faculty members, and try to learn as much as you can.

9 chapter

OTHER OPTIONS AFTER HIGH SCHOOL

Thirty years ago, most young people went directly to work after high school. Today, most young people first go to school for more training, but the majority don't go to traditional four-year colleges.

ACCORDING TO SHANNON MCBRIDE, Director of the Golden Crescent Tech Prep Partnership in Victoria, Texas, "Only 40 percent of high school graduates attempt to go to a four-year college, and of those, only 25 percent get their degree. And of that 25 percent, only 37 percent use the degree they got in that area."

So why aren't the remaining 60 percent of students choosing a traditional four-year college? The reasons are as varied as the students. Life events can often interfere with plans to attend college. Responsibilities to a family may materialize that make it impossible to delay earning an income for four years. One may have to work and go to school. And traditional colleges demand certain conventions, behaviors, and attitudes that don't fit every kind of person. Some people need a lot of physical activity to feel satisfied, while others just aren't interested in spending day after day sitting, reading, memorizing, and analyzing. Years of strict time management and postponed rewards are more than they can stand.

If any of these reasons ring true with you, there are still postsecondary options for you, all of which will not only allow you to pursue further education but also will train you for a career. Let's take a look at some of these educational directions you can follow.

DISTANCE LEARNING

As a future college student, can you picture yourself in any of these scenarios?

1. You need some information, but the only place to find it is at a big state university. Trouble is, it's hundreds of miles away. No problem. You simply go to your local community college and hook up electronically with the university. Voila! The resources are brought to you.

2. That ten-page paper is due in a few days, but you still have some last-minute questions to ask the professor before you turn it in. Only one problem: you won't be able to see the professor until after the paper is due. Being a night owl, you also want to work on it when your roommate is asleep. Not to worry. Since you have the professor's e-mail address, just like all the other students in the class, you simply e-mail your question to her. She replies. You get your answer, finish the paper, and even turn it in electronically.

3. After graduating from high school, you can't go to college right away, but your employer has a neat hook up with a college that offers courses via the Internet. During your lunch hours, you and several of your work buddies log in to a class and get college credit.

Not too long ago, if you'd offered these scenarios to high school graduates as real possibilities, they would have thought you were a sci-fi freak. Distance education was not common at all—or if it was, it usually meant getting courses via snail mail or on videotape. Well, today you are in the right place at the right time. Distance education is a reality for countless high school graduates.

What distance education now means is that you can access educational programs and not have to physically be in a classroom on a campus. Through such technologies as cable or satellite television, videotapes and audiotapes, fax, computer modem, computer conferencing and videoconferencing, and other means of electronic delivery, the classroom comes to you—sometimes even if you're sitting in your room in your bunny slippers and it's 2 in the morning.

Distance learning expands the reach of the classroom by using various technologies to deliver university resources to off-campus sites, transmit college courses into the workplace, and enable you to view class lectures in the comfort of your home.

Where and How Can I Take Distance Learning Courses?

The technology for new, cheaper telecommunications technology is getting better all the time, and there is a growing demand for education by people who can't afford either the time or money to be a full-time, on-campus student. To fill that demand, educational networks also are growing and changing how and when you can access college courses.

Most states have established new distance learning systems to advance the delivery of instruction to schools, postsecondary institutions, and state government agencies. Colleges and universities are collaborating with commercial telecommunications entities, including online information services such as America Online and cable and telephone companies, to provide education to far-flung student constituencies. Professions such as law, medicine, and accounting, as well as knowledge-based industries, are utilizing telecommunications networks for the transmission of customized higher education programs to working professionals, technicians, and managers.

Ways in Which Distance Learning May Be Offered:

- **Credit courses.** In general, if these credit courses are completed successfully, they may be applied toward a degree.

- **Noncredit courses and courses offered for professional certification.** These programs can help you acquire specialized knowledge in a concentrated, time-efficient manner and stay on top of the latest developments in your field. They provide a flexible way for you to prepare for a new career or study for professional licensure and certification. Many of these university programs are created in cooperation with professional and trade associations so that courses are based on real-life workforce needs, and the practical skills learned are immediately applicable in the field.

What Else Does Distance Learning Offer?

Distance learning comes in a variety of colors and flavors. Along with traditional college degrees, you can earn professional certification or continuing education credits (CEUs) in a particular field.

Professional Certification

Certificate programs often focus on employment specializations, such as hazardous waste management or electronic publishing, and can be helpful to those seeking to advance or change careers. Also, many states mandate continuing education for professionals such as teachers, nursing home administrators, or accountants. Distance learning offers a convenient way for many individuals to meet professional certification requirements. Health care, engineering, and education are just a few of the many professions that take advantage of distance learning to help their professionals maintain certification.

Many colleges offer a sequence of distance learning courses in a specific field of a profession. For instance, within the engineering profession, certificate programs in computer integrated manufacturing, systems engineering, test and evaluation, and waste management education and research consortium are offered via distance learning.

Business offerings include distance learning certification in information technology, total quality management, and health services management.

Within the field of education, you'll find distance learning certificate programs in areas such as early reading instruction and special education for the learning handicapped. There are opportunities for you to earn degrees at a distance at the associate, baccalaureate, and graduate levels. Two-year community college students are now able to earn baccalaureate degrees—without relocating—by transferring to distance learning programs offered by four-year universities. Corporations are forming partnerships with universities to bring college courses to worksites and encourage employees to continue their education. Distance learning is especially popular among people who want to earn their degree part-time while continuing to work full-time. Although on-campus residencies are sometimes required for certain distance learning degree programs, they generally can be completed while employees are on short-term leave or vacation.

Continuing Education Units (CEUs)

If you choose to take a course on a noncredit basis, you may be able to earn continuing education units (CEUs). The CEU system is a nationally recognized system to provide a standardized measure for accumulating, transferring, and recognizing participation in continuing education programs. One CEU is defined as 10 contact hours of participation in an organized continuing education experience under responsible sponsorship, capable direction, and qualified instruction.

The Way Distance Learning Works

Enrolling in a distance learning course may simply involve filling out a registration form, making sure that you have access to the equipment needed, and

paying the tuition and fees by check, money order, or credit card. In these cases, your applications may be accepted without entrance examinations or proof of prior educational experience.

Other courses may involve educational prerequisites and access to equipment not found in all geographic locations. Some institutions offer detailed information about individual courses, such as a course outline, upon request. If you have access to the Internet and simply wish to review course descriptions, you may be able to peruse an institution's course catalogs electronically by accessing the institution's home page on the Web.

Time Requirements

Some courses allow you to enroll at your convenience and work at your own pace. Others closely adhere to a traditional classroom schedule. Specific policies and time limitations pertaining to withdrawals, refunds, transfers, and renewal periods can be found in the institutional catalog.

Admission to a Degree Program

If you plan to enter a degree program, you should consult the academic advising department of the institution of your choice to learn about entrance requirements and application procedures. You may find it necessary to develop a portfolio of your past experiences and of your accomplishments that may have resulted in college-level learning.

How Do I Communicate with My Instructor?

Student-faculty exchanges occur using electronic communication (through fax and e-mail). Many institutions offer their distance learning students access to toll-free numbers so students can talk to their professors or teaching assistants without incurring any long-distance charges.

Responses to your instructor's comments on your lessons, requests for clarification of comments, and all other exchanges between you and your instructor will take time. Interaction with your instructor—whether by computer, phone, or letter—is important, and you must be willing to take the initiative.

COMMUNITY COLLEGES

Two-year colleges—better known as community colleges—are often called "the people's colleges." With their open-door policies (admission is open to individuals with a high school diploma or its equivalent), community colleges provide access to higher education for millions of Americans who might otherwise be excluded from higher education. Community college students are diverse, of all ages, races, and economic backgrounds. While many community college students enroll full-time, an equally large number attend on a part-time basis so they can fulfill employment and family commitments as they advance their education.

Today, there are more than 1,100 community colleges in the United States. They enroll more than 5.6 million students, who represent 45 percent of all undergraduates in the United States. Nearly 55 percent of all first-time freshmen begin their higher education in a community college.

Community colleges can also be referred to as either technical or junior colleges, and they may either be under public or independent control. What unites these two-year colleges is that they are regionally accredited, postsecondary institutions, whose highest credential awarded is the associate degree. With few exceptions, community colleges offer a comprehensive curriculum, which includes transfer, technical, and continuing education programs.

Important Factors in a Community College Education

The student who attends a community college can count on receiving quality instruction in a supportive learning community. This setting frees the student to pursue his or her own goals, nurture special talents, explore new fields of learning, and develop the capacity for lifelong learning.

From the student's perspective, four characteristics capture the essence of community colleges:

- They are community-based institutions that work in close partnership with high schools, community groups, and employers in extending high-quality programs at convenient times and places.

- Community colleges are cost effective. Annual tuition and fees at public community colleges average approximately half those at public four-year colleges and less than 15 percent of private four-year institutions. In addition, since most community colleges are generally close to their students' homes, these students can also save a significant amount of money on the room, board, and transportation expenses traditionally associated with a college education.

- They provide a caring environment, with faculty members who are expert instructors, known for excellent teaching and for meeting students at the point of their individual needs, regardless of age, sex, race, current job status, or previous academic preparation. Community

A SCHOLARSHIP FOR CAREER COLLEGE STUDENTS

The Imagine America Scholarship can help those who dream of a career but might not be able to achieve it through traditional college education.

What Is the Imagine America Scholarship?

Introduced in 1998 by the Career Training Foundation, the Imagine America Scholarship aims to reduce the growing "skills gap" in America. Any graduating high school senior can be considered for selection for one of the two scholarships awarded to his or her high school. The Imagine America Scholarship gives 10,000 graduating high school seniors scholarships of $1,000 to be used at more than 300 participating career colleges and schools across the country.

You Can Participate in the Imagine America Scholarship If:

- **You attend any private postsecondary institution that is accredited by an agency recognized by the U.S. Department of Education.**

- **You are graduating from high school this year.**

To find out more about the Imagine America Scholarship Program, talk to your high school counselor or visit www.petersons.com/cca for more information.

colleges join a strong curriculum with a broad range of counseling and career services that are intended to assist students in making the most of their educational opportunities.

- Many offer comprehensive programs, including transfer curricula in such liberal arts programs as chemistry, psychology, and business management, that lead directly to a baccalaureate degree and career programs that prepare students for employment or assist those already employed to upgrade their skills. For those students who need to strengthen their academic skills, community colleges also offer a wide range of developmental programs in mathematics, languages, and learning skills, designed to prepare the student for success in college studies.

Getting to Know Your Two-Year College

The best way to learn about your college is to visit in person. During a campus visit, be prepared to ask a lot

of questions. Talk to students, faculty members, administrators, and counselors about the college and its programs, particularly those in which you have a special interest. Ask about available certificates and associate degrees. Don't be shy. Do what you can to dig below the surface. Ask college officials about the transfer rate to four-year colleges. If a college emphasizes student services, find out what particular assistance is offered, such as educational or career guidance. Colleges are eager to provide you with the information you need to make informed decisions.

The Money Factor

For many students, the decision to attend a community college is often based on financial factors. If you aren't sure what you want to do or what talents you have, community colleges allow you the freedom to explore different career interests at a low cost. For those students who can't afford the cost of university tuition, community colleges let them take care of their basic classes before transferring to a four-year institution. Many two-year colleges can now offer you instruction in your own home through cable television or public broadcast stations or through home study courses that can save both time and money. Look into all your options, and be sure to add up all the costs of attending various colleges before deciding which is best for you.

Working and Going to School

Many two-year college students maintain full-time or part-time employment while they earn their degrees. Over the past decades, a steadily growing number of students have chosen to attend community colleges while they fulfill family and employment responsibilities. To enable these students to balance the demands of home, work, and school, most community colleges offer classes at night and on weekends.

For the full-time student, the usual length of time it takes to obtain an associate degree is two years. However, your length of study will depend on the course load you take: the fewer credits you earn each

MOST POPULAR MAJORS FOR COMMUNITY COLLEGE GRADS

The American Association of Community Colleges conducted a survey in the year 2000 to see what the most popular majors for community college students were. The top 15 majors and their average starting salaries follow:

MAJOR	AVERAGE STARTING SALARY
1. Registered Nursing	$32,757
2. General Computer Technologies	$34,242
3. Computer Networking	$38,767
4. Engineering–Electric/Electronics	$29, 464
5. Computer Technician/Networking	$36,092
6. Manufacturing Technology	$30,291
7. Radiology Technology	$32,478
8. Digital Media	$35,409
9. Computer Programming	$30,838
10. General Skilled Trades	$25,598
11. Law Enforcement	$27,975
12. Dental Hygiene	$41,907
13. Computer-Aided Design	$27,968
14. Automotive	$29,305
15. General Allied Health	$24,781

term, the longer it will take you to earn a degree. To assist you in moving more quickly to your degree, many community colleges now award credit through examination or for equivalent knowledge gained through relevant life experiences. Be certain to find out the credit options that are available to you at the college in which you are interested. You may discover that it will take less time to earn a degree than you first thought.

Preparation for Transfer

Studies have repeatedly shown that students who first attend a community college and then transfer to a four-year college or university do at least as well academically as the students who entered the four-year institutions as freshmen. Most community colleges have agreements with nearby four-year institutions to make transfer of credits easier. If you are thinking of transferring, be sure to meet with a counselor or faculty adviser before choosing your courses. You will want to map out a course of study with transfer in mind. Make sure you also find out the credit-transfer requirements of the four-year institution you might want to attend.

New Career Opportunities

Community colleges realize that many entering students are not sure about the field in which they want to focus their studies or the career they would like to pursue. Often, students discover fields and careers they never knew existed. Community colleges have the resources to help students identify areas of career interest and to set challenging occupational goals.

Once a career goal is set, you can be confident that a community college will provide job-relevant, quality occupation and technical education. About half of the students who take courses for credit at community colleges do so to prepare for employment or to acquire or upgrade skills for their current job. Especially helpful in charting a career path is the assistance of a counselor or a faculty adviser, who can discuss job opportunities in your chosen field and help you map out your course of study.

In addition, since community colleges have close ties to their communities, they are in constant contact with leaders in business, industry, organized labor, and public life. Community colleges work with these individuals and their organizations to prepare students for direct entry into the world of work. For example, some community colleges have established partnerships with local businesses and industries to provide specialized training programs. Some also provide the academic portion of apprenticeship training, while others offer extensive job-shadowing and cooperative education opportunities. Be sure to examine all of the career-preparation opportunities offered by the community colleges in which you are interested.

VOCATIONAL/CAREER COLLEGES

Career education is important for every employee as technology continues to change, and the traditional large employers are facing serious downsizing. No one is immune from this downsizing. From the largest employers, such as the U.S. military, defense contractors, IBM, aviation, and health care, down to the company with one and two employees, issues of keeping up with technology and producing goods and services cheaper, faster and at less cost requires—indeed demands—a skilled, world-class workforce. In good or bad economic times, you will always have a distinct advantage if you have a demonstrable skill and can be immediately productive while continuing to learn and improve. If you know how to use technology, work collaboratively, and find creative solutions, you will always be in demand.

Career colleges offer scores of opportunities to learn the technical skills required by many of today's and tomorrow's top jobs. This is especially true in the areas of computer and information technology, health care, and hospitality (culinary arts, travel and tourism, and hotel and motel management). Career colleges range in size from those with a handful of students to universities with thousands enrolled. They are located in every state in the nation and share one common objective—to prepare students for a successful career in the world of work through a focused, intensive

SNAPSHOT OF A CAREER COLLEGE STUDENT

Katrina Dew
Network Systems Administration
Silicon Valley College
Fremont, California

WHAT I LIKE ABOUT BEING A CAREER STUDENT:

"Career colleges are for fast-track-oriented students who want to get out in the work field and still feel that they have an appropriate education."

ABOUT KATRINA

Right after high school, Katrina headed for junior college, but she felt like she was spinning her wheels. She wanted something that was goal-oriented. Community college offered too many options. She needed to be focused in one direction.

At first, Katrina thought she would become a physical therapist. Then she realized how much schooling she would need to begin working. Turning to the computer field, she saw some definite benefits. For one, she had messed around with them in high school. She could get a degree and get out in two years. She saw that computer careers are big and getting bigger. Plus, there weren't a lot of women in that field, which signaled more potential for her. But before she switched schools, she visited the career college, talked to students, and sat in on lectures. She really liked the way the teachers related to their students. Along with her technical classes, she's taken algebra, psychology, English composition, and management communication.

Nicholas Cecere
Automotive Techniques Management
Education America/Vale Technical Institute
Blairsville, Pennsylvania

WHAT I LIKE ABOUT BEING A CAREER STUDENT:

"I compare career college to a magnifying glass that takes the sun and focuses it. You learn just what you need to learn."

ABOUT NICHOLAS

Nicholas has completely repainted his 1988 Mercury Topaz, redone all the brakes, put in a brand-new exhaust system, and lots of smaller stuff here and there. But he says that's nothing compared to the completely totaled cars some of his classmates haul into the school. Talk about hands-on: they're able to completely restore them while going through the program.

Nicholas didn't always have gasoline running through his veins. In fact, he just recently discovered how much he likes automotives. After graduating from high school, he went to a community college, and after one semester, he left to work at a personal care home. Standing over a sink of dirty dishes made him realize he wanted more than just a job. He started thinking about what he wanted to do and visited a few schools, including the body shop where his brother worked. Where others might see twisted car frames, Nicholas saw opportunity and enrolled in the program.

curriculum. America's career colleges are privately owned and operated for-profit companies. Instead of using tax support to operate, career colleges pay taxes. Because career colleges are businesses, they must be responsive to the workforce needs of their communities or they will cease to exist.

Generally, these schools prepare you for a specific career. Some will require you to take academic courses such as English or history. Others will relate every class you take to a specific job, such as computer-aided drafting or interior design. Some focus specifically on business or technical fields. Bob Sullivan, a career counselor at East Brunswick High School in East Brunswick, New Jersey, points out that the negative side to this kind of education is that if you haven't carefully researched what you want to do, you could waste a lot of time and money. "There's no room for exploration or finding yourself as opposed to a community college where you can go to find yourself and feel your way around," he explains.

So how do you find the right career college for you? A good place to start is knowing generally what you want to do. You don't have to know the fine details of your goals, but you should have a broad idea, such as a career in allied health or business or computing. Once you make that decision, most career colleges will help you define your initial decisions.

After you've crossed that hurdle, the rest is easy. Since professional training is the main purpose of career colleges, its graduates are the best measure of a school's success. Who hires the graduates? How do their jobs relate to the education they received? Career colleges should be able to provide that data to prospective students. "Career colleges have a different customer than other institutions," notes Stephen Friedheim, President of ESS College of Business in Dallas, Texas. In addition to focusing on the needs of their students, career colleges also want to ensure they meet the needs of the employers who are hiring their graduates. "The assumption is that if you can please the employer, you will please the student," Friedheim explains.

Checking the credentials of a career college is one of the most important steps you should take in your career college search. Though not every career college has to be accredited, it is a sign that the college has gone through a process that ensures quality. It also means that students can qualify for federal grant and loan programs. Furthermore, you should see if the college has met the standards from professional training organizations. In fields such as court reporting and health-related professions, those criteria mean a lot.

FINANCIAL AID OPTIONS FOR CAREER AND COMMUNITY COLLEGES

The financial aid process is basically the same for students attending a community college, a career college, or a technical institute as it is for students attending a four-year college. However, there are some details that can make the difference between getting the maximum amount of financial aid and only scraping by.

As with four-year students, the federal government is still your best source of financial aid. Most community colleges and career and technical schools participate in federal financial aid programs. To get detailed information about federal financial aid programs and how to apply for them, read through Chapter 7: "Financial Aid Dollars and Sense." Here are some quick tips on where to look for education money.

Investigate federal financial aid programs. You should definitely check out a Federal Pell Grant, which is a need-based grant available to those who can't pay the entire tuition themselves. The Federal Supplemental Educational Opportunity Grant (FSEOG) is for those students with exceptional financial need. You also can take advantage of the Federal Work-Study programs that provide jobs for students with financial aid eligibility to work in return for part of their tuition. Many two-year institutions offer work-study, but the number of jobs tends to be limited. Also, federal loans make up a substantial part of financial aid for two-year students. Student loans, which have lower interest rates, may be sponsored by the institution or federally sponsored, or they may be available through commercial financial institutions.

WHAT TO LOOK FOR IN A CAREER COLLEGE

A tour of the college is a must! While visiting the campus, do the following:

- **Get a full explanation of the curriculum, including finding out how you will be trained.**

- **Take a physical tour of the classrooms and laboratories and look for cleanliness, modern equipment/computers, and size of classes. Observe the activity in classes: are students engaged in class, and are lectures dynamic?**

- **Ask about employment opportunities after graduation. What are the placement rates (most current) and list of employers? Inquire about specific placement assistance: resume preparation, job leads, etc. Look for "success stories" on bulletin boards, placement boards, and newsletters.**

- **Find out about tuition and other costs associated with the program. Ask about the financial aid assistance provided to students.**

- **Find out if an externship is part of the training program. How are externships assigned? Does the student have any input as to externship assignment?**

- **Ask if national certification and registration in your chosen field is available upon graduation.**

- **Inquire about the college's accreditation and certification.**

- **Also find out the associations and organizations the college belongs to. Ask what awards or honors the college has achieved.**

- **Ask if the college utilizes an advisory board to develop employer relationships.**

- **Ask about the rules and regulations. What GPA must be maintained? What is the attendance policy? What are grounds for termination? What is the refund policy if the student drops or is terminated? Is there a dress code? What are the holidays of the college?**

Source: Arizona College of Allied Health, Phoenix, Arizona

They are basically the same as those for the traditional four-year college student, such as the Federal Perkins Loan and the Subsidized and Unsubsidized Federal Stafford Student Loans. In fact, some private career colleges and technical institutes only offer federal loans. You also can find more specific information about federal loans in Chapter 7.

Don't overlook scholarships. What many two-year students don't realize is that they could be eligible for scholarships. Regrettably, many make the assumption that scholarships are only for very smart students attending prestigious universities. You'd be surprised to learn how many community and career colleges have scholarships. It's critical to talk to the financial aid office of each school you plan to attend to find out what scholarships might be available. The Imagine America scholarship program is offered to students who attend select career colleges around the country. See "A Scholarship for Career College Students" on page 95 for more information.

Check in with your state. Two-year students should find out how their states can help them pay for tuition. Every state in the union has some level of state financial aid that goes to community college students. The amounts are dependent on which state you live in, and most are in the form of grants.

APPRENTICESHIPS

Some students like working with their hands and have the skill, patience, and temperament to become expert mechanics, carpenters, or electronic repair technicians. If you think you'd enjoy a profession like this and feel that college training isn't for you, then you might want to think about a job that requires apprenticeship training.

To stay competitive, America needs highly skilled workers. But if you're looking for a soft job, forget it. An apprenticeship is no snap. It demands hard work and has tough competition, so you've got to have the will to see it through. An apprenticeship is a program formally agreed upon between a worker and an employer where the employee learns a skilled trade through classroom work and on-the-job training. Apprenticeship programs vary in length, pay, and intensity among the various trades. A person completing an apprenticeship program generally becomes a journeyperson (skilled craftsperson) in that trade.

The advantages of apprenticeships are numerous. First and foremost, an apprenticeship leads to a lasting lifetime skill. As a highly trained worker, you can take

BUREAU OF APPRENTICESHIP AND TRAINING OFFICES

National Office:

**U.S. Department of Labor
Frances Perkins Building
200 Constitution Avenue, NW
Washington, D.C. 20210**

**Northeast Regional Office
Suite 1815 East
170 South Independence Mall West
Philadelphia, Pennsylvania 19106**

**Southern Regional Office
Room 6T71
61 Forsyth Street, SW
Atlanta, Georgia 30303**

**Midwestern Regional Office
Room 656
230 South Dearborn Street
Chicago, Illinois**

**Southwestern Regional Office
Room 317
Federal Building
525 Griffin Street
Dallas, Texas 75202**

**Western Regional Office
Room 465721
U.S. Custom House
19th Street
Denver, Colorado 80202**

your skill anywhere you decide to go. The more creative, exciting, and challenging jobs are put in the hands of the fully skilled worker, the all-around person who knows his or her trade inside out.

Skilled workers advance much faster than those who are semiskilled or whose skills are not broad enough to equip them to assume additional responsibilities in a career. Those who complete an apprenticeship have also acquired the skills and judgment that are necessary to go into business for themselves if they choose.

What to Do if You're Interested in an Apprenticeship

If you want to begin an apprenticeship, you have to be at least 16 years old, and you must fill out an application for employment. These applications may be available year-round or at certain times during the year, depending on the trade you're interested in. Because an apprentice must be trained in an area where work actually exists and where a certain pay scale is guaranteed upon completion of the program, the wait for application acceptance may be pretty long in areas of low employment. This standard works to your advantage, however. Just think: you wouldn't want to spend one to six years of your life learning a job where no work exists or where the wage is the same as, or just a little above, that of common laborer.

Federal regulations prohibit anyone under the age of 16 from being considered for an apprenticeship. Some programs require a high school degree or certain course work. Other requirements may include passing certain aptitude tests, proof of physical ability to perform the duties of the trade, and possession of a valid driver's license.

Once you have met the basic program entrance requirements, you'll be interviewed and awarded points on your interest in the trade, your attitude toward work in general, and personal traits, such as appearance, sincerity, character, and habits. Openings are awarded to those who have achieved the most points.

If you're considering an apprenticeship, the best sources of assistance and information are vocational or career counselors, local state employment security agencies, field offices of state apprenticeship agencies, and regional offices of the Bureau of Apprenticeship and Training (BAT). Apprenticeships are usually registered with the BAT or a state apprenticeship council. Some apprenticeships are not registered at all, although that doesn't necessarily mean that the program isn't valid. To find out if a certain apprenticeship is legitimate, contact your state's apprenticeship agency or a regional office of the BAT. Addresses and phone numbers for these regional offices are listed above. You can also visit the Bureau's Web site at www.doleta.gov/atels_bat.

THE MILITARY OPTION

Bet you didn't know that the United States military is the largest employer in the country. There's got to be a good reason that so many people get their paychecks from Uncle Sam.

SHOULD I OR SHOULDN'T I WORK FOR THE LARGEST EMPLOYER IN THE U.S.?

Every year, thousands of young people pursue a military career and enjoy the benefits it offers. Yet thousands more consider joining the military and decide against it. Their reasons vary, but many choose not to enlist because they lack knowledge of what a career in the military can offer. Others simply mistrust recruiters based on horror stories they've heard. Sadly, many make the decision against joining the military without ever setting foot in the recruiting office.

But if you are an informed "shopper," you will be able to make an informed choice about whether the military is right for you.

People rarely buy anything based on their needs: Instead, they buy based on their emotions. We see it on a daily basis in advertising, from automobiles to soft drinks. We rarely see an automobile commercial that gives statistics about how the car is engineered, how long it will last, the gas mileage, and other technical specifications. Instead, we see people driving around and having a good time.

The reason for this is that advertising agencies know that you will probably buy something based on how you feel rather than what you think. Because of this tendency to buy with emotion rather than reason, it is important to separate the feelings from the facts. That way, you can base your decision about whether to join the military primarily on the facts.

There are two big questions that you must answer before you can come to any conclusions. First, is the military right for me, and second, if the first answer is yes, which branch is right for me?

Suppose that you have to decide whether to buy a new car or repair your current car. The first choice you make will determine your next course of action. You will have to weigh the facts to determine if you will purchase a new car or not. Once you've decided to buy a car rather than repair your old one, you must then decide exactly what make and model will best suit your needs.

NO HYPE, JUST THE FACTS

So you didn't wake up one morning and know for sure that you're going to join the Navy. One minute you think you'd like the Army, but then you talk to your cousin who convinces you to follow him into the Air Force. But then the neighbor down the street is a Marine, and he's gung ho for you to join up with them. What to do?

Well, a helpful Web site is the answer. Go to www.spear.navy.mil/profile for some really straightforward and non-partisan information about each branch of the military. You'll be able to compare the benefits that each service offers plus pick up other helpful tips and information. The Web site is designed specifically for high school students considering the military.

"Normally the first question we get from people interested in the Air Force is 'What does the Air Force have to offer me?' But I back off and ask them about their qualifications. Sometimes it's easier to go to an Ivy League school than to join the Air Force because of our stringent requirements."

**Master Sergeant Timothy Little
United States Air Force**

You should make a list of the reasons why you want to join the military before you ever set foot in the recruiter's office. Whether your list is long—containing such items as money for college, job security, opportunity to travel, technical training, and good pay—or contains only one item, such as having full-time employment, the number of items on your list is not what's important. What is important is that you are able to satisfy those reasons, or primary motivators.

Whatever your list contains, the first course of action is to collect your list of reasons to join the military and put them in order of importance to you. This process, known as rank-ordering, will help you determine if you should proceed with the enlistment process.

"Take two people with the same qualifications who are looking for jobs. The person with the Army background will be that much more competitive. That's due to the fact that he or she is disciplined and knows how to act without being told what to do."

Staff Sergeant Max Burda
United States Army

Rank-ordering your list is a simple process of deciding which motivators are most important to you and then listing them in order of importance. List your most important motivator as number one, your next most important as number two, and so on.

If we apply the car-buying scenario here, your primary motivators may be finding a car that costs under $20,000, has a four-cylinder engine, gets at least 30 miles to the gallon, has leather interior, is available in blue, and has a sunroof. If you put those motivators in rank order, your list might look something like this:

1. Costs under $20,000

2. Gets at least 30 mpg

3. Has a sunroof

4. Has leather interior

5. Available in blue

You'll notice that the number one, or most important, motivator in this case is cost, while the last, or least important, motivator is color. The more important the motivator, the less likely you'll be willing to settle for something different or to live without it altogether.

After you've rank-ordered your motivators, go down your list and determine whether those motivators can be met by enlisting in the military. If you find that all your motivators can be met by enlisting, that's great; but even if only some of your motivators can be met, you may still want to consider it. Seldom does a product meet all our needs and wants.

CHOOSING WHICH BRANCH TO JOIN

"If you like to travel, we offer more than anyone else. The longest you're under-way is generally two to three weeks, with three to four days off in every port and one day on the ship. Prior to pulling in, you can even set up tours."

Chief Petty Officer Keith Horst
United States Navy

If you are seriously considering joining the military, you probably have checked out at least two of the branches. Check them all out, even if it means just requesting literature and reviewing it. A word of caution though: Brochures do not tell the complete story, and it is very difficult to base your decision either for or against a military branch on the contents of a brochure alone. Would you buy a car based solely on the information contained in a brochure? Probably not!

"I tell people that you get paid the same in all the services, and the benefits are the same. What's different about each branch is the environment."

Sergeant Ian Bonnell, Infantry Sergeant
United States Marines

I'M JOINING THE AIR FORCE

It didn't take Brian Filipek long to decide he wanted to join the Air Force. But that's if you don't count the times he talked to people who had served in the Air Force or the research he did on the Internet to gather information—and that was before he even set foot inside the recruiter's office. By the time an Air Force recruiter responded to a card Brian had sent in, he was pretty sure he liked what he'd seen so far. "The recruiter didn't have to do any work to convince me," says Brian. After that, it was a matter of going through the pre-qualifying process, like whether he met the height and weight qualifications, and the security forms he had to fill out.

After he enlisted, Brian didn't stop gathering information. Long before he was sent to Basic Training, he found out about Warrior Week, which is held on one of the last weeks in Basic Training. He was already looking forward to it. "I'm an outdoors kind of person," he says. "I want to do the obstacle course and ropes course."

Though the idea of testing his endurance and strength appeals to him, being away from family will be hard. "Granted, your food is cooked for you, but you're still on your own," he says. However, he knows that it's worth it to achieve his goal of education and free job training. Brian acknowledges that the military is not for everyone, but as far as he's concerned, he's sure he's made the right choice.

Brian Filipek, Enlistee
U.S. Air Force

The process of choosing the right branch of the military for you is basically the same process that you used to determine if joining the military was right for you. You should start with your list of primary motivators and use the "yes/no" method to determine whether each branch can meet all or some of those motivators. Once you've determined which branch or branches can best meet your motivators, it's time to compare those branches. Remember to look for the negative aspects as well as the motivators of each of the branches as you compare.

After making your comparisons, you may still find yourself with more than one choice. What do you do then? You could flip a coin, but that's not the wisest idea! Instead, look at some of these factors:

Length of enlistment—Some branches may require a longer term for offering the same benefits that you could receive from another branch.

Advanced pay grade—You may be entitled to an advanced rank in some branches based on certain enlistment options.

"In the Army, you can get training in everything from culinary arts to truck driving and all the way to aviation mechanics, military intelligence, and computer networking."
Staff Sergeant Max Burda
United States Army

Length and type of training—How long will your training take? Usually the longer the training, the more in-depth and useful it is. You'll also want to consider how useful the training will be once you've left the military.

Enlistment bonuses—Be careful when using an enlistment bonus as the only factor in deciding which branch to choose. If it comes down to a tie between two branches and only one offers a bonus, it's not a bad reason to choose that branch.

Additional pay and allowances—There may be additional pay you'd be entitled to that can only be offered by a particular branch. For instance, if you join the Navy, you may be entitled to Sea Pay and Submarine Pay, something obviously not available if you join the Air Force.

Ability to pursue higher education—While all the military branches offer educational benefits, you must consider when you will be able to take advantage of these benefits. If your job requires 12-hour shifts and has you out in the field a lot, when will you be able to attend classes?

"Everyone in the Navy learns how to fight a fire. You get qualified in First Aid and CPR. That's mandatory for every sailor. The only jobs we don't have in the Navy are veterinarians, forest rangers, and rodeo stars."
Chief Petty Officer Keith Horst
United States Navy

Once you have considered these factors, and perhaps some of your own, you should be able to decide which branch is right for you. If you still haven't been able to select one branch over another, though, consider the following:

- Ask your recruiter if you can speak to someone who has recently joined.

- If there is a base nearby, you may be able to get a tour to look at its facilities.

- If you are well versed in Internet chat rooms, you may want to look for ones that cater to military members—then ask a lot of questions.

- Talk to friends and family members who are currently serving in the military. Be careful, however, not to talk to people who have been out of the military for a while, as they probably aren't familiar with today's military. Also, avoid people who left the military under less-than-desirable conditions (for example, someone who was discharged from Basic Training for no compatibility).

If you choose to continue with processing for enlistment, your next step will probably be to take the Armed Services Vocational Aptitude Battery (ASVAB).

THE ASVAB

The ASVAB, a multiple-aptitude battery designed for use with students in their junior or senior year in high school or in a postsecondary school, was developed to yield results useful to both students and the military. The military uses the results to determine the qualifications of young people for enlistment and to help place them in military occupational programs. Schools use ASVAB test results to assist their students in developing future educational and career plans.

Frequently Asked Questions about the ASVAB

What is the Armed Services Vocational Aptitude Battery (ASVAB)?

The ASVAB, sponsored by the Department of Defense, is a multi-aptitude test battery consisting of ten short individual tests covering Word Knowledge, Paragraph Comprehension, Arithmetic Reasoning, Mathematic Knowledge, General Science, Auto and Shop Information, Mechanical Comprehension, Electronics Information, Numerical Operations, and Coding Speed. Your ASVAB results provide scores for each individual test, as well as three academic composite scores—Verbal, Math, and Academic Ability—and two career exploration composite scores.

Why should I take the ASVAB?

As a high school student nearing graduation, you are faced with important career choices. Should you go on to college, technical, or vocational school? Would it be better to enter the job market? Should you consider a military career? Your ASVAB scores are measures of aptitude. Your composite scores measure your aptitude for higher academic learning and give you ideas for career exploration.

When and where is the ASVAB given?

ASVAB is administered annually or semiannually at more than 14,000 high schools and postsecondary schools in the United States.

Is there a charge or fee to take the ASVAB?

ASVAB is administered at no cost to the school or to the student.

How long does it take to complete the ASVAB?

ASVAB testing takes approximately 3 hours. If you miss class, it will be with your school's approval.

If I wish to take the ASVAB but my school doesn't offer it (or I missed it), what should I do?

See your school counselor. In some cases, arrangements may be made for you to take it at another high school. Your counselor should call 800-323-0513 (toll-free) for additional information.

How do I find out what my scores mean and how to use them?

Your scores will be provided to you on a report called the ASVAB Student Results Sheet. Along with your scores, you should receive a copy of *Exploring*

Careers: The ASVAB Workbook, which contains information that will help you understand your ASVAB results and show you how to use them for career exploration. Test results are returned to participating schools within thirty days.

What is a passing score on the ASVAB?

No one "passes" or "fails" the ASVAB. The ASVAB enables you to compare your scores to those of other students at your grade level.

If I take the ASVAB, am I obligated to join the military?

No. Taking the ASVAB does not obligate you to the military in any way. You are free to use your test results in whatever manner you wish. You may use the ASVAB results for up to two years for military enlistment if you are a junior, a senior, or a

postsecondary school student. The military services encourage all young people to finish high school before joining the armed forces.

If I am planning to go to college, should I take the ASVAB?

Yes. ASVAB results provide you with information that can help you determine your capacity for advanced academic education. You can also use your ASVAB results, along with other personal information, to identify areas for career exploration.

Should I take the ASVAB if I plan to become a commissioned officer?

Yes. Taking the ASVAB is a valuable experience for any student who aspires to become a military officer. The aptitude information you receive could assist you in career planning.

Should I take the ASVAB if I am considering entering the Reserve or National Guard?

Yes. These military organizations also use the ASVAB for enlistment purposes.

What should I do if a service recruiter contacts me?

You may be contacted by a service recruiter before you graduate. If you want to learn about the many opportunities available through the military service, arrange for a follow-up meeting. However, you are under no obligation to the military as a result of taking the ASVAB.

Is the ASVAB administered other than in the school testing program?

Yes. ASVAB is also used in the regular military enlistment program. It is administered at approximately sixty-five Military Entrance Processing Stations located throughout the United States. Each year, hundreds of thousands of young men and women who are interested in enlisting in the uniformed services (Army, Navy, Air Force, Marines, and Coast Guard) but who did not take the ASVAB while in school are examined and processed at these military stations.

Is any special preparation necessary before taking the ASVAB?

Yes. A certain amount of preparation is required for taking any examination. Whether it is an athletic competition or a written test, preparation is a *must* in order to achieve the best results. Your test scores reflect not only your ability but also the time and effort in preparing for the test. The uniformed services use ASVAB to help determine a person's qualification for enlistment and to help indicate the vocational areas for which the person is best suited. Achieving your maximum score will increase your vocational opportunities. So take practice tests to prepare.

BASIC TRAINING: WHAT HAVE I GOTTEN MYSELF INTO?

The main objective of Basic Training is to transform civilians into well-disciplined military personnel in a matter of weeks. Performing such a monumental task takes a lot of hard work, both mentally and physically. For most people, Basic Training ends with a parade on graduation day. For others, though, it ends somewhere short of graduation. It is those "horror stories" that make Basic Training probably the one biggest fear, or anxiety, for those considering military enlistment.

Unlike the boot camp you may have heard about from your Uncle Louie or seen on television, today's Basic Training doesn't include the verbal and physical abuse of yesterday. All of the military branches are ensuring that new enlistees are treated fairly and with dignity. Not that enlistees aren't yelled at (because they are); however, the vulgarity and demeaning verbal attacks are a thing of the past. There are, from time to time, incidents involving instructors who contradict the military's policies. These violations, however, receive a lot of attention, are thoroughly investigated, and usually end up with disciplinary action taken against those involved in the abuse.

I SURVIVED BASIC TRAINING

Although Michael Hipszky was eager to join the Navy, it didn't take long for doubts about his decision to hit him. While he was riding the bus to the Navy's Basic Training facility, he asked himself THE QUESTION—"Why am I putting myself through this mess?" Recalls Michael, "It crosses everyone's mind. As far as I know, in my division, everyone had the same thought. 'I want to go home.' Those first few days are intense."

He figures it's because you lose control the minute you walk through the door on the first day of Basic Training. Someone's telling you (in a very loud voice) how to stand at attention, how to stand in line, how to do just about everything. "So many things go through your head," says Michael. He soon found that if he followed three rules, life got a whole lot easier:

1. KEEP YOUR MOUTH SHUT. "Your mouth is your biggest problem," he warns, "talking when you aren't supposed to and saying dumb things."

2. PAY ATTENTION TO DETAIL. "They'll say things like, 'Grab the door knob, turn it half to the right, and go through.' A lot of people will just pull it open and get yelled at. They teach you how to fold your clothes and clean the head (toilet). Everything is paying attention to detail," Michael advises.

3. DON'T THINK FOR YOURSELF. "Wait to be told what to do," Michael says, recalling the time his group was handed a form and told to wait until ordered to fill it out. Many saw that the form was asking for information like name, date, and division and began filling it out, only to get in trouble because they didn't wait.

Having been through Basic Training, he now knows that every little thing—from folding T-shirts the exact way he'd been told to do (arms folded in), to sweeping the floor, to marching—is all part of the training process. "You don't realize it until you're done," he says.

Despite all the yelling and push-ups, Michael values the training he got in the classes. He learned how to put out different kinds of fires, how to manage his money, how to identify aircraft—even etiquette. And that's just for starters.

His lowest point was about halfway through Basic, which, he found out, usually happens for everyone at the same time. "The first half of Basic, everything is so surreal. Then you get halfway through, and finishing up Basic seems so far away. You're always busy, whether you're stenciling your clothes or marching. You march a lot," he says. But then he reached his highest point, which was pass-in review at the end of the training and winning awards. He knew he'd done well. Looking into his future with the Navy, Michael says, "I want to see the world and have the experiences that the Navy can give you." Having finished Basic Training, he's well on his way.

Airman Michael Hipszky
United States Navy

"A lot of kids are worried about Marine boot camp. They've seen movies or heard stories. Boot camp is not set up to make you fail. It's challenging, but that's the purpose of it. You're learning that no matter what life throws at you, you will be able to improvise, adapt, and overcome."

Sergeant Ian Bonnell, Infantry Sergeant United States Marines

If you are still uncertain of which branch you'd like to join, do not allow the type of Basic Training you'll receive to be your only deciding factor. If, for example, the Marine Corps meets all your needs and is clearly your first choice, do not select the Air Force because its Basic Training seems easier. Conversely, if the Air Force is clearly your first choice, do not select the Marine Corps because it has the "toughest" Basic Training, and you want to prove you are up to the challenge. Basic Training is a means to transform you from civilian life to military life. It happens in a relatively short period of time compared to the entire length of your enlistment.

Some Words on Getting through Basic Training

No matter what you may have heard or read elsewhere, there are no secrets to getting through Basic Training; only common sense and preparation will get you through. Here are some do's and don'ts that should help you survive Basic Training for any of the services. Although following these guidelines will not ensure your success at Basic Training, your chances for success will be greatly improved by following them.

Before Arriving at Basic Training

DO:

- Start an exercise program
- Maintain a sensible diet
- Stay out of trouble (pay any traffic fines promptly before leaving for Basic Training)
- Ensure that all of your financial obligations are in order

- Bring the required items that you'll be told to bring
- Give up smoking

DON'T:

- Skip preparing yourself physically because you think that Basic Training will whip you into shape
- Abuse drugs and/or alcohol
- Have a big send-off party and get drunk the night before you leave for Basic Training
- Leave home with open tickets, summonses, or warrants
- Get yourself into heavy debt (such as buying a new car)
- Bring any prohibited items
- Have your hair cut in a radical manner (This includes having your head shaved. Men will receive a "very close" haircut shortly after arriving at Basic Training.)
- Have any part of your body pierced, tattooed, or otherwise altered

PAYING FOR COLLEGE THROUGH THE ARMED SERVICES

You can take any of the following three paths into the armed services—all of which provide opportunities for financial assistance for college.

Enlisted personnel

All five branches of the armed services offer college-credit courses on base. Enlisted personnel can also take college courses at civilian colleges while on active duty.

"In the Air Force, you're not only getting an education, but also experience. You could go to school for a degree in avionics technology, but in the Air Force, you get the teaching and the experience— real-world, hands-on experience—that makes your education marketable."

Master Sergeant Timothy Little United States Air Force

ROTC

More than 40,000 college students participate in Reserve Officers' Training Corps (ROTC). Two-, three-, and four-year ROTC scholarships are available to outstanding students. You can try ROTC at no obligation for two years or, if you have a four-year scholarship, for one year. Normally, all ROTC classes, uniforms, and books are free. ROTC graduates are required to serve in the military for a set period of time, either full-time on active duty or part-time in the Reserve or National Guard. Qualifying graduates can delay their service to go to graduate or professional school first.

Officer Candidate School

Openings at the U.S. service academies are few, so it pays to get information early. Every student is on a full scholarship, but free does not mean easy—these intense programs train graduates to meet the demands of leadership and success.

West Point. The U.S. Army Academy offers a broad-based academic program with nineteen majors in twenty-five fields of study. Extensive training and leadership experience go hand in hand with academics.

Annapolis. The U.S. Naval Academy is a unique blend of tradition and state-of-the-art technology. Its core curriculum includes eighteen major fields of study, and classroom work is supported by practical experience in leadership and professional operations.

Air Force Academy. The U.S. Air Force Academy prepares and motivates cadets for careers as Air Force officers. The academy offers a B.S. degree in twenty-six majors. Graduates receive a reserve commission as a second lieutenant in the Air Force.

Coast Guard Academy. This broad-based education, which leads to a B.S. degree in eight technical or professional majors, includes a thorough grounding in the professional skills necessary for the Coast Guard's work.

WHAT'S MY JOB?—OH, I JUST DRIVE AN ARMORED CARRIER AROUND

Justin Platt thought maybe he would join the Army, but first he had a few doubts to overcome. A big one was his reluctance to be away from friends and family. Another one was the overseas duty—something he definitely didn't want. But his desire to get his foot in the door of medical training won out. When he found out that he could get an education in the Army to become a nurse, his fears flew out the window, and Justin joined the Army. He's glad he did.

Stationed at Fort Carson in Colorado, Justin's been through Basic Training and is on his first stint of active duty working in—you guessed it—the medical field. "I work in an aid station, which is like a mini hospital," he says. He's the one who does the screening for anyone in his battalion who comes into sick call. Okay, it's from 5 a.m. to 7 a.m., but Justin doesn't mind.

Justin's job on active duty doesn't just consist of handing out Band-Aids and cough drops. He's also learning how to drive an armored carrier—not your usual medical training. But in the field, Army medics have to be able to pick up the wounded, which means knowing how to drive what he describes as a souped-up SUV—only instead of tires, it has tracks.

Justin plans to get enough rank to go from green to gold—enlisted to officer. "I'll have to take additional college courses to get a four-year degree," he says. It'll take him about seven years, including his Army duty. Not bad for someone who once had doubts about joining the military.

Private First Class Justin Platt

Fort Carson, Colorado

Financing Higher Education through the U.S. Armed Forces

The U.S. military provides a number of options to help students and their parents get financial aid for postsecondary education.

The Montgomery G.I. Bill

Available to enlistees in all branches of the service, the G.I. Bill pays up to $23,400 toward education costs at any accredited two- or four-year college or vocational school, for up to ten years after discharge.

There are two options under the bill:

1. **Active Duty.** If you serve on active duty, you will allocate $1,200 of your pay ($100 a month for twelve months) to your education fund.

Then, under the G.I. Bill, the federal government pays out up to $23,400.

2. **Reserve Duty.** If you join a Reserve unit, you can receive up to $9,180 to offset your education costs.

You can visit the Veteran's Affairs Web page at www.va.gov.

The Department of Defense

The U.S. Department of Defense offers a large number of education benefits to those enrolled in the U.S. military or employed by the Department of Defense, including scholarships, grants, tuition assistance, and internships. Visit their Web site at http://web.lmi.org/edugate for complete information.

Tuition Assistance

All branches of the military pay up to 75 percent of tuition for full-time, active-duty enlistees who take courses at community colleges or by correspondence during their tours of duty. Details vary by service.

The Community College of the Air Force

Members of the armed forces can convert their technical training and military experience into academic credit, earning an associate degree, an occupational instructor's certificate, or a trade school certificate. Participants receive an official transcript from this fully accredited program. You can visit the Community College of the Air Force on line at www.au.af.mil/au/ccaf.

Educational Loan-Repayment Program

The Armed Services can help repay government-insured and other approved loans. One third of the loan will be repaid for each year served on active duty.

Other Forms of Tuition Assistance

Each branch of the military offers its own education incentives. To find out more, check with a local recruiting office.

YOU AND THE WORKPLACE

SOME OF YOU WILL GO TO COLLEGE

first and then look for jobs. Some of you might work for a

few years and then go to college. And many of you will go

immediately into the workplace and bypass college altogeth-

er. Whenever you become an employee, you'll want to know

what you can do to succeed on the job and move to both

higher levels of responsibility and more pay.

Chapter 11

JUMP INTO WORK

Almost everyone ends up in the workplace at some point. No matter when you plan to receive that first full-time paycheck, there are some things you'll need to do to prepare yourself for the world of work.

AT EACH GRADE LEVEL, there are specific steps you should take regardless of whether or not you plan to attend college immediately following high school. In fact, college and career timelines should coincide, according to guidance counselors and career specialists, and students should take college-preparatory courses, even if they aren't planning on attending college.

THE CAREER TIMELINE

The following timeline will help you meet college requirements and still prepare for work. In an effort to make sure that you are adequately preparing for both school and work, incorporate these five steps into your career/college timeline:

1. **Take an aptitude test.** You can do this as early as the sixth grade, but even if you're in high school now, it's not too late. By doing so, you will begin to get a feel for what areas you might be good at and enjoy. Your guidance counselor should have a test in his or her office for you to take, or you can try the ASVAB (see page 105). Thousands of high school students take this test every year to discover possible career paths—and taking the ASVAB doesn't require you to join the military!

2. **Beginning in middle school, you should start considering what your options are after high school.** However, if you're only starting to think about this in high school, that's okay, too. Keep a notebook of information gathered from field trips, job-shadowing experiences, mentoring programs, and career fairs to help you make sense of the possibilities open to you. This process should continue through high school. Many schools offer job shadowing and internship programs for students to explore different vocational avenues. Take advantage of these opportunities if you can. Too often, students don't explore the workplace until after they've taken the courses necessary to enter a particular profession, only to discover it wasn't the career they dreamed of after all.

3. **No later than the tenth grade, visit a vocational center to look at the training programs offered.** Some public school systems send students to vocational and career program centers for career exploration.

4. **During your junior and senior years, be**

TAKING A BREAK BETWEEN HIGH SCHOOL AND COLLEGE

Because of the soaring costs of college tuition today, college is no longer a place to "find yourself." It is a costly investment in your future. The career you choose to pursue may or may not require additional education; your research will determine whether or not it's required or preferred. If you decide not to attend college immediately after high school, however, don't consider it to be a closed door. Taking some time off between high school and college is considered perfectly acceptable by employers. Many students simply need a break after thirteen years of schooling. Most experts agree that it's better to be ready and prepared for college; many adults get more out of their classes after they've had a few years to mature.

Source: Street Smart Career Guide: A Step-by-Step Program for Your Career Development.

sure to create a portfolio of practice resumes, writing samples, and a list of work skills. This portfolio should also include your high school transcript and letters of recommendation. It will serve as a valuable reference tool when it comes time to apply for jobs.

5. **By tenth or eleventh grade, you should begin focusing on a specific career path.** More employers today are looking for employees who have both the education and work experience that relates to the career field for which they're interviewing. If you are looking for part-time employment, you should consider jobs that pertain to your field of study. Until you start interacting with people in the field, you won't have a realistic feel of what's involved in that profession. It adds to the importance of the learning. If you're planning on heading into the workplace right after high school, take a look at the previous two pages for a list of careers that don't require a four-year degree.

WRITING YOUR RESUME

Resumes are a critical part of getting a job. Chances are you'll have to submit one before you get interviewed. A resume is an introduction of your skills to a potential employer. For that reason, your resume must stand out in a crowd because some employers receive dozens of resumes in the mail each week. A resume that is too long, cluttered, or disorganized may find its way to the "circular file," also known as the trash can. You can avoid this hazard by creating a resume that is short, presentable, and easy to read.

Remember that a resume is a summary of who you are and an outline of your experiences, skills, and goals. While writing it, you may discover some talents that you weren't aware you had and that will help boost your confidence for the job search.

Begin by collecting facts about yourself, including where you went to high school, your past and present jobs, activities, interests, and leadership

(Continued on page 117)

roles. Next to the individual activities, write down what responsibilities you had. For example, something as simple as babysitting requires the ability to settle disagreements and supervise others.

Next, decide on how you would like to format your resume. Most hiring managers expect to see one of two types of resumes: chronological or functional. The chronological resume is the most traditional, supplying the reader with a sequential listing (from present to past) of your accomplishments. Because the emphasis here is on past employment experience, high school and college students with little or no employment history might want to avoid this type. A functional resume, on the other hand, highlights a person's abilities rather than his or her work history. Entry-level candidates who want to focus on skills rather than credentials should consider using a functional resume.

CAREERS WITHOUT A FOUR-YEAR DEGREE

Some students spend a few years in the workplace before going to college. Others begin their career with a high school diploma, a vocational certificate, or up to two years of education or training after high school.

With that in mind, sometimes it's easier to know what you don't want than what you do want. Take a look at the list below, and check off the careers that interest you. Perhaps you've thought of something you'd like to do that isn't on this list. Well, don't dump your hopes. There are many different levels of training and education that can lead you to the career of your dreams. Since this list is not all-inclusive, you should check with your high school counselor or go on line to research the training you'll need to achieve the job or career you want—without a four-year degree.

Then talk to your guidance counselor, teacher, librarian, or career counselor for more information about the careers on the list below or those you've researched on your own.

AGRICULTURE AND NATURAL RESOURCES

High school/vocational diploma
- ❏ Fisher
- ❏ Groundskeeper
- ❏ Logger
- ❏ Pest Controller

Up to two years beyond high school
- ❏ Fish and Game Warden
- ❏ Tree Surgeon

APPLIED ARTS (VISUAL)

High school/vocational diploma
- ❏ Floral Arranger
- ❏ Merchandise Displayer
- ❏ Painter (artist)

Up to two years beyond high school
- ❏ Cartoonist
- ❏ Commercial Artist
- ❏ Fashion Designer
- ❏ Interior Decorator
- ❏ Photographer

APPLIED ARTS (WRITTEN AND SPOKEN)

High school/vocational diploma
- ❏ Proofreader

Up to two years beyond high school
- ❏ Advertising copywriter
- ❏ Legal assistant

BUSINESS MACHINE/COMPUTER OPERATION

High school/vocational diploma
- ❏ Data Entry
- ❏ Statistical Clerk
- ❏ Telephone Operator
- ❏ Typist

Up to two years beyond high school
- ❏ Computer Operator
- ❏ Motion Picture Projectionist
- ❏ Word Processing Machine Operator

CONSTRUCTION AND MAINTENANCE

High school/vocational diploma
- ❏ Bricklayer
- ❏ Construction Laborer
- ❏ Elevator Mechanic
- ❏ Floor Covering Installer
- ❏ Heavy Equipment Operator
- ❏ Janitor
- ❏ Maintenance Mechanic

Up to two years beyond high school
- ❏ Building Inspector
- ❏ Carpenter

- ❏ Electrician
- ❏ Insulation Worker
- ❏ Lather
- ❏ Painter (construction)
- ❏ Pipefitter
- ❏ Plumber
- ❏ Roofer
- ❏ Sheet Metal Worker
- ❏ Structural Steel Worker
- ❏ Tile Setter

CRAFTS AND RELATED SERVICES

High school/vocational diploma
- ❏ Baker/Cook/Chef
- ❏ Butcher
- ❏ Furniture Upholsterer
- ❏ Housekeeper (hotel)
- ❏ Tailor/Dressmaker

Up to two years beyond high school
- ❏ Dry Cleaner
- ❏ Jeweler
- ❏ Locksmith
- ❏ Musical Instrument Repairer

CREATIVE/PERFORMING ARTS

High school/vocational diploma
- ❏ Singer
- ❏ Stunt Performer

Up to two years beyond high school
- ❏ Actor/Actress
- ❏ Dancer/Choreographer
- ❏ Musician
- ❏ Writer/Author

EDUCATION AND RELATED SERVICES

High school/vocational diploma
- ❏ Nursery School Attendant
- ❏ Teacher's Aide

ENGINEERING AND RELATED TECHNOLOGIES

High school/vocational diploma
- ❏ Biomedical Equipment Technician
- ❏ Laser Technician

Up to two years beyond high school
- ❏ Aerospace Engineer Technician
- ❏ Broadcast Technician
- ❏ Chemical Laboratory Technician
- ❏ Civil Engineering Technician
- ❏ Computer Programmer
- ❏ Computer Service Technician
- ❏ Electronic Technician
- ❏ Energy Conservation Technician

- ❏ Industrial Engineering Technician
- ❏ Laboratory Tester
- ❏ Mechanical Engineering Technician
- ❏ Metallurgical Technician
- ❏ Pollution Control Technician
- ❏ Quality Control Technician
- ❏ Robot Technician
- ❏ Surveyor (land)
- ❏ Technical Illustrator
- ❏ Tool Designer
- ❏ Weather Observer

FINANCIAL TRANSACTIONS

High school/vocational diploma
- ❏ Accounting Clerk
- ❏ Bank Teller
- ❏ Cashier
- ❏ Payroll Clerk
- ❏ Travel Agent

Up to two years beyond high school
- ❏ Bookkeeper
- ❏ Loan Officer

HEALTH CARE (GENERAL)

High school/vocational diploma
- ❏ Dental Assistant
- ❏ Medical Assistant
- ❏ Nursing/Psychiatric Aide

Up to two years beyond high school
- ❏ Dietetic Technician
- ❏ Nurse (practical)
- ❏ Nurse (registered)
- ❏ Optometric Assistant
- ❏ Physical Therapist's Assistant
- ❏ Physician's Assistant
- ❏ Recreation Therapist

HEALTH-CARE SPECIALTIES AND TECHNOLOGIES

High school/vocational diploma
- ❏ Dialysis Technician

Up to two years beyond high school
- ❏ Dental Hygienist
- ❏ Dental Laboratory Technician
- ❏ EEG Technologist
- ❏ EKG Technician
- ❏ Emergency Medical Technician
- ❏ Medical Laboratory Technician
- ❏ Medical Technologist
- ❏ Nuclear Medicine Technologist
- ❏ Operating Room Technician
- ❏ Optician

- ❑ Radiation Therapy Technologist
- ❑ Radiologic Technologist
- ❑ Respiratory Therapist
- ❑ Sonographer

HOME/BUSINESS EQUIPMENT REPAIR
High school/vocational diploma
- ❑ Air-Conditioning/Refrigeration/ Heating Mechanic
- ❑ Appliance Servicer
- ❑ Coin Machine Mechanic
Up to two years beyond high school
- ❑ Communications Equipment Mechanic
- ❑ Line Installer/Splicer
- ❑ Office Machine Servicer
- ❑ Radio/TV Repairer
- ❑ Telephone Installer

INDUSTRIAL EQUIPMENT OPERATIONS AND REPAIR
High school/vocational diploma
- ❑ Assembler
- ❑ Blaster
- ❑ Boilermaker
- ❑ Coal Equipment Operator
- ❑ Compressor House Operator
- ❑ Crater
- ❑ Dock Worker
- ❑ Forging Press Operator
- ❑ Furnace Operator
- ❑ Heat Treater
- ❑ Machine Tool Operator
- ❑ Material Handler
- ❑ Miner
- ❑ Sailor
- ❑ Sewing Machine Operator
Up to two years beyond high school
- ❑ Bookbinder
- ❑ Compositor/Typesetter
- ❑ Electronic Equipment Repairer
- ❑ Electroplater
- ❑ Firefighter
- ❑ Instrument Mechanic
- ❑ Lithographer
- ❑ Machine Repairer
- ❑ Machinist
- ❑ Millwright
- ❑ Molder
- ❑ Nuclear Reactor Operator
- ❑ Patternmaker
- ❑ Photoengraver
- ❑ Power House Mechanic
- ❑ Power Plant Operator
- ❑ Printing Press Operator
- ❑ Stationery Engineer
- ❑ Tool and Die Maker
- ❑ Water Plant Operator
- ❑ Welder
- ❑ Wire Drawer

MANAGEMENT AND PLANNING
High school/vocational diploma
- ❑ Administrative Assistant

- ❑ Food Service Supervisor
- ❑ Postmaster
- ❑ Service Station Manager
Up to two years beyond high school
- ❑ Benefits Manager
- ❑ Building Manager
- ❑ Caterer
- ❑ Contractor
- ❑ Credit Manager
- ❑ Customer Service Coordinator
- ❑ Employment Interviewer
- ❑ Executive Housekeeper
- ❑ Funeral Director
- ❑ Hotel/Motel Manager
- ❑ Importer/Exporter
- ❑ Insurance Manager
- ❑ Manager (small business)
- ❑ Office Manager
- ❑ Personnel Manager
- ❑ Restaurant/Bar Manager
- ❑ Store Manager
- ❑ Supermarket Manager

MARKETING AND SALES
High school/vocational diploma
- ❑ Auctioneer
- ❑ Bill Collector
- ❑ Driver (route)
- ❑ Fashion Model
- ❑ Product Demonstrator
- ❑ Salesperson (general)
- ❑ Sample Distributor
Up to two years beyond high school
- ❑ Claims Adjuster
- ❑ Insurance Worker
- ❑ Manufacturer's Representative
- ❑ Real Estate Agent
- ❑ Sales Manager
- ❑ Travel Agent
- ❑ Travel Guide

PERSONAL AND CUSTOMER SERVICE
High school/vocational diploma
- ❑ Barber
- ❑ Bartender
- ❑ Beautician
- ❑ Child-care Worker
- ❑ Counter Attendant
- ❑ Dining Room Attendant
- ❑ Electrologist
- ❑ Flight Attendant
- ❑ Host/Hostess
- ❑ Houseparent
- ❑ Manicurist
- ❑ Parking Lot Attendant
- ❑ Porter
- ❑ Private Household Worker
- ❑ Waiter/Waitress

RECORDS AND COMMUNICATIONS
High school/vocational diploma
- ❑ Billing Clerk
- ❑ Clerk (general)

- ❑ File Clerk
- ❑ Foreign Trade Clerk
- ❑ Hotel Clerk
- ❑ Meter Reader
- ❑ Postal Clerk
- ❑ Receptionist
- ❑ Stenographer
Up to two years beyond high school
- ❑ Court Reporter
- ❑ Legal Secretary
- ❑ Library Assistant
- ❑ Library Technician
- ❑ Medical Records Technician
- ❑ Medical Secretary
- ❑ Personnel Assistant
- ❑ Secretary
- ❑ Travel Clerk

SOCIAL AND GOVERNMENT
High school/vocational diploma
- ❑ Corrections Officer
- ❑ Police Officer
- ❑ Security Guard
- ❑ Store Detective
Up to two years beyond high school
- ❑ Detective (police)
- ❑ Hazardous Waste Technician
- ❑ Recreation Leader
- ❑ Personal/Customer Services

STORAGE AND DISPATCHING
High school/vocational diploma
- ❑ Dispatcher
- ❑ Mail Carrier
- ❑ Railroad Conductor
- ❑ Shipping/Receiving Clerk
- ❑ Stock Clerk
- ❑ Tool Crib Attendant
- ❑ Warehouse Worker
Up to two years beyond high school
- ❑ Warehouse Supervisor

VEHICLE OPERATION AND REPAIR
High school/vocational diploma
- ❑ Automotive Painter
- ❑ Bus Driver
- ❑ Chauffeur
- ❑ Diesel Mechanic
- ❑ Farm Equipment Mechanic
- ❑ Forklift Operator
- ❑ Heavy Equipment Mechanic
- ❑ Locomotive Engineer
- ❑ Railroad Braker
- ❑ Refuse Collector
- ❑ Service Station Attendant
- ❑ Taxicab Driver
- ❑ Truck Driver
Up to two years beyond high school
- ❑ Aircraft Mechanic
- ❑ Airplane Pilot
- ❑ Auto Body Repairer
- ❑ Automotive Mechanic
- ❑ Garage Supervisor
- ❑ Motorcycle Mechanic

Parts of a Resume

At the very least, your resume should include the following components:

Heading: Centered at the top of the page should be your name, address, phone number, and e-mail address.

Objective: In one sentence, tell the employer what type of work you are looking for.

Education: Beginning with your most recent school or program, include the date (or expected date) of completion, the degree or certificate earned, and the address of the institution. Don't overlook any workshops or seminars, self-study, or on-the-job training in which you have been involved. If any courses particularly lend themselves to the type of work you'd be doing on that job, include them. Mention grade point averages and class rank when they are especially impressive.

Skills and abilities: Until you've actually listed these on paper, you can easily overlook many of them. They may be as varied as the ability to work with computers or being captain of the girl's basketball team.

Work experience: If you don't have any, skip this section. If you do, begin with your most recent employer and include the date you left the job, your job title, the company name, and the company address. If you are still employed there, simply enter your start date and "to present" for the date. Include notable accomplishments for each job. High school and college students with little work experience shouldn't be shy about including summer, part-time, and volunteer jobs, such as lifeguarding, babysitting, delivering pizzas, or volunteering at the local parks and recreation department.

Personal: Here's your opportunity to include your special talents and interests as well as notable accomplishments or experiences.

SAMPLE FUNCTIONAL RESUME

Michele A. Thomas
3467 Main Street
Atlanta, Georgia 30308
404-555-3423
E-mail: mthomas_987654321@yahoo.com

OBJECTIVE

Seeking a sales position in the wireless phone industry

EDUCATION

High School Diploma, June 2003

John F. Kennedy High School, Atlanta, Georgia

SKILLS

Computer literate, IBM: MS Works, MS Word, WordPerfect, Netscape; Macintosh: MS Word, Excel

ACTIVITIES/LEADERSHIP

Student Government secretary, 2002–2003

Key Club vice president, 2001–2002

Future Business Leaders of America

AWARDS

Varsity Swim Club (Captain; MVP Junior, Senior; Sportsmanship Award)
Outstanding Community Service Award, 2002

EXPERIENCE

Sales Clerk, The Limited, Atlanta, Georgia; part-time, September 2001 to present

Cashier, Winn-Dixie Supermarkets, Atlanta, Georgia, Summers 2000 and 2001

INTERESTS

Swimming, reading, computers

REFERENCES

Available upon request

References: Most experts agree that it's best to simply state that references are available upon request. However, if you do decide to list names, addresses, and phone numbers, limit yourself to no more than three. Make sure you inform any people whom you have listed that they may be contacted. Take a look at the sample resume on the previous page, and use it as a model when you create your resume.

SAMPLE COVER LETTER

Take a look at how this student applied the facts outlined in her resume to the job she's applying for in the cover letter below. You can use this letter to help you get started on your own cover letters. Text that appears in all caps below indicates the kind of information you need to include in that section. Before you send your letter, proofread it for mistakes and ask a parent or friend you trust to look it over as well.

(DATE)
June 29, 2003

(YOUR ADDRESS)
3467 Main Street
Atlanta, Georgia 30308
E-mail: mthomas_987654321@yahoo.com
Phone: 404-555-6721

(PERSON—BY NAME—TO WHOM YOU'RE SENDING THE LETTER)
Mr. Charles E. Pence
Manager, Human Resources
NexAir Wireless
20201 East Sixth Street
Atlanta, Georgia 30372

Dear Mr. Pence:

(HOW YOU HEARD OF THE POSITION)
Your job announcement in the Atlanta Gazette for an entry-level sales position asked for someone who has both computer and sales skills. (SOMETHING EXTRA THAT WILL INTEREST THE READER) My training and past job experience fit both of those categories. I also bring an enthusiasm and desire to begin my career in a communications firm such as NexAir.

(WHAT PRACTICAL SKILLS YOU CAN BRING TO THE POSITION)
A few weeks ago, I graduated from John F. Kennedy High School here in Atlanta. While in school, I concentrated on gaining computer skills on both IBM and Macintosh machines and participated in organizations such as the Key Club, in which I was vice president, and the Future Business Leaders of America.

(RELATE PAST EXPERIENCE TO DESIRED JOB)
As you will see from my resume, I worked as a cashier at Winn-Dixie Supermarket for two summers and am currently employed as a sales clerk at The Limited. From these two positions, I have gained valuable customer service skills and an attention to detail, qualities which I'm sure are of utmost importance to you as you make your hiring decision.

I would very much like to interview for the position and am available at your convenience. I look forward to hearing from you soon.

Sincerely,

Michele A. Thomas

Resume-Writing Tips

These tips will help as you begin constructing your resume:

- Keep the resume short and simple. Although senior executives may use as many as two or three pages, recent graduates should limit themselves to one page.

- Capitalize headings.

- Keep sentences short; avoid writing in paragraphs.

- Use language that is simple, not flowery or complex.

- Be specific, and offer examples when appropriate.

- Emphasize achievements.

- Be honest.

- Don't include information about salary or wages.

- Use high-quality, white, beige, or gray, 8½" × 11" paper.

- Make good use of white space by leaving adequate side and top margins on the paper.

- Make what you write presentable, using good business style and typing it on a computer or word processor.

- Because your resume should be a reflection of your personality, write it yourself.

- Avoid gimmicks such as colored paper, photos, or clip art.

- Make good use of bullets or asterisks, underlining, and bold print.

- Proofread your work, and have someone you trust proofread it also.

- Be neat and accurate.

- Never send a resume without a cover letter.

The Cover Letter

Every resume should be accompanied by a cover letter. This is often the most crucial part of your job search because the letter will be the first thing that a potential employer reads. When you include a cover letter, you're showing the employer that you care enough to take the time to address him or her personally and that you are genuinely interested in the job.

Always call the company and verify the name and title of the person to whom you are addressing the letter. Although you will want to keep your letter brief, introduce yourself and begin with a statement that will catch the reader's attention. Indicate the position you are applying for and mention if someone referred you or if you are simply responding to a newspaper ad. Draw attention to yourself by including something that will arouse the employer's curiosity about your experience and accomplishments. A cover letter should request something, most commonly an interview. Sign and date your letter. Then follow up with a phone call a few days after you're sure the letter has been received. Persistence pays. The sample cover letter on the next page can help you as you begin writing your cover letter.

JOB HUNTING 101

High school is a time for taking classes and learning, developing relationships with others, becoming involved in extracurricular activities that teach valuable life skills, and generally preparing for college or a job. Regardless of where you're headed after high school, you need to learn how to create a favorable impression. That can mean setting some clear, attainable goals for yourself, putting them down on paper in the form of a resume and cover letter, and convincing interviewers that you are, indeed, the person for whom they are looking. In short, learn how to sell yourself. A brief course in Job Hunting 101 will help you do just that.

Marketing Yourself

You can use several approaches to market yourself successfully. Networking, the continual process of contacting friends and relatives, is a great way to get information about job openings. Seventy-five percent of the job openings in this country are not advertised but are filled by friends, relatives, and acquaintances of people who already work there. From the employer's perspective, there is less risk associated with hiring someone recommended by an employee than by hiring someone unknown. Networking is powerful. Everyone has a primary network of people they know and talk to frequently. Those acquaintances know and talk to networks of their own, thereby creating a secondary network for you and multiplying the number of individuals who know what you're looking for in a job.

Broadcasting is another marketing method in which you gather a list of companies that interest you and then mail them letters asking for job interviews. Although the rate of return on your mailings is small, two thirds of all job hunters use this approach, and half of those who use it find a job. You will increase your response rate by addressing your letter to a particular person—the one who has the power to hire you—and by following up with a phone call a few days after the letter has been received. To obtain the manager's name, simply call the company and ask the receptionist for the person's name, job title, and correct spelling. Good resources for finding potential employers include referrals, community agencies, job fairs, newspaper ads, trade directories, trade journals, state indexes, the local chamber of commerce, the Yellow Pages, and the Web. See page 121 for a listing of career Web resources. These tips can help as you begin hunting for the perfect job.

- Job-hunting is time intensive. Do your homework, and take it seriously by using every opportunity available to you.

- Prepare yourself for the fact that there will be far more rejections than acceptances.

- Consider taking a temporary job while you continue the job hunt. It will help pay the bills and give you new skills to boost your resume at the same time.

- Research the activities of potential employers, and show that you have studied them when you're being interviewed.

- Keep careful records of all contacts and follow-up activities.

- Don't ignore any job leads—act on every tip you get.

- Stay positive.

With all these thoughts in mind, you should be ready to begin the process of making people believe in you, and that's a major part of being successful in your job hunt.

THE JOB INTERVIEW

You can prevent some of the preinterview jitters by adequately preparing. Remember that you have nothing to lose and that you, too, are doing the choosing. Just as you are waiting and hoping to be offered a job, you have the option of choosing whether or not to accept an offer. It's all right to feel somewhat anxious, but keep everything in perspective. This is an adventure, and you are in control. Most important, remember to be yourself. With all of this in mind, consider some of the following points of the interview process.

- Speak up during the interview, and furnish the interviewer with the information he or she needs in order to make an informed decision. It is especially impressive if you can remember the names of people to whom you've been introduced. People like to be called by name, and it shows that you took the initiative to remember them.

- Always arrive a few minutes early for the interview, and look your best. The way you act and dress tells the interviewer plenty about your attitude and personality. Sloppy dress, chewing gum, and cigarettes have no place at an interview and will probably cut your interview short. Instead, dress professionally and appropriately for the job. Avoid heavy makeup, short skirts, jeans, and untidy or flashy clothing of any kind. Although a business suit may be appropriate for certain jobs, a person who is applying for an outdoor position should probably interview in clean, neatly pressed dress slacks and a golf shirt or a skirt and blouse.

The best way to prepare for the interview is to practice. Have a friend or relative play the role of the interviewer, and go over some of the most commonly asked questions. Learn as much as you can about the company you're interviewing with—it pays to do your homework. When you show a potential employer that you've taken the time and initiative to learn about his or her company, you're showing that you will be a motivated and hardworking employee. Employers fear laziness and minimal effort, looking instead for workers who don't always have to be told what to do and when to do it.

Here is a list of interview questions you can expect to have to answer:

- **Tell me a little bit about yourself.** This is your chance to pitch your qualifications for the job in two minutes. Provide a few details about your education, previous jobs you've held, and extracurricular activities that relate to the position that you're interviewing for.

- **Are you at your best when working alone or in a group?** The safest answer is "Both." Most companies today cluster their employees into work groups, so you will need strong interpersonal skills. However, on occasion, you may be required to work on projects alone.

- **What did you like the most about your last job? What did you dislike the most about it?** Always accentuate the positives in an interview, so focus primarily on what you liked. Also be honest about what you disliked, but then explain how facing the negatives helped you grow as an employee.

- **What are your career goals?** Be sure you've done some research on the company and industry before your interview. When this question comes up, talk realistically about how far you believe your skills and talents will take you and what actions you plan to take to ensure this happens, such as pursuing more education.

- **Do you have any questions for me?** Absolutely! See "Asking Questions" below.

FINDING JOBS ON THE WEB

As we mentioned, you can find jobs through your network of friends, family, and acquaintances; through classified ads in the newspaper; and through career Web pages. Here is a listing of popular Web sites that not only offer job search technology but also information on resume writing, interviewing, and other important career advice.

www.monster.com   **www.careerbuilder.com**

www.hotjobs.com   **www.vault.com**

Take the time to prepare some answers to these commonly asked questions. For instance, if you haven't set at least one career goal for yourself, do it now. Be ready to describe it to the interviewer. Likewise, you should be able to talk about your last job, including what you liked the most and the least. Adapt your answers so they apply to the job for which you are presently interviewing. Other questions that might be asked include:

- What qualifications do you have?
- Why do you want to work for us?
- Do you enjoy school? Why or why not?
- Do you plan to continue your education?
- What do you plan to be doing for work five years from now?
- What motivates you to do a good job?

If you are seeking a job as a manager, you might respond by saying you liked the varied responsibilities of your past job. Recall that you enjoyed the unexpected challenges and flexible schedule. And when describing what you liked least, make sure you respond with some function or area of responsibility that has nothing to do with the responsibilities of the job you hope to get.

More than likely, the first question you'll be asked is to tell the interviewer something about yourself. This is your chance to "toot your horn," but don't ramble. You might ask the interviewer specifically what he or she would like to hear about: your educational background or recent experiences and responsibilities in your present or last job. After he or she chooses, stick to the basics; the next move belongs to the interviewer.

When asked about personal strengths and weaknesses, given that the question is two parts, begin with a weakness so you can end on a strong note with your strengths. Again, try to connect your description of a strength or weakness with the requirements for the job. Naturally, it wouldn't be wise to reveal a serious weakness about yourself, but you can mention how you have changed your shortcomings. You might say, "I like to get my work done fast, but I consciously try to slow down a little to make sure I'm careful and accurate." When it comes to strengths, don't exaggerate, but don't sell yourself short.

Asking Questions

You can ask questions, too. In fact, the interviewer expects you to ask questions to determine if the job is right for you, just as he or she will be trying to find out if you'll be successful working for his or her company. When you ask questions, it shows that you're interested and want to learn more. When the type of question you ask indicates that you've done your homework regarding the job and the company, your interviewer will be impressed. Avoid asking questions about salary or fringe benefits, anything adversarial, or questions that show you have a negative opinion of the company. It's all right to list your questions on a piece of paper; it's the quality of the question that's important, not whether you can remember it. Here are a few sample questions that you should consider asking if the topics don't come up in your interview:

- What kind of responsibilities come with this job?
- How is the department organized?
- What will be the first project for the new hire to tackle?
- What is a typical career advancement path for a person in this position?
- Who will the supervisor be for this position, and can I meet him or her?
- What is the office environment like? Is it casual or corporate?
- When do you expect to reach a hiring decision?

SAMPLE THANK-YOU LETTER

After you've interviewed for a job, it's important to reiterate your interest in the position by sending a thank-you letter to those who interviewed you. Take a look at Michele's letter to the manager she interviewed with at NexAir. You can use this letter as a model when the time comes for you to write some thank-you letters.

July 17, 2003

Michele A. Thomas
3467 Main Street
Atlanta, Georgia 30308
E-mail: mthomas_987654321@yahoo.com
Phone: 404-555-6721

Mr. Charles E. Pence
Manager, Human Resources
NexAir Wireless
20201 East Sixth Street
Atlanta, Georgia 30372

Dear Mr. Pence:

It was a pleasure meeting with you Monday to discuss the sales opportunity at NexAir's downtown location. After learning more about the position, it is clear to me that with my background and enthusiasm, I would be an asset to your organization.

As we discussed, my experiences as a cashier at Winn-Dixie Supermarket and as a sales clerk at The Limited have provided me with the basic skills necessary to perform the responsibilities required of a sales representative at NexAir. I believe that with my ability to learn quickly and communicate effectively, I can help NexAir increase sales of its wireless products.

Thank you for the opportunity to interview with your organization. If there is any additional information I can provide about myself, please do not hesitate to call me. I look forward to hearing your decision soon.

Sincerely,

Michele A. Thomas

Following Up

After the interview, follow up with a thank-you note to the interviewer. Not only is it a thoughtful gesture, it triggers the interviewer's memory about you and shows that you have a genuine interest in the job. Your thank-you note should be written in a business letter format and should highlight the key points in your interview. The sample thank-you note above can help.

During the interview process, remember that you will not appeal to everyone who interviews you. If your first experience doesn't work out, don't get discouraged. Keep trying.

WHAT EMPLOYERS EXPECT FROM EMPLOYEES

As part of the National City Bank personnel team in Columbus, Ohio, Rose Graham works with Cooperative Business Education (CBE) coordinators in the area who are trying to place high school students in the workplace. When asked what skills she looks for in potential employees, she quickly replies that basic communication skills are at the top of her list. She stresses, "The ability to construct a sentence and put together words cannot be overemphasized." She cites knowledge of the personal computer, with good keyboarding skills, as essential.

In an article published in the *Nashville Business Journal*, Donna Cobble of Staffing Solutions outlined these basic skills for everyday life in the workplace:

Communication: Being a good communicator not only means having the ability to express oneself properly in the English language, but it also means being a good listener. If you feel inferior in any of these areas, it's a good idea to sign up for a public speaking class, read books on the subject, and borrow techniques from professional speakers.

Organization: Organization is the key to success in any occupation or facet of life. The ability to plan, prioritize, and complete a task in a timely fashion is a valuable skill. Check out the next section for tips on improving your time-management skills.

Problem solving: Companies are looking for creative problem solvers, people who aren't afraid to act on a situation and follow through with their decision. Experience and practice play a major role in your ability to determine the best solution. You can learn these techniques by talking with others about how they solve problems as well as observing others in the problem-solving process.

Sensitivity: In addition to being kind and courteous to their fellow workers, employees need to be sensitive to a coworker's perspective. That might mean putting yourself in the other person's shoes to gain a better understanding of that person's feelings. Employers look for individuals who are able to work on a team instead of those concerned only with their own personal gain.

Judgment: Although closely related to problem solving, good judgment shows up on many different levels in the workplace. It is the ability of a person to assess a situation, weigh the options, consider the risks, and make the necessary decision. Good judgment is built on experience and self-confidence.

Concentration: Concentration is the ability to focus on one thing at a time. Learning to tune out distractions and relate solely to the task at hand is a valuable asset for anyone.

Cooperation: Remember that you're being paid to do a job, so cooperate.

Honesty: Dishonesty shows up in many different ways, ranging from stealing time or property to divulging company secrets. Stay honest.

Initiative: Don't always wait to be told exactly what to do. Show some initiative and look around to see what needs to be done next.

Willingness to learn: Be willing to learn how things are done at the company instead of doing things the way you want to do them.

Dependability: Arrive at work on time every day, and meet your deadlines.

Enthusiasm: Although not every task you're assigned will be stimulating, continue to show enthusiasm for your work at all times.

Acceptance of criticism: Corrective criticism is necessary for any employee to learn how things should be done. Employees who view criticism as a way to improve themselves will benefit from it.

Loyalty: There is no place for negativity in the workplace. You simply won't be happy working for an employer to whom you're not loyal.

Never fail to show pride in your work, the place where you work, and your appearance. By making these traits a part of your personality and daily performance, you will demonstrate that you are a cut above other employees with equal or better qualifications.

JUMPING ON THE SALARY FAST-TRACK

So the job offer comes, and it's time to talk about money. Unless you are an undiscovered genius, you most likely will start near the bottom of the salary scale if you're heading straight to the workplace after graduating from high school. There's not much room to negotiate a salary since you probably won't be able to say, "Well, I've done this, this, and this. I know what my experience is worth." You will find that most people hiring first-time employees will have a "take-it-or-leave-it" attitude about salary offers. However, according to Amryl Ward, a human resources consultant who has been hiring employees for more than twenty-five years in various human resource positions, there are some things that entry-level employees can do to make themselves more easily hired and, once hired, to get themselves on the fast-track toward more pay.

1. **As you interview for the job, be prepared to tell a potential employer why you're worth hiring.** "Bring your skills to the table," says Ward. For instance, you might not think that the job you had during the summer at that big office supply store did anything more than earn you spending money.

On the contrary, you learned valuable skills, such as how to be part of a team and how to deal with customers. What about that after-school office job you had? You learned how to answer the phones and how to work with certain software. Think carefully about the jobs you had in high school and what you learned from them. Those are called transferable skills.

2. **Once you're hired, be willing to do more than just what the job requires.** Sure, you may be frying fries at the start. But if you come in early and stay late, if you pitch in to help another employee with his or her job, or if you voluntarily clean up the counters and sweep the floor, that says to management, "This employee is a winner. Let's keep him or her in mind the next time a promotion comes up." Soon, you might be managing a crew, then the store.

ON THE JOB

Once you snag that perfect job, there's no time to rest easy. You need to keep your manager happy and instill trust in your coworkers. And at the same time you're doing this, you'll want to watch out for yourself, keep yourself happy, and stay ahead of the learning curve. Here are some ways for you to do just that.

Minding Your Office Etiquette

Okay, so maybe you didn't know which was the salad fork at your cousin Sally's wedding reception. Most likely, though, you can name a few basic rules of etiquette, like not chewing with your mouth open at the dinner table. Now, what about when it comes to the manners you're supposed to have in the workplace? That usually draws a blank if you've never worked in an office setting. How would you know what's the right way to answer the phone or talk to your boss or customers?

Shannon McBride, of the Golden Crescent Tech Prep School to Career Partnership in Victoria, Texas, has seen many students come through his program and land good jobs. He's also seen many of them succeed because they knew how to present themselves in a professional situation. Unfortunately, he can also relate stories of high school graduates who had no clue how to act in the workplace. They didn't realize that when they're working in an office with a group of people, they have to go out of their way to get along and follow the unwritten rules of that workplace. They didn't realize that the office is not the place to make personal statements about their individuality in how they dress or in how they conduct themselves that conflict with the environment.

McBride says that means you'll have to size up how others are dressing and match what the office is geared to. For instance, if you work in a business office, most likely you'd wear slacks and a button-down shirt or a nice skirt and top. If you worked in a golf pro shop, you'd wear a golf shirt and shorts. "As much as you want to be an individual," says McBride, "you have to fit in when you're in a business setting. If you want an adult job, you have to act like an adult."

A lot of young people don't grasp how important office etiquette is and blow it off as just some silly rules imposed by adults. But McBride cautions that not following the norms of office etiquette can make or break a job. You can have all the technical talent and know all the latest software applications, but if you're not up on how people dress, talk, and conduct business, your job probably won't last very long. When it comes to getting a job, McBride warns, "First impressions are so important. Bad office etiquette can hurt that first impression." The best advice that we can give is that if you're not sure what the policy is about answering phones, using e-mail or the Internet on the job, or dress codes, you should ask your boss. He or she won't steer you wrong and will be pleased that you were concerned enough to ask.

Finding a Friendly Face at Work

There you are on the first day of a new job. Everyone looks like they know what they're doing while you stand there feeling really dumb. Even for the most seasoned employee, those first few weeks on the job are tough. Of course, everyone else looks like they know what they're doing because they've been doing it for quite some time. Wouldn't it be nice, though, if you had someone to help you adjust? Someone who would give you those little inside tips everyone else learns with experience. Someone to caution you about things that could go wrong or to give you a heads-up when you're doing something that could lead to a reprimand. If you look around the office, you'll find such a person, says Robert Fait, Career Counselor and Instructional Specialist, who is associated with Career and Technology Education in the Katy Independent School district in Katy, Texas.

You might not realize that such a person is a mentor, but in the strict definition of the word, that's what he or she is. Or, as Fait puts it, "Mentors are role models who are willing to assist others with personal education and career goal setting and planning. This caring person shares a listening ear, a comforting shoulder, and an understanding heart." In other words, a mentor is someone who will make you feel comfortable in a new working environment, show you the procedures, and, in the end, help you become more productive.

Unless the company you're working for has a formal mentoring program, mentors don't come with huge signs around their necks that read, "Look here. I'm a mentor. Ask me anything." You have to look for them. Fait advises new employees to look closely at their coworkers and take notice of who demonstrates positive behavior, has strong work habits, and seems trustworthy. Those are the people to approach. "Such workers are usually willing to share their knowledge and insights with others," says Fait.

Who knows? Given some time, you could become a mentor yourself after you've been on the job for a while. Maybe you'll be able to help some new employee who looks kind of bewildered and in need of a friendly hand because you'll remember what it was like to be the new person.

12 Chapter

SURVIVAL SKILLS

Whether you're headed to college or work, you're going to come face to face with some intimidating stuff after graduation.

YOUR LEVEL OF STRESS will most likely increase due to the demands of your classes or job and to your exposure to alcohol or drugs; various forms of conflict will rise, and you're going to have to keep up with your own health and nutrition. Seem daunting? It's really not if you keep a level head about you and stick to your core values. This section will help you work through the muddier side of life after high school.

SKILLS TO MAKE YOU STRESS-HARDY

Jump out of bed and into the shower. What to wear? Throw that on. Yuck—what's that stain? "Mom, where are my clean socks?" Tick, tock. No time to grab a bite if you want to make the homeroom bell. Skid around the corner and race for the classroom just as the final bell rings. Whoops, forgot your bio book. Sports, clubs, job, homework, friends on the phone, and finally (sigh) sleep.

Sound like your life? If you're like most high school students, that description probably hits pretty close to home. So now we'll take your already hectic schedule and throw in the fact that you'll soon be graduating and have to figure out what to do with your life. Can you say "stress"?

Some people say that stress actually motivates them to perform better, but we won't talk about those perfect people. For most of you, stress means that you

may snap at the dog, slam a few doors, get mad at your mom, and feel down. Maybe you'll even have physical symptoms—stomach disturbances, rapid heartbeat, sweaty palms, dizziness. The list goes on. Not a good place to be when you're dealing with a huge list of things to do, plus graduation is staring you in the face.

How to handle stress has been written about countless times, but out of all the advice that's out there, a few simple pointers can really help you prevent the sweaty palms and nauseated feeling in the pit of your stomach.

- **French fries out, good food in.** Eat at least one hot, balanced meal a day. Healthy, as in veggies, fruits, meats, cheese, grains. Read further along in this section for more information about nutrition and health.

- **Sleep.** Seven, eight, ten hours a day. Easier said than done, but well worth it. Sleep will not only get you through high school but also your college and career lives, and it will help you stop feeling like such a frazzled bunch of nerve endings.

- **Hug your dog, cat, rabbit, friend, or mom.** Loneliness breeds stress because then all you've got is yourself and those stressed-out thoughts zooming around in your head.

- **Get with friends.** That takes time, but being with people you like and doing fun things eases stress—as long as you don't overdo it.

- **Exercise.** This does not include running down the hall to make the bell. We're talking 20 minutes of heart-pounding perspiration at least three times a week. It's amazing what a little sweat can do to relax you. Believe it or not, good posture helps too.

- **Don't smoke, drink, or use excessive amounts of caffeine.** Whoever told you that partying is the way to relieve stress got it all wrong. Nicotine and alcohol actually take away the things your body needs to fight stress.

- **Simplify your expenses.** Money can be a big stress factor. Think of ways to eliminate where you're spending money so that the money you have doesn't have to be stretched so far. Be creative. Share resources. Sell items you no longer use. Maybe put off buying something you've been wanting.

- **Let your feelings out of your head.** It takes time and energy to keep them bottled up inside. Have regular conversations with your parents and siblings so that minor annoyances can be solved when they're still small.

- **Organize your time.** As in prioritizing and dealing with one small part of your life instead of trying to solve everything in one shot. Read on for more information about time management. This is just a teaser.

- **Lighten up.** When you've graduated and are into whatever it is you'll end up doing, you'll look back and realize that this was a teensy little part of your life. So look on the bright side. The decisions you'll be making about your future are heavy, but they won't be cut in stone. You can change them if they don't work out.

Stress Busters

Most people get stressed when things are out of control—too many things to do, too many decisions to make, or too much information to digest. If you add not having enough time, enough money, or enough energy to get it all done, you have the perfect recipe for stress.

In the space below, identify what's causing you stress:

_____
_____
_____
_____
_____
_____

Then, choose from these three stress-busting options:

1. **Alter the situation.** Some things you can't control, some things you can. Change the ones you can. If you have too much on your plate and can't possibly do it all, push a few things aside. There's got to be something on the list you can get rid of. (And no, homework is not an acceptable answer.) Maybe you need to be able to say no to extra demands. Concentrate on what is important. Make a list of your priorities from the most important to the least, and work your way down.

2. **Avoid the situation—for now.** Step back and ask, "Is this really a problem? Do I really need to solve it now?" This doesn't mean you should procrastinate on things that need to get done. Think of this stress buster as buying some time, taking a break, catching your breath, getting advice, and airing out the situation so that you can deal with it when you're more prepared to handle it.

3. **Accept the situation.** How you perceive your circumstances has a lot to do with how you make decisions about them. Put whatever is stressing you in the perspective of the big picture. How will this really affect me next year or even ten years from now? Look at your circumstances through the lens of your personal values. Think about what feels right to you, not someone else.

Quick Fixes for Stressful Moments

So, you've done all the things we talked about earlier in this section, and you're still feeling like you're being pulled in a million directions. If your stress thermometer has hit the top, use these quick fixes to help calm you down.

- Make the world slow down for a bit. Take a walk. Take a shower. Listen to some soothing music.

- Breathe deeply. Get in tune with the rhythm of your own breathing. Lie or sit down for 15 minutes and just concentrate on relaxing.

- Relax those little knots of tension. Start at your head and work down to your toes.

- Close your eyes and clear your mind. Oops, there comes that nagging thought. Out, out, out. Get rid of the clutter. Imagine yourself in your favorite place: the beach, under a tree, whatever works.

- Close the door to your bedroom, and let out a blood-curdling scream. Walt Whitman knew what he was talking about when he said, "I sound my barbaric yawp over the roofs of the world." Just let your family know what you're doing so they don't come running to your room in fear. You'll be amazed at how much better you feel.

- When all else fails, watch a funny movie. Read the comics. Get in a giggly frame of mind. Those big challenges will quickly be brought down to size.

WINNING THE TIME MANAGEMENT GAME

What is the value of time? Six dollars an hour? The price of a scholarship because the application is a day late? Time can be a very expensive resource or something you can use to your advantage. Even if you recognize the value of time, managing it is a challenge.

When you live with enough time, life is relaxed and balanced. In order to find that balance, you have to prioritize and plan. Decide what you want and what is important to you. Organize logically and schedule realistically. Overcome obstacles. Change bad habits. Simplify and streamline. Save time when you can.

Sound impossible? It's not easy, but you can do it. The secret is held in a Chinese proverb: The wisdom of life is the elimination of nonessentials.

It's All about Control

The good thing about time is that much of it is yours to do with as you wish. You may feel out of control and as if you must run to keep up with the conflicting demands and expectations of your life. But we all have the same number of hours in each day. The key is in how we spend them. The following tips are designed to help you spend your time wisely and to keep you in control of your life.

Prepare a list of your goals and the tasks necessary to accomplish them. This could be by day, week, month, semester, or even year. You may also want to break the list into sections, such as friends and family, school, work, sports, health and fitness, home, personal development, and college preparation.

Prioritize based on time-sensitive deadlines. Use a grading system to code how important each task is. A is "Do It Now," B is "Do It Soon," C is "Do It Later." Understand the difference between "important" and "urgent."

Be realistic about how much you can really do. Analyze how you spend your time now. What can you cut? How much time do you truly have for each task?

Think ahead. How many times have you underestimated how long it will take to do something? Plan for roadblocks, and give yourself some breathing space.

Accept responsibility. Once you decide to do something, commit yourself to it. That doesn't mean that a task that was on the "A" list can't be moved to the "C" list. But be consistent and specific about what you want to accomplish.

Divide and conquer. You may need to form a committee, delegate tasks to your parents, or ask for help from a friend. That is why it is called time management.

Take advantage of your personal prime time. Don't schedule yourself to get up and do homework at 6 a.m.

if you are a night owl. It won't work. Instead, plan complex tasks when you are most efficient.

Avoid procrastination. There are a million ways to procrastinate. And not one of them is a good reason if you really want to get something done. Have you ever noticed that you always find time to do the things you enjoy?

Do the most unpleasant task first. Get it over with. Then it will be all downhill from there.

Don't over-prepare. That is just another way to procrastinate.

Learn to say no to the demands on your time that you cannot afford.

Be enthusiastic, and share your goals with others.

If you set too many goals at once, you will overwhelm yourself from the start. Remember, what is important is the quality of the time you spend on a task, not the quantity. It doesn't make any difference if you study for 10 hours if you don't recall a thing you've reviewed. The overall goal is to be productive, efficient, and effective, not just busy. You'll also need to pace yourself. All work and no play makes for an unbalanced person.

Use all the benefits of modern technology to help you manage time. You can save lots of time by using a fax, e-mail, or voice mail. If you don't already use a day planner or calendar, you would be wise to invest in one. Write in all the important deadlines, and refer to it often. Block out commitments you know you have so you won't over-schedule yourself. When you do over-schedule yourself or underestimate the time it takes to accomplish a task, learn from your mistakes. But don't get too down on yourself. Give yourself a pep talk every now and then to keep yourself positive and motivated.

MOVING OUT ON YOUR OWN?

As you consider moving away from home either to a college dorm or your own place, some pretty wonderful expectations of what it will be like no doubt will come floating into your head. No more parental rules. On your own. Making your own decisions. Hamburgers forever. Coming and going when you want to. Oops, what's this? Looks like you're out of clothes to wear. No more cereal bowls—they're all in the sink, and they're dirty. Out of milk and the refrigerator's empty. Yikes! What happened to all those warm, fuzzy thoughts about freedom?

Sure, it's nice to be able to come and go as you please, but before you get too far into that pleasant—and unrealistic—mind mode, here are some thoughts you might want to consider as you make plans to become independent. Ozzie Hashley, a guidance counselor at Clinton Community Schools in Clinton, Michigan, works with juniors and seniors in high school. Here is what he says to inform students about the realities of independent life.

1. If you rent your own place, have you thought about the extra charges in addition to the rent? Says Hashley, "Many students think only of paying the rent. They don't realize that they'll be responsible for utilities in many cases. Or the money it will take to wash and dry your clothes."

2. Subsisting on hamburgers and fries sounds yummy, but as you watch a fast food diet eat its way into your paycheck, you'll most likely think about cooking up something yourself. What will you cook? Who will buy the food? More importantly, who will do the dishes? Dividing up the responsibilities of preparing food is a big aspect of being on your own, especially when sharing a living space.

3. Medical insurance may not be on your mind as you prepare to graduate—you're probably on your parent's insurance plans right now. However, once you are established as an independent person at age 18 and you're living on your own, insurance becomes a big consideration. If you need health care and don't have medical insurance, the bills will be big. So when

you get a job, make sure that you have medical coverage. If you're going off to college after high school, you'll most likely be covered under your parent's insurance until age 23.

4. There's no one to tell you when to come home when you're on your own. There's also no one to tell you that you're really disorganized when it comes to managing your time. Time management might not sound like a big deal now, but when you have to juggle all the facets of being independent— your job, taking care of your living space and car, your social life—then being able to manage time becomes an important part of life.

5. Managing your money moves into a whole other realm when you are on your own. You have to make sure you have enough to pay the rent, your car loan, and insurance, not to mention that movie you wanted to see, the CD you wanted to buy, or those funky jeans you saw at the mall last week. If you want to eat at the end of the month, budgeting will become an important part of your new independent vocabulary. Ask your parents or an adult you trust to help you set up your budget. Also learn how to balance your checkbook. It's a lot easier to manage your money when you keep track of how much you have in your bank account and how much you spend!

DRUGS AND ALCOHOL: ARE YOU AT RISK?

At risk? Wait a minute. How could you be at risk when the legal drinking age in all fifty states is 21? Chances are, if you're reading this, you're not 21 yet. It's also illegal to smoke or buy any tobacco product before age 18, and possession of any drug for recreational use is illegal, period. So if you drink alcohol before age 21; smoke or buy cigarettes, cigars,

or chewing tobacco before age 18; or take any illegal drugs, you could:

- Be arrested for driving under the influence (DUI)
- Be convicted
- Be required to pay steep fines
- Have your driving privileges suspended
- Get kicked out of school (that's any kind of school, college included)
- Get fired
- Go to jail
- Have a criminal record

A criminal record . . . so what?

Consider this true story. A 29-year-old man who recently received his graduate degree in business was offered a job with a major Fortune-100 corporation. We're talking big bucks, stock options, reserved parking space—the whole nine yards. When the company did a background check and found that he was arrested for a DUI during his freshman year of college, they rescinded their offer. The past can and will come back to haunt you. Let's not even think about what would happen down the line if you decide to run for public office.

Think about why you might want to try drinking or doing drugs. For fun? To forget your troubles? To be cool? Are your reasons good enough? Remember the consequences before you make a decision.

How Can I Say No without Looking like a Geek?

"It takes a lot more guts to stay sober, awake, and aware than to just get high, get numb, and learn nothing about life," says one former user. "Laugh at people who suggest you drink or take drugs, and then avoid them like the plague."

Friends worth having will respect your decision to say no. And girls—if a guy pressures you to drink or get high, ditch him pronto. You can vice-versa that for guys, too. According to the National Institute on Drug Abuse (NIDA), alcohol and club drugs like GHB or Rohypnol (roofies) make you an easy target for date rape.

The Nitty Gritty

Along with the temporary pleasure they may give you, all drugs (including club drugs, alcohol, and nicotine) have a downside. Alcohol, for example, is a depressant. Even one drink slows down the part of your brain that controls your reasoning. So your judgment gets dull just when you're wondering, "Should I drive my friends home? Should I talk to this guy? Should I have another drink?"

Your body needs about an hour to burn up the alcohol in one drink. Nothing, including coffee, will sober you up any faster. Here's what "one drink" means: one shot of hard liquor (straight or mixed in a cocktail), one glass of wine, one 12-ounce beer, or one wine cooler.

Alcohol helps smart people make bad decisions. In fact, many drugs make you believe that you're thinking even more clearly than usual. Well, guess what? You aren't. Depending on what drug you take, how much, and what you do while you're on it, you're also risking confusion, nausea, headache, sleep problems, depression, paranoia, rape (especially "date rape"), unwanted pregnancy, sexually transmitted diseases (STDs) ranging from herpes to HIV/AIDS, having a baby with a birth defect, memory impairment, persistent psychosis, lung damage, cancer, injuring or killing someone else, and death.

Take a moment now, when your brain is razor sharp, to decide if those consequences are worth the

DID YOU KNOW...

... that nicotine is as addictive as cocaine and heroin, according to the American Cancer Society?

... that drinking a lot of alcohol fast can kill you on the spot, according to Keystone College?

... that MDMA (Ecstasy, X, Adam, Clarity, Lover's Speed), according to NIDA, may permanently damage your memory?

DO I HAVE A PROBLEM?

Take the quiz below to see if you're in real trouble with drugs or alcohol.

1. **Do you look forward to drinking or using drugs?**

2. **Do most of your friends drink or do drugs?**

3. **Do you keep a secret supply of alcohol or drugs?**

4. **Can you drink a lot without appearing drunk?**

5. **Do you "power-hit" to get high faster, by binge-drinking, funneling, or slamming?**

6. **Do you ever drink or do drugs alone, including in a group where no one else is doing so?**

7. **Do you ever drink or use drugs when you hadn't planned to?**

8. **Do you ever have blackouts where you can't remember things that happened when you were drunk or high?**

If you answered yes to any of these questions, you probably need help. If you have a friend who fits the picture, find a respectful way to bring up your concerns. Don't be surprised if he or she tells you to back off—but don't give up, either. If someone in your family has an alcohol or drug problem, be aware that you may be prone to the same tendency.

Source: Keystone College, La Plume, Pennsylvania

escape you get for 20 minutes one night. You may be saying, "Oh, come on. Only addicts have problems like that." Getting drunk or high doesn't necessarily mean that you're an alcoholic or an addict—but it always means a loss of control.

"So much of addiction is about denial," says one member of Alcoholics Anonymous. "I just didn't think I looked or acted or thought or smelled or lied or cheated or failed like an alcoholic or addict. It was when the drugs and alcohol use started to cause problems in multiple areas of my life that I began to think the problem might reside with me. Friends leaving—in disgust—was what opened my eyes."

Where Can I Get Help?

If you think you have a problem, or if you think a friend has a problem, try Alcoholics Anonymous or Narcotics Anonymous. If you're not sure, ask yourself the questions in "Do I Have a Problem?" on the top of this page.

Talk to any adult you trust: maybe your doctor, a clergy member, a counselor, or your parents. Health clinics and hospitals offer information and treatment. The American Cancer Society can help you quit smoking. These are only a few places to turn—check out the Yellow Pages and the Web for more.

Alcoholics Anonymous
212-870-3400
www.aa.org

American Cancer Society
800-ACS-2345
www.cancer.org

Narcotics Anonymous
818-773-9999
www.na.org

So, that's the straight stuff. You're at a tough but wonderful age, when your life is finally your own and your decisions really matter. Think about what you value most—and then make your choices.

CONFLICT: HOW TO AVOID IT AND DEFUSE IT

You're walking along and you see a group of kids up ahead . . . and suddenly you're afraid. Or you're about to talk to someone you have a disagreement with, and already you're tense. Or your boyfriend's jealousy is spooking you. What should you do?

All of these situations involve potential conflicts that could get out of hand. Even if you never get into a violent situation, you'll face conflicts with others, as we all do. Learning to spot the warning signs of violence and to handle conflicts well will bring you lifelong benefits.

What's Your Style?

What do you do when you're faced with a potential conflict? Do you try to get away, no matter what? Do you find yourself bowing to pressure from others? Do you feel like you have to stand and fight, even if you don't want to? Do you wish you had some new ways to handle conflict?

Different situations call for different strategies. First, let's talk about situations where violence is a

real possibility. Most of us get a bad feeling before things get violent, but too often, we ignore the feeling. Trust your gut feeling! And whether you're on the street or in school, Fred Barfoot of the Crime Prevention Association of Philadelphia suggests that you keep in mind these tips for avoiding violence:

- Walk like you're in charge and you know where you're going.

- Stick to lighted areas.

- Travel with a trusted friend when possible. On campus, get an escort from security at night. Loners are targets.

- If a person or group up ahead makes you nervous, cross the street immediately—and calmly—as if you'd intended to anyway.

- Call out to an imaginary friend, "Hey, Joe! Wait up!" and then run toward your "friend," away from whoever is scaring you.

- Go right up to the nearest house and ring the bell. Pretend you're expected: "Hey Joe, it's me!" You can explain later.

- If someone threatens you physically, scream.

- If someone assaults you, scream, kick where it hurts, scratch—anything.

- Don't ever get in a car with someone you don't know well or trust, even if you've seen that person around a lot.

- Strike up a conversation with an innocent bystander if you feel threatened by someone else, just to make yourself less vulnerable for a few minutes.

- Wear a whistle around your neck or carry a personal alarm or pepper spray.

- If someone mugs you, hand over your purse, wallet, jewelry—whatever he or she asks for. None of it is worth your life.

- Don't go along with something your gut says is wrong, no matter who says it's okay.

Remember that it's not a sign of weakness to back down if someone's egging you on to fight. Bill Tomasco, principal of Furness High School in Philadelphia, says that pressure from other kids to fight creates much of the violence in schools. If you're being pushed to fight, show true strength: Know that your opponent has a good side too, speak only to that good side, and don't give in to the pressure of the crowd.

Are You Safe at Home?

Locking doors and windows makes sense—but sometimes the danger lies within. A lot of violence occurs in abusive relationships, says Amy Gottlieb, a marriage family therapist intern at the California Family Counseling Center in Encino. To find out if you're at risk, ask yourself whether your partner, roommate, or family member:

- Uses jealousy to justify controlling you
- Puts you down, humiliates you, or pulls guilt trips on you
- Threatens to reveal your secrets or tells lies about you
- Makes all the decisions
- Frightens you, especially if it's on purpose
- Threatens you in any way
- Makes light of abusive behavior or says you provoked it

If any of these things are going on in your relationship, talk about it to an adult you trust, and ask for help.

Talking It Out

If your instincts tell you to get away from a situation, do it. But you can resolve many actual or potential conflicts face to face and gracefully so that everyone walks away feeling good. Read on for some tips on handling conflict from Kare Anderson, a communications expert in Sausalito, California.

Most of us make the mistake of reacting quickly, thinking only of our own needs, and not listening, says Anderson. Try doing the opposite. First and foremost, think about what you really want from the situation, and keep your goal in mind the whole time. But bring up the other person's concerns first. Then, discuss how the situation affects you both. Offer a solution that will benefit you both—and only then talk about how your solution addresses your own needs.

When the other person is talking, really listen—don't just come up with retorts in your head. Always show that you've heard the person before you give your response, especially if you're talking with someone of a different sex, size, or race. Those differences can distract us so much that we actually hear less. If you're female, you may need to s-l-o-w yourself down. Say less than you think you need to. Guys, don't shut down altogether—keep the communication going.

Even if the other person acts like a jerk, be gracious and respectful. Ask questions instead of criticizing. Let someone save face instead of looking like a fool. If you insult or embarrass someone, you may never have that person's full attention again. In short, treat the other person as you'd like to be treated.

What should you do if you're really angry? One teen said, "Thinking about things calms me down." Another said, "Once in a while, we have to cool off for a day and then come back to the discussion." Anger almost always covers up fear. What are you afraid of? Is the reward you want out of this negotiation bigger than your fear? Focus on that reward. Don't forget to breathe—long, slow breaths.

Think about these strategies often, so you'll be more likely to use them when a situation gets hot, instead of just reacting blindly. Use them to plan for negotiations ahead of time, too. Learning to resolve problems with people takes most of us a lifetime—get a jump on it now!

THE LOWDOWN ON SEXUAL HARASSMENT

Has someone ever looked at you, talked to you, or touched you in a way that gave you the creeps, made you self-conscious about your body, or created a sexual mood when it wasn't appropriate? And did you begin to dread seeing this person because he or she just wouldn't quit?

If so, you've encountered sexual harassment. Sexual harassment is inappropriate behavior that

- is happening to you because of your sex

- is unwanted (you don't like it)

- is objectively offensive (to a hypothetical "reasonable" man or woman)

- is either severe, persistent, or pervasive

- interferes with your work or school experience

Paul Edison, a domestic and sexual violence prevention educator in Portland, Oregon, says that mostly—just as with crimes like rape—men harass women. But teenage girls are a bit more likely than older women to sexually harass someone, more girl-on-girl harassment goes on with teens, and guys get harassed, too. In some of the most brutal cases coming to light now, gay men (or men perceived to be gay) are the targets.

People who sexually harass others fall into three camps, says Edison. Some just seem to be misguided and insensitive. Others get turned on by harassing someone. And a third group does it to intimidate—for example, to drive someone away from a job or just to make them feel bad about themselves.

So What Do I Do if Someone's Harassing Me?

Experts in self-defense say the best technique is to name the behavior that's bugging you and request that it stop. You might say, "Your hand is on my knee. Please remove it." If the person doesn't quit, you might try writing a letter spelling out what's bothering you and requesting that the person stop—this way, you've confronted the situation directly and you also have a record of your complaint.

But here's the good news, says Edison: You are not expected to handle harassment on your own, especially if the person harassing you is in a position of authority over you, such as a teacher, sergeant, or boss. The authorities at your school or your job should handle it—but they can't do that unless you tell them what's going on.

If you file a complaint, be prepared to describe what happened, when, and where. And make sure you report your concerns to someone who has clear authority to handle sexual harassment complaints, such as the principal or the personnel director.

Often, the person harassing you will stop as soon as he or she gets the clear message that the behavior isn't okay with you, especially if your complaint goes to someone higher up as well. Edison notes that most harassment cases don't end up involving lawyers and lawsuits. You may choose, in serious cases, to register your complaint with the Office of Civil Rights (if you're being harassed at school) or the Equal Employment Opportunity Commission (if you're being harassed at work). You can also file your complaint on different levels at the same time: for example, with your school and the police.

You have the legal right to a school and workplace free from discrimination based on your race, color, religion, sex, national origin, and—depending on where you live, as state and local laws vary—your sexual orientation. You have the right to protection from retaliation if you file a complaint of harassment. So don't be afraid to report a situation if it truly offends you and interferes with your life.

What if I'm Just Being Hypersensitive?

If someone's words or actions make you uncomfortable, that's all the reason you need to ask that person to stop the behavior, no matter how innocent the behavior may be. Trust your feelings—especially if you find you're trying to convince yourself that nothing is wrong.

What Will Happen to the Person Who Has Been Harassing Me?

If your complaint is successfully handled, says Edison, the main thing that will happen is that the person will stop harassing you. People aren't "charged" with sexual harassment unless their behavior includes criminal conduct. But your harasser may face disciplinary action, loss of privileges, suspension, expulsion, lawsuits, or criminal action, depending on the severity of his or her behavior.

How Can I Avoid Harassing Someone?

Sometimes the line between harmless flirting, joking, or complimenting and harassment is pretty thin. How can you stay on the right side of that line?

First, pay attention to your own motives. Be honest with yourself. Do you enjoy watching someone get uncomfortable when you say or do certain things? Do you feel angry with the person for some reason? Do you enjoy exercising your authority over this person in some way? Do you find yourself obsessing about the person? If any of these are true, whatever you're saying or doing probably isn't harmless.

Even if your motives seem harmless to you, be extraordinarily careful about whom and how you touch. You may be comfortable touching people casually—perhaps you'll touch someone's hand or shoulder in conversation—but remember that other people's boundaries may differ from yours.

Pay attention to the person's reactions to you. Are you getting clear green signals when you do or say things around this person, or does the person seem to shrink away from you? Does the person shut down or seem upset when you do or say certain things? Of course, if someone's told you clearly that she or he doesn't like it when you do or say certain things, apologize and stop at once. And remember, no means no.

So, if you're faced with something that feels like sexual harassment, remember to trust your feelings, convey them clearly, and get help promptly if you need it.

STAYING HEALTHY IN SPITE OF YOURSELF

When someone—like your mom—asks if you're eating right, do you ever want to say, "Hey, have you looked at my life lately? Do you see a lot of time there for eating right?" Well, how about exercise—are you getting enough? "Yeah, right. I bench-press my backpack when I'm not doing wind sprints to my next class," may be how you reply.

If you're feeling like you can't escape your stress and fatigue, you might be surprised by how much better you'll feel if you keep active and don't just eat junk. Your workload will seem easier. You'll sleep better. You'll look fantastic. And you can stay healthy—even if your time and money are in short supply.

But Really, Who Has Time to Exercise?

As one teen says, "Schoolwork gets in the way, and then I want to relax when I have a moment that isn't filled with schoolwork." You can make time for anything, if you choose to. But if you aren't athletic by nature or your school or work keeps you going nonstop, exercise is the first thing to go out the window.

However, you don't have to become a gym rat or run miles to get enough exercise. Longer workouts are great if you do them consistently, but you're better off getting little bits of regular exercise than just doing a huge workout every so often or never doing anything. And by "little bits," we mean 15- to 20-minute chunks. Add that to a fast walk to the bus, a frenzied private dance session in your room, or running up the stairs instead of taking the elevator, and you're exercising!

Regardless of how you choose to pump that muscle in the middle of your chest, the important thing is that you're doing something. You'll not only feel better about yourself, but you'll have increased energy to do other things, like study, go to work, or go out with friends.

What Does "Eating Right" Mean Anyway?

Eating right means eating a balance of good foods in moderate amounts. Your diet needn't be complicated or expensive. Dr. Michele Wilson, a specialist in adolescent medicine at the Children's Hospital of Philadelphia, notes that a teen's diet should be heavy in grains—especially whole grains—and light in sugars and fats. It should include a lot of fruits and vegetables and provide you with plenty of protein, calcium, vitamin A, B vitamins, iron, and zinc. Sound complicated?

Well, what's complicated about a bean burrito with cheese? How about pasta with vegetables, meat, or both in the sauce? A banana or some cantaloupe? Stir-fried vegetables with tofu? Carrot sticks with peanut butter? Yogurt? Cereal with milk and fruit? All of these are cheap, quick to make, and great for you.

One teen swears by microwaveable veggie burgers and adds, "Staying away from deep-fried anything is a good plan." Try to avoid things like chips and sweets, says Dr. Wilson, adding that if you're a vegetarian—and especially if you don't eat dairy products or fish—you should make sure you're getting enough protein and iron. And no matter what your diet, drink water—eight glasses a day.

As Long as I'm in Control of What I Eat, I'm Okay, Right?

That depends. Of course, having no control over what you eat is a problem. But "in control" can be good or bad. How severely do you control what and how you eat? Are you obsessed with getting thinner? Do people who love you tell you that you're too thin, and do you take that as a compliment? Do you ever binge secretly or make yourself throw up after a meal? If any of

these are true, you may be suffering from anorexia or bulimia.

According to the National Association of Anorexia Nervosa and Associated Disorders (ANAD), eating disorders affect about 7 million women and 1 million men in this country and can lead to serious health problems—even death. "The thing that convinced me to get help was fear—I had to be hospitalized, as I was literally dying from my anorexia," says one woman. Most Americans who are anorexic or bulimic developed their eating disorders in their teens.

We asked some women being treated for eating disorders what they used to see when they looked in the mirror. "Total ugliness," said one. "The smallest dimple in my flesh looked immense," said another. And a third said, "I got rid of the mirrors because they would set me off to where I wouldn't eat for days." Their advice to teens struggling with an eating disorder? "Treat yourself as you wish your parents had treated you," "Ask people you feel close to not to discuss your weight with you," and "Find ways outside of yourself to feel in control." Above all—get help! That means going to someone you trust, whether it be a parent, relative, sibling, friend, doctor, or teacher. Or call ANAD's national hotline at 847-831-3438 for a listing of support groups and referrals in your area.

So if I Eat Right and Exercise, I'm Healthy?

Well, probably. But Dr. Wilson suggests that you keep a few other things in mind too. If you smoke, drink, or do drugs, you're asking for trouble. Aside from their many scarier side effects, all these habits can steal nutrients that you need. If all this sounds like the recipe for a dull and totally uncool life, remember that feeling and looking great are never boring and that vomiting (or dying) after downing the most tequilas in the fastest time looks really uncool. If you're making short-term decisions that will hurt you in the long run, take some time to figure out why. Good health is priceless—just ask any grandparent.

Part 4

APPENDICIES

NOW THAT YOU HAVE DECIDED what types of opportunities you wish to pursue after graduation, you need a jumping-off point for getting more information. The appendices that follow will provide you with additional data to help you with your decision-making process.

NOTE: Because of Peterson's comprehensive editorial review and because all material comes directly from institution or organization officials, we believe that the information presented in these appendices is accurate. Nonetheless, errors and omissions are possible in a data collection and processing endeavor of this scope. You should check with the specific institution or organization at the time of application to verify pertinent data that may have changed since the publication of this book.

4-YEAR COLLEGES AND UNIVERSITIES

Alabama

Alabama Agricultural and
Mechanical University
4900 Meridian Street
Normal, AL 35762
800-553-0816
www.aamu.edu

Alabama State University
915 South Jackson Street
Montgomery, AL 36101-0271
800-253-5037
www.alasu.edu

American College of
Computer & Information
Sciences
2101 Magnolia Avenue,
Suite 207
Birmingham, AL 35205
800-767-AICS
www.accis.edu

Andrew Jackson University
10 Old Montgomery Highway
Birmingham, AL 35209
205-871-9288
www.aju.edu

Athens State University
300 North Beaty Street
Athens, AL 35611-1902
800-522-0272
www.athens.edu

Auburn University
Auburn University, AL 36849
800-AUBURN9
www.auburn.edu

Auburn University
Montgomery
PO Box 244023
Montgomery, AL 36124-4023
334-244-3000
www.aum.edu

Birmingham-Southern
College
900 Arkadelphia Road
Birmingham, AL 35254
800-523-5793
www.bsc.edu

Columbia Southern
University
24847 Commercial Avenue,
PO Box 3110
Orange Beach, AL 36561
800-977-8449
www.columbiasouthern.edu

Concordia College
1804 Green Street,
PO Box 1329
Selma, AL 36701
334-874-5700

Education America,
Southeast College of
Technology, Mobile
828 Downtowner Loop West
Mobile, AL 36609-5404
800-866-0850
www.educationamerica.com

Faulkner University
5345 Atlanta Highway
Montgomery, AL 36109-3398
800-879-9816
www.faulkner.edu

Heritage Christian University
PO Box HCU
Florence, AL 35630
800-367-3565
www.hcu.edu

Huntingdon College
1500 East Fairview Avenue
Montgomery, AL 36106-2148
800-763-0313
www.huntingdon.edu

Jacksonville State University
700 Pelham Road North
Jacksonville, AL 36265-1602
800-231-5291
www.jsu.edu

Judson College
302 Bibb Street, PO Box 120
Marion, AL 36756
800-447-9472
home.judson.edu

Miles College
PO Box 3800
Birmingham, AL 35208
205-929-1000

Oakwood College
7000 Adventist Boulevard
Huntsville, AL 35896
256-726-7000
www.oakwood.edu

Samford University
800 Lakeshore Drive
Birmingham, AL 35229-0002
800-888-7218
www.samford.edu

Southeastern Bible College
3001 Highway 280 East
Birmingham, AL 35243-4181
205-970-9200
www.sebc.edu

Southern Christian
University
1200 Taylor Road
Montgomery, AL 36117
800-351-4040
www.southernchristian.edu

Spring Hill College
4000 Dauphin Street
Mobile, AL 36608-1791
800-SHC-6704
www.shc.edu

Stillman College
PO Drawer 1430, 3600
Stillman Boulevard
Tuscaloosa, AL 35403-9990
800-841-5722
www.stillman.edu

Talladega College
627 West Battle Street
Talladega, AL 35160-2354
800-633-2440
www.talladega.edu

Troy State University
University Avenue
Troy, AL 36082
334-670-3000
www.troyst.edu

Troy State University Dothan
PO Box 8368
Dothan, AL 36304-0368
334-983-6556
www.tsud.edu

Troy State University
Montgomery
PO Drawer 4419
Montgomery, AL 36103-4419
800-355-TSUM
www.tsum.edu

Tuskegee University
Tuskegee, AL 36088
800-622-6531
www.tusk.edu

The University of Alabama
Tuscaloosa, AL 35487
800-933-BAMA
www.ua.edu

The University of Alabama at
Birmingham
Birmingham, AL 35294
205-934-4011
www.uab.edu

The University of Alabama in
Huntsville
301 Sparkman Drive
Huntsville, AL 35899
800-UAH-CALL
www.uah.edu

The University of West
Alabama
Livingston, AL 35470
800-621-8044
www.uwa.edu

University of Mobile
PO Box 13220
Mobile, AL 36663-0220
800-946-7267
www.umobile.edu

University of Montevallo
Station 6001
Montevallo, AL 35115
800-292-4349
www.montevallo.edu

University of North Alabama
University Station
Florence, AL 35632-0001
800-TALKUNA
www.una.edu

University of South Alabama
307 University Boulevard
Mobile, AL 36688-0002
800-872-5247
www.southalabama.edu

Virginia College at
Birmingham
65 Bagby Drive
Birmingham, AL 35209
205-802-1200
www.vc.edu

Alaska

Alaska Bible College
Box 289
Glennallen, AK 99588-0289
907-822-3201
www.akbible.edu

Alaska Pacific University
4101 University Drive
Anchorage, AK 99508-4672
907-561-1266
www.alaskapacific.edu

Sheldon Jackson College
801 Lincoln Street
Sitka, AK 99835-7699
907-747-5222
www.sj-alaska.edu

University of Alaska
Anchorage
3211 Providence Drive
Anchorage, AK 99508-8060
907-786-1800
www.uaa.alaska.edu

University of Alaska
Fairbanks
PO Box 757480
Fairbanks, AK 99775-7480
907-474-7211
www.uaf.edu

University of Alaska
Southeast
11120 Glacier Highway
Juneau, AK 99801
907-465-6457
www.jun.alaska.edu

Arizona

American Indian College of
the Assemblies of God, Inc.
10020 North Fifteenth Ave
Phoenix, AZ 85021-2199
602-944-3335

Arizona State University
Tempe, AZ 85287
480-965-9011
www.asu.edu

Arizona State University East
7001 East Williams Field Rd.
Mesa, AZ 85212
480-727-3278
www.east.asu.edu

Arizona State University West
PO Box 37100, 4701 W
Thunderbird Rd
Phoenix, AZ 85069-7100
602-543-5500
www.west.asu.edu

The Art Institute of Phoenix
2233 West Dunlap Avenue
Phoenix, AZ 85021-2859
602-678-4300
www.aipx.edu

Collins College: A School of
Design and Technology
1140 South Priest Drive
Tempe, AZ 85281-5206
480-966-3000
www.collinscollege.edu

DeVry Institute of Technology
2149 West Dunlap Avenue
Phoenix, AZ 85021-2995
602-870-9222
www.devry-phx.edu

Education America, Tempe
Campus
875 West Elliot Road,
Suite 216
Tempe, AZ 85284
480-834-1000
educationamerica.com

Embry-Riddle Aeronautical
University
3200 Willow Creek Road
Prescott, AZ 86301-3720
928-708-3728
www.embryriddle.edu

Grand Canyon University
3300 W Camelback Road,
PO Box 11097
Phoenix, AZ 85061-1097
602-249-3300
www.grand-canyon.edu

International Baptist College
2150 East Southern Avenue
Tempe, AZ 85282
480-838-7070

Mesa State College
1100 North Avenue
Grand Junction, CO 81501
970-248-1020
www.mesastate.edu

Metropolitan College of
Court Reporting
4640 East Elwood Street,
Suite 12
Phoenix, AZ 85040
602-955-5900
www.metropolitancollege.edu

Northcentral University
600 East Gurley Street #E
Prescott, AZ 86301
520-541-7777
www.ncu.edu

Northern Arizona University
Box 4132
Flagstaff, AZ 86011
520-523-9011
www.nau.edu

Prescott College
220 Grove Avenue
Prescott, AZ 86301-2990
520-778-2090
www.prescott.edu

Southwestern College
2625 East Cactus Road
Phoenix, AZ 85032-7042
602-992-6101
www.southwesterncollege.edu

University of Advancing
Computer Technology
2625 West Baseline Road
Tempe, AZ 85283-1042
602-383-8228
www.uact.edu

The University of Arizona
Tucson, AZ 85721
520-621-2211
www.arizona.edu

University of
Phoenix–Phoenix Campus
4635 East Elwood Street
Phoenix, AZ 85040-1958
480-557-2000
www.phoenix.edu

University of
Phoenix–Southern Arizona
Campus
5099 East Grant Road
Tucson, AZ 85712
520-881-6512
www.phoenix.edu

Western International
University
9215 North Black Canyon
Highway
Phoenix, AZ 85021-2718
602-943-2311
www.wintu.edu

Arkansas

Arkansas Baptist College
1600 Bishop Street
Little Rock, AR 72202-6067
501-374-7856
www.arbaptcoll.edu

Arkansas State University
PO Box 10
State University, AR 72467
870-972-2100
www.astate.edu

Arkansas Tech University
Russellville, AR 72801-2222
479-968-0389
www.atu.edu

Central Baptist College
1501 College Avenue
Conway, AR 72032-6470
800-205-6872
www.cbc.edu

Harding University
900 East Center
Searcy, AR 72149-0001
800-477-4407
www.harding.edu

Henderson State University
1100 Henderson Street
Arkadelphia, AR 71999-0001
800-228-7333
www.hsu.edu

Hendrix College
1600 Washington Avenue
Conway, AR 72032-3080
800-277-9017
www.hendrix.edu

John Brown University
2000 West University Street
Siloam Springs, AR
72761-2121
877-JBU-INFO
www.jbu.edu

Lyon College
PO Box 2317
Batesville, AR 72503-2317
800-423-2542
www.lyon.edu

Ouachita Baptist University
410 Ouachita Street
Arkadelphia, AR 71998-0001
870-245-5000
www.obu.edu

Philander Smith College
812 West 13th Street
Little Rock, AR 72202-3799
800-446-6772
www.philander.edu

Southern Arkansas
University–Magnolia
100 East University
Magnolia, AR 71753
870-235-4000
www.saumag.edu

University of Arkansas
Fayetteville, AR 72701-1201
800-377-8632
www.uark.edu

University of Arkansas at Little Rock
2801 South University Ave
Little Rock, AR 72204-1099
501-569-3000
www.ualr.edu

University of Arkansas at Monticello
Monticello, AR 71656
870-367-6811
www.uamont.edu

University of Arkansas at Pine Bluff
1200 North University Drive
Pine Bluff, AR 71601-2799
870-543-8000

University of Arkansas for Medical Sciences
4301 West Markham
Little Rock, AR 72205-7199
501-686-5000
www.uams.edu

University of Central Arkansas
201 Donaghey Avenue
Conway, AR 72035-0001
501-450-5000
www.uca.edu

University of the Ozarks
415 North College Avenue
Clarksville, AR 72830-2880
800-264-8636
www.ozarks.edu

Williams Baptist College
60 West Fulbright Avenue
Walnut Ridge, AR 72476
800-722-4434
wbcoll.edu

California

Academy of Art College
79 New Montgomery Street
San Francisco, CA 94105-3410
415-274-2200
www.academyart.edu

Alliant International University
10455 Pomerado Road
San Diego, CA 92131-1799
858-271-4300
www.usiu.edu

American InterContinental University
12655 West Jefferson Blvd
Los Angeles, CA 90066
310-302-2000
www.aiuniv.edu

Antioch University Los Angeles
13274 Fiji Way
Marina del Rey, CA 90292-7090
310-578-1080
www.antiochla.edu

Antioch University Santa Barbara
801 Garden Street
Santa Barbara, CA 93101-1581
805-962-8179
www.antiochsb.edu

Argosy University-Los Angeles
3745 Chapman Avenue, Suite 100
Orange, CA 92868
714-940-0025
www.sarasota.edu

Armstrong University
1608 Webster Street
Oakland, CA 94612
510-835-7900
www.armstrong-u.edu

Art Center College of Design
1700 Lida Street
Pasadena, CA 91103-1999
626-396-2200
www.artcenter.edu

The Art Institute of California
10025 Mesa Rim Road
San Diego, CA 92121
858-546-0602
www.aica.artinstitutes.edu

Art Institute of Southern California
2222 Laguna Canyon Road
Laguna Beach, CA 92651-1136
949-376-6000
www.aisc.edu

Art Institutes International at San Francisco
1170 Market Street
San Francisco, CA 94102-4908
415-865-0198
www.aisf.artinstitutes.edu

Azusa Pacific University
901 East Alosta Avenue, PO Box 7000
Azusa, CA 91702-7000
626-815-6000
www.apu.edu

Bethany College of the Assemblies of God
800 Bethany Drive
Scotts Valley, CA 95066-2820
831-438-3800
www.bethany.edu

Bethesda Christian University
730 North Euclid Street
Anaheim, CA 92801
714-517-1945
www.bcu.edu

Biola University
13800 Biola Avenue
La Mirada, CA 90639-0001
562-903-6000
www.biola.edu

Brooks Institute of Photography
801 Alston Road
Santa Barbara, CA 93108-2399
805-966-3888
www.brooks.edu

California Baptist University
8432 Magnolia Avenue
Riverside, CA 92504-3206
909-689-5771
www.calbaptist.edu

California Christian College
4881 East University Avenue
Fresno, CA 93703-3533
559-251-4215
www.calchristiancollege.org

California College for Health Sciences
2423 Hoover Avenue
National City, CA 91950-6605
619-477-4800
www.cchs.edu

California College of Arts and Crafts
1111 Eighth Street
San Francisco, CA 94107
415-703-9500
www.ccac-art.edu

California Institute of Integral Studies
1453 Mission Street
San Francisco, CA 94103
415-575-6100
www.ciis.edu

California Institute of Technology
1200 East California Boulevard
Pasadena, CA 91125-0001
626-395-6811
www.caltech.edu

California Institute of the Arts
24700 McBean Parkway
Valencia, CA 91355-2340
661-255-1050
www.calarts.edu

California Lutheran University
60 West Olsen Road
Thousand Oaks, CA 91360-2787
805-492-2411
www.clunet.edu

California Maritime Academy
PO Box 1392, 200 Maritime Academy Drive
Vallejo, CA 94590-0644
707-654-1000
www.csum.edu

California National University for Advanced Studies
16909 Parthenia Street
North Hills, CA 91343
818-830-2411
www.cnuas.edu

California Polytechnic State University, San Luis Obispo
San Luis Obispo, CA 93407
805-756-1111
www.calpoly.edu

California State Polytechnic University, Pomona
3801 West Temple Avenue
Pomona, CA 91768-2557
909-869-7659
www.csupomona.edu

California State University San Marcos
San Marcos, CA 92096-0001
760-750-4000
ww2.csusm.edu

California State University,
Bakersfield
9001 Stockdale Highway
Bakersfield, CA 93311-1099
661-664-2011
www.csubak.edu

California State University,
Chico
400 West First Street
Chico, CA 95929-0722
530-898-6116
www.csuchico.edu

California State University,
Dominguez Hills
1000 East Victoria Street
Carson, CA 90747-0001
310-243-3300
www.csudh.edu

California State University,
Fresno
5241 North Maple Avenue
Fresno, CA 93740-8027
559-278-4240
www.csufresno.edu

California State University,
Fullerton
PO Box 34080
Fullerton, CA 92834-9480
714-278-2011
www.fullerton.edu

California State University,
Hayward
25800 Carlos Bee Boulevard
Hayward, CA 94542-3000
510-885-3000
www.csuhayward.edu

California State University,
Long Beach
1250 Bellflower Boulevard
Long Beach, CA 90840
562-985-4111
www.csulb.edu

California State University,
Los Angeles
5151 State University Drive
Los Angeles, CA 90032-8530
323-343-3000
www.calstatela.edu

California State University,
Monterey Bay
100 Campus Center
Seaside, CA 93955-8001
831-582-3000
www.monterey.edu

California State University,
Northridge
18111 Nordhoff Street
Northridge, CA 91330
818-677-1200
www.csun.edu

California State University,
Sacramento
6000 J Street
Sacramento, CA 95819-6048
916-278-6011
www.csus.edu

California State University,
San Bernardino
5500 University Parkway
San Bernardino, CA
92407-2397
909-880-5000
www.csusb.edu

California State University,
Stanislaus
801 West Monte Vista Avenue
Turlock, CA 95382
209-667-3122
www.csustan.edu

Chapman University
One University Drive
Orange, CA 92866
714-997-6815
www.chapman.edu

Charles R. Drew University of
Medicine and Science
1731 East 120th Street
Los Angeles, CA 90059
323-563-4800
www.cdrewu.edu

Christian Heritage College
2100 Greenfield Drive
El Cajon, CA 92019-1157
619-441-2200
www.christianheritage.edu

Claremont McKenna College
500 East 9th Street
Claremont, CA 91711
909-621-8000
www.claremontmckenna.edu

Cleveland Chiropractic
College-Los Angeles Campus
590 North Vermont Avenue
Los Angeles, CA 90004-2196
323-660-6166
www.clevelandchiropractic.edu

Cogswell Polytechnical
College
1175 Bordeaux Drive
Sunnyvale, CA 94089-1299
408-541-0100
www.cogswell.edu

Coleman College
7380 Parkway Drive
La Mesa, CA 91942-1532
619-465-3990
www.coleman.edu

Columbia
College–Hollywood
18618 Oxnard Street
Tarzana, CA 91356
818-345-8414
www.columbiacollege.edu

Concordia University
1530 Concordia West
Irvine, CA 92612-3299
949-854-8002
www.cui.edu

Design Institute of San Diego
8555 Commerce Avenue
San Diego, CA 92121-2685
858-566-1200

DeVry Institute of Technology
22801 West Roscoe Blvd
West Hills, CA 91304
801-713-8111
www.wh.devry.edu

DeVry Institute of Technology
6600 Dumbarton Circle
Fremont, CA 94555
510-574-1100
www.fre.devry.edu

DeVry Institute of Technology
3880 Kilroy Airport Way
Long Beach, CA 90806
562-427-0861
www.lb.devry.edu

DeVry Institute of Technology
901 Corporate Center Drive
Pomona, CA 91768-2642
909-622-8866
www.pom.devry.edu

Dominican School of
Philosophy and Theology
2401 Ridge Road
Berkeley, CA 94709-1295
510-849-2030
www.dspt.edu

Dominican University of
California
50 Acacia Avenue
San Rafael, CA 94901-2298
415-457-4440
www.dominican.edu

Education America
University
123 Camino de la Reina,
North Building, Suite 100
San Diego, CA 92108
619-686-8600

Emmanuel Bible College
1605 East Elizabeth Street
Pasadena, CA 91104
626-791-2575
www.emmanuelbiblecollege.
edu

Fresno Pacific University
1717 South Chestnut Avenue
Fresno, CA 93702-4709
559-453-2000
www.fresno.edu

Golden Gate University
536 Mission Street
San Francisco, CA
94105-2968
415-442-7000
www.ggu.edu

Harvey Mudd College
301 East 12th Street
Claremont, CA 91711-5994
909-621-8000
www.hmc.edu

Holy Names College
3500 Mountain Boulevard
Oakland, CA 94619-1699
510-436-1000
www.hnc.edu

Hope International University
2500 East Nutwood Avenue
Fullerton, CA 92831-3138
714-879-3903
www.hiu.edu

Humboldt State University
1 Harpst Street
Arcata, CA 95521-8299
707-826-3011
www.humboldt.edu

Humphreys College
6650 Inglewood Avenue
Stockton, CA 95207-3896
209-478-0800
www.humphreys.edu

Institute of Computer Technology
3200 Wilshire Boulevard, # 400
Los Angeles, CA 90010-1308
213-381-3333
www.ictcollege.edu

Interior Designers Institute
1061 Camelback Road
Newport Beach, CA 92660
949-675-4451
www.idi.edu/main.html

International Technological University
1650 Warburton Avenue
Santa Clara, CA 95050
408-556-9010
www.itu.edu

John F. Kennedy University
12 Altarinda Road
Orinda, CA 94563-2603
925-254-0200
www.jfku.edu

La Sierra University
4700 Pierce Street
Riverside, CA 92515-8247
909-785-2000
www.lasierra.edu

LIFE Bible College
1100 Covina Boulevard
San Dimas, CA 91773-3298
909-599-5433
www.lifebible.edu

Lincoln University
401 15th Street
Oakland, CA 94612
510-628-8010
www.lincolnuca.edu

Loma Linda University
Loma Linda, CA 92350
909-558-1000
www.llu.edu

Loyola Marymount University
One LMU Drive
Los Angeles, CA 90045-2659
310-338-2700

The Master's College and Seminary
21726 Placerita Canyon Road
Santa Clarita, CA 91321-1200
661-259-3540
www.masters.edu

Menlo College
1000 El Camino Real
Atherton, CA 94027-4301
650-688-3753
www.menlo.edu

Mills College
5000 MacArthur Boulevard
Oakland, CA 94613-1000
510-430-2255
www.mills.edu

Mount St. Mary's College
12001 Chalon Road
Los Angeles, CA 90049-1599
310-954-4000
www.msmc.la.edu

Mt. Sierra College
101 East Huntington Drive
Monrovia, CA 91016
626-873-2144
www.mtsierra.edu

Musicians Institute
1655 North McCadden Place
Hollywood, CA 90028
323-462-1384

The National Hispanic University
14271 Story Road
San Jose, CA 95127-3823
408-254-6900
www.nhu.edu

National University
11255 North Torrey Pines Rd.
La Jolla, CA 92037-1011
619-563-7100
www.nu.edu

New College of California
50 Fell Street
San Francisco, CA 94102-5206
415-241-1300
www.newcollege.edu

Newschool of Architecture & Design
1249 F Street
San Diego, CA 92101-6634
619-235-4100
www.newschoolarch.edu

Northwestern Polytechnic University
117 Fourier Avenue
Fremont, CA 94539-7482
510-657-5911
www.npu.edu

Notre Dame de Namur University
1500 Ralston Avenue
Belmont, CA 94002-1997
650-593-1601
www.cnd.edu

Occidental College
1600 Campus Road
Los Angeles, CA 90041-3314
323-259-2500
www.oxy.edu

Otis College of Art and Design
9045 Lincoln Boulevard
Los Angeles, CA 90045-9785
310-665-6800
www.otisart.edu

Pacific Oaks College
5 Westmoreland Place
Pasadena, CA 91103
626-397-1300
www.pacificoaks.edu

Pacific States University
1516 South Western Avenue
Los Angeles, CA 90006
323-731-2383
www.psuca.edu

Pacific Union College
One Angwin Avenue
Angwin, CA 94508-9707
707-965-6311
www.puc.edu

Patten College
2433 Coolidge Avenue
Oakland, CA 94601-2699
510-261-8500
www.diac.com/~patten

Pepperdine University
24255 Pacific Coast Highway
Malibu, CA 90263-0002
310-506-4000
www.pepperdine.edu

Pitzer College
1050 North Mills Avenue
Claremont, CA 91711-6101
909-621-8000
www.pitzer.edu

Point Loma Nazarene University
3900 Lomaland Drive
San Diego, CA 92106-2899
619-849-2200
www.ptloma.edu

Pomona College
550 North College Avenue
Claremont, CA 91711
909-621-8000
www.pomona.edu

Saint Mary's College of California
1928 Saint Mary's Road
Moraga, CA 94556
925-631-4000
www.stmarys-ca.edu

Samuel Merritt College
370 Hawthorne Avenue
Oakland, CA 94609-3108
510-869-6511
www.samuelmerritt.edu

San Diego State University
5500 Campanile Drive
San Diego, CA 92182
619-594-5200
www.sdsu.edu

San Francisco Art Institute
800 Chestnut Street
San Francisco, CA 94133
415-771-7020
www.sfai.edu

San Francisco Conservatory of Music
1201 Ortega Street
San Francisco, CA 94122-4411
415-564-8086
www.sfcm.edu

San Francisco State University
1600 Holloway Avenue
San Francisco, CA 94132-1722
415-338-1100
www.sfsu.edu

San Jose Christian College
790 South Twelfth Street
San Jose, CA 95112-2381
408-278-4300
www.sjchristiancol.edu

San Jose State University
One Washington Square
San Jose, CA 95192-0001
408-924-1000
www.sjsu.edu

Santa Clara University
500 El Camino Real
Santa Clara, CA 95053
408-554-4000
www.scu.edu

Scripps College
1030 Columbia Avenue
Claremont, CA 91711-3948
909-621-8000
www.scrippscol.edu

Shasta Bible College
2980 Hartnell Avenue
Redding, CA 96002
530-221-4275
www.shasta.edu

Simpson College and
Graduate School
2211 College View Drive
Redding, CA 96003-8606
530-224-5600
www.simpsonca.edu

Sonoma State University
1801 East Cotati Avenue
Rohnert Park, CA 94928-3609
707-664-2880
www.sonoma.edu

Southern California Bible
College & Seminary
2075 East Madison Avenue
El Cajon, CA 92019
619-442-9841
www.scbcs.edu

Southern California Institute
of Architecture
350 Merrick Street
Los Angeles, CA 90013
213-613-2200
www.sciarc.edu

St. John's Seminary College
5118 Seminary Road
Camarillo, CA 93012-2599
805-482-2755
www.west.net/~sjsc

Stanford University
Stanford, CA 94305-9991
650-723-2300
www.stanford.edu

Thomas Aquinas College
10000 North Ojai Road
Santa Paula, CA 93060-9980
805-525-4417
www.thomasaquinas.edu

Touro University
International
Suite 102, 10542 Calle Lee
Los Alamitos, CA 90720
714-816-0366
www.tourouniversity.edu

University of California,
Berkeley
Berkeley, CA 94720-1500
510-642-6000
www.berkeley.edu

University of California,
Davis
One Shields Avenue
Davis, CA 95616
530-752-1011
www.ucdavis.edu

University of California,
Irvine
Irvine, CA 92697
949-824-5011
www.uci.edu

University of California,
Los Angeles
405 Hilgard Avenue
Los Angeles, CA 90095
310-825-4321
www.ucla.edu

University of California,
Riverside
900 University Avenue
Riverside, CA 92521-0102
909-787-1012
www.ucr.edu

University of California,
San Diego
9500 Gilman Drive
La Jolla, CA 92093
858-534-2230
www.ucsd.edu

University of California,
Santa Barbara
Santa Barbara, CA 93106
805-893-8000
www.ucsb.edu

University of California,
Santa Cruz
1156 High Street
Santa Cruz, CA 95064
831-459-0111
www.ucsc.edu

University of Judaism
15600 Mulholland Drive
Bel Air, CA 90077-1599
310-476-9777
www.uj.edu

University of La Verne
1950 Third Street
La Verne, CA 91750-4443
909-593-3511
www.ulv.edu

University of Phoenix–
Northern California Campus
7901 Stoneridge Drive,
Suite 100
Pleasanton, CA 94588
877-4-STUDENT
www.phoenix.edu

University of Phoenix–
Sacramento Campus
1760 Creekside Oaks Drive,
Suite 100
Sacramento, CA 95833
800-266-2107
www.phoenix.edu

University of Phoenix–
San Diego Campus
3890 Murphy Canyon Road,
Suite 100
San Diego, CA 92123
888-UOP-INFO
www.phoenix.edu

University of Phoenix–
Southern California Campus
10540 Talbert Avenue, West
Building, Suite 100
Fountain Valley, CA 92708
800-GO-TO-UOP
www.phoenix.edu

University of Redlands
1200 E. Colton Avenue,
PO Box 3080
Redlands, CA 92373-0999
909-793-2121
www.redlands.edu

University of San Diego
5998 Alcala Park
San Diego, CA 92110-2492
619-260-4600
www.sandiego.edu

University of San Francisco
2130 Fulton Street
San Francisco, CA 94117-1080
415-422-6886
www.usfca.edu

University of Southern
California
University Park Campus
Los Angeles, CA 90089
213-740-2311
www.usc.edu

University of the Pacific
3601 Pacific Avenue
Stockton, CA 95211-0197
209-946-2011
www.uop.edu

University of West
Los Angeles
1155 West Arbor Vitae Street
Inglewood, CA 90301-2902
310-342-5200
www.uwla.edu

Vanguard University of
Southern California
55 Fair Drive
Costa Mesa, CA 92626-6597
714-556-3610
www.vanguard.edu

Westmont College
955 La Paz Road
Santa Barbara, CA
93108-1099
805-565-6000
www.westmont.edu

Westwood College of
Aviation Technology–
Los Angeles
8911 Aviation Boulevard
Inglewood, CA 90301-2904
310-337-4444
www.westwood.edu

Whittier College
13406 E Philadelphia Street
Whittier, CA 90608-0634
562-907-4200
www.whittier.edu

Woodbury University
7500 Glenoaks Boulevard
Burbank, CA 91504-1099
818-767-0888
www.woodbury.edu

Yeshiva Ohr Elchonon
Chabad/West Coast
Talmudical Seminary
7215 Waring Avenue
Los Angeles, CA 90046-7660
213-937-3763

Colorado

Adams State College
208 Edgemont Boulevard
Alamosa, CO 81102
719-587-7011
www.adams.edu

The Art Institute of Colorado
1200 Lincoln Street
Denver, CO 80203
303-837-0825
www.aic.artinstitutes.edu

Colorado Christian University
180 South Garrison Street
Lakewood, CO 80226-7499
303-202-0100
www.ccu.edu

The Colorado College
14 East Cache La Poudre
Colorado Springs, CO
80903-3294
719-389-6000
www.coloradocollege.edu

Colorado School of Mines
1500 Illinois Street
Golden, CO 80401-1887
303-273-3000
www.mines.edu

Colorado State University
Fort Collins, CO 80523-0015
970-491-1101
www.colostate.edu

Colorado Technical University
4435 North Chestnut Street
Colorado Springs, CO
80907-3896
719-598-0200
www.coloradotech.edu

Colorado Technical University
Denver Campus
5775 Denver Tech Center Blvd
Greenwood Village, CO 80111
303-694-6600
www.coloradotech.edu

Denver Technical College
925 South Niagara Street
Denver, CO 80224-1658
303-329-3000
www.den.devry.edu

Denver Technical College at
Colorado Springs
225 South Union Boulevard
Colorado Springs, CO
80910-3138
719-632-3000
www.dtc.edu

DeVry Institute of Technology
225 South Union Boulevard
Colorado Springs, CO 80910
719-632-3000
www.cs.devry.edu

Education America, Colorado
Springs Campus
6050 Erin Park Drive, #250
Colorado Springs, CO 80918
719-532-1234

Education America,
Denver Campus
11011 West 6th Avenue
Lakewood, CO 80215-0090
303-445-0500

Fort Lewis College
1000 Rim Drive
Durango, CO 81301-3999
970-247-7010
www.fortlewis.edu

Johnson & Wales University
7150 Montview Boulevard
Denver, CO 80220
303-256-9300
www.jwu.edu

Jones International
University
9697 East Mineral Avenue
Englewood, CO 80112
303-784-8045
www.jonesinternational.edu

Metropolitan State College of
Denver
PO Box 173362
Denver, CO 80217-3362
303-556-3018
www.mscd.edu

Naropa University
2130 Arapahoe Avenue
Boulder, CO 80302-6697
303-444-0202
www.naropa.edu

National American University
5125 North Academy Blvd
Colorado Springs, CO 80918
719-277-0588

National American University
1325 South Colorado Blvd,
Suite 100
Denver, CO 80222
303-758-6700

Nazarene Bible College
1111 Academy Park Loop
Colorado Springs, CO
80910-3704
719-884-5000
www.nbc.edu

Regis University
3333 Regis Boulevard
Denver, CO 80221-1099
303-458-4100
www.regis.edu

Rocky Mountain College of
Art & Design
6875 East Evans Avenue
Denver, CO 80224-2329
303-753-6046
www.rmcad.edu

Teikyo Loretto Heights
University
3001 South Federal Blvd
Denver, CO 80236-2711
303-937-4200

United States Air Force
Academy
HQ USAFA/XPR,
2304 Cadet Drive, Suite 200
USAF Academy, CO
80840-5025
719-333-1818
www.usafa.edu/rr

University of Colorado at
Boulder
Boulder, CO 80309
303-492-1411
www.colorado.edu

University of Colorado at
Colorado Springs
PO Box 7150
Colorado Springs, CO
80933-7150
719-262-3000
www.uccs.edu

University of Colorado at
Denver
PO Box 173364
Denver, CO 80217-3364
303-556-2400
www.cudenver.edu

University of Colorado
Health Sciences Center
4200 East Ninth Avenue
Denver, CO 80262
303-399-1211
www.uchsc.edu

University of Denver
University Park,
2199 South University Park
Denver, CO 80208
303-871-2000
www.du.edu

University of Northern
Colorado
Greeley, CO 80639
970-351-1890
www.unco.edu

University of Phoenix–
Colorado Campus
10004 Park Meadows Drive
Lone Tree, CO 80124
303-755-9090
www.phoenix.edu

University of Phoenix–
Southern Colorado Campus
5475 Tech Center, Suite 130
Colorado Springs, CO 80919
719-599-5282
www.phoenix.edu

University of Southern
Colorado
2200 Bonforte Boulevard
Pueblo, CO 81001-4901
719-549-2100
www.uscolo.edu

Western State College of
Colorado
600 North Adams Street
Gunnison, CO 81231
970-943-0120
www.western.edu

Westwood College of
Technology–Denver North
7350 North Broadway
Denver, CO 80221-3653
303-426-7000
www.westwood.edu

Yeshiva Toras Chaim
Talmudical Seminary
1400 Quitman Street
Denver, CO 80204-1415
303-629-8200

Connecticut

Albertus Magnus College
700 Prospect Street
New Haven, CT 06511-1189
203-773-8550
www.albertus.edu

Beth Benjamin Academy of
Connecticut
132 Prospect Street
Stamford, CT 06901-1202
203-325-4351

Central Connecticut State
University
1615 Stanley Street
New Britain, CT 06050-4010
860-832-3200
www.ccsu.edu

Charter Oak State College
55 Paul Manafort Drive
New Britain, CT 06053-2142
860-832-3800
www.charteroak.edu

Connecticut College
270 Mohegan Avenue
New London, CT 06320-4196
860-447-1911
www.connecticutcollege.edu

Eastern Connecticut State
University
83 Windham Street
Willimantic, CT 06226-2295
860-465-5000
www.easternct.edu

Fairfield University
1073 North Benson Road
Fairfield, CT 06430-5195
203-254-4000
www.fairfield.edu

Hartford College for Women
1265 Asylum Avenue
Hartford, CT 06105-2299
860-768-5600

Holy Apostles College and
Seminary
33 Prospect Hill Road
Cromwell, CT 06416-2005
860-632-3000
www.holy-apostles.org

Lyme Academy of Fine Arts
84 Lyme Street
Old Lyme, CT 06371
860-434-5232
www.lymeacademy.edu

Paier College of Art, Inc.
20 Gorham Avenue
Hamden, CT 06514-3902
203-287-3030
www.paierart.com

Quinnipiac University
275 Mount Carmel Avenue
Hamden, CT 06518-1940
203-582-8200
www.quinnipiac.edu

Sacred Heart University
5151 Park Avenue
Fairfield, CT 06432-1000
203-371-7999
www.sacredheart.edu

Saint Joseph College
1678 Asylum Avenue
West Hartford, CT 06117-2700
860-232-4571
www.sjc.edu

Southern Connecticut State
University
501 Crescent Street
New Haven, CT 06515-1355
203-392-5200
www.southernct.edu

Teikyo Post University
800 Country Club Road
Waterbury, CT 06723-2540
203-596-4500
teikyopost.edu

Trinity College
300 Summit Street
Hartford, CT 06106-3100
860-297-2000
www.trincoll.edu

United States Coast Guard
Academy
15 Mohegan Avenue
New London, CT 06320-8100
860-444-8444
www.cga.edu

University of Bridgeport
380 University Avenue
Bridgeport, CT 06601
203-576-4000
www.bridgeport.edu

University of Connecticut
Storrs, CT 06269
860-486-2000
www.uconn.edu

University of Hartford
200 Bloomfield Avenue
West Hartford, CT 06117-1599
860-768-4100
www.hartford.edu

University of New Haven
300 Orange Avenue
West Haven, CT 06516-1916
203-932-7000
www.newhaven.edu

Wesleyan University
Middletown, CT 06459-0260
860-685-2000
www.wesleyan.edu

Western Connecticut State
University
181 White Street
Danbury, CT 06810-6885
203-837-8200
www.wcsu.edu

Yale University
New Haven, CT 06520
203-432-4771
www.yale.edu

Delaware

Delaware State University
1200 North DuPont Highway
Dover, DE 19901-2277
302-739-4924
www.dsc.edu

Goldey-Beacom College
4701 Limestone Road
Wilmington, DE 19808-1999
302-998-8814
goldey.gbc.edu

United States Open
University
6 Denny Road, Suite 301
Wilmington, DE 19809
302-778-0300
www.open.edu

University of Delaware
Newark, DE 19716
302-831-2000
www.udel.edu

Wesley College
120 North State Street
Dover, DE 19901-3875
302-736-2300
www.wesley.edu

Wilmington College
320 DuPont Highway
New Castle, DE 19720-6491
302-328-9401
www.wilmcoll.edu

District of Columbia

American University
4400 Massachusetts Avenue,
NW
Washington, DC 20016-8001
202-885-1000
www.american.edu

The Catholic University of
America
Cardinal Station
Washington, DC 20064
202-319-5000
www.cua.edu

Corcoran College of Art and
Design
500 17th Street NW
Washington, DC 20006-4804
202-639-1800
www.corcoran.edu

Gallaudet University
800 Florida Avenue, NE
Washington, DC 20002-3625
202-651-5000
www.gallaudet.edu

Georgetown University
37th and O Street, NW
Washington, DC 20057
202-687-5055
www.georgetown.edu

The George Washington
University
2121 Eye Street, NW
Washington, DC 20052
202-994-1000
www.gwu.edu

Howard University
2400 Sixth Street, NW
Washington, DC 20059-0002
202-806-6100
www.howard.edu

Potomac College
4000 Chesapeake Street, NW
Washington, DC 20016
202-686-0876
www.potomac.edu

Southeastern University
501 I Street, SW
Washington, DC 20024-2788
202-488-8162
www.seu.edu

Strayer University
1025 15th Street, NW
Washington, DC 20005-2603
202-408-2400
www.strayer.edu

Trinity College
125 Michigan Avenue, NE
Washington, DC 20017-1094
202-884-9000
www.trinitydc.edu

University of the District of
Columbia
4200 Connecticut Avenue, NW
Washington, DC 20008-1175
202-274-5000
www.udc.edu

Florida

American College of
Prehospital Medicine
7552 Navarre Parkway, Suite 1
Navarre, FL 32566-7312
800-735-2276
www.acpm.edu

American InterContinental
University
8151 West Peters Road,
Suite 1000
Plantation, FL 33324
954-835-0939
www.aiufl.edu

Argosy University-Sarasota
5250 17th Street
Sarasota, FL 34235-8246
941-379-0404
www.argosyu.edu

The Baptist College of Florida
5400 College Drive
Graceville, FL 32440-1898
800-328-2660
www.baptistcollege.edu

Barry University
11300 Northeast Second Ave
Miami Shores, FL 33161-6695
800-695-2279
www.barry.edu

Bethune-Cookman College
640 Dr Mary McLeod
Bethune Blvd
Daytona Beach, FL
32114-3099
800-448-0228
www.bethune.cookman.edu

Carlos Albizu University,
Miami Campus
2173 NW 99th Avenue
Miami, FL 33172-2209
800-672-3246
www.albizu.edu

Clearwater Christian College
3400 Gulf-to-Bay Boulevard
Clearwater, FL 33759-4595
800-348-4463
www.clearwater.edu

DeVry University
4000 Millenia Boulevard
Orlando, FL 32839
407-370-3131
www.orl.devry.edu

Eckerd College
4200 54th Avenue South
St. Petersburg, FL 33711
800-456-9009
www.eckerd.edu

Edward Waters College
1658 Kings Road
Jacksonville, FL 32209-6199
904-355-3030
www.ewc.edu

Embry-Riddle Aeronautical
University
600 South Clyde Morris Blvd
Daytona Beach, FL
32114-3900
800-862-2416
www.embryriddle.edu

Embry-Riddle Aeronautical
University,
Extended Campus
600 South Clyde Morris Blvd
Daytona Beach, FL
32114-3900
800-862-2416
www.embryriddle.edu

Everglades College
1500 NW 49th Street,
Suite 600
Ft. Lauderdale, FL 33309
954-772-2655
www.evergladescollege.edu

Flagler College
PO Box 1027
St. Augustine, FL 32085-1027
800-304-4208
www.flagler.edu

Florida Agricultural and
Mechanical University
Tallahassee, FL 32307-3200
850-599-3000
www.famu.edu

Florida Atlantic University
777 Glades Road,
PO Box 3091
Boca Raton, FL 33431-0991
800-299-4FAU
www.fau.edu

Florida Christian College
1011 Bill Beck Boulevard
Kissimmee, FL 34744-5301
407-847-8966
www.fcc.edu

Florida College
119 North Glen Arven Avenue
Temple Terrace, FL 33617
800-326-7655
www.flcoll.edu

Florida Gulf Coast University
10501 FGCU Boulevard South
Fort Myers, FL 33965-6565
800-590-3428
www.fgcu.edu

Florida Institute of Technology
150 West University Blvd
Melbourne, FL 32901-6975
800-888-4348
www.fit.edu

Florida International
University
University Park
Miami, FL 33199
305-348-2000
www.fiu.edu

Florida Memorial College
15800 NW 42nd Avenue
Miami-Dade, FL 33054
800-822-1362
www.fmc.edu/main.cfm

Florida Metropolitan
University–Brandon Campus
3924 Coconut Palm Drive
Tampa, FL 33619
813-621-0041
www.fmu.edu

Florida Metropolitan
University–Fort Lauderdale
Campus
1040 Bayview Drive
Fort Lauderdale, FL
33304-2522
800-468-0168
www.fmu.edu

Florida Metropolitan
University–Jacksonville
Campus
8226 Phillips Highway
Jacksonville, FL 32256
888-741-4271
www.cci.edu

Florida Metropolitan
University–Lakeland Campus
995 East Memorial
Boulevard, Suite 110
Lakeland, FL 33801
863-686-1444
www.cci.edu

Florida Metropolitan
University–Melbourne
Campus
2401 North Harbor City Blvd
Melbourne, FL 32935-6657
321-253-2929
www.fmu.edu

Florida Metropolitan
University–North Orlando
Campus
5421 Diplomat Circle
Orlando, FL 32810-5674
800-628-5870
www.fmu.edu

Florida Metropolitan
University–Pinellas Campus
2471 McMullen Booth Road,
Suite 200
Clearwater, FL 33759
800-353-FMUS
www.fmu.edu

Florida Metropolitan
University–South Orlando
Campus
2411 Sand Lake Road
Orlando, FL 32809
www.fmu.edu

Florida Metropolitan
University–Tampa Campus
3319 West Hillsborough Ave
Tampa, FL 33614-5899
813-879-6000
www.cci.edu

Florida Southern College
111 Lake Hollingsworth Drive
Lakeland, FL 33801-5698
800-274-4131
www.flsouthern.edu

Florida State University
Tallahassee, FL 32306
850-644-2525
www.fsu.edu

Hobe Sound Bible College
PO Box 1065
Hobe Sound, FL 33475-1065
800-881-5534

International Academy of
Design & Technology
5225 Memorial Highway
Tampa, FL 33634-7350
800-ACADEMY
www.academy.edu

International College
2655 Northbrooke Drive
Naples, FL 34119
800-466-8017
www.internationalcollege.edu

International Fine Arts
College
1737 North Bayshore Drive
Miami, FL 33132-1121
800-225-9023
www.ifac.edu

Jacksonville University
2800 University Blvd North
Jacksonville, FL 32211-3394
800-225-2027
www.ju.edu

Johnson & Wales University
1701 Northeast 127th Street
North Miami, FL 33181
800-232-2433
www.jwu.edu

Jones College
5353 Arlington Expressway
Jacksonville, FL 32211-5540
904-743-1122
www.jones.edu

Lynn University
3601 North Military Trail
Boca Raton, FL 33431-5598
800-544-8035
www.lynn.edu

New College of Florida
5700 North Tamiami Trail
Sarasota, FL 34243-2197
941-359-4700
www.ncf.edu

New World School of the Arts
300 NE 2nd Avenue
Miami, FL 33132
305-237-3135
www.mdcc.edu/nwsa

Northwood University,
Florida Campus
2600 North Military Trail
West Palm Beach, FL
33409-2911
800-458-8325
www.northwood.edu

Nova Southeastern
University
3301 College Avenue
Fort Lauderdale, FL
33314-7721
800-541-6682
www.nova.edu

Palm Beach Atlantic
University
901 South Flagler Dr,
PO Box 24708
West Palm Beach, FL
33416-4708
800-238-3998
www.pbac.edu

Ringling School of Art and
Design
2700 North Tamiami Trail
Sarasota, FL 34234-5895
800-255-7695
www.rsad.edu

Rollins College
1000 Holt Avenue
Winter Park, FL 32789-4499
407-646-2000
www.rollins.edu

Saint Leo University
PO Box 6665
Saint Leo, FL 33574-6665
800-334-5532
www.saintleo.edu

Schiller International
University
453 Edgewater Drive
Dunedin, FL 34698-7532
800-336-4133
www.schiller.edu

Southeastern College of the
Assemblies of God
1000 Longfellow Boulevard
Lakeland, FL 33801-6099
800-500-8760
www.secollege.edu

St. John Vianney College
Seminary
2900 Southwest 87th Avenue
Miami, FL 33165-3244
305-223-4561

St. Thomas University
16400 Northwest 32nd Ave
Miami, FL 33054-6459
800-367-9010
www.stu.edu

Stetson University
421 North Woodland Blvd
DeLand, FL 32720-3781
800-688-0101
www.stetson.edu

Talmudic College of Florida
1910 Alton Road
Miami Beach, FL 33139
305-534-7050

Trinity Baptist College
800 Hammond Boulevard
Jacksonville, FL 32221
800-786-2206
www.tbc.edu

Trinity College of Florida
2430 Welbilt Boulevard
New Port Richey, FL 34655
888-776-4999
www.trinitycollege.edu

University of Central Florida
4000 Central Florida Blvd
Orlando, FL 32816
407-823-2000
www.ucf.edu

University of Florida
Gainesville, FL 32611
352-392-3261
www.ufl.edu

University of Miami
University of Miami Branch
Coral Gables, FL 33124
305-284-2211
www.miami.edu

University of North Florida
4567 St. Johns Bluff Rd South
Jacksonville, FL 32224-2645
904-620-1000
www.unf.edu

University of Phoenix–Fort
Lauderdale Campus
600 North Pine Island Road,
Suite 500
Plantation, FL 33324-1393
800-228-7240
www.phoenix.edu

University of
Phoenix–Jacksonville
Campus
4500 Salisbury Road,
Suite 200
Jacksonville, FL 32216-0959
800-228-7240
www.phoenix.edu

University of Phoenix–
Orlando Campus
2290 Lucien Way, Suite 400
Maitland, FL 32751
800-228-7240
www.phoenix.edu

University of Phoenix–Tampa
Campus
100 Tampa Oaks Boulevard,
Suite 200
Tampa, FL 33637-1920
800-228-7240
www.phoenix.edu

University of South Florida
4202 East Fowler Avenue
Tampa, FL 33620-9951
813-974-2011
www.usf.edu

The University of Tampa
401 West Kennedy Boulevard
Tampa, FL 33606-1490
888-646-2438
www.ut.edu

University of West Florida
11000 University Parkway
Pensacola, FL 32514-5750
850-474-2000
uwf.edu

Warner Southern College
5301 US Highway 27 South
Lake Wales, FL 33853-8725
863-638-1426
www.warner.edu

Webber International
University
PO Box 96,
1200 North Scenic Highway
Babson Park, FL 33827-0096
800-741-1844
www.webber.edu

Georgia

Agnes Scott College
141 East College Avenue
Decatur, GA 30030-3797
800-868-8602
www.agnesscott.edu

Albany State University
504 College Drive
Albany, GA 31705-2717
229-430-4600
asuweb.asurams.edu/asu

American InterContinental
University
3330 Peachtree Road, NE
Atlanta, GA 30326-1016
888-999-4248
www.aiuniv.edu

American InterContinental
University
500 Embassy Row,
6600 Peachtree-Dunwoody Rd
Atlanta, GA 30328
800-255-6839
www.aiuniv.edu

Armstrong Atlantic State
University
11935 Abercorn Street
Savannah, GA 31419-1997
800-633-2349
www.armstrong.edu

Atlanta Christian College
2605 Ben Hill Road
East Point, GA 30344-1999
800-776-1ACC
www.acc.edu

Atlanta College of Art
1280 Peachtree Street, NE
Atlanta, GA 30309-3582
800-832-2104
www.aca.edu

Augusta State University
2500 Walton Way
Augusta, GA 30904-2200
706-737-1400
www.aug.edu

Beacon College and
Graduate School
6003 Veterans Parkway
Columbus, GA 31909
706-323-5364
www.beacon.edu

Berry College
PO Box 490159
Mount Berry, GA 30149-0159
800-237-7942
www.berry.edu

Beulah Heights Bible College
892 Berne Street, SE,
PO Box 18145
Atlanta, GA 30316
888-777-BHBC
www.beulah.org

Brenau University
One Centennial Circle
Gainesville, GA 30501-3697
800-252-5119
www.brenau.edu

Brewton-Parker College
Highway 280
Mt. Vernon, GA 30445-0197
800-342-1087
www.bpc.edu

Clark Atlanta University
223 James P. Brawley Dr, SW
Atlanta, GA 30314
800-688-3228
www.cau.edu

Clayton College & State
University
5900 North Lee Street
Morrow, GA 30260-0285
770-961-3400
www.clayton.edu

Columbus State University
4225 University Avenue
Columbus, GA 31907-5645
866-264-2035
www.colstate.edu

Covenant College
14049 Scenic Highway
Lookout Mountain, GA 30750
706-820-1560
www.covenant.edu

Dalton State College
213 North College Drive
Dalton, GA 30720-3797
800-829-4436
www.daltonstate.edu

DeVry University
2555 Northwinds Parkway
Alpharetta, GA 30004
770-521-4900
www.atl.devry.edu/alpharetta

DeVry University
250 North Arcadia Avenue
Decatur, GA 30030-2198
800-221-4771
www.atl.devry.edu

Emmanuel College
PO Box 129, 181 Springs St
Franklin Springs, GA
30639-0129
706-245-7226
www.emmanuel-college.edu

Emory University
1380 South Oxford Road
Atlanta, GA 30322-1100
800-727-6036
www.emory.edu

Fort Valley State University
1005 State University Drive
Fort Valley, GA 31030-4313
800-248-7343
www.fvsu.edu

Georgia Baptist College of
Nursing of Mercer University
274 Boulevard, NE
Atlanta, GA 30312
800-551-8835
www.nursing.mercer.edu

Georgia College & State
University
Hancock Street
Milledgeville, GA 31061
478-445-5004
www.gcsu.edu

Georgia Institute of
Technology
225 North Avenue, NW
Atlanta, GA 30332-0001
404-894-2000
www.gatech.edu

Georgia Southern University
PO Box 8055
Statesboro, GA 30460
912-681-5611
www.gasou.edu

Georgia Southwestern State
University
800 Wheatley Street
Americus, GA 31709-4693
800-338-0082
www.gsw.edu

Georgia State University
University Plaza
Atlanta, GA 30303-3083
404-651-2000
www.gsu.edu

Kennesaw State University
1000 Chastain Road
Kennesaw, GA 30144-5591
770-423-6000
www.kennesaw.edu

LaGrange College
601 Broad Street
LaGrange, GA 30240-2999
800-593-2885
www.lgc.edu

Life University
1269 Barclay Circle
Marietta, GA 30060-2903
770-426-2600
www.life.edu

Luther Rice Bible College and
Seminary
3038 Evans Mill Road
Lithonia, GA 30038-2454
800-442-1577
www.lrs.edu

Macon State College
100 College Station Drive
Macon, GA 31206-5144
800-272-7619
www.maconstate.edu

Medical College of Georgia
1120 Fifteenth Street
Augusta, GA 30912
706-721-0211
www.mcg.edu

Mercer University
1400 Coleman Avenue
Macon, GA 31207-0003
800-840-8577
www.mercer.edu

Morehouse College
830 Westview Drive, SW
Atlanta, GA 30314
800-851-1254
www.morehouse.edu

Morris Brown College
643 Martin Luther King Jr Dr,
NW
Atlanta, GA 30314-4140
404-739-1000
www.morrisbrown.edu

North Georgia College &
State University
Dahlonega, GA 30597-1001
800-498-9581
www.ngcsu.edu

Oglethorpe University
4484 Peachtree Road, NE
Atlanta, GA 30319-2797
800-428-4484
www.oglethorpe.edu

Paine College
1235 15th Street
Augusta, GA 30901-3182
800-476-7703
www.paine.edu

Piedmont College
PO Box 10, 165 Central Ave
Demorest, GA 30535-0010
800-277-7020
www.piedmont.edu

Reinhardt College
7300 Reinhardt College Circle
Waleska, GA 30183-2981
87-REINHARDT
www.reinhardt.edu

Savannah College of Art and
Design
342 Bull Street, PO Box 3146
Savannah, GA 31402-3146
800-869-7223
www.scad.edu

Savannah State University
2319 Falligant Avenue
Savannah, GA 31404
800-788-0478
www.savstate.edu

Shorter College
315 Shorter Avenue
Rome, GA 30165
800-868-6980
www.shorter.edu

South University
709 Mall Boulevard
Savannah, GA 31406-4805
912-201-8000
www.southuniversity.edu

Southern Polytechnic State
University
1100 South Marietta Parkway
Marietta, GA 30060-2896
800-635-3204
www.spsu.edu

Spelman College
350 Spelman Lane, SW
Atlanta, GA 30314-4399
800-982-2411
www.spelman.edu

State University of West
Georgia
1600 Maple Street
Carrollton, GA 30118
770-836-6500
www.westga.edu

Thomas University
1501 Millpond Road
Thomasville, GA 31792-7499
800-538-9784
www.thomasu.edu

Toccoa Falls College
PO Box 777
Toccoa Falls, GA 30598-1000
800-868-3257
www.toccoafalls.edu

University of Georgia
Athens, GA 30602
706-542-3000
www.uga.edu

University of Phoenix-Atlanta
Campus
7000 Central Parkway,
Suite 1700
Atlanta, GA 30328
678-731-0555
www.phoenix.edu

Valdosta State University
1500 North Patterson Street
Valdosta, GA 31698
800-618-1878
www.valdosta.edu

Wesleyan College
4760 Forsyth Road
Macon, GA 31210-4462
800-447-6610
www.wesleyancollege.edu

Hawaii

Brigham Young
University–Hawaii
55-220 Kulanui Street
Laie, HI 96762-1294
808-293-3211
www.byuh.edu

Chaminade University of
Honolulu
3140 Waialae Avenue
Honolulu, HI 96816-1578
808-735-4711
www.chaminade.edu

Education America, Honolulu
Campus
1111 Bishop Street, Suite 400
Honolulu, HI 96813
808-942-1000

Hawai`i Pacific University
1166 Fort Street
Honolulu, HI 96813-2785
808-544-0200
www.hpu.edu

International College and
Graduate School
20 Dowsett Avenue
Honolulu, HI 96817
808-595-4247
home.hawaii.rr.com/
international/icgs.html

University of Hawaii at Hilo
200 West Kawili Street
Hilo, HI 96720-4091
808-974-7311
www.uhh.hawaii.edu

University of Hawaii at
Manoa
2444 Dole Street
Honolulu, HI 96822
808-956-8111
www.uhm.hawaii.edu

University of Hawaii–
West Oahu
96-129 Ala Ike
Pearl City, HI 96782-3366
808-454-4700

University of Phoenix–
Hawaii Campus
827 Fort Street
Honolulu, HI 96813
866-2-ENROLL
www.phoenix.edu

Idaho

Albertson College of Idaho
2112 Cleveland Boulevard
Caldwell, ID 83605-4494
208-459-5011
www.albertson.edu

Boise Bible College
8695 West Marigold Street
Boise, ID 83714-1220
208-376-7731
www.boisebible.edu

Boise State University
1910 University Drive
Boise, ID 83725-0399
208-426-1011
www.boisestate.edu

Idaho State University
741 South 7th Avenue
Pocatello, ID 83209
208-282-0211
www.isu.edu

Lewis-Clark State College
500 Eighth Avenue
Lewiston, ID 83501-2698
208-792-5272
www.lcsc.edu

Northwest Nazarene University
623 Holly Street
Nampa, ID 83686-5897
208-467-8011
www.nnu.edu

University of Idaho
875 Perimeter Drive
Moscow, ID 83844-2282
208-885-6111
www.its.uidaho.edu/uihome

Illinois

American Academy of Art
332 South Michigan Ave,
Suite 300
Chicago, IL 60604-4302
312-461-0600
www.aaart.edu

American InterContinental
University Online
2895 Greenspoint Parkway,
Suite 400
Hoffman Estates, IL 60195
847-585-2002
www.aiu-online.com

Augustana College
639 38th Street
Rock Island, IL 61201-2296
309-794-7000
www.augustana.edu

Aurora University
347 South Gladstone Avenue
Aurora, IL 60506-4892
630-892-6431
www.aurora.edu

Benedictine University
5700 College Road
Lisle, IL 60532-0900
630-829-6000
www.ben.edu

Blackburn College
700 College Avenue
Carlinville, IL 62626-1498
217-854-3231

Blessing-Rieman College of
Nursing
Broadway at 11th Street,
POB 7005
Quincy, IL 62305-7005
217-228-5520
www.brcn.edu

Bradley University
1501 West Bradley Avenue
Peoria, IL 61625-0002
309-676-7611
www.bradley.edu

Chicago State University
9501 South King Drive
Chicago, IL 60628
773-995-2000
www.csu.edu

Christian Life College
400 East Gregory Street
Mount Prospect, IL 60056
847-259-1840

Columbia College Chicago
600 South Michigan Avenue
Chicago, IL 60605-1996
312-663-1600
www.colum.edu

Concordia University
7400 Augusta Street
River Forest, IL 60305-1499
708-771-8300
www.curf.edu

DePaul University
1 East Jackson Boulevard
Chicago, IL 60604-2287
312-362-8000
www.depaul.edu

DeVry Institute of Technology
18624 West Creek Drive
Tinley Park, IL 60477
708-342-3100
www.tp.devry.edu

DeVry Institute of Technology
3300 North Campbell Avenue
Chicago, IL 60618-5994
773-929-8500
www.chi.devry.edu

DeVry Institute of Technology
1221 North Swift Road
Addison, IL 60101-6106
630-953-1300
www.dpg.devry.edu

Dominican University
7900 West Division Street
River Forest, IL 60305-1099
708-366-2490
www.dom.edu

Dr. William M. Scholl College
of Podiatric Medicine
1001 North Dearborn Street
Chicago, IL 60610-2856
312-280-2880
finchcms.edu/scholl

East-West University
816 South Michigan Avenue
Chicago, IL 60605-2103
312-939-0111

Eastern Illinois University
600 Lincoln Avenue
Charleston, IL 61920-3099
217-581-5000
www.eiu.edu

Elmhurst College
190 Prospect Avenue
Elmhurst, IL 60126-3296
630-617-3500
www.elmhurst.edu

Eureka College
300 East College Avenue
Eureka, IL 61530-1500
309-467-3721
www.eureka.edu

Finch University of Health
Sciences/The Chicago
Medical School
3333 Green Bay Road
North Chicago, IL
60064-3095
847-578-3000
www.finchcms.edu

Governors State University
One University Parkway
University Park, IL
60466-0975
708-534-5000
www.govst.edu

Greenville College
315 East College, PO Box 159
Greenville, IL 62246-0159
618-664-2800
www.greenville.edu

Harrington Institute of
Interior Design
410 South Michigan Avenue
Chicago, IL 60605-1496
312-939-4975
www.interiordesign.edu

Hebrew Theological College
7135 North Carpenter Road
Skokie, IL 60077-3263
847-982-2500
www.htcnet.edu

Illinois College
1101 West College Avenue
Jacksonville, IL 62650-2299
217-245-3000
www.ic.edu

The Illinois Institute of Art
350 North Orleans
Chicago, IL 60654
312-280-3500
www.ilia.aii.edu

The Illinois Institute of Art-
Schaumburg
1000 Plaza Drive
Schaumburg, IL 60173
847-619-3450
www.ilis.artinstitutes.edu

Illinois Institute of Technology
3300 South Federal Street
Chicago, IL 60616-3793
312-567-3000
www.iit.edu

Illinois State University
Normal, IL 61790-2200
309-438-2111
www.ilstu.edu

Illinois Wesleyan University
PO Box 2900
Bloomington, IL 61702-2900
309-556-1000
www.iwu.edu

International Academy of
Design & Technology
One North State Street,
Suite 400
Chicago, IL 60602-9736
312-980-9200
www.iamd.edu

Judson College
1151 North State Street
Elgin, IL 60123-1498
847-695-2500
www.judson-il.edu

Kendall College
2408 Orrington Avenue
Evanston, IL 60201-2899
847-866-1300
www.kendall.edu

Knox College
2 East South Street
Galesburg, IL 61401
309-341-7000
www.knox.edu

Lake Forest College
555 North Sheridan Road
Lake Forest, IL 60045-2399
847-234-3100
www.lakeforest.edu

Lakeview College of Nursing
903 North Logan Avenue
Danville, IL 61832
217-443-5238
www.lakeviewcol.edu

Lewis University
Route 53
Romeoville, IL 60446
815-838-0500
www.lewisu.edu

Lincoln Christian College
100 Campus View Drive
Lincoln, IL 62656-2167
217-732-3168
www.lccs.edu

Loyola University Chicago
820 North Michigan Avenue
Chicago, IL 60611-2196
773-274-3000
www.luc.edu

MacMurray College
447 East College Avenue
Jacksonville, IL 62650
217-479-7000
www.mac.edu

McKendree College
701 College Road
Lebanon, IL 62254-1299
618-537-4481
www.mckendree.edu

Millikin University
1184 West Main Street
Decatur, IL 62522-2084
217-424-6211
www.millikin.edu

Monmouth College
700 East Broadway
Monmouth, IL 61462-1998
309-457-2311
www.monm.edu

Moody Bible Institute
820 North LaSalle Boulevard
Chicago, IL 60610-3284
312-329-4000
www.moody.edu

NAES College
2838 West Peterson Avenue
Chicago, IL 60659-3813
773-761-5000

National-Louis University
2840 Sheridan Road
Evanston, IL 60201-1796
847-475-1100
www.nl.edu

North Central College
30 North Brainard St,
PO Box 3063
Naperville, IL 60566-7063
630-637-5100
www.noctrl.edu

North Park University
3225 West Foster Avenue
Chicago, IL 60625-4895
773-244-6200
www.northpark.edu

Northeastern Illinois
University
5500 North St Louis Avenue
Chicago, IL 60625-4699
773-583-4050
www.neiu.edu

Northern Illinois University
De Kalb, IL 60115-2854
815-753-1000
www.niu.edu

Northwestern University
Evanston, IL 60208
847-491-3741
www.northwestern.edu

Olivet Nazarene University
One University Avenue
Bourbonnais, IL 60914-2271
815-939-5011
www.olivet.edu

Principia College
One Maybeck Place
Elsah, IL 62028-9799
618-374-2131
www.prin.edu/college

Quincy University
1800 College Avenue
Quincy, IL 62301-2699
217-222-8020
www.quincy.edu

Robert Morris College
401 South State Street
Chicago, IL 60605
312-935-6800
www.rmcil.edu

Rockford College
5050 East State Street
Rockford, IL 61108-2393
815-226-4000
www.rockford.edu

Roosevelt University
430 South Michigan Avenue
Chicago, IL 60605-1394
312-341-3500
www.roosevelt.edu

Rush University
600 South Paulina
Chicago, IL 60612-3832
312-942-5000
www.rushu.rush.edu

Saint Anthony College of
Nursing
5658 East State Street
Rockford, IL 61108-2468
815-395-5091
www.sacn.edu

Saint Francis Medical Center
College of Nursing
511 NE Greenleaf Street
Peoria, IL 61603-3783
309-655-2596
www.sfmccon.edu

Saint Xavier University
3700 West 103rd Street
Chicago, IL 60655-3105
773-298-3000
www.sxu.edu

School of the Art Institute of
Chicago
37 South Wabash
Chicago, IL 60603-3103
312-899-5100
www.artic.edu/saic

Shimer College
PO Box 500
Waukegan, IL 60079-0500
847-623-8400
www.shimer.edu

Southern Illinois University
Carbondale
Carbondale, IL 62901-6806
618-453-2121
www.siuc.edu

Southern Illinois University
Edwardsville
Edwardsville, IL 62026-0001
618-650-2000
www.siue.edu

St. Augustine College
1333-1345 West Argyle
Chicago, IL 60640-3501
773-878-8756
www.staugustinecollege.edu

St. John's College
421 North Ninth Street
Springfield, IL 62702-5317
217-525-5628
www.st-johns.org/
collegeofnursing

Telshe Yeshiva–Chicago
3535 West Foster Avenue
Chicago, IL 60625-5598
773-463-7738

Trinity Christian College
6601 West College Drive
Palos Heights, IL
60463-0929
708-597-3000
www.trnty.edu

Trinity College of Nursing
and Schools of Allied Health
555 6th Street, Suite 300
Moline, IL 61265-1216
309-779-7700
www.trinitycollegeqc.edu/HO
ME/index.htm

Trinity International
University
2065 Half Day Road
Deerfield, IL 60015-1284
847-945-8800
www.tiu.edu

University of Chicago
5801 Ellis Avenue
Chicago, IL 60637-1513
773-702-1234
www.uchicago.edu

University of Illinois at
Chicago
601 South Morgan Street
Chicago, IL 60607-7128
312-996-7000
www.uic.edu

University of Illinois at
Springfield
PO Box 19243
Springfield, IL 62794-9243
217-206-6600
www.uis.edu

University of Illinois at
Urbana–Champaign
601 East John Street
Champaign, IL 61820
217-333-1000
www.uiuc.edu

University of St. Francis
500 Wilcox Street
Joliet, IL 60435-6169
815-740-3360
www.stfrancis.edu

VanderCook College of Music
3140 South Federal Street
Chicago, IL 60616-3731
312-225-6288
www.vandercook.edu

West Suburban College of
Nursing
3 Erie Court
Oak Park, IL 60302
708-763-6530

Western Illinois University
1 University Circle
Macomb, IL 61455-1390
309-295-1414
www.wiu.edu

Wheaton College
501 East College Avenue
Wheaton, IL 60187-5593
630-752-5000
www.wheaton.edu

Indiana

Anderson University
1100 East Fifth Street
Anderson, IN 46012-3495
765-649-9071
www.anderson.edu

Ball State University
2000 University Avenue
Muncie, IN 47306-1099
765-289-1241
www.bsu.edu

Bethel College
1001 West McKinley Avenue
Mishawaka, IN 46545-5591
219-259-8511
www.bethelcollege.edu

Butler University
4600 Sunset Avenue
Indianapolis, IN 46208-3485
317-940-8000
www.butler.edu

Calumet College of Saint
Joseph
2400 New York Avenue
Whiting, IN 46394-2195
219-473-7770
www.ccsj.edu

Crossroads Bible College
601 North Shortridge Road
Indianapolis, IN 46219
317-352-8736

DePauw University
313 South Locust Street
Greencastle, IN 46135-0037
765-658-4800
www.depauw.edu

Earlham College
801 National Road West
Richmond, IN 47374-4095
765-983-1200
www.earlham.edu

Franklin College of Indiana
501 East Monroe
Franklin, IN 46131-2598
317-738-8000
www.franklincoll.edu

Goshen College
1700 South Main Street
Goshen, IN 46526-4794
219-535-7000
www.goshen.edu

Grace College
200 Seminary Drive
Winona Lake, IN
46590-1294
219-372-5100
www.grace.edu

Hanover College
PO Box 108
Hanover, IN 47243-0108
812-866-7000
www.hanover.edu

Huntington College
2303 College Avenue
Huntington, IN 46750-1299
219-356-6000
www.huntington.edu

Indiana Institute of
Technology
1600 East Washington Blvd
Fort Wayne, IN 46803-1297
219-422-5561
www.indtech.edu

Indiana State University
210 North Seventh Street
Terre Haute, IN 47809-1401
812-237-6311
web.indstate.edu

Indiana University
Bloomington
Bloomington, IN 47405
812-855-4848
www.iub.edu

Indiana University East
2325 Chester Boulevard
Richmond, IN 47374-1289
765-973-8200
www.indiana.edu

Indiana University Kokomo
PO Box 9003
Kokomo, IN 46904-9003
765-453-2000
www.indiana.edu

Indiana University Northwest
3400 Broadway
Gary, IN 46408-1197
219-980-6500
www.indiana.edu

Indiana University South Bend
1700 Mishawaka Avenue,
PO Box 7111
South Bend, IN 46634-7111
219-237-4872
www.indiana.edu

Indiana University Southeast
4201 Grant Line Road
New Albany, IN 47150-6405
812-941-2000
www.indiana.edu

Indiana University–Purdue
University Fort Wayne
2101 East Coliseum Blvd
Fort Wayne, IN 46805-1499
219-481-6100
www.ipfw.edu

Indiana University–Purdue
University Indianapolis
355 North Lansing
Indianapolis, IN 46202-2896
317-274-5555
www.indiana.edu

Indiana Wesleyan University
4201 South Washington St
Marion, IN 46953-4974
765-674-6901
www.indwes.edu

Manchester College
604 College Avenue
North Manchester, IN
46962-1225
219-982-5000
www.manchester.edu

Marian College
3200 Cold Spring Road
Indianapolis, IN 46222-1997
317-955-6000
www.marian.edu

Martin University
2171 Avondale Place,
PO Box 18567
Indianapolis, IN 46218-3867
317-543-3235

Oakland City University
143 North Lucretia Street
Oakland City, IN 47660-1099
812-749-4781
www.oak.edu

Purdue University
West Lafayette, IN 47907
765-494-4600
www.purdue.edu

Purdue University Calumet
2200 169th Street
Hammond, IN 46323-2094
219-989-2400
www.calumet.purdue.edu

Purdue University North
Central
1401 South US Highway 421
Westville, IN 46391-9542
219-785-5200
www.purduenc.edu

Rose-Hulman Institute of
Technology
5500 Wabash Avenue
Terre Haute, IN 47803-3920
812-877-1511
www.rose-hulman.edu

Saint Joseph's College
PO Box 850
Rensselaer, IN 47978
219-866-6000
www.saintjoe.edu

Saint Mary's College
Notre Dame, IN 46556
219-284-4000
www.saintmarys.edu

Saint Mary-of-the-Woods
College
Saint Mary-of-the-Woods,
IN 47876
812-535-5151
www.smwc.edu

Taylor University
236 West Reade Avenue
Upland, IN 46989-1001
765-998-2751
www.tayloru.edu

Taylor University, Fort Wayne
Campus
1025 West Rudisill Boulevard
Fort Wayne, IN 46807-2197
219-744-8600
www.tayloru.edu/fw

Tri-State University
1 University Avenue
Angola, IN 46703-1764
219-665-4100
www.tristate.edu

University of Evansville
1800 Lincoln Avenue
Evansville, IN 47722-0002
812-479-2000
www.evansville.edu

University of Indianapolis
1400 East Hanna Avenue
Indianapolis, IN 46227-3697
317-788-3368
www.uindy.edu

University of Notre Dame
Notre Dame, IN 46556
219-631-5000
www.nd.edu

University of Saint Francis
2701 Spring Street
Fort Wayne, IN 46808-3994
219-434-3100
www.sf.edu

University of Southern
Indiana
8600 University Boulevard
Evansville, IN 47712-3590
812-464-8600
www.usi.edu

Valparaiso University
651 South College Avenue
Valparaiso, IN 46383-6493
219-464-5000
www.valpo.edu

Wabash College
PO Box 352
Crawfordsville, IN
47933-0352
765-361-6100
www.wabash.edu

Iowa

Allen College
1825 Logan Avenue
Waterloo, IA 50703
319-226-2000
www.allencollege.edu

Briar Cliff University
3303 Rebecca Street
Sioux City, IA 51104-2100
712-279-5321
www.briarcliff.edu

Buena Vista University
610 West Fourth Street
Storm Lake, IA 50588
712-749-2351
www.bvu.edu

Central College
812 University Street
Pella, IA 50219-1999
641-628-9000
www.central.edu

Clarke College
1550 Clarke Drive
Dubuque, IA 52001-3198
563-588-6300
www.clarke.edu

Coe College
1220 1st Avenue, NE
Cedar Rapids, IA
52402-5070
319-399-8000
www.coe.edu

Cornell College
600 First Street West
Mount Vernon, IA
52314-1098
319-895-4000
www.cornellcollege.edu

Des Moines University
Osteopathic Medical Center
3200 Grand Avenue
Des Moines, IA 50312-4104
515-271-1400
www.dsmu.edu

Divine Word College
102 Jacoby Drive SW
Epworth, IA 52045-0380
563-876-3353
www.dwci.edu

Dordt College
498 4th Avenue, NE
Sioux Center, IA 51250-1697
712-722-6000
www.dordt.edu

Drake University
2507 University Avenue
Des Moines, IA 50311-4516
515-271-2011
www.drake.edu

Emmaus Bible College
2570 Asbury Road
Dubuque, IA 52001-3097
319-588-8000
www.emmaus.edu

Faith Baptist Bible College
and Theological Seminary
1900 Northwest 4th Street
Ankeny, IA 50021-2152
515-964-0601
www.faith.edu

Graceland University
1 University Place
Lamoni, IA 50140
641-784-5000
www2.graceland.edu

Grand View College
1200 Grandview Avenue
Des Moines, IA 50316-1599
515-263-2800
www.gvc.edu

Grinnell College
Grinnell, IA 50112-1690
641-269-4000
www.grinnell.edu

Hamilton Technical College
1011 East 53rd Street
Davenport, IA 52807-2653
319-386-3570
www.hamiltontechcollege.com

Iowa State University of
Science and Technology
Ames, IA 50011
515-294-4111
www.iastate.edu

Iowa Wesleyan College
601 North Main Street
Mount Pleasant, IA
52641-1398
319-385-8021
www.iwc.edu

Loras College
1450 Alta Vista
Dubuque, IA 52004-0178
563-588-7100
www.loras.edu

Luther College
700 College Drive
Decorah, IA 52101-1045
319-387-2000
www.luther.edu

Maharishi University of
Management
1000 North 4th Street
Fairfield, IA 52557
641-472-7000
www.mum.edu

Mercy College of Health
Sciences
928 Sixth Avenue
Des Moines, IA 50309-1239
515-643-3180
www.mchs.edu

Morningside College
1501 Morningside Avenue
Sioux City, IA 51106-1751
712-274-5000
www.morningside.edu

Mount Mercy College
1330 Elmhurst Drive, NE
Cedar Rapids, IA
52402-4797
319-363-8213
www.mtmercy.edu

Mount St. Clare College
400 North Bluff Boulevard,
PO Box 2967
Clinton, IA 52733-2967
319-242-4023
www.clare.edu

Northwestern College
101 Seventh Street, SW
Orange City, IA 51041-1996
712-737-7000
www.nwciowa.edu

Palmer College of
Chiropractic
1000 Brady Street
Davenport, IA 52803-5287
563-884-5000
www.palmer.edu

Simpson College
701 North C Street
Indianola, IA 50125-1297
515-961-6251
www.simpson.edu

St. Ambrose University
518 West Locust Street
Davenport, IA 52803-2898
563-333-6000
www.sau.edu

University of Dubuque
2000 University Avenue
Dubuque, IA 52001-5099
563-589-3000
www.dbq.edu

The University of Iowa
Iowa City, IA 52242-1316
319-335-3500
www.uiowa.edu

University of Northern Iowa
1222 West 27th Street
Cedar Falls, IA 50614
319-273-2311
www.uni.edu

Upper Iowa University
605 Washington Street,
Box 1857
Fayette, IA 52142-1857
563-425-5200
www.uiu.edu

Wartburg College
222 Ninth Street, NW,
PO Box 1003
Waverly, IA 50677-0903
319-352-8200
www.wartburg.edu

William Penn University
201 Trueblood Avenue
Oskaloosa, IA 52577-1799
641-673-1001
www.wmpenn.edu

Kansas

Baker University
Box 65
Baldwin City, KS
66006-0065
785-594-6451
www.bakeru.edu

Barclay College
607 North Kingman
Haviland, KS 67059-0288
620-862-5252
www.barclaycollege.edu

Benedictine College
1020 North 2nd Street
Atchison, KS 66002-1499
913-367-5340
www.benedictine.edu

Bethany College
421 North First Street
Lindsborg, KS 67456-1897
785-227-3311
www.bethanylb.edu

Bethel College
300 East 27th Street
North Newton, KS 67117
316-283-2500
www.bethelks.edu

Central Christian College of
Kansas
1200 South Main,
PO Box 1403
McPherson, KS 67460-5799
620-241-0723
www.centralchristian.edu

Emporia State University
1200 Commercial Street
Emporia, KS 66801-5087
620-341-1200
www.emporia.edu

Fort Hays State University
600 Park Street
Hays, KS 67601-4099
785-628-4000
www.fhsu.edu

Friends University
2100 West University Street
Wichita, KS 67213
316-295-5000
www.friends.edu

Haskell Indian Nations
University
155 Indian Avenue, #5031
Lawrence, KS 66046-4800
785-749-8404

Kansas State University
Manhattan, KS 66506
785-532-6011
www.ksu.edu

Kansas Wesleyan University
100 East Claflin
Salina, KS 67401-6196
785-827-5541
www.kwu.edu

Manhattan Christian College
1415 Anderson Avenue
Manhattan, KS 66502-4081
785-539-3571
www.mccks.edu

McPherson College
1600 East Euclid,
PO Box 1402
McPherson, KS 67460-1402
620-241-0731
www.mcpherson.edu

MidAmerica Nazarene
University
2030 East College Way
Olathe, KS 66062-1899
913-782-3750
www.mnu.edu

Newman University
3100 McCormick Avenue
Wichita, KS 67213-2097
316-942-4291
www.newmanu.edu

Ottawa University
1001 South Cedar
Ottawa, KS 66067-3399
785-242-5200
www.ottawa.edu

Pittsburg State University
1701 South Broadway
Pittsburg, KS 66762
620-231-7000
www.pittstate.edu

Saint Mary College
4100 South Fourth Street
Trafficway
Leavenworth, KS
66048-5082
913-682-5151
www.smcks.edu

Southwestern College
100 College Street
Winfield, KS 67156-2499
620-229-6000
www.sckans.edu

Sterling College
PO Box 98
Sterling, KS 67579-0098
620-278-2173
www.sterling.edu

Tabor College
400 South Jefferson
Hillsboro, KS 67063
620-947-3121
www.tabor.edu

University of Kansas
Lawrence, KS 66045
785-864-2700
www.ku.edu

Washburn University of
Topeka
1700 SW College Avenue
Topeka, KS 66621
785-231-1010
www.washburn.edu

Wichita State University
1845 North Fairmount
Wichita, KS 67260
316-978-3456
www.wichita.edu

Kentucky

Alice Lloyd College
100 Purpose Road
Pippa Passes, KY 41844
606-368-2101
www.alc.edu

Asbury College
1 Macklem Drive
Wilmore, KY 40390-1198
800-888-1818
www.asbury.edu

Bellarmine University
2001 Newburg Road
Louisville, KY 40205-0671
800-274-4723
www.bellarmine.edu

Berea College
Berea, KY 40404
800-326-5948
www.berea.edu

Brescia University
717 Frederica Street
Owensboro, KY 42301-3023
877-BRESCIA
www.brescia.edu

Campbellsville University
1 University Drive
Campbellsville, KY
42718-2799
800-264-6014
www.campbellsvil.edu

Centre College
600 West Walnut Street
Danville, KY 40422-1394
800-423-6236
www.centre.edu

Clear Creek Baptist Bible
College
300 Clear Creek Road
Pineville, KY 40977-9754
606-337-3196
www.ccbbc.edu

Cumberland College
6178 College Station Drive
Williamsburg, KY 40769-1372
800-343-1609
cc.cumber.edu

Eastern Kentucky University
521 Lancaster Avenue
Richmond, KY 40475-3102
859-622-1000
www.eku.edu

Georgetown College
400 East College Street
Georgetown, KY 40324-1696
800-788-9985
www.georgetowncollege.edu

Kentucky Christian College
100 Academic Parkway
Grayson, KY 41143-2205
800-522-3181
www.kcc.edu

Kentucky Mountain Bible
College
PO Box 10
Vancleve, KY 41385-0010
800-879-KMBC
www.kmbc.edu

Kentucky State University
400 East Main Street
Frankfort, KY 40601
800-325-1716
www.kysu.edu

Kentucky Wesleyan College
3000 Frederica Street, PO
Box 1039
Owensboro, KY 42302-1039
270-926-3111
www.kwc.edu

Lindsey Wilson College
210 Lindsey Wilson Street
Columbia, KY 42728-1298
800-264-0138
www.lindsey.edu

Mid-Continent College
99 Powell Road East
Mayfield, KY 42066-9007
270-247-8521
www.midcontinent.edu

Midway College
512 East Stephens Street
Midway, KY 40347-1120
800-755-0031
www.midway.edu

Morehead State University
University Boulevard
Morehead, KY 40351
800-585-6781
www.moreheadstate.edu

Murray State University
PO Box 9
Murray, KY 42071-0009
800-272-4678
www.murraystate.edu

Northern Kentucky
University
Louie B Nunn Drive
Highland Heights, KY 41099
800-637-9948
www.nku.edu

Pikeville College
147 Sycamore Street
Pikeville, KY 41501
866-232-7700
www.pc.edu

Southern Baptist Theological
Seminary
2825 Lexington Road
Louisville, KY 40280-0004
502-897-4011
www.sbts.edu

Spalding University
851 South Fourth Street
Louisville, KY 40203-2188
800-896-8941
www.spalding.edu

Sullivan University
3101 Bardstown Road
Louisville, KY 40205
502-456-6504
www.sullivan.edu

Thomas More College
333 Thomas More Parkway
Crestview Hills, KY
41017-3495
800-825-4557
www.thomasmore.edu

Transylvania University
300 North Broadway
Lexington, KY 40508-1797
800-872-6798
www.transy.edu

Union College
310 College Street
Barbourville, KY 40906-1499
800-489-8646
www.unionky.edu

University of Kentucky
Lexington, KY 40506-0032
859-257-9000
www.uky.edu

University of Louisville
2301 South Third Street
Louisville, KY 40292-0001
800-334-8635
www.louisville.edu

Western Kentucky University
1 Big Red Way
Bowling Green, KY
42101-3576
270-745-0111
www.wku.edu

Louisiana

Centenary College of
Louisiana
2911 Centenary Blvd,
PO Box 41188
Shreveport, LA 71134-1188
800-234-4448
www.centenary.edu

Dillard University
2601 Gentilly Boulevard
New Orleans, LA 70122-3097
504-283-8822

Grambling State University
PO Box 607
Grambling, LA 71245
318-247-3811
www.gram.edu

Grantham College of
Engineering
34641 Grantham College Rd
Slidell, LA 70460-6815
800-955-2527
www.grantham.edu

Louisiana College
1140 College Drive
Pineville, LA 71359-0001
800-487-1906
www.lacollege.edu

Louisiana State University
and Agricultural and
Mechanical College
Baton Rouge, LA 70803
225-578-3202
www.lsu.edu

Louisiana State University
Health Sciences Center
433 Bolivar Street
New Orleans, LA 70112-2223
504-568-4808
www.lsumc.edu

Louisiana State University in
Shreveport
1 University Place
Shreveport, LA 71115-2399
318-797-5000
www.lsus.edu

Louisiana Tech University
PO Box 3168
Ruston, LA 71272
800-528-3241
www.latech.edu

Loyola University New
Orleans
6363 Saint Charles Avenue
New Orleans, LA 70118-6195
800-4-LOYOLA
www.loyno.edu

McNeese State University
4205 Ryan Street
Lake Charles, LA 70609
800-622-3352
www.mcneese.edu

New Orleans Baptist
Theological Seminary
3939 Gentilly Boulevard
New Orleans, LA 70126-4858
800-662-8701
www.nobts.edu

Nicholls State University
906 East First Street
Thibodaux, LA 70310
877-NICHOLLS
www.nicholls.edu

Northwestern State
University of Louisiana
350 Sam Sibley Drive
Natchitoches, LA 71497
800-327-1903
www.nsula.edu

Our Lady of Holy Cross
College
4123 Woodland Drive
New Orleans, LA 70131-7399
800-259-7744
www.olhcc.edu

Saint Joseph Seminary
College
Saint Benedict, LA 70457
504-892-1800
www.stjosephabbey.org

Southeastern Louisiana
University
Hammond, LA 70402
800-222-7358
www.selu.edu

Southern University and
Agricultural and Mechanical
College
Baton Rouge, LA 70813
800-256-1531
www.subr.edu

Southern University at New
Orleans
6400 Press Drive
New Orleans, LA 70126-1009
504-286-5000
www.suno.edu

Tulane University
6823 St Charles Avenue
New Orleans, LA 70118-5669
800-873-9283
www.tulane.edu

University of Louisiana at
Lafayette
104 University Circle,
PO Box 42651
Lafayette, LA 70504
337-482-1000
www.louisiana.edu

University of Louisiana at
Monroe
700 University Avenue
Monroe, LA 71209-0001
800-372-5127
www.ulm.edu

University of New Orleans
Lake Front
New Orleans, LA 70148
888-514-4275
www.uno.edu

University of
Phoenix–Louisiana Campus
1 Galleria Boulevard,
Suite 725
Metairie, LA 70001-2082
800-228-7240
www.phoenix.edu

Xavier University of
Louisiana
1 Drexel Drive
New Orleans, LA 70125-1098
504-486-7411
www.xula.edu

Maine

Bates College
Andrews Road
Lewiston, ME 04240-6028
207-786-6255
www.bates.edu

Bowdoin College
5000 College Station
Brunswick, ME 04011
207-725-3000
www.bowdoin.edu

Colby College
Mayflower Hill
Waterville, ME 04901-8840
207-872-3000
www.colby.edu

College of the Atlantic
105 Eden Street
Bar Harbor, ME 04609-1198
207-288-5015
www.coa.edu

Husson College
One College Circle
Bangor, ME 04401-2999
207-941-7000
www.husson.edu

Maine College of Art
97 Spring Street
Portland, ME 04101-3987
207-775-3052
www.meca.edu

Maine Maritime Academy
Castine, ME 04420
207-326-4311
www.mainemaritime.edu

New England School of
Communications
1 College Circle
Bangor, ME 04401-2999
207-941-7176
www.nescom.org

Saint Joseph's College
278 Whites Bridge Road
Standish, ME 04084-5263
207-892-6766
www.sjcme.edu

Thomas College
180 West River Road
Waterville, ME 04901-5097
207-859-1111
www.thomas.edu

Unity College
90 Quaker Hill Road
Unity, ME 04988
207-948-3131
www.unity.edu

University of Maine
Orono, ME 04469
207-581-1110
www.umaine.edu

University of Maine at
Augusta
46 University Drive
Augusta, ME 04330-9410
207-621-3000
www.uma.maine.edu

University of Maine at
Farmington
224 Main Street
Farmington, ME 04938-1990
207-778-7000
www.umf.maine.edu

University of Maine at Fort
Kent
23 University Drive
Fort Kent, ME 04743-1292
207-834-7500
www.umfk.maine.edu

University of Maine at
Machias
9 O'Brien Avenue
Machias, ME 04654-1321
207-255-1200
www.umm.maine.edu

University of Maine at
Presque Isle
181 Main Street
Presque Isle, ME 04769-2888
207-768-9400
www.umpi.maine.edu

University of New England
Hills Beach Road
Biddeford, ME 04005-9526
207-283-0171
www.une.edu

University of Southern
Maine
96 Falmouth Street,
PO Box 9300
Portland, ME 04104-9300
207-780-4141
www.usm.maine.edu

Maryland

Baltimore Hebrew University
5800 Park Heights Avenue
Baltimore, MD 21215-3996
410-578-6900
www.bhu.edu

Baltimore International
College
Commerce Exchange,
17 Commerce Street
Baltimore, MD 21202-3230
410-752-4710
www.bic.edu

Bowie State University
14000 Jericho Park Road
Bowie, MD 20715-9465
301-860-4000
www.bowiestate.edu

Capitol College
11301 Springfield Road
Laurel, MD 20708-9759
301-369-2800
www.capitol-college.edu

College of Notre Dame of
Maryland
4701 North Charles Street
Baltimore, MD 21210-2476
410-435-0100
www.ndm.edu

Columbia Union College
7600 Flower Avenue
Takoma Park, MD
20912-7796
301-891-4000
www.cuc.edu

Coppin State College
2500 West North Avenue
Baltimore, MD 21216-3698
410-383-5400
www.coppin.edu

Frostburg State University
101 Braddock Road
Frostburg, MD 21532-1099
301-687-4000
www.frostburg.edu

Goucher College
1021 Dulaney Valley Road
Baltimore, MD 21204-2794
410-337-6000
www.goucher.edu

Griggs University
PO Box 4437,
12501 Old Columbia Pk
Silver Spring, MD
20914-4437
301-680-6570
www.griggs.edu

Hood College
401 Rosemont Avenue
Frederick, MD 21701-8575
301-663-3131
www.hood.edu

Johns Hopkins University
3400 North Charles Street
Baltimore, MD 21218-2699
410-516-8000
www.jhu.edu

Loyola College in Maryland
4501 North Charles Street
Baltimore, MD 21210-2699
410-617-2000
www.loyola.edu

Maple Springs Baptist Bible
College and Seminary
4130 Belt Road
Capitol Heights, MD 20743
301-736-3631

Maryland Institute, College of
Art
1300 Mount Royal Avenue
Baltimore, MD 21217-4191
410-669-9200
www.mica.edu

Morgan State University
1700 East Cold Spring Lane
Baltimore, MD 21251
443-885-3333
www.morgan.edu

Mount Saint Mary's College
and Seminary
16300 Old Emmitsburg Road
Emmitsburg, MD
21727-7799
301-447-6122
www.msmary.edu

Ner Israel Rabbinical College
Mount Wilson Lane
Baltimore, MD 21208
410-484-7200

Peabody Conservatory of
Music of The Johns Hopkins
University
1 East Mount Vernon Place
Baltimore, MD 21202-2397
410-659-8150
www.peabody.jhu.edu

St. John's College
PO Box 2800
Annapolis, MD 21404
410-263-2371
www.sjca.edu

St. Mary's College of
Maryland
18952 East Fisher Road
St. Mary's City, MD
20686-3001
301-862-0200
www.smcm.edu

Salisbury University
1101 Camden Avenue
Salisbury, MD 21801-6837
410-543-6000
www.ssu.edu

Sojourner-Douglass College
500 North Caroline Street
Baltimore, MD 21205-1814
410-276-0306
sdc.edu

Towson University
8000 York Road
Towson, MD   21252-0001
410-704-2000
www.towson.edu

United States Naval
Academy
121 Blake Road
Annapolis, MD   21402-5000
410-293-1000
www.usna.edu

University of Baltimore
1420 North Charles Street
Baltimore, MD   21201-5779
410-837-4200
www.ubalt.edu

University of Maryland
Eastern Shore
Princess Anne, MD
21853-1299
410-651-2200
www.umes.edu

University of Maryland
University College
3501 University Blvd East
Adelphi, MD   20783
301-985-7000
www.umuc.edu

University of Maryland,
Baltimore County
1000 Hilltop Circle
Baltimore, MD   21250-5398
410-455-1000
www.umbc.edu

University of Maryland,
College Park
College Park, MD   20742
301-405-1000
www.maryland.edu

University of Phoenix–
Maryland Campus
8830 Stanford Boulevard,
Suite 100
Columbia, MD   21045
410-536-7144
www.phoenix.edu

Villa Julie College
Green Spring Valley Road
Stevenson, MD   21153
410-486-7000
www.vjc.edu

Washington Bible College
6511 Princess Garden Pkwy
Lanham, MD   20706-3599
301-552-1400
www.bible.edu

Washington College
300 Washington Avenue
Chestertown, MD
21620-1197
410-778-2800
www.washcoll.edu

Western Maryland College
2 College Hill
Westminster, MD
21157-4390
410-848-7000
www.wmdc.edu

Massachusetts

American International
College
1000 State Street
Springfield, MA 01109-3189
413-737-7000
www.aic.edu

Amherst College
PO Box 5000
Amherst, MA 01002-5000
413-542-2000
www.amherst.edu

Anna Maria College
Sunset Lane
Paxton, MA 01612
508-849-3300
www.annamaria.edu

The Art Institute of Boston at
Lesley University
700 Beacon Street
Boston, MA 02215-2598
617-585-6600
www.aiboston.edu

Assumption College
500 Salisbury Street
Worcester, MA 01609-1296
508-767-7000
www.assumption.edu

Atlantic Union College
PO Box 1000
South Lancaster, MA
01561-1000
978-368-2000
www.atlanticuc.edu

Babson College
Babson Park, MA 02457-0310
781-235-1200
www.babson.edu

Bay Path College
588 Longmeadow Street
Longmeadow, MA
01106-2292
413-565-1000
www.baypath.edu

Becker College
61 Sever Street
Worcester, MA 01609
508-791-9241
www.beckercollege.edu

Bentley College
175 Forest Street
Waltham, MA 02452-4705
781-891-2000
www.bentley.edu

Berklee College of Music
1140 Boylston Street
Boston, MA 02215-3693
617-266-1400
www.berklee.edu

Boston Architectural Center
320 Newbury Street
Boston, MA 02115-2795
617-585-0200
www.the-bac.edu

Boston College
140 Commonwealth Avenue
Chestnut Hill, MA 02467-3800
617-552-8000
www.bc.edu

The Boston Conservatory
8 The Fenway
Boston, MA 02215
617-536-6340
www.bostonconservatory.edu

Boston University
Boston, MA 02215
617-353-2000
www.bu.edu

Brandeis University
415 South Street
Waltham, MA 02454-9110
781-736-2000
www.brandeis.edu

Bridgewater State College
Bridgewater, MA 02325-0001
508-531-1200
www.bridgew.edu

Cambridge College
1000 Massachusetts Avenue
Cambridge, MA 02138-5304
617-868-1000
www.cambridge.edu

Clark University
950 Main Street
Worcester, MA 01610-1477
508-793-7711
www.clarku.edu

College of the Holy Cross
1 College Street
Worcester, MA 01610-2395
508-793-2011
www.holycross.edu

Curry College
1071 Blue Hill Avenue
Milton, MA 02186-9984
617-333-0500
www.curry.edu

Eastern Nazarene College
23 East Elm Avenue
Quincy, MA 02170-2999
617-745-3000
www.enc.edu

Elms College
291 Springfield Street
Chicopee, MA 01013-2839
413-594-2761
www.elms.edu

Emerson College
120 Boylston Street
Boston, MA 02116-4624
617-824-8500
www.emerson.edu

Emmanuel College
400 The Fenway
Boston, MA 02115
617-277-9340
www.emmanuel.edu

Endicott College
376 Hale Street
Beverly, MA 01915-2096
978-927-0585
www.endicott.edu

Fitchburg State College
160 Pearl Street
Fitchburg, MA 01420-2697
978-345-2151
www.fsc.edu

Framingham State College
100 State Street,
PO Box 9101
Framingham, MA 01701-9101
508-620-1220
www.framingham.edu

Gordon College
255 Grapevine Road
Wenham, MA 01984-1899
978-927-2300
www.gordon.edu

Hampshire College
893 West Street
Amherst, MA 01002
413-549-4600
www.hampshire.edu

Harvard University
Cambridge, MA 02138
617-495-1000
www.harvard.edu

Hebrew College
160 Herrick Road
Newton Centre, MA 02459
617-559-8600
www.hebrewcollege.edu

Hellenic College
50 Goddard Avenue
Brookline, MA 02445-7496
617-731-3500
www.hchc.edu

Lasell College
1844 Commonwealth Avenue
Newton, MA 02466-2709
617-243-2000
www.lasell.edu

Lesley University
29 Everett Street
Cambridge, MA 02138-2790
617-868-9600
www.lesley.edu

Massachusetts College of Art
621 Huntington Avenue
Boston, MA 02115-5882
617-879-7000
www.massart.edu

Massachusetts College of
Liberal Arts
375 Church Street
North Adams, MA
01247-4100
413-662-5000
www.mcla.edu

Massachusetts College of
Pharmacy and Health
Sciences
179 Longwood Avenue
Boston, MA 02115-5896
617-732-2800
www.mcp.edu

Massachusetts Institute of
Technology
77 Massachusetts Avenue
Cambridge, MA 02139-4307
617-253-1000
web.mit.edu

Massachusetts Maritime
Academy
101 Academy Drive
Buzzards Bay, MA
02532-1803
508-830-5000
www.mma.mass.edu

Merrimack College
315 Turnpike Street
North Andover, MA
01845-5800
978-837-5000
www.merrimack.edu

Montserrat College of Art
23 Essex Street, Box 26
Beverly, MA 01915
978-922-8222
www.montserrat.edu

Mount Holyoke College
50 College Street
South Hadley, MA 01075
413-538-2000
www.mtholyoke.edu

Mount Ida College
777 Dedham Street
Newton Center, MA
02459-3310
617-928-4500
www.mountida.edu

New England Conservatory
of Music
290 Huntington Avenue
Boston, MA 02115-5000
617-585-1100
www.
newenglandconservatory.edu

Nichols College
PO Box 5000
Dudley, MA 01571-5000
508-213-1560
www.nichols.edu

Northeastern University
360 Huntington Avenue
Boston, MA 02115-5096
617-373-2000
www.neu.edu

Pine Manor College
400 Heath Street
Chestnut Hill, MA 02467
617-731-7000
www.pmc.edu

Regis College
235 Wellesley Street
Weston, MA 02493
781-768-7000
www.regiscollege.edu

Saint John's Seminary
College of Liberal Arts
197 Foster Street
Brighton, MA 02135-4644
617-746-5450

Salem State College
352 Lafayette Street
Salem, MA 01970-5353
978-542-6000
www.salemstate.edu

School of the Museum of
Fine Arts
230 The Fenway
Boston, MA 02115
617-267-6100
www.smfa.edu

Simmons College
300 The Fenway
Boston, MA 02115
617-521-2000
www.simmons.edu

Simon's Rock College of Bard
84 Alford Road
Great Barrington, MA
01230-9702
413-528-0771
www.simons-rock.edu

Smith College
Northampton, MA 01063
413-584-2700
www.smith.edu

Springfield College
263 Alden Street
Springfield, MA 01109-3797
413-748-3000
www.spfldcol.edu

Stonehill College
320 Washington Street
Easton, MA 02357-5510
508-565-1000
www.stonehill.edu

Suffolk University
8 Ashburton Place
Boston, MA 02108-2770
617-573-8000
www.suffolk.edu

Tufts University
Medford, MA 02155
617-628-5000
www.tufts.edu

University of Massachusetts
Amherst
Amherst, MA 01003
413-545-0111
www.umass.edu

University of Massachusetts
Boston
100 Morrissey Boulevard
Boston, MA 02125-3393
617-287-5000
www.umb.edu

University of Massachusetts
Dartmouth
285 Old Westport Road
North Dartmouth, MA
02747-2300
508-999-8000
www.umassd.edu

University of Massachusetts
Lowell
1 University Avenue
Lowell, MA 01854-2881
978-934-4000
www.uml.edu

University of Phoenix–
Boston Campus
150 Grossman Drive
Braintree, MA 02184
781-843-0844
www.phoenix.edu

Wellesley College
106 Central Street
Wellesley, MA 02481
781-283-1000
www.wellesley.edu

Wentworth Institute of
Technology
550 Huntington Avenue
Boston, MA 02115-5998
617-989-4590
www.wit.edu

Western New England
College
1215 Wilbraham Road
Springfield, MA 01119-2654
413-782-3111
www.wnec.edu

Westfield State College
Western Avenue
Westfield, MA 01086
413-572-5300
www.wsc.ma.edu

Wheaton College
East Main Street
Norton, MA 02766
508-285-7722
www.wheatoncollege.edu

Wheelock College
200 The Riverway
Boston, MA 02215
617-879-2000
www.wheelock.edu

Williams College
988 Main Street
Williamstown, MA 01267
413-597-3131
www.williams.edu

Worcester Polytechnic
Institute
100 Institute Road
Worcester, MA 01609-2280
508-831-5000
www.wpi.edu

Worcester State College
486 Chandler Street
Worcester, MA 01602-2597
508-929-8000
www.worcester.edu

Michigan

Adrian College
110 South Madison Street
Adrian, MI 49221-2575
517-265-5161
www.adrian.edu

Albion College
611 East Porter Street
Albion, MI 49224-1831
517-629-1000
www.albion.edu

Alma College
614 West Superior Street
Alma, MI 48801-1599
989-463-7111
www.alma.edu

Andrews University
Berrien Springs, MI 49104
616-471-7771
www.andrews.edu

Aquinas College
1607 Robinson Road, SE
Grand Rapids, MI
49506-1799
616-459-8281
www.aquinas.edu

Ave Maria College
300 West Forest Avenue
Ypsilanti, MI 48197
734-482-4519
www.avemaria.edu

Baker College of Auburn Hills
1500 University Drive
Auburn Hills, MI 48326-1586
248-340-0600
www.baker.edu

Baker College of Cadillac
9600 East 13th Street
Cadillac, MI 49601
231-876-3100
www.baker.edu

Baker College of Clinton
Township
34950 Little Mack Avenue
Clinton Township, MI
48035-4701
810-791-6610
www.baker.edu

Baker College of Flint
1050 West Bristol Road
Flint, MI 48507-5508
810-767-7600
www.baker.edu

Baker College of Jackson
2800 Springport Road
Jackson, MI 49202
517-789-6123
www.baker.edu

Baker College of Muskegon
1903 Marquette Avenue
Muskegon, MI 49442-3497
231-777-8800
www.baker.edu

Baker College of Owosso
1020 South Washington St
Owosso, MI 48867-4400
989-729-3300
www.baker.edu

Baker College of Port Huron
3403 Lapeer Road
Port Huron, MI 48060-2597
810-985-7000
www.baker.edu

Calvin College
3201 Burton Street, SE
Grand Rapids, MI
49546-4388
616-957-6000
www.calvin.edu

Central Michigan University
Mount Pleasant, MI 48859
989-774-4000
www.cmich.edu

Cleary College
3601 Plymouth Road
Ann Arbor, MI 48105-2659
734-332-4477
www.cleary.edu

College for Creative Studies
201 East Kirby
Detroit, MI 48202-4034
313-664-7400
www.ccscad.edu

Concordia University
4090 Geddes Road
Ann Arbor, MI 48105-2797
734-995-7300
www.cuaa.edu

Cornerstone University
1001 East Beltline Ave, NE
Grand Rapids, MI
49525-5897
616-949-5300
www.cornerstone.edu

Davenport University
415 East Fulton
Grand Rapids, MI 49503
616-451-3511
www.davenport.edu

Davenport University
27500 Dequindre Road
Warren, MI 48092-5209
810-558-8700
www.davenport.edu

Davenport University
220 East Kalamazoo
Lansing, MI 48933-2197
517-484-2600
www.davenport.edu

Davenport University
4801 Oakman Boulevard
Dearborn, MI 48126-3799
313-581-4400
www.davenport.edu

Davenport University
4123 West Main Street
Kalamazoo, MI 49006-2791
616-382-2835
www.davenport.edu

Eastern Michigan University
Ypsilanti, MI 48197
734-487-1849
www.emich.edu

Ferris State University
901 South State Street
Big Rapids, MI 49307
231-591-2000
www.ferris.edu

Finlandia University
601 Quincy Street
Hancock, MI 49930-1882
906-482-5300
www.suomi.edu

Grace Bible College
1011 Aldon Street SW,
PO Box 910
Grand Rapids, MI
49509-0910
616-538-2330
www.gbcol.edu

Grand Valley State University
1 Campus Drive
Allendale, MI 49401-9403
616-895-6611
www.gvsu.edu

Great Lakes Christian College
6211 West Willow Highway
Lansing, MI 48917-1299
517-321-0242
www.glcc.edu

Hillsdale College
33 East College Street
Hillsdale, MI 49242-1298
517-437-7341
www.hillsdale.edu

Hope College
141 East 12th Street,
PO Box 9000
Holland, MI 49422-9000
616-395-7000
www.hope.edu

Kalamazoo College
1200 Academy Street
Kalamazoo, MI 49006-3295
616-337-7000
www.kzoo.edu

Kendall College of Art and
Design of Ferris State
University
111 Division Avenue North
Grand Rapids, MI
49503-3194
616-451-2787
www.kcad.edu

Kettering University
1700 West Third Avenue
Flint, MI 48504-4898
810-762-9500
www.kettering.edu

Lake Superior State
University
650 W Easterday Avenue
Sault Sainte Marie, MI
49783-1626
906-632-6841
www.lssu.edu

Lawrence Technological
University
21000 West Ten Mile Road
Southfield, MI 48075-1058
248-204-4000
www.ltu.edu

Madonna University
36600 Schoolcraft Road
Livonia, MI 48150-1173
734-432-5300
www.munet.edu

Marygrove College
8425 West McNichols Road
Detroit, MI 48221-2599
313-927-1200
www.marygrove.edu

Michigan State University
East Lansing, MI 48824
517-355-1855
www.msu.edu

Michigan Technological
University
1400 Townsend Drive
Houghton, MI 49931-1295
906-487-1885
www.mtu.edu

Northern Michigan
University
1401 Presque Isle Avenue
Marquette, MI 49855-5301
906-227-1000
www.nmu.edu

Northwood University
4000 Whiting Drive
Midland, MI 48640-2398
989-837-4200
www.northwood.edu

Oakland University
Rochester, MI 48309-4401
248-370-2100
www.oakland.edu

Olivet College
320 South Main Street
Olivet, MI 49076-9701
616-749-7000
www.olivetcollege.edu

Reformed Bible College
3333 East Beltline, NE
Grand Rapids, MI
49525-9749
616-222-3000
www.reformed.edu

Rochester College
800 West Avon Road
Rochester Hills, MI
48307-2764
248-218-2000
www.rc.edu

Sacred Heart Major Seminary
2701 Chicago Boulevard
Detroit, MI 48206-1799
313-883-8500

Saginaw Valley State
University
7400 Bay Road
University Center, MI 48710
989-790-4000
www.svsu.edu

Saint Mary's College of Ave
Maria University
3535 Indian Trail
Orchard Lake, MI
48324-1623
248-682-1885

Siena Heights University
1247 East Siena Heights Dr
Adrian, MI 49221-1796
517-263-0731
www.sienahts.edu

Spring Arbor University
106 East Main Street
Spring Arbor, MI
49283-9799
517-750-1200
www.arbor.edu

University of Detroit Mercy
4001 W McNichols Rd,
PO Box 19900
Detroit, MI 48219-0900
313-993-1000
www.udmercy.edu

University of Michigan
Ann Arbor, MI 48109
734-764-1817
www.umich.edu

University of
Michigan–Dearborn
4901 Evergreen Road
Dearborn, MI 48128-1491
313-593-5000
www.umd.umich.edu

University of Michigan–Flint
303 East Kearsley Street
Flint, MI 48502-1950
810-762-3000
www.flint.umich.edu

University of Phoenix–Grand
Rapids Campus
3351 Claystone SE, Suite 200
Grand Rapids, MI 49546
888-345-9699
www.phoenix.edu

University of Phoenix–Metro
Detroit Campus
5480 Corporate Drive,
Suite 260
Troy, MI 48098
800-834-2438
www.phoenix.edu

Walsh College of
Accountancy and Business
Administration
3838 Livernois Road,
PO Box 7006
Troy, MI 48007-7006
248-689-8282
www.walshcollege.edu

Wayne State University
656 West Kirby Street
Detroit, MI 48202
313-577-2424
www.wayne.edu

Western Michigan University
1903 West Michigan Avenue
Kalamazoo, MI 49008-5202
616-387-1000
www.wmich.edu

William Tyndale College
35700 West Twelve Mile Road
Farmington Hills, MI
48331-3147
248-553-7200
www.williamtyndale.edu

Yeshiva Geddolah of Greater
Detroit Rabbinical College
24600 Greenfield
Oak Park, MI 48237-1544
810-968-3360

Minnesota

Augsburg College
2211 Riverside Avenue
Minneapolis, MN
55454-1351
612-330-1000
www.augsburg.edu

Bemidji State University
1500 Birchmont Drive, NE
Bemidji, MN 56601-2699
218-755-2000
www.bemidjistate.edu

Bethel College
3900 Bethel Drive
St. Paul, MN 55112-6999
651-638-6400
www.bethel.edu

Capella University
222 South Ninth Street
Minneapolis, MN 55402
612-339-8650
www.capellauniversity.edu

Carleton College
One North College Street
Northfield, MN 55057-4001
507-646-4000
www.carleton.edu

College of Saint Benedict
37 South College Avenue
Saint Joseph, MN
56374-2091
320-363-5011
www.csbsju.edu

College of St. Catherine
2004 Randolph Avenue
St. Paul, MN 55105-1789
651-690-6000
www.stkate.edu

The College of St.
Scholastica
1200 Kenwood Avenue
Duluth, MN 55811-4199
218-723-6000
www.css.edu

College of Visual Arts
344 Summit Avenue
St. Paul, MN 55102-2124
651-224-3416
www.cva.edu

Concordia College
901 South 8th Street
Moorhead, MN 56562
218-299-4000
www.concordiacollege.edu

Concordia University
275 Syndicate Street North
St. Paul, MN 55104-5494
651-641-8278
www.csp.edu

Crown College
6425 County Road 30
St. Bonifacius, MN
55375-9002
952-446-4100
www.crown.edu

Gustavus Adolphus College
800 West College Avenue
St. Peter, MN   56082-1498
507-933-8000
www.gustavus.edu

Hamline University
1536 Hewitt Avenue
St. Paul, MN   55104-1284
651-523-2800
www.hamline.edu

Macalester College
1600 Grand Avenue
St. Paul, MN   55105-1899
651-696-6000
www.macalester.edu

Martin Luther College
1995 Luther Court
New Ulm, MN   56073
507-354-8221
www.mlc-wels.edu

Mayo School of Health-
Related Sciences
200 First Street, SW
Rochester, MN   55905
507-284-3293
www.mayo.edu/hrs/hrs.htm

Metropolitan State University
700 East 7th Street
St. Paul, MN   55106-5000
651-772-7777
www.metrostate.edu

Minneapolis College of Art
and Design
2501 Stevens Avenue South
Minneapolis, MN
55404-4347
612-874-3700
www.mcad.edu

Minnesota Bible College
920 Mayowood Road, SW
Rochester, MN   55902-2382
507-288-4563
www.mnbc.edu

Minnesota State University
Moorhead
1104 7th Avenue South
Moorhead, MN   56563-0002
218-236-2011
www.mnstate.edu

Minnesota State University,
Mankato
228 Wiecking Center
Mankato, MN   56001
507-389-2463
www.mnsu.edu

National American
University–St. Paul Campus
1380 Energy Lane, Suite 13
St. Paul, MN   55108-9952
651-644-1265
www.nationalcollege.edu

North Central University
910 Elliot Avenue
Minneapolis, MN
55404-1322
612-332-3491
www.northcentral.edu

Northwestern College
3003 Snelling Avenue North
St. Paul, MN   55113-1598
651-631-5100
www.nwc.edu

Oak Hills Christian College
1600 Oak Hills Road, SW
Bemidji, MN   56601-8832
218-751-8670
www.oakhills.edu

Pillsbury Baptist Bible
College
315 South Grove
Owatonna, MN   55060-3097
507-451-2710
www.pillsbury.edu

Saint John's University
Collegeville, MN   56321
320-363-2011
www.csbsju.edu

Saint Mary's University of
Minnesota
700 Terrace Heights
Winona, MN   55987-1399
507-452-4430
www.smumn.edu

Southwest State University
1501 State Street
Marshall, MN   56258-1598
507-537-7021
www.southwest.msus.edu

St. Cloud State University
720 4th Avenue South
St. Cloud, MN   56301-4498
320-255-2244
www.stcloudstate.edu

St. Olaf College
1520 St Olaf Avenue
Northfield, MN   55057-1098
507-646-2222
www.stolaf.edu

University of Minnesota,
Crookston
2900 University Avenue
Crookston, MN   56716-5001
218-281-6510
www.crk.umn.edu

University of Minnesota,
Duluth
10 University Drive
Duluth, MN   55812-2496
218-726-8000
www.d.umn.edu

University of Minnesota,
Morris
600 East 4th Street
Morris, MN   56267-2134
320-589-2211
www.mrs.umn.edu

University of Minnesota,
Twin Cities Campus
100 Church Street, SE
Minneapolis, MN
55455-0213
612-625-5000
www.umn.edu/tc

University of St. Thomas
2115 Summit Avenue
St. Paul, MN   55105-1096
651-962-5000
www.stthomas.edu

Winona State University
PO Box 5838
Winona, MN   55987-5838
507-457-5000
www.winona.msus.edu

Mississippi

Alcorn State University
1000 ASU Drive
Alcorn State, MS 39096-7500
800-222-6790
www.alcorn.edu

Belhaven College
1500 Peachtree Street
Jackson, MS 39202-1789
800-960-5940
www.belhaven.edu

Blue Mountain College
PO Box 160
Blue Mountain, MS
38610-9509
800-235-0136
www.bmc.edu

Delta State University
Highway 8 West
Cleveland, MS 38733-0001
800-468-6378
www.deltast.edu

Jackson State University
1400 John R Lynch Street
Jackson, MS 39217
800-848-6817
www.jsums.edu

Magnolia Bible College
PO Box 1109
Kosciusko, MS 39090-1109
601-289-2896

Millsaps College
1701 North State Street
Jackson, MS 39210-0001
800-352-1050
www.millsaps.edu

Mississippi College
200 South Capitol Street
Clinton, MS 39058
800-738-1236

Mississippi State University
Mississippi State, MS 39762
662-325-2323
www.msstate.edu

Mississippi University for
Women
Box W-1600
Columbus, MS 39701-9998
877-GO 2 THE W
www.muw.edu

Mississippi Valley State
University
14000 Highway 82 West
Itta Bena, MS 38941-1400
662-254-9041
www.mvsu.edu

Rust College
150 Rust Avenue
Holly Springs, MS
38635-2328
888-886-8492
www.rustcollege.edu

Southeastern Baptist College
4229 Highway 15 North
Laurel, MS 39440-1096
601-426-6346

Tougaloo College
500 West County Line Road
Tougaloo, MS 39174
888-42GALOO
www.tougaloo.edu

University of Mississippi
University, MS 38677
662-915-7211
www.olemiss.edu

University of Mississippi
Medical Center
2500 North State Street
Jackson, MS 39216-4505
601-984-1000
umc.edu

University of Southern
Mississippi
2701 Hardy Street
Hattiesburg, MS 39406
601-266-7011
www.usm.edu

Wesley College
PO Box 1070
Florence, MS 39073-1070
800-748-9972
www.wesleycollege.com

William Carey College
498 Tuscan Avenue
Hattiesburg, MS 39401-5499
601-318-6051
www.wmcarey.edu

Missouri

Avila College
11901 Wornall Road
Kansas City, MO 64145-1698
816-942-8400
www.avila.edu

Baptist Bible College
628 East Kearney
Springfield, MO 65803-3498
417-268-6060
www.bbcnet.edu/bbgst.html

Calvary Bible College and
Theological Seminary
15800 Calvary Road
Kansas City, MO 64147-1341
816-322-0110
www.calvary.edu

Central Bible College
3000 North Grant Avenue
Springfield, MO 65803-1096
417-833-2551
www.cbcag.edu

Central Christian College of
the Bible
911 Urbandale Drive East
Moberly, MO 65270-1997
660-263-3900
www.cccb.edu

Central Methodist College
411 Central Methodist Square
Fayette, MO 65248-1198
660-248-3391
www.cmc.edu

Central Missouri State
University
PO Box 800
Warrensburg, MO 64093
660-543-4111
www.cmsu.edu

Cleveland Chiropractic
College-Kansas City Campus
6401 Rockhill Road
Kansas City, MO 64131-1181
816-501-0100
www.cleveland.edu

College of the Ozarks
PO Box 17
Point Lookout, MO 65726
417-334-6411
www.cofo.edu

Columbia College
1001 Rogers Street
Columbia, MO 65216-0002
573-875-8700
www.ccis.edu

Conception Seminary
College
PO Box 502
Conception, MO 64433-0502
660-944-2218
www.conceptionabbey.edu

Culver-Stockton College
1 College Hill
Canton, MO 63435-1299
217-231-6000
www.culver.edu

Deaconess College of
Nursing
6150 Oakland Avenue
St. Louis, MO 63139-3215
314-768-3044
www.deaconess.edu

DeVry Institute of Technology
11224 Holmes Road
Kansas City, MO 64131-3698
816-941-0430
www.kc.devry.edu

Drury University
900 North Benton Avenue
Springfield, MO 65802-3791
417-873-7879
www.drury.edu

Evangel University
1111 North Glenstone
Springfield, MO 65802-2191
417-865-2811
www.evangel.edu

Fontbonne College
6800 Wydown Boulevard
St. Louis, MO 63105-3098
314-862-3456
www.fontbonne.edu

Global University of the
Assemblies of God
1211 South Glenstone Ave
Springfield, MO 65804
417-862-9533
www.globaluniversity.edu

Hannibal-LaGrange College
2800 Palmyra Road
Hannibal, MO 63401-1999
573-221-3675
www.hlg.edu

Harris-Stowe State College
3026 Laclede Avenue
St. Louis, MO 63103-2136
314-340-3366
www.hssc.edu

Jewish Hospital College of
Nursing and Allied Health
306 South Kingshighway
St. Louis, MO 63110-1091
314-454-7055
jhconah.org

Kansas City Art Institute
4415 Warwick Boulevard
Kansas City, MO 64111-1874
816-472-4852
www.kcai.edu

Kansas City College of Legal
Studies
402 East Bannister Road,
Suite A
Kansas City, MO 64131
816-444-2232
www.metropolitancollege.edu

Lester L. Cox College of
Nursing and Health Sciences
1423 North Jefferson
Springfield, MO 65802
417-269-3401
www.coxnet.org/coxcollege/
default.cfm

Lincoln University
820 Chestnut
Jefferson City, MO 65102
573-681-5000
www.lincolnu.edu

Lindenwood University
209 South Kingshighway
St. Charles, MO 63301-1695
636-949-2000
www.lindenwood.edu

Logan University-College of
Chiropractic
1851 Schoettler Road,
Box 1065
Chesterfield, MO
63006-1065
636-227-2100
www.logan.edu

Maryville University of Saint
Louis
13550 Conway Road
St. Louis, MO 63141-7299
314-529-9300
www.maryville.edu

Messenger College
PO Box 4050
Joplin, MO 64803
417-624-7070

Missouri Baptist College
One College Park Drive
St. Louis, MO 63141-8660
314-434-1115
www.mobap.edu

Missouri Southern State
College
3950 East Newman Road
Joplin, MO 64801-1595
417-625-9300
www.mssc.edu

Missouri Tech
1167 Corporate Lake Drive
St. Louis, MO 63132-1716
314-569-3600
www.motech.edu

Missouri Valley College
500 East College
Marshall, MO 65340-3197
660-831-4000
www.moval.edu

Missouri Western State
College
4525 Downs Drive
St. Joseph, MO 64507-2294
816-271-4200
www.mwsc.edu

National American University
4200 Blue Ridge Boulevard
Kansas City, MO 64133-1612
816-353-4554
www.national.edu

Northwest Missouri State
University
800 University Drive
Maryville, MO   64468-6001
660-562-1212
www.nwmissouri.edu

Ozark Christian College
1111 North Main Street
Joplin, MO   64801-4804
417-624-2518
www.occ.edu

Park University
8700 NW River Park Drive
Parkville, MO   64152-3795
816-741-2000
www.park.edu

Research College of Nursing
2316 East Meyer Boulevard
Kansas City, MO   64132
816-276-4700

Rockhurst University
1100 Rockhurst Road
Kansas City, MO   64110-2561
816-501-4000
www.rockhurst.edu

Saint Louis University
221 North Grand Boulevard
St. Louis, MO   63103-2097
314-977-2222
imagine.slu.edu

Saint Luke's College
4426 Wornall Road
Kansas City, MO   64111
816-932-2233
www.saint-lukes.org

Southeast Missouri State
University
One University Plaza
Cape Girardeau, MO
63701-4799
573-651-2000
www.semo.edu

Southwest Baptist University
1600 University Avenue
Bolivar, MO   65613-2597
417-328-5281
www.sbuniv.edu

Southwest Missouri State
University
901 South National
Springfield, MO   65804-0094
417-836-5000
www.smsu.edu

St. Louis Christian College
1360 Grandview Drive
Florissant, MO   63033-6499
314-837-6777
www.slcc4ministry.edu

St. Louis College of
Pharmacy
4588 Parkview Place
St. Louis, MO   63110-1088
314-367-8700
www.stlcop.edu

Stephens College
1200 East Broadway
Columbia, MO   65215-0002
573-442-2211
www.stephens.edu

Truman State University
100 East Normal Street
Kirksville, MO   63501-4221
660-785-4000
www.truman.edu

University of
Missouri–Columbia
305 Jesse Hall
Columbia, MO   65211
573-882-2121
www.missouri.edu

University of
Missouri–Kansas City
5100 Rockhill Road
Kansas City, MO   64110-2499
816-235-1000
www.umkc.edu

University of Missouri–Rolla
1870 Miner Circle
Rolla, MO   65409-0910
573-341-4111
www.umr.edu

University of Missouri–
St. Louis
8001 Natural Bridge Road
St. Louis, MO   63121-4499
314-516-5000
www.umsl.edu

University of Phoenix–
Saint Louis Campus
Riverport Executive Center II,
13801 Riverport Drive,
Suite 102
St. Louis, MO   63043
314-298-9755
www.phoenix.edu

Washington University in
St. Louis
1 Brookings Drive
St. Louis, MO   63130-4899
314-935-5000
www.wustl.edu

Webster University
470 East Lockwood Avenue
St. Louis, MO   63119-3194
314-968-6900
www.webster.edu

Westminster College
501 Westminster Avenue
Fulton, MO   65251-1299
573-642-3361
www.westminster-mo.edu

William Jewell College
500 College Hill
Liberty, MO   64068-1843
816-781-7700
www.jewell.edu

William Woods University
One University Avenue
Fulton, MO   65251-2388
573-642-2251
www.williamwoods.edu

Montana

Carroll College
1601 North Benton Avenue
Helena, MT   59625-0002
406-447-4300
www.carroll.edu

Montana State University–
Billings
1500 North 30th Street
Billings, MT   59101-0298
406-657-2011
www.msubillings.edu

Montana State
University–Bozeman
Bozeman, MT   59717
406-994-0211
www.montana.edu

Montana State University–
Northern
PO Box 7751
Havre, MT   59501-7751
406-265-3700
www.msun.edu

Montana Tech of The
University of Montana
1300 West Park Street
Butte, MT   59701-8997
406-496-4101
www.mtech.edu

Rocky Mountain College
1511 Poly Drive
Billings, MT   59102-1796
406-657-1000
www.rocky.edu

University of Great Falls
1301 Twentieth Street South
Great Falls, MT   59405
406-761-8210
www.ugf.edu

The University of Montana–
Missoula
Missoula, MT   59812-0002
406-243-0211
www.umt.edu

The University of Montana–
Western
710 South Atlantic
Dillon, MT   59725-3598
406-683-7011
www.umwesten.edu

Nebraska

Bellevue University
1000 Galvin Road South
Bellevue, NE   68005-3098
402-291-8100
www.bellevue.edu

Chadron State College
1000 Main Street
Chadron, NE   69337
308-432-6000
www.csc.edu

Clarkson College
101 South 42nd Street
Omaha, NE   68131-2739
402-552-3100
www.clarksoncollege.edu

College of Saint Mary
1901 South 72nd Street
Omaha, NE   68124-2377
402-399-2400
www.csm.edu

Concordia University
800 North Columbia Avenue
Seward, NE   68434-1599
402-643-3651
www.cune.edu

Creighton University
2500 California Plaza
Omaha, NE   68178-0001
402-280-2700
www.creighton.edu

Dana College
2848 College Drive
Blair, NE 68008-1099
402-426-9000
www.dana.edu

Doane College
1014 Boswell Avenue
Crete, NE 68333-2430
402-826-2161
www.doane.edu

Grace University
1311 South Ninth Street
Omaha, NE 68108
402-449-2800
www.graceuniversity.edu

Hastings College
800 North Turner Avenue
Hastings, NE 68901-7696
402-463-2402
www.hastings.edu

Midland Lutheran College
900 North Clarkson Street
Fremont, NE 68025-4200
402-721-5480
www.mlc.edu

Nebraska Christian College
1800 Syracuse Avenue
Norfolk, NE 68701-2458
402-379-5000
www.nechristian.edu

Nebraska Methodist College
8501 West Dodge Road
Omaha, NE 68114-3426
402-354-4863
www.methodistcollege.edu

Nebraska Wesleyan
University
5000 Saint Paul Avenue
Lincoln, NE 68504-2796
402-466-2371
www.nebrwesleyan.edu

Peru State College
PO Box 10
Peru, NE 68421
402-872-3815
www.peru.edu

Union College
3800 South 48th Street
Lincoln, NE 68506-4300
402-488-2331
www.ucollege.edu

University of Nebraska at
Kearney
905 West 25th Street
Kearney, NE 68849-0001
308-865-8441

University of Nebraska at
Omaha
6001 Dodge Street
Omaha, NE 68182
402-554-2800
www.unomaha.edu

University of Nebraska
Medical Center
Nebraska Medical Center
Omaha, NE 68198
402-559-4000
www.unmc.edu

University of Nebraska–
Lincoln
14th and R Streets
Lincoln, NE 68588
402-472-7211
www.unl.edu

Wayne State College
1111 Main Street
Wayne, NE 68787
402-375-7000
www.wsc.edu

York College
1125 East 8th Street
York, NE 68467
402-363-5600
www.york.edu

Nevada

Morrison University
140 Washington Street
Reno, NV 89503-5600
775-323-4145
www.morrison.edu

Sierra Nevada College
999 Tahoe Boulevard
Incline Village, NV 89451
775-831-1314
www.sierranevada.edu

University of Nevada,
Las Vegas
4505 Maryland Parkway
Las Vegas, NV 89154-9900
702-895-3011
www.unlv.edu

University of Nevada, Reno
Reno, NV 89557
775-784-1110
www.unr.edu

University of Phoenix–
Nevada Campus
333 North Rancho Drive,
Suite 300
Las Vegas, NV 89106
702-638-7868
www.phoenix.edu

New Hampshire

Colby-Sawyer College
100 Main Street
New London, NH 03257-4648
603-526-3000
www.colby-sawyer.edu

Daniel Webster College
20 University Drive
Nashua, NH 03063-1300
603-577-6000
www.dwc.edu

Dartmouth College
Hanover, NH 03755
603-646-1110
www.dartmouth.edu

Franklin Pierce College
College Road, PO Box 60
Rindge, NH 03461-0060
603-899-4000
www.fpc.edu

Keene State College
229 Main Street
Keene, NH 03435
603-352-1909
www.keene.edu

Magdalen College
511 Kearsarge Mountain Rd
Warner, NH 03278
603-456-2656
www.magdalen.edu

New England College
7 Main Street
Henniker, NH 03242-3293
603-428-2211
www.nec.edu

New Hampshire Institute of
Art
148 Concord Street
Manchester, NH 03104-4158
603-623-0313
www.nhia.edu

Plymouth State College
17 High Street
Plymouth, NH 03264-1595
603-535-5000
www.plymouth.edu

Rivier College
420 Main Street
Nashua, NH 03060-5086
603-888-1311
www.rivier.edu

Saint Anselm College
100 Saint Anselm Drive
Manchester, NH 03102-1310
603-641-7000
www.anselm.edu

Southern New Hampshire
University
2500 North River Road
Manchester, NH 03106-1045
603-668-2211
www.snhu.edu

Thomas More College of
Liberal Arts
6 Manchester Street
Merrimack, NH 03054-4818
603-880-8308
www.thomasmorecollege.edu

University of New
Hampshire
Durham, NH 03824
603-862-1234
www.unh.edu

University of New
Hampshire at Manchester
400 Commercial Street
Manchester, NH 03101-1113
603-641-4321
www.unh.edu/unhm

University System College
for Lifelong Learning
125 North State Street
Concord, NH 03301
603-228-3000
www.cll.edu

White Pines College
40 Chester Street
Chester, NH 03036-4331
603-887-4401
www.whitepines.edu

New Jersey

Beth Medrash Govoha
617 Sixth Street
Lakewood, NJ 08701-2797
732-367-1060

Bloomfield College
467 Franklin Street
Bloomfield, NJ 07003-9981
973-748-9000
www.bloomfield.edu

Caldwell College
9 Ryerson Avenue
Caldwell, NJ   07006-6195
973-618-3000
www.caldwell.edu

Centenary College
400 Jefferson Street
Hackettstown, NJ
07840-2100
908-852-1400
www.centenarycollege.edu

The College of New Jersey
PO Box 7718
Ewing, NJ   08628
609-771-1855
www.tcnj.edu

College of Saint Elizabeth
2 Convent Road
Morristown, NJ   07960-6989
973-290-4000
www.st-elizabeth.edu

DeVry College of Technology
630 US Highway 1
North Brunswick, NJ
08902-3362
732-435-4880
www.nj.devry.edu

Drew University
36 Madison Avenue
Madison, NJ   07940-1493
973-408-3000
www.drew.edu

Fairleigh Dickinson
University, Florham-
Madison Campus
285 Madison Avenue
Madison, NJ   07940-1099
973-443-8500
www.fdu.edu

Fairleigh Dickinson
University,
Teaneck–Hackensack Campus
1000 River Road
Teaneck, NJ   07666-1914
201-692-2000
www.fdu.edu

Felician College
262 South Main Street
Lodi, NJ   07644-2198
201-559-6000
www.felician.edu

Georgian Court College
900 Lakewood Avenue
Lakewood, NJ   08701-2697
732-364-2200
www.georgian.edu

Kean University
1000 Morris Avenue
Union, NJ   07083
908-527-2000
www.kean.edu

Monmouth University
400 Cedar Avenue
West Long Branch, NJ
07764-1898
732-571-3400
www.monmouth.edu

Montclair State University
1 Normal Avenue
Upper Montclair, NJ
07043-1624
973-655-4000
www.montclair.edu

New Jersey City University
2039 Kennedy Boulevard
Jersey City, NJ   07305-1597
201-200-2000
www.njcu.edu/core.htm

New Jersey Institute of
Technology
University Heights
Newark, NJ   07102-1982
973-596-3000
www.njit.edu

Princeton University
Princeton, NJ   08544-1019
609-258-3000
www.princeton.edu

Rabbinical College of
America
226 Sussex Avenue,
PO Box 1996
Morristown, NJ   07962-1996
973-267-9404

Ramapo College of New
Jersey
505 Ramapo Valley Road
Mahwah, NJ   07430-1680
201-684-7500
www.ramapo.edu

The Richard Stockton College
of New Jersey
PO Box 195, Jimmie Leeds Rd
Pomona, NJ   08240-0195
609-652-1776
www.stockton.edu

Rider University
2083 Lawrenceville Road
Lawrenceville, NJ
08648-3001
609-896-5000
www.rider.edu

Rowan University
201 Mullica Hill Road
Glassboro, NJ   08028-1701
856-256-4500
www.rowan.edu

Rutgers, The State University
of New Jersey, Camden
311 North Fifth Street
Camden, NJ   08102-1401
856-225-1766
camden-www.rutgers.edu

Rutgers, The State University
of New Jersey, New
Brunswick
New Brunswick, NJ
08901-1281
732-932-4636
www.rutgers.edu

Rutgers, The State University
of New Jersey, Newark
Newark, NJ   07102
973-353-1766
info.rutgers.edu/newark

Saint Peter's College
2641 Kennedy Boulevard
Jersey City, NJ   07306-5997
201-915-9000
www.spc.edu

Seton Hall University
400 South Orange Avenue
South Orange, NJ
07079-2697
973-761-9000
www.shu.edu

Stevens Institute of
Technology
Castle Point on Hudson
Hoboken, NJ   07030
201-216-5000
www.stevens-tech.edu

Talmudical Academy of New
Jersey
Route 524
Adelphia, NJ   07710
732-431-1600

Thomas Edison State College
101 West State Street
Trenton, NJ   08608-1176
609-984-1100
www.tesc.edu

Westminster Choir College of
Rider University
101 Walnut Lane
Princeton, NJ   08540-3899
609-921-7100
westminster.rider.edu

William Paterson University
of New Jersey
300 Pompton Road
Wayne, NJ   07470-8420
973-720-2000
www.wpunj.edu

New Mexico

College of Santa Fe
1600 Saint Michael's Drive
Santa Fe, NM 87505-7634
505-473-6011
www.csf.edu

College of the Southwest
6610 Lovington Highway
Hobbs, NM 88240-9129
505-392-6561
www.csw.edu

Eastern New Mexico
University
Portales, NM 88130
505-562-1011
www.enmu.edu

Metropolitan College of
Court Reporting
1717 Louisiana Blvd NE,
Suite 207
Albuquerque, NM 87110-7027
505-888-3400
www.metropolitancollege.edu

National American University
1202 Pennsylvania Ave, NE
Albuquerque, NM 87110
505-265-7517

Nazarene Indian Bible
College
2315 Markham Road, SW
Albuquerque, NM 87105
505-877-0240

New Mexico Highlands
University
PO Box 9000
Las Vegas, NM 87701
505-454-3000
www.nmhu.edu

New Mexico Institute of
Mining and Technology
801 Leroy Place
Socorro, NM 87801
505-835-5011
www.nmt.edu

New Mexico State University
PO Box 30001
Las Cruces, NM 88003-8001
505-646-0111
www.nmsu.edu

St. John's College
1160 Camino Cruz Blanca
Santa Fe, NM 87501-4599
505-984-6000
www.sjcsf.edu

University of New Mexico
Albuquerque, NM
87131-2039
505-277-0111
www.unm.edu

University of Phoenix–New
Mexico Campus
7471 Pan American Freeway NE
Albuquerque, NM 87109
505-821-4800
www.phoenix.edu

Western New Mexico
University
PO Box 680
Silver City, NM 88062-0680
505-538-6011
www.wnmu.edu

New York

Adelphi University
South Avenue
Garden City, NY 11530
516-877-3000
www.adelphi.edu

Albany College of Pharmacy
of Union University
106 New Scotland Avenue
Albany, NY 12208-3425
518-445-7200
www.acp.edu

Alfred University
One Saxon Drive
Alfred, NY 14802-1205
607-871-2111
www.alfred.edu

Audrey Cohen College
75 Varick Street
New York, NY 10013-1919
212-343-1234
www.audreycohen.edu

Bard College
Ravine Road, PO Box 5000
Annandale-on-Hudson, NY
12504
845-758-6822
www.bard.edu

Barnard College
3009 Broadway
New York, NY 10027-6598
212-854-5262
Fax: 212-854-6220
www.barnard.edu

Bernard M. Baruch College
of the City University of
New York
17 Lexington Avenue
New York, NY 10010-5585
212-802-2000
www.baruch.cuny.edu

Beth HaMedrash Shaarei
Yosher Institute
4102-10 Sixteenth Avenue
Brooklyn, NY 11204
718-854-2290

Beth Hatalmud Rabbinical
College
2127 Eighty-second Street
Brooklyn, NY 11214
718-259-2525

Boricua College
3755 Broadway
New York, NY 10032-1560
212-694-1000

Briarcliffe College
1055 Stewart Avenue
Bethpage, NY 11714
516-918-3600
www.briarcliffe.edu

Brooklyn College of the City
University of New York
2900 Bedford Avenue
Brooklyn, NY 11210-2889
718-951-5000
www.brooklyn.cuny.edu

Canisius College
2001 Main Street
Buffalo, NY 14208-1098
716-883-7000
www.canisius.edu

Cazenovia College
22 Sullivan Street
Cazenovia, NY 13035-1084
315-655-7000
www.cazcollege.edu

Central Yeshiva Tomchei
Tmimim-Lubavitch
841-853 Ocean Parkway
Brooklyn, NY 11230
718-434-0784

City College of the City
University of New York
160 Convent Avenue
New York, NY 10031-9198
212-650-7000
www.ccny.cuny.edu

Clarkson University
Potsdam, NY 13699
315-268-6400
www.clarkson.edu

Colgate University
13 Oak Drive
Hamilton, NY 13346-1386
315-228-1000
www.colgate.edu

College of Aeronautics
8601 23rd Avenue
Flushing, NY 11369-1037
718-429-6600
www.aero.edu

The College of Insurance
101 Murray Street
New York, NY 10007-2165
212-962-4111
www.tci.edu

College of Mount Saint
Vincent
6301 Riverdale Avenue
Riverdale, NY 10471-1093
718-405-3200
www.cmsv.edu

The College of New Rochelle
29 Castle Place
New Rochelle, NY
10805-2308
914-632-5300
cnr.edu

The College of Saint Rose
432 Western Avenue
Albany, NY 12203-1419
518-454-5111
www.strose.edu

College of Staten Island of
the City University of
New York
2800 Victory Boulevard
Staten Island, NY
10314-6600
718-982-2000
www.csi.cuny.edu

Columbia College
116th Street and Broadway
New York, NY 10027
212-854-1754
www.columbia.edu

Columbia University, School
of General Studies
2970 Broadway
New York, NY 10027-6939
212-854-2772

Columbia University,
The Fu Foundation School
of Engineering and Applied
Science
500 West 120th Street
New York, NY 10027
212-854-1754
www.columbia.edu

Concordia College
171 White Plains Road
Bronxville, NY 10708-1998
914-337-9300
www.concordia-ny.edu

Cooper Union for the
Advancement of Science
and Art
30 Cooper Square
New York, NY 10003-7120
212-353-4100
www.cooper.edu

Cornell University
Ithaca, NY 14853-0001
607-255-2000
www.cornell.edu

The Culinary Institute
of America
1946 Campus Drive
Hyde Park, NY 12538-1499
845-452-9600
www.ciachef.edu

D'Youville College
320 Porter Avenue
Buffalo, NY 14201-1084
716-881-3200
www.dyc.edu

Daemen College
4380 Main Street
Amherst, NY 14226-3592
716-839-3600
www.daemen.edu

Darkei Noam Rabbinical
College
2822 Avenue J
Brooklyn, NY 11210
718-338-6464

DeVry Institute of Technology
30-20 Thomson Avenue
Long Island City, NY 11101
718-361-0004
www.ny.devry.edu

Dominican College
470 Western Highway
Orangeburg, NY 10962-1210
845-359-7800
www.dc.edu

Dowling College
Idle Hour Boulevard
Oakdale, NY 11769-1999
631-244-3000
www.dowling.edu

Elmira College
One Park Place
Elmira, NY 14901
607-735-1800
www.elmira.edu

Eugene Lang College, New
School University
65 West 11th Street
New York, NY 10011-8601
212-229-5600
www.newschool.edu

Excelsior College
7 Columbia Circle
Albany, NY 12203-5159
518-464-8500
www.excelsior.edu

Fashion Institute of
Technology
Seventh Avenue at 27th St
New York, NY 10001-5992
212-217-7999
www.fitnyc.suny.edu

Five Towns College
305 North Service Road
Dix Hills, NY 11746-6055
631-424-7000
www.fivetowns.edu

Fordham University
441 East Fordham Road
New York, NY 10458
718-817-1000
www.fordham.edu

Globe Institute of Technology
291 Broadway, Second Floor
New York, NY 10007
212-349-4330
www.globe.edu

Hamilton College
198 College Hill Road
Clinton, NY 13323-1296
315-859-4011
www.hamilton.edu

Hartwick College
West Street, PO Box 4020
Oneonta, NY 13820-4020
607-431-4200
www.hartwick.edu

Hilbert College
5200 South Park Avenue
Hamburg, NY 14075-1597
716-649-7900
www.hilbert.edu

Hobart and William Smith
Colleges
Geneva, NY 14456-3397
315-781-3000
www.hws.edu

Hofstra University
100 Hofstra University
Hempstead, NY 11549
516-463-6600
www.hofstra.edu

Holy Trinity Orthodox
Seminary
PO Box 36
Jordanville, NY 13361
315-858-0945
www.hts.edu

Houghton College
One Willard Avenue
Houghton, NY 14744
716-567-9200
www.houghton.edu

Hunter College of the City
University of New York
695 Park Avenue
New York, NY 10021-5085
212-772-4000
www.hunter.cuny.edu

Iona College
715 North Avenue
New Rochelle, NY
10801-1890
914-633-2000
www.iona.edu

Ithaca College
100 Job Hall
Ithaca, NY 14850-7020
607-274-3011
www.ithaca.edu

Jewish Theological Seminary
of America
3080 Broadway
New York, NY 10027-4649
212-678-8000
www.jtsa.edu

John Jay College of Criminal
Justice of the City University
of New York
899 Tenth Avenue
New York, NY 10019-1093
212-237-8000
www.jjay.cuny.edu

The Juilliard School
60 Lincoln Center Plaza
New York, NY 10023-6588
212-799-5000
www.juilliard.edu

Kehilath Yakov Rabbinical
Seminary
206 Wilson Street
Brooklyn, NY 11211-7207
718-963-1212

Keuka College
Keuka Park, NY 14478-0098
315-279-5000
www.keuka.edu

Kol Yaakov Torah Center
29 West Maple Avenue
Monsey, NY 10952-2954
914-425-3863
horizons.edu

Laboratory Institute of
Merchandising
12 East 53rd Street
New York, NY 10022-5268
212-752-1530
www.limcollege.edu

Le Moyne College
1419 Salt Springs Road
Syracuse, NY 13214-1399
315-445-4100
www.lemoyne.edu

Lehman College of the City
University of New York
250 Bedford Park Blvd West
Bronx, NY 10468-1589
718-960-8000
www.lehman.cuny.edu

Long Island University,
Brentwood Campus
100 Second Avenue
Brentwood, NY 11717
631-273-5112
www.liunet.edu/cwis/brent/
brent.htm

Long Island University,
Brooklyn Campus
One University Plaza
Brooklyn, NY 11201-8423
718-488-1000
www.liu.edu

Long Island University, C.W.
Post Campus
720 Northern Boulevard
Brookville, NY 11548-1300
516-299-2000
www.cwpost.liunet.edu/cwis/
cwp/post.html

Long Island University,
Southampton College
239 Montauk Highway
Southampton, NY
11968-4198
631-283-4000
www.southampton.liu.edu

Long Island University,
Southampton College,
Friends World
239 Montauk Highway
Southampton, NY 11968
631-287-8464
www.southampton.liu.edu/
fw

Machzikei Hadath Rabbinical
College
5407 Sixteenth Avenue
Brooklyn, NY 11204-1805
718-854-8777

Manhattan College
Manhattan College Parkway
Riverdale, NY 10471
718-862-8000
www.manhattan.edu

Manhattan School of Music
120 Claremont Avenue
New York, NY 10027-4698
212-749-2802
www.msmnyc.edu

Manhattanville College
2900 Purchase Street
Purchase, NY 10577-2132
914-694-2200
www.mville.edu

Mannes College of Music,
New School University
150 West 85th Street
New York, NY 10024-4402
212-580-0210
www.mannes.edu

Marist College
3399 North Road
Poughkeepsie, NY
12601-1387
845-575-3000
www.marist.edu

Marymount College
100 Marymount Avenue
Tarrytown, NY   10591-3796
914-631-3200
www.marymt.edu

Marymount Manhattan
College
221 East 71st Street
New York, NY   10021-4597
212-517-0400
www.marymount.mmm.edu

Medaille College
18 Agassiz Circle
Buffalo, NY   14214-2695
716-884-3281
www.medaille.edu

Medgar Evers College of the
City University of New York
1650 Bedford Avenue
Brooklyn, NY   11225-2298
718-270-4900
www.mec.cuny.edu

Mercy College
555 Broadway
Dobbs Ferry, NY   10522-1189
914-693-4500
www.mercynet.edu

Mesivta of Eastern Parkway
Rabbinical Seminary
510 Dahill Road
Brooklyn, NY   11218-5559
718-438-1002

Mesivta Tifereth Jerusalem of
America
145 East Broadway
New York, NY   10002-6301
212-964-2830

Mesivta Torah Vodaath
Rabbinical Seminary
425 East Ninth Street
Brooklyn, NY   11218-5299
718-941-8000

Mirrer Yeshiva
1795 Ocean Parkway
Brooklyn, NY   11223-2010
718-645-0536

Molloy College
1000 Hempstead Avenue
Rockville Centre, NY
11571-5002
516-678-5000

Mount Saint Mary College
330 Powell Avenue
Newburgh, NY   12550-3494
845-561-0800
www.msmc.edu

Nazareth College of
Rochester
4245 East Avenue
Rochester, NY   14618-3790
716-389-2525
www.naz.edu

New School Bachelor of Arts,
New School University
66 West 12th Street
New York, NY   10011-8603
212-229-5600
www.newschool.edu

New York Institute of
Technology
PO Box 8000
Old Westbury, NY
11568-8000
516-686-7516
www.nyit.edu

New York School of Interior
Design
170 East 70th Street
New York, NY   10021-5110
212-472-1500
www.nysid.edu

New York University
70 Washington Square South
New York, NY   10012-1019
212-998-1212
www.nyu.edu

Niagara University
Niagara University, NY
14109
716-285-1212
www.niagara.edu

Nyack College
One South Boulevard
Nyack, NY   10960-3698
845-358-1710
www.nyackcollege.edu

Ohr Hameir Theological
Seminary
Furnace Woods Road
Peekskill, NY   10566
914-736-1500

Ohr Somayach/Joseph
Tanenbaum Educational
Center
PO Box 334, 244 Route 306
Monsey, NY   10952-0334
914-425-1370

Pace University
One Pace Plaza
New York, NY   10038
212-346-1200
www.pace.edu

Parsons School of Design,
New School University
66 Fifth Avenue
New York, NY   10011-8878
212-229-8900
www.parsons.edu

Paul Smith's College of Arts
and Sciences
PO Box 265
Paul Smiths, NY   12970-0265
518-327-6000
www.paulsmiths.edu

Plattsburgh State University
of New York
101 Broad Steet
Plattsburgh, NY   12901-2681
518-564-2000
www.plattsburgh.edu

Polytechnic University,
Brooklyn Campus
Six Metrotech Center
Brooklyn, NY   11201-2990
718-260-3600
www.poly.edu

Practical Bible College
PO Box 601
Bible School Park, NY
13737-0601
607-729-1581
www.practical.edu

Pratt Institute
200 Willoughby Avenue
Brooklyn, NY   11205-3899
718-636-3600
www.pratt.edu

Purchase College, State
University of New York
735 Anderson Hill Road
Purchase, NY   10577-1400
914-251-6000
www.purchase.edu

Queens College of the City
University of New York
65-30 Kissena Boulevard
Flushing, NY   11367-1597
718-997-5000
www.qc.edu

Rabbinical Academy Mesivta
Rabbi Chaim Berlin
1605 Coney Island Avenue
Brooklyn, NY   11230-4715
718-377-0777

Rabbinical College Beth
Shraga
28 Saddle River Road
Monsey, NY   10952-3035
914-356-1980

Rabbinical College Bobover
Yeshiva B'nei Zion
1577 Forty-eighth Street
Brooklyn, NY   11219
718-438-2018

Rabbinical College Ch'san
Sofer
1876 Fiftieth Street
Brooklyn, NY   11204
718-236-1171

Rabbinical College of Long
Island
201 Magnolia Boulevard
Long Beach, NY   11561-3305
516-431-7414

Rabbinical Seminary Adas
Yereim
185 Wilson Street
Brooklyn, NY   11211-7206
718-388-1751

Rabbinical Seminary M'kor
Chaim
1571 Fifty-fifth Street
Brooklyn, NY   11219
718-851-0183

Rabbinical Seminary of
America
92-15 Sixty-ninth Avenue
Forest Hills, NY   11375
718-268-4700

Rensselaer Polytechnic
Institute
110 8th Street
Troy, NY   12180-3590
518-276-6000
www.rpi.edu

Roberts Wesleyan College
2301 Westside Drive
Rochester, NY   14624-1997
716-594-6000
www.roberts.edu

Rochester Institute of
Technology
One Lomb Memorial Drive
Rochester, NY   14623-5698
716-475-2411
www.rit.edu

Russell Sage College
45 Ferry Street
Troy, NY   12180-4115
518-244-2000
www.sage.edu/html/rsc/
welcome.html

Sarah Lawrence College
1 Mead Way
Bronxville, NY   10708
914-337-0700
www.slc.edu

School of Visual Arts
209 East 23rd Street
New York, NY   10010-3994
212-592-2000
www.schoolofvisualarts.edu

Sh'or Yoshuv Rabbinical
College
1526 Central Avenue
Far Rockaway, NY
11691-4002
718-327-2048

Siena College
515 Loudon Road
Loudonville, NY   12211-1462
518-783-2300
www.siena.edu

Skidmore College
815 North Broadway
Saratoga Springs, NY
12866-1632
518-580-5000
www.skidmore.edu

St. Bonaventure University
Route 417
St. Bonaventure, NY
14778-2284
716-375-2000
www.sbu.edu

St. Francis College
180 Remsen Street
Brooklyn Heights, NY
11201-4398
718-522-2300
www.stfranciscollege.edu

St. John Fisher College
3690 East Avenue
Rochester, NY   14618-3597
716-385-8000
www.sjfc.edu

St. John's University
8000 Utopia Parkway
Jamaica, NY   11439
718-990-6161
www.stjohns.edu

St. Joseph's College,
New York
245 Clinton Avenue
Brooklyn, NY   11205-3688
718-636-6800
www.sjcnj.edu

St. Joseph's College, Suffolk
Campus
155 West Roe Boulevard
Patchogue, NY   11772-2399
631-447-3200
www.sjcny.edu

St. Lawrence University
Canton, NY   13617-1455
315-229-5011
www.stlawu.edu

St. Thomas Aquinas College
125 Route 340
Sparkill, NY   10976
845-398-4000
www.stac.edu

State University of New York
at Albany
1400 Washington Avenue
Albany, NY   12222-0001
518-442-3300
www.albany.edu

State University of New York
at Binghamton
PO Box 6000
Binghamton, NY
13902-6000
607-777-2000
www.binghamton.edu

State University of New York
at Farmingdale
Route 110
Farmingdale, NY   11735
631-420-2000
www.farmingdale.edu

State University of New York
at New Paltz
75 South Manheim
Boulevard
New Paltz, NY   12561
845-257-2121
www.newpaltz.edu

State University of New York
at Oswego
Oswego, NY   13126
315-312-2500
www.oswego.edu

State University of New York
College at Brockport
350 New Campus Drive
Brockport, NY   14420-2997
716-395-2211
www.brockport.edu

State University of New York
College at Buffalo
1300 Elmwood Avenue
Buffalo, NY   14222-1095
716-878-4000
Fax: 716-878-6100
www.buffalostate.edu

State University of New York
College at Cortland
PO Box 2000
Cortland, NY   13045
607-753-2011
www.cortland.edu

State University of New York
College at Fredonia
Fredonia, NY   14063-1136
716-673-3111
www.fredonia.edu

State University of New York
College at Geneseo
1 College Circle
Geneseo, NY   14454-1401
716-245-5211
www.geneseo.edu

State University of New York
College at Old Westbury
PO Box 210
Old Westbury, NY
11568-0210
516-876-3000
www.oldwestbury.edu

State University of New York
College at Oneonta
Ravine Parkway
Oneonta, NY   13820-4015
607-436-3500
www.oneonta.edu

State University of New York
College at Potsdam
44 Pierrepont Avenue
Potsdam, NY   13676
315-267-2000
www.potsdam.edu

State University of New York
College of Agriculture and
Technology
at Cobleskill
Cobleskill, NY   12043
518-255-5011
www.cobleskill.edu

State University of New York
College of Environmental
Science and Forestry
1 Forestry Drive
Syracuse, NY   13210-2779
315-470-6500
www.esf.edu

State University of New York
College of Technology at
Canton
Cornell Drive
Canton, NY   13617
315-386-7011
www.canton.edu

State University of New York
Empire State College
1 Union Avenue
Saratoga Springs, NY
12866-4391
518-587-2100
www.esc.edu

State University of New York
Health Science Center at
Brooklyn
450 Clarkson Avenue
Brooklyn, NY   11203-2098
718-270-1000
www.downstate.edu

State University of New York
Institute of Technology at
Utica/Rome
PO Box 3050
Utica, NY   13504-3050
315-792-7100
www.sunyit.edu

State University of New York
Maritime College
6 Pennyfield Avenue
Throggs Neck, NY
10465-4198
718-409-7200
www.sunymaritime.edu

State University of New York
Upstate Medical University
750 East Adams Street
Syracuse, NY   13210-2334
315-464-5540
www.upstate.edu

Stony Brook University, State
University of New York
Nicolls Road
Stony Brook, NY   11794
631-689-6000
www.sunysb.edu

Syracuse University
Syracuse, NY   13244-0003
315-443-1870
www.syracuse.edu

Talmudical Institute of
Upstate New York
769 Park Avenue
Rochester, NY   14607-3046
716-473-2810

Talmudical Seminary Oholei
Torah
667 Eastern Parkway
Brooklyn, NY   11213-3310
718-774-5050

Torah Temimah Talmudical
Seminary
507 Ocean Parkway
Brooklyn, NY   11218-5913
718-853-8500

Touro College
27-33 West 23rd Street
New York, NY   10010
212-463-0400
www.touro.edu

Union College
Schenectady, NY
12308-2311
518-388-6000
www.union.edu

United States Merchant
Marine Academy
300 Steamboat Road
Kings Point, NY   11024-1699
516-773-5000
www.usmma.edu

United States Military
Academy
600 Thayer Road
West Point, NY   10996
845-938-4011
www.usma.edu

United Talmudical Seminary
82 Lee Avenue
Brooklyn, NY   11211-7900
718-963-9260

University at Buffalo, The
State University of New York
Capen Hall
Buffalo, NY   14260
716-645-2000
www.buffalo.edu

University of Rochester
Wilson Boulevard
Rochester, NY   14627-0250
716-275-2121
www.rochester.edu

Utica College of Syracuse
University
1600 Burrstone Road
Utica, NY   13502-4892
315-792-3111
www.utica.edu

Vassar College
124 Raymond Avenue
Poughkeepsie, NY   12604
845-437-7000
www.vassar.edu

Wadhams Hall Seminary-
College
6866 State Highway 37
Ogdensburg, NY   13669
315-393-4231
www.wadhams.edu

Wagner College
1 Campus Road
Staten Island, NY
10301-4495
718-390-3100
www.wagner.edu

Webb Institute
Crescent Beach Road
Glen Cove, NY   11542-1398
516-671-2213
www.webb-institute.edu

Wells College
Aurora, NY   13026
315-364-3266
www.wells.edu

Yeshiva Derech Chaim
1573 39th Street
Brooklyn, NY   11218
718-438-3070

Yeshiva Karlin Stolin
Rabbinical Institute
1818 Fifty-fourth Street
Brooklyn, NY   11204
718-232-7800

Yeshiva of Nitra Rabbinical
College
Pines Bridge Road
Mount Kisco, NY   10549
718-384-5460

Yeshiva Shaar Hatorah
Talmudic Research Institute
117-06 84th Avenue
Kew Gardens, NY
11418-1469
718-846-1940

Yeshiva University
500 West 185th Street
New York, NY   10033-3201
212-960-5400
www.yu.edu

Yeshivat Mikdash Melech
1326 Ocean Parkway
Brooklyn, NY   11230-5601
718-339-1090

Yeshivath Viznitz
Phyllis Terrace, PO Box 446
Monsey, NY   10952
914-356-1010

Yeshivath Zichron Moshe
Laurel Park Road
South Fallsburg, NY   12779
914-434-5240

York College of the City
University of New York
94-20 Guy R Brewer Blvd
Jamaica, NY   11451-0001
718-262-2000
www.york.cuny.edu

North Carolina

Appalachian State University
Boone, NC 28608
828-262-2000
www.appstate.edu

Barber-Scotia College
145 Cabarrus Avenue, West
Concord, NC 28025-5187
800-610-0778
www.barber-scotia.edu

Barton College
PO Box 5000
Wilson, NC 27893-7000
800-345-4973
www.barton.edu

Belmont Abbey College
100 Belmont-Mt. Holly Road
Belmont, NC 28012-1802
888-BAC-0110
www.belmontabbeycollege.
edu

Bennett College
900 East Washington Street
Greensboro, NC 27401-3239
336-273-4431
www.bennett.edu

Brevard College
400 North Broad Street
Brevard, NC 28712-3306
800-527-9090
www.brevard.edu

Campbell University
Buies Creek, NC 27506
800-334-4111
www.campbell.edu

Catawba College
2300 West Innes Street
Salisbury, NC 28144-2488
800-CATAWBA
www.catawba.edu

Chowan College
PO Box 1848
Murfreesboro, NC 27855
800-488-4101
www.chowan.edu

Davidson College
PO Box 5000
Davidson, NC 28035-5000
800-768-0380
www.davidson.edu

Duke University
Durham, NC 27708-0586
919-684-8111
www.duke.edu

East Carolina University
East Fifth Street
Greenville, NC 27858-4353
252-328-6131
www.ecu.edu

Elizabeth City State
University
1704 Weeksville Road
Elizabeth City, NC 27909-7806
800-347-3278
www.ecsu.edu

Elon University
2700 Campus Box
Elon, NC 27244-2010
800-334-8448
www.elon.edu

Fayetteville State University
1200 Murchison Road
Fayetteville, NC 28301-4298
800-222-2594
www.uncfsu.edu

Gardner-Webb University
PO Box 997
Boiling Springs, NC 28017
800-253-6472
www.gardner-webb.edu

Greensboro College
815 West Market Street
Greensboro, NC 27401-1875
800-346-8226
www.gborocollege.edu

Guilford College
5800 West Friendly Avenue
Greensboro, NC 27410-4173
800-992-7759
www.guilford.edu

Heritage Bible College
PO Box 1628
Dunn, NC 28335-1628
910-892-3178
www.pfwb.org/non-frames/
hbc/index.htm

High Point University
University Station, Montlieu Ave
High Point, NC 27262-3598
800-345-6993
www.highpoint.edu

John Wesley College
2314 North Centennial Street
High Point, NC 27265-3197
336-889-2262
www.johnwesley.edu

Johnson C. Smith University
100 Beatties Ford Road
Charlotte, NC 28216-5398
800-782-7303
www.jcsu.edu

Lees-McRae College
PO Box 128
Banner Elk, NC 28604-0128
800-280-4562
www.lmc.edu

Lenoir-Rhyne College
7th Avenue and 8th Street, NE
Hickory, NC 28603
800-277-5721
www.lrc.edu

Livingstone College
701 West Monroe Street
Salisbury, NC 28144-5298
800-835-3435
www.livingstone.edu

Mars Hill College
PO Box 370
Mars Hill, NC 28754
800-543-1514
www.mhc.edu

Meredith College
3800 Hillsborough Street
Raleigh, NC 27607-5298
800-MEREDITH
www.meredith.edu

Methodist College
5400 Ramsey Street
Fayetteville, NC 28311-1420
800-488-7110
www.methodist.edu

Montreat College
PO Box 1267
Montreat, NC 28757-1267
828-669-8012
www.montreat.edu

Mount Olive College
634 Henderson Street
Mount Olive, NC 28365
919-658-2502
www.mountolivecollege.edu

North Carolina Agricultural
and Technical State
University
1601 East Market Street
Greensboro, NC 27411
336-334-7500
www.ncat.edu

North Carolina Central
University
1801 Fayetteville Street
Durham, NC 27707-3129
919-560-6100
www.nccu.edu

North Carolina School of the
Arts
1533 South Main Street,
PO Box 12189
Winston-Salem, NC
27127-2188
336-770-3399
www.ncarts.edu

North Carolina State
University
Raleigh, NC 27695
919-515-2011
www.ncsu.edu

North Carolina Wesleyan
College
3400 North Wesleyan Blvd
Rocky Mount, NC 27804-8677
800-488-6292
www.ncwc.edu

Peace College
15 East Peace Street
Raleigh, NC 27604-1194
800-PEACE-47
www.peace.edu

Pfeiffer University
PO Box 960
Misenheimer, NC 28109-0960
800-338-2060
www.pfeiffer.edu

Piedmont Baptist College
716 Franklin Street
Winston-Salem, NC
27101-5197
800-937-5097
www.pbc.edu

Queens University of
Charlotte
1900 Selwyn Avenue
Charlotte, NC 28274-0002
800-849-0202
www.queens.edu

Roanoke Bible College
715 North Poindexter Street
Elizabeth City, NC 27909-4054
800-RBC-8980
www.roanokebible.edu

Saint Augustine's College
1315 Oakwood Avenue
Raleigh, NC 27610-2298
800-948-1126
www.st-aug.edu

Salem College
PO Box 10548
Winston-Salem, NC
27108-0548
800-327-2536
www.salem.edu

Shaw University
118 East South Street
Raleigh, NC 27601-2399
800-214-6683
www.shawuniversity.edu

St. Andrews Presbyterian
College
1700 Dogwood Mile
Laurinburg, NC 28352-5598
800-763-0198
www.sapc.edu

The University of North
Carolina at Asheville
One University Heights
Asheville, NC 28804-3299
800-531-9842
www.unca.edu

The University of North
Carolina at Chapel Hill
Chapel Hill, NC 27599
919-962-2211
www.unc.edu

The University of North
Carolina at Charlotte
9201 University City Blvd
Charlotte, NC 28223-0001
704-687-2000
www.uncc.edu

The University of North
Carolina at Greensboro
1000 Spring Garden Street
Greensboro, NC 27412-5001
336-334-5000
www.uncg.edu

The University of North
Carolina at Pembroke
One University Drive,
PO Box 1510
Pembroke, NC 28372-1510
800-949-uncp
www.uncp.edu

The University of North
Carolina at Wilmington
601 South College Road
Wilmington, NC 28403-3297
800-228-5571
www.uncwil.edu

Wake Forest University
Reynolda Station
Winston-Salem, NC 27109
336-758-5000
www.wfu.edu

Warren Wilson College
PO Box 9000
Asheville, NC 28815-9000
800-934-3536
www.warren-wilson.edu

Western Carolina University
Cullowhee, NC 28723
877-WCU4YOU
www.wcu.edu

Wingate University
PO Box 159
Wingate, NC 28174-0159
800-755-5550
www.wingate.edu

Winston-Salem State
University
601 Martin Luther King Jr Dr
Winston-Salem, NC
27110-0003
800-257-4052
www.wssu.edu

North Dakota

Dickinson State University
8th Avenue West and 3rd St
West
Dickinson, ND 58601-4896
701-483-2507
www.dsu.nodak.edu

Jamestown College
6000 College Lane
Jamestown, ND 58405
701-252-3467
www.jc.edu

Mayville State University
330 3rd Street, NE
Mayville, ND 58257-1299
701-786-2301
www.masu.nodak.edu

Medcenter One College of
Nursing
512 North 7th Street
Bismarck, ND 58501-4494
701-323-6271
www.medcenterone.com/
nursing/nursing.htm

Minot State University
500 University Avenue West
Minot, ND 58707-0002
701-858-3000
www.minotstateu.edu

North Dakota State
University
University Station,
PO Box 5454
Fargo, ND 58105-5454
701-231-8011
www.ndsu.edu

Trinity Bible College
50 South 6th Avenue
Ellendale, ND 58436-7150
701-349-3621

University of Mary
7500 University Drive
Bismarck, ND 58504-9652
701-255-7500
www.umary.edu

University of North Dakota
Grand Forks, ND 58202
701-777-2011
www.und.edu

Valley City State University
101 College Street, SW
Valley City, ND 58072
701-845-7990
www.vcsu.nodak.edu

Ohio

Antioch College
795 Livermore Street
Yellow Springs, OH
45387-1697
937-754-5000
www.antioch-college.edu

Antioch University McGregor
800 Livermore Street
Yellow Springs, OH
45387-1609
937-769-1800
www.mcgregor.edu

Art Academy of Cincinnati
1125 Saint Gregory Street
Cincinnati, OH 45202-1799
513-721-5205
www.artacademy.edu

Ashland University
401 College Avenue
Ashland, OH 44805-3702
419-289-4142
www.ashland.edu

Baldwin-Wallace College
275 Eastland Road
Berea, OH 44017-2088
440-826-2900
www.bw.edu

Bluffton College
280 West College Avenue
Bluffton, OH 45817-1196
419-358-3000
www.bluffton.edu

Bowling Green State
University
Bowling Green, OH 43403
419-372-2531
www.bgsu.edu

Bryant and Stratton College
1700 East 13th Street
Cleveland, OH 44114-3203
216-771-1700
www.bryantstratton.edu

Case Western Reserve
University
10900 Euclid Avenue
Cleveland, OH 44106
216-368-2000
www.cwru.edu

Capital University
2199 East Main Street
Columbus, OH 43209-2394
614-236-6011
www.capital.edu

Cedarville University
251 North Main Street
Cedarville, OH 45314-0601
937-766-2211
www.cedarville.edu

Central State University
1400 Brush Row Road,
PO Box 1004
Wilberforce, OH 45384
937-376-6011
www.centralstate.edu

Cincinnati Bible College and
Seminary
2700 Glenway Avenue,
PO Box 04320
Cincinnati, OH 45204-3200
513-244-8100
www.cincybible.edu

Circleville Bible College
1476 Lancaster Pike,
PO Box 458
Circleville, OH 43113-9487
740-474-8896
www.biblecollege.edu

Cleveland College of Jewish
Studies
26500 Shaker Boulevard
Beachwood, OH 44122-7116
216-464-4050
www.ccjs.edu

The Cleveland Institute of Art
11141 East Boulevard
Cleveland, OH 44106-1700
216-421-7000
www.cia.edu

Cleveland Institute of Music
11021 East Boulevard
Cleveland, OH 44106-1776
216-791-5000
www.cim.edu

Cleveland State University
1983 East 24th Street
Cleveland, OH 44115
216-687-2000
www.csuohio.edu

College of Mount St. Joseph
5701 Delhi Road
Cincinnati, OH 45233-1670
513-244-4200
www.msj.edu

The College of Wooster
1189 Beall Avenue
Wooster, OH 44691-2363
330-263-2000
www.wooster.edu

Columbus College of Art and
Design
107 North Ninth Street
Columbus, OH 43215-1758
614-224-9101
www.ccad.edu

David N. Myers College
112 Prospect Avenue
Cleveland, OH 44115-1096
216-696-9000
www.dnmyers.edu

Defiance College
701 North Clinton Street
Defiance, OH 43512-1610
419-784-4010
www.defiance.edu

Denison University
Granville, OH 43023
740-587-0810
www.denison.edu

DeVry Institute of Technology
1350 Alum Creek Drive
Columbus, OH 43209-2705
614-253-7291

Franciscan University of
Steubenville
1235 University Boulevard
Steubenville, OH
43952-1763
740-283-3771
www.franuniv.edu

Franklin University
201 South Grant Avenue
Columbus, OH 43215-5399
614-797-4700
www.franklin.edu

God's Bible School and
College
1810 Young Street
Cincinnati, OH 45210-1599
513-721-7944

Heidelberg College
310 East Market Street
Tiffin, OH 44883-2462
419-448-2000
www.heidelberg.edu

Hiram College
Box 67
Hiram, OH 44234-0067
330-569-3211
www.hiram.edu

John Carroll University
20700 North Park Boulevard
University Heights, OH
44118-4581
216-397-1886
www.jcu.edu

Kent State University
PO Box 5190
Kent, OH 44242-0001
330-672-3000
www.kent.edu

Kenyon College
Gambier, OH 43022-9623
740-427-5000
www.kenyon.edu

Lake Erie College
391 West Washington Street
Painesville, OH 44077-3389
440-352-3361
www.lec.edu

Lourdes College
6832 Convent Boulevard
Sylvania, OH 43560-2898
419-885-3211
www.lourdes.edu

Malone College
515 25th Street, NW
Canton, OH 44709-3897
330-471-8100
www.malone.edu

Marietta College
215 Fifth Street
Marietta, OH 45750-4000
740-376-4643
www.marietta.edu

Miami University
Oxford, OH 45056
513-529-1809
www.muohio.edu

Mount Carmel College of
Nursing
127 South Davis Avenue
Columbus, OH 43222
614-234-5800

Mount Union College
1972 Clark Avenue
Alliance, OH 44601-3993
330-821-5320
www.muc.edu

Mount Vernon Nazarene
College
800 Martinsburg Road
Mount Vernon, OH
43050-9500
740-397-9000
www.mvnc.edu

Muskingum College
163 Stormont Street
New Concord, OH 43762
740-826-8211
www.muskingum.edu

Notre Dame College
4545 College Road
South Euclid, OH
44121-4293
216-381-1680
www.ndc.edu

Oberlin College
173 West Lorain Street
Oberlin, OH 44074
440-775-8121
www.oberlin.edu

Ohio Dominican College
1216 Sunbury Road
Columbus, OH 43219-2099
614-253-2741
www.odc.edu

Ohio Northern University
525 South Main
Ada, OH 45810-1599
419-772-2000
www.onu.edu

The Ohio State University
190 North Oval Mall
Columbus, OH 43210
614-292-6446
www.osu.edu

The Ohio State University at
Lima
4240 Campus Drive
Lima, OH 45804-3576
419-221-1641
www.ohio-state.edu

The Ohio State University at
Marion
1465 Mount Vernon Avenue
Marion, OH 43302-5695
740-389-6786
www.ohio-state.edu

The Ohio State University–
Mansfield Campus
1680 University Drive
Mansfield, OH 44906-1599
419-755-4011
www.ohio-state.edu

The Ohio State University–
Newark Campus
1179 University Drive
Newark, OH 43055-1797
740-366-3321
www.ohio-state.edu

Ohio University
Athens, OH 45701-2979
740-593-1000
www.ohio.edu

Ohio University–Chillicothe
571 West Fifth Street,
PO Box 629
Chillicothe, OH 45601-0629
740-774-7200
www.ohio.edu/chillicothe

Ohio University–Eastern
45425 National Road
St. Clairsville, OH
43950-9724
740-695-1720

Ohio University–Lancaster
1570 Granville Pike
Lancaster, OH 43130-1097
740-654-6711

Ohio University–Southern
Campus
1804 Liberty Avenue
Ironton, OH 45638-2214
740-533-4600
www.ohiou.edu

Ohio University–Zanesville
1425 Newark Road
Zanesville, OH 43701-2695
740-453-0762
www.zanesvile.ohiou.edu

Ohio Wesleyan University
61 South Sandusky Street
Delaware, OH 43015
740-368-2000
web.owu.edu

Otterbein College
1 Otterbein College
Westerville, OH 43081
614-890-3000
www.otterbein.edu

Pontifical College
Josephinum
7625 North High Street
Columbus, OH 43235-1498
614-885-5585
www.pcj.edu

Shawnee State University
940 Second Street
Portsmouth, OH 45662-4344
740-354-3205
www.shawnee.edu

Tiffin University
155 Miami Street
Tiffin, OH 44883-2161
419-447-6442
www.tiffin.edu

The Union Institute
440 East McMillan Street
Cincinnati, OH 45206-1925
513-861-6400
www.tui.edu

The University of Akron
302 Buchtel Common
Akron, OH 44325-0001
330-972-7111
www.uakron.edu

University of Cincinnati
2624 Clifton Avenue
Cincinnati, OH 45221
513-556-6000
www.uc.edu

University of Dayton
300 College Park
Dayton, OH 45469-1300
937-229-1000
www.udayton.edu

The University of Findlay
1000 North Main Street
Findlay, OH 45840-3653
419-422-8313
www.findlay.edu

University of Phoenix–Ohio
Campus
5005 Rockside Road,
Suite 325
Independence, OH 44131
216-447-9144
www.phoenix.edu

University of Rio Grande
218 North College Avenue
Rio Grande, OH 45674
740-245-5353
www.rio.edu

University of Toledo
2801 West Bancroft
Toledo, OH 43606-3398
419-530-4242
www.utoledo.edu

Urbana University
579 College Way
Urbana, OH 43078-2091
937-484-1301
www.urbana.edu

Ursuline College
2550 Lander Road
Pepper Pike, OH 44124-4398
440-449-4200
www.ursuline.edu

Walsh University
2020 Easton Street, NW
North Canton, OH
44720-3396
330-499-7090
www.walsh.edu

Wilberforce University
1055 North Bickett Road
Wilberforce, OH 45384
937-376-2911
www.wilberforce.edu

Wilmington College
Pyle Center Box 1185
Wilmington, OH   45177
937-382-6661
www.wilmington.edu

Wittenberg University
PO Box 720
Springfield, OH   45501-0720
937-327-6231
www.wittenberg.edu

Wright State University
3640 Colonel Glenn Highway
Dayton, OH   45435
937-775-3333
www.wright.edu

Xavier University
3800 Victory Parkway
Cincinnati, OH   45207
513-745-3000
www.xu.edu

Youngstown State University
One University Plaza
Youngstown, OH
44555-0001
330-742-3000
www.ysu.edu

Oklahoma

American Christian College
and Seminary
4300 Highline Boulevard,
Suite 202
Oklahoma City, OK   73108
405-945-0100
www.abcs.edu

Cameron University
2800 West Gore Boulevard
Lawton, OK   73505-6377
580-581-2200
www.cameron.edu

East Central University
1100 East 14th Street
Ada, OK   74820-6899
580-332-8000
www.ecok.edu

Hillsdale Free Will Baptist
College
PO Box 7208
Moore, OK   73153-1208
405-912-9000
www.hc.edu

Langston University
Langston, OK   73050
405-466-2231
www.lunet.edu

Metropolitan College
4528 South Sheridan Road,
Suite 105
Tulsa, OK   74145-1011
918-627-9300
www.metropolitancollege.edu

Metropolitan College
2901 North Classen
Boulevard, Suite 200
Oklahoma City, OK   73106
405-528-5000
www.metropolitancollege.edu

Mid-America Bible College
3500 Southwest 119th Street
Oklahoma City, OK
73170-4504
405-691-3800
www.mabc.edu

Northeastern State
University
600 North Grand
Tahlequah, OK   74464-2399
918-456-5511
www.nsuok.edu

Northwestern Oklahoma
State University
709 Oklahoma Boulevard
Alva, OK   73717-2799
580-327-1700
www.nwosu.edu

Oklahoma Baptist University
500 West University
Shawnee, OK   74804
405-275-2850
www.okbu.edu

Oklahoma Christian
University
PO Box 11000
Oklahoma City, OK
73136-1100
405-425-5000
www.oc.edu

Oklahoma City University
2501 North Blackwelder
Oklahoma City, OK
73106-1402
405-521-5000
www.okcu.edu

Oklahoma Panhandle State
University
PO Box 430
Goodwell, OK   73939-0430
580-349-2611
www.opsu.edu

Oklahoma State University
Stillwater, OK   74078
405-744-5000
www.okstate.edu

Oklahoma Wesleyan
University
2201 Silver Lake Road
Bartlesville, OK   74006-6299
918-333-6151
www.okwu.edu

Oral Roberts University
7777 South Lewis Avenue
Tulsa, OK   74171-0001
918-495-6161
www.oru.edu

Rogers State University
1701 West Will Rogers Blvd
Claremore, OK   74017-3252
918-343-7777
www.rsu.edu

Southeastern Oklahoma
State University
Fifth and University
Durant, OK   74701-0609
580-745-2000
www.sosu.edu

Southern Nazarene
University
6729 Northwest 39th Expwy
Bethany, OK   73008
405-789-6400
www.snu.edu

Southwestern College of
Christian Ministries
PO Box 340
Bethany, OK   73008-0340
405-789-7661
www.sccm.edu

Southwestern Oklahoma
State University
100 Campus Drive
Weatherford, OK
73096-3098
580-772-6611
www.swosu.edu

St. Gregory's University
1900 West MacArthur Drive
Shawnee, OK   74804-2499
405-878-5100
www.sgc.edu

University of Central
Oklahoma
100 North University Drive
Edmond, OK   73034-5209
405-974-2000
www.ucok.edu

University of Oklahoma
660 Parrington Oval
Norman, OK   73019-0390
405-325-0311
www.ou.edu

University of Oklahoma
Health Sciences Center
PO Box 26901
Oklahoma City, OK   73190
405-271-4000
www.uokhsc.edu

University of Phoenix–
Oklahoma City Campus
6501 North Broadway,
Suite 100
Oklahoma City, OK   73116
405-842-8007
www.phoenix.edu

University of Phoenix–Tulsa
Campus
10810 East 45th Street,
Suite 103
Tulsa, OK   74146
918-622-4877
www.phoenix.edu

University of Science and
Arts of Oklahoma
1727 West Alabama
Chickasha, OK   73018
405-224-3140
www.usao.edu

University of Tulsa
600 South College Avenue
Tulsa, OK   74104-3189
918-631-2000
www.utulsa.edu

Oregon

The Art Institute of Portland
2000 Southwest Fifth Avenue
Portland, OR 97201-4907
503-228-6528
www.aipd.artinstitutes.edu

Cascade College
9101 East Burnside Street
Portland, OR 97216-1515
503-255-7060
www.cascade.edu

Concordia University
2811 Northeast Holman
Portland, OR 97211-6099
503-288-9371
www.cu-portland.edu

Eastern Oregon University
1 University Boulevard
La Grande, OR 97850-2899
541-962-3672
www.eou.edu

Eugene Bible College
2155 Bailey Hill Road
Eugene, OR 97405-1194
541-485-1780
www.ebc.edu

George Fox University
414 North Meridian
Newberg, OR 97132-2697
503-538-8383
www.georgefox.edu

Lewis & Clark College
0615 SW Palatine Hill Road
Portland, OR 97219-7899
503-768-7000
www.lclark.edu

Linfield College
900 SE Baker Street
McMinnville, OR 97128-6894
503-434-2200
www.linfield.edu

Marylhurst University
PO Box 261
Marylhurst, OR 97036-0261
503-636-8141
www.marylhurst.edu

Mount Angel Seminary
Saint Benedict, OR 97373
503-845-3951

Multnomah Bible College
and Biblical Seminary
8435 Northeast Glisan Street
Portland, OR 97220-5898
503-255-0332
www.multnomah.edu

Northwest Christian College
828 East 11th Avenue
Eugene, OR 97401-3745
541-343-1641
www.nwcc.edu

Oregon College of Art & Craft
8245 Southwest Barnes Road
Portland, OR 97225
503-297-5544
www.ocac.edu

Oregon Health & Science
University
3181 SW Sam Jackson Park Rd
Portland, OR 97201-3098
503-494-8311
www.ohsu.edu

Oregon Institute of
Technology
3201 Campus Drive
Klamath Falls, OR 97601-8801
541-885-1000
www.oit.edu

Oregon State University
Corvallis, OR 97331
541-737-1000
osu.orst.edu

Pacific Northwest College of
Art
1241 NW Johnson Street
Portland, OR 97209
503-226-4391
www.pnca.edu

Pacific University
2043 College Way
Forest Grove, OR 97116-1797
503-357-6151
www.pacificu.edu

Portland State University
PO Box 751
Portland, OR 97207-0751
503-725-3000
www.pdx.edu

Reed College
3203 Southeast Woodstock
Boulevard
Portland, OR 97202-8199
503-771-1112
www.reed.edu

Southern Oregon University
1250 Siskiyou Boulevard
Ashland, OR 97520
541-552-7672
www.sou.edu

University of Oregon
Eugene, OR 97403
541-346-3111
www.uoregon.edu

University of
Phoenix–Oregon Campus
13221 SW 68th Parkway,
Suite 500
Portland, OR 97223
503-670-0590
www.phoenix.edu

University of Portland
5000 North Willamette
Boulevard
Portland, OR 97203-5798
503-943-7911
www.up.edu

Warner Pacific College
2219 Southeast 68th Avenue
Portland, OR 97215-4099
503-517-1000
www.warnerpacific.edu

Western Baptist College
5000 Deer Park Drive, SE
Salem, OR 97301-9392
503-581-8600
www.wbc.edu

Western Oregon University
345 North Monmouth Ave
Monmouth, OR 97361-1394
503-838-8000
www.wou.edu

Western States Chiropractic
College
2900 Northeast 132nd Ave
Portland, OR 97230-3099
503-256-3180
www.wschiro.edu

Willamette University
900 State Street
Salem, OR 97301-3931
503-370-6300
www.willamette.edu

Pennsylvania

Albright College
13th and Bern Sreets,
PO Box 15234
Reading, PA   19612-5234
610-921-2381
www.albright.edu

Allegheny College
520 North Main Street
Meadville, PA   16335
814-332-3100
www.allegheny.edu

Alvernia College
400 Saint Bernardine Street
Reading, PA   19607-1799
610-796-8200
www.alvernia.edu

Arcadia University
450 South Easton Road
Glenside, PA   19038-3295
215-572-2900
www.arcadia.edu

Baptist Bible College of
Pennsylvania
538 Venard Road
Clarks Summit, PA
18411-1297
570-586-2400
www.bbc.edu

Bloomsburg University of
Pennsylvania
400 East Second Street
Bloomsburg, PA   17815-1905
570-389-4000
www.bloomu.edu

Bryn Athyn College of the
New Church
PO Box 717
Bryn Athyn, PA   19009-0717
215-938-2543
www.newchurch.edu/college

Bryn Mawr College
101 North Merion Avenue
Bryn Mawr, PA   19010-2899
610-526-5000
www.brynmawr.edu

Bucknell University
Lewisburg, PA   17837
570-577-2000
www.bucknell.edu

Cabrini College
610 King of Prussia Road
Radnor, PA   19087-3698
610-902-8100
www.cabrini.edu

California University of
Pennsylvania
250 University Avenue
California, PA   15419-1394
724-938-4000
www.cup.edu

Carlow College
3333 Fifth Avenue
Pittsburgh, PA   15213-3165
412-578-6005
www.carlow.edu

Carnegie Mellon University
5000 Forbes Avenue
Pittsburgh, PA   15213-3891
412-268-2000
www.cmu.edu

Cedar Crest College
100 College Drive
Allentown, PA   18104-6196
610-437-4471
www.cedarcrest.edu

Chatham College
Woodland Road
Pittsburgh, PA   15232-2826
412-365-1100
www.chatham.edu

Chestnut Hill College
9601 Germantown Avenue
Philadelphia, PA 19118-2693
215-248-7000
www.chc.edu

Cheyney University of
Pennsylvania
Cheyney and Creek Roads
Cheyney, PA 19319
610-399-2000
www.cheyney.edu

Clarion University of
Pennsylvania
Clarion, PA 16214
814-393-2000
www.clarion.edu

College Misericordia
301 Lake Street
Dallas, PA 18612-1098
570-674-6400
www.miseri.edu

The Curtis Institute of Music
1726 Locust Street
Philadelphia, PA 19103-6107
215-893-5252

Delaware Valley College
700 East Butler Avenue
Doylestown, PA 18901-2697
215-345-1500
www.devalcol.edu

DeSales University
2755 Station Avenue
Center Valley, PA
18034-9568
610-282-1100
www.desales.edu

Dickinson College
PO Box 1773
Carlisle, PA 17013-2896
717-243-5121
www.dickinson.edu

Drexel University
3141 Chestnut Street
Philadelphia, PA 19104-2875
215-895-2000
www.drexel.edu

Duquesne University
600 Forbes Avenue
Pittsburgh, PA 15282-0001
412-396-6000
www.duq.edu

East Stroudsburg University
of Pennsylvania
200 Prospect Street
East Stroudsburg, PA
18301-2999
570-422-3211
www.esu.edu

Eastern College
1300 Eagle Road
St. Davids, PA 19087-3696
610-341-5800
www.eastern.edu

Edinboro University of
Pennsylvania
Edinboro, PA 16444
814-732-2000
www.edinboro.edu

Elizabethtown College
1 Alpha Drive
Elizabethtown, PA
17022-2298
717-361-1000
www.etown.edu

Franklin and Marshall
College
PO Box 3003
Lancaster, PA 17604-3003
717-291-3911
www.fandm.edu

Gannon University
University Square
Erie, PA 16541-0001
814-871-7000
www.gannon.edu

Geneva College
3200 College Avenue
Beaver Falls, PA 15010-3599
724-846-5100
www.geneva.edu

Gettysburg College
300 North Washington Street
Gettysburg, PA 17325-1483
717-337-6000
www.gettysburg.edu

Gratz College
7605 Old York Road
Melrose Park, PA 19027
215-635-7300
www.gratzcollege.edu

Grove City College
100 Campus Drive
Grove City, PA 16127-2104
724-458-2000
www.gcc.edu

Gwynedd-Mercy College
Sumneytown Pike
Gwynedd Valley, PA
19437-0901
215-646-7300
www.gmc.edu

Haverford College
370 Lancaster Avenue
Haverford, PA 19041-1392
610-896-1000
www.haverford.edu

Holy Family College
Grant and Frankford Avenues
Philadelphia, PA 19114-2094
215-637-7700
www.hfc.edu

Immaculata College
1145 King Road, Box 500
Immaculata, PA 19345-0500
610-647-4400
www.immaculata.edu

Indiana University of
Pennsylvania
Indiana, PA 15705-1087
724-357-2100
www.iup.edu

Juniata College
1700 Moore Street
Huntingdon, PA 16652-2119
814-641-3000
www.juniata.edu

King's College
133 North River Street
Wilkes-Barre, PA 18711-0801
570-208-5900
www.kings.edu

Kutztown University of
Pennsylvania
PO Box 730
Kutztown, PA 19530-0730
610-683-4000
www.kutztown.edu

La Roche College
9000 Babcock Boulevard
Pittsburgh, PA 15237-5898
412-367-9300
www.laroche.edu

La Salle University
1900 West Olney Avenue
Philadelphia, PA 19141-1199
215-951-1000
www.lasalle.edu

Lafayette College
Easton, PA 18042-1798
610-330-5000
www.lafayette.edu

Lancaster Bible College
901 Eden Road,
PO Box 83403
Lancaster, PA 17608-3403
717-569-7071
www.lbc.edu

Lebanon Valley College
101 North College Avenue
Annville, PA 17003-1400
717-867-6100
www.lvc.edu

Lehigh University
27 Memorial Drive West
Bethlehem, PA 18015-3094
610-758-3000
www.lehigh.edu

Lincoln University
PO Box 179
Lincoln University, PA 19352
610-932-8300
www.lincoln.edu

Lock Haven University of
Pennsylvania
North Fairview Street
Lock Haven, PA 17745-2390
570-893-2011
www.lhup.edu

Lycoming College
700 College Place
Williamsport, PA 17701-5192
570-321-4000
www.lycoming.edu

Mansfield University of
Pennsylvania
Academy Street
Mansfield, PA 16933
570-662-4000
www.mansfield.edu

Marywood University
2300 Adams Avenue
Scranton, PA 18509-1598
570-348-6211
www.marywood.edu

MCP Hahnemann University
245 North 15th Street
Philadelphia, PA 19102-1192
215-762-7000
www.mcphu.edu

Mercyhurst College
501 East 38th Street
Erie, PA 16546
814-824-2000
www.mercyhurst.edu

Messiah College
One College Avenue
Grantham, PA 17027
717-766-2511
www.messiah.edu

Millersville University of
Pennsylvania
PO Box 1002
Millersville, PA 17551-0302
717-872-3011
www.millersville.edu

Moore College of Art and
Design
20th and the Parkway
Philadelphia, PA 19103
215-568-4515
www.moore.edu

Moravian College
1200 Main Street
Bethlehem, PA 18018-6650
610-861-1300
www.moravian.edu

Mount Aloysius College
7373 Admiral Peary Highway
Cresson, PA 16630-1999
814-886-4131
www.mtaloy.edu

Muhlenberg College
2400 Chew Street
Allentown, PA 18104-5586
484-664-3100
www.muhlenberg.edu

Neumann College
One Neumann Drive
Aston, PA 19014-1298
610-459-0905
www.neumann.edu

Peirce College
1420 Pine Street
Philadelphia, PA 19102-4699
215-545-6400
www.peirce.edu

Pennsylvania College of
Technology
One College Avenue
Williamsport, PA 17701-5778
570-326-3761
www.pct.edu

Pennsylvania School of Art &
Design
204 North Prince Street,
PO Box 59
Lancaster, PA 17608-0059
717-396-7833
www.psad.edu

The Pennsylvania State
University Abington College
1600 Woodland Road
Abington, PA 19001-3918
215-881-7300
www.psu.edu

The Pennsylvania State
University Altoona College
3000 Ivyside Park
Altoona, PA 16601-3760
814-949-5000
www.psu.edu

Pennsylvania State
University at Erie, The
Behrend College
Station Road
Erie, PA 16563
814-898-6000
www.psu.edu

The Pennsylvania State
University Berks Campus of
the Berks–Lehigh Valley
College
Tulpehocken Road,
PO Box 7009
Reading, PA 19610-6009
610-396-6000
www.psu.edu

The Pennsylvania State
University Harrisburg
Campus of the Capital
College
777 West Harrisburg Pike
Middletown, PA 17057-4898
717-948-6000
www.psu.edu

The Pennsylvania State
University Lehigh Valley
Campus of the Berks-Lehigh
Valley College
8380 Mohr Lane
Fogelsville, PA 18051-9999
610-285-5000
www.psu.edu

The Pennsylvania State
University Schuylkill Campus
of the Capital College
200 University Drive
Schuylkill Haven, PA
17972-2208
570-385-6000
www.psu.edu

The Pennsylvania State
University University Park
Campus
201 Old Main
University Park, PA
16802-1503
814-865-4700
www.psu.edu

Philadelphia Biblical
University
200 Manor Avenue
Langhorne, PA 19047-2990
215-752-5800
www.pbu.edu

Philadelphia University
School House Lane and
Henry Avenue
Philadelphia, PA 19144-5497
215-951-2700
www.philau.edu

Point Park College
201 Wood Street
Pittsburgh, PA 15222-1984
412-391-4100
www.ppc.edu

Robert Morris University
881 Narrows Run Road
Moon Township, PA
15108-1189
412-262-8200
www.rmu.edu

Rosemont College
1400 Montgomery Avenue
Rosemont, PA 19010-1699
610-527-0200
www.rosemont.edu

St. Charles Borromeo
Seminary, Overbrook
100 East Wynnewood Road
Wynnewood, PA 19096
610-667-3394

Saint Francis University
PO Box 600,
117 Evergreen Drive
Loretto, PA 15940-0600
814-472-3000
www.sfcpa.edu

Saint Joseph's University
5600 City Avenue
Philadelphia, PA 19131-1395
610-660-1000
www.sju.edu

Saint Vincent College
300 Fraser Purchase Road
Latrobe, PA 15650-2690
724-539-9761
www.stvincent.edu

Seton Hill College
Seton Hill Drive
Greensburg, PA 15601
724-834-2200
www.setonhill.edu

Shippensburg University of
Pennsylvania
1871 Old Main Drive
Shippensburg, PA
17257-2299
717-477-7447
www.ship.edu

Slippery Rock University of
Pennsylvania
Slippery Rock, PA 16057
724-738-9000
www.sru.edu

Susquehanna University
514 University Avenue
Selinsgrove, PA 17870
570-374-0101
www.susqu.edu

Swarthmore College
500 College Avenue
Swarthmore, PA 19081-1397
610-328-8000
www.swarthmore.edu

Talmudical Yeshiva of
Philadelphia
6063 Drexel Road
Philadelphia, PA 19131-1296
215-473-1212

Temple University
1801 North Broad Street
Philadelphia, PA 19122-6096
215-204-7000
www.temple.edu

Thiel College
75 College Avenue
Greenville, PA 16125-2181
724-589-2000
www.thiel.edu

Thomas Jefferson University
Eleventh and Walnut Streets
Philadelphia, PA 19107
215-955-6000
www.tju.edu

The University of Scranton
Scranton, PA 18510
570-941-7400
www.scranton.edu

The University of the Arts
320 South Broad Street
Philadelphia, PA 19102-4944
215-717-6000
www.uarts.edu

University of Pennsylvania
34th and Walnut Streets
Philadelphia, PA 19104
215-898-5000
www.upenn.edu

University of
Phoenix–Philadelphia
Campus
170 South Warner Road,
Suite 200
Wayne, PA 19087
610-989-0880
www.phoenix.edu

University of
Phoenix–Pittsburgh Campus
Penn Center West Four, Suite
100, Mail Stop: 10-1651
Pittsburgh, PA 15276
412-747-9000
www.phoenix.edu

University of Pittsburgh
4200 Fifth Avenue
Pittsburgh, PA 15260
412-624-4141
www.pitt.edu

University of Pittsburgh at
Bradford
300 Campus Drive
Bradford, PA 16701-2812
814-362-7500
www.upb.pitt.edu

University of Pittsburgh at
Greensburg
1150 Mount Pleasant Road
Greensburg, PA 15601-5860
724-837-7040
www.pitt.edu/~upg

University of Pittsburgh at
Johnstown
450 Schoolhouse Road
Johnstown, PA 15904-2990
814-269-7000
info.pitt.edu/~upjweb

University of the Sciences in
Philadelphia
600 South 43rd Street
Philadelphia, PA 19104-4495
215-596-8800
www.usip.edu

Ursinus College
Box 1000, Main Street
Collegeville, PA 19426-1000
610-409-3000
www.ursinus.edu

Valley Forge Christian
College
1401 Charlestown Road
Phoenixville, PA 19460-2399
610-935-0450
www.vfcc.edu

Villanova University
800 Lancaster Avenue
Villanova, PA 19085-1699
610-519-4500
www.villanova.edu

Washington & Jefferson
College
60 South Lincoln Street
Washington, PA 15301-4801
724-222-4400
www.washjeff.edu

Waynesburg College
51 West College Street
Waynesburg, PA 15370-1222
724-627-8191
www.waynesburg.edu

West Chester University of
Pennsylvania
University Avenue and
High Street
West Chester, PA 19383
610-436-1000
www.wcupa.edu

Westminster College
319 South Market Street
New Wilmington, PA
16172-0001
724-946-8761
www.westminster.edu

Widener University
One University Place
Chester, PA 19013-5792
610-499-4000
www.widener.edu

Wilkes University
170 South Franklin St, PO
Box 111
Wilkes-Barre, PA
18766-0002
570-408-5000
www.wilkes.edu

Wilson College
1015 Philadelphia Avenue
Chambersburg, PA
17201-1285
717-264-4141
www.wilson.edu

Yeshiva Beth Moshe
930 Hickory Street,
PO Box 1141
Scranton, PA 18505-2124
717-346-1747

York College of Pennsylvania
York, PA 17405-7199
717-846-7788
www.ycp.edu

Rhode Island

Brown University
Providence, RI 02912
401-863-1000
www.brown.edu

Bryant College
1150 Douglas Pike
Smithfield, RI 02917-1284
401-232-6000
www.bryant.edu

Johnson & Wales University
8 Abbott Park Place
Providence, RI 02903-3703
401-598-1000
www.jwu.edu

Providence College
River Avenue and Eaton St
Providence, RI 02918
401-865-1000
www.providence.edu

Rhode Island College
600 Mount Pleasant Avenue
Providence, RI 02908-1924
401-456-8000
www.ric.edu

Rhode Island School of
Design
2 College Street
Providence, RI 02903-2784
401-454-6100
www.risd.edu

Roger Williams University
1 Old Ferry Road
Bristol, RI 02809
401-253-1040
www.rwu.edu

Salve Regina University
100 Ochre Point Avenue
Newport, RI 02840-4192
401-847-6650
www.salve.edu

University of Rhode Island
Kingston, RI 02881
401-874-1000
www.uri.edu

South Carolina

Allen University
1530 Harden Street
Columbia, SC 29204
803-254-4165

Anderson College
316 Boulevard
Anderson, SC 29621-4035
800-542-3594
www.ac.edu

Benedict College
1600 Harden Street
Columbia, SC 29204
803-256-4220
www.benedict.edu

Charleston Southern
University
PO Box 118087
Charleston, SC 29423-8087
800-947-7474
www.charlestonsouthern.edu

The Citadel, The Military
College of South Carolina
171 Moultrie Street
Charleston, SC 29409
800-868-1842
www.citadel.edu

Claflin University
700 College Avenue, NE
Orangeburg, SC 29115
803-531-2860

Clemson University
Clemson, SC 29634
864-656-3311
www.clemson.edu

Coastal Carolina University
PO Box 261954
Conway, SC 29528-6054
800-277-7000
www.coastal.edu

Coker College
300 East College Avenue
Hartsville, SC 29550
800-950-1908
www.coker.edu

College of Charleston
66 George Street
Charleston, SC 29424-0001
843-953-5507
www.cofc.edu

Columbia College
1301 Columbia College Drive
Columbia, SC 29203-5998
800-277-1301
www.columbiacollegesc.edu

Columbia International
University
PO Box 3122
Columbia, SC 29230-3122
800-777-2227
www.ciu.edu

Converse College
580 East Main Street
Spartanburg, SC 29302-0006
800-766-1125
www.converse.edu

Erskine College
2 Washington Street,
PO Box 338
Due West, SC 29639
800-241-8721
www.erskine.edu

Francis Marion University
PO Box 100547
Florence, SC 29501-0547
800-368-7551
www.fmarion.edu

Furman University
3300 Poinsett Highway
Greenville, SC 29613
864-294-2000
www.furman.edu

Johnson & Wales University
701 East Bay Street
Charleston, SC 29403
800-868-1522
www.jwu.edu

Lander University
320 Stanley Avenue
Greenwood, SC 29649-2099
888-452-6337
www.lander.edu

Limestone College
1115 College Drive
Gaffney, SC 29340
800-795-7151
www.limestone.edu

Medical University of South
Carolina
171 Ashley Avenue
Charleston, SC 29425-0002
843-792-2300
www.musc.edu

Morris College
100 West College Street
Sumter, SC 29150-3599
888-853-1345
www.morris.edu

Newberry College
2100 College Street
Newberry, SC 29108-2197
800-845-4955
www.newberry.edu

North Greenville College
PO Box 1892
Tigerville, SC 29688-1892
800-468-6642
www.ngc.edu

Presbyterian College
503 South Broad Street
Clinton, SC 29325
800-476-7272
www.presby.edu

South Carolina State
University
300 College Street Northeast
Orangeburg, SC 29117-0001
800-260-5956
www.scsu.edu

Southern Methodist College
541 Broughton Stret,
PO Box 1027
Orangeburg, SC 29116-1027
803-534-7826
www.southernmethodistcol-
lege.org

Southern Wesleyan
University
907 Wesleyan Drive,
PO Box 1020
Central, SC 29630-1020
800-289-1292
www.swu.edu

University of South Carolina
Columbia, SC 29208
803-777-7000
www.sc.edu

University of South Carolina
Aiken
471 University Parkway
Aiken, SC 29801-6309
888-WOW-USCA
www.usca.edu

University of South Carolina
Spartanburg
800 University Way
Spartanburg, SC 29303-4999
800-277-8727
www.uscs.edu

Voorhees College
1411 Voorhees Road
Denmark, SC 29042
800-446-6250
www.voorhees.edu

Winthrop University
701 Oakland Avenue
Rock Hill, SC 29733
800-763-0230
www.winthrop.edu

Wofford College
429 North Church Street
Spartanburg, SC 29303-3663
864-597-4000
www.wofford.edu

South Dakota

Augustana College
2001 South Summit Avenue
Sioux Falls, SD 57197
605-274-0770
www.augie.edu

Black Hills State University
1200 University Street
Spearfish, SD 57799
605-642-6011
www.bhsu.edu

Colorado Technical University
Sioux Falls Campus
3901 West 59th Street
Sioux Falls, SD 57108
605-361-0200
www.colotechu.edu

Dakota State University
820 North Washington
Madison, SD 57042-1799
605-256-5111
www.dsu.edu

Dakota Wesleyan University
1200 West University Avenue
Mitchell, SD 57301-4398
605-995-2600
www.dwu.edu

Huron University
333 9th Street SW
Huron, SD 57350-2798
605-352-8721
www.huron.edu

Mount Marty College
1105 West 8th Street
Yankton, SD 57078-3724
605-668-1011
www.mtmc.edu

National American University
321 Kansas City Street
Rapid City, SD 57701
605-394-4800
www.national.edu

National American
University–Sioux Falls
Branch
2801 South Kiwanis Avenue
Sioux Falls, SD 57105-4293
605-334-5430

Northern State University
1200 South Jay Street
Aberdeen, SD 57401-7198
605-626-3011
www.northern.edu

Oglala Lakota College
490 Piya Wiconi Road
Kyle, SD 57752-0490
605-455-2321
www.olc.edu

Presentation College
1500 North Main Street
Aberdeen, SD 57401-1299
605-225-1634
www.presentation.edu

Sinte Gleska University
PO Box 490
Rosebud, SD 57570-0490
605-747-2263
www.sinte.indian.com

South Dakota School of
Mines and Technology
501 East Saint Joseph
Rapid City, SD 57701-3995
605-394-2511
www.sdsmt.edu

South Dakota State
University
PO Box 2201
Brookings, SD 57007
605-688-4151
www.sdstate.edu

University of Sioux Falls
1101 West 22nd Street
Sioux Falls, SD 57105-1699
605-331-5000
www.usiouxfalls.edu

University of South Dakota
414 East Clark Street
Vermillion, SD 57069-2390
605-677-5011
www.usd.edu

Tennessee

American Baptist College of
American Baptist Theological
Seminary
1800 Baptist World Center Dr
Nashville, TN 37207
615-228-7877

Aquinas College
4210 Harding Road
Nashville, TN 37205-2005
615-297-7545
www.aquinas-tn.edu

Austin Peay State University
601 College Street
Clarksville, TN 37044-0001
800-844-2778
www.apsu.edu

Baptist Memorial College of
Health Sciences
1003 Monroe Avenue
Memphis, TN 38104
800-796-7171
www.bmhcc.org/bchs/
index.asp

Belmont University
1900 Belmont Boulevard
Nashville, TN 37212-3757
800-56E-NROL
www.belmont.edu

Bethel College
325 Cherry Avenue
McKenzie, TN 38201
731-352-4000
www.bethel-college.edu

Bryan College
PO Box 7000
Dayton, TN 37321-7000
800-277-9522
www.bryan.edu

Carson-Newman College
1646 Russell Avenue
Jefferson City, TN 37760
800-678-9061
www.cn.edu

Christian Brothers University
650 East Parkway South
Memphis, TN 38104-5581
800-288-7576
www.cbu.edu

Crichton College
6655 Winchester Road,
PO Box 757830
Memphis, TN 38175-7830
800-960-9777
www.crichton.edu

Cumberland University
One Cumberland Square
Lebanon, TN 37087-3554
800-467-0562
www.cumberland.edu

East Tennessee State
University
807 University Parkway
Johnson City, TN 37614
800-462-3878
www.etsu.edu

Fisk University
1000 17th Avenue North
Nashville, TN 37208-3051
800-443-FISK
www.fisk.edu

Free Will Baptist Bible
College
3606 West End Avenue
Nashville, TN 37205-2498
800-763-9222
www.fwbbc.edu

Freed-Hardeman University
158 East Main Street
Henderson, TN 38340-2399
800-630-3480
www.fhu.edu

Johnson Bible College
7900 Johnson Drive
Knoxville, TN 37998-1001
800-827-2122
www.jbc.edu

King College
1350 King College Road
Bristol, TN 37620-2699
800-362-0014
www.king.edu

Lambuth University
705 Lambuth Boulevard
Jackson, TN 38301
800-526-2884
www.lambuth.edu

Lane College
545 Lane Avenue
Jackson, TN 38301-4598
800-960-7533
www.lanecollege.edu

Lee University
PO Box 3450
Cleveland, TN 37320-3450
800-LEE-9930
www.leeuniversity.edu

LeMoyne-Owen College
807 Walker Avenue
Memphis, TN 38126-6595
901-774-9090
www.lemoyne-owen.edu

Lincoln Memorial University
Cumberland Gap Parkway
Harrogate, TN 37752-1901
800-325-0900
www.lmunet.edu

Lipscomb University
3901 Granny White Pike
Nashville, TN 37204-3951
800-333-4358
www.lipscomb.edu

Martin Methodist College
433 West Madison Street
Pulaski, TN 38478-2716
800-467-1273
www.martinmethodist.edu

Maryville College
502 East Lamar Alexander Pkwy
Maryville, TN 37804-5907
800-597-2687
www.maryvillecollege.edu

Memphis College of Art
Overton Park, 1930 Poplar Ave
Memphis, TN 38104-2764
800-727-1088
www.mca.edu

Middle Tennessee State
University
1301 East Main Street
Murfreesboro, TN 37132
800-433-MTSU
www.mtsu.edu

Milligan College
PO Box 500
Milligan College, TN 37682
423-461-8700
www.milligan.edu

O'More College of Design
423 South Margin Street
Franklin, TN 37064-2816
615-794-4254
www.omorecollege.edu

Rhodes College
2000 North Parkway
Memphis, TN 38112-1690
800-844-5969
www.rhodes.edu

Southern Adventist
University
PO Box 370
Collegedale, TN 37315-0370
800-768-8437
www.southern.edu

Tennessee State University
3500 John A Merritt Blvd
Nashville, TN 37209-1561
615-963-5000
www.tnstate.edu

Tennessee Technological
University
North Dixie Avenue
Cookeville, TN 38505
800-255-8881
www.tntech.edu

Tennessee Temple University
1815 Union Avenue
Chattanooga, TN 37404-3587
800-553-4050

Tennessee Wesleyan College
PO Box 40
Athens, TN 37371-0040
800-PICK-TWC
www.twcnet.edu

Trevecca Nazarene
University
333 Murfreesboro Road
Nashville, TN 37210-2877
888-210-4TNU
www.trevecca.edu

Tusculum College
60 Shiloh Road
Greeneville, TN 37743-9997
800-729-0256
www.tusculum.edu

Union University
1050 Union University Drive
Jackson, TN 38305-3697
800-33-UNION
www.uu.edu

The University of Memphis
Memphis, TN 38152
901-678-2000
www.memphis.edu

University of the South
735 University Avenue
Sewanee, TN 37383-1000
800-522-2234
www.sewanee.edu

The University of Tennessee
Knoxville, TN 37996
865-974-1000
www.tennessee.edu

The University of Tennessee
at Chattanooga
615 McCallie Avenue
Chattanooga, TN 37403-2598
423-425-4111
www.utc.edu

The University of Tennessee
at Martin
University Street
Martin, TN 38238-1000
800-829-8861
www.utm.edu

The University of Tennessee
Health Science Center
800 Madison Avenue
Memphis, TN 38163-0002
901-448-5500
www.utmem.edu

Vanderbilt University
Nashville, TN 37240-1001
800-288-0432
www.vanderbilt.edu

Watkins College of Art and
Design
100 Powell Place
Nashville, TN 37204
615-383-4848
www.watkins.edu

Texas

Abilene Christian University
ACU Box 29100
Abilene, TX 79699-9100
915-674-2000
www.acu.edu

Amberton University
1700 Eastgate Drive
Garland, TX 75041-5595
972-279-6511
www.amberton.edu

Angelo State University
2601 West Avenue N
San Angelo, TX 76909
915-942-2555
www.angelo.edu

Arlington Baptist College
3001 West Division
Arlington, TX 76012-3425
817-461-8741
www.abconline.edu

Austin College
900 North Grand Avenue
Sherman, TX 75090-4400
903-813-2000
www.austinc.edu

Austin Graduate School of
Theology
1909 University Avenue
Austin, TX 78705-5610
512-476-2772
www.austingrad.edu

Baptist Missionary
Association Theological
Seminary
1530 East Pine Street
Jacksonville, TX 75766-5407
903-586-2501
www.geocities.com/athens/
acropolis/3386

Baylor University
Waco, TX 76798
254-710-1011
www.baylor.edu

The Criswell College
4010 Gaston Avenue
Dallas, TX 75246-1537
214-821-5433
www.criswell.edu

College of Biblical
Studies–Houston
6000 Dale Carnegie Drive
Houston, TX 77036
713-785-5995
www.cbshouston.edu

Concordia University at
Austin
3400 Interstate 35 North
Austin, TX 78705-2799
512-486-2000
www.concordia.edu

Dallas Baptist University
3000 Mountain Creek Pkwy
Dallas, TX 75211-9299
214-333-7100
www.dbu.edu

Dallas Christian College
2700 Christian Parkway
Dallas, TX 75234-7299
972-241-3371
www.dallas.edu

DeVry Institute of Technology
4800 Regent Boulevard
Irving, TX 75063-2439
972-929-6777
www.dal.devry.edu

East Texas Baptist University
1209 North Grove
Marshall, TX 75670-1498
903-935-7963
www.etbu.edu

Hardin-Simmons University
2200 Hickory Street
Abilene, TX 79698-0001
915-670-1000

Houston Baptist University
7502 Fondren Road
Houston, TX 77074-3298
281-649-3000
www.hbu.edu

Howard Payne University
1000 Fisk Street
Brownwood, TX 76801-2715
915-646-2502
www.hputx.edu

Huston-Tillotson College
900 Chicon Street
Austin, TX 78702-2795
512-505-3000
www.htc.edu

Jarvis Christian College
PO Box 1470
Hawkins, TX 75765-1470
903-769-5700
www.jarvis.edu

Lamar University
4400 Martin Luther King
Parkway
Beaumont, TX 77710
409-880-7011
www.lamar.edu

LeTourneau University
PO Box 7001
Longview, TX 75607-7001
903-233-3000
www.letu.edu

Lubbock Christian University
5601 19th Street
Lubbock, TX 79407-2099
806-796-8800

McMurry University
South 14th and Sayles
Abilene, TX 79697
915-793-3800
www.mcm.edu

Midwestern State University
3410 Taft Boulevard
Wichita Falls, TX 76308
940-397-4000
www.mwsu.edu

Northwood University, Texas
Campus
1114 West FM 1382
Cedar Hill, TX 75104-1204
972-291-1541
www.northwood.edu

Our Lady of the Lake
University of San Antonio
411 Southwest 24th Street
San Antonio, TX 78207-4689
210-434-6711
www.ollusa.edu

Paul Quinn College
3837 Simpson-Stuart Road
Dallas, TX 75241-4331
214-376-1000
www.pqc.edu

Prairie View A&M University
PO Box 188, University Dr,
FM 1098
Prairie View, TX 77446-0188
936-857-3311
www.pvamu.edu

Rice University
PO Box 1892
Houston, TX 77251-1892
713-348-0000
www.rice.edu

Sam Houston State
University
Huntsville, TX 77341
936-294-1111
www.shsu.edu

Schreiner University
2100 Memorial Boulevard
Kerrville, TX 78028-5697
830-896-5411
www.schreiner.edu

Southern Methodist
University
6425 Boaz
Dallas, TX 75275
214-768-2000
www. smu.edu

Southwest Texas State
University
601 University Drive
San Marcos, TX 78666
512-245-2111
www.swt.edu

Southwestern Adventist
University
PO Box 567
Keene, TX 76059
817-645-3921
www.swau.edu

Southwestern Assemblies of
God University
1200 Sycamore Street
Waxahachie, TX 75165-2397
972-937-4010
www.sagu.edu

Southwestern Christian
College
Box 10, 200 Bowser Street
Terrell, TX 75160
972-524-3341
www.swcc.edu

Southwestern University
1001 East University Avenue
Georgetown, TX 78626
512-863-6511
www.southwestern.edu

St. Edward's University
3001 South Congress Avenue
Austin, TX 78704-6489
512-448-8400
www.stedwards.edu

St. Mary's University of San
Antonio
1 Camino Santa Maria
San Antonio, TX 78228-8507
210-436-3011
www.stmarytx.edu

Stephen F. Austin State
University
1936 North Street
Nacogdoches, TX 75962
936-468-2011
www.sfasu.edu

Sul Ross State University
East Highway 90
Alpine, TX 79832
915-837-8011
www.sulross.edu

Tarleton State University
Box T-0001, Tarleton Station
Stephenville, TX 76402
254-968-9000
www.tarleton.edu

Texas A&M International
University
5201 University Boulevard
Laredo, TX 78041-1900
956-326-2001
www.tamiu.edu

Texas A&M University
College Station, TX 77843
979-845-3211
www.tamu.edu

Texas A&M University at
Galveston
PO Box 1675
Galveston, TX 77553-1675
409-740-4400
www.tamug.tamu.edu

Texas A&M University
System Health Science
Center
John B. Connally Building,
301 Tarrow Street, Suite 319
College Station, TX
77840-7896
409-458-6475
tamushsc.tamu.edu

Texas A&M
University–Commerce
PO Box 3011
Commerce, TX 75429-3011
903-886-5081
www.tamu-commerce.edu

Texas A&M
University–Corpus Christi
6300 Ocean Drive
Corpus Christi, TX 78412-
5503
361-825-5700
www.tamucc.edu

Texas A&M
University–Kingsville
West Santa Gertrudis
Kingsville, TX 78363
361-593-2111
www.tamuk.edu

Texas A&M
University–Texarkana
PO Box 5518
Texarkana, TX 75505-5518
903-223-3000
www.tamut.edu

Texas Chiropractic College
5912 Spencer Highway
Pasadena, TX 77505-1699
281-487-1170
www.txchiro.edu

Texas Christian University
2800 South University Drive
Fort Worth, TX 76129-0002
817-257-7000
www.tcu.edu

Texas College
2404 North Grand Avenue,
PO Box 4500
Tyler, TX 75712-4500
903-593-8311
http://168.44.174.253

Texas Lutheran University
1000 West Court Street
Seguin, TX 78155-5999
830-372-8000
www.tlu.edu

Texas Southern University
3100 Cleburne
Houston, TX 77004-4584
713-313-7011
www.tsu.edu

Texas Tech University
Lubbock, TX 79409
806-742-2011
www.ttu.edu

Texas Wesleyan University
1201 Wesleyan Street
Fort Worth, TX 76105-1536
817-531-4444
www.txwesleyan.edu

Texas Woman's University
304 Administration Drive
Denton, TX 76201
940-898-2000
www.twu.edu

Trinity University
715 Stadium Drive
San Antonio, TX 78212-7200
210-999-7011
www.trinity.edu

University of Dallas
1845 East Northgate Drive
Irving, TX 75062-4736
972-721-5000
www.udallas.edu

University of Houston
4800 Calhoun Road
Houston, TX 77204
713-743-1000
www.uh.edu

University of Houston–Clear
Lake
2700 Bay Area Boulevard
Houston, TX 77058-1098
281-283-7600
www.cl.uh.edu

University of
Houston–Downtown
One Main Street
Houston, TX 77002-1001
713-221-8000
www.uhd.edu

University of Houston–
Victoria
3005 North Ben Wilson Street
Victoria, TX 77901-4450
361-570-4848
www.vic.uh.edu

University of Mary Hardin-
Baylor
900 College Street
Belton, TX 76513
254-295-8642
www.umhb.edu

University of North Texas
PO Box 311277
Denton, TX 76203
940-565-2000
www.unt.edu

University of Phoenix–Dallas/
Ft. Worth Campus
Churchill Tower, 12400 Coit
Road, Suite 100
Dallas, TX 75251
972-385-1055
www.phoenix.edu

University of Phoenix–
Houston Campus
11451 Katy Freeway,
Suite 200
Houston, TX 77079
281-596-0363
www.phoenix.edu

University of St. Thomas
3800 Montrose Boulevard
Houston, TX 77006-4696
713-522-7911
www.stthom.edu

University of the Incarnate
Word
4301 Broadway
San Antonio, TX 78209-6397
210-829-6000
www.uiw.edu

The University of Texas at
Arlington
Arlington, TX 76019
817-272-2011
www.uta.edu

The University of Texas at
Austin
Austin, TX 78712-1111
512-471-3434
www.utexas.edu

The University of Texas at
Brownsville
80 Fort Brown
Brownsville, TX 78520-4991
956-544-8200
www.utb.edu

The University of Texas at
Dallas
PO Box 830688
Richardson, TX 75083-0688
972-883-2111
www.utdallas.edu

The University of Texas at
El Paso
500 West University Avenue
El Paso, TX 79968-0001
915-747-5000
www.utep.edu

The University of Texas at
San Antonio
6900 North Loop 1604 West
San Antonio, TX 78249-0617
210-458-4011
www.utsa.edu

The University of Texas at
Tyler
3900 University Boulevard
Tyler, TX 75799-0001
903-566-7000
www.uttyler.edu

The University of Texas
Health Science Center at
Houston
PO Box 20036
Houston, TX 77225-0036
713-500-3333
www.uth.tmc.edu

The University of Texas
Health Science Center at
San Antonio
7703 Floyd Curl Drive
San Antonio, TX 78229-3900
210-567-7000
www.uthscsa.edu

The University of Texas
Medical Branch
301 University Boulevard
Galveston, TX 77555
409-772-1011
www.utmb.edu

The University of Texas of the
Permian Basin
4901 East University
Odessa, TX 79762-0001
915-552-2020
www.utpb.edu

The University of Texas
Southwestern Medical
Center at Dallas
5323 Harry Hines Boulevard
Dallas, TX 75390
214-648-3111
www.swmed.edu

The University of Texas–
Pan American
1201 West University Drive
Edinburg, TX 78539-2999
956-381-2011
www.panam.edu

Wayland Baptist University
1900 West Seventh Street
Plainview, TX 79072-6998
806-296-5521
www.wbu.edu

West Texas A&M University
2501 4th Avenue
Canyon, TX 79016-0001
806-651-2000
www.wtamu.edu

Wiley College
711 Wiley Avenue
Marshall, TX 75670-5199
903-927-3300
www.wileyc.edu

Utah

Brigham Young University
Provo, UT 84602-1001
801-378-1211
www.byu.edu

Southern Utah University
351 West Center
Cedar City, UT 84720-2498
435-586-7700
www.suu.edu

University of Phoenix–Utah
Campus
5251 Green Street
Salt Lake City, UT 84123
801-263-1444
www.phoenix.edu

University of Utah
201 South University Street
Salt Lake City, UT 84112-1107
801-581-7200
www.utah.edu

Utah State University
Old Main Hill
Logan, UT 84322
435-797-1000
www.usu.edu

Weber State University
1001 University Circle
Ogden, UT 84408-1001
801-626-6000
weber.edu

Western Governors
University
2040 East Murray Holladay,
Suite 106
Salt Lake City, UT 84117
801-274-3280
www.wgu.edu

Westminster College
1840 South 1300 East
Salt Lake City, UT 84105-3697
801-484-7651
www.wcslc.edu

Vermont

Bennington College
Bennington, VT 05201
802-442-5401
www.bennington.edu

Burlington College
95 North Avenue
Burlington, VT 05401-2998
802-862-9616
www.burlcol.edu

Castleton State College
Castleton, VT 05735
802-468-5611
www.castleton.edu

Champlain College
PO Box 670
Burlington, VT 05402-0670
802-860-2700
www.champlain.edu

College of St. Joseph
71 Clement Road
Rutland, VT 05701-3899
802-773-5900
www.csj.edu

Goddard College
123 Pitkin Road
Plainfield, VT 05667-9432
802-454-8311
www.goddard.edu

Green Mountain College
One College Circle
Poultney, VT 05764-1199
802-287-8000
www.greenmtn.edu

Johnson State College
337 College Hill
Johnson, VT 05656-9405
802-635-2356
www.jsc.vsc.edu

Lyndon State College
PO Box 919
Lyndonville, VT 05851-0919
802-626-6200
www.lsc.vsc.edu

Marlboro College
PO Box A, South Road
Marlboro, VT 05344
802-257-4333
www.marlboro.edu

Middlebury College
Middlebury, VT 05753-6002
802-443-5000
www.middlebury.edu

Norwich University
158 Harmon Drive
Northfield, VT 05663
802-485-2000
www.norwich.edu

Saint Michael's College
One Winooski Park
Colchester, VT 05439
802-654-2000
www.smcvt.edu

Southern Vermont College
982 Mansion Drive
Bennington, VT 05201-6002
802-442-5427
www.svc.edu

Sterling College
PO Box 72
Craftsbury Common, VT
05827-0072
802-586-7711
www.sterlingcollege.edu

University of Vermont
Burlington, VT 05405
802-656-3131
www.uvm.edu

Vermont Technical College
PO Box 500
Randolph Center, VT 05061-
0500
802-728-1000
www.vtc.edu

Virginia

American Military University
9104-P Manassas Drive
Manassas, VA   20111
703-330-5398
www.amunet.edu

The Art Institute of
Washington
1820 North Fort Meyer Drive,
Ground Floor
Arlington, VA   22209
703-358-9550
www.aiw.artinstitutes.edu

Averett University
420 West Main Street
Danville, VA   24541-3692
434-791-5600
www.averett.edu

Bluefield College
3000 College Drive
Bluefield, VA   24605-1799
540-326-3682
www.bluefield.edu

Bridgewater College
402 East College Street
Bridgewater, VA   22812-1599
540-828-8000
www.bridgewater.edu

Christendom College
134 Christendom Drive
Front Royal, VA   22630-5103
540-636-2900
www.christendom.edu

Christopher Newport
University
1 University Place
Newport News, VA
23606-2998
757-594-7000
www.cnu.edu

The College of William and
Mary
PO Box 8795
Williamsburg, VA
23187-8795
757-221-4000
www.wm.edu

Community Hospital of
Roanoke Valley–College of
Health Sciences
PO Box 13186
Roanoke, VA   24031-3186
540-985-8483
www.chs.edu

DeVry Institute of Technology
Century Building II,
Suite 1100,
2361 Jefferson Davis Hwy
Arlington, VA   22202
866-338-7932
www.crys.devry.edu

Eastern Mennonite
University
1200 Park Road
Harrisonburg, VA
22802-2462
540-432-4000
www.emu.edu

Emory & Henry College
PO Box 947
Emory, VA   24327-0947
540-944-4121
www.ehc.edu

Ferrum College
PO Box 1000
Ferrum, VA   24088-9001
540-365-2121
www.ferrum.edu

George Mason University
4400 University Drive
Fairfax, VA   22030-4444
703-993-1000
www.gmu.edu

Hampden-Sydney College
PO Box 667
Hampden-Sydney, VA   23943
804-223-6000
www.hsc.edu

Hampton University
Hampton, VA   23668
757-727-5000
www.hamptonu.edu

Hollins University
PO Box 9603
Roanoke, VA   24020-1603
540-362-6000
www.hollins.edu

James Madison University
800 South Main Street
Harrisonburg, VA   22807
540-568-6211
www.jmu.edu

Liberty University
1971 University Boulevard
Lynchburg, VA   24502
804-582-2000
www.liberty.edu

Longwood College
201 High Street
Farmville, VA   23909-1800
804-395-2000
www.longwood.edu

Lynchburg College
1501 Lakeside Drive
Lynchburg, VA   24501-3199
804-544-8100
www.lynchburg.edu

Mary Baldwin College
201 East Frederick Street
Staunton, VA   24401-3610
540-887-7000
www.mbc.edu

Mary Washington College
1301 College Avenue
Fredericksburg, VA
22401-5358
540-654-1000
www.mwc.edu

Marymount University
2807 North Glebe Road
Arlington, VA   22207-4299
703-522-5600
www.marymount.edu

Norfolk State University
700 Park Avenue
Norfolk, VA   23504
757-823-8600
www.nsu.edu

Old Dominion University
5215 Hampton Boulevard
Norfolk, VA   23529
757-683-3000
www.odu.edu

Radford University
PO Box 6890, RU Station
Radford, VA   24142
540-831-5000
www.radford.edu

Randolph-Macon College
PO Box 5005
Ashland, VA   23005-5505
804-752-7200
www.rmc.edu

Randolph-Macon Woman's
College
2500 Rivermont Avenue
Lynchburg, VA   24503-1526
804-947-8000
www.rmwc.edu

Roanoke College
221 College Lane
Salem, VA   24153-3794
540-375-2500
www.roanoke.edu

Saint Paul's College
115 College Drive
Lawrenceville, VA
23868-1202
804-848-3111
www.saintpauls.edu

Shenandoah University
1460 University Drive
Winchester, VA   22601-5195
540-665-4500
www.su.edu

Southern Virginia College
One College Hill Drive
Buena Vista, VA   24416
540-261-8400
www.southernvirginia.edu

Sweet Briar College
US Route 29 North
Sweet Briar, VA   24595
804-381-6100
www.sbc.edu

University of Richmond
28 Westhampton Way
University of Richmond, VA
23173
804-289-8000
www.richmond.edu

University of Virginia
Charlottesville, VA   22903
434-924-0311
www.virginia.edu

The University of Virginia's
College at Wise
1 College Avenue
Wise, VA   24293
540-328-0100
www.uvawise.edu

Virginia Commonwealth
University
901 West Franklin Street
Richmond, VA   23284-9005
804-828-0100
www.vcu.edu

Virginia Intermont College
1013 Moore Street
Bristol, VA   24201-4298
540-669-6101
www.vic.edu

Virginia Military Institute
Lexington, VA   24450
540-464-7207
www.vmi.edu

Virginia Polytechnic Institute
and State University
Blacksburg, VA   24061
540-231-6000

Virginia State University
1 Hayden Drive
Petersburg, VA   23806-0001
804-524-5000
www.vsu.edu

Virginia Union University
1500 North Lombardy Street
Richmond, VA   23220-1170
804-257-5600

Virginia Wesleyan College
1584 Wesleyan Drive
Norfolk, VA   23502-5599
757-455-3200
www.vwc.edu

Washington and Lee
University
Lexington, VA   24450-0303
540-463-8400
www.wlu.edu

World College
5193 Shore Drive, Suite 105
Virginia Beach, VA
23455-2500
757-464-4600

Washington

Antioch University Seattle
2326 Sixth Avenue
Seattle, WA 98121-1814
206-441-5352
www.antiochsea.edu

Bastyr University
14500 Juanita Drive, NE
Kenmore, WA 98028-4966
425-823-1300
www.bastyr.edu

Central Washington
University
400 East 8th Avenue
Ellensburg, WA 98926-7463
509-963-1111
www.cwu.edu

City University
11900 NE First Street
Bellevue, WA 98005
425-637-1010
www.cityu.edu

Cornish College of the Arts
710 East Roy Street
Seattle, WA 98102-4696
206-323-1400
www.cornish.edu

DeVry Institute of Technology
3600 South 34th Way
Federal Way, WA 98001
253-943-2800
www.sea.devry.edu

Eastern Washington
University
526 5th Street
Cheney, WA 99004-2431
509-359-6200
www.ewu.edu

The Evergreen State College
2700 Evergreen Parkway, NW
Olympia, WA 98505
360-866-6000
www.evergreen.edu

Gonzaga University
502 East Boone Avenue
Spokane, WA 99258
509-328-4220
www.gonzaga.edu

Henry Cogswell College
3002 Colby Avenue
Everett, WA 98201
425-258-3351
www.henrycogswell.edu

Heritage College
3240 Fort Road
Toppenish, WA 98948-9599
509-865-8500
www.heritage.edu

The Leadership Institute of
Seattle
14506 Juanita Drive, NE
Kenmore, WA 98028-4966
425-939-8100
www.lios.org

Northwest College
PO Box 579
Kirkland, WA 98083-0579
425-822-8266
www.nwcollege.edu

Northwest College of Art
16464 State Highway 305
Poulsbo, WA 98370
360-779-9993
www.nca.edu

Pacific Lutheran University
Tacoma, WA 98447
253-531-6900
www.plu.edu

Puget Sound Christian
College
410 4th Avenue North
Edmonds, WA 98020-3171
425-775-8686

Saint Martin's College
5300 Pacific Avenue, SE
Lacey, WA 98503-7500
360-491-4700
www.stmartin.edu

Seattle Pacific University
3307 Third Avenue West
Seattle, WA 98119-1997
206-281-2000
www.spu.edu

Seattle University
900 Broadway
Seattle, WA 98122
206-296-6000
www.seattleu.edu

Trinity Lutheran College
4221 228th Avenue, SE
Issaquah, WA 98029-9299
425-392-0400
www.tlc.edu

University of
Phoenix–Washington
Campus
7100 Fort Dent Way,
Suite 100
Seattle, WA 98188
877-877-4867
www.phoenix.edu

University of Puget Sound
1500 North Warner Street
Tacoma, WA 98416
253-879-3100
www.ups.edu

University of Washington
Seattle, WA 98195
206-543-2100
www.washington.edu

Walla Walla College
204 South College Avenue
College Place, WA 99324-1198
509-527-2615
www.wwc.edu

Washington State University
Pullman, WA 99164
509-335-3564
www.wsu.edu

Western Washington
University
516 High Street
Bellingham, WA 98225-5996
360-650-3000
www.wwu.edu

Whitman College
345 Boyer Avenue
Walla Walla, WA 99362-2083
509-527-5111
www.whitman.edu

Whitworth College
300 West Hawthorne Road
Spokane, WA 99251-0001
509-777-1000
www.whitworth.edu

West Virginia

Alderson-Broaddus College
1 College Hill
Philippi, WV   26416
304-457-1700
www.ab.edu

Appalachian Bible College
PO Box ABC
Bradley, WV   25818
304-877-6428
www.abc.edu

Bethany College
Main Street
Bethany, WV   26032
304-829-7000
www.bethanywv.edu

Bluefield State College
219 Rock Street
Bluefield, WV   24701-2198
304-327-4000
www.bluefield.wvnet.edu

Concord College
Vermillion Street,
PO Box 1000
Athens, WV   24712-1000
304-384-3115
www.concord.edu

Davis & Elkins College
100 Campus Drive
Elkins, WV 26241-3996
304-637-1900
www.dne.edu

Fairmont State College
1201 Locust Avenue
Fairmont, WV 26554
304-367-4000
www.fscwv.edu

Glenville State College
200 High Street
Glenville, WV 26351-1200
304-462-7361
www.glenville.edu

Marshall University
400 Hal Greer Boulevard
Huntington, WV 25755
304-696-3170
www.marshall.edu

Mountain State University
PO Box AG
Beckley, WV 25802-2830
304-253-7351
www.mountainstate.edu

Ohio Valley College
One Campus View Drive
Vienna, WV 26105-8000
304-865-6000
www.ovc.edu

Salem International
University
223 West Main Street,
PO Box 500
Salem, WV 26426-0500
304-782-5011
www.salemiu.edu

Shepherd College
PO Box 3210
Shepherdstown, WV
25443-3210
304-876-5000
www.shepherd.edu

University of Charleston
2300 MacCorkle Avenue, SE
Charleston, WV 25304-1099
304-357-4800
www.uchaswv.edu

West Liberty State College
PO Box 295
West Liberty, WV 26074
304-336-5000
www.wlsc.wvnet.edu

West Virginia State College
Post Office Box 1000
Institute, WV 25112-1000
304-766-3000
www.wvsc.edu

West Virginia University
University Avenue
Morgantown, WV 26506
304-293-0111
www.wvu.edu

West Virginia University
Institute of Technology
405 Fayette Pike
Montgomery, WV 25136
304-442-3071
www.wvutech.edu

West Virginia Wesleyan
College
59 College Avenue
Buckhannon, WV 26201
304-473-8000
www.wvwc.edu

Wheeling Jesuit University
316 Washington Avenue
Wheeling, WV 26003-6295
304-243-2000
www.wju.edu

Wisconsin

Alverno College
3400 South 43rd Street,
PO Box 343922
Milwaukee, WI 53234-3922
414-382-6000
www.alverno.edu

Bellin College of Nursing
725 South Webster Ave,
PO Box 23400
Green Bay, WI 54305-3400
920-433-3560
www.bcon.edu

Beloit College
700 College Street
Beloit, WI 53511-5596
608-363-2000
www.beloit.edu

Cardinal Stritch University
6801 North Yates Road
Milwaukee, WI 53217-3985
414-410-4000
www.stritch.edu

Carroll College
100 North East Avenue
Waukesha, WI 53186-5593
262-547-1211
www.cc.edu

Carthage College
2001 Alford Park Drive
Kenosha, WI 53140-1994
262-551-8500
www.carthage.edu

Columbia College of Nursing
2121 East Newport Avenue
Milwaukee, WI 53211-2952
414-961-3530
www.ccon.edu

Concordia University
Wisconsin
12800 North Lake Shore Dr
Mequon, WI 53097-2402
262-243-5700
www.cuw.edu

Edgewood College
1000 Edgewood College Dr
Madison, WI 53711-1997
608-663-4861
www.edgewood.edu

Lakeland College
PO Box 359
Sheboygan, WI 53082-0359
920-565-2111
www.lakeland.edu

Lawrence University
PO Box 599
Appleton, WI 54912-0599
920-832-7000
www.lawrence.edu

Maranatha Baptist Bible
College
745 West Main Street
Watertown, WI 53094
920-261-9300
www.mbbc.edu

Marian College of Fond du
Lac
45 South National Avenue
Fond du Lac, WI 54935-4699
920-923-7600
www.mariancollege.edu

Marquette University
PO Box 1881
Milwaukee, WI 53201-1881
414-288-7250
www.marquette.edu

Milwaukee Institute of Art
and Design
273 East Erie Street
Milwaukee, WI 53202-6003
414-276-7889
www.miad.edu

Milwaukee School of
Engineering
1025 North Broadway
Milwaukee, WI 53202-3109
414-277-7300
www.msoe.edu

Mount Mary College
2900 North Menomonee
River Parkway
Milwaukee, WI 53222-4597
414-258-4810
www.mtmary.edu

Mount Senario College
1500 College Avenue West
Ladysmith, WI 54848-2128
715-532-5511
www.mountsenario.edu

Northland College
1411 Ellis Avenue
Ashland, WI 54806-3925
715-682-1699
www.northland.edu

Ripon College
300 Seward Street,
PO Box 248
Ripon, WI 54971
920-748-8115
www.ripon.edu

Silver Lake College
2406 South Alverno Road
Manitowoc, WI 54220-9319
920-684-6691
www.sl.edu

St. Norbert College
100 Grant Street
De Pere, WI 54115-2099
920-337-3181
www.snc.edu

University of Wisconsin–Eau
Claire
PO Box 4004
Eau Claire, WI 54702-4004
715-836-2637
www.uwec.edu

University of
Wisconsin–Green Bay
2420 Nicolet Drive
Green Bay, WI 54311-7001
920-465-2000
www.uwgb.edu

University of Wisconsin–
La Crosse
1725 State Street
La Crosse, WI 54601-3742
608-785-8000
www.uwlax.edu

University of Wisconsin–
Madison
500 Lincoln Drive
Madison, WI 53706-1380
608-262-1234
www.wisc.edu

University of Wisconsin–
Milwaukee
PO Box 413
Milwaukee, WI 53201-0413
414-229-1122
www.uwm.edu

University of Wisconsin–
Oshkosh
800 Algoma Boulevard
Oshkosh, WI 54901
920-424-1234
www.uwosh.edu

University of Wisconsin–
Parkside
900 Wood Road, Box 2000
Kenosha, WI 53141-2000
262-595-2345
www.uwp.edu

University of Wisconsin–
Platteville
1 University Plaza
Platteville, WI 53818-3099
608-342-1491
www.uwplatt.edu

University of Wisconsin–
River Falls
410 South Third Street
River Falls, WI 54022-5001
715-425-3911
www.uwrf.edu

University of Wisconsin–
Stevens Point
2100 Main Street
Stevens Point, WI
54481-3897
715-346-0123
www.uwsp.edu

University of Wisconsin–
Stout
Menomonie, WI 54751
715-232-1122
www.uwstout.edu

University of Wisconsin–
Superior
Belknap and Catlin,
PO Box 2000
Superior, WI 54880-4500
715-394-8101
www.uwsuper.edu

University of Wisconsin–
Whitewater
800 West Main Street
Whitewater, WI 53190-1790
262-472-1234
www.uww.edu

Viterbo University
815 South Ninth Street
La Crosse, WI 54601-4797
608-796-3000
www.viterbo.edu

Wisconsin Lutheran College
8800 West Bluemound Road
Milwaukee, WI 53226-9942
414-443-8800
www.wlc.edu

Wyoming

University of Wyoming
Laramie, WY 82071
307-766-1121
www.uwyo.edu

2-YEAR COLLEGES AND UNIVERSITIES

Alabama

Alabama Southern
Community College
PO Box 2000
Monroeville, AL 36461
334-575-3156
www.ascc.edu

Bessemer State Technical
College
PO Box 308
Bessemer, AL 35021-0308
205-428-6391
www.bessemertech.com

Bevill State Community
College
PO Box 800
Sumiton, AL 35148
205-648-3271
www.bevillst.cc.al.us

Bishop State Community
College
351 North Broad Street
Mobile, AL 36603-5898
334-690-6801
www.bscc.cc.al.us

Calhoun Community College
PO Box 2216
Decatur, AL 35609-2216
256-306-2500
www.calhoun.cc.al.us

Central Alabama Community
College
PO Box 699
Alexander City, AL
35011-0699
256-234-6346
www.cacc.cc.al.us

Chattahoochee Valley
Community College
2602 College Drive
Phenix City, AL 36869-7928
334-291-4900
www.cvcc.cc.al.us

Community College of the Air
Force
130 West Maxwell Boulevard
Maxwell Air Force Base, AL
36112-6613
334-953-2794

Douglas MacArthur State
Technical College
PO Drawer 910
Opp, AL 36467
334-493-3573

Enterprise State Junior
College
PO Box 1300
Enterprise, AL 36331-1300
334-347-2623
www.esjc.cc.al.us

Gadsden State Community
College
PO Box 227
Gadsden, AL 35902-0227
256-549-8200
www.gadsdenst.cc.al.us

George C. Wallace
Community College
Route 6, Box 62
Dothan, AL 36303-9234
334-983-3521
dns1.wallace.edu

George Corley Wallace State
Community College
PO Box 2530
Selma, AL 36702-2530
334-876-9227

Harry M. Ayers State Technical
College
PO Box 1647
Anniston, AL 36202-1647
256-835-5400
www.ayers.cc.al.us

Herzing College
280 West Valley Avenue
Birmingham, AL 35209
205-916-2800
www.herzing.edu/
birmingham

ITT Technical Institute
500 Riverhills Business Park
Birmingham, AL 35242
205-991-5410

J. F. Drake State Technical
College
3421 Meridian Street North
Huntsville, AL 35811-1584
256-539-8161
www.dstc.cc.al.us

James H. Faulkner State
Community College
1900 Highway 31 South
Bay Minette, AL 36507
334-580-2100
www.faulkner.cc.al.us

Jefferson Davis Community
College
PO Box 958
Brewton, AL 36427-0958
334-867-4832
www.jdcc.net

Jefferson State Community
College
2601 Carson Road
Birmingham, AL 35215-3098
205-853-1200
www.jscc.cc.al.us

John M. Patterson State
Technical College
3920 Troy Highway
Montgomery, AL
36116-2699
334-288-1080
www.jptech.cc.al.us

Lawson State Community
College
3060 Wilson Road, SW
Birmingham, AL 35221-1798
205-925-2515

Lurleen B. Wallace Junior
College
PO Box 1418
Andalusia, AL 36420-1418
334-222-6591

Marion Military Institute
1101 Washington Street
Marion, AL 36756
334-683-2306
www.marion-institute.org

Northeast Alabama
Community College
PO Box 159
Rainsville, AL 35986-0159
256-228-6001

Northwest-Shoals
Community College
PO Box 2545
Muscle Shoals, AL 35662
256-331-5200
www.nwscc.cc.al.us

Prince Institute of
Professional Studies
7735 Atlanta Highway
Montgomery, AL 36117-4231
334-271-1670
www.princeinstitute.com

Reid State Technical College
PO Box 588
Evergreen, AL 36401-0588
334-578-1313
www.rstc.cc.al.us

Shelton State Community
College
9500 Old Greensboro Road
Tuscaloosa, AL 35405
205-391-2211
www.shelton.cc.al.us

Snead State Community
College
220 N Walnut Street,
PO Drawer D
Boaz, AL 35957-0734
256-593-5120
www.snead.cc.al.us

South University
122 Commerce Street
Montgomery, AL
36104-2538
334-263-1013
www.southcollege.edu

Southern Union State
Community College
PO Box 1000, Roberts Street
Wadley, AL 36276
256-395-2211
www.suscc.cc.al.us

Trenholm State Technical
College
1225 Air Base Blvd,
PO Box 9000
Montgomery, AL
36108-3105
334-832-9000

Virginia College at Huntsville
2800-A Bob Wallace Avenue
Huntsville, AL 35805
256-533-7387

Wallace State Community
College
PO Box 2000
Hanceville, AL 35077-2000
256-352-8000
wallacestatehanceville.edu

Alaska

Charter College
2221 East Northern Lights
Boulevard, Suite 120
Anchorage, AK 99508-4157
Phone: 907-277-1000
www.chartercollege.org

University of Alaska
Anchorage, Kenai Peninsula
College
34820 College Drive
Soldotna, AK 99669-9798
Phone: 907-262-0300
www.uaa.alaska.edu/kenai

University of Alaska
Anchorage, Kodiak College
117 Benny Benson Drive
Kodiak, AK 99615-6643
Phone: 907-486-4161
www.koc.alaska.edu

University of Alaska
Anchorage, Matanuska-
Susitna College
PO Box 2889
Palmer, AK 99645-2889
Phone: 907-745-9774
www.uaa.alaska.edu/matsu/
msc.htm

University of Alaska
Southeast, Ketchikan
Campus
2600 7th Avenue
Ketchikan, AK 99901-5798
Phone: 907-225-6177
www.ketch.alaska.edu

University of Alaska
Southeast, Sitka Campus
1332 Seward Avenue
Sitka, AK 99835-9418
Phone: 907-747-6653
www.uas-sitka.net

University of Alaska, Prince
William Sound Community
College
PO Box 97
Valdez, AK 99686-0097
Phone: 907-834-1600
www.uaa.alaska.edu/pwscc/h
ome.html

Arizona

Apollo College–Phoenix, Inc.
8503 North 27th Avenue
Phoenix, AZ 85051
Phone: 602-864-1571
www.apollocollege.com

Apollo College–Tri-City, Inc.
630 West Southern Avenue
Mesa, AZ 85210-5004
Phone: 480-831-6585
www.apollocollege.com

Apollo College–Tucson, Inc.
3870 North Oracle Road
Tucson, AZ 85705-3227
Phone: 520-888-5885
www.apollocollege.com

Apollo College–Westside, Inc.
2701 West Bethany Home Rd
Phoenix, AZ 85017
Phone: 602-433-1333
www.apollocollege.com

Arizona Automotive Institute
6829 North 46th Avenue
Glendale, AZ 85301-3597
Phone: 602-934-7273
www.azautoinst.com

Arizona Institute of Business
& Technology
6049 North 43rd Avenue
Phoenix, AZ 85019
Phone: 602-242-6265
www.aibt.edu

Arizona Western College
PO Box 929
Yuma, AZ 85366-0929
Phone: 928-317-6000
www.awc.cc.az.us

Central Arizona College
8470 North Overfield Road
Coolidge, AZ 85228-9779
Phone: 520-426-4444
www.cac.cc.az.us

Chandler-Gilbert Community
College
2626 East Pecos Road
Chandler, AZ 85225-2479
Phone: 480-732-7000
www.cgc.maricopa.edu

Chaparral College
4585 East Speedway, No 204
Tucson, AZ 85712
Phone: 520-327-6866
www.chap-col.edu

Cochise College
4190 West Highway 80
Douglas, AZ 85607-9724
Phone: 520-364-7943
www.cochise.cc.az.us

Cochise College
901 North Columbo
Sierra Vista, AZ 85635-2317
Phone: 520-515-0500
www.cochise.cc.az.us

Coconino Community
College
3000 North 4th Street,
Suite 17, PO Box 80000
Flagstaff, AZ 86003
Phone: 520-527-1222

Diné College
PO Box 98
Tsaile, AZ 86556
Phone: 520-724-6600
crystal.ncc.cc.nm.us

Eastern Arizona College
PO Box 769
Thatcher, AZ 85552-0769
Phone: 520-428-8322
www.easternarizona.com

Estrella Mountain
Community College
3000 North Dysart Road
Avondale, AZ   85323-1000
Phone: 602-935-8000
www.emc.maricopa.edu

GateWay Community College
108 North 40th Street
Phoenix, AZ   85034-1795
Phone: 602-392-5000
www.gwc.maricopa.edu

Glendale Community College
6000 West Olive Avenue
Glendale, AZ   85302-3090
Phone: 623-845-3000
www.gc.maricopa.edu

High-Tech Institute
1515 East Indian School Road
Phoenix, AZ   85014-4901
Phone: 602-279-9700
www.high-techinstitute.com

ITT Technical Institute
4837 East McDowell Road
Phoenix, AZ   85008-4292
Phone: 602-252-2331

ITT Technical Institute
1455 West River Road
Tucson, AZ   85704
Phone: 520-408-7488
www.itt-tech.edu

Lamson College
1126 North Scottsdale Road,
Suite 17
Tempe, AZ   85281
Phone: 480-898-7000
www.lamsoncollege.com

Mesa Community College
1833 West Southern Avenue
Mesa, AZ   85202-4866
Phone: 602-461-7000

Mohave Community College
1971 Jagerson Avenue
Kingman, AZ   86401
Phone: 520-757-4331
www.mohave.cc.az.us

Northland Pioneer College
PO Box 610
Holbrook, AZ   86025-0610
Phone: 520-524-7600
www.northland.cc.az.us

Paradise Valley Community
College
18401 North 32nd Street
Phoenix, AZ   85032-1200
Phone: 602-787-6500
www.pvc.maricopa.edu

Phoenix College
1202 West Thomas Road
Phoenix, AZ   85013-4234
Phone: 602-264-2492
www.pc.maricopa.edu

Pima Community College
4905 East Broadway
Tucson, AZ   85709-1010
Phone: 520-206-4666
www.pima.edu

Pima Medical Institute
3350 East Grant Road
Tucson, AZ   85716
Phone: 520-326-1600
www.pimamedical.com

Pima Medical Institute
957 South Dobson Road
Mesa, AZ   85202
Phone: 602-644-0267
www.pimamedical.com

Rhodes College
2525 West Beryl Avenue
Phoenix, AZ   85021
Phone: 602-942-4141
rhodes-college.com

Rio Salado College
2323 West 14th Street
Tempe, AZ   85281-6950
Phone: 480-517-8000
www.rio.maricopa.edu

Scottsdale Community
College
9000 East Chaparral Road
Scottsdale, AZ   85256-2626
Phone: 602-423-6000
www.sc.maricopa.edu

Scottsdale Culinary Institute
8100 East Camelback Road,
Suite 1001
Scottsdale, AZ   85251-3940
Phone: 480-990-3773
www.scichefs.com

South Mountain Community
College
7050 South Twenty-fourth St
Phoenix, AZ   85040
Phone: 602-243-8000
www.smc.maricopa.edu

The Art Center
2525 North Country Club Rd
Tucson, AZ   85716-2505
Phone: 520-325-0123
www.theartcenter.edu

The Bryman School
4343 North 16th Street
Phoenix, AZ   85016-5338
Phone: 602-274-4300
www.hightechschools.com

The Paralegal Institute, Inc.
2933 West Indian School Rd
Phoenix, AZ   85017
Phone: 602-212-0501
www.theparalegalinstitute.
com

The Refrigeration School
4210 East Washington Street
Phoenix, AZ   85034-1816
Phone: 602-275-7133
www.refrigerationschool.
com

Universal Technical Institute
3121 West Weldon Avenue
Phoenix, AZ   85017-4599
Phone: 602-264-4164
www.uticorp.com

Yavapai College
1100 East Sheldon Street
Prescott, AZ   86301-3297
Phone: 520-445-7300
www.yavapai.cc.az.us

Arkansas

Arkansas State University–
Beebe
PO Box 1000
Beebe, AR   72012-1000
501-882-3600
www.asub.arknet.edu

Arkansas State University–
Mountain Home
1600 South College Street
Mountain Home, AR   72653
870-508-6100
www.asumh.edu

Arkansas State University–
Newport
7648 Victory Boulevard
Newport, AR   72112
870-512-7800
www.asun.arknet.edu

Black River Technical College
Highway 304 East,
PO Box 468
Pocahontas, AR   72455
870-892-4565

Cossatot Technical College of
the University of Arkansas
PO Box 960
DeQueen, AR   71832
870-584-4471
ctc.tec.ar.us

Crowley's Ridge College
100 College Drive
Paragould, AR   72450-9731
870-236-6901
www.crc.paragould.ar.us

East Arkansas Community
College
1700 Newcastle Road
Forrest City, AR   72335-2204
870-633-4480

Education America,
Southeast College of
Technology, Little Rock
Campus
8901 Kanis Road
Little Rock, AR   72205
501-312-0007

Garland County Community
College
101 College Drive
Hot Springs, AR   71913
501-760-4222
www.gccc.cc.ar.us

ITT Technical Institute
4520 South University
Little Rock, AR   72204
501-565-5550
www.itt-tech.edu

Mid-South Community
College
2000 West Broadway
West Memphis, AR   72301
870-733-6722
www.mscc.cc.ar.us

Mississippi County
Community College
PO Box 1109
Blytheville, AR   72316-1109
870-762-1020

North Arkansas College
1515 Pioneer Drive
Harrison, AR   72601
870-743-3000
pioneer.northark.net

NorthWest Arkansas
Community College
One College Drive
Bentonville, AR   72712
501-636-9222
www.nwacc.cc.ar.us

Ouachita Technical College
PO Box 816, One College Cr
Malvern, AR   72104
501-332-3658
www.otc.tec.ar.us

Ozarka College
PO Box 10
Melbourne, AR   72556
870-368-7371
ozarka.edu

Phillips Community College
of the University of Arkansas
PO Box 785
Helena, AR   72342-0785
870-338-6474
www.pccua.cc.ar.us

Pulaski Technical College
3000 West Scenic Drive
North Little Rock, AR   72118
501-771-1000
www.ptc.tec.ar.us

Rich Mountain Community
College
1100 College Drive
Mena, AR   71953
501-394-7622
www.rmcc.cc.ar.us

South Arkansas Community
College
PO Box 7010
El Dorado, AR   71731-7010
870-862-8131
seminole.saccw.cc.ar.us

Southeast Arkansas College
1900 Hazel Street
Pine Bluff, AR   71603
870-543-5900
www.seark.org

Southern Arkansas
University Tech
SAU Tech Station, 100 Carr Rd
Camden, AR   71701
870-574-4500
www.sautech.edu

University of Arkansas at
Fort Smith
PO Box 3649
Fort Smith, AR   72913-3649
501-788-7000
www.westark.edu

University of Arkansas
Community College at
Batesville
PO Box 3350
Batesville, AR   72503
870-793-7581
www.uaccb.cc.ar.us

University of Arkansas
Community College at Hope
PO Box 140
Hope, AR   71801-0140
870-777-5722
www.uacch.cc.ar.us

University of Arkansas
Community College at
Morrilton
One Bruce Street
Morrilton, AR   72110
501-354-2465
www.state.ar.us/pjc

California

Allan Hancock College
800 South College Drive
Santa Maria, CA   93454-6399
Phone: 805-922-6966
www.hancock.cc.ca.us

American Academy of
Dramatic Arts/Hollywood
1336 North La Brea Avenue
Hollywood, CA   90028
Phone: 323-464-2777
www.aada.org

American River College
4700 College Oak Drive
Sacramento, CA   95841-4286
Phone: 916-484-8011
www.arc.losrios.cc.ca.us

Antelope Valley College
3041 West Avenue K
Lancaster, CA   93536-5426
Phone: 661-722-6300
www.avc.edu

Bakersfield College
1801 Panorama Drive
Bakersfield, CA   93305-1299
Phone: 661-395-4011
www.kccd.cc.ca.us

Barstow College
2700 Barstow Road
Barstow, CA   92311-6699
Phone: 760-252-2411
www.barstow.cc.ca.us

Brooks College
4825 East Pacific Coast
Highway
Long Beach, CA   90804-3291
Phone: 562-498-2441
Fax: 562-597-7412
www.brookscollege.edu/

Butte College
3536 Butte Campus Drive
Oroville, CA   95965-8399
Phone: 530-895-2511
Fax: 530-895-2345

Cañada College
4200 Farm Hill Boulevard
Redwood City, CA
94061-1099
Phone: 650-306-3100
www.canadacollege.net

Cabrillo College
6500 Soquel Drive
Aptos, CA   95003-3194
Phone: 831-479-6100
www.cabrillo.cc.ca.us

California College of
Technology
4330 Watt Avenue, Suite 400
Sacramento, CA   95660
Phone: 916-649-8168
www.californiacollegetech.
com

California Culinary Academy
625 Polk Street
San Francisco, CA
94102-3368
Phone: 415-771-3500
www.baychef.com

California Design College
3440 Wilshire Boulevard,
Seventh Floor
Los Angeles, CA   90010
Phone: 213-251-3636
www.cdc.edu

Cerritos College
11110 Alondra Boulevard
Norwalk, CA   90650-6298
Phone: 562-860-2451
www.cerritos.edu

Cerro Coso Community
College
3000 College Heights Blvd
Ridgecrest, CA   93555-9571
Phone: 760-384-6100
www.cc.cc.ca.us

Chabot College
25555 Hesperian Boulevard
Hayward, CA   94545-5001
Phone: 510-723-6600
www.chabot.cc.ca.us

Chaffey College
5885 Haven Avenue
Rancho Cucamonga, CA
91737-3002
Phone: 909-987-1737
www.chaffey.cc.ca.us

Citrus College
1000 West Foothill Boulevard
Glendora, CA   91741-1899
Phone: 626-963-0323
www.citrus.cc.ca.us

City College of San Francisco
50 Phelan Avenue
San Francisco, CA
94112-1821
Phone: 415-239-3000
www.ccsf.org

Coastline Community
College
11460 Warner Avenue
Fountain Valley, CA
92708-2597
Phone: 714-546-7600
www.coastline.cccd.edu

College of Alameda
555 Atlantic Avenue
Alameda, CA   94501-2109
Phone: 510-522-7221
www.peralta.cc.ca.us

College of Marin
835 College Avenue
Kentfield, CA   94904
Phone: 415-457-8811
www.marin.cc.ca.us

College of Oceaneering
272 South Fries Avenue
Wilmington, CA   90744-6399
Phone: 310-834-2501
www.diveco.com

College of San Mateo
1700 West Hillsdale Blvd
San Mateo, CA   94402-3784
Phone: 650-574-6161
www.gocsm.net

College of the Canyons
26455 Rockwell Canyon Road
Santa Clarita, CA
91355-1899
Phone: 661-259-7800
www.coc.cc.ca.us

College of the Desert
43-500 Monterey Avenue
Palm Desert, CA   92260-9305
Phone: 760-346-8041
www.desert.cc.ca.us

College of the Redwoods
7351 Tompkins Hill Road
Eureka, CA   95501-9300
Phone: 707-476-4100

College of the Sequoias
915 South Mooney Blvd
Visalia, CA 93277-2234
Phone: 559-730-3700
www.sequoias.cc.ca.us

College of the Siskiyous
800 College Avenue
Weed, CA 96094-2899
Phone: 530-938-4461
www.siskiyous.edu

Columbia College
11600 Columbia College Dr
Sonora, CA 95370
Phone: 209-588-5100

Compton Community
College
1111 East Artesia Boulevard
Compton, CA 90221-5393
Phone: 310-900-1600

Contra Costa College
2600 Mission Bell Drive
San Pablo, CA 94806-3195
Phone: 510-235-7800
www.contracosta.cc.ca.us

Copper Mountain College
6162 Rotary Way
Joshua Tree, CA 92252
Phone: 760-366-3791
www.cmccd.cc.ca.us

Cosumnes River College
8401 Center Parkway
Sacramento, CA 95823-5799
Phone: 916-691-7451
www.wserver.crc.losrios.cc.
ca.us

Crafton Hills College
11711 Sand Canyon Road
Yucaipa, CA 92399-1799
Phone: 909-794-2161

Cuesta College
PO Box 8106
San Luis Obispo, CA
93403-8106
Phone: 805-546-3100
www.cuesta.org

Cuyamaca College
900 Rancho San Diego Pkwy
El Cajon, CA 92019-4304
Phone: 619-660-4000
www.cuyamaca.net

Cypress College
9200 Valley View
Cypress, CA 90630-5897
Phone: 714-484-7000
www.cypress.cc.ca.us

D-Q University
PO Box 409
Davis, CA 95617-0409
Phone: 530-758-0470

De Anza College
21250 Stevens Creek Blvd
Cupertino, CA 95014-5793
Phone: 408-864-5678
www.deanza.fhda.edu

Deep Springs College
HC 72, Box 45001
Deep Springs, CA
89010-9803
Phone: 760-872-2000
www.deepsprings.edu

Diablo Valley College
321 Golf Club Road
Pleasant Hill, CA
94523-1544
Phone: 925-685-1230
www.dvc.edu

Don Bosco College of
Science and Technology
1151 San Gabriel Boulevard
Rosemead, CA 91770-4299
Phone: 626-940-2000
www.boscotech.org

East Los Angeles College
1301 Avenida Cesar Chavez
Monterey Park, CA
91754-6001
Phone: 323-265-8650
www.elac.cc.ca.us

El Camino College
16007 Crenshaw Boulevard
Torrance, CA 90506-0001
Phone: 310-532-3670

Empire College
3035 Cleveland Avenue
Santa Rosa, CA 95403
Phone: 707-546-4000
www.empcol.com

Evergreen Valley College
3095 Yerba Buena Road
San Jose, CA 95135-1598
Phone: 408-274-7900

Fashion Careers of California
College
1923 Morena Boulevard
San Diego, CA 92110
Phone: 619-275-4700
www.fashioncollege.com

Fashion Institute of Design
and Merchandising,
Los Angeles
919 South Grand Avenue
Los Angeles, CA 90015-1421
Phone: 213-624-1200
www.fidm.com

Fashion Institute of Design
and Merchandising,
San Diego Campus
1010 Second Avenue,
Suite 200
San Diego, CA 92101-4903
Phone: 619-235-2049
www.fidm.com

Fashion Institute of Design
and Merchandising,
San Francisco Campus
55 Stockton Street
San Francisco, CA
94108-5829
Phone: 415-675-5200
www.fidm.com

Feather River Community
College District
570 Golden Eagle Avenue
Quincy, CA 95971-9124
Phone: 530-283-0202
www.frcc.cc.ca.us

Foothill College
12345 El Monte Road
Los Altos Hills, CA
94022-4599
Phone: 650-949-7777
www.foothillcollege.org

Foundation College
5353 Mission Center Road,
Suite 100
San Diego, CA 92108-1306
Phone: 619-683-3273
www.foundationcollege.org

Fresno City College
1101 East University Avenue
Fresno, CA 93741-0002
Phone: 559-442-4600
www.scccd.cc.ca.us

Fullerton College
321 East Chapman Avenue
Fullerton, CA 92832-2095
Phone: 714-992-7000
www.fullcoll.edu

Gavilan College
5055 Santa Teresa Boulevard
Gilroy, CA 95020-9599
Phone: 408-847-1400
www.gavilan.cc.ca.us

Glendale Community College
1500 North Verdugo Road
Glendale, CA 91208-2894
Phone: 818-240-1000
www.glendale.cc.ca.us

Golden West College
PO Box 2748,
15744 Golden West Street
Huntington Beach, CA
92647-2748
Phone: 714-892-7711
www.gwc.cccd.edu

Grossmont College
8800 Grossmont College Dr
El Cajon, CA 92020-1799
Phone: 619-644-7000

Hartnell College
156 Homestead Avenue
Salinas, CA 93901-1697
Phone: 831-755-6700

Heald College Concord
5130 Commercial Circle
Concord, CA 94520
Phone: 925-228-5800
www.heald.edu

Heald College, School of
Business
2150 John Glenn Drive
Concord, CA 94520-5618
Phone: 510-827-1300

Heald College, School of
Business
1450 North Main Street
Salinas, CA 93906
Phone: 408-443-1700
www.heald.edu

Heald College, School of
Business
1605 East March Lane
Stockton, CA 95210
Phone: 209-477-1114

Heald College, School of
Business
2425 Mendocino Avenue
Santa Rosa, CA 95403-3116
Phone: 707-525-1300

Heald College, Schools of
Business and Technology
341 Great Mall Parkway
Milpitas, CA 95035
Phone: 408-934-4900
www.heald.edu

Heald College, Schools of
Business and Technology
255 West Bullard Avenue
Fresno, CA 93704-1706
Phone: 559-438-4222
www.heald.edu

Heald College, Schools of
Business and Technology
2910 Prospect Park Drive
Rancho Cordova, CA
95670-6005
Phone: 916-638-1616
www.heald.edu

Heald College, Schools of
Business and Technology
Seven Sierra Gate Plaza
Roseville, CA 95678
Phone: 916-789-8600
www.heald.edu

Heald College, Schools of
Business and Technology
24301 Southland Drive,
Suite 500
Hayward, CA 94545-1557
Phone: 510-783-2100
www.heald.edu

Heald College, Schools of
Business and Technology
350 Mission Street
San Francisco, CA
94105-2206
Phone: 415-808-3000
www.heald.edu

Imperial Valley College
PO Box 158, 380 East Aten Rd
Imperial, CA 92251-0158
Phone: 760-352-8320
www.imperial.cc.ca.us

Irvine Valley College
5500 Irvine Center Drive
Irvine, CA 92620-4399
Phone: 949-451-5100
www.ivc.cc.ca.us

ITT Technical Institute
16916 South Harlan Road
Lathrop, CA 95330
Phone: 209-858-0077
www.itt-tech.edu

ITT Technical Institute
10863 Gold Center Drive
Rancho Cordova, CA
95670-6034
Phone: 916-851-3900
www.itt-tech.edu

ITT Technical Institute
630 East Brier Drive,
Suite 150
San Bernardino, CA
92408-2800
Phone: 909-889-3800
www.itt-tech.edu

ITT Technical Institute
5104 Old Ironsides Drive
Santa Clara, CA 95050
Phone: 408-496-0655
www.itt-tech.edu

ITT Technical Institute
3979 Trust Way
Hayward, CA 94545
Phone: 510-785-8522

ITT Technical Institute
2051 Solar Drive, Suite 150
Oxnard, CA 93030
Phone: 805-988-0143

ITT Technical Institute
1530 West Cameron Avenue
West Covina, CA 91790-2711
Phone: 626-960-8681
www.itt-tech.edu

ITT Technical Institute
20050 South Vermont Avenue
Torrance, CA 90502
Phone: 310-380-1555
www.itt-tech.edu

ITT Technical Institute
525 North Muller Street
Anaheim, CA 92801-9938
Phone: 714-535-3700
www.itt-tech.edu

ITT Technical Institute
12669 Encinitas Avenue
Sylmar, CA 91342-3664
Phone: 818-364-5151
www.itt-tech.edu

ITT Technical Institute
9680 Granite Ridge Drive,
Suite 100
San Diego, CA 92123
Phone: 858-571-8500
www.itt-tech.edu

Kelsey Jenney College
201 A Street
San Diego, CA 92101
Phone: 619-233-7418
www.kelsey-jenney.com

Lake Tahoe Community
College
One College Drive
South Lake Tahoe, CA
96150-4524
Phone: 530-541-4660
www.ltcc.cc.ca.us

Laney College
900 Fallon Street
Oakland, CA 94607-4893
Phone: 510-834-5740
laney.peralta.cc.ca.us

Las Positas College
3033 Collier Canyon Road
Livermore, CA 94550-7650
Phone: 925-373-5800
www.clpccd.cc.ca.us/lpc

Lassen Community College
District
Highway 139, PO Box 3000
Susanville, CA 96130
Phone: 530-257-6181
www.lassen.cc.ca.us

Long Beach City College
4901 East Carson Street
Long Beach, CA 90808-1780
Phone: 562-938-4111
de.lbcc.cc.ca.us

Los Angeles City College
855 North Vermont Avenue
Los Angeles, CA 90029-3590
Phone: 323-953-4000
www.lacc.cc.ca.us

Los Angeles County College
of Nursing and Allied Health
1200 N State St, Muir Hall,
Rm 114
Los Angeles, CA 90033-1084
Phone: 213-226-4911

Los Angeles Harbor College
1111 Figueroa Place
Wilmington, CA 90744-2397
Phone: 310-522-8200
www.lahc.cc.ca.us

Los Angeles Mission College
13356 Eldridge Avenue
Sylmar, CA 91342-3245
Phone: 818-364-7600
www.lamission.cc.ca.us

Los Angeles Pierce College
6201 Winnetka Avenue
Woodland Hills, CA
91371-0001
Phone: 818-347-0551
www.lapc.cc.ca.us

Los Angeles Southwest
College
1600 West Imperial Highway
Los Angeles, CA 90047-4810
Phone: 323-241-5225

Los Angeles Trade-Technical
College
400 West Washington Blvd
Los Angeles, CA 90015-4108
Phone: 213-744-9500

Los Angeles Valley College
5800 Fulton Avenue
Valley Glen, CA 91401-4096
Phone: 818-947-2600
www.lavc.cc.ca.us

Los Medanos College
2700 East Leland Road
Pittsburg, CA 94565-5197
Phone: 925-439-2181

Maric College
3666 Kearny Villa Road
San Diego, CA 92123-1995
Phone: 858-279-4500
www.mariccollege.edu

Marymount College, Palos
Verdes, California
30800 Palos Verdes Drive
East
Rancho Palos Verdes, CA
90275-6299
Phone: 310-377-5501
www.marymountpv.edu

Mendocino College
PO Box 3000
Ukiah, CA 95482-0300
Phone: 707-468-3000
www.mendocino.cc.ca.us

Merced College
3600 M Street
Merced, CA 95348-2898
Phone: 209-384-6000

Merritt College
12500 Campus Drive
Oakland, CA 94619-3196
Phone: 510-531-4911

MiraCosta College
One Barnard Drive
Oceanside, CA 92056-3899
Phone: 760-757-2121
www.miracosta.cc.ca.us

Mission College
3000 Mission College
Boulevard
Santa Clara, CA 95054-1897
Phone: 408-988-2200
www.wvmccd.cc.ca.us/mc

Modesto Junior College
435 College Avenue
Modesto, CA 95350-5800
Phone: 209-575-6498
mjc.yosemite.cc.ca.us

Monterey Peninsula College
980 Fremont Street
Monterey, CA 93940-4799
Phone: 831-646-4000
www.mpc.edu

Moorpark College
7075 Campus Road
Moorpark, CA 93021-1695
Phone: 805-378-1400
www.moorpark.cc.ca.us

Mt. San Antonio College
1100 North Grand Avenue
Walnut, CA 91789-1399
Phone: 909-594-5611
www.mtsac.edu

Mt. San Jacinto College
1499 North State Street
San Jacinto, CA 92583-2399
Phone: 909-487-6752
www.msjc.cc.ca.us

MTI College
2011 West Chapman Avenue,
Suite 100
Orange, CA 92868-2632
Phone: 714-385-1132

MTI College of Business and
Technology
5221 Madison Avenue
Sacramento, CA 95841
Phone: 916-339-1500
www.mticollege.com

Napa Valley College
2277 Napa-Vallejo Highway
Napa, CA 94558-6236
Phone: 707-253-3000
www.nvc.cc.ca.us

Ohlone College
43600 Mission Boulevard
Fremont, CA 94539-5884
Phone: 510-659-6000
www.ohlone.cc.ca.us

Orange Coast College
2701 Fairview Road,
PO Box 5005
Costa Mesa, CA 92628-5005
Phone: 714-432-0202
www.orangecoastcollege.
com

Oxnard College
4000 South Rose Avenue
Oxnard, CA 93033-6699
Phone: 805-986-5800
www.oxnard.cc.ca.us

Palo Verde College
811 West Chanslorway
Blythe, CA 92225-1118
Phone: 760-922-6168
www.paloverde.cc.ca.us

Palomar College
1140 West Mission Road
San Marcos, CA 92069-1487
Phone: 760-744-1150
www.palomar.edu

Pasadena City College
1570 East Colorado Blvd
Pasadena, CA 91106-2041
Phone: 626-585-7123
www.paccd.cc.ca.us

Pima Medical Institute
780 Bay Boulevard
Chula Vista, CA 91910
Phone: 619-425-3200

Platt College
3700 Inland Empire
Boulevard, Suite 400
Ontario, CA 91764
Phone: 909-941-9410
www.plattcollege.edu

Platt College
3901 MacArthur Boulevard
Newport Beach, CA 92660
Phone: 949-833-2300
www.plattcollege.edu

Platt College
10900 East 183rd Street,
Suite 290
Cerritos, CA 90703-5342
Phone: 562-809-5100
www.platt.edu

Platt College San Diego
6250 El Cajon Boulevard
San Diego, CA 92115-3919
Phone: 619-265-0107
www.platt.edu

Platt College–Los Angeles,
Inc
7470 North Figueroa Street
Los Angeles, CA 90041-1717
Phone: 323-258-8050
www.plattcollege.edu

Porterville College
100 East College Avenue
Porterville, CA 93257-6058
Phone: 559-791-2200
www.pc.cc.ca.us

Professional Golfers Career
College
PO Box 892319
Temecula, CA 92589
Phone: 909-693-2963

Queen of the Holy Rosary
College
PO Box 3908
Mission San Jose, CA
94539-0391
Phone: 510-657-2468
www.msjdominicans.org/col-
lege.html

Reedley College
995 North Reed Avenue
Reedley, CA 93654-2099
Phone: 559-638-3641
www.rc.cc.ca.us

Rhodes College
9616 Archibald Avenue,
Suite 100
Rancho Cucamonga, CA
91730
Phone: 909-484-4311
rhodes-college.com

Rio Hondo College
3600 Workman Mill Road
Whittier, CA 90601-1699
Phone: 562-692-0921
www.rh.cc.ca.us

Riverside Community
College
4800 Magnolia Avenue
Riverside, CA 92506-1299
Phone: 909-222-8000
www.rccd.cc.ca.us

Sacramento City College
3835 Freeport Boulevard
Sacramento, CA 95822-1386
Phone: 916-558-2111
www.scc.losrios.cc.ca.us

Saddleback College
28000 Marguerite Parkway
Mission Viejo, CA
92692-3697
Phone: 949-582-4500
www.saddleback.cc.ca.us

Salvation Army College for
Officer Training
30840 Hawthorne Boulevard
Rancho Palos Verdes, CA
90275
Phone: 310-377-0481

San Bernardino Valley
College
701 South Mt Vernon Avenue
San Bernardino, CA
92410-2748
Phone: 909-888-6511

San Diego City College
1313 Twelfth Avenue
San Diego, CA 92101-4787
Phone: 619-388-3400
www.city.sdccd.cc.ca.us

San Diego Golf Academy
1910 Shadowridge Drive,
Suite 111
Vista, CA 92083
Phone: 760-734-1208
www.sdgagolf.com

San Diego Mesa College
7250 Mesa College Drive
San Diego, CA 92111-4998
Phone: 619-388-2600
www.sdmesa.sdccd.cc.ca.us

San Diego Miramar College
10440 Black Mountain Road
San Diego, CA 92126-2999
Phone: 619-536-7800
www.miramar.sdccd.cc.ca.us

San Francisco College of
Mortuary Science
1598 Dolores Street
San Francisco, CA
94110-4927
Phone: 415-824-1313
www.sfcms.org

San Joaquin Delta College
5151 Pacific Avenue
Stockton, CA 95207-6370
Phone: 209-954-5151
www.deltacollege.org

San Joaquin Valley College
8400 West Mineral King
Avenue
Visalia, CA 93291
Phone: 559-651-2500
www.sjvc.com

San Jose City College
2100 Moorpark Avenue
San Jose, CA 95128-2799
Phone: 408-298-2181
www.sjcc.edu

Santa Ana College
1530 West 17th Street
Santa Ana, CA 92706-3398
Phone: 714-564-6000
www.rsccd.org

Santa Barbara City College
721 Cliff Drive
Santa Barbara, CA
93109-2394
Phone: 805-965-0581
www.sbcc.net

Santa Monica College
1900 Pico Boulevard
Santa Monica, CA
90405-1628
Phone: 310-434-4000
www.smc.edu

Santa Rosa Junior College
1501 Mendocino Avenue
Santa Rosa, CA 95401-4395
Phone: 707-527-4011
www.santarosa.edu

Santiago Canyon College
8045 East Chapman Avenue
Orange, CA 92869
Phone: 714-564-4000
www.sccollege.org

Sequoia Institute
200 Whitney Place
Fremont, CA 94539-7663
Phone: 510-490-6900
www.sequoiainstitute.com

Shasta College
PO Box 496006
Redding, CA 96049-6006
Phone: 530-225-4600
www.shastacollege.edu

Sierra College
5000 Rocklin Road
Rocklin, CA 95677-3397
Phone: 916-624-3333
www.sierra.cc.ca.us

Silicon Valley College
41350 Christy Street
Fremont, CA 94538
Phone: 510-623-9966
www.siliconvalley.edu

Silicon Valley College
6201 San Ignacio Boulevard
San Jose, CA 95119
Phone: 408-360-0840
www.siliconvalley.edu

Silicon Valley College
2800 Mitchell Drive
Walnut Creek, CA 94598
Phone: 925-280-0235
www.siliconvalley.edu

Skyline College
3300 College Drive
San Bruno, CA 94066-1698
Phone: 650-738-4100
skylinecollege.net

Solano Community College
4000 Suisun Valley Road
Suisun, CA 94585-3197
Phone: 707-864-7000
www.solano.cc.ca.us

Southern California College
of Business and Law
595 West Lambert Road
Brea, CA 92821-3909
Phone: 714-256-8830

Southern California Institute
of Technology
1900 West Crescent Avenue,
Building B
Anaheim, CA 92801
Phone: 714-520-5552

Southwestern College
900 Otay Lakes Road
Chula Vista, CA 91910-7299
Phone: 619-421-6700
www.swc.cc.ca.us

Taft College
29 Emmons Park Drive
Taft, CA 93268-2317
Phone: 661-763-7700
www.taft.cc.ca.us

The Art Institute of Los
Angeles
2900 31st Street
Santa Monica, CA
90405-3035
Phone: 310-752-4700
www.aila.aii.edu

Ventura College
4667 Telegraph Road
Ventura, CA 93003-3899
Phone: 805-654-6400
www.ventura.cc.ca.us

Victor Valley College
18422 Bear Valley Road
Victorville, CA 92392-5849
Phone: 760-245-4271
www.vvcconline.com

Vista Community College
2020 Milvia Street, 3rd Floor
Berkeley, CA 94704-5102
Phone: 510-981-2800
www.peralta.cc.ca.us

West Hills Community
College
300 Cherry Lane
Coalinga, CA 93210-1399
Phone: 559-935-0801
www.westhills.cc.ca.us

West Los Angeles College
4800 Freshman Drive
Culver City, CA 90230-3519
Phone: 310-287-4200
www.wlac.cc.ca.us

West Valley College
14000 Fruitvale Avenue
Saratoga, CA 95070-5698
Phone: 408-867-2200
www.westvalley.edu

Western Institute of Science
and Health
130 Avram Avenue
Rohnert Park, CA 94928
Phone: 707-664-9267
www.westerni.org

Yuba College
2088 North Beale Road
Marysville, CA 95901-7699
Phone: 530-741-6700
www.yuba.cc.ca.us

Colorado

Aims Community College
Box 69
Greeley, CO 80632-0069
Phone: 970-330-8008
www.aims.edu

Arapahoe Community
College
5900 South Santa Fe Drive,
PO Box 9002
Littleton, CO 80160-9002
Phone: 303-797-4222
www.arapahoe.edu

Bel–Rea Institute of Animal
Technology
1681 South Dayton Street
Denver, CO 80231-3048
Phone: 303-751-8700
www.bel-rea.com

Blair College
828 Wooten Road
Colorado Springs, CO 80915
Phone: 719-574-1082
www.cci.edu

Cambridge College
12500 East Iliff Avenue, # 100
Aurora, CO 80014
Phone: 303-338-9700
www.hightechschools.com

CollegeAmerica–Denver
1385 South Colorado Blvd
Denver, CO 80222-1912
Phone: 303-691-9756
www.collegeamerica.com

CollegeAmerica–Fort Collins
4601 South Mason Street
Fort Collins, CO 80525-3740
Phone: 970-223-6060
www.collegeamerica.com

Colorado Mountain College,
Alpine Campus
1330 Bob Adams Drive
Steamboat Springs, CO
80487
Phone: 970-870-4444
www.coloradomtn.edu

Colorado Mountain College,
Spring Valley Campus
3000 County Road 114
Glenwood Springs, CO
81601
Phone: 970-945-7481
www.coloradomtn.edu

Colorado Mountain College,
Timberline Campus
901 South Highway 24
Leadville, CO 80461
Phone: 719-486-2015
www.coloradomtn.edu

Colorado Northwestern
Community College
500 Kennedy Drive
Rangely, CO 81648-3598
Phone: 970-675-2261
www.cncc.cc.co.us

Colorado School of Trades
1575 Hoyt Street
Lakewood, CO 80215-2996
Phone: 303-233-4697
schooloftrades.com

Community College of
Aurora
16000 East Centre Tech Pkwy
Aurora, CO 80011-9036
Phone: 303-360-4700
www.cca.cccoes.edu

Community College of
Denver
PO Box 173363
Denver, CO 80217-3363
Phone: 303-556-2600
www.ccd.rightchoice.org

Denver Academy of Court
Reporting
7290 Samuel Drive, Suite 200
Denver, CO 80221-2792
Phone: 303-427-5292
www.dacr.com

Denver Automotive and
Diesel College
460 South Lipan Street
Denver, CO 80223-2025
Phone: 303-722-5724
www.denverautodiesel.com

Front Range Community
College
3645 West 112th Avenue
Westminster, CO
80031-2105
Phone: 303-466-8811
frcc.cc.co.us

Institute of Business &
Medical Careers
1609 Oakridge Drive,
Suite 102
Fort Collins, CO 80525
Phone: 970-223-2669

IntelliTec College
772 Horizon Drive
Grand Junction, CO 81506
Phone: 970-245-8101

IntelliTec College
2315 East Pikes Peak Avenue
Colorado Springs, CO
80909-6030
Phone: 719-632-7626

IntelliTec Medical Institute
2345 North Academy
Boulevard
Colorado Springs, CO 80909
Phone: 719-596-7400

ITT Technical Institute
500 East 84th Avenue,
Suite B12
Thornton, CO 80229
Phone: 303-288-4488
www.itt-tech.edu

Lamar Community College
2401 South Main Street
Lamar, CO 81052-3999
Phone: 719-336-2248

Morgan Community College
17800 County Road 20
Fort Morgan, CO 80701-
4399
Phone: 970-542-3100
www.mcc.cccoes.edu

Northeastern Junior College
100 College Drive
Sterling, CO 80751-2399
Phone: 970-521-6600
www.nejc.cc.co.us

Otero Junior College
1802 Colorado Avenue
La Junta, CO 81050-3415
Phone: 719-384-6831

Parks College
9065 Grant Street
Denver, CO 80229-4339
Phone: 303-457-2757
www.cci.edu

Pikes Peak Community
College
5675 South Academy Blvd
Colorado Springs, CO
80906-5498
Phone: 719-576-7711
www.ppcc.cccoes.edu

Pima Medical Institute
1701 West 72nd Avenue, #130
Denver, CO 80221
Phone: 303-426-1800
www.pimamedical.com

Platt College
3100 South Parker Road,
Suite 200
Aurora, CO 80014-3141
Phone: 303-369-5151
www.plattcolorado.edu

Pueblo Community College
900 West Orman Avenue
Pueblo, CO 81004-1499
Phone: 719-549-3200
www.pcc.cccoes.edu

Red Rocks Community
College
13300 West 6th Avenue
Lakewood, CO 80228-1255
Phone: 303-988-6160

Trinidad State Junior College
600 Prospect
Trinidad, CO 81082-2396
Phone: 719-846-5011
www.tsjc.cccoes.edu

Westwood College of
Aviation Technology–Denver
10851 West 120th Avenue
Broomfield, CO 80021-3465
Phone: 303-466-1714
www.westwood.edu

Connecticut

Asnuntuck Community
College
170 Elm Street
Enfield, CT 06082-3800
860-253-3000
www.asctc.commnet.edu

Briarwood College
2279 Mount Vernon Road
Southington, CT 06489-1057
860-628-4751
www.briarwood.edu

Capital Community College
61 Woodland Street
Hartford, CT 06105-2354
860-520-7800
webster.commnet.edu

Gateway Community College
60 Sargent Drive
New Haven, CT 06511-5918
203-285-2000
www.gwctc.commnet.edu

Gibbs College
142 East Avenue
Norwalk, CT 06851-5754
203-838-4173
www.gibbscollege.com

Goodwin College
745 Burnside Avenue
East Hartford, CT 06108
860-528-4111
www.goodwincollege.org

Housatonic Community
College
900 Lafayette Boulevard
Bridgeport, CT 06604-4704
203-332-5000
www.hctc.commnet.edu

International College of
Hospitality Management,
César
101 Wykeham Road
Washington, CT 06793-1300
860-868-9555
www.ichm.ritz.edu

Manchester Community
College
PO Box 1046
Manchester, CT 06045-1046
860-647-6000
www.mctc.commnet.edu

Middlesex Community
College
100 Training Hill Road
Middletown, CT 06457-4889
860-343-5800
www.mxctc.commnet.edu

Mitchell College
437 Pequot Avenue
New London, CT 06320-4498
860-701-5000

Naugatuck Valley Community
College
750 Chase Parkway
Waterbury, CT 06708-3000
203-575-8040
www.nvcc.commnet.edu

Northwestern Connecticut
Community College
Park Place East
Winsted, CT 06098-1798
860-738-6300
www.commnet.edu/nwctc

Norwalk Community College
188 Richards Avenue
Norwalk, CT 06854-1655
203-857-7000
www.ncc.commnet.edu

Quinebaug Valley
Community College
742 Upper Maple Street
Danielson, CT 06239-1440
860-774-1130
www.qvcc.commnet.edu

St. Vincent's College
2800 Main Street
Bridgeport, CT 06606-4292
203-576-5235

Three Rivers Community
College
Mahan Drive
Norwich, CT 06360
860-886-1931
www.trctc.commnet.edu

Tunxis Community College
271 Scott Swamp Road
Farmington, CT 06032-3026
860-677-7701
www.tunxis.commnet.edu

Delaware

Delaware Technical &
Community College,
Stanton/Wilmington Campus
400 Stanton-Christiana Road
Newark, DE 19713
302-454-3900
www.dtcc.edu

Delaware Technical &
Community College, Jack F.
Owens Campus
PO Box 610, Route 18
Georgetown, DE 19947
302-856-5400
www.dtcc.edu

Delaware Technical &
Community College, Terry
Campus
100 Campus Drive
Dover, DE 19901
302-857-1000
www.dtcc.edu/terry

Florida

The Academy
3131 Flightline Drive
Lakeland, FL 33811-2836
863-648-2004
www.theacademy.net

ATI Career Training Center
1 NE 19th Street
Miami, FL 33132
305-573-1600
www.aticareertraining.com

ATI Career Training Center
3501 NW 9th Avenue
Oakland Park, FL
33309-9612
954-563-5899
www.aticareertraining.com

ATI Career Training Center
Electronics Campus
2880 NW 62nd Street
Fort Lauderdale, FL
33309-9731
954-973-4760
www.aticareertraining.com

ATI Health Education Center
1395 NW 167th Street,
Suite 200
Miami, FL 33169-5742
305-628-1000
www.aticareertraining.com

Atlantic Coast Institute
5225 West Broward Blvd
Fort Lauderdale, FL 33317
954-581-2223
www.atlanticcoastinstitute.
com

Brevard Community College
1519 Clearlake Road
Cocoa, FL 32922-6597
321-632-1111
www.brevard.cc.fl.us

Broward Community College
225 East Las Olas Boulevard
Fort Lauderdale, FL
33301-2298
954-475-6500
www.broward.cc.fl.us

Central Florida Community
College
PO Box 1388
Ocala, FL 34478-1388
352-854-2322
www.cfcc.cc.fl.us

Chipola Junior College
3094 Indian Circle
Marianna, FL 32446-3065
850-526-2761

City College
1401 West Cypress Creek Rd
Fort Lauderdale, FL 33309
954-492-5353
www.citycollege.edu

College for Professional
Studies
1801 Clint Moore Road,
Suite 215
Boca Raton, FL 33487
561-994-2522
www.kaplancollege.edu

Cooper Career Institute
2247 Palm Beach Lakes Blvd,
Suite 110
West Palm Beach, FL 33409
561-640-6999
www.lawfirms-ww.com/
services/cooper.htm

Daytona Beach Community
College
PO Box 2811
Daytona Beach, FL
32120-2811
386-255-8131
www.dbcc.cc.fl.us

Edison Community College
PO Box 60210
Fort Myers, FL 33906-6210
941-489-9300
www.edison.edu

Education America, Tampa
Technical Institute,
Jacksonville
7011 A.C. Skinner Parkway
Jacksonville, FL 32256
904-296-3435

Education America, Tampa
Technical Institute, Pinellas
Campus
8550 Ulmerton Road
Largo, FL 33771
727-532-1999

Education America, Tampa
Technical Institute, Tampa
Campus
2410 East Busch Boulevard
Tampa, FL 33612-8410
813-932-0701
www.tampatech.edu

Florida Community College
at Jacksonville
501 West State Street
Jacksonville, FL 32202-4030
904-632-3000
www.fccj.org

Florida Computer & Business
School
1321 Southwest 107 Avenue,
Suite 201B
Miami, FL 33174
305-553-6065
www.floridacomputer.com

Florida Culinary Institute
2400 Metrocenter Boulevard
West Palm Beach, FL 33407
561-688-2001

Florida Hospital College of
Health Sciences
800 Lake Estelle Drive
Orlando, FL 32803
407-303-7747
www.fhchs.edu

Florida Keys Community
College
5901 College Road
Key West, FL 33040-4397
305-296-9081
www.firn.edu/fkcc

Florida National College
4206 West 12th Avenue
Hialeah, FL 33012
305-821-3333
www.fnc.edu

Florida Technical College
1819 North Semoran Blvd
Orlando, FL 32807-3546
407-678-5600
www.flatech.edu

Florida Technical College
8711 Lone Star Road
Jacksonville, FL 32211
904-724-2229
www.flatech.edu

Florida Technical College
1450 South Woodland
Boulevard, 3rd Floor
DeLand, FL 32720
904-734-3303
www.flatech.edu

Florida Technical College
298 Havendale Boulevard
Auburndale, FL 33823
863-967-8822
www.flatech.edu

Full Sail Real World
Education
3300 University Boulevard
Winter Park, FL 32792-7437
407-679-6333
www.fullsail.com

Gulf Coast Community
College
5230 West Highway 98
Panama City, FL 32401-1058
850-769-1551
www.gc.cc.fl.us

Herzing College
1300 North Semoran
Boulevard, Suite 103
Orlando, FL 32807
407-380-6315
www.herzing.edu

Herzing College
1270 North Wickham Road,
Suite 51
Melbourne, FL 32935
321-255-9232
www.herzing.edu

Hillsborough Community
College
PO Box 31127
Tampa, FL 33631-3127
813-253-7000
www.hcc.cc.fl.us

Indian River Community
College
3209 Virginia Avenue
Fort Pierce, FL 34981-5596
561-462-4700
www.ircc.cc.fl.us

Institute of Career Education
1750 45th Street
West Palm Beach, FL
33407-2192
561-881-0220

ITT Technical Institute
3401 South University Drive
Fort Lauderdale, FL
33328-2021
954-476-9300
www.itt-tech.edu

ITT Technical Institute
7955 NW 12th Street
Miami, FL 33126
305-477-3080
www.itt-tech.edu

ITT Technical Institute
2600 Lake Lucien Drive,
Suite 140
Maitland, FL 32751-7234
407-660-2900
www.itt-tech.edu

ITT Technical Institute
6600-10 Youngerman Circle
Jacksonville, FL 32244-6630
904-573-9100
www.itt-tech.edu

ITT Technical Institute
4809 Memorial Highway
Tampa, FL 33634-7151
813-885-2244
www.itt-tech.edu

Keiser College
1800 W International Spdwy,
Bldg 3
Daytona Beach, FL 32114
904-274-5060
www.keisercollege.cc.fl.us

Keiser College
900 South Babcock Street
Melbourne, FL 32901-1461
321-255-2255
www.keisercollege.cc.fl.us

Keiser College
1500 Northwest 49th Street
Fort Lauderdale, FL 33309
954-776-4456
www.keisercollege.cc.fl.us

Keiser College
1700 Halstead Boulevard
Tallahassee, FL 32308
850-906-9494
www.keisercollege.cc.fl.us

Keiser College
332 Sarasota Quay
Sarasota, FL 34236
941-954-0954
www.keisercollege.cc.fl.us

Lake City Community
College
Route 19, Box 1030
Lake City, FL 32025-8703
386-752-1822
www.lakecity.cc.fl.us

Lake-Sumter Community
College
9501 US Highway 441
Leesburg, FL 34788-8751
352-787-3747
www.lscc.cc.fl.us

Manatee Community College
5840 26th Street West,
PO Box 1849
Bradenton, FL 34206-7046
941-752-5000
www.mcc.cc.fl.us

Miami-Dade Community
College
300 Northeast Second Ave
Miami, FL 33132-2296
305-237-3000
www.mdcc.edu

New England Institute of
Technology at Palm Beach
2410 Metro Centre Boulevard
West Palm Beach, FL 33407
561-842-8324
newenglandtech.com

North Florida Community
College
1000 Turner Davis Drive
Madison, FL 32340-1602
850-973-2288
www.nflcc.cc.fl.us

Okaloosa-Walton Community
College
100 College Boulevard
Niceville, FL 32578-1295
850-678-5111
www.owcc.cc.fl.us

Palm Beach Community
College
4200 Congress Avenue
Lake Worth, FL 33461-4796
561-967-7222
www.pbcc.cc.fl.us

Pasco-Hernando Community
College
10230 Ridge Road
New Port Richey, FL
34654-5199
727-847-2727
www.pasco-hernandocc.com

Pensacola Junior College
1000 College Boulevard
Pensacola, FL 32504-8998
850-484-1000
www.pjc.cc.fl.us

Peoples College
233 Academy Drive,
PO Box 421768
Kissimmee, FL 34742-1768
407-847-4444

Polk Community College
999 Avenue H, NE
Winter Haven, FL
33881-4299
863-297-1000
www.polk.cc.fl.us

Prospect Hall School of
Business
2620 Hollywood Boulevard
Hollywood, FL 33020
954-923-8100
www.prospect.edu

Santa Fe Community College
3000 Northwest 83rd Street
Gainesville, FL 32606-6200
352-395-5000
www.santafe.cc.fl.us

Seminole Community
College
100 Weldon Boulevard
Sanford, FL 32773-6199
407-328-4722
www.seminole.cc.fl.us

South Florida Community
College
600 West College Drive
Avon Park, FL 33825-9356
863-453-6661
www.sfcc.cc.fl.us

South University
1760 North Congress Avenue
West Palm Beach, FL 33409
561-697-9200
www.southcollege.edu

Southern College
5600 Lake Underhill Road
Orlando, FL 32807-1699
407-273-1000
www.southerncollege.org

Southwest Florida College
Suite 200, 1685 Medical Lane
Fort Myers, FL 33907
941-939-4766
www.swfc.edu

St. Johns River Community
College
5001 Saint Johns Avenue
Palatka, FL 32177-3897
904-312-4200
www.sjrcc.cc.fl.us

St. Petersburg College
PO Box 13489
St. Petersburg, FL
33733-3489
727-341-3600
www.spjc.edu

Tallahassee Community
College
444 Appleyard Drive
Tallahassee, FL 32304-2895
850-201-6200
www.tallahassee.cc.fl.us

Valencia Community College
PO Box 3028
Orlando, FL 32802-3028
407-299-5000
www.valencia.cc.fl.us

Webster College
1530 SW Third Avenue
Ocala, FL 34474
352-629-1941

Webster College
2127 Grand Boulevard
Holiday, FL 34690
727-942-0069
www.webstercollege.com

Webster Institute of
Technology
3910 US Highway 301 North,
Suite 200
Tampa, FL 33619-1259
813-620-1446
www.websterinstitute.com

Georgia

Abraham Baldwin
Agricultural College
2802 Moore Highway
Tifton, GA 31794-2601
912-386-3236
stallion.aback.peachnet.edu

Andrew College
413 College Street
Cuthbert, GA 31740-1395
912-732-2171
www.andrewcollege.edu

The Art Institute of Atlanta
6600 Peachtree Dunwoody
Road, 100 Embassy Row
Atlanta, GA 30328
770-394-8300
www.aia.artinstitute.edu

Asher School of Business
4975 Jimmy Carter
Boulevard, Suite 600
Norcross, GA 30093
770-638-0121
www.asbaec.com

Ashworth College
430 Technology Parkway
Norcross, GA 30092
770-729-8400
www.ashworthcollege.com

Athens Technical College
800 US Highway 29 North
Athens, GA 30601-1500
706-355-5000
www.aati.edu

Atlanta Metropolitan College
1630 Metropolitan Parkway,
SW
Atlanta, GA 30310-4498
404-756-4000
www.atlm.peachnet.edu

Atlanta Technical College
1560 Metropolitan Parkway
Atlanta, GA 30310
404-756-3700
www.atlantatech.org

Augusta Technical College
3200 Augusta Tech Drive
Augusta, GA 30906
706-771-4000
www.augusta.tec.ga.us

Bainbridge College
2500 East Shotwell Street
Bainbridge, GA 31717
229-248-2500
www.bbc.peachnet.edu

Bauder College
Phipps Plaza,
3500 Peachtree Rd, NE
Atlanta, GA 30326
404-237-7573
www.bauder.edu

Central Georgia Technical
College
3300 Macon Tech Drive
Macon, GA 31206-3628
912-757-3400
www.macon.tec.ga.us

Chattahoochee Technical
College
980 South Cobb Drive
Marietta, GA 30060
770-528-4500
www.chat-tec.com

Coastal Georgia Community
College
3700 Altama Avenue
Brunswick, GA 31520-3644
912-264-7235
www.cgcc.peachnet.edu

Columbus Technical College
928 Manchester Expressway
Columbus, GA 31904-6572
706-649-1800
www.columbustech.org

Coosa Valley Technical
Institute
One Maurice Culberson Dr
Rome, GA 30161
706-295-6963
www.coosa.tec.ga.us

Darton College
2400 Gillionville Road
Albany, GA 31707-3098
229-430-6740
www.dartnet.peachnet.edu

DeKalb Technical College
495 North Indian Creek Drive
Clarkston, GA 30021-2397
404-297-9522
www.dekalb.tec.ga.us

East Georgia College
131 College Circle
Swainsboro, GA 30401-2699
478-289-2000
www.ega.peachnet.edu

Emory University, Oxford
College
100 Hamill Street,
PO Box 1418
Oxford, GA 30054
770-784-8888
www.emory.edu/OXFORD

Flint River Technical College
1533 US highway 19 South
Thomaston, GA 30286
706-646-6148
www.flint.tec.ga.us

Floyd College
PO Box 1864
Rome, GA 30162-1864
706-802-5000
www.fc.peachnet.edu

Gainesville College
PO Box 1358
Gainesville, GA 30503-1358
770-718-3639
www.gc.peachnet.edu

Georgia Military College
201 East Greene Street
Milledgeville, GA 31061-
3398
478-445-2700
www.gmc.cc.ga.us

Georgia Perimeter College
3251 Panthersville Road
Decatur, GA 30034-3897
404-244-5090
www.gpc.peachnet.edu

Gordon College
419 College Drive
Barnesville, GA 30204-1762
770-358-5000
www.gdn.peachnet.edu

Griffin Technical College
501 Varsity Road
Griffin, GA 30223
770-228-7348
www.griftec.org

Gupton-Jones College of
Funeral Service
5141 Snapfinger Woods Dr
Decatur, GA 30035-4022
770-593-2257
www.gupton-jones.edu

Gwinnett Technical College
PO Box 1505
Lawrenceville, GA
30046-1505
770-962-7580
www.gwinnett-tech.org

Herzing College
3355 Lenox Road, Suite 100
Atlanta, GA 30326
404-816-4533
www.herzing.edu/atlanta

Interactive College of
Technology
5303 New Peachtree Road
Chamblee, GA 30341
770-216-2960
www.ict-ils.edu

Middle Georgia College
1100 Second Street, SE
Cochran, GA 31014-1599
912-934-6221
www.mgc.peachnet.edu

Middle Georgia Technical
College
80 Cohen Walker Drive
Warner Robbins, GA 31088
912-988-6800
www.mgti.org

Northwestern Technical
College
265 Bicentennial Trail
Rock Springs, GA 30739
706-764-3510
www.northwestern.tec.ga.us

Ogeechee Technical College
One Joe Kennedy Boulevard
Statesboro, GA 30458
912-681-5500
www.ogeechee.tec.ga.us

Savannah Technical College
5717 White Bluff Road
Savannah, GA 31405
912-351-6362
www.savannah.tec.ga.us

South Georgia College
100 West College Park Drive
Douglas, GA 31533-5098
912-389-4510
www.sgc.peachnet.edu

Southwest Georgia Technical
College
15689 US 19 North
Thomasville, GA 31792
229-225-4096
www.swgtc.edu

Truett-McConnell College
100 Alumni Drive
Cleveland, GA 30528
706-865-2134
www.truett.cc.ga.us

Waycross College
2001 South Georgia Parkway
Waycross, GA 31503-9248
912-285-6133
www.way.peachnet.edu

West Central Technical College
997 South Highway 16
Carrollton, GA 30116
770-836-6800
www.carroll.tec.ga.us

West Georgia Technical College
303 Fort Drive
LaGrange, GA 30240
706-845-4323
www.westga.tec.ga.us

Young Harris College
PO Box 98
Young Harris, GA 30582-0098
706-379-3111
www.yhc.edu

Hawaii

Hawaii Business College
33 South King Street, Fourth Floor
Honolulu, HI 96813-4316
Phone: 808-524-4014
www.hbc.edu

Hawaii Community College
200 West Kawili Street
Hilo, HI 96720-4091
Phone: 808-974-7611
www.hawcc.hawaii.edu

Hawaii Tokai International College
2241 Kapiolani Boulevard
Honolulu, HI 96826-4310
Phone: 808-983-4100
www.tokai.edu

Heald College, Schools of Business and Technology
1500 Kapiolani Boulevard
Honolulu, HI 96814-3797
Phone: 808-955-1500
www.heald.edu

Honolulu Community College
874 Dillingham Boulevard
Honolulu, HI 96817-4598
Phone: 808-845-9211
www.hcc.hawaii.edu

Kapiolani Community College
4303 Diamond Head Road
Honolulu, HI 96816-4421
Phone: 808-734-9111

Kauai Community College
3-1901 Kaumualii Highway
Lihue, HI 96766-9591
Phone: 808-245-8311
www.kauaicc.hawaii.edu

Leeward Community College
96-045 Ala Ike
Pearl City, HI 96782-3393
Phone: 808-455-0011
www.lcc.hawaii.edu

Maui Community College
310 Kaahumanu Avenue
Kahului, HI 96732
Phone: 808-984-3500
mauicc.hawaii.edu

TransPacific Hawaii College
5257 Kalanianaole Highway
Honolulu, HI 96821-1884
Phone: 808-377-5402
www.transpacific.org

Windward Community College
45-720 Keaahala Road
Kaneohe, HI 96744-3528
Phone: 808-235-7400
www.wcc.hawaii.edu

Idaho

American Institute of Health Technology, Inc.
1200 North Liberty Road
Boise, ID 83704
Phone: 208-377-8080
www.aiht.com

Brigham Young University–Idaho
Rexburg, ID 83460-1650
Phone: 208-496-2011
www.byui.edu

College of Southern Idaho
PO Box 1238
Twin Falls, ID 83303-1238
Phone: 208-733-9554
www.csi.edu

Eastern Idaho Technical College
1600 South 25th East
Idaho Falls, ID 83404-5788
Phone: 208-524-3000
www.eitc.edu

ITT Technical Institute
12302 West Explorer Drive
Boise, ID 83713
Phone: 208-322-8844
www.itt-tech.edu

North Idaho College
1000 West Garden Avenue
Coeur d'Alene, ID 83814-2199
Phone: 208-769-3300
www.nic.edu

Illinois

Black Hawk College
6600 34th Avenue
Moline, IL 61265-5899
309-796-5000
www.bhc.edu

Career Colleges of Chicago
11 East Adams Street, 2nd Floor
Chicago, IL 60603-6301
312-895-6300
www.careerchi.com

Carl Sandburg College
2400 Tom L. Wilson Blvd
Galesburg, IL 61401-9576
309-344-2518
www.csc.cc.il.us

City Colleges of Chicago, Harold Washington College
30 East Lake Street
Chicago, IL 60601-2449
312-553-5600
www.ccc.edu

City Colleges of Chicago, Harry S Truman College
1145 West Wilson Avenue
Chicago, IL 60640-5616
773-907-4700
www.ccc.edu/truman

City Colleges of Chicago, Kennedy-King College
6800 South Wentworth Ave
Chicago, IL 60621-3733
773-602-5000

City Colleges of Chicago, Malcolm X College
1900 West Van Buren Street
Chicago, IL 60612-3145
312-850-7000
cccweb.ccc.edu/malcolmx

City Colleges of Chicago, Olive-Harvey College
10001 South Woodlawn Ave
Chicago, IL 60628-1645
773-291-6100
www.ccc.edu

City Colleges of Chicago, Richard J. Daley College
7500 South Pulaski Road
Chicago, IL 60652-1242
773-838-7500
cccweb.cc.edu/daley/home.htm

City Colleges of Chicago, Wilbur Wright College
4300 North Narragansett Ave
Chicago, IL 60634-1591
773-777-7900
www.ccc.edu/wright

College of DuPage
425 Fawell Boulevard
Glen Ellyn, IL 60137-6599
630-942-2800
www.cod.edu

College of Lake County
19351 West Washington St
Grayslake, IL 60030-1198
847-223-6601
www.clc.cc.il.us

The College of Office Technology
1514-20 West Division Street, Second Floor
Chicago, IL 60622
773-278-0042

The Cooking and Hospitality Institute of Chicago
361 West Chestnut
Chicago, IL 60610-3050
312-944-0882
www.chicnet.org

Danville Area Community College
2000 East Main Street
Danville, IL 61832-5199
217-443-3222
www.dacc.cc.il.us

Elgin Community College
1700 Spartan Drive
Elgin, IL 60123-7193
847-697-1000
www.elgin.cc.il.us

Gem City College
PO Box 179
Quincy, IL 62306-0179
217-222-0391

Heartland Community College
1500 West Raab Road
Normal, IL 61761
309-268-8000
www.hcc.cc.il.us

Highland Community College
2998 West Pearl City Road
Freeport, IL 61032-9341
815-235-6121
www.highland.cc.il.us

Illinois Central College
One College Drive
East Peoria, IL 61635-0001
309-694-5011
www.icc.cc.il.us

Illinois Eastern Community
Colleges, Frontier
Community College
Frontier Drive
Fairfield, IL 62837-2601
618-842-3711
www.iecc.cc.il.us./fcc

Illinois Eastern Community
Colleges, Lincoln Trail
College
11220 State Highway 1
Robinson, IL 62454
618-544-8657
www.iecc.cc.il.us/ltc

Illinois Eastern Community
Colleges, Olney Central
College
305 North West Street
Olney, IL 62450
618-395-7777
www.iecc.cc.il.us/occ

Illinois Eastern Community
Colleges, Wabash Valley
College
2200 College Drive
Mount Carmel, IL
62863-2657
618-262-8641
www.iecc.cc.il.us/wvc

Illinois Valley Community
College
815 North Orlando Smith Ave
Oglesby, IL 61348-9692
815-224-2720
www.ivcc.edu

ITT Technical Institute
7040 High Grove Boulevard
Burr Ridge, IL 60521
630-455-6470
www.itt-tech.edu

ITT Technical Institute
1401 Feehanville Drive
Mount Prospect, IL 60056
847-375-8800
www.itt-tech.edu

ITT Technical Institute
600 Holiday Plaza Drive
Matteson, IL 60443
708-747-2571
www.itt-tech.edu

John A. Logan College
700 Logan College Road
Carterville, IL 62918-9900
618-985-3741
www.jal.cc.il.us

John Wood Community
College
150 South 48th Street
Quincy, IL 62301-9147
217-224-6500
www.jwcc.edu

Joliet Junior College
1215 Houbolt Road
Joliet, IL 60431-8938
815-729-9020
www.jjc.cc.il.us

Kankakee Community
College
PO Box 888
Kankakee, IL 60901-0888
815-933-0345

Kaskaskia College
27210 College Road
Centralia, IL 62801-7878
618-545-3000
www.kc.cc.il.us

Kishwaukee College
21193 Malta Road
Malta, IL 60150
815-825-2086
kish.cc.il.us

Lake Land College
5001 Lake Land Boulevard
Mattoon, IL 61938-9366
217-234-5253
www.lakeland.cc.il.us

Lewis and Clark Community
College
5800 Godfrey Road
Godfrey, IL 62035-2466
618-466-3411
www.lc.cc.il.us

Lexington College
10840 South Western Avenue
Chicago, IL 60643-3294
773-779-3800

Lincoln College
715 West Raab Road
Normal, IL 61761
309-452-0500
www.lincoln.mclean.il.us

Lincoln College
300 Keokuk Street
Lincoln, IL 62656-1699
217-732-3155
www.lincolncollege.com

Lincoln Land Community
College
5250 Shepherd Road,
PO Box 19256
Springfield, IL 62794-9256
217-786-2200
www.llcc.cc.il.us

MacCormac College
506 South Wabash Avenue
Chicago, IL 60605-1667
312-922-1884
www.maccormac.edu

McHenry County College
8900 US Highway 14
Crystal Lake, IL 60012-2761
815-455-3700
www.mchenry.cc.il.us

Midstate College
411 West Northmoor Road
Peoria, IL 61614
309-692-4092
www.midstate.edu

Moraine Valley Community
College
10900 South 88th Avenue
Palos Hills, IL 60465-0937
708-974-4300
www.moraine.cc.il.us

Morrison Institute of
Technology
701 Portland Avenue
Morrison, IL 61270-0410
815-772-7218
www.morrison.tech.il.us

Morton College
3801 South Central Avenue
Cicero, IL 60804-4398
708-656-8000
www.morton.cc.il.us

Northwestern Business
College
4829 North Lipps Avenue
Chicago, IL 60630-2298
773-777-4220
northwesternbc.edu

Oakton Community College
1600 East Golf Road
Des Plaines, IL 60016-1268
847-635-1600
www.oakton.edu

Parkland College
2400 West Bradley Avenue
Champaign, IL 61821-1899
217-351-2200
www.parkland.cc.il.us

Prairie State College
202 South Halsted Street
Chicago Heights, IL
60411-8226
708-709-3500
www.prairie.cc.il.us

Ravenswood Hospital
Medical Center–Henry J.
Kutsch College of Nursing
2318 West Irving Park Road
Chicago, IL 60618
773-463-9191
www.advocatehealth.com/
rhmccon

Rend Lake College
468 North Ken Gray Parkway
Ina, IL 62846-9801
618-437-5321
www.rlc.cc.il.us

Richland Community College
One College Park
Decatur, IL 62521-8513
217-875-7200
www.richland.cc.il.us

Rock Valley College
3301 North Mulford Road
Rockford, IL 61114-5699
815-654-4250
www.rvc.cc.il.us

Rockford Business College
730 North Church Street
Rockford, IL 61103
815-965-8616
www.rbcsuccess.com

Sanford-Brown College
3237 West Chain of Rocks Rd
Granite City, IL 62040
618-931-0300
www.sanford-brown.edu

Sauk Valley Community
College
173 Illinois Route 2
Dixon, IL 61021
815-288-5511
www.svcc.edu

Shawnee Community
College
8364 Shawnee College Road
Ullin, IL 62992-9725
618-634-3200
www.shawnee.cc.il.us

South Suburban College
15800 South State Street
South Holland, IL
60473-1270
708-596-2000
www.ssc.cc.il.us

Southeastern Illinois College
3575 College Road
Harrisburg, IL 62946-4925
618-252-5400
www.sic.cc.il.us

Southwestern Illinois College
2500 Carlyle Road
Belleville, IL 62221-5899
618-235-2700
www.southwestern.cc.il.us

Spoon River College
23235 North County 22
Canton, IL 61520-9801
309-647-4645
www.spoonrivercollege.net

Springfield College in Illinois
1500 North Fifth Street
Springfield, IL 62702-2694
217-525-1420
www.sci.edu

Triton College
2000 5th Avenue
River Grove, IL 60171-9983
708-456-0300
www.triton.cc.il.us

Waubonsee Community
College
Route 47 at Harter Road
Sugar Grove, IL 60554-9799
630-466-7900
www.wcc.cc.il.us

William Rainey Harper
College
1200 West Algonquin Road
Palatine, IL 60067-7398
847-925-6000
www.harpercollege.com

Worsham College of
Mortuary Science
495 Northgate Parkway
Wheeling, IL 60090-2646
847-808-8444
www.worshamcollege.com

Indiana

Ancilla College
Union Road, PO Box 1
Donaldson, IN 46513
219-936-8898
www.ancilla.edu

College of Court Reporting
111 West Tenth Street,
Suite 111
Hobart, IN 46342
219-942-1459

Commonwealth Business
College
325 East US Highway 20
Michigan City, IN 46360
219-877-3100
www.cbcaec.com

Commonwealth Business
College
1000 East 80th Place,
Suite 101, N
Merrillville, IN 46410
219-769-3321
www.cbcaec.com

Holy Cross College
PO Box 308
Notre Dame, IN 46556-0308
219-239-8400
www.hcc-nd.edu

Indiana Business College
5460 Victory Drive, Suite 100
Indianapolis, IN 46203
317-783-5100
www.ibcschools.com

Indiana Business College
802 North Meridian Street
Indianapolis, IN 46204-1108
317-264-5656
www.ibcschools.com

Indiana Business College
3175 South Third Place
Terre Haute, IN 47802
812-232-4458
www.ibcschools.com

Indiana Business College
140 East 53rd Street
Anderson, IN 46103
756-644-7514
www.ibcschools.com

Indiana Business College
4601 Theatre Drive
Evansville, IN 47715-4601
812-476-6000
www.ibcschools.com

Indiana Business College
6413 North Clinton Street
Fort Wayne, IN 46825
219-471-7667
www.ibcschools.com

Indiana Business College
411 West Riggin Road
Muncie, IN 47303
765-288-8681
www.ibcschools.com

Indiana Business College
2 Executive Drive
Lafayette, IN 47905
765-447-9550
www.ibcschools.com

Indiana Business College
830 North Miller Avenue
Marion, IN 46952-2338
765-662-7497
www.ibcschools.com

Indiana Business College
2222 Poshard Drive
Columbus, IN 47203-1843
812-379-9000
www.ibcschools.com

International Business
College
7205 Shadeland Station
Indianapolis, IN 46256
317-841-6400
www.intlbusinesscollege.
com

International Business
College
3811 Illinois Road
Fort Wayne, IN 46804-1298
219-459-4500
www.bradfordschools.com

ITT Technical Institute
4919 Coldwater Road
Fort Wayne, IN 46825-5532
219-484-4107
www.itt-tech.edu

ITT Technical Institute
9511 Angola Court
Indianapolis, IN 46268-1119
317-875-8640
www.itt-tech.edu

ITT Technical Institute
10999 Stahl Road
Newburgh, IN 47630-7430
812-858-1600
www.itt-tech.edu

Ivy Tech State
College–Central Indiana
1 West 26th Street,
PO Box 1763
Indianapolis, IN 46206-1763
317-921-4800
www.ivytech.edu

Ivy Tech State
College–Columbus
4475 Central Avenue
Columbus, IN 47203-1868
812-372-9925
www.ivytech.edu

Ivy Tech State College–East
Central
4301 South Cowan Road,
PO Box 3100
Muncie, IN 47302-9448
765-289-2291
www.ivytech.edu

Ivy Tech State College–
Kokomo
1815 East Morgan St,
PO Box 1373
Kokomo, IN 46903-1373
765-459-0561
www.ivytech.edu

Ivy Tech State College–
Lafayette
3101 South Creasy Lane
Lafayette, IN 47905-5266
765-772-9100
www.ivytech.edu

Ivy Tech State College–North
Central
220 Dean Johnson Boulevard
South Bend, IN 46601
219-289-7001
www.ivytech.edu

Ivy Tech State
College–Northeast
3800 North Anthony Blvd
Fort Wayne, IN 46805-1430
219-482-9171
www.ivytech.edu

Ivy Tech State
College–Northwest
1440 East 35th Avenue
Gary, IN 46409-1499
219-981-1111
www.ivytech.edu

Ivy Tech State
College–Southcentral
8204 Highway 311
Sellersburg, IN 47172-1829
812-246-3301
www.ivytech.edu

Ivy Tech State College–
Southeast
590 Ivy Tech Drive,
PO Box 209
Madison, IN   47250-1883
812-265-4028
www.ivy.tec.in.us

Ivy Tech State College–
Southwest
3501 First Avenue
Evansville, IN   47710-3398
812-426-2865
www.ivytech.edu

Ivy Tech State College–
Wabash Valley
7999 US Highway 41, South
Terre Haute, IN   47802
812-299-1121
www.ivytech.edu

Ivy Tech State College–
Whitewater
2325 Chester Boulevard
Richmond, IN   47374-1220
765-966-2656
www.ivytech.edu

Lincoln Technical Institute
1201 Stadium Drive
Indianapolis, IN   46202-2194
317-632-5553
www.lincolntech.com

Michiana College
4422 East State Boulevard
Fort Wayne, IN   46815
219-484-4400
www.michiana.com

Michiana College
1030 East Jefferson Blvd
South Bend, IN   46617-3123
219-237-0774
www.michianacollege.com

Mid-America College of
Funeral Service
3111 Hamburg Pike
Jeffersonville, IN   47130-
9630
812-288-8878

Professional Careers Institute
7302 Woodland Drive
Indianapolis, IN   46278
317-299-6001
www.pcicareers.com

Sawyer College
6040 Hohman Avenue
Hammond, IN   46320
219-931-0436
www.sawyercollege.com

Vincennes University
1002 North First Street
Vincennes, IN   47591-5202
812-888-8888
www.vinu.edu

Vincennes University–Jasper
Campus
850 College Avenue
Jasper, IN   47546-9393
812-482-3030
www.vinu.edu/vujc.htm

Iowa

AIB College of Business
2500 Fleur Drive
Des Moines, IA   50321-1799
515-244-4221
www.aib.edu

Clinton Community College
1000 Lincoln Boulevard
Clinton, IA   52732-6299
563-244-7001
www.eiccd.cc.ia.us/ccc

Des Moines Area Community
College
2006 South Ankeny Blvd
Ankeny, IA   50021-8995
515-964-6200
www.dmacc.cc.ia.us

Ellsworth Community
College
1100 College Avenue
Iowa Falls, IA   50126-1199
641-648-4611
www.iavalley.cc.ia.us/ecc

Hamilton College
1924 D Street SW
Cedar Rapids, IA   52404
319-363-0481
www.hamiltonia.edu

Hawkeye Community
College
PO Box 8015
Waterloo, IA   50704-8015
319-296-2320
www.hawkeye.cc.ia.us

Indian Hills Community
College
525 Grandview Avenue,
Building #1
Ottumwa, IA   52501-1398
641-683-5111

Iowa Central Community
College
330 Avenue M
Fort Dodge, IA   50501-5798
515-576-7201
www.iccc.cc.ia.us

Iowa Lakes Community
College
19 South 7th Street
Estherville, IA   51334-2295
712-362-2604
www.ilcc.cc.ia.us

Iowa Western Community
College
2700 College Road, Box 4-C
Council Bluffs, IA   51502
712-325-3200
www.iwcc.cc.ia.us

Kaplan College
1801 East Kimberly Road,
Suite 1
Davenport, IA   52807-2095
563-355-3500
www.kaplancollegeia.com

Kirkwood Community
College
PO Box 2068
Cedar Rapids, IA
52406-2068
319-398-5411
www.kirkwood.cc.ia.us

Marshalltown Community
College
3700 South Center Street
Marshalltown, IA
50158-4760
515-752-7106
voyager.iavalley.cc.ia.us/mcc

Muscatine Community
College
152 Colorado Street
Muscatine, IA   52761-5396
563-288-6001
www.eicc.org

North Iowa Area Community
College
500 College Drive
Mason City, IA   50401-7299
641-423-1264
www.niacc.com

Northeast Iowa Community
College
Box 400
Calmar, IA   52132-0480
563-562-3263
www.nicc.edu

Northwest Iowa Community
College
603 West Park Street
Sheldon, IA   51201-1046
712-324-5061
www.nwicc.cc.ia.us

Scott Community College
500 Belmont Road
Bettendorf, IA   52722-6804
563-441-4001
www.eiccd.cc.ia.us/scc

Southeastern Community
College, North Campus
1500 West Agency Street,
PO Box 180
West Burlington, IA
52655-0180
319-752-2731
www.secc.cc.ia.us

Southeastern Community
College, South Campus
335 Messenger Road,
PO Box 6007
Keokuk, IA   52632-6007
319-524-3221
www.secc.cc.ia.us

Southwestern Community
College
1501 West Townline Street
Creston, IA   50801
641-782-7081
www.swcc.cc.ia.us

St. Luke's College of Nursing
and Health Sciences
2720 Stone Park Boulevard
Sioux City, IA   51104
712-279-3149
www.stlukes.org/college/sn_c
ollege.htm

Waldorf College
106 South 6th Street
Forest City, IA   50436-1713
641-585-2450
www.waldorf.edu

Western Iowa Tech
Community College
4647 Stone Avenue,
PO Box 5199
Sioux City, IA   51102-5199
712-274-6400
www.witcc.cc.ia.us

2-Year Colleges and Universities

Kansas

Allen County Community College
1801 North Cottonwood St
Iola, KS 66749-1607
316-365-5116
www.allencc.net

Barton County Community College
245 Northeast 30th Road
Great Bend, KS 67530-9283
620-792-2701
www.barton.cc.ks.us

The Brown Mackie College
2106 South 9th Street
Salina, KS 67401-2810
785-825-5422
www.bmcaec.com

The Brown Mackie College–Olathe Campus
100 East Santa Fe, Suite 300
Olathe, KS 66061
913-768-1900
www.bmcaec.com

Butler County Community College
901 South Haverhill Road
El Dorado, KS 67042-3280
316-321-2222
www.buccc.cc.ks.us

Cloud County Community College
2221 Campus Drive,
PO Box 1002
Concordia, KS 66901-1002
785-243-1435
www.cloudccc.cc.ks.us

Coffeyville Community College
400 West 11th Street
Coffeyville, KS 67337-5063
620-251-7700
www.ccc.cc.ks.us

Colby Community College
1255 South Range
Colby, KS 67701-4099
785-462-3984
www.colbycc.org

Cowley County Community College and Area Vocational–Technical School
125 South Second,
PO Box 1147
Arkansas City, KS
67005-1147
620-442-0430
www.cowley.cc.ks.us

Dodge City Community College
2501 North 14th Avenue
Dodge City, KS 67801-2399
620-225-1321

Donnelly College
608 North 18th Street
Kansas City, KS 66102-4298
913-621-6070
www.donnelly.cc.ks.us

Education America, Topeka Technical College, Topeka Campus
1620 N.W. Gage Boulevard
Topeka, KS 66618
785-232-5858

Fort Scott Community College
2108 South Horton
Fort Scott, KS 66701
316-223-2700
www.ftscott.cc.ks.us

Garden City Community College
801 Campus Drive
Garden City, KS 67846-6399
316-276-7611
www.gccc.cc.ks.us

Hesston College
Box 3000
Hesston, KS 67062-2093
620-327-4221
www.hesston.edu

Highland Community College
606 West Main Street
Highland, KS 66035
785-442-6000

Hutchinson Community College and Area Vocational School
1300 North Plum Street
Hutchinson, KS 67501-5894
620-665-3500
www.hutchcc.edu

Independence Community College
Brookside Drive and
College Avenue, PO Box 708
Independence, KS
67301-0708
316-331-4100
www.indy.cc.ks.us

Johnson County Community College
12345 College Boulevard
Overland Park, KS
66210-1299
913-469-8500
www.johnco.cc.ks.us

Kansas City Kansas Community College
7250 State Avenue
Kansas City, KS 66112-3003
913-334-1100
www.kckcc.cc.ks.us

Labette Community College
200 South 14th Street
Parsons, KS 67357-4299
620-421-6700
www.labette.cc.ks.us

Neosho County Community College
800 West 14th Street
Chanute, KS 66720-2699
620-431-2820
www.neosho.cc.ks.us

Pratt Community College and Area Vocational School
348 NE State Route 61
Pratt, KS 67124-8317
316-672-5641
www.pcc.cc.ks.us

Seward County Community College
Box 1137
Liberal, KS 67905-1137
620-624-1951
www.sccc.cc.ks.us

Kentucky

Ashland Community College
1400 College Drive
Ashland, KY 41101-3683
606-329-2999
www.ashlandcc.org

Daymar College
3361 Buckland Square
Owensboro, KY 42301
270-926-4040
www.daymarcollege.com

Draughons Junior College
2424 Airway Drive
Bowling Green, KY 42103
270-843-6750
www.draughons.org

Elizabethtown Community College
600 College Street Road
Elizabethtown, KY
42701-3081
270-769-2371
www.uky.edu/
communitycolleges/eli

Hazard Community College
1 Community College Drive
Hazard, KY 41701-2403
606-436-5721
www.hazcc.uky.edu

Henderson Community College
2660 South Green Street
Henderson, KY 42420-4623
270-827-1867

Hopkinsville Community College
PO Box 2100
Hopkinsville, KY 42241-2100
270-886-3921
www.hopcc.kctcs.net

Institute of Electronic Technology
509 South 30th Street,
PO Box 8252
Paducah, KY 42001
502-444-9676

ITT Technical Institute
10509 Timberwood Circle,
Suite 100
Louisville, KY 40223-5392
502-327-7424
www.itt-tech.edu

Jefferson Community College
109 East Broadway
Louisville, KY 40202-2005
502-584-0181
www.jctc.kctcs.net

Kentucky Career Institute
PO Box 143,
8095 Connector Drive
Florence, KY 41022-0143
859-371-9393
www.kcicareer.com

Louisville Technical Institute
3901 Atkinson Square Drive
Louisville, KY 40218-4528
502-456-6509
www.louisvilletech.com

Madisonville Community
College
2000 College Drive
Madisonville, KY
42431-9185
270-821-2250
www.madcc.kctcs.net

Maysville Community
College
1755 US 68
Maysville, KY 41056
606-759-7141
www.maycc.kctcs.net

National College of Business
& Technology
139 South Killarney Lane
Richmond, KY 40475
859-623-8956
www.ncbt.edu

National College of Business
& Technology
288 South Mayo Trail, Suite 2
Pikeville, KY 41501
606-432-5477
www.ncbt.edu/index2.shtml

National College of Business
& Technology
3950 Dixie Highway
Louisville, KY 40216
502-447-7634
www.ncbt.edu/index2.shtml

National College of Business
& Technology
115 East Lexington Avenue
Danville, KY 40422
859-236-6991
www.ncbt.edu

National College of Business
& Technology
628 East Main Street
Lexington, KY 40508-2312
859-253-0621
www.ncbt.edu

National College of Business
& Technology
7627 Ewing Boulevard
Florence, KY 41042
859-525-6510
www.ncbt.edu

Owensboro Community
College
4800 New Hartford Road
Owensboro, KY 42303-1899
270-686-4400
www.owecc.net/main

Paducah Community College
PO Box 7380
Paducah, KY 42002-7380
502-554-9200
www.pccky.com

Prestonsburg Community
College
One Bert T Combs Drive
Prestonsburg, KY
41653-1815
606-886-3863
www.prestonsburgcc.com

RETS Electronic Institute
300 High Rise Drive
Louisville, KY 40213
502-968-7191

RETS Medical and Business
Istitute
4001 Ft. Cambell Boulevard
Hopkinsville, KY 42240
270-886-1302

Somerset Community
College
808 Monticello Street
Somerset, KY 42501-2973
606-679-8501
www.somcc.kctcs.net

Southeast Community
College
700 College Road
Cumberland, KY 40823-1099
606-589-2145
www.soucc.kctcs.net

Southern Ohio College,
Northern Kentucky Campus
309 Buttermilk Pike
Fort Mitchell, KY 41017-2191
859-341-5627
www.aecsoc.com

Southwestern College of
Business
2929 South Dixie Highway
Crestview Hills, KY 41017
606-341-6633
home.fuse.net/scb

Spencerian College
4627 Dixie Highway
Louisville, KY 40216
502-447-1000

Spencerian College–
Lexington
2355 Harrodsburg Road
Lexington, KY 40504
859-223-9608
www.spencerian.edu

St. Catharine College
2735 Bardstown Road
St. Catharine, KY
40061-9499
859-336-5082
www.sccky.edu

University of Kentucky,
Lexington Community
College
Cooper Drive
Lexington, KY 40506-0235
859-257-4872
www.uky.edu/lcc

Louisiana

Baton Rouge School of
Computers
9255 Interline Avenue
Baton Rouge, LA
70809-1971
504-923-2525
www.brsc.net

Bossier Parish Community
College
2719 Airline Drive North
Bossier City, LA 71111-5801
318-746-9851
www.bpcc.cc.la.us

Camelot Career College
2742 Wooddale Boulevard
Baton Rouge, LA 70805
228-201-0580

Cameron College
2740 Canal Street
New Orleans, LA 70119
504-821-5881

Culinary Arts Institute of
Louisiana
427 Lafayette Street
Baton Rouge, LA 70802
225-343-6233
www.caila.com

Delgado Community College
501 City Park Avenue
New Orleans, LA 70119-4399
504-483-4400
www.dcc.edu

Delta College of Arts and
Technology
7380 Exchange Place
Baton Rouge, LA
70806-3851
504-928-7770

Delta School of Business &
Technology
517 Broad Street
Lake Charles, LA 70601
337-439-5765
www.deltatech-lc.com

Education America,
Remington College, Baton
Rouge Campus
1900 North Lobdell
Baton Rouge, LA 70806
225-922-3990

Education America,
Remington College, Lafayette
Campus
303 Rue Louis XIV
Lafayette, LA 70508
337-981-4010
www.educationamerica.com

Education America,
Southeast College of
Technology, New Orleans
Campus
321 Veterans Memorial Blvd
Metairie, LA 70005
504-831-8889
www.educationamerica.com

Elaine P. Nunez Community
College
3710 Paris Road
Chalmette, LA 70043-1249
504-680-2240
www.nunez.cc.la.us

Herzing College
2400 Veterans Boulevard
Kenner, LA 70062
504-733-0074
www.herzing.edu

ITT Technical Institute
140 James Drive E
St. Rose, LA 70087
504-463-0338
www.itt-tech.edu

Louisiana State University at
Alexandria
8100 Highway 71 South
Alexandria, LA 71302-9121
318-445-3672
www.lsua.edu

Louisiana State University at
Eunice
PO Box 1129
Eunice, LA 70535-1129
337-457-7311
www.lsue.edu

Louisiana Technical
College–Acadian Campus
1933 West Hutchinson Ave
Crowley, LA 70526
337-788-7521
www.acadian.tec.la.us

Louisiana Technical
College–Alexandria Campus
4311 South MacArthur
Alexandria, LA 71307-5698
318-487-5398

Louisiana Technical
College–Ascension Campus
9697 Airline Highway
Sorrento, LA 70778-3007
225-675-5398

Louisiana Technical
College–Avoyelles Campus
508 Choupique Street
Cottonport, LA 71327
318-876-2401

Louisiana Technical
College–Bastrop Campus
729 Kammell Street
Bastrop, LA 71221-1120
318-283-0836

Louisiana Technical
College–Baton Rouge
Campus
3250 North Acadian Thruway
East
Baton Rouge, LA 70805
225-359-9204
www.brti.tec.la.us

Louisiana Technical
College–Charles B. Coreil
Campus
1124 Vocational Drive,
PO Box 296
Ville Platte, LA 70586-0296
318-363-2197

Louisiana Technical College–
Delta Ouachita Campus
609 Vocational Parkway,
West, Ouachita Industrial Pk
West Monroe, LA
71292-9064
318-397-6100

Louisiana Technical
College–Evangeline Campus
600 South Martin Luther
King Drive
St. Martinville, LA 70582
318-394-6466

Louisiana Technical College–
Florida Parishes Campus
PO Box 1300
Greensburg, LA 70441
225-222-4251

Louisiana Technical College–
Folkes Campus
3337 Highway 10
Jackson, LA 70748
225-634-2636

Louisiana Technical College–
Gulf Area Campus
1115 Clover Street
Abbeville, LA 70510
318-893-4984

Louisiana Technical College–
Hammond Campus
111 Pride Avenue
Hammond, LA 70401
504-543-4120

Louisiana Technical College–
Huey P. Long Campus
303 South Jones Street
Winnfield, LA 71483
318-628-4342

Louisiana Technical College–
Jefferson Campus
5200 Blaire Drive
Metairie, LA 70001
504-736-7072

Louisiana Technical College–
L.E. Fletcher Campus
310 St. Charles Street
Hourma, LA 70361-5033
504-857-3655
ltcslc1.southla.tec.la.us

Louisiana Technical College–
Lafayette Campus
1101 Bertrand Drive
Lafayette, LA 70502-4909
318-262-5962

Louisiana Technical College–
LaFourche Campus
1425 Tiger Drive
Thibodaux, LA 70302-1831
504-447-0924

Louisiana Technical College–
Lamar Salter Campus
15014 Lake Charles Highway
Leesville, LA 71446
318-537-3135

Louisiana Technical College–
Mansfield Campus
943 Oxford Road
Mansfield, LA 71052
318-872-2243
www.lctcs.state.la.us/
mansfield/index.html

Louisiana Technical College–
Morgan Smith Campus
1230 North Main Street
Jennings, LA 70546-1327
318-824-4811

Louisiana Technical College–
Natchitoches Campus
6587 Highway 1, Bypass
Natchitoches, LA 71457
318-357-3162

Louisiana Technical College–
North Central Campus
605 North Boundary West
Farmerville, LA 71241
318-368-3179
www.lctcs.state.la.us

Louisiana Technical College–
Northeast Louisiana Campus
1710 Warren Street
Winnsboro, LA 71295
318-485-2163

Louisiana Technical College–
Northwest Louisiana Campus
814 Constable Street
Minden, LA 71058-0835
318-371-3035

Louisiana Technical College–
Oakdale Campus
Old Pelican Highway
Oakdale, LA 71463
318-335-3944

River Parishes Campus
PO Drawer AQ
Reserve, LA 70084
504-536-4418

Louisiana Technical College–
Sabine Valley Campus
1255 Fisher Road
Many, LA 71449
318-256-4101
www.sabine.tec.la.us

Louisiana Technical College–
Shelby M. Jackson Campus
PO Box 1465
Ferriday, LA 71334
318-757-6501

Louisiana Technical College–
Shreveport-Bossier Campus
2010 North Market Street
Shreveport, LA 71137-8527
318-676-7811

Louisiana Technical College–
Sidney N. Collier Campus
3727 Louisa Street
New Orleans, LA 70126
504-942-8333
www.collier.tec.la.us

Louisiana Technical College–
Slidell Campus
1000 Canulette Road
Slidell, LA 70459-0827
504-646-6430

Louisiana Technical College–
Sowela Campus
3820 J. Bennett Johnston Ave
Lake Charles, LA
70616-6950
318-491-2698

Louisiana Technical
College–Sullivan Campus
1710 Sullivan Drive
Bogalusa, LA 70427
504-732-6640

Louisiana Technical College–
T.H. Harris Campus
332 East South Street
Opelousas, LA 70570
318-948-0239

Louisiana Technical College–
Tallulah Campus
Old Highway 65 South
Tallulah, LA 71284-1740
318-574-4820

Louisiana Technical College–
Teche Area Campus
PO Box 11057
New Iberia, LA 70562-1057
318-373-0011

Louisiana Technical College–
West Jefferson Campus
475 Manhattan Boulevard
Harvey, LA 70058
504-361-6464

Louisiana Technical College–
Young Memorial Campus
900 Youngs Road
Morgan City, LA 70381
504-380-2436
www.youngmemorial.com

MedVance Institute
4173 Government Street
Baton Rouge, LA 70806
225-338-9085
www.medvance.org

Our Lady of the Lake College
7434 Perkins Road
Baton Rouge, LA 70808
225-768-1700
www.ololcollege.edu

Southern University at
Shreveport
3050 Martin Luther King, Jr. Dr
Shreveport, LA 71107
318-674-3300

Maine

Andover College
901 Washington Avenue
Portland, ME 04103-2791
207-774-6126
www.andovercollege.com

Beal College
629 Main Street
Bangor, ME 04401-6896
207-947-4591
www.bealcollege.com

Central Maine Medical
Center School of Nursing
300 Main Street
Lewiston, ME 04240-0305
207-795-2840
www.cmmcson.org

Central Maine Technical
College
1250 Turner Street
Auburn, ME 04210-6498
207-755-5100
www.cmtc.net

Eastern Maine Technical
College
354 Hogan Road
Bangor, ME 04401-4206
207-941-4600
www.emtc.org

Kennebec Valley Technical
College
92 Western Avenue
Fairfield, ME 04937-1367
207-453-5000
www.kvtc.net

Mid-State College
88 East Hardscrabble Road
Auburn, ME 04210-8888
207-783-1478
www.midstatecollege.com

Northern Maine Technical
College
33 Edgemont Drive
Presque Isle, ME 04769-2016
207-768-2700
www.nmtc.net

Southern Maine Technical
College
Fort Road
South Portland, ME 04106
207-767-9500
www.smtc.net

Washington County Technical
College
RR#1, Box 22C River Road
Calais, ME 04619
207-454-1000

York County Technical
College
112 College Drive
Wells, ME 04090
207-646-9282
www.yctc.net

Maryland

Allegany College of
Maryland
12401 Willowbrook Road, SE
Cumberland, MD 21502-2596
301-784-5000
www.ac.cc.md.us

Anne Arundel Community
College
101 College Parkway
Arnold, MD 21012-1895
410-647-7100
www.aacc.cc.md.us

Baltimore City Community
College
2901 Liberty Heights Avenue
Baltimore, MD 21215-7893
410-462-8000
www.bccc.state.md.us

Carroll Community College
1601 Washington Road
Westminster, MD 21157
410-386-8000
www.carroll.cc.md.us

Cecil Community College
One Seahawk Drive
North East, MD 21901-1999
410-287-6060
www.cecil.cc.md.us

Chesapeake College
PO Box 8
Wye Mills, MD 21679-0008
410-822-5400
www.chesapeake.edu

College of Southern
Maryland
8730 Mitchell Road,
PO Box 910
La Plata, MD 20646-0910
301-934-2251
www.csm.cc.md.us

The Community College of
Baltimore County–Catonsville
Campus
800 South Rolling Road
Baltimore, MD 21228-5381
410-455-6050
www.ccbc.cc.md.us

The Community College of
Baltimore County–Dundalk
Campus
7200 Sollers Point Road
Baltimore, MD 21222-4694
410-282-6700
www.ccbc.cc.md.us

The Community College of
Baltimore County–Essex
Campus
7201 Rossville Boulevard
Baltimore, MD 21237-3899
410-682-6000
www.ccbc.cc.md.us

Frederick Community College
7932 Opossumtown Pike
Frederick, MD 21702-2097
301-846-2400
www.fcc.cc.md.us

Garrett Community College
687 Mosser Road,
PO Box 151
McHenry, MD 21541-0151
301-387-3000
garrett.gcc.cc.md.us

Hagerstown Business
College
18618 Crestwood Drive
Hagerstown, MD 21742-2797
301-739-2670
www.
hagerstownbusinesscol.org

Hagerstown Community
College
11400 Robinwood Drive
Hagerstown, MD 21742-6590
301-790-2800
www.hcc.cc.md.us

Harford Community College
401 Thomas Run Road
Bel Air, MD 21015-1698
410-836-4000
www.harford.cc.md.us

Howard Community College
10901 Little Patuxent Parkway
Columbia, MD 21044-3197
410-772-4800
www.howardcc.edu

Maryland College of Art and
Design
10500 Georgia Avenue
Silver Spring, MD 20902-4111
301-649-4454
www.mcadmd.org

Montgomery College
900 Hungerford Drive
Rockville, MD 20850
301-279-5000
www.montgomerycollege.
org

Prince George's Community
College
301 Largo Road
Largo, MD 20774-2199
301-336-6000
pgweb.pg.cc.md.us

Wor-Wic Community College
32000 Campus Drive
Salisbury, MD 21804
410-334-2800
www.worwic.cc.md.us

Massachusetts

Baptist Bible College East
950 Metropolitan Avenue
Boston, MA 02136
617-364-3510
www.bbceast.edu

Bay State College
122 Commonwealth Avenue
Boston, MA 02116-2975
617-236-8000
www.baystate.edu

Benjamin Franklin Institute of
Technology
41 Berkeley Street
Boston, MA 02116-6296
617-423-4630
www.fib.edu

Berkshire Community
College
1350 West Street
Pittsfield, MA 01201-5786
413-499-4660
cc.berkshire.org

Bristol Community College
777 Elsbree Street
Fall River, MA 02720-7395
508-678-2811
www.bristol.mass.edu

Bunker Hill Community
College
250 New Rutherford Avenue
Boston, MA 02129
617-228-2000
www.bhcc.state.ma.us

Cape Cod Community
College
2240 Iyanough Road
West Barnstable, MA
02668-1599
508-362-2131
www.capecod.mass.edu

Dean College
99 Main Street
Franklin, MA 02038-1994
508-541-1900
www.dean.edu

Fisher College
118 Beacon Street
Boston, MA 02116-1500
617-236-8800
www.fisher.edu

Greenfield Community
College
1 College Drive
Greenfield, MA 01301-9739
413-775-1000
www.gcc.mass.edu

Holyoke Community College
303 Homestead Avenue
Holyoke, MA 01040-1099
413-538-7000
www.hcc.mass.edu

ITT Technical Institute
10 Forbes Road
Woburn, MA 01801
781-937-8324
www.itt-tech.edu

ITT Technical Institute
333 Providence Highway
Norwood, MA 02062
781-278-7200
www.itt-tech.edu

Katharine Gibbs School
126 Newbury Street
Boston, MA 02116-2904
617-578-7100
www.katharinegibbs.com

Labouré College
2120 Dorchester Avenue
Boston, MA 02124-5698
617-296-8300
www.labourecollege.com

Marian Court College
35 Little's Point Road
Swampscott, MA 01907-2840
781-595-6768
www.mariancourt.edu

Massachusetts Bay
Community College
50 Oakland Street
Wellesley Hills, MA 02481
781-239-3000
www.mbcc.mass.edu

Massasoit Community
College
1 Massasoit Boulevard
Brockton, MA 02302-3996
508-588-9100
www.massasoit.mass.edu

Middlesex Community
College
Springs Road
Bedford, MA 01730-1655
781-280-3200
www.middlesex.cc.ma.us

Mount Wachusett
Community College
444 Green Street
Gardner, MA 01440-1000
978-632-6600
www.mwcc.mass.edu

New England College of
Finance
1 Lincoln Plaza
Boston, MA 02111-2645
617-951-2350
www.finance.edu

New England Institute of Art
& Communications
10 Brookline Place West
Brookline, MA 02445
617-267-7910
www.masscomm.edu

Newbury College
129 Fisher Avenue
Brookline, MA 02445
617-730-7000
www.newbury.edu

North Shore Community
College
1 Ferncroft Road
Danvers, MA 01923-4093
978-762-4000
www.nscc.cc.ma.us

Northern Essex Community
College
100 Elliott Street
Haverhill, MA 01830
978-556-3000
www.necc.mass.edu

Quincy College
34 Coddington Street
Quincy, MA 02169-4522
617-984-1600
www.quincycollege.com

Quinsigamond Community
College
670 West Boylston Street
Worcester, MA 01606-2092
508-853-2300
www.qcc.mass.edu

Roxbury Community College
1234 Columbus Avenue
Roxbury Crossing, MA
02120-3400
617-427-0060
www.rcc.mass.edu

Springfield Technical
Community College
1 Armory Square
Springfield, MA 01105-1296
413-781-7822
www.stcc.mass.edu

Urban College of Boston
178 Tremont Street
Boston, MA 02111
617-292-4723
www.urbancollegeof-
boston.org

Michigan

Alpena Community College
666 Johnson Street
Alpena, MI 49707-1495
989-356-9021
alpenacc.org

Bay de Noc Community
College
2001 North Lincoln Road
Escanaba, MI 49829-2511
906-786-5802
www.baydenoc.cc.mi.us

Bay Mills Community
College
12214 West Lakeshore Drive
Brimley, MI 49715
906-248-3354
www.bmcc.org

Davenport University
3555 East Patrick Road
Midland, MI 48642
517-835-5588
www.davenport.edu

Delta College
1961 Delta Road
University Center, MI 48710
989-686-9000
www.delta.edu

Glen Oaks Community
College
62249 Shimmel Road
Centreville, MI 49032-9719
616-467-9945
www.glenoaks.cc.mi.us

Gogebic Community College
E-4946 Jackson Road
Ironwood, MI 49938
906-932-4231
www.gogebic.cc.mi.us

Grand Rapids Community
College
143 Bostwick Avenue, NE
Grand Rapids, MI
49503-3201
616-234-4000
www.grcc.cc.mi.us

Henry Ford Community
College
5101 Evergreen Road
Dearborn, MI 48128-1495
313-845-9615
www.henryford.cc.mi.us

ITT Technical Institute
4020 Sparks Drive, SE
Grand Rapids, MI 49546
616-956-1060
www.itt-tech.edu

ITT Technical Institute
1522 East Big Beaver Road
Troy, MI 48083-1905
248-524-1800
www.itt-tech.edu

Jackson Community College
2111 Emmons Road
Jackson, MI 49201-8399
517-787-0800
www.jackson.cc.mi.us

Kalamazoo Valley
Community College
PO Box 4070
Kalamazoo, MI 49003-4070
616-372-5000
www.kvcc.edu

Kellogg Community College
450 North Avenue
Battle Creek, MI 49017-3397
616-965-3931
www.kellogg.cc.mi.us

Kirtland Community College
10775 North St Helen Road
Roscommon, MI
48653-9699
989-275-5000
kosmo.kirtland.cc.mi.us/dis-
tancelearning

Lake Michigan College
2755 East Napier
Benton Harbor, MI
49022-1899
616-927-8100

Lansing Community College
PO Box 40010
Lansing, MI 48901-7210
517-483-1957
www.lansing.cc.mi.us

Lewis College of Business
17370 Meyers Road
Detroit, MI 48235-1423
313-862-6300
www.lewiscollege.edu

Macomb Community College
14500 Twelve Mile Road
Warren, MI 48093-3896
810-445-7000
www.macomb.cc.mi.us

Mid Michigan Community
College
1375 South Clare Avenue
Harrison, MI 48625-9447
989-386-6622
www.midmich.cc.mi.us

Monroe County Community
College
1555 South Raisinville Road
Monroe, MI 48161-9047
734-242-7300
www.monroe.cc.mi.us

Montcalm Community
College
2800 College Drive
Sidney, MI 48885-9723
517-328-2111
www.montcalm.cc.mi.us

Mott Community College
1401 East Court Street
Flint, MI 48503-2089
810-762-0200
www.mcc.edu

Muskegon Community
College
221 South Quarterline Road
Muskegon, MI 49442-1493
616-773-9131

North Central Michigan
College
1515 Howard Street
Petoskey, MI 49770-8717
231-348-6600
www.ncmc.cc.mi.us

Northwestern Michigan
College
1701 East Front Street
Traverse City, MI
49686-3061
231-995-1000
www.nmc.edu

Oakland Community College
2480 Opdyke Road
Bloomfield Hills, MI
48304-2266
248-341-2000
www.occ.cc.mi.us

Schoolcraft College
18600 Haggerty Road
Livonia, MI 48152-2696
734-462-4400
www.schoolcraft.cc.mi.us

Southwestern Michigan
College
58900 Cherry Grove Road
Dowagiac, MI 49047-9793
616-782-1000
www.smc.cc.mi.us

St. Clair County Community
College
323 Erie Street, PO Box 5015
Port Huron, MI 48061-5015
810-984-3881
www.stclair.cc.mi.us

Washtenaw Community
College
4800 East Huron River Drive,
PO Box D-1
Ann Arbor, MI 48106
734-973-3300
www.wccnet.org

Wayne County Community
College District
801 West Fort Street
Detroit, MI 48226-3010
313-496-2600
www.wccc.edu

West Shore Community
College
PO Box 277,
3000 North Stiles Road
Scottville, MI 49454-0277
231-845-6211
www.westshore.cc.mi.us

Minnesota

Academy College
3050 Metro Drive, Suite 200
Minneapolis, MN 55425
952-851-0066
www.academyeducation.
com

Alexandria Technical College
1601 Jefferson Street
Alexandria, MN 56308-3707
320-762-0221
www.alextech.org

Anoka-Hennepin Technical
College
1355 West Highway 10
Anoka, MN 55303
612-576-4700
www.ank.tec.mn.us

Anoka-Ramsey Community
College
11200 Mississippi Blvd, NW
Coon Rapids, MN
55433-3470
763-427-2600
www.anokaramsey.mnscu.
edu

Anoka-Ramsey Community
College, Cambridge Campus
300 Polk Street South
Cambridge, MN 55008-5706
763-689-7000
www.an.cc.mn.us

Argosy University-Twin Cities
5503 Green Valley Drive
Bloomington, MN
55437-1003
612-844-0064
www.medicalinstitute.org

The Art Institutes
International Minnesota
15 South 9th Street
Minneapolis, MN
55402-3137
612-332-3361
www.aim.aii.edu

Bethany Lutheran College
700 Luther Drive
Mankato, MN 56001-6163
507-344-7000
www.blc.edu

Brown Institute
1440 Northland Drive
Mendota Heights, MN
55120
651-905-3400
www.brown-institute.com

Central Lakes College
501 West College Drive
Brainerd, MN 56401-3904
218-855-8000
www.clc.cc.mn.us

Century Community and
Technical College
3300 Century Avenue North
White Bear Lake, MN 55110
651-779-3200
www.century.cc.mn.us

College of St. Catherine–
Minneapolis
601 25th Avenue South
Minneapolis, MN
55454-1494
651-690-7700
www.stkate.edu

Dakota County Technical
College
1300 East 145th Street
Rosemount, MN 55068
651-423-8000
www.dctc.mnscu.edu

Duluth Business University
412 West Superior Street
Duluth, MN 55802
218-722-4000
www.dbumn.com

Dunwoody Institute
818 Dunwoody Boulevard
Minneapolis, MN 55403
612-374-5800
www.dunwoody.tec.mn.us

Fergus Falls Community
College
1414 College Way
Fergus Falls, MN
56537-1009
218-739-7500
www.ff.cc.mn.us

Fond du Lac Tribal and
Community College
2101 14th Street
Cloquet, MN 55720
218-879-0800
www.fdl.cc.mn.us

Globe College
7166 North 10th Street
Oakdale, MN 55128
651-730-5100
www.globecollege.com

Hennepin Technical College
9000 Brooklyn Boulevard
Brooklyn Park, MN 55445
763-425-3800
www.htc.mnscu.edu

Herzing College, Minneapolis
Drafting School Campus
5700 West Broadway
Minneapolis, MN 55428
763-535-3000
www.herzing.edu

Hibbing Community College
1515 East 25th Street
Hibbing, MN 55746-3300
218-262-7200
www.hcc.mnscu.edu

Inver Hills Community
College
2500 East 80th Street
Inver Grove Heights, MN
55076-3224
651-450-8500
www.ih.cc.mn.us

Itasca Community College
1851 Highway 169 East
Grand Rapids, MN 55744
218-327-4460
www.it.cc.mn.us

Lake Superior College
2101 Trinity Road
Duluth, MN 55811
218-733-7600
www.lsc.cc.mn.us

Lakeland Medical–Dental
Academy
1402 West Lake Street
Minneapolis, MN
55408-2682
612-827-5656
www.lakelandacademy.com

Mesabi Range Community
and Technical College
1001 Chestnut Street West
Virginia, MN 55792-3448
218-741-3095
www.mr.mnscu.edu

Minneapolis Business
College
1711 West County Road B
Roseville, MN 55113
612-636-7406
www.mplsbusinesscollege.
com

Minneapolis Community and
Technical College
1501 Hennepin Avenue
Minneapolis, MN
55403-1779
612-341-7000
www.mctc.mnscu.edu

Minnesota School of
Business
1401 West 76th Street
Richfield, MN 55423
612-861-2000
www.msbcollege.com

Minnesota State College–
Southeast Technical
1250 Homer Road,
PO Box 409
Winona, MN 55987
507-453-2700

Minnesota West Community
and Technical College
1314 North Hiawatha Avenue
Pipestone, MN 56164
507-825-6800
www.mnwest.mnscu.edu

Music Tech
304 Washington Ave North
Minneapolis, MN
55401-1315
612-338-0175
www.musictech.com

NEI College of Technology
825 41st Avenue, NE
Columbia Heights, MN
55421-2974
763-781-4881
www.neicollege.org

Normandale Community
College
9700 France Avenue South
Bloomington, MN
55431-4399
952-487-8200
www.nr.cc.mn.us

North Hennepin Community
College
7411 85th Avenue North
Minneapolis, MN
55445-2231
763-424-0702
www.nh.cc.mn.us

Northland Community and
Technical College
1101 Highway One East
Thief River Falls, MN 56701
218-681-0701
www.northland.cc.mn.us

Northwest Technical College
150 2nd Street SW, Suite B,
PO Box 309
Perham, MN 56573
218-374-6982
www.ntc-online.com

Northwest Technical Institute
11995 Singletree Lane
Eden Prairie, MN
55344-5351
952-944-0080
www.nw-ti.com

Pine Technical College
900 4th Street SE
Pine City, MN 55063
320-629-5100
www.ptc.tec.mn.us

Rainy River Community
College
1501 Highway 71
International Falls, MN
56649
218-285-7722
www.rrcc.mnscu.edu

Rasmussen College Eagan
3500 Federal Drive
Eagan, MN 55122-1346
651-687-9000
www.rasmussen.edu

Rasmussen College Mankato
501 Holly Lane
Mankato, MN 56001-6803
507-625-6556
www.rasmussen.edu

Rasmussen College
Minnetonka
12450 Wayzata Boulevard,
Suite 315
Minnetonka, MN
55305-1928
952-545-2000
www.rasmussen.edu

Rasmussen College St. Cloud
226 Park Avenue South
St. Cloud, MN 56301-3713
320-251-5600
www.rasmussen.edu

Ridgewater College
PO Box 1097
Willmar, MN 56201-1097
320-235-5114
www.ridgewater.mnscu.edu

Riverland Community
College
1900 8th Avenue, NW
Austin, MN 55912
507-433-0600
netco.tec.mn.us/~rivercc

Rochester Community and
Technical College
851 30th Avenue, SE
Rochester, MN 55904-4999
507-285-7210
www.roch.edu

South Central Technical
College
1920 Lee Boulevard
North Mankato, MN 56003
507-389-7200
www.sctc.mnscu.edu

St. Cloud Technical College
1540 Northway Drive
St. Cloud, MN 56303-1240
320-654-5000
sctcweb.tec.mn.us

St. Paul Technical College
235 Marshall Avenue
St. Paul, MN 55102-1800
651-221-1300
www.sptc.tec.mn.us

Vermilion Community
College
1900 East Camp Street
Ely, MN 55731-1996
218-365-7200
www.vcc.mnscu.edu

Mississippi

Antonelli College
480 East Woodrow Wilson Dr
Jackson, MS   39216
601-362-9991
www.antonellicollege.com

Antonelli College
1500 North 31st Avenue
Hattiesburg, MS   39401
601-583-4100
www.antonellic.com

Coahoma Community
College
3240 Friars Point Road
Clarksdale, MS   38614-9799
662-627-2571
www.ccc.cc.ms.us

Copiah-Lincoln Community
College
PO Box 649
Wesson, MS   39191-0649
601-643-5101
www.colin.cc.ms.us

Copiah-Lincoln Community
College–Natchez Campus
11 Co-Lin Circle
Natchez, MS   39120-8446
601-442-9111
www.colin.cc.ms.us

East Central Community
College
PO Box 129
Decatur, MS   39327-0129
601-635-2111
www.eccc.cc.ms.us

East Mississippi Community
College
PO Box 158
Scooba, MS   39358-0158
662-476-8442

Hinds Community College
PO Box 1100
Raymond, MS   39154-1100
601-857-5261
www.hinds.cc.ms.us

Holmes Community College
PO Box 369
Goodman, MS   39079-0369
601-472-2312
www.holmes.cc.ms.us

Itawamba Community
College
602 West Hill Street
Fulton, MS   38843
601-862-8000

Jones County Junior College
900 South Court Street
Ellisville, MS   39437-3901
601-477-4000
www.jcjc.cc.ms.us

Mary Holmes College
Highway 50 West,
PO Drawer 1257
West Point, MS   39773-1257
601-494-6820

Meridian Community College
910 Highway 19 North
Meridian, MS   39307
601-483-8241
www.mcc.cc.ms.us

Mississippi Delta Community
College
PO Box 668
Moorhead, MS   38761-0668
662-246-6322

Mississippi Gulf Coast
Community College
PO Box 548
Perkinston, MS   39573-0548
601-928-5211
www.mgccc.cc.ms.us

Northeast Mississippi
Community College
101 Cunningham Boulevard
Booneville, MS   38829
662-728-7751
www.necc.cc.ms.us

Northwest Mississippi
Community College
4975 Highway 51 North
Senatobia, MS   38668-1701
601-562-3200
www.nwcc.cc.ms.us

Pearl River Community
College
101 Highway 11 North
Poplarville, MS   39470
601-403-1000
www.prcc.cc.ms.us

Southwest Mississippi
Community College
College Drive
Summit, MS   39666
601-276-2000
www.smcc.cc.ms.us

Virginia College at Jackson
5360 I-55 North
Jackson, MS   39211
601-977-0960
www.vc.edu

Wood College
PO Box 289
Mathiston, MS   39752-0289
662-263-5352
www.wood.cc.ms.us

Missouri

Blue River Community
College
1501 West Jefferson Street
Blue Springs, MO   64015
816-655-6000
www.kcmetro.cc.mo.us/bluer
iver/brhome.html

Cottey College
1000 West Austin
Nevada, MO   64772-2700
417-667-8181
www.cottey.edu

Crowder College
601 Laclede
Neosho, MO   64850-9160
417-451-3223
www.crowdercollege.net

East Central College
PO Box 529
Union, MO   63084-0529
636-583-5193
www.ecc.cc.mo.us

Electronics Institute
15329 Kensington Avenue
Kansas City, MO   64147-1212
816-331-5700

Hickey College
940 West Port Plaza, Suite 101
St. Louis, MO   63146
314-434-2212
www.hickeycollege.com

ITT Technical Institute
13505 Lakefront Drive
Earth City, MO   63045-1412
314-298-7800
www.itt-tech.edu

ITT Technical Institute
1930 Meyer Drury Drive
Arnold, MO   63010
636-464-6600
www.itt-tech.edu

Jefferson College
1000 Viking Drive
Hillsboro, MO   63050-2441
636-797-3000
www.jeffco.edu

Linn State Technical College
One Technology Drive
Linn, MO   65051-9606
573-897-5000
www.linnstate.edu

Longview Community
College
500 Southwest Longview Rd
Lee's Summit, MO
64081-2105
816-672-2000
www.kcmetro.cc.mo.us

Maple Woods Community
College
2601 Northeast Barry Road
Kansas City, MO   64156-1299
816-437-3000
www.kemetro.cc.mo.us/mapl
ewoods/mwhome.html

Metro Business College
1732 North Kings Highway
Cape Girardeau, MO   63701
573-334-9181
www.metrobusinesscollege.
edu

Mineral Area College
PO Box 1000
Park Hills, MO   63601-1000
573-431-4593
www.mac.cc.mo.us

Missouri College
10121 Manchester Road
St. Louis, MO   63122-1583
314-821-7700
www.mocollege.com

Moberly Area Community
College
101 College Avenue
Moberly, MO   65270-1304
660-263-4110
www.macc.cc.mo.us

North Central Missouri
College
1301 Main Street
Trenton, MO   64683-1824
660-359-3948
www.ncmc.cc.mo.us

Ozarks Technical Community
College
PO Box 5958
Springfield, MO   65801
417-895-7000
www.otc.cc.mo.us

Patricia Stevens College
330 North Fourth Street,
Suite 306
St. Louis, MO   63102
314-421-0949
www.patriciastevenscollege.
com

Penn Valley Community
College
3201 Southwest Trafficway
Kansas City, MO   64111
816-759-4000
www.kcmetro.cc.mo.us/
pennvalley/pvhome.html

Ranken Technical College
4431 Finney Avenue
St. Louis, MO   63113
314-371-0236
www.ranken.org

Rhodes College
1010 West Sunshine
Springfield, MO   65807-2488
417-864-7220
rhodes-college.com

Saint Charles Community
College
4601 Mid Rivers Mall Drive
St. Peters, MO   63376-0975
636-922-8000
www.stchas.edu

Sanford-Brown College
1203 Smizer Mill Road
Fenton, MO   63026
636-349-4900
www.sanford-brown.edu

Sanford-Brown College
75 Village Square
Hazelwood, MO   63042
314-731-1101

Sanford-Brown College
3555 Franks Drive
St. Charles, MO   63301
314-949-2620

Sanford-Brown College
520 East 19th Avenue
North Kansas City, MO
64116
816-472-7400
www.sanford-brown.edu/
default.htm

Southwest Missouri State
University–West Plains
128 Garfield
West Plains, MO   65775
417-255-7255
www.wp.smsu.edu

St. Louis Community College
at Florissant Valley
3400 Pershall Road
St. Louis, MO   63135-1499
314-595-4200
www.198.209.221.102

St. Louis Community College
at Forest Park
5600 Oakland Avenue
St. Louis, MO   63110-1316
314-644-9100
www.stlcc.cc.mo.us

St. Louis Community College
at Meramec
11333 Big Bend Boulevard
Kirkwood, MO   63122-5720
314-984-7500
www.stlcc.cc.mo.us/mc

State Fair Community
College
3201 West 16th Street
Sedalia, MO   65301-2199
660-530-5800
www.sfcc.cc.mo.us

Three Rivers Community
College
2080 Three Rivers Boulevard
Poplar Bluff, MO   63901-2393
573-840-9600
www.trcc.cc.mo.us

Vatterott College
3925 Industrial Drive
St. Ann, MO   63074-1807
314-428-5900
www.vatterott-college.edu

Wentworth Military Academy
and Junior College
1880 Washington Avenue
Lexington, MO   64067
660-259-2221
www.wma1880.org

Montana

Blackfeet Community College
PO Box 819
Browning, MT   59417-0819
Phone: 406-338-5441
www.montana.edu/wwwbcc

Dawson Community College
Box 421
Glendive, MT   59330-0421
Phone: 406-377-3396
www.dawson.cc.mt.us

Dull Knife Memorial College
PO Box 98
Lame Deer, MT   59043-0098
Phone: 406-477-6215
www.dkmc.cc.mt.us

Flathead Valley Community
College
777 Grandview Drive
Kalispell, MT   59901-2622
Phone: 406-756-3822
www.fvcc.cc.mt.us

Fort Belknap College
PO Box 159
Harlem, MT   59526-0159
Phone: 406-353-2607
www.montana.edu/wwwse/
fbc/fbc.html

Fort Peck Community College
PO Box 398
Poplar, MT   59255-0398
Phone: 406-768-5551
www.fpcc.cc.mt.us

Helena College of Technology
of The University of Montana
1115 North Roberts Street
Helena, MT   59601
Phone: 406-444-6800
www.hct.umontana.edu

Little Big Horn College
Box 370
Crow Agency, MT
59022-0370
Phone: 406-638-2228

Miles Community College
2715 Dickinson
Miles City, MT   59301-4799
Phone: 406-234-3031
www.mcc.cc.mt.us

Montana State University–
Great Falls College of
Technology
2100 16th Avenue, South
Great Falls, MT   59405
Phone: 406-771-4300
www.msugf.edu

Salish Kootenai College
PO Box 117
Pablo, MT   59855-0117
Phone: 406-675-4800
www.skc.edu

Stone Child College
RR1, Box 1082
Box Elder, MT   59521
Phone: 406-395-4313

Nebraska

Central Community
College–Columbus Campus
4500 63rd Street,
PO Box 1027
Columbus, NE   68602-1027
402-564-7132
www.cccneb.edu

Central Community College–
Grand Island Campus
PO Box 4903
Grand Island, NE
68802-4903
308-398-4222
Fax: 308-398-7398
www.cccneb.edu

Central Community College–
Hastings Campus
PO Box 1024
Hastings, NE   68902-1024
402-463-9811
www.cccneb.edu

ITT Technical Institute
9814 M Street
Omaha, NE   68127-2056
402-331-2900
www.itt-tech.edu

Lincoln School of Commerce
1821 K Street, PO Box 82826
Lincoln, NE   68501-2826
402-474-5315
www.lscadvantage.com

Little Priest Tribal College
PO Box 270
Winnebago, NE   68071
402-878-2380
www.lptc.cc.ne.us

Metropolitan Community
College
PO Box 3777
Omaha, NE   68103-0777
402-457-2400
www.mccneb.edu

Mid-Plains Community
College Area
601 West State Farm Road
North Platte, NE   69101
308-535-3600
www.mpcca.cc.ne.us

Nebraska College of
Business
3350 North 90th Street
Omaha, NE 68134
402-572-8500
www.ncbedu.com

Nebraska Indian Community
College
PO Box 428
Macy, NE 68039-0428
402-837-5078
www.thenicc.org

Northeast Community
College
801 East Benjamin Ave,
PO Box 469
Norfolk, NE 68702-0469
402-371-2020
alpha.necc.cc.ne.us

Omaha College of Health
Careers
225 North 80th Street
Omaha, NE 68114
402-392-1300

Southeast Community
College, Beatrice Campus
4771 W. Scott Road
Beatrice, NE 68310-7042
402-228-3468
www.college.sccm.cc.ne.us/
3a.htm

Southeast Community
College, Lincoln Campus
8800 O Street
Lincoln, NE 68520-1299
402-471-3333
www.college.secc.cc.ne.us

Southeast Community
College, Milford Campus
600 State Street
Milford, NE 68405-9397
402-761-2131
www.college.sccm.cc.ne.us

Western Nebraska
Community College
1601 East 27th Street
Scottsbluff, NE 69361
308-635-3606
wncc.net

Nevada

Career College of Northern
Nevada
1195-A Corporate Boulevard
Reno, NV 89502
Phone: 775-856-2266
www.ccnn4u.com

Community College of
Southern Nevada
3200 East Cheyenne Avenue
North Las Vegas, NV
89030-4296
Phone: 702-651-4000
www.ccsn.nevada.edu

Great Basin College
1500 College Parkway
Elko, NV 89801-3348
Phone: 775-738-8493

Heritage College
3305 Spring Mountain Road,
Suite 7
Las Vegas, NV 89102
Phone: 702-368-2338
www.heritage-college.com

ITT Technical Institute
168 Gibson Road
Henderson, NV 89014
Phone: 702-558-5404
www.itt-tech.edu

Las Vegas College
4100 West Flamingo Road,
Suite 2100
Las Vegas, NV 89103-3926
Phone: 702-368-6200
www.cci.edu

Truckee Meadows
Community College
7000 Dandini Boulevard
Reno, NV 89512-3901
Phone: 775-673-7000
www.tmcc.edu

Western Nevada Community
College
2201 West College Parkway
Carson City, NV 89703-7316
Phone: 775-445-3000
www.wncc.nevada.edu

New Hampshire

Hesser College
3 Sundial Avenue
Manchester, NH 03103-7245
603-668-6660
www.hesser.edu

McIntosh College
23 Cataract Avenue
Dover, NH 03820-3990
603-742-1234
www.mcintoshcollege.com

New Hampshire Community
Technical College,
Berlin/Laconia
2020 Riverside Drive
Berlin, NH 03570-3717
603-752-1113
www.berl.tec.nh.us

New Hampshire Community
Technical College,
Manchester
1066 Front Street
Manchester, NH 03102-8518
603-668-6706
www.manc.tec.nh.us

New Hampshire Community
Technical College, Nashua/
Claremont
505 Amherst Street
Nashua, NH 03063-1026
603-882-6923
www.nashua.tec.nh.us

New Hampshire Technical
Institute
11 Institute Drive
Concord, NH 03301-7412
603-271-6484
www.nhti.net

New Jersey

Assumption College for
Sisters
350 Bernardsville Road
Mendham, NJ 07945-0800
973-543-6528
www.acscollegeforsisters.org

Atlantic Cape Community
College
5100 Black Horse Pike
Mays Landing, NJ
08330-2699
609-625-1111
www.atlantic.edu

Bergen Community College
400 Paramus Road
Paramus, NJ 07652-1595
201-447-7100
www.bergen.cc.nj.us

Berkeley College
44 Rifle Camp Road,
PO Box 440
West Paterson, NJ
07424-3353
973-278-5400
www.berkeleycollege.edu

Brookdale Community
College
765 Newman Springs Road
Lincroft, NJ 07738-1597
732-842-1900
www.brookdale.cc.nj.us

Burlington County College
Route 530
Pemberton, NJ 08068-1599
609-894-9311
www.bcc.edu

Camden County College
PO Box 200
Blackwood, NJ 08012-0200
856-227-7200
www.camdencc.edu

County College of Morris
214 Center Grove Road
Randolph, NJ 07869-2086
973-328-5000
www.ccm.edu

Cumberland County College
PO Box 1500, College Drive
Vineland, NJ 08362-1500
856-691-8600
www.cccnj.net

Essex County College
303 University Avenue
Newark, NJ 07102-1798
973-877-3000
www.essex.edu

Gloucester County College
1400 Tanyard Road
Sewell, NJ 08080
856-468-5000
www.gccnj.edu

Hudson County Community
College
25 Journal Square
Jersey City, NJ 07306
201-656-2020
www.hudson.cc.nj.us

Mercer County Community
College
1200 Old Trenton Road,
PO Box B
Trenton, NJ 08690-1004
609-586-4800
www.mccc.edu

Middlesex County College
2600 Woodbridge Avenue,
PO Box 3050
Edison, NJ 08818-3050
732-548-6000
www.middlesex.cc.nj.us

Ocean County College
College Drive, PO Box 2001
Toms River, NJ 08754-2001
732-255-0400
www.ocean.cc.nj.us

Passaic County Community
College
One College Boulevard
Paterson, NJ 07505-1179
973-684-6800
www.pccc.cc.nj.us

Raritan Valley Community
College
PO Box 3300
Somerville, NJ 08876-1265
908-526-1200
www.raritanval.edu

Salem Community College
460 Hollywood Avenue
Carneys Point, NJ
08069-2799
856-299-2100
www.salem.cc.nj.us

Somerset Christian College
10 Liberty Square
Zarephath, NJ 08890-9035
732-356-1595
www.zarephath.edu

Sussex County Community
College
1 College Hill
Newton, NJ 07860
973-300-2100
www.sussex.cc.nj.us

Union County College
1033 Springfield Avenue
Cranford, NJ 07016-1528
908-709-7000
www.ucc.edu

Warren County Community
College
475 Route 57 West
Washington, NJ 07882-4343
908-689-1090
www.warren.cc.nj.us

New Mexico

Albuquerque Technical
Vocational Institute
525 Buena Vista, SE
Albuquerque, NM
87106-4096
Phone: 505-224-3000
www.tvi.cc.nm.us

Clovis Community College
417 Schepps Boulevard
Clovis, NM 88101-8381
Phone: 505-769-2811
www.clovis.cc.nm.us

Doña Ana Branch
Community College
MSC-3DA, Box 30001,
3400 South Espina Street
Las Cruces, NM 88003-8001
Phone: 505-527-7500
dabcc-www.nmsu.edu

Eastern New Mexico
University–Roswell
PO Box 6000
Roswell, NM 88202-6000
Phone: 505-624-7000
www.enmu.edu/roswell/
buchanaj/ENMU-R

Institute of American Indian
Arts
83 Avan Nu Po Road
Santa Fe, NM 87508
Phone: 505-424-2300
www.iaiancad.org

ITT Technical Institute
5100 Masthead, NE
Albuquerque, NM
87109-4366
Phone: 505-828-1114
www.itt-tech.edu

Luna Community College
PO Box 1510
Las Vegas, NM 87701
Phone: 505-454-2500
www.lvti.cc.nm.us

Mesa Technical College
911 South Tenth Street
Tucumcari, NM 88401
Phone: 505-461-4413
www.mesatc.cc.nm.us

New Mexico Junior College
5317 Lovington Highway
Hobbs, NM 88240-9123
Phone: 505-392-4510
www.nmjc.cc.nm.us

New Mexico Military Institute
101 West College Boulevard
Roswell, NM 88201-5173
Phone: 505-622-6250
www.nmmi.cc.nm.us

New Mexico State
University–Alamogordo
2400 North Scenic Drive
Alamogordo, NM
88311-0477
Phone: 505-439-3600
alamo.nmsu.edu

New Mexico State
University–Carlsbad
1500 University Drive
Carlsbad, NM 88220-3509
Phone: 505-234-9200
cavern.nmsu.edu

New Mexico State
University–Grants
1500 3rd Street
Grants, NM 87020-2025
Phone: 505-287-7981

Northern New Mexico
Community College
921 Paseo de Oñate
Española, NM 87532
Phone: 505-747-2100
www.nnm.cc.nm.us

Pima Medical Institute
2201 San Pedro NE,
Building 3, Suite 100
Albuquerque, NM 87110
Phone: 505-881-1234
www.pimamedical.com

San Juan College
4601 College Boulevard
Farmington, NM 87402-4699
Phone: 505-326-3311
www.sjc.cc.nm.us

Santa Fe Community College
6401 Richards Avenue
Santa Fe, NM 87505-4887
Phone: 505-428-1000
www.santa-fe.cc.nm.us

Southwestern Indian
Polytechnic Institute
9169 Coors, NW, Box 10146
Albuquerque, NM
87184-0146
Phone: 505-346-2347
www.sipi.bia.edu

The Art Center
5041 Indian School Road, NE,
Suite 100
Albuquerque, NM 87110
Phone: 505-254-7575
www.theartcenter.edu

University of New Mexico–
Gallup
200 College Road
Gallup, NM 87301-5603
Phone: 505-863-7500
www.gallup.unm.edu

University of New Mexico–
Los Alamos Branch
4000 University Drive
Los Alamos, NM
87544-2233
Phone: 505-662-5919

University of New Mexico–
Valencia Campus
280 La Entrada
Los Lunas, NM 87031-7633
Phone: 505-925-8500

New York

Adirondack Community
College
640 Bay Road
Queensbury, NY 12804
518-743-2200
www.sunyacc.edu

American Academy
McAllister Institute of Funeral
Service
450 West 56th Street
New York, NY 10019-3602
212-757-1190

American Academy of
Dramatic Arts
120 Madison Avenue
New York, NY 10016-7004
212-686-9244
www.aada.org

Berkeley College
3 East 43rd Street
New York, NY 10017-4604
212-986-4343
www.berkeleycollege.edu

Berkeley College
99 Church Street
White Plains, NY 10601
914-694-1122
www.berkeleycollege.edu

Borough of Manhattan
Community College of the
City University of New York
199 Chambers Street
New York, NY 10007-1097
212-346-8000
www.bmcc.cuny.edu

Bramson ORT College
69-30 Austin Street
Forest Hills, NY 11375-4239
718-261-5800
www.bramsonort.org

Bronx Community College of
the City University of
New York
University Avenue & West
181st Street
Bronx, NY 10453
718-289-5100
www.bcc.cuny.edu

Broome Community College
PO Box 1017
Binghamton, NY 13902-1017
607-778-5000
www.sunybroome.edu

Bryant and Stratton Business
Institute
150 Bellwood Drive
Rochester, NY 14606
716-720-0660
www.bryantstratton.edu

Bryant and Stratton Business
Institute
953 James Street
Syracuse, NY 13203-2502
315-472-6603
Fax: 315-474-4383
www.bryantstratton.edu

Bryant and Stratton Business
Institute
1214 Abbott Road
Lackawanna, NY 14218-1989
716-821-9331
www.bryantstratton.edu

Bryant and Stratton Business
Institute
1225 Jefferson Road
Rochester, NY 14623-3136
716-292-5627
www.bryantstratton.edu

Bryant and Stratton Business
Institute
1259 Central Avenue
Albany, NY 12205-5230
518-437-1802
www.bryantstratton.edu

Bryant and Stratton Business
Institute
Suite 400, 465 Main Street
Buffalo, NY 14203
716-884-9120
www.bryantstratton.edu

Bryant and Stratton Business
Institute, Amherst Campus
40 Hazelwood Drive
Amherst, NY 14228
716-691-0012
www.bryantstratton.edu

Bryant and Stratton Business
Institute, North Campus
8687 Carling Road
Liverpool, NY 13090-1315
315-652-6500
www.bryantstratton.edu

Catholic Medical Center of
Brooklyn and Queens School
of Nursing
175-05 Horace Harding
Expressway
Fresh Meadows, NY 11365
718-357-0500

Cayuga County Community
College
197 Franklin Street
Auburn, NY 13021-3099
315-255-1743
www.cayuga-cc.edu

Clinton Community College
136 Clinton Point Drive
Plattsburgh, NY 12901-9573
518-562-4200
clintoncc.suny.edu

Cochran School of Nursing
967 North Broadway
Yonkers, NY 10701
914-964-4283
www.riversidehealth.org

Columbia-Greene
Community College
4400 Route 23
Hudson, NY 12534-0327
518-828-4181
Fax: 518-828-8543
www.sunycgcc.edu

Corning Community College
One Academic Drive
Corning, NY 14830-3297
607-962-9011
Fax: 607-962-9456
www.corning-cc.edu

Crouse Hospital School of
Nursing
736 Irving Avenue
Syracuse, NY 13210
315-470-7481
www.crouse.org/son/home.
htm

Dorothea Hopfer School of
Nursing at The Mount Vernon
Hospital
53 Valentine Street
Mount Vernon, NY 10550
914-664-8000

Dutchess Community College
53 Pendell Road
Poughkeepsie, NY
12601-1595
845-431-8000
www.sunydutchess.edu

Ellis Hospital School of
Nursing
1101 Nott Street
Schenectady, NY 12308
518-243-4471
www.ehson.org

Elmira Business Institute
303 North Main Street
Elmira, NY 14901
607-733-7177
www.ebi-college.com

Erie Community College, City
Campus
121 Ellicott Street
Buffalo, NY 14203-2698
716-851-1001
www.sunyerie.edu

Erie Community College,
North Campus
6205 Main Street
Williamsville, NY 14221-7095
716-851-1002
www.sunyerie.edu

Erie Community College,
South Campus
4041 Southwestern Blvd
Orchard Park, NY 14127-2199
716-851-1003
Fax: 716-648-9953
www.sunyerie.edu

Eugenio Marìa de Hostos
Community College of the
City University of New York
500 Grand Concourse
Bronx, NY 10451
718-518-4444
www.hostos.cuny.edu

Finger Lakes Community
College
4355 Lakeshore Drive
Canandaigua, NY 14424-8395
716-394-3500
www.flcc.edu

Fiorello H. LaGuardia
Community College of the
City University of New York
31-10 Thomson Avenue
Long Island City, NY
11101-3071
718-482-7200
www.lagcc.cuny.edu

Fulton-Montgomery
Community College
2805 State Highway 67
Johnstown, NY 12095-3790
518-762-4651
fmcc.suny.edu

Genesee Community College
1 College Road
Batavia, NY 14020-9704
716-343-0055
www.sunygenesee.cc.ny.us

Helene Fuld College of
Nursing of North General
Hospital
1879 Madison Avenue
New York, NY 10035-2709
212-423-1000

Herkimer County Community
College
Reservoir Road
Herkimer, NY 13350
315-866-0300
www.hccc.ntcnet.com

Hudson Valley Community
College
80 Vandenburgh Avenue
Troy, NY 12180-6096
518-629-4822
www.hvcc.edu

Institute of Design and
Construction
141 Willoughby Street
Brooklyn, NY 11201-5317
718-855-3661
www.idcbrooklyn.org

Interboro Institute
450 West 56th Street
New York, NY 10019-3602
212-399-0091
www.interboro.com

Island Drafting and Technical
Institute
128 Broadway
Amityville, NY 11787
631-691-8733
www.islanddrafting.com

ITT Technical Institute
235 Greenfield Parkway
Liverpool, NY 13088
315-461-8000
www.itt-tech.edu

ITT Technical Institute
2295 Millersport Highway,
PO Box 327
Getzville, NY 14068
716-689-2200
www.itt-tech.edu

ITT Technical Institute
13 Airline Drive
Albany, NY 12205
518-452-9300
www.itt-tech.edu

Jamestown Business College
7 Fairmount Avenue, Box 429
Jamestown, NY 14702-0429
716-664-5100
www.jbcny.org

Jamestown Community
College
525 Falconer Street
Jamestown, NY 14701-1999
716-665-5220
www.sunyjcc.edu

Jefferson Community
College
1220 Coffeen Street
Watertown, NY 13601
315-786-2200
www.sunyjefferson.edu

Katharine Gibbs School
200 Park Avenue
New York, NY 10166-0005
212-867-9300
www.katharinegibbs.com

Katharine Gibbs School
320 South Service Road
Melville, NY 11747-3785
631-370-3300
www.gibbsmelville.com

Kingsborough Community
College of the City University
of New York
2001 Oriental Blvd,
Manhattan Beach
Brooklyn, NY 11235
718-368-5000
www.kbcc.cuny.edu

Long Island Business
Institute
6500 Jericho Turnpike
Commack, NY 11725
631-499-7100
www.libinstitute.com

Long Island College Hospital
School of Nursing
397 Hicks Street
Brooklyn, NY 11201-5940
718-780-1953

Maria College
700 New Scotland Avenue
Albany, NY 12208-1798
518-438-3111
www.mariacollege.org

Mildred Elley
800 New Louden Road
Latham, NY 12110
518-786-0855

Mohawk Valley Community
College
1101 Sherman Drive
Utica, NY 13501-5394
315-792-5400
www.mvcc.edu

Monroe College
Monroe College Way
Bronx, NY 10468-5407
718-933-6700
www.monroecoll.edu

Monroe College
434 Main Street
New Rochelle, NY 10801
914-632-5400
www.monroecoll.edu

Monroe Community College
1000 East Henrietta Road
Rochester, NY 14623-5780
716-292-2000
www.monroecc.edu

Nassau Community College
1 Education Drive
Garden City, NY 11530-6793
516-572-7500
www.sunynassau.edu

New York Career Institute
15 Park Row, 4th Floor
New York, NY 10038-2301
212-962-0002
www.nyci.com

New York City Technical
College of the City University
of New York
300 Jay Street
Brooklyn, NY 11201-2983
718-260-5000
www.nyctc.cuny.edu

The New York College for
Wholistic Health Education &
Research
6801 Jericho Turnpike,
Suite 300
Syosset, NY 11791-4413
516-364-0808
www.nycollege.edu

New York Restaurant School
75 Varick Street, 16th Floor
New York, NY 10013
212-226-5500
www.nyrs.artinstitutes.edu

Niagara County Community
College
3111 Saunders Settlement Rd
Sanborn, NY 14132-9460
716-614-6222

North Country Community
College
20 Winona Avenue,
PO Box 89
Saranac Lake, NY 12983-0089
518-891-2915
www.nccc.edu

Olean Business Institute
301 North Union Street
Olean, NY 14760-2691
716-372-7978

Onondaga Community
College
4941 Onondaga Road
Syracuse, NY 13215-2099
315-498-2622
www.sunyocc.edu

Orange County Community
College
115 South Street
Middletown, NY 10940-6437
914-344-6222
www.orange.cc.ny.us

Phillips Beth Israel School of
Nursing
310 East 22nd Street,
9th Floor
New York, NY 10010-5702
212-614-6110
www.wehealny.org/bischool
of nursing

Plaza Business Institute
74-09 37th Avenue
Jackson Heights, NY
11372-6300
718-779-1430
www.plazacollege.edu

Queensborough Community
College of the City University
of New York
222-05 56th Avenue
Bayside, NY 11364
718-631-6262
www.qcc.cuny.edu

Rochester Business Institute
1630 Portland Avenue
Rochester, NY 14621
716-266-0430
www.rochester-institute.com

Rockland Community College
145 College Road
Suffern, NY 10901-3699
914-574-4000
www.sunyrockland.edu

Sage College of Albany
140 New Scotland Avenue
Albany, NY 12208-3425
518-292-1730
www.sage.edu/SCA

Saint Joseph's Hospital
Health Center School of
Nursing
206 Prospect Avenue
Syracuse, NY 13203
315-448-5040
www.sjhsyr.org/nursing

Samaritan Hospital School of
Nursing
2215 Burdett Avenue
Troy, NY 12180
518-271-3285

Schenectady County
Community College
78 Washington Avenue
Schenectady, NY 12305-2294
518-381-1200
www.sunysccc.edu

Simmons Institute of Funeral
Service
1828 South Avenue
Syracuse, NY 13207
315-475-5142
www.simmonsinstitute.com

State University of New York
College of Agriculture and
Technology at Morrisville
PO Box 901
Morrisville, NY 13408-0901
315-684-6000
www.morrisville.edu

State University of New York
College of Environmental
Science & Forestry, Ranger
School
PO Box 48, 257 Ranger
School Road
Wanakena, NY 13695
315-848-2566
www.esf.edu

State University of New York
College of Technology at
Alfred
Alfred, NY 14802
607-587-4111
www.alfredstate.edu

State University of New York College of Technology at Delhi
Main Street
Delhi, NY 13753
607-746-4000
www.delhi.edu

Suffolk County Community College
533 College Road
Selden, NY 11784-2899
631-451-4110
www.sunysuffolk.edu

Sullivan County Community College
112 College Road
Loch Sheldrake, NY 12759
845-434-5750
www.sullivan.suny.edu

Taylor Business Institute
269 West 40th Street
New York, NY 10018
212-643-2020

TCI-The College for Technology
320 West 31st Street
New York, NY 10001-2705
212-594-4000
www.tciedu.com

Tompkins Cortland Community College
170 North Street, PO Box 139
Dryden, NY 13053-0139
607-844-8211
www.sunytccc.edu

Trocaire College
360 Choate Avenue
Buffalo, NY 14220-2094
716-826-1200
Fax: 716-826-4704
www.trocaire.edu

Ulster County Community College
Stone Ridge, NY 12484
914-687-5000
www.ulster.cc.ny.us

Utica School of Commerce
201 Bleecker Street
Utica, NY 13501-2280
315-733-2307
www.uscny.com

Villa Maria College of Buffalo
240 Pine Ridge Road
Buffalo, NY 14225-3999
716-896-0700
www.villa.edu

Westchester Business Institute
325 Central Avenue,
PO Box 710
White Plains, NY 10602
914-948-4442
www.wbi.org

Westchester Community College
75 Grasslands Road
Valhalla, NY 10595-1698
914-785-6600
www.sunywcc.edu

Wood Tobe–Coburn School
8 East 40th Street
New York, NY 10016
212-686-9040
www.woodtobecoburn.com

North Carolina

Alamance Community College
PO Box 8000
Graham, NC 27253-8000
336-578-2002
www.alamance.cc.nc.us

Asheville-Buncombe Technical Community College
340 Victoria Road
Asheville, NC 28801-4897
828-254-1921
www.asheville.cc.nc.us

Beaufort County Community College
PO Box 1069
Washington, NC 27889-1069
252-946-6194
www.beaufort.cc.nc.us

Bladen Community College
PO Box 266
Dublin, NC 28332-0266
910-862-2164
www.bladen.cc.nc.us

Blue Ridge Community College
College Drive
Flat Rock, NC 28731-9624
828-692-3572
www.blueridge.cc.nc.us

Brunswick Community College
PO Box 30
Supply, NC 28462-0030
910-755-7300
www.brunswick.cc.nc.us

Cabarrus College of Health Sciences
431 Copperfield Blvd, NE
Concord, NC 28025-2405
704-783-1555
www.cabarruscollege.edu

Caldwell Community College and Technical Institute
2855 Hickory Boulevard
Hudson, NC 28638-2397
828-726-2200
www.cccti.com

Cape Fear Community College
411 North Front Street
Wilmington, NC 28401-3993
910-251-5100
www.cfcc.wilmington.net

Carolinas College of Health Sciences
PO Box 32861,
1200 Blythe Blvd
Charlotte, NC 28232-2861
704-355-5043
www.carolinascollege.org

Carteret Community College
3505 Arendell Street
Morehead City, NC 28557-2989
252-247-6000
gofish.carteret.cc.nc.us

Catawba Valley Community College
2550 Highway 70 SE
Hickory, NC 28602-9699
828-327-7000
www.cvcc.cc.nc.us

Cecils College
1567 Patton Avenue
Asheville, NC 28806
828-252-2486
www.cecilscollege.com

Central Carolina Community College
1105 Kelly Drive
Sanford, NC 27330-9000
919-775-5401
www.ccarolina.cc.nc.us

Central Piedmont Community College
PO Box 35009
Charlotte, NC 28235-5009
704-330-2722
www.cpcc.cc.nc.us

Cleveland Community College
137 South Post Road
Shelby, NC 28152
704-484-4000
www.cleveland.cc.nc.us

Coastal Carolina Community College
444 Western Boulevard
Jacksonville, NC 28546-6899
910-455-1221
www.coastal.cc.nc.us

College of The Albemarle
PO Box 2327
Elizabeth City, NC 27906-2327
252-335-0821

Craven Community College
800 College Court
New Bern, NC 28562-4984
252-638-4131
www.craven.cc.nc.us

Davidson County Community College
PO Box 1287
Lexington, NC 27293-1287
336-249-8186
www.davidson.cc.nc.us

Durham Technical Community College
1637 Lawson Street
Durham, NC 27703-5023
919-686-3300
www.dtcc.cc.nc.us

Edgecombe Community College
2009 West Wilson Street
Tarboro, NC 27886-9399
252-823-5166
www.edgecombe.cc.nc.us

Fayetteville Technical Community College
PO Box 35236
Fayetteville, NC 28303-0236
910-678-8400
www.fayetech.cc.nc.us

Forsyth Technical Community College
2100 Silas Creek Parkway
Winston-Salem, NC 27103-5197
336-723-0371
www.forsyth.tec.nc.us

Gaston College
201 Highway 321 South
Dallas, NC   28034-1499
704-922-6200
www.gastoncollege.org

Guilford Technical
Community College
PO Box 309
Jamestown, NC   27282-0309
336-334-4822
technet.gtcc.cc.nc.us

Halifax Community College
PO Drawer 809
Weldon, NC   27890-0809
252-536-2551
www.hcc.cc.nc.us

Haywood Community
College
185 Freedlander Drive
Clyde, NC   28721-9453
828-627-2821
www.haywood.cc.nc.us

Isothermal Community
College
PO Box 804
Spindale, NC   28160-0804
828-286-3636
www.isothermal.cc.nc.us

James Sprunt Community
College
PO Box 398
Kenansville, NC   28349-0398
910-296-2400
www.sprunt.com

Johnston Community
College
PO Box 2350
Smithfield, NC   27577-2350
919-934-3051
www.johnston.cc.nc.us

Lenoir Community College
PO Box 188
Kinston, NC   28502-0188
252-527-6223
lenoir.cc.nc.us

Louisburg College
501 North Main Street
Louisburg, NC   27549-2399
919-496-2521
www.louisburg.edu

Martin Community College
1161 Kehukee Park Road
Williamston, NC   27892
252-792-1521
www.martin.cc.nc.us

Mayland Community College
PO Box 547
Spruce Pine, NC   28777-0547
828-765-7351
www.mayland.cc.nc.us

McDowell Technical
Community College
Route 1, Box 170
Marion, NC   28752-9724
828-652-6021
www.mcdowelltech.cc.nc.us

Mitchell Community College
500 West Broad
Statesville, NC   28677-5293
704-878-3200
www.mitchell.cc.nc.us

Montgomery Community
College
PO Box 787
Troy, NC   27371-0787
910-576-6222
www.montgomery.cc.nc.us

Nash Community College
PO Box 7488
Rocky Mount, NC
27804-0488
252-443-4011
www.nash.cc.nc.us

Pamlico Community College
PO Box 185
Grantsboro, NC   28529-0185
252-249-1851

Piedmont Community
College
PO Box 1197
Roxboro, NC   27573-1197
336-599-1181
www.piedmont.cc.nc.us

Pitt Community College
Highway 11 South,
PO Drawer 7007
Greenville, NC   27835-7007
252-321-4200
www.pitt.cc.nc.us

Randolph Community
College
PO Box 1009
Asheboro, NC   27204-1009
336-633-0200

Richmond Community
College
PO Box 1189
Hamlet, NC   28345-1189
910-582-7000
www.richmond.cc.nc.us

Roanoke-Chowan
Community College
109 Community College Rd
Ahoskie, NC   27910
252-862-1200
www.roanoke.cc.nc.us

Robeson Community College
Highway 301 North,
PO Box 1420
Lumberton, NC   28359-1420
910-738-7101
www.robeson.cc.nc.us

Rockingham Community
College
PO Box 38
Wentworth, NC   27375-0038
336-342-4261
www.rcc.cc.nc.us

Rowan-Cabarrus Community
College
PO Box 1595
Salisbury, NC   28145-1595
704-637-0760
www.rccc.cc.nc.us

Sampson Community
College
PO Box 318
Clinton, NC   28329-0318
910-592-8081
www.sampson.cc.nc.us

Sandhills Community
College
3395 Airport Road
Pinehurst, NC   28374-8299
910-692-6185
www.sandhills.cc.nc.us

South Piedmont Community
College
PO Box 126
Polkton, NC   28135-0126
704-272-7635
www.southpiedmont.org

Southeastern Baptist
Theological Seminary
PO Box 1889
Wake Forest, NC
27588-1889
919-556-3101
www.sebts.edu

Southeastern Community
College
PO Box 151
Whiteville, NC   28472-0151
910-642-7141
www.southeastern.cc.nc.us

Southwestern Community
College
447 College Drive
Sylva, NC   28779
828-586-4091
www.southwest.cc.nc.us

Stanly Community College
141 College Drive
Albemarle, NC   28001-7458
704-982-0121
www.stanly.cc.nc.us

Surry Community College
PO Box 304
Dobson, NC   27017-0304
336-386-8121
www.surry.cc.nc.us.

Tri-County Community
College
4600 East US 64
Murphy, NC   28906-7919
828-837-6810
www.tccc.cc.nc.us

Vance-Granville Community
College
PO Box 917
Henderson, NC   27536-0917
252-492-2061
www.vgcc.cc.nc.us

Wake Technical Community
College
9101 Fayetteville Road
Raleigh, NC   27603-5696
919-662-3400
www.wake.tec.nc.us

Wayne Community College
PO Box 8002
Goldsboro, NC   27533-8002
919-735-5151
www.wayne.cc.nc.us

Western Piedmont
Community College
1001 Burkemont Avenue
Morganton, NC   28655-4511
828-438-6000
www.wp.cc.nc.us

Wilkes Community College
1328 Collegiate Drive, PO
Box 120
Wilkesboro, NC   28697
336-838-6100
www.wilkes.cc.nc.us

Wilson Technical Community
College
902 Herring Avenue,
PO Box 4305
Wilson, NC 27893-3310
252-291-1195
www.wilsontech.cc.nc.us

North Dakota

Bismarck State College
PO Box 5587
Bismarck, ND 58506-5587
701-224-5400
www.bismarckstate.com

Cankdeska Cikana
Community College
PO Box 269
Fort Totten, ND 58335-0269
701-766-4415

Fort Berthold Community
College
PO Box 490
New Town, ND 58763-0490
701-627-4738
www.fort-berthold.cc.nd.us

Lake Region State College
1801 College Drive North
Devils Lake, ND 58301-1598
701-662-1600
www.lrsc.nodak.edu

Minot State University–
Bottineau Campus
105 Simrall Boulevard
Bottineau, ND 58318-1198
701-228-2277
www.misu-b.nodak.edu

North Dakota State College
of Science
800 North Sixth Street
Wahpeton, ND 58076
701-671-2401
www.ndscs.nodak.edu

Sitting Bull College
1341 92nd Street
Fort Yates, ND 58538-9701
701-854-3861
www.sittingbull.edu

Turtle Mountain Community
College
Box 340
Belcourt, ND 58316-0340
701-477-7862
www.turtle-mountain.cc.nd.us

United Tribes Technical
College
3315 University Drive
Bismarck, ND 58504-7596
701-255-3285

Williston State College
Box 1326
Williston, ND 58802-1326
701-774-4200
www.wsc.nodak.edu

Ohio

Antonelli College
124 East Seventh Street
Cincinnati, OH 45202-2592
513-241-4338
www.antonellic.com

The Art Institute of Cincinnati
1171 East Kemper Road
Cincinnati, OH 45246
513-751-1206
www.
theartinstituteofcincinnati.com

Belmont Technical College
120 Fox Shannon Place
St. Clairsville, OH
43950-9735
740-695-9500
www.belmont.cc.oh.us

Bohecker's Business College
326 East Main Street
Ravenna, OH 44266
330-297-7319

Bowling Green State
University–Firelands College
One University Drive
Huron, OH 44839-9791
419-433-5560
www.bgsu.edu/colleges/
firelands

Bradford School
6170 Busch Boulevard
Columbus, OH 43229-2507
614-846-9410
www.
bradfordschoolcolumbus.com

Bryant and Stratton College
27557 Chardon Road
Willoughby Hills, OH 44092
440-944-6800
www.bryantstratton.edu

Bryant and Stratton College
12955 Snow Road
Parma, OH 44130-1013
216-265-3151
www.bryantstratton.edu

Central Ohio Technical
College
1179 University Drive
Newark, OH 43055-1767
740-366-1351
www.cotc.tec.oh.us

Chatfield College
20918 State Route 251
St. Martin, OH 45118-9705
513-875-3344
www.chatfield.edu

Cincinnati College of
Mortuary Science
645 West North Bend Road
Cincinnati, OH 45224-1462
513-761-2020
www.ccms.edu

Cincinnati State Technical and
Community College
3520 Central Parkway
Cincinnati, OH 45223-2690
513-569-1500
www.cinstate.cc.oh.us

Clark State Community
College
570 East Leffel Lane,
PO Box 570
Springfield, OH 45501-0570
937-325-0691
www.clark.cc.oh.us

Cleveland Institute of
Electronics
1776 East Seventeenth Street
Cleveland, OH 44114-3636
216-781-9400
www.cie-wc.edu

College of Art Advertising
4343 Bridgetown Road
Cincinnati, OH 45211-4427
513-574-1010

Columbus State Community
College
Box 1609
Columbus, OH 43216-1609
614-287-2400
www.cscc.edu

Cuyahoga Community
College
700 Carnegie Avenue
Cleveland, OH 44115-2878
216-987-6000
www.tri-c.cc.oh.us

Davis College
4747 Monroe Street
Toledo, OH 43623-4307
419-473-2700

Edison State Community
College
1973 Edison Drive
Piqua, OH 45356-9253
937-778-8600
www.edison.cc.oh.us

Education America,
Remington College,
Cleveland Campus
14445 Broadway Avenue
Cleveland, OH 44125
216-475-7520

ETI Technical College
1320 West Maple Street, NW
North Canton, OH
44720-2854
330-494-1214
www.etitech.com

ETI Technical College of Niles
2076 Youngstown-Warren Rd
Niles, OH 44446-4398
330-652-9919
www.eti-college.com

Gallipolis Career College
1176 Jackson Pike, Suite 312
Gallipolis, OH 45631
740-446-4367
www.
gallipoliscareercollege.com

Hocking College
3301 Hocking Parkway
Nelsonville, OH 45764-9588
740-753-3591
www.hocking.edu

Hondros College
4140 Executive Parkway
Westerville, OH 43081-3855
614-508-7277
www.hondroscollege.com

International College of
Broadcasting
6 South Smithville Road
Dayton, OH 45431-1833
937-258-8251
www.icbroadcasting.com

ITT Technical Institute
1030 North Meridian Road
Youngstown, OH
44509-4098
330-270-1600
www.itt-tech.edu

ITT Technical Institute
4750 Wesley Avenue
Norwood, OH 45212
513-531-8300
www.itt-tech.edu

ITT Technical Institute
14955 Sprague Road
Strongsville, OH 44136
440-234-9091
www.itt-tech.edu

ITT Technical Institute
3325 Stop 8 Road
Dayton, OH 45414-3425
937-454-2267
www.itt-tech.edu

Jefferson Community
College
4000 Sunset Boulevard
Steubenville, OH
43952-3598
740-264-5591
www.jeffersoncc.org

Kent State University,
Ashtabula Campus
3325 West 13th Street
Ashtabula, OH 44004-2299
440-964-3322
www.ashtabula.kent.edu

Kent State University, East
Liverpool Campus
400 East 4th Street
East Liverpool, OH
43920-3497
330-385-3805
www.kenteliv.kent.edu

Kent State University,
Geauga Campus
14111 Claridon-Troy Road
Burton, OH 44021-9500
440-834-4187
www.geauga.kent.edu

Kent State University, Salem
Campus
2491 State Route 45 South
Salem, OH 44460-9412
330-332-0361
www.salem.kent.edu

Kent State University, Stark
Campus
6000 Frank Avenue, NW
Canton, OH 44720-7599
330-499-9600
www.stark.kent.edu

Kent State University,
Trumbull Campus
4314 Mahoning Avenue, NW
Warren, OH 44483-1998
330-847-0571
www.trumbull.kent.edu

Kent State University,
Tuscarawas Campus
330 University Drive, NE
New Philadelphia, OH
44663-9403
330-339-3391
www.tusc.kent.edu

Kettering College of Medical
Arts
3737 Southern Boulevard
Kettering, OH 45429-1299
937-296-7201
www.kcma.edu

Lakeland Community College
7700 Clocktower Drive
Kirtland, OH 44094-5198
440-953-7000
www.lakeland.cc.oh.us

Lima Technical College
4240 Campus Drive
Lima, OH 45804-3597
419-221-1112
www.ltc.tec.oh.us

Lorain County Community
College
1005 Abbe Road, North
Elyria, OH 44035
440-365-5222
www.lorainccc.edu

Marion Technical College
1467 Mount Vernon Avenue
Marion, OH 43302-5694
740-389-4636
www.mtc.tec.oh.us

Mercy College of Northwest
Ohio
2221 Madison Avenue
Toledo, OH 43624
419-251-1279
www.mercycollege.edu

Miami University–Hamilton
Campus
1601 Peck Boulevard
Hamilton, OH 45011-3399
513-785-3000
www.ham.muohio.edu

Miami University–
Middletown Campus
4200 East University
Boulevard
Middletown, OH 45042-3497
513-727-3200
www.mid.muohio.edu

Miami–Jacobs College
PO Box 1433
Dayton, OH 45401-1433
937-461-5174
www.miamijacobs.edu

Muskingum Area Technical
College
1555 Newark Road
Zanesville, OH 43701-2626
740-454-2501
www.matc.tec.oh.us

North Central State College
2441 Kenwood Circle, PO
Box 698
Mansfield, OH 44901-0698
419-755-4800
www.ncstate.tec.oh.us

Northwest State Community
College
22-600 State Route 34
Archbold, OH 43502-9542
419-267-5511
www.nscc.cc.oh.us

Ohio Business College
1907 North Ridge Road
Lorain, OH 44055
440-277-0021
www.obc-lorain.com

Ohio Institute of
Photography and Technology
2029 Edgefield Road
Dayton, OH 45439-1917
937-294-6155
www.oipt.com

The Ohio State University
Agricultural Technical
Institute
1328 Dover Road
Wooster, OH 44691
330-264-3911
www.ati.ohio-state.edu

Ohio Valley Business College
16808 St. Clair Avenue,
PO Box 7000
East Liverpool, OH 43920
330-385-1070

Owens Community College
PO Box 10000
Toledo, OH 43699-1947
419-661-7000
www.owens.cc.oh.us

Owens Community College
300 Davis Street
Findlay, OH 45840
419-423-6827
www.owens.cc.oh.us

Professional Skills Institute
20 Arco Drive
Toledo, OH 43607
419-531-9610
www.proskills.com

RETS Tech Center
555 East Alex Bell Road
Centerville, OH 45459
937-433-3410
www.retstechenter.com

Sinclair Community College
444 West Third Street
Dayton, OH 45402-1460
937-512-2500
www.sinclair.edu

Southeastern Business
College
1855 Western Avenue
Chillicothe, OH 45601-1038
740-774-6300
www.careersohio.com

Southern Ohio College,
Cincinnati Campus
1011 Glendale-Milford Road
Cincinnati, OH 45215
513-771-2424
www.socaec.com

Southern Ohio College,
Findlay Campus
1637 Tiffin Avenue
Findlay, OH 45840
419-423-2211

Southern Ohio College,
Northeast Campus
2791 Mogadore Road
Akron, OH 44312-1596
330-733-8766

Southern State Community
College
100 Hobart Drive
Hillsboro, OH 45133-9487
937-393-3431
soucc.southern.cc.oh.us

Southwestern College of
Business
9910 Princeton-Glendale Rd
Cincinnati, OH 45246-1122
513-874-0432

Southwestern College of
Business
631 South Breiel Boulevard
Middletown, OH 45044-5113
513-423-3346

Southwestern College of
Business
632 Vine Street, Suite 200
Cincinnati, OH 45202-4304
513-421-3212

Southwestern College of
Business
225 West First Street
Dayton, OH 45402-3003
937-224-0061

Stark State College of
Technology
6200 Frank Avenue, NW
Canton, OH 44720-7299
330-494-6170
www.stark.cc.oh.us

Stautzenberger College
5355 Southwyck Boulevard
Toledo, OH 43614
419-866-0261
www.stautzen.com

Technology Education
College
288 South Hamilton Road
Columbus, OH 43213-2087
614-759-7700
www.teccollege.com

Terra State Community
College
2830 Napoleon Road
Fremont, OH 43420-9670
419-334-8400
www.terra.cc.oh.us

Trumbull Business College
3200 Ridge Road
Warren, OH 44484
330-369-3200
www.tbc-trumbullbusiness.
com

The University of Akron–
Wayne College
1901 Smucker Road
Orrville, OH 44667-9192
330-683-2010
www.wayne.uakron.edu

University of Cincinnati
Clermont College
4200 Clermont College Drive
Batavia, OH 45103-1785
513-732-5200

University of Cincinnati
Raymond Walters College
9555 Plainfield Road
Cincinnati, OH 45236-1007
513-745-5600

University of Northwestern
Ohio
1441 North Cable Road
Lima, OH 45805-1498
419-227-3141
www.unoh.edu

Virginia Marti College of
Fashion and Art
11724 Detroit Avenue,
PO Box 580
Lakewood, OH 44107-3002
216-221-8584
www.virginiamarticollege.
com

Washington State
Community College
710 Colegate Drive
Marietta, OH 45750-9225
740-374-8716
www.wscc.edu

West Side Institute of
Technology
9801 Walford Avenue
Cleveland, OH 44102-4797
216-651-1656

Wright State University,
Lake Campus
7600 State Route 703
Celina, OH 45822-2921
419-586-0300
www.wright.lake.edu

Oklahoma

Bacone College
2299 Old Bacone Road
Muskogee, OK 74403-1597
918-683-4581
www.bacone.edu

Carl Albert State College
1507 South McKenna
Poteau, OK 74953-5208
918-647-1200
www.casc.cc.ok.us

Connors State College
Route 1 Box 1000
Warner, OK 74469-9700
918-463-2931
www.connors.cc.ok.us

Eastern Oklahoma State
College
1301 West Main
Wilburton, OK 74578-4999
918-465-2361
www.eosc.cc.ok.us

Murray State College
One Murray Campus
Tishomingo, OK 73460-3130
580-371-2371
www.msc.cc.ok.us

Northeastern Oklahoma
Agricultural and Mechanical
College
200 I Street, NE
Miami, OK 74354-6434
918-542-8441
www.neoam.cc.ok.us

Northern Oklahoma College
1220 East Grand Avenue,
PO Box 310
Tonkawa, OK 74653-0310
580-628-6200

Oklahoma City Community
College
7777 South May Avenue
Oklahoma City, OK
73159-4419
405-682-1611
www.okc.cc.ok.us

Oklahoma State University,
Oklahoma City
900 North Portland
Oklahoma City, OK
73107-6120
405-947-4421
www.osuokc.edu

Oklahoma State University,
Okmulgee
1801 East Fourth Street
Okmulgee, OK 74447-3901
918-756-6211
www.osu-okmulgee.edu

Redlands Community
College
1300 South Country Club Rd
El Reno, OK 73036-5304
405-262-2552
www.redlands.cc.net

Rose State College
6420 Southeast 15th Street
Midwest City, OK
73110-2799
405-733-7311
www.rose.cc.ok.us

Seminole State College
PO Box 351
Seminole, OK 74818-0351
405-382-9950

Southwestern Oklahoma
State University at Sayre
409 East Mississippi Street
Sayre, OK 73662-1236
580-928-5533

Spartan School of
Aeronautics
8820 East Pine Street,
PO Box 582833
Tulsa, OK 74158-2833
918-836-6886
www.spartan.edu

Tulsa Community College
6111 East Skelly Drive
Tulsa, OK 74135-6198
918-595-7000
www.tulsa.cc.ok.us

Western Oklahoma State
College
2801 North Main Street
Altus, OK 73521-1397
580-477-2000
www.western.cc.ok.us

Oregon

Blue Mountain Community
College
2411 Northwest Carden
Avenue, PO Box 1000
Pendleton, OR 97801-1000
Phone: 541-276-1260
www.bmcc.cc.or.us

Central Oregon Community
College
2600 Northwest College Way
Bend, OR 97701-5998
Phone: 541-383-7700
www.cocc.edu

Chemeketa Community
College
PO Box 14007
Salem, OR 97309-7070
Phone: 503-399-5000
www.chemeketa.edu

Clackamas Community
College
19600 South Molalla Avenue
Oregon City, OR 97045-7998
Phone: 503-657-6958
www.clackamas.cc.or.us

Clatsop Community College
1653 Jerome
Astoria, OR 97103-3698
Phone: 503-325-0910
www.clatsopcollege.com

Heald College, Schools of
Business and Technology
625 SW Broadway, 2nd Floor
Portland, OR 97205
Phone: 503-229-0492
www.heald.edu

ITT Technical Institute
6035 Northeast 78th Court
Portland, OR 97218-2854
Phone: 503-255-6500
Fax: 503-255-6135
www.itt-tech.edu

Lane Community College
4000 East 30th Avenue
Eugene, OR 97405-0640
Phone: 541-747-4501
www.lanecc.edu

Linn-Benton Community
College
6500 Southwest Pacific Blvd
Albany, OR 97321
Phone: 541-917-4999
www.lbcc.cc.or.us

Mt. Hood Community
College
26000 Southeast Stark Street
Gresham, OR 97030-3300
Phone: 503-491-6422
www.mhcc.cc.or.us

Pioneer Pacific College
27501 Southwest Parkway Ave
Wilsonville, OR 97070
Phone: 503-682-3903
www.pioneerpacificcollege.
com

Portland Community College
PO Box 19000
Portland, OR 97280-0990
Phone: 503-244-6111
www.pcc.edu

Rogue Community College
3345 Redwood Highway
Grants Pass, OR 97527-9298
Phone: 541-956-7500
www.rogue.cc.or.us

Southwestern Oregon
Community College
1988 Newmark Avenue
Coos Bay, OR 97420-2912
Phone: 541-888-2525
www.southwestern.cc.or.us

Treasure Valley Community
College
650 College Boulevard
Ontario, OR 97914-3423
Phone: 541-889-6493
www.tvcc.cc.or.us

Umpqua Community College
PO Box 967
Roseburg, OR 97470-0226
Phone: 541-440-4600
www.umpqua.cc.or.us

Western Business College
425 Southwest Washington
Portland, OR 97204
Phone: 503-222-3225

Pennsylvania

Academy of Medical Arts and
Business
2301 Academy Drive
Harrisburg, PA 17112-1012
717-545-4747
www.acadcampus.com

Allentown Business School
1501 Lehigh Street
Allentown, PA 18103-3880
610-791-5100
www.chooseabs.com

Antonelli Institute
300 Montgomery Avenue
Erdenheim, PA 19038
215-836-2222
www.antonelli.org

Bradley Academy for the
Visual Arts
1409 Williams Road
York, PA 17402-9012
717-755-2300
www.bradley-acad.com

The Art Institute of
Philadelphia
1622 Chestnut Street
Philadelphia, PA 19103-5198
215-567-7080
www.aiph.artinstitutes.edu

The Art Institute of Pittsburgh
420 Boulevard of the Allies
Pittsburgh, PA 15219
412-263-6600
www.aip.aii.edu

Berean Institute
1901 West Girard Avenue
Philadelphia, PA 19130-1599
215-763-4833

Berks Technical Institute
2205 Ridgewood Road
Wyomissing, PA 19610-1168
610-372-1722
www.berkstech.com

Bradford School
707 Grant Street, Gulf Tower
Pittsburgh, PA 15219
412-391-6710
www.bradfordschoolpgh.
com

Bucks County Community
College
275 Swamp Road
Newtown, PA 18940-1525
215-968-8000
www.bucks.edu

Business Institute of
Pennsylvania
335 Boyd Drive
Sharon, PA 16146
724-983-0700
www.biop.com

Butler County Community
College
College Drive, PO Box 1203
Butler, PA 16003-1203
724-287-8711
bc3.cc.pa.us

Cambria County Area
Community College
PO Box 68
Johnstown, PA 15907-0068
814-532-5300
www.ccacc.cc.pa.us

Cambria-Rowe Business
College
221 Central Avenue
Johnstown, PA 15902-2494
814-536-5168
www.crbc.net

Central Pennsylvania College
College Hill Road
Summerdale, PA 17093-0309
717-732-0702
www.centralpenn.edu

CHI Institute, RETS Campus
1991 Lawrence Road,
Suite 42
Broomall, PA 19008
610-353-7630

CHI Institute
520 Street Road
Southampton, PA 18966-3747
215-357-5100
www.chitraining.com

Churchman Business School
355 Spring Garden Street
Easton, PA 18042-3592
610-258-5345
www.churchman4u.com

Commonwealth Technical
Institute
727 Goucher Street
Johnstown, PA 15905-3092
814-255-8200
www.hgac.org

Community College of
Allegheny County
800 Allegheny Avenue
Pittsburgh, PA 15233-1894
412-323-2323
www.ccac.edu

Community College of
Beaver County
One Campus Drive
Monaca, PA 15061-2588
724-775-8561
www.ccbc.cc.pa.us

Community College of
Philadelphia
1700 Spring Garden Street
Philadelphia, PA 19130-3991
215-751-8000
www.ccp.cc.pa.us

Consolidated School of
Business
2124 Ambassador Circle
Lancaster, PA 17603
717-394-6211
www.csb.edu

Consolidated School of
Business
1605 Clugston Road
York, PA 17404
717-764-9550
www.csb.edu

Dean Institute of Technology
1501 West Liberty Avenue
Pittsburgh, PA 15226-1103
412-531-4433
home.earthlink.net/~deantech

Delaware County Community
College
901 South Media Line Road
Media, PA 19063-1094
610-359-5000
www.dccc.edu

Douglas School of Business
130 Seventh Street
Monessen, PA 15062
724-684-3684
www.douglas-school.com

DuBois Business College
1 Beaver Drive
DuBois, PA 15801-2401
814-371-6920
www.dbcollege.com

Duff's Business Institute
110 Ninth Street
Pittsburgh, PA 15222-3618
412-261-4520
www.cci.edu

Electronic Institutes
19 Jamesway Plaza
Middletown, PA 17057-4851
717-944-2731
www.ei.tec.pa.us

Erie Business Center, Main
246 West Ninth Street
Erie, PA 16501-1392
814-456-7504
www.eriebc.com

Erie Business Center South
170 Cascade Galleria
New Castle, PA 16101-3950
724-658-9066
www.eriebc.com

Erie Institute of Technology
2221 Peninsula Drive
Erie, PA 16506-2954
814-838-2711
www.erieinst.com

Harcourt Learning Direct
Center for Degree Studies
925 Oak Street
Scranton, PA 18515
570-342-7701
www.harcourt-learning.com

Harcum College
750 Montgomery Avenue
Bryn Mawr, PA 19010-3476
610-525-4100
www.harcum.edu

Harrisburg Area Community
College
1 HACC Drive
Harrisburg, PA 17110-2999
717-780-2300
www.hacc.edu

Hussian School of Art
1118 Market Street
Philadelphia, PA 19107-3679
215-981-0900
www.hussianart.edu

ICM School of Business &
Medical Careers
10 Wood Street at Fort Pitt Blvd
Pittsburgh, PA 15222-1977
412-261-2647
www.icmschools.com

Information Computer
Systems Institute
2201 Hangar Place
Allentown, PA 18103-9504
610-264-8029
www.icsinstitute.com

International Academy of
Design & Technology
555 Grant Street
Pittsburgh, PA 15219
412-391-4197
www.iadtpitt.com

ITT Technical Institute
5020 Louise Drive
Mechanicsburg, PA 17055
717-691-9263
www.itt-tech.edu

ITT Technical Institute
105 Mall Boulevard
Monroeville, PA 15146
412-856-5920
www.itt-tech.edu

ITT Technical Institute
Eight Parkway Centre
Pittsburgh, PA 15220
412-937-9150
www.itt-tech.edu

Johnson Technical Institute
3427 North Main Avenue
Scranton, PA 18508-1495
570-342-6404
www.jti.org

Keystone College
One College Green
La Plume, PA 18440
570-945-5141
www.keystone.edu

Lackawanna College
501 Vine Street
Scranton, PA 18509
570-961-7810
www.ljc.edu

Lansdale School of Business
201 Church Road
North Wales, PA 19454-4148
215-699-5700
www.lsbonline.com

Laurel Business Institute
11-15 Penn Street
Uniontown, PA 15401
724-439-4900
www.laurelbusiness.net

Lehigh Carbon Community
College
4525 Education Park Drive
Schnecksville, PA 18078-2598
610-799-2121
www.lccc.edu

Lincoln Technical Institute
5151 Tilghman Street
Allentown, PA 18104-3298
610-398-5300
www.lincolntech.com

Lincoln Technical Institute
9191 Torresdale Avenue
Philadelphia, PA 19136-1595
215-335-0800

Lord Fairfax Community
College
PO Box 47
Middletown, VA 22645-0047
540-868-7000
www.lf.cc.va.us

Luzerne County Community
College
1333 South Prospect Street
Nanticoke, PA 18634-9804
570-740-0300
www.luzerne.edu

Manor College
700 Fox Chase Road
Jenkintown, PA 19046
215-885-2360
www.manor.edu

McCann School of Business
Main and Pine Streets
Mahanoy City, PA 17948
717-773-1820
www.mccannschool.com

Median School of Allied
Health Careers
125 7th Street
Pittsburgh, PA 15222-3400
412-391-7021
www.medianschool.com

Montgomery County
Community College
340 DeKalb Pike
Blue Bell, PA 19422-0796
215-641-6300
www.mc3.edu

New Castle School of Trades
New Castle Youngstown
Road, Route 422 RD1
Pulaski, PA 16143-9721
724-964-8811
www.ncstrades.com

Newport Business Institute
945 Greensburg Road
Lower Burrell, PA 15068-3929
724-339-7542
www.akvalley.com/newport

Newport Business Institute
941 West Third Street
Williamsport, PA 17701-5855
570-326-2869
www.akvalley.com/newport

Northampton County Area
Community College
3835 Green Pond Road
Bethlehem, PA 18020-7599
610-861-5300
www.northampton.edu

Northwest Pennsylvania
Technical Institute
150 East Front Street,
Suite 200
Erie, PA 16507
814-452-1122
www.penn.org

Oakbridge Academy of Arts
1250 Greensburg Road
Lower Burrell, PA 15068
724-335-5336
www.akvalley.com/oakbridge

Orleans Technical Institute-
Center City Campus
1845 Walnut Street, Suite 700
Philadelphia, PA 19103-4707
215-854-1853
www.jevs.org

Pace Institute
606 Court Street
Reading, PA 19601
610-375-1212
www.paceinstitute.com

Penn Commercial Business
and Technical School
82 South Main Street
Washington, PA 15301-6822
724-222-5330
www.penn-commercial.com

Pennco Tech
3815 Otter Street
Bristol, PA 19007-3696
215-824-3200

Pennsylvania Institute of
Culinary Arts
717 Liberty Avenue
Pittsburgh, PA 15222-3500
412-566-2433
www.paculinary.com

Pennsylvania Institute of
Technology
800 Manchester Avenue
Media, PA 19063-4098
610-892-1500
www.pit.edu

The Pennsylvania State
University Beaver Campus of
the Commonwealth College
100 University Drive
Monaca, PA 15061
724-773-3500
www.psu.edu

The Pennsylvania State
University Delaware County
Campus of the
Commonwealth College
25 Yearsley Mill Road
Media, PA 19063-5596
610-892-1350
www.psu.edu

The Pennsylvania State
University DuBois Campus of
the Commonwealth College
College Place
DuBois, PA 15801-3199
814-375-4700
www.psu.edu

The Pennsylvania State
University Fayette Campus of
the Commonwealth College
1 University Drive,
PO Box 519
Uniontown, PA 15401-0519
724-430-4100
www.psu.edu

The Pennsylvania State
University Hazleton Campus
of the Commonwealth
College
Hazleton, PA 18201-1291
570-450-3000
www.psu.edu

The Pennsylvania State
University McKeesport
Campus of the
Commonwealth College
4000 University Drive
McKeesport, PA 15132-7698
412-675-9000
www.psu.edu

The Pennsylvania State
University Mont Alto
Campus of the
Commonwealth College
Campus Drive
Mont Alto, PA 17237-9703
717-749-6000
www.psu.edu

The Pennsylvania State
University New Kensington
Campus of the
Commonwealth College
3550 7th Street Road, RT 780
New Kensington, PA
15068-1798
724-334-5466
www.nk.psu.edu

The Pennsylvania State
University Shenango
Campus of the
Commonwealth College
147 Shenango Avenue
Sharon, PA 16146-1537
724-983-2814
www.psu.edu

The Pennsylvania State
University Wilkes-Barre
Campus of the
Commonwealth College
PO PSU
Lehman, PA 18627-0217
570-675-2171
www.psu.edu

The Pennsylvania State
University Worthington
Scranton Campus of the
Commonwealth College
120 Ridge View Drive
Dunmore, PA 18512-1699
570-963-2500
www.psu.edu

The Pennsylvania State
University York Campus of
the Commonwealth College
1031 Edgecomb Avenue
York, PA 17403-3298
717-771-4000
www.psu.edu

Pittsburgh Institute of
Aeronautics
PO Box 10897
Pittsburgh, PA 15236-0897
412-462-9011
Fax: 412-466-0513
www.piainfo.org

Pittsburgh Institute of
Mortuary Science,
Incorporated
5808 Baum Boulevard
Pittsburgh, PA 15206-3706
412-362-8500
www.p-i-m-s.com

Pittsburgh Technical Institute
635 Smithfield Street
Pittsburgh, PA 15222-2560
412-809-5100
www.pittsburghtechnical.
com

Reading Area Community
College
PO Box 1706
Reading, PA 19603-1706
610-372-4721
www.racc.cc.pa.us

The Restaurant School
4207 Walnut Street
Philadelphia, PA 19104-3518
215-222-4200
www.therestaurantschool.
com

Schuylkill Institute of
Business and Technology
171 Red Horse Road
Pottsville, PA 17901
570-622-4835
www.sibtinpa.com

South Hills School of
Business & Technology
508 58th Street
Atloona, PA 16602
814-944-6134
www.southhills.edu

South Hills School of
Business & Technology
480 Waupelani Drive
State College, PA 16801-4516
814-234-7755
www.southhills.edu

Thaddeus Stevens College of
Technology
750 East King Street
Lancaster, PA 17602-3198
717-299-7730
www.stevenstech.org

Thompson Institute
5650 Derry Street
Harrisburg, PA 17111-3518
717-564-4112
www.thompsoninstitute.org

Triangle Tech, Inc.–DuBois
School
PO Box 551
DuBois, PA 15801-0551
814-371-2090
www.triangle-tech.com

Triangle Tech, Inc.–
Erie School
2000 Liberty Street
Erie, PA 16502-2594
814-453-6016
www.triangle-tech.com

Triangle Tech, Inc.–
Greensburg Center
222 East Pittsburgh Street,
Suite A
Greensburg, PA 15601-3304
724-832-1050
www.triangle-tech.com

Triangle Tech, Inc.
1940 Perrysville Avenue
Pittsburgh, PA 15214-3897
412-359-1000
www.triangle-tech.com

Tri-State Business Institute
5757 West 26th Street
Erie, PA 16506
814-838-7673

University of Pittsburgh at
Titusville
PO Box 287
Titusville, PA 16354
814-827-4400
www.upt.pitt.edu

Vale Technical Institute
135 West Market Street
Blairsville, PA 15717-9989
724-459-9500
www.educationamerica.com

Valley Forge Military College
1001 Eagle Road
Wayne, PA 19087-3695
610-989-1200
www.vfmac.edu

Western School of Health
and Business Careers
421 Seventh Avenue
Pittsburgh, PA 15219-1907
412-281-2600
www.westernschool.com

Westmoreland County
Community College
400 Armbrust Road
Youngwood, PA 15697-1895
724-925-4000
www.westmoreland.cc.pa.us

The Williamson Free School
of Mechanical Trades
106 South New Middletown Rd
Media, PA 19063
610-566-1776
www.libertynet.org/wiltech

York Technical Institute
1405 Williams Road
York, PA 17402-9017
717-757-1100
www.yti.edu

Yorktowne Business Institute
West Seventh Avenue
York, PA 17404
717-846-5000
www.ybi.edu

Rhode Island

Community College of
Rhode Island
400 East Avenue
Warwick, RI 02886-1807
401-825-1000
www.ccri.cc.ri.us

New England Institute of
Technology
2500 Post Road
Warwick, RI 02886-2244
401-739-5000
www.neit.edu

South Carolina

Aiken Technical College
PO Drawer 696
Aiken, SC 29802-0696
803-593-9231
www.aik.tec.sc.us

Central Carolina Technical
College
506 North Guignard Drive
Sumter, SC 29150-2499
803-778-1961
www.sum.tec.sc.us

Columbia Junior College
3810 Main Street
Columbia, SC 29203-6400
803-799-9082
cjcsc.com

Denmark Technical College
Solomon Blatt Boulevard,
Box 327
Denmark, SC 29042-0327
803-793-5100

Florence-Darlington Technical
College
PO Box 100548
Florence, SC 29501-0548
843-661-8324
www.flo.tec.sc.us

Forrest Junior College
601 East River Street
Anderson, SC 29624
864-225-7653
www.forrestcollege.com

Greenville Technical College
PO Box 5616
Greenville, SC 29606-5616
864-250-8000
www.greenvilletech.com

Horry-Georgetown Technical
College
2050 Highway 501,
PO Box 261966
Conway, SC 29528-6066
843-347-3186
www.hor.tec.sc.us

ITT Technical Institute
One Marcus Drive, Building 4
Greenville, SC 29615-4818
864-288-0777
www.itt-tech.edu

Midlands Technical College
PO Box 2408
Columbia, SC 29202-2408
803-738-1400
www.midlandstech.com

Northeastern Technical
College
PO Drawer 1007
Cheraw, SC 29520-1007
843-921-6900
www.northeasterntech.org

Orangeburg-Calhoun
Technical College
3250 St Matthews Road, NE
Orangeburg, SC 29118-8299
803-536-0311
www.octech.org

Piedmont Technical College
PO Box 1467
Greenwood, SC 29648-1467
864-941-8324
www.piedmont.tec.sc.us

Spartanburg Methodist
College
1200 Textile Road
Spartanburg, SC
29301-0009
864-587-4000
www.smcsc.edu

Spartanburg Technical
College
PO Box 4386
Spartanburg, SC
29305-4386
864-591-3600
www.spt.tec.sc.us

Technical College of the
Lowcountry
921 Ribaut Road,
PO Box 1288
Beaufort, SC 29901-1288
843-525-8324
www.tcl-tec-sc-us.org

Tri-County Technical College
PO Box 587, 7900 Highway 76
Pendleton, SC 29670-0587
864-646-8361

Trident Technical College
PO Box 118067
Charleston, SC 29423-8067
843-574-6111
tridenttech.org

University of South Carolina
Beaufort
801 Carteret Street
Beaufort, SC 29902-4601
843-521-4100
www.sc.edu/beaufort

University of South Carolina
Lancaster
PO Box 889
Lancaster, SC 29721-0889
803-313-7471
www.sc.edu/lancaster

University of South Carolina
Salkehatchie
PO Box 617
Allendale, SC 29810-0617
803-584-3446

University of South Carolina
Sumter
200 Miller Road
Sumter, SC 29150-2498
803-775-8727
www.uscsumter.edu

University of South Carolina
Union
PO Drawer 729
Union, SC 29379-0729
864-427-3681
web.csd.sc.edu:80/union/info.
html

Williamsburg Technical
College
601 Martin Luther King, Jr Ave
Kingstree, SC 29556-4197
843-355-4110
www.williamsburgtech.com

York Technical College
452 South Anderson Road
Rock Hill, SC 29730-3395
803-327-8000
www.yorktech.com

South Dakota

Kilian Community College
224 North Phillips Avenue
Sioux Falls, SD 57104-6014
605-336-1711
kcc.cc.sd.us

Lake Area Technical Institute
230 11th Street Northeast
Watertown, SD 57201
605-882-5284
www.lati.tec.sd.us

Mitchell Technical Institute
821 North Capital
Mitchell, SD 57301
605-995-3024
mti.tec.sd.us

Si Tanka College
435 North Elm Street,
Box 220
Eagle Butte, SD 57625
605-964-6044
www.sitanka.com

Sisseton-Wahpeton
Community College
Old Agency Box 689
Sisseton, SD 57262
605-698-3966
swcc.cc.sd.us/cc.htm

Southeast Technical Institute
2320 N. Career Ave.
Sioux Falls, SD 57107-1301
605-367-7624
sti.tec.sd.us

Western Dakota Technical
Institute
800 Mickelson Drive
Rapid City, SD 57703
605-394-4034
www.westerndakotatech.org

Tennessee

American Academy of
Nutrition, College of
Nutrition
1204 -D Kenesaw, Sequoyah
Hills Center
Knoxville, TN   37919-7736
865-524-8079
www.nutritioneducation.com

Chattanooga State Technical
Community College
4501 Amnicola Highway
Chattanooga, TN   37406-1097
423-697-4400
www.cstcc.cc.tn.us

Cleveland State Community
College
PO Box 3570
Cleveland, TN   37320-3570
423-472-7141
www.clscc.cc.tn.us

Columbia State Community
College
PO Box 1315
Columbia, TN   38402-1315
931-540-2722
www.coscc.cc.tn.us

Draughons Junior College
1860 Wilma Rudolph Blvd
Clarksville, TN   37040
931-552-7600

Draughons Junior College
340 Plus Park Boulevard
Nashville, TN   37217
615-361-7555
www.draughons.org

Dyersburg State Community
College
1510 Lake Road
Dyersburg, TN   38024
731-286-3200
www.dscc.cc.tn.us

Education America,
Southeast College of
Technology, Memphis
Campus
2731 Nonconnah Boulevard,
Suite 160
Memphis, TN   38132-2131
901-291-4200
www.educationamerica.com

Electronic Computer
Programming College
3805 Brainerd Road
Chattanooga, TN   37411-3798
423-624-0077

Hiwassee College
225 Hiwassee College Drive
Madisonville, TN   37354
423-442-2001
www.hiwassee.edu

ITT Technical Institute
1255 Lynnfield Road, Suite 92
Memphis, TN   38119
901-762-0556
www.itt.tech.edu

ITT Technical Institute
441 Donelson Pike
Nashville, TN   37214
615-889-8700
www.itt-tech.edu

ITT Technical Institute
10208 Technology Drive
Knoxville, TN   37932
865-671-2800
www.itt-tech.edu

Jackson State Community
College
2046 North Parkway
Jackson, TN   38301-3797
901-424-3520
www.jscc.cc.tn.us

John A. Gupton College
1616 Church Street
Nashville, TN   37203-2920
615-327-3927
www.guptoncollege.com

Knoxville Business College
720 North Fifth Avenue
Knoxville, TN   37917
865-524-3043
www.kbcollege.edu

MedVance Institute
1065 East 10th Street
Cookeville, TN   38501-1907
931-526-3660
www.medvance.org

Mid-America Baptist
Theological Seminary
PO Box 381528
Germantown, TN
38183-1528
901-751-8453
www.mabts.edu

Miller-Motte Business
College
1820 Business Park Drive
Clarksville, TN   37040
931-553-0071

Motlow State Community
College
PO Box 8500
Lynchburg, TN   37352-8500
931-393-1500
www.mscc.cc.tn.us

Nashville Auto Diesel College
1524 Gallatin Road
Nashville, TN   37206-3298
615-226-3990
www.nadcedu.com

Nashville State Technical
Institute
120 White Bridge Road
Nashville, TN   37209-4515
615-353-3333
www.nsti.tec.tn.us

National College of Business
& Technology
Suite 200, 5042 Linbar Drive
Nashville, TN   37211
615-333-3344
www.ncbt.edu

North Central Institute
168 Jack Miller Boulevard
Clarksville, TN   37042
931-431-9700
www.nci.edu

Northeast State Technical
Community College
PO Box 246
Blountville, TN   37617-0246
423-323-3191
www.nstcc.cc.tn.us

Nossi College of Art
907 Two Mile Parkway,
Suite E-6
Goodlettsville, TN
37072-2319
615-851-1088
www.nossi.com

Pellissippi State Technical
Community College
PO Box 22990
Knoxville, TN   37933-0990
865-694-6400
www.pstcc.cc.tn.us

Roane State Community
College
276 Patton Lane
Harriman, TN   37748-5011
865-354-3000
www.rscc.cc.tn.us

Southwest Tennessee
Community College
PO Box 780
Memphis, TN   38101-0780
901-333-7822
www.stcc.cc.tn.us

Tennessee Institute of
Electronics
3203 Tazewell Pike
Knoxville, TN   37918-2530
865-688-9422
www.tie1.com

Volunteer State Community
College
1480 Nashville Pike
Gallatin, TN   37066-3188
615-452-8600
www.vscc.cc.tn.us

Walters State Community
College
500 South Davy Crockett
Parkway
Morristown, TN   37813-6899
423-585-2600
www.wscc.cc.tn.us

Watkins College of Art and
Design
100 Powell Place
Nashville, TN   37204
615-383-4848
www.watkins.edu

Texas

Alvin Community College
3110 Mustang Road
Alvin, TX   77511-4898
281-331-6111
www.alvin.cc.tx.us

Amarillo College
PO Box 447
Amarillo, TX   79178-0001
806-371-5000
www.actx.edu

Angelina College
PO Box 1768
Lufkin, TX   75902-1768
409-639-1301
www.angelina.cc.tx.us

The Art Institute of Dallas
Two NorthPark, 8080 Park
Lane, Suite 100
Dallas, TX   75231-9959
214-692-8080
www.aid.edu

The Art Institute of Houston
1900 Yorktown
Houston, TX   77056-4115
713-623-2040
www.aih.aii.edu

Austin Business College
2101 IH-35 South, Third Floor
Austin, TX   78741
512-447-9415
www.austinbusinesscollege.
org

Austin Community College
5930 Middle Fiskville Road
Austin, TX   78752-4390
512-223-7000
www.austin.cc.tx.us

Blinn College
902 College Avenue
Brenham, TX   77833-4049
979-830-4000
www.blinncol.edu

Border Institute of
Technology
9611 Acer Avenue
El Paso, TX   79925-6744
915-593-7328
www.bitelp.com

Brazosport College
500 College Drive
Lake Jackson, TX
77566-3199
979-230-3000
www.brazosport.cc.tx.us

Brookhaven College
3939 Valley View Lane
Farmers Branch, TX
75244-4997
972-860-4700
www.dcccd.edu/bhc/bhc-
home.htm

Cedar Valley College
3030 North Dallas Avenue
Lancaster, TX   75134-3799
972-860-8201
www.dcccd.edu

Center for Advanced Legal
Studies
3910 Kirby Drive, Suite 200
Houston, TX   77098-4151
713-529-2778
www.paralegalpeople.com

Central Texas College
PO Box 1800
Killeen, TX   76540-1800
254-526-7161
www.ctcd.cc.tx.us

Cisco Junior College
Box 3, Route 3
Cisco, TX   76437-9321
254-442-2567
www.cisco.cc.tx.us

Clarendon College
PO Box 968
Clarendon, TX   79226-0968
806-874-3571

Coastal Bend College
3800 Charco Road
Beeville, TX   78102-2197
361-358-2838
www.cbc.cc.tx.us

The College of Saint Thomas
More
3020 Lubbock Street
Fort Worth, TX   76109-2323
817-923-8459
www.cstm.edu

College of the Mainland
1200 Amburn Road
Texas City, TX   77591-2499
409-938-1211

Collin County Community
College District
4800 Preston Park Boulevard
Plano, TX   75093-8309
972-758-3800
www.ccccd.edu/ccccd.html

Commonwealth Institute of
Funeral Service
415 Barren Springs Drive
Houston, TX   77090
281-873-0262
www.commonwealthinst.org

Computer Career Center
6101 Montana Avenue
El Paso, TX   79925
915-779-8031

Court Reporting Institute of
Dallas
8585 North Stemmons
Freeway, Suite 200 North
Dallas, TX   75247
214-350-9722
www.crid.com

Dallas Institute of Funeral
Service
3909 South Buckner
Boulevard
Dallas, TX   75227
214-388-5466

Del Mar College
101 Baldwin Boulevard
Corpus Christi, TX
78404-3897
361-698-1200
www.delmar.edu

Eastfield College
3737 Motley Drive
Mesquite, TX   75150-2099
972-860-7100
www.efc.dcccd.edu

Education America, Dallas
Campus
1800 East Gate Drive
Garland, TX   75041
972-686-7878

Education America, Fort
Worth Campus
300 East Loop 820
Fort Worth, TX   76112
817-451-0017

Education America, Houston
Campus
9421 West Sam Houston
Parkway
Houston, TX   77099
713-773-2500

El Centro College
Main and Lamar Streets
Dallas, TX   75202-3604
214-860-2037
www.ecc.dcccd.edu

El Paso Community College
PO Box 20500
El Paso, TX   79998-0500
915-831-2000
www.epcc.edu

Frank Phillips College
Box 5118
Borger, TX   79008-5118
806-274-5311
www.fpc.cc.tx.us

Galveston College
4015 Avenue Q
Galveston, TX   77550-7496
409-763-6551
www.gc.edu

Grayson County College
6101 Grayson Drive
Denison, TX   75020-8299
903-465-6030
www.grayson.edu

Hallmark Institute of
Aeronautics
8901 Wetmore Road
San Antonio, TX   78216
210-826-1000

Hallmark Institute of
Technology
10401 IH 10 West
San Antonio, TX   78230-1737
210-690-9000
www.hallmarkinstitute.com

Hill College of the Hill Junior
College District
PO Box 619
Hillsboro, TX   76645-0619
254-582-2555
www.hill-college.cc.tx.us

Houston Community College
System
3100 Main Street
Houston, TX   77002-9330
713-718-2000
www.hccs.cc.tx.us

Howard College
1001 Birdwell Lane
Big Spring, TX   79720
915-264-5000
www.hc.cc.tx.us

ITT Technical Institute
2222 Bay Area Boulevard
Houston, TX   77058
281-486-2630
www.itt-tech.edu

ITT Technical Institute
15621 Blue Ash Drive,
Suite 160
Houston, TX   77090-5821
281-873-0512
www.itt-tech.edu

ITT Technical Institute
6330 East Highway 290,
Suite 150
Austin, TX   78723-1061
512-467-6800
www.itt-tech.edu

ITT Technical Institute
551 Ryan Plaza Drive
Arlington, TX   76011
817-794-5100
www.itt-tech.edu

ITT Technical Institute
2950 South Gessner
Houston, TX   77063-3751
713-952-2294
www.itt-tech.edu

ITT Technical Institute
2101 Waterview Parkway
Richardson, TX 75080
972-690-9100
www.itt-tech.edu

ITT Technical Institute
5700 Northwest Parkway
San Antonio, TX 78249-3303
210-694-4612
www.itt-tech.edu

Jacksonville College
105 B J Albritton Drive
Jacksonville, TX 75766-4759
903-586-2518
www.grocities.com/
collegepark/library/3135

KD Studio
2600 Stemmons Freeway,
#117
Dallas, TX 75207
214-638-0484
www.kdstudio.com

Kilgore College
1100 Broadway Boulevard
Kilgore, TX 75662-3299
903-984-8531
www.kilgore.cc.tx.us

Kingwood College
20000 Kingwood Drive
Kingwood, TX 77339-3801
281-312-1600
kcweb.nhmccd.cc.tx.us

Lamar Institute of Technology
PO Box 10043
Beaumont, TX 77710
409-880-8321
theinstitute.lamar.edu

Lamar State College–Orange
410 Front Street
Orange, TX 77630-5899
409-883-7750
hal.lamar.edu/~orange

Lamar State College–
Port Arthur
PO Box 310
Port Arthur, TX 77641-0310
409-983-4921
www.pa.lamar.edu/

Laredo Community College
West End Washington Street
Laredo, TX 78040-4395
956-722-0521
www.Laredo.cc.tx.us

Lee College
PO Box 818
Baytown, TX 77522-0818
281-427-5611
www.lee.edu

Lon Morris College
800 College Avenue
Jacksonville, TX 75766-2900
903-589-4000
www.lonmorris.edu

McLennan Community
College
1400 College Drive
Waco, TX 76708-1499
254-299-8000
www.mclennan.cc.tx.us

Midland College
3600 North Garfield
Midland, TX 79705-6399
915-685-4500
www.midland.cc.tx.us

Montgomery College
3200 College Park Drive
Conroe, TX 77384
936-273-7000
wwwmc.nhmccd.edu

Mountain View College
4849 West Illinois Avenue
Dallas, TX 75211-6599
214-860-8600
www.mvc.dcccd.edu

MTI College of Business and
Technology
1275 Space Park Drive
Houston, TX 77058
281-333-3363
www.mtitexas.com

MTI College of Business and
Technology
7277 Regency Square
Boulevard
Houston, TX 77036-3163
713-974-7181
www.mtitexas.com

Navarro College
3200 West 7th Avenue
Corsicana, TX 75110-4899
903-874-6501
www.nav.cc.tx.us

North Central Texas College
1525 West California Street
Gainesville, TX 76240-4699
940-668-7731
www.nctc.cc.tx.us

North Harris College
2700 W. W. Thorne Drive
Houston, TX 77073-3499
281-618-5400
www.nhmccd.edu

North Lake College
5001 North MacArthur Blvd
Irving, TX 75038-3899
972-273-3000
www.nlc.dcccd.edu

Northeast Texas Community
College
PO Box 1307
Mount Pleasant, TX
75456-1307
903-572-1911
www.ntcc.cc.tx.us

Odessa College
201 West University Avenue
Odessa, TX 79764-7127
915-335-6400
www.odessa.edu

Palo Alto College
1400 West Villaret
San Antonio, TX 78224-2499
210-921-5000
www.accd.ed/pac/pacmain/
pachp.htm

Panola College
1109 West Panola Street
Carthage, TX 75633-2397
903-693-2000
www.panola.cc.tx.us

Paris Junior College
2400 Clarksville Street
Paris, TX 75460-6298
903-785-7661
www.paris.cc.tx.us

Ranger College
College Circle
Ranger, TX 76470
254-647-3234
www.ranger.cc.tx.us

Richland College
12800 Abrams Road
Dallas, TX 75243-2199
972-238-6106

San Antonio College
1300 San Pedro Avenue
San Antonio, TX 78212-4299
210-733-2000

San Jacinto College Central
Campus
8060 Spencer Highway,
PO Box 2007
Pasadena, TX 77501-2007
281-476-1501
www.sjcd.cc.tx.us

San Jacinto College North
Campus
5800 Uvalde Street
Houston, TX 77049-4599
281-458-4050
www.sjcd.cc.tx.us

San Jacinto College South
Campus
13735 Beamer Road
Houston, TX 77089-6099
281-484-1900
www.sjcd.cc.tx.us

South Plains College
1401 South College Avenue
Levelland, TX 79336-6595
806-894-9611
www.spc.cc.tx.us

South Texas Community
College
3201 West Pecan
McAllen, TX 78501
956-631-4922
www.stcc.cc.tx.us

Southwest School of
Electronics
5424 Highway 290 West,
Suite 200
Austin, TX 78735-8800
512-892-2640

Southwest Texas Junior
College
2401 Garner Field Road
Uvalde, TX 78801-6297
830-278-4401
www.swtjc.cc.tx.us

St. Philip's College
1801 Martin Luther King Dr
San Antonio, TX 78203-2098
210-531-3200
www.accd.edu/spc

Tarrant County College
District
1500 Houston Street
Fort Worth, TX 76102-6599
817-515-5100
www.tcjc.cc.tx.us

Temple College
2600 South First Street
Temple, TX 76504-7435
254-298-8282
www.templejc.edu

Texarkana College
2500 North Robison Road
Texarkana, TX 75599-0001
903-838-4541
www.tc.cc.tx.us

Texas Culinary Academy
6020 Dillard Circle
Austin, TX 78752
512-323-2511
www.txca.com

Texas Southmost College
80 Fort Brown
Brownsville, TX 78520-4991
956-544-8200

Texas State Technical College
300 College Drive
Sweetwater, TX 79556-4108
915-235-7300
www.sweetwater.tstc.edu

Texas State Technical
College–Harlingen
1902 North Loop 499
Harlingen, TX 78550-3697
956-364-4000
www.harlingen.tstc.edu

Texas State Technical
College–Waco
3801 Campus Drive
Waco, TX 76705-1695
254-799-3611
www.tstc.edu

Tomball College
30555 Tomball Parkway
Tomball, TX 77375-4036
281-351-3300
www.tc.nhmccd.cc.tx.us

Trinity Valley Community
College
100 Cardinal Drive
Athens, TX 75751-2765
903-677-TVCC
www.tvcc.cc.tx.us

Tyler Junior College
PO Box 9020
Tyler, TX 75711-9020
903-510-2200
www.tyler.cc.tx.us

Universal Technical Institute
721 Lockhaven Drive
Houston, TX 77073-5598
281-443-6262
www.uticorp.com

Vernon Regional Junior
College
4400 College Drive
Vernon, TX 76384-4092
940-552-6291
www.vrjc.cc.tx.us

Victoria College
2200 East Red River
Victoria, TX 77901-4494
361-573-3291
www.vc.cc.tx.us

Wade College
Suite M5120,
International Apparel Mart,
PO Box 586343
Dallas, TX 75258-6343
214-637-3530
www.wadecollege.com

Weatherford College
225 College Park Avenue
Weatherford, TX 76086-5699
817-594-5471
www.wc.edu

Western Technical Institute
1000 Texas Avenue
El Paso, TX 79901-1536
915-532-3737
www.wti-ep.com

Western Technical Institute
4710 Alabama Street
El Paso, TX 79930-2610
915-566-9621
www.wti-ep.com

Western Texas College
6200 College Avenue
Snyder, TX 79549-6105
915-573-8511
www.wtc.cc.tx.us

Wharton County Junior
College
911 Boling Highway
Wharton, TX 77488-3298
979-532-4560
www.wcjc.cc.tx.us

Utah

Certified Careers Institute
1455 West 2200 South,
Suite 200
Salt Lake City, UT 84119
Phone: 801-973-7008
www.cciutah.edu

College of Eastern Utah
451 East 400 North
Price, UT 84501-2699
Phone: 435-637-2120
www.ceu.edu

Dixie State College of Utah
225 South 700 East
St. George, UT 84770-3876
Phone: 435-652-7500
www.dixie.edu

ITT Technical Institute
920 West Levoy Drive
Murray, UT 84123-2500
Phone: 801-263-3313
www.itt-tech.edu

LDS Business College
411 East South Temple Street
Salt Lake City, UT
84111-1392
Phone: 801-524-8100
www.ldsbc.edu

Mountain West College
3280 West 3500 South
West Valley City, UT 84119
Phone: 801-840-4800
www.mwcollege.com

Salt Lake Community
College
PO Box 30808
Salt Lake City, UT
84130-0808
Phone: 801-957-4111
www.slcc.edu

Snow College
150 East College Avenue
Ephraim, UT 84627-1203
Phone: 435-283-7000
www.snow.edu

Stevens-Henager College
2168 Washington Boulevard
Ogden, UT 84401-1420
Phone: 801-394-7791
www.stevenshenager.com

Utah Career College
1902 West 7800 South
West Jordan, UT 84088
Phone: 801-304-4224
www.utahcollege.com

Utah Valley State College
800 West 1200 South Street
Orem, UT 84058-5999
Phone: 801-222-8000
www.uvsc.edu

Vermont

Community College of
Vermont
PO Box 120
Waterbury, VT 05676-0120
802-241-3535
www.ccv.vsc.edu

Landmark College
River Road South
Putney, VT 05346
802-387-4767
www.landmarkcollege.org

New England Culinary
Institute
250 Main Street
Montpelier, VT 05602-9720
802-223-6324
www.neculinary.com

Woodbury College
660 Elm Street
Montpelier, VT 05602
802-229-0516
www.woodbury-college.edu

Virginia

Blue Ridge Community
College
PO Box 80
Weyers Cave, VA 24486-0080
540-234-9261
www.br.cc.va.us

Bryant and Stratton College,
Richmond
8141 Hull Street Road
Richmond, VA 23235-6411
804-745-2444
www.bryantstratton.edu

Bryant and Stratton College,
Virginia Beach
301 Centre Pointe Drive
Virginia Beach, VA
23462-4417
757-499-7900
www.bryantstratton.edu

Central Virginia Community
College
3506 Wards Road
Lynchburg, VA 24502-2498
804-832-7600
www.cv.cc.va.us

Dabney S. Lancaster
Community College
100 Dabney Drive,
PO Box 1000
Clifton Forge, VA 24422
540-863-2800
www.dl.cc.va.us

Danville Community College
1008 South Main Street
Danville, VA 24541-4088
804-797-2222
www.dc.cc.va.us

Dominion College
933 Reservoir Street
Harrisonburg, VA 22801
540-433-6977
www.dominioncollege.com

Dominion College
5372 Fallowater Lane, Suite B
Roanoke, VA 24014
540-776-8381
www.dominioncollege.org

Eastern Shore Community
College
29300 Lankford Highway
Melfa, VA 23410-3000
757-787-5900
www.es.cc.va.us

ECPI Technical College
800 Moorefield Park Drive
Richmond, VA 23236
804-330-5533
www.ecpi.edu

ECPI Technical College
5234 Airport Road
Roanoke, VA 24012
540-563-8080
www.ecpi.edu

ECPI College of Technology
1919 Commerce Drive
Hampton, VA 23666
757-838-9191
www.ecpi.edu

ECPI College of Technology
5555 Greenwich Road
Virginia Beach, VA 23462
757-671-7171
www.ecpi.edu

Germanna Community
College
2130 Germanna Highway
Locust Grove, VA 22508-2102
540-727-3000
www.so.cc.va.us

ITT Technical Institute
863 Glenrock Road, Suite 100
Norfolk, VA 23502-3701
757-466-1260
www.itt-tech.edu

ITT Technical Institute
300 Gateway Centre Parkway
Richmond, VA 23235
804-330-4992
www.itt-tech.edu

Johnson & Wales University
2428 Almeda Avenue,
Suite 316
Norfolk, VA 23513
757-853-3508
www.jwu.edu

John Tyler Community
College
13101 Jefferson Davis Hwy
Chester, VA 23831-5316
804-796-4000
www.jt.cc.va.us

J. Sargeant Reynolds
Community College
PO Box 85622
Richmond, VA 23285-5622
804-371-3000
www.jsr.cc.va.us

Mountain Empire
Community College
PO Drawer 700
Big Stone Gap, VA
24219-0700
540-523-2400
www.me.cc.va.us

National College of Business
& Technology
100 Logan Street,
PO Box 629
Bluefield, VA 24605-1405
540-326-3621
www.ncbt.edu

National College of Business
& Technology
51 B Burgess Road
Harrisonburg, VA 22801-9709
540-432-0943
www.ncbt.edu

National College of Business
& Technology
734 Main Street
Danville, VA 24541-1819
804-793-6822
www.ncbt.edu

National College of Business
& Technology
300A Piedmont Avenue
Bristol, VA 24201
540-669-5333
www.ncbt.edu/index2.shtml

National College of Business
& Technology
104 Candlewood Court
Lynchburg, VA 24502-2653
804-239-3500
www.ncbt.edu/index2.shtml

National College of Business
& Technology
1819 Emmet Street
Charlottesville, VA 22901
804-295-0136
www.ncbt.edu

National College of Business
& Technology
10 Church Street, PO Box 232
Martinsville, VA 24114
540-632-5621
www.ncbt.edu

National College of Business
& Technology
1813 East Main Street
Salem, VA 24153
540-986-1800
www.ncbt.edu/index2.shtml

New River Community
College
PO Box 1127
Dublin, VA 24084-1127
540-674-3600
www.nr.cc.va.us

Northern Virginia Community
College
4001 Wakefield Chapel Road
Annandale, VA 22003-3796
703-323-3000
www.nv.cc.va.us

Patrick Henry Community
College
PO Box 5311
Martinsville, VA 24115-5311
540-638-8777
www.ph.cc.va.us

Paul D. Camp Community
College
PO Box 737,
100 North College Drive
Franklin, VA 23851-0737
757-569-6700
www.pc.cc.va.us

Piedmont Virginia
Community College
501 College Drive
Charlottesville, VA
22902-7589
804-977-3900
www.pvcc.cc.va.us

Rappahannock Community
College
12745 College Drive
Glenns, VA 23149-2616
804-758-6700
www.rcc.cc.va.us

Richard Bland College of The
College of William and Mary
11301 Johnson Road
Petersburg, VA 23805-7100
804-862-6100
www.rbc.edu

Southside Virginia
Community College
109 Campus Drive
Alberta, VA 23821-9719
804-949-1000
www.sv.cc.va.us

Southwest Virginia
Community College
PO Box SVCC
Richlands, VA 24641-1101
540-964-2555
www.sw.vccs.edu

Stratford University
7777 Leesburg Pike,
Suite 100 South
Falls Church, VA 22043
703-821-8570
www.stratford.edu

Thomas Nelson Community
College
PO Box 9407
Hampton, VA 23670-0407
757-825-2700
www.tncc.cc.va.us

Tidewater Community
College
121 College Place
Norfolk, VA 23510
757-822-1122
www.tc.cc.va.us

Virginia Highlands
Community College
PO Box 828
Abingdon, VA 24212-0828
540-676-5484
www.vh.cc.va.us

Virginia Western Community
College
PO Box 14007
Roanoke, VA 24038
540-857-7311
www.vw.cc.va.us

Wytheville Community
College
1000 East Main Street
Wytheville, VA 24382-3308
540-223-4700
www.wd.dd.va.us

Washington

Bates Technical College
1101 South Yakima Avenue
Tacoma, WA 98405-4895
Phone: 253-596-1500
www.bates.ctc.edu

Bellevue Community College
3000 Landerholm Circle, SE
Bellevue, WA 98007-6484
Phone: 425-564-1000
www.bcc.ctc.edu

Bellingham Technical College
3028 Lindbergh Avenue
Bellingham, WA 98225
Phone: 360-738-0221
www.beltc.ctc.edu

Big Bend Community
College
7662 Chanute Street
Moses Lake, WA 98837-3299
Phone: 509-762-5351
www.bbcc.ctc.edu

Cascadia Community College
Suite 102, 19017 120th Ave,
NE
Bothell, WA 98011
Phone: 425-398-5400
www.cascadia.ctc.edu

Centralia College
600 West Locust
Centralia, WA 98531-4099
Phone: 360-736-9391
centralia.ctc.edu

Clark College
1800 East McLoughlin Blvd
Vancouver, WA 98663-3598
Phone: 360-992-2000
www.clark.edu

Clover Park Technical College
4500 Steilacoom Blvd, SW
Lakewood, WA 98499
Phone: 253-589-5678
www.cptc.ctc.edu

Columbia Basin College
2600 North 20th Avenue
Pasco, WA 99301-3397
Phone: 509-547-0511
www.cbc2.org

Court Reporting Institute
929 North 130th Street,
Suite 2
Seattle, WA 98133
Phone: 206-363-8300

Crown College
8739 South Hosmer
Tacoma, WA 98444-1836
Phone: 253-531-3123
www.crowncollege.edu

Edmonds Community
College
20000 68th Avenue West
Lynnwood, WA 98036-5999
Phone: 425-640-1500
www.edcc.edu

Everett Community College
2000 Tower Street
Everett, WA 98201-1327
Phone: 425-388-9100
www.evcc.ctc.edu

Grays Harbor College
1620 Edward P Smith Drive
Aberdeen, WA 98520-7599
Phone: 360-532-9020
ghc.ctc.edu

Green River Community
College
12401 Southeast 320th Street
Auburn, WA 98092-3699
Phone: 253-833-9111
www.greenriver.ctc.edu

Highline Community College
PO Box 98000
Des Moines, WA 98198-9800
Phone: 206-878-3710
www.hcc.ctc.edu

ITT Technical Institute
2525 223rd Street, SE,
Canyon Park East
Bothell, WA 98021
Phone: 425-485-0303
www.itt-tech.edu

ITT Technical Institute
12720 Gateway Drive,
Suite 100
Seattle, WA 98168-3333
Phone: 206-244-3300
www.itt-tech.edu

ITT Technical Institute
1050 North Argonne Road
Spokane, WA 99212-2682
Phone: 509-926-2900
www.itt-tech.edu

Lake Washington Technical
College
11605 132nd Avenue NE
Kirkland, WA 98034-8506
Phone: 425-739-8100

Lower Columbia College
PO Box 3010
Longview, WA 98632-0310
Phone: 360-577-2300
lcc.ctc.edu

North Seattle Community
College
9600 College Way North
Seattle, WA 98103-3599
Phone: 206-527-3600
nsccux.sccd.ctc.edu

Northwest Aviation College
506 23rd, NE
Auburn, WA 98002
Phone: 253-854-4960
www.afsnac.com

Northwest Indian College
2522 Kwina Road
Bellingham, WA 98226
Phone: 360-676-2772
www.nwic.edu

Olympic College
1600 Chester Avenue
Bremerton, WA 98337-1699
Phone: 360-792-6050
www.oc.ctc.edu/~oc

Peninsula College
1502 East Lauridsen Blvd
Port Angeles, WA
98362-2779
Phone: 360-452-9277
www.pc.ctc.edu

Pierce College
9401 Farwest Drive, SW
Lakewood, WA 98498-1999
Phone: 253-964-6500
www.pierce.ctc.edu

Pima Medical Institute
1627 Eastlake Avenue East
Seattle, WA 98102
Phone: 206-322-6100
www.pimamedical.com

Renton Technical College
3000 NE Fourth Street
Renton, WA 98056-4195
Phone: 425-235-2352
www.renton-tc.ctc.edu

Seattle Central Community
College
1701 Broadway
Seattle, WA 98122-2400
Phone: 206-587-3800
edison.sccd.ctc.edu/sccc.html

Shoreline Community
College
16101 Greenwood Avenue N
Seattle, WA 98133-5696
Phone: 206-546-4101
www.shoreline.ctc.edu

Skagit Valley College
2405 College Way
Mount Vernon, WA
98273-5899
Phone: 360-416-7600
www.svc.ctc.edu

South Puget Sound
Community College
2011 Mottman Road, SW
Olympia, WA 98512-6292
Phone: 360-754-7711
www.spscc.ctc.edu

South Seattle Community
College
6000 16th Avenue, SW
Seattle, WA 98106-1499
Phone: 206-764-5300
www.sccd.ctc.edu

Spokane Community College
1810 North Greene Street
Spokane, WA 99217-5399
Phone: 509-533-7000
www.scc.spokane.cc.wa.us

Spokane Falls Community
College
3410 West Fort George
Wright Drive
Spokane, WA 99224-5288
Phone: 509-533-3500
www.sfcc.spokane.cc.wa.us

Tacoma Community College
6501 South 19th Street
Tacoma, WA 98466
Phone: 253-566-5000
Fax: 253-566-5376
www.tacoma.ctc.edu

The Art Institute of Seattle
2323 Elliott Avenue
Seattle, WA 98121-1642
Phone: 206-448-0900
www.ais.edu

Walla Walla Community
College
500 Tausick Way
Walla Walla, WA 99362-9267
Phone: 509-522-2500
www.wallawalla.cc

Wenatchee Valley College
1300 Fifth Street
Wenatchee, WA 98801-1799
Phone: 509-662-1651
www.wvc.ctc.edu

Whatcom Community
College
237 West Kellogg Road
Bellingham, WA 98226-8003
Phone: 360-676-2170
Fax: 360-676-2171
www.whatcom.ctc.edu

Yakima Valley Community
College
PO Box 22520
Yakima, WA 98907-2520
Phone: 509-574-4600
www.yvcc.cc.wa.us

West Virginia

Huntington Junior College of
Business
900 Fifth Avenue
Huntington, WV 25701-2004
304-697-7550
www.htgnjrcollege.com

Mountain State College
1508 Spring Street
Parkersburg, WV 26101-3993
304-485-5487
www.mountainstate.org

National Institute of
Technology
5514 Big Tyler Road
Cross Lanes, WV 25313-1390
304-776-6290

Potomac State College of
West Virginia University
Fort Avenue
Keyser, WV 26726-2698
304-788-6800
www.pscvax.psc.wvnet.edu

Southern West Virginia
Community and Technical
College
PO Box 2900
Mount Gay, WV 25637-2900
304-792-7098
www.southern.wvnet.edu

West Virginia Business
College
1052 Main Street
Wheeling, WV 26003
304-232-0361

West Virginia University at
Parkersburg
300 Campus Drive
Parkersburg, WV 26101-9577
304-424-8000
www.wvup.wvnet.edu

West Virginia Junior College
1000 Virginia Street East
Charleston, WV 25301-2817
304-345-2820
www.wvjc.com

West Virginia Junior College
148 Willey Street
Morgantown, WV 26505-5521
304-296-8282

West Virginia Northern
Community College
1704 Market Street
Wheeling, WV 26003-3699
304-233-5900
www.northern.wvnet.edu

Wisconsin

Blackhawk Technical College
PO Box 5009
Janesville, WI 53547-5009
608-758-6900
www.blackhawktech.org

Bryant and Stratton College
1300 North Jackson Street
Milwaukee, WI 53202-2608
414-276-5200
www.bryantstratton.edu

Chippewa Valley Technical
College
620 West Clairemont Avenue
Eau Claire, WI 54701-6162
715-833-6200
www.chippewa.tec.wi.us

College of Menominee
Nation
PO Box 1179
Keshena, WI 54135
715-799-5600
www.menominee.com

Fox Valley Technical College
1825 North Bluemound, PO
Box 2277
Appleton, WI 54912-2277
920-735-5600
www.foxvalley.tec.wi.us

Gateway Technical College
3520 30th Avenue
Kenosha, WI 53144-1690
262-656-6900
www.gateway.tec.wi.us

Herzing College
5218 East Terrace Drive
Madison, WI 53718
608-249-6611
www.herzing.edu

ITT Technical Institute
6300 West Layton Avenue
Greenfield, WI 53220-4612
414-282-9494
www.itt-tech.edu

ITT Technical Institute
470 Security Boulevard
Green Bay, WI 54313
920-662-9000
www.itt-tech.edu

Lac Courte Oreilles Ojibwa
Community College
13466 West Trepania Road
Hayward, WI 54843-2181
715-634-4790
www.geocities.com/athens/
acropolis/4551

Lakeshore Technical College
1290 North Avenue
Cleveland, WI 53015-1414
920-458-4183
www.gotoltc.com

Madison Area Technical
College
3550 Anderson Street
Madison, WI 53704-2599
608-246-6100
madison.tec.wi.us

Madison Media Institute
2702 Agriculture Drive,
Suite 1
Madison, WI 53718
608-829-2728
www.madisonmedia.com

Mid-State Technical College
500 32nd Street North
Wisconsin Rapids, WI
54494-5599
715-422-5300
www.midstate.tec.wi.us

Milwaukee Area Technical
College
700 West State Street
Milwaukee, WI 53233-1443
414-297-6600

Moraine Park Technical
College
235 North National Ave,
PO Box 1940
Fond du Lac, WI 54936-1940
920-922-8611
www.mptc.tec.wi.us

Nicolet Area Technical
College
Box 518
Rhinelander, WI 54501-0518
715-365-4410
www.nicoletcollege.com

Northcentral Technical
College
1000 West Campus Drive
Wausau, WI 54401-1899
715-675-3331
www.northcentral.tec.wi.us

Northeast Wisconsin
Technical College
2740 W Mason Street,
PO Box 19042
Green Bay, WI 54307-9042
920-498-5400
www.nwtc.tec.wi.us

Southwest Wisconsin
Technical College
1800 Bronson Boulevard
Fennimore, WI 53809-9778
608-822-3262
www.southwest.tec.wi.us

University of Wisconsin–
Baraboo/Sauk County
1006 Connie Road
Baraboo, WI 53913-1015
608-356-8351
www.baraboo-sauk.uwc.edu

University of Wisconsin–
Barron County
1800 College Drive
Rice Lake, WI 54868-2497
715-234-8176
www.barron.uwc.edu

University of Wisconsin–
Fond du Lac
400 University Drive
Fond du Lac, WI 54935
920-929-3600
www.fdl.uwc.edu

University of Wisconsin–
Fox Valley
1478 Midway Road
Menasha, WI 54952
920-832-2600
www.fox.uwc.edu

University of Wisconsin–
Manitowoc
705 Viebahn Street
Manitowoc, WI 54220-6699
920-683-4700

University of Wisconsin–
Marathon County
518 South Seventh Avenue
Wausau, WI 54401-5396
715-261-6100
mthwww.uwc.edu

University of Wisconsin–
Marinette
750 West Bay Shore
Marinette, WI 54143-4299
715-735-4300
www.uwc.edu/mnt

University of Wisconsin–
Marshfield/Wood County
2000 West 5th Street
Marshfield, WI 54449
715-389-6500

University of Wisconsin–
Richland
1200 Highway 14 West
Richland Center, WI 53581
608-647-6186
richland.uwc.edu

University of Wisconsin–
Rock County
2909 Kellogg Avenue
Janesville, WI 53546-5699
608-758-6565
rock.uwc.edu

University of Wisconsin–
Sheboygan
1 University Drive
Sheboygan, WI 53081-4789
920-459-6600
www.sheboygan.uwc.edu

University of Wisconsin–
Washington County
400 University Drive
West Bend, WI 53095-3699
262-335-5200
washington.uwc.edu

University of Wisconsin–
Waukesha
1500 University Drive
Waukesha, WI 53188-2799
414-521-5200
waukesha.uwc.edu

Waukesha County Technical
College
800 Main Street
Pewaukee, WI 53072-4601
414-691-5566
www.wctconline.com

Western Wisconsin Technical
College
304 6th Street North,
PO Box C-908
La Crosse, WI 54602-0908
608-785-9200
www.western.tec.wi.us

Wisconsin Indianhead
Technical College, Ashland
Campus
2100 Beaser Avenue
Ashland, WI 54806-3607
715-682-4591
www.witc.tec.wi.us

Wisconsin Indianhead
Technical College,
New Richmond Campus
1019 South Knowles Avenue
New Richmond, WI
54017-1738
715-246-6561
www.witc.tec.wi.us

Wisconsin Indianhead
Technical College, Rice Lake
Campus
1900 College Drive
Rice Lake, WI 54868-2435
715-234-7082
www.witc.tec.wi.us

Wisconsin Indianhead
Technical College, Superior
Campus
600 North 21st Street
Superior, WI 54880-5207
715-394-6677

Wyoming

Casper College
125 College Drive
Casper, WY 82601-4699
Phone: 307-268-2110
www.cc.whecn.edu

Central Wyoming College
2660 Peck Avenue
Riverton, WY 82501-2273
Phone: 307-855-2000
www.cwc.cc.wy.us

Eastern Wyoming College
3200 West C Street
Torrington, WY 82240-1699
Phone: 307-532-8200
ewcweb.cc.wy.us

Laramie County Community
College
1400 East College Drive
Cheyenne, WY 82007-3299
Phone: 307-778-5222
lccc.cc.wy.us

Northwest College
231 West 6th Street
Powell, WY 82435-1898
Phone: 307-754-6000
www.nwc.cc.wy.us

Sheridan College
PO Box 1500
Sheridan, WY 82801-1500
Phone: 307-674-6446
www.sc.cc.wy.us

Western Wyoming
Community College
PO Box 428
Rock Springs, WY
82902-0428
Phone: 307-382-1600
www.wwcc.cc.wy.us

Wyoming Technical Institute
4373 North Third Street
Laramie, WY 82072-9519
Phone: 307-742-3776
www.wyotech.com

VOCATIONAL AND TECHNICAL COLLEGES

Alabama

Charles Academy of Beauty
Culture
2986 Eslava Creek Pky
Mobile, AL 36606
251-478-6401

Chattahoochee Valley
Community College
2602 College Drive
Phenix City, AL 36869-7928
334-291-4939

Education America,
Southeast College of
Technology, Mobile Campus
828 Downtowner Loop West
Mobile, AL 36609-5404
251-343-8200 Ext. 221

Gadsden Business College
1805 Hillyer Robinson
Industrial Parkway Suite B
Anniston, AL 36207
256-831-3838

Gadsden Business College
3225 Rainbow Drive,
Suite 246
Rainbow City, AL 35906
256-442-2805

Gadsden State Community
College
PO Box 227
Gadsden, AL 35902-0227
256-549-8210

Gaither and Company Beauty
College
414 East Willow Street
Scottsboro, AL 35768
256-259-1001

Herzing College
280 West Valley Avenue
Birmingham, AL 35209-4816
205-916-2800

Holland School for Jewelers
1034 Dawson Avenue,
PO Box 882
Selma, AL 36701

ITT Technical Institute
500 Riverhills Business Park
Birmingham, AL 35242
205-991-5410

Jefferson State Community
College
2601 Carson Road
Birmingham, AL 35215-3098
205-856-7991

Medical Institute
914 N. Mckenzie St.
Foley, AL 36535
251-970-1460

Northwest-Shoals
Community College
PO Box 2545
Muscle Shoals, AL 35662
256-331-5462

Snead State Community
College
220 N Walnut Street,
PO Drawer D
Boaz, AL 35957-0734
256-840-4107

South University
122 Commerce Street
Montgomery, AL 36104
334-263-1013

Spring Hill College
4000 Dauphin Street
Mobile, AL 36608-1791
251-380-3092

Virginia College at
Birmingham
PO Box 19249
Birmingham, AL 35219-9249
205-802-1200 Ext. 207

Wallace Community College-
Sparks Campus
PO Drawer 580
Eufaula, AL 36027
334-687-3543 Ext. 4270

Alaska

Alaska Vocational Institute
210 Ferry Way, Suite 200
Juneau, AK 99801

Alaska Vocational Technical
Center
PO Box 889
Seward, AK 99664
907-224-4153

Career Academy
1415 East Tudor Road
Anchorage, AK 99507-1033
907-563-7575

Charter College
2221 East Northern Lights
Boulevard, Suite 120
Anchorage, AK 99508-4140
907-777-1341

Shear Allusions 2000, A
Training Salon
44539 Sterling Highway
The Blazy Mall
Soldotna, AK 99669
907-262-6525

Arizona

Academy of Radio
Broadcasting
4914 East McDowell Rd, #107
Phoenix, AZ 85008
602-267-8001

Alta Center For
Communication Arts
9014 North 23rd Avenue,
Suite 1
Phoenix, AZ 85021
888-729-4954

Apollo College-Phoenix, Inc.
8503 North 27th Avenue
Phoenix, AZ 85051
602-864-1571

Apollo College-Tri-City, Inc.
630 West Southern Avenue
Mesa, AZ 85210-5004
480-831-6585

Apollo College-Tucson, Inc.
3870 North Oracle Road
Tucson, AZ 85705
520-888-5885

Apollo College-Westside, Inc.
2701 West Bethany Home Rd
Phoenix, AZ 85017
602-433-1333 Ext. 251

Arizona Automotive Institute
6829 North 46th Avenue
Glendale, AZ 85301
623-934-7273

Arizona College of Allied
Health
1940 West Indian School Rd
Phoenix, AZ 85015
602-222-9300

Arizona Paralegal Training
Program
111 West Monroe Street,
Suite 800
Phoenix, AZ 85003
602-252-2171

The Art Institute of Phoenix
2233 West Dunlap Avenue
Phoenix, AZ 85021
800-474-2479

The Bryman School
2250 West Peoria Avenue
Phoenix, AZ 85029
602-274-4300

Chaparral College
4585 East Speedway
Boulevard, Suite 204
Tucson, AZ 85712
520-327-6866

Charles of Italy Beauty
College
1987 McCulloch Boulevard
Lake Havasu City, AZ 86403

Collins College: A School of
Design and Technology
1140 South Priest Drive
Tempe, AZ 85281-5206
480-966-3000

Conservatory of Recording
Arts and Sciences
2300 East Broadway Road
Tempe, AZ 85282
800-562-6383

DeVoe College of Beauty
750 Bartow Drive
Sierra Vista, AZ 85635
520-458-8660

Education America, Tempe
Campus
875 West Elliot Road
Tempe, AZ 85284
480-834-1000

GateWay Community College
108 North 40th Street
Phoenix, AZ 85034-1795
602-392-5194

High-Tech Institute
1515 East Indian School Road
Phoenix, AZ 85014-4901
602-279-9700

High-Tech Institute
2250 West Peoria Avenue
Phoenix, AZ 85029
602-279-9700

International Academy of
Hair Design
4415 South Rural Road,
Suite 2
Tempe, AZ 85282

International Import/Export
Institute
2432 West Peoria, Suite 1026
Phoenix, AZ 85029
602-648-5750

ITT Technical Institute
1455 West River Road
Tucson, AZ 85704
520-408-7488

ITT Technical Institute
4837 East McDowell Road
Phoenix, AZ 85008-4292
602-231-0871

Metropolitan College of
Court Reporting
4640 East Elwood Street,
Suite 12
Phoenix, AZ 85040
602-955-5900

Mohave Community College
1971 Jagerson Avenue
Kingman, AZ 86401
520-757-0898

Motorcycle Mechanics
Institute
2844 West Deer Valley Road
Phoenix, AZ 85027-2399
623-869-9644

Northern Arizona College of
Health Careers
5200 East Cortland
Boulevard, Suite A19
Flagstaff, AZ 86004
928-526-0763

Northland Pioneer College
PO Box 610
Holbrook, AZ 86025-0610
928-536-6257

Pima Medical Institute
957 South Dobson
Mesa, AZ 85202
480-345-7777

The Refrigeration School
4210 East Washington Street
Phoenix, AZ 85034
602-275-7133

Rhodes College
2525 West Beryl Avenue
Phoenix, AZ 85021-1641
602-942-4141

Scottsdale Culinary Institute
8100 East Camelback Road,
Suite 1001
Scottsdale, AZ 85251-3940
602-990-3773

Universal Technical Institute
3121 West Weldon Avenue
Phoenix, AZ 85017
602-264-4164

University of Phoenix-
Phoenix Campus
4605 East Elwood Street
Phoenix, AZ 85040
480-557-2000

University of Phoenix-
Southern Arizona Campus
5099 East Grant Road, #120
Tucson, AZ 85712
520-881-6512

Arkansas

Arkansas College of
Barbering and Hair Design
200 Washington Avenue
North Little Rock, AR
72114-5615

Cossatot Technical College of
the University of Arkansas
PO Box 960
DeQueen, AR 71832
870-584-4471

Crowley's Ridge Technical
Institute
PO Box 925
Forrest City, AR 72336-0925
870-633-5411 Ext. 13

East Arkansas Community
College
1700 Newcastle Road
Forrest City, AR 72335-2204
870-633-4480 Ext. 219

Education America,
Southeast College of
Technology,
Little Rock Campus
8901 Kanis Road
Little Rock, AR 72205
501-312-0007

Fayetteville Beauty College
1200 North College Avenue
Fayetteville, AR 72703
501-442-5181

ITT Technical Institute
4520 South University Ave
Little Rock, AR 72204-9925
501-565-5550

Mid-South Community
College
2000 West Broadway
West Memphis, AR 72301
870-733-6722

Northwest Technical Institute
PO Box A
Springdale, AR 72765-2000
501-751-8824 Ext. 105

Ouachita Technical College
PO Box 816, One College Cr
Malvern, AR 72104
501-332-3658 Ext. 1118

Ozarka College
PO Box 10
Melbourne, AR 72556
870-368-7371 Ext. 209

Quapaw Technical Institute
PO Box 3950
Hot Springs, AR 71914
501-767-3534

Searcy Beauty College
1004 South Main Street
Searcy, AR 72143
501-268-6300

Southern Arkansas
University Tech
SAU Tech Station
Camden, AR 71701
870-574-4558

California

Academy of Art College
79 New Montgomery Street
San Francisco, CA 94105
415-263-7757

Academy of Radio
Broadcasting
16052 Beach Boulevard,
Suite 263
Huntington Beach, CA 92647
714-842-0100

The Advanced Career
College
41765 N. 12th St. Ste. B.
West Palmdale, CA 93551
661-948-4141

American Career College,
Inc.
4021 Rosewood Avenue
Los Angeles, CA 90004
323-666-7555

American InterContinental
University
12655 West Jefferson Blvd
Los Angeles, CA 90066
888-248-7390

Andon College
1201 North El Dorado Street
Stockton, CA 95202
209-462-8777

Andon College
1700 McHenry Village Way
Modesto, CA 95350
209-571-8777

Antelope Valley College
3041 West Avenue K
Lancaster, CA 93536-5426
661-722-6338

The Art Institute of California
10025 Mesa Rim Road
San Diego, CA 92121-2913
866-275-2422 Ext. 3117

The Art Institute of
Los Angeles
2900 31st Street
Santa Monica, CA
90405-3035
310-752-4700

Art Institute of Los Angeles-
Orange County
3601 West Sunflower Avenue
Santa Ana, CA 92704
888-549-3055

Art Institutes International at San Francisco
1170 Market Street
San Francisco, CA 94102
888-493-3261

Asian-American International Beauty College
7871 Westminster Boulevard
Westminster, CA 92683
714-891-0508

Bethany College of the Assemblies of God
800 Bethany Drive
Scotts Valley, CA 95066-2820
831-438-3800 Ext. 1400

Brooks College
4825 East Pacific Coast Hwy
Long Beach, CA 90804
800-421-3775 Ext. 271

Brooks Institute of Photography
801 Alston Road
Santa Barbara, CA 93108-2399
805-966-3888

Bryman College
1045 West Redondo Beach Boulevard, Suite 275
Gardena, CA 90247
310-527-7105 Ext. 102

Bryman College
12446 Putnam Street
Whittier, CA 90602
562-945-9191

Bryman College
1245 South Winchester Boulevard, Suite 102
San Jose, CA 95128
408-246-4171

Bryman College
22336 Main Street
Hayward, CA 94541
510-582-9500

Bryman College
3000 South Robertson Boulevard, 3rd Floor
Los Angeles, CA 90034
310-840-5777

Bryman College
3208 Rosemead Boulevard, Suite 100
El Monte, CA 91731
626-573-5470

Bryman College
3460 Wilshire Boulevard, Suite 500
Los Angeles, CA 90010
213-388-9950

Bryman College
511 North Brookhurst Street, Suite 300
Anaheim, CA 92801
714-953-6500

Bryman College
520 North Euclid Avenue
Ontario, CA 91762-3591
909-984-5027

Bryman College
814 Mission Street, Suite 500
San Francisco, CA 94103
415-777-2500

Bryan College of Court Reporting
2333 Beverly Boulevard
Los Angeles, CA 90057
213-484-8850

California College for Health Sciences
2423 Hoover Avenue
National City, CA 91950-6605
619-477-4800 Ext. 301

California College of Technology
4330 Watt Avenue, Suite 400
Sacramento, CA 95660
916-649-8168

California Motel Training
801 Riverside Avenue, Suite 104
Roseville, CA 95678

California Paramedical and Technical College
4550 La Sierra Avenue
Riverside, CA 92505-2907
909-687-9006

California Paramedical and Technical College
3745 Long Beach Boulevard
Long Beach, CA 90807-3377
562-427-4217

California School of Culinary Arts
521 East Green Street
Pasadena, CA 91101
888-900-2433 Ext. 1352

California Vocational College
3951 Balboa Street
San Francisco, CA 94121
415-668-0103

Career Networks Institute
986 Town & Country Road
Orange, CA 92868-4714
714-568-1566

Central Coast College
480 South Main Street
Salinas, CA 93901
831-753-6660

City College of San Francisco
50 Phelan Avenue
San Francisco, CA 94112-1821
415-239-3285

Coleman College
1284 West San Marcos Blvd
San Marcos, CA 92069
760-747-3990

Coleman College
7380 Parkway Drive
La Mesa, CA 91942
619-465-3990 Ext. 131

Computer Training Academy
235 Charcot Avenue
San Jose, CA 95131
408-441-6990 Ext. 112

Concorde Career Institute
570 W. 4th St. Ste. 107
San Bernardino, CA 92401
714-884-8891

Concord University School of Law
1133 Westwood Boulevard, Suite 2010
Los Angeles, CA 90024
800-439-4794

De Anza College
21250 Stevens Creek Blvd
Cupertino, CA 95014-5793

Dell'Arte School of Physical Theatre
PO Box 816
Blue Lake, CA 95525
541-488-9180

Detective Training Institute
PO Box 909
San Juan Capistrano, CA 92693

Education America University
123 Camino De La Reina, Suite 100
San Diego, CA 92108
619-686-8600 Ext. 202

Empire College
3035 Cleveland Avenue
Santa Rosa, CA 95403
707-546-4000

Galen College of California, Inc.
1604 Ford Avenue, Suite 10
Modesto, CA 95350
209-527-5084

Galen College of California, Inc.
3908 West Caldwell Avenue, Suite A
Visalia, CA 93277
559-732-5200

Galen College of California, Inc.
1325 North Wishon Avenue
Fresno, CA 93728
559-264-9700

Gemological Institute of America, Inc.
550 South Hill Street, Suite 901
Los Angeles, CA 90013
213-833-0115

Gemological Institute of America, Inc.
5345 Armada Drive
Carlsbad, CA 92008
760-603-4001

Glendale Career College
1015 Grandview Avenue
Glendale, CA 91201
818-243-1131

Glendale Career College-Oceanside
Tri-City Medical Center, 4002 Vista Way
Oceanside, CA 92056
760-945-9896

Harbor Medical College
1231 Cabrillo Avenue, Suite 201
Torrance, CA 90501
310-320-3200

Heald College, Schools of
Business and Technology
255 West Bullard Avenue
Fresno, CA 93704-1706
559-438-4222 Ext. 4134

High-Tech Institute
1111 Howe Avenue, #250
Sacramento, CA 95825
916-929-9700

Institute for Business and
Technology
2550 Scott Boulevard
Santa Clara, CA 95050
408-727-1060

International Air Academy,
Inc.
2980 Inland Empire
Boulevard
Ontario, CA 91764-4804
909-989-5222 Ext. 224

ITT Technical Institute
630 East Brier Drive,
Suite 150
San Bernardino, CA 92408-
2800
909-889-3800

ITT Technical Institute
9680 Granite Ridge Drive
San Diego, CA 92123-2662
858-571-8500

ITT Technical Institute
10863 Gold Center Drive
Rancho Cordova, CA
95670-6034
916-851-3900

ITT Technical Institute
Lake Marriott Business
Center, 5104 Old Ironside
Santa Clara, CA 95054
408-496-0655

ITT Technical Institute
20050 South Vermont Avenue
Torrance, CA 90502
310-380-1555 Ext. 105

ITT Technical Institute
12669 Encinitas Avenue
Sylmar, CA 91342-3664
818-364-5151

ITT Technical Institute
2051 North Solar Drive,
Suite 150
Oxnard, CA 93030
805-988-0143

ITT Technical Institute
525 North Muller Avenue
Anaheim, CA 92801
714-535-3700

ITT Technical Institute
3979 Trust Way, Britannia
Point Eden
Hayward, CA 94545
510-785-8522 Ext. 23

ITT Technical Institute
16916 South Harlan Road
Lathrop, CA 95330
209-858-0077

ITT Technical Institute
1530 West Cameron Avenue
West Covina, CA 91790-2767
626-960-8681

Kensington College
2428 North Grand Avenue,
Suite D
Santa Ana, CA 92705

Las Positas College
3033 Collier Canyon Road
Livermore, CA 94550-7650
501-373-5800

Loving Hands Institute of
Healing Arts
639 11th Street
Fortuna, CA 95540-2346
707-725-9627

Maric College
3666 Kearny Villa Road,
Suite 100
San Diego, CA 92123
858-279-4500

Maric College
2030 University Drive
Vista, CA 92083
760-630-1555

Marinello School of Beauty
1226 University Avenue
San Diego, CA 92103
800-648-3413

Martinez Adult School
600 F Street
Martinez, CA 94553-3298
925-228-3276 Ext. 230

Mendocino College
PO Box 3000
Ukiah, CA 95482-0300
707-468-3101

Modern Technology College
6180 Laurel Canyon
Boulevard, #101
North Hollywood, CA 91606
818-763-2563 Ext. 223

MTI Business College of
Stockton Inc.
6006 North El Dorado Street
Stockton, CA 95207-4349
209-957-3030 Ext. 314

National Career Education
6060 Sunrise Vista Drive
Citrus Heights, CA 95610
916-969-4900

National Institute of
Technology
236 East Third Street
Long Beach, CA 90802
562-437-0501

New School of Architecture &
Design
1249 F Street
San Diego, CA 92101-6634
619-235-4100 Ext. 103

North-West College
134 W. Holt Avenue
Pomona, CA 91768
626-960-5046

North-West College
2121 W. Garvey Avenue
West Covina, CA 91790
626-960-5046

North-West College
530 E. Union Street
Pasadena, CA 91101

North-West College
124 S. Glendale Avenue
Glendale, CA 91205
818-242-0205

Orange Coast College
2701 Fairview Road,
PO Box 5005
Costa Mesa, CA 92628-5005
714-432-5773

Pacific College of Oriental
Medicine
7445 Mission Valley Road,
Suite 105
San Diego, CA 92108
619-574-6909

Pacific School of Massage
and Healing Arts
44800 Fish Rock Road
Gualala, CA 95445
707-884-3138

Platt College
3700 Inland Empire Blvd
Ontario, CA 91764
909-941-9410

Platt College
3901 MacArthur Boulevard
Newport Beach, CA 92660
949-833-2300

Platt College-Los Angeles, Inc
7470 North Figueroa Street
Los Angeles, CA 90041-1717
323-258-8050

Platt College San Diego
6250 El Cajon Boulevard
San Diego, CA 92115-3919
619-265-0107

Rhodes College
9616 Archilbald Avenue,
Suite 100
Rancho Cucamonga, CA
91730
909-484-4311

Sacramento City College
3835 Freeport Boulevard
Sacramento, CA 95822-1386
916-558-2438

San Joaquin Valley College
10641 Church Street
Rancho Cucamonga, CA
91730
909-948-7582

San Joaquin Valley College
295 East Sierra Avenue
Fresno, CA 93710-3616
559-229-7800

San Joaquin Valley College
8400 West Mineral King Ave
Visalia, CA 93291-9283
559-651-2500

San Joaquin Valley College
4985 East Anderson Avenue
Fresno, CA 93727
559-453-0123

Santa Barbara Business
College
5266 Hollister Avenue
Santa Barbara, CA 93111
805-967-9677

Santa Barbara Business
College
305 East Plaza Drive
Santa Maria, CA 93454
805-922-8256

Santa Barbara Business
College
211 South Real Road
Bakersfield, CA 93309
805-835-1100

Silicon Valley College
2800 Mitchell Road
Walnut Creek, CA 94598
925-280-0235

Silicon Valley College
41350 Christy Street
Fremont, CA 94538
510-623-9966

Silicon Valley College
6201 San Ignacio Avenue
San Jose, CA 95119
408-360-0840

Simi Valley Adult School
3192 Los Angeles Avenue
Simi Valley, CA 93065
805-579-6200

Skadron College
295 East Caroline, Suite D
San Bernardino, CA 92408
909-783-8810

Spectrum Community
Services, Inc.
1435 Grove Way
Hayward, CA 94546
510-881-0300 Ext. 227

Travel-World College and
Agency
2990 South Sepulveda
Boulevard, Suite 205
West Los Angeles, CA 90064
310-479-6093

United Education Corp
3380 Shelby Street, Suite 150
Ontario, CA 91764
909-476-2424

United Education
Corporation
7335 Van Nuys Boulevard
Van Nuys, CA 91405
818-756-1200

United Education Corp
1323 6th Avenue
San Diego, CA 92101
619-544-9800

United Education
Corporation
6812 Pacific Boulevard
Huntington Park, CA 90255
323-277-8000

United Education
Corporation
310 3rd Avenue, Suite C6/C7
Chula Vista, CA 91910
619-409-4111

United Education
Corporation
295 East Caroline Street,
Suite E
San Bernardino, CA 92408
909-554-1999

United Education
Corporation
3727 West 6th Street
Los Angeles, CA 90020
213-427-3700

Universal Technical Institute
15530 6th Street, Suite #110
Rancho Cucamonga, CA
91730
909-484-1929

University of Phoenix-
Northern California Campus
7901 Stoneridge Drive,
Suite 100
Pleasanton, CA 94588
877-478-8336

University of Phoenix-
Sacramento Campus
1760 Creekside Oaks Drive,
#100
Sacramento, CA 95833
800-266-2107

University of Phoenix-
San Diego Campus
11682 El Camino Real,
2nd Floor
San Diego, CA 92130
888-867-4636

University of Phoenix-
Southern California Campus
10540 Talbert Avenue, #120
Fountain Valley, CA 92708
800-468-6867

Valley Travel College
1368 W. Herndon Ste. 101
Fresno, CA 93711
559-436-1027

Western Career College
380 Civic Drive, Suite 300
Pleasant Hill, CA 94523
925-609-6650

Western Career College
8909 Folsom Boulevard
Sacramento, CA 95826
916-361-1660 Ext. 615

Westwood College of
Aviation Technology-
Los Angeles
8911 Aviation Boulevard
Inglewood, CA 90301
310-642-5440 Ext. 203

Westwood College of
Technology-Anaheim
2461 West La Palma Avenue
Anaheim, CA 92801
714-226-9990 Ext. 100

Westwood College of
Technology-Inland Empire
20 West 7th Street
Upland, CA 91786
909-931-7550 Ext. 100

Westwood College of
Technology-Los Angeles
3460 Wilshire, Suite 700
Los Angeles, CA 90010
213-739-9999 Ext. 100

Colorado

Americana Beauty College II
3650 Austin Bluffs Parkway,
Suite 174
Colorado Springs, CO 80918
719-598-4188

The Art Institute of Colorado
1200 Lincoln Street
Denver, CO 80203
800-275-2420

Bel-Rea Institute of Animal
Technology
1681 South Dayton Street
Denver, CO 80231-3048
303-751-8700

Cambridge College
12500 East Iliff Avenue
Aurora, CO 80014
303-338-9700

CollegeAmerica
1385 South Colorado
Boulevard, 5th Floor
Denver, CO 80222
303-691-9756

Colorado School of Trades
1575 Hoyt Street
Lakewood, CO 80215-2996
303-233-4697 Ext. 16

Denver Automotive and
Diesel College
460 South Lipan Street,
PO Box 9366
Denver, CO 80223-9960
303-722-5724

Denver Career College
1401 19th Street
Denver, CO 80202-1213
303-295-0550

Education America, Colorado
Springs Campus
6050 Erin Park Drive,
Suite 250
Colorado Springs, CO
80918-3401
719-532-1234

Education America, Denver
Campus
11011 West 6th Avenue
Lakewood, CO 80215-5501
303-445-0500

Institute of Business and
Medical Careers
1609 Oakridge Drive,
Suite 102
Fort Collins, CO 80525

International Guide Academy
Inc.
PMB 318, 2888 Bluff Street
Boulder, CO 80301
303-530-3420

ITT Technical Institute
500 East 84 Avenue
Thornton, CO 80229-5338
303-288-4488

Johnson & Wales University
7150 Montview Boulevard
Denver, CO 80220
303-256-9300

Otero Junior College
1802 Colorado Avenue
La Junta, CO 81050-3415
719-384-6831

Parks College
9065 Grant Street
Denver, CO 80229
303-457-2757

Parks College
6 Abilene Street
Aurora, CO 80011
303-367-2757

Platt College
3100 South Parker Road,
Suite 200
Aurora, CO 80014-3141
303-369-5151

Real Estate College of
Colorado
33 Inverness Place
Durango, CO 81301

Rocky Mountain College of
Art & Design
6875 East Evans Avenue
Denver, CO 80224-2359
303-753-6046

Sage Technical Services
365 South Main Street
Brighton, CO 80601
800-867-9856

Sage Technical Services
764 Horizon Drive, Suite 201
Grand Junction, CO 81506

Technical Trades Institute
2315 East Pikes Peak Avenue
Colorado Springs, CO
80909-6030
719-632-7626

T. H. Pickens Technical Center
500 Airport Boulevard
Aurora, CO 80011
303-344-4910 Ext. 27935

Trinidad State Junior
College-Valley Campus
1011 Main Street
Alamosa, CO 81101
719-589-1513

University of Phoenix-
Colorado Campus
10004 Park Meadows Drive
Lone Tree, CO 80124
303-755-9090

University of Phoenix-
Southern Colorado Campus
5475 Tech Center Drive,
Suite 130
Colorado Springs, CO 80919
719-599-5282 Ext. 114

Westwood College of
Aviation Technology-Denver
10851 West 120th Avenue
Broomfield, CO 80021-3465
303-466-1714

Westwood College of
Technology-Denver North
7350 North Broadway
Denver, CO 80221-3653
303-426-7000 Ext. 100

Westwood College of
Technology-Denver South
3150 South Sheridan Blvd
Denver, CO 80227
303-934-1122 Ext. 100

Connecticut

Academy of Learning-
Waterbury
720 Wolcott Street
Waterbury, CT 06705-1335
203-574-4342

Connecticut Center for
Massage Therapy
25 Sylvan Road, South
Westport, CT 06880
877-292-2268

Connecticut Culinary Institute
Talcott Plaza,
230 Farmington Avenue
Farmington, CT 06032
800-762-4337

Connecticut Institute of Hair
Design
1000 Main Street
East Hartford, CT 06108
860-528-5032

Katherine Gibbs College
148 East Avenue
Norwalk, CT 06851
203-838-4173 Ext. 301

Naugatuck Valley Community
College
750 Chase Parkway
Waterbury, CT 06708-3000
203-575-8078

Norwalk Community College
188 Richards Avenue
Norwalk, CT 06854-1655
203-857-7060 Ext. 7060

St. Vincent's College
2800 Main Street
Bridgeport, CT 06606-4292
203-576-5519

University of Bridgeport
380 University Avenue
Bridgeport, CT 06601
203-576-4552

Westlawn Institute of Marine
Technology, Inc.
733 Summer Street
Stamford, CT 06901

Worldtek Travel School
111 Water Street
New Haven, CT 06511

Delaware

Delaware College of Art and
Design
600 N. Market St.
Wilmington, DE 19801
302-622-8867 Ext. 110

Harrison Career Institute
631 West Newport Pike
Wilmington, DE 19804
302-999-7827

Schilling-Douglas School of
Hair Design
70 Amstel Avenue
Newark, DE 19711
302-737-5100 Ext. 11

District of
Columbia

Harrison Center for Career
Education (YWCA)
624 Ninth Street, NW,
Fourth Floor
Washington, DC 20001

Potomac College
4000 Chesapeake Street, NW
Washington, DC 20016
202-686-0876

Strayer University
1025 15th Street, NW
Washington, DC 20005
202-408-2400

Strayer University at Takoma
Park
6830 Laurel Street, NW
Washington, DC 20012
202-722-8100

Florida

The Academy
3131 Flightline Drive
Lakeland, FL 33811

Advanced Career Training
7660 Phillips Highway,
Suite 14
Jacksonville, FL 32256
904-737-6911

American Institute of
Diamond Cutting, Inc.
1287 East Newport Center Dr,
#202
Deerfield Beach, FL 33442
954-574-0833

American InterContinental
University
8151 West Peters Road,
Suite 1000
Plantation, FL 33324
888-757-4422

American Travel Institute
2908 Lakeview Drive
Fern Park, FL 32730
407-331-7443 Ext. 209

The Art Institute of Fort
Lauderdale
1799 Southeast 17th Street
Fort Lauderdale, FL
33316-3000
954-463-3000 Ext. 420

ATI Career Training Center
1 Northeast 19th Street
Miami, FL 33132
305-573-1600

ATI Career Training Center
3501 Northwest 9th Avenue
Oakland Park, FL 33309-5900
954-563-5899

ATI Career Training Center
Electronics Campus
2880 Northwest 62nd Street
Fort Lauderdale, FL
33309-9731
954-973-4760

ATI Health Education Center
Plaza Executive Center, 1395
Northwest 167th Street,
Miami, FL 33169-5745
305-628-1000

Atlantic Coast Institute
5225 West Broward
Boulevard
Fort Lauderdale, FL 33317
954-581-2223

Atlantic Vocational-Technical Center
4700 Coconut Creek Parkway
Coconut Creek, FL 33063
954-977-2083

Barbara Brennan School of Healing
500 Northeast Spanish River Boulevard, Suite 108
Boca Raton, FL 33431-4559
800-924-2564

Charles F. Chapman School of Seamanship, Inc.
4343 SE St. Lucie Boulevard
Stuart, FL 34997-9982
800-225-2841

ConCorde Career Institute
1960 Arlington Expressway, Suite 120
Jacksonville, FL 32211-7429
904-725-0525

Daytona Beach Community College
PO Box 2811
Daytona Beach, FL 32120-2811
386-255-8131 Ext. 5537

Education America, Tampa Technical Institute, Jacksonville Campus
7011 A.C. Skinner Parkway, Suite 140
Jacksonville, FL 32256
904-296-3435

Education America, Tampa Technical Institute, Pinellas Campus
8550 Ulmerton Road, Unit 100
Largo, FL 33771
727-532-1999

Education America, Tampa Technical Institute, Tampa Campus
2410 East Busch Boulevard
Tampa, FL 33612
800-992-4850 Ext. 211

First Coast Technical Institute
2980 Collins Avenue
St. Augustine, FL 32095-1919
904-829-1056

Florida College of Natural Health
1751 Mound Street, Suite G-100
Sarasota, FL 34236
941-954-8999

Florida College of Natural Health
2001 West Sample Road, Suite 100
Pompano Beach, FL 33064
954-975-6400

Florida College of Natural Health
7925 Northwest 12th Street, Suite 201
Miami, FL 33126
305-597-9599

Florida College of Natural Health
887 East Altamonte Drive
Altamonte Springs, FL 32701
407-261-0319

Florida Computer & Business School
1321 Southwest 107th Avenue, Suite 201B
Miami, FL 33174
305-553-6065

Florida Metropolitan University-Brandon Campus
3924 Coconut Palm Drive
Tampa, FL 33619
813-621-0041

Florida Metropolitan University-Fort Lauderdale Campus
1040 Bayview Drive
Fort Lauderdale, FL 33304
954-568-1600 Ext. 68

Florida Metropolitan University-Jacksonville Campus
8226 Phillips Highway
Jacksonville, FL 32256
904-731-4949

Florida Metropolitan University-Lakeland Campus
995 East Memorial Boulevard, Suite 110
Lakeland, FL 33801-1919
863-686-1444 Ext. 101

Florida Metropolitan University-Melbourne Campus
2401 North Harbor City Blvd
Melbourne, FL 32935
321-253-2929 Ext. 11

Florida Metropolitan University-North Orlando Campus
5421 Diplomat Circle
Orlando, FL 32810
407-628-5870 Ext. 108

Florida Metropolitan University-Pinellas Campus
2471 McMullen Booth Road
Clearwater, FL 33759
725-2688 Ext. 146

Florida Metropolitan University-South Orlando Campus
2411 Sand Lake Road
Orlando, FL 32809
407-851-2525

Florida Metropolitan University-Tampa Campus
3319 West Hillsborough Avenue
Tampa, FL 33614
813-879-6000

Florida School of Dog Grooming, Inc.
2315 North A Street
Tampa, FL 33609
813-254-2213

Florida School of Massage
6421 SW 13th Street
Gainesville, FL 32608-5419

Florida Technical College
1450 South Woodland Blvd
DeLand, FL 32720
386-734-3303

Florida Technical College
1819 North Semoran Blvd
Orlando, FL 32807
407-678-5600

Florida Technical College
298 Havendale Boulevard
Auburndale, FL 33823
863-967-8822

Florida Technical College
8711 Lone Star Road
Jacksonville, FL 32211
904-724-2229

Full Sail Real World Education
3300 University Boulevard
Winter Park, FL 32792-7429
407-679-0100

Herzing College
1595 South Semoran Boulevard, Suite 1501
Orlando, FL 32792-5509
407-478-0500

High-Tech Institute
1000 Woodcock Road
Orlando, FL 32803
407-673-9900

Hillsborough Community College
PO Box 31127
Tampa, FL 33631-3127
813-253-7022

Indian River Community College
3209 Virginia Avenue
Fort Pierce, FL 34981-5596
561-462-4745

Institute of Legal & Medical Professions
1600 Sarno Road, Suite 107
Melbourne, FL 32935
321-242-7555

International Academy of Design & Technology
5225 Memorial Highway
Tampa, FL 33634
813-881-0007 Ext. 8036

International Academy of Design & Technology
5959 Lake Ellenor Drive
Orlando, FL 32809
877-753-0007

International School of Beauty, Inc.
7127 US Highway 19
New Port Richey, FL 34652

ITT Technical Institute
2600 Lake Lucien Drive, Suite 140
Maitland, FL 32751-9754
407-660-2900 Ext. 18

ITT Technical Institute
3401 South University Drive
Fort Lauderdale, FL 33328
954-476-9300

ITT Technical Institute
4809 Memorial Highway
Tampa, FL 33634-7350
813-885-2244

ITT Technical Institute
6600 Youngerman Circle,
Suite 10
Jacksonville, FL 32244
904-573-9100

ITT Technical Institute
7955 Northwest 12th Street,
Suite 119
Miami, FL 33126
305-477-3080 Ext. 120

Johnson & Wales University
1701 Northeast 127th Street
North Miami, FL 33181
305-892-7600

Keiser Career Institute
12520 Pines Boulevard
Pembroke Pines, FL 33027
954-252-0002

Keiser Career Institute
9468 South US 1
Port St. Lucie, FL 34952
561-398-9990

Keiser College
1500 Northwest 49th Street
Fort Lauderdale, FL
33309-9722
954-776-4456

Keiser College
1700 Halstead Boulevard
Tallahassee, FL 32309
850-906-9494

Keiser College
1800 Business Park Blvd
Daytona Beach, FL 32114
904-274-5060

Keiser College
3515 Aviation Drive
Lakeland, FL 33811
863-701-7789

Keiser College
6151 Lake Osprey Drive
Sarasota, FL 34240
941-907-3900

Keiser College
8505 Mills Drive
Miami, FL 33183
305-596-2226

La Belle Beauty School
775 West 49th Street, Bay 5
Hialeah, FL 33012
305-558-0562

Manatee Community College
5840 26th Street West,
PO Box 1849
Bradenton, FL 34206-7046
941-752-5031

Marine Mechanics Institute
9751 Delegates Drive
Orlando, FL 32837-9835
407-240-2422

National School of
Technology, Inc.
4410 West 16th Avenue,
Suite 52
Hialeah, FL 33012
305-558-9500

National School of
Technology, Inc.
16150 Northeast 17 Avenue
North Miami Beach, FL
33162
305-949-9500

National School of
Technology, Inc.
9020 Southwest 137th Ave,
Suite 200
Miami, FL 33186
305-386-9900 Ext. 112

New England Institute of
Technology at Palm Beach
1126 53rd Court
West Palm Beach, FL 33407

North Florida Community
College
1000 Turner Davis Drive
Madison, FL 32340-1602
850-973-1622

Pasco-Hernando Community
College
10230 Ridge Road
New Port Richey, FL
34654-5199
727-816-3261

Phoenix East Aviation, Inc.
561 Pearl Harbor Drive
Daytona Beach, FL 32114
904-258-0703

Regional Airline Academy
Deland Airport, 1200
Flightline Boulevard, Suite 10
Deland, FL 32724
866-709-4892

South University
1760 North Congress Avenue
West Palm Beach, FL 33409
561-697-9200

Southwest Florida College
10210 Highland Manor Drive,
Suite 200
Tampa, FL 33610
813-630-4401

Southwest Florida College
1685 Medical Lane
Fort Myers, FL 33907
941-939-4766

Sunstate Academy of Hair
Design
2418 Colonial Boulevard
Fort Myers, FL 33907-1491
941-278-1311

Tulsa Welding School
3500 Southside Boulevard
Jacksonville, FL 32216
904-646-9353

Ultrasound Diagnostic
School
10255 Fortune Parkway,
Unit 501
Jacksonville, FL 32256
904-363-6221

Ultrasound Diagnostic
School
4780 North State Road 7,
#100-E
Lauderdale Lakes, FL
33319-5860
954-942-6551

Ultrasound Diagnostic
School
5701 East Hillsborough Ave
Tampa, FL 33610
813-621-0072

University of Phoenix-Fort
Lauderdale Campus
600 North Pine Island Road,
Suite 500
Plantation, FL 33324
954-382-5303

University of Phoenix-
Jacksonville Campus
8131 Baymeadows Circle
West, Suite 101
Jacksonville, FL 32256
904-636-6645

University of Phoenix-
Orlando Campus
2290 Lucien Way, Suite 400
Maitland, FL 32751
407-667-0555

University of Phoenix-Tampa
Campus
100 Tampa Oaks Boulevard,
Suite 200
Tampa, FL 33637
813-977-1449

Webster College
2221 Southwest 19th Avenue
Ocala, FL 34474
352-629-1941

Webster College
2127 Grand Boulevard
Holiday, FL 34691
727-942-0069

Webster Institute of
Technology
3910 US Highway 301 North,
Suite 200
Tampa, FL 33619-1259
813-620-1446

Georgia

Advanced Career Training
1 Corporate Square,
Suite 110
Atlanta, GA 30329
404-321-2929

Advanced Career Training
7165 Georgia Highway 85
Riverdale, GA 30274
770-991-9356

American InterContinental
University
3330 Peachtree Road, NE
Atlanta, GA 30326
888-999-4248

American InterContinental
University
6600 Peachtree-Dunwoody
Road, 500 Embassy Row
Atlanta, GA 30328
800-353-1744

The Art Institute of Atlanta
6600 Peachtree Dunwoody
Road, 100 Embassy Row
Atlanta, GA 30328
770-394-8300

Bauder College
Phipps Plaza,
3500 Peachtree Rd
Atlanta, GA 30326
404-237-7573 Ext. 223

Beauty College of America
1171 Main St.
Forest Park, GA 30297
404-361-4098

Coastal Georgia Community
College
3700 Altama Avenue
Brunswick, GA 31520-3644
912-264-7253

Cobb Beauty College, Inc.
3096 Cherokee Street
Kennesaw, GA 30144-2828
770-424-6915

Columbus Technical College
928 Manchester Expressway
Columbus, GA 31904-6572
706-649-0652

Computer-Ed Institute
2359 Windy Hill Road
Marietta, GA 30067-8550
770-226-0056

Computer-Ed Institute
5675 Jimmy Carter
Boulevard, Suite 100
Norcross, GA 30071
678-966-9411 Ext. 230

Georgia Medical Institute
101 Marietta Street, NW,
6th Floor
Atlanta, GA 30303
404-525-1111

Georgia Medical Institute-
Jonesboro
6431 Tara Boulevard
Jonesboro, GA 30236
770-603-0000

Georgia Medical Institute-
Marietta
1395 South Marietta Parkway,
Building 500, Suite 202
Marietta, GA 30067
770-428-6303

Grady Health System
80 Butler Street, SE,
PO Box 26095
Atlanta, GA 30335-3801
404-616-3611

Gwinnett College
4230 Highway 29, Suite 11
Lilburn, GA 30047

Herzing College
3355 Lenox Road, Suite 100
Atlanta, GA 30326
404-816-4533

Kerr Business College
2528 Centerwest Parkway,
Building A
Augusta, GA 30909
706-738-5046

Lacarme School of
Cosmetology
6254 Memorial Drive,
Suite M
Stone Mountain, GA 30083
770-879-6673

Medix School
2108 Cobb Parkway
Smyrna, GA 30080
770-980-0002

National Center for
Montessori Education-
Atlanta
2175 Norcross-Tucker Road
Norcross, GA 30071
770-434-5931

National Institute of
Technology
1706 Northeast Expressway
Atlanta, GA 30329
404-327-8787

NCPT, Inc.
100 Embassy Row
Atlanta, GA 30328
770-730-8553 Ext. 2532

North Georgia Technical
College
Georgia Highway 197, North,
PO Box 65
Clarkesville, GA 30523
706-754-7725

Roffler-Moler Hairstyling
College
1311 Roswell Road
Marietta, GA 30062
770-565-3285

Southeastern Beauty School
PO Box 12483
Columbus, GA 31917-2483
706-687-1054 Ext. 1

South University
709 Mall Boulevard
Savannah, GA 31406-6912
912-691-6000

Ultrasound Diagnostic
School
1140 Hammond Drive,
Suite 1150-A
Atlanta, GA 30328
770-350-0009

Hawaii

Education America, Honolulu
Campus
1111 Bishop Street, Suite 400
Honolulu, HI 96813
808-942-1000

Hawaii Business College
33 South King Street,
4th Floor
Honolulu, HI 96813
808-524-4014

Hawaii Institute of Hair
Design
71 South Hotel Street
Honolulu, HI 96813-3112
808-533-6596

Heald College, Schools of
Business and Technology
1500 Kapiolani Boulevard
Honolulu, HI 96814-3797
808-955-1500 Ext. 512

Hollywood Beauty College
99-084 Kauhale Street,
Building A
Aiea, HI 96701

Honolulu Community
College
874 Dillingham Boulevard
Honolulu, HI 96817-4598
808-845-9129

Institute of Body
Therapeutics
PO Box 11777
Lahaina, HI 96761

Kauai Community College
3-1901 Kaumualii Highway
Lihue, HI 96766-9591
808-245-8225

New York Technical Institute
of Hawaii
1375 Dillingham Boulevard
Honolulu, HI 96817-4415
808-841-5827

Travel Institute of the Pacific
1314 Sourth King Street,
Suite 1164
Honolulu, HI 96814-4401
808-591-2708

University of Phoenix-Hawaii
Campus
827 Fort Street
Honolulu, HI 96813
866-236-7655

Idaho

Aero Technicians, Inc.
Rexburg Airport, PO Box 7
Rexburg, ID 83440
208-245-4446

American Institute of Health
Technology
1200 North Liberty Street
Boise, ID 83704
208-377-8080 Ext. 22

Eastern Idaho Technical
College
1600 South 25th East
Idaho Falls, ID 83404-5788
208-524-3000 Ext. 3371

Headmasters School of Hair
Design II
602 Main Street
Lewiston, ID 83501
208-743-1512

ITT Technical Institute
12302 West Explorer Drive
Boise, ID 83713-1529
208-322-8844

Mr. Juan's College of Hair
Design
577 Lynwood Mall
Twin Falls, ID 83301
208-733-7777

Sage Technical Services
207 South 34th Avenue
Caldwell, ID 83605
800-858-6304

Sage Technical Services
1420 East 3rd Avenue
Post Falls, ID 83854
800-400-0079

The School of Hairstyling
257 North Main Street
Pocatello, ID 83204

Shadow Mountain Business
Careers
11911 Ustick Road
Boise, ID 83706

Illinois

The Academy of Dog
Grooming Arts
1900 South Arlington
Heights Road
Arlington Heights, IL 60005
847-228-5700

Altamore School of
Cosmetology
7904 North Second Street
Machesney Park, IL 61115

American Academy of Art
332 South Michigan Avenue
Chicago, IL 60604
312-461-0600

American InterContinental
University Online
2895 Greenspoint Parkway,
Suite 400
Hoffman Estates, IL 60195
847-585-3709

Cain's Barber College
365 East 51st Street
Chicago, IL 60615-3510
773-536-4441 Ext. 18

Career Colleges of Chicago
11 East Adams Street,
2nd Floor
Chicago, IL 60603-6301
312-895-6317

The Chubb Institute
270 West North Avenue
Villa Park, IL 60181
630-993-6121

College of DuPage
425 22nd Street
Glen Ellyn, IL 60137-6599
630-942-2800

College of Lake County
19351 West Washington St
Grayslake, IL 60030-1198
847-543-2061

The Cooking and Hospitality
Institute of Chicago
361 West Chestnut
Chicago, IL 60610-3050
877-828-7772

Coyne American Institute
1235 West Fullerton Avenue
Chicago, IL 60614-2186
773-935-2520 Ext. 230

Educators of Beauty
211 East Third Street
Sterling, IL 61081
815-625-0247

Environmental Technical
Institute
1101 West Thorndale Avenue
Itasca, IL 60143-1334
630-285-9100 Ext. 206

Environmental Technical
Institute-Blue Island Campus
13010 South Division Street
Blue Island, IL 60406-2606
708-385-0707

Fox College
4201 West 93rd Street
Oak Lawn, IL 60453
708-636-7700

Illinois Eastern Community
Colleges, Olney Central
College
305 North West Street
Olney, IL 62450
618-395-7777 Ext. 2005

The Illinois Institute of Art
350 North Orleans, Suite 136
Chicago, IL 60654-1593
800-351-3450

The Illinois Institute of Art-
Schaumburg
1000 Plaza Drive
Schaumburg, IL 60173
800-314-3450

International Academy of
Design & Technology
1 North State Street, #400
Chicago, IL 60602-9736
312-980-9200

ITT Technical Institute
7040 High Grove Boulevard
Burr Ridge, IL 60527
630-455-6470

ITT Technical Institute
1401 Feehanville Drive
Mount Prospect, IL 60056
847-375-8800

ITT Technical Institute
600 Holiday Plaza Drive
Matteson, IL 60443
708-747-2571

John A. Logan College
700 Logan College Road
Carterville, IL 62918-9900

La' James College of
Hairstyling
485 42nd Avenue
East Moline, IL 61244
309-755-1313

Lake Land College
5001 Lake Land Boulevard
Mattoon, IL 61938-9366
217-234-5377

Lewis and Clark Community
College
5800 Godfrey Road
Godfrey, IL 62035-2466
618-468-5100

Lincoln Technical Institute
8317 West North Avenue
Melrose Park, IL 60160

MacCormac College
506 South Wabash Avenue
Chicago, IL 60605-1667
312-922-1884 Ext. 204

Midwest Institute of
Technology
3712 West Montrose Avenue
Chicago, IL 60618
773-478-0119

Moraine Valley Community
College
10900 South 88th Avenue
Palos Hills, IL 60465-0937
708-974-2110

Oakton Community College
1600 East Golf Road
Des Plaines, IL 60016-1268
847-635-1629

Olympia College
9811 Woods Drive
Skokie, IL 60077
847-470-0277

Parkland College
2400 West Bradley Avenue
Champaign, IL 61821-1899
217-351-2236

Professionals Choice Hair
Design Academy
2719 West Jefferson Street
Joliet, IL 60435

Rockford Business College
730 North Church Street
Rockford, IL 61103
815-965-8616 Ext. 13

Sanford-Brown College
3237 West Chain of Rocks Rd
Granite City, IL 62040
618-931-0300

Southwestern Illinois College
2500 Carlyle Road
Belleville, IL 62221-5899

Triton College
2000 5th Avenue
River Grove, IL 60171-9983
708-456-0300 Ext. 3130

Undergraduate School of
Cosmetology
300 West Carpenter Street
Springfield, IL 62702

Universal Technical Institute,
Inc.
601 Regency Drive
Glendale Heights, IL
60139-2208
630-529-2662

The Vanderschmidt School
4825 North Scott Street,
Suite 76
Schiller Park, IL 60176

Westwood College
7125 Janes Avenue,
Suite 100
Woodridge, IL 60517
630-434-8244 Ext. 100

Westwood College of
Technology-O'Hare
4825 North Scott Street,
Suite 100
Schiller Park, IL 60176
847-928-1710 Ext. 100

Westwood College of
Technology-River Oaks
80 River Oaks Center,
Suite 102
Calumet City, IL 60409
708-832-1988 Ext. 100

Indiana

Alexandria School of
Scientific Therapeutics
809 South Harrison Street,
PO Box 287
Alexandria, IN 46001
800-622-8756

Honors Beauty College, Inc.
1315 E. 86th
Indianapolis, IN 46240
317-465.9837

Horizon Career College
8315 Virginia Street, A
Merrillville, IN 46410
219-756-6811

Indiana Business College
2222 Poshard Drive
Columbus, IN 47203
812-379-9000

Indiana Business College
6413 North Clinton Street
Fort Wayne, IN 46825
219-471-7667

Indiana Business College
4601 Theater Drive
Evansville, IN 47715
812-476-6000

Indiana Business College
802 North Meridian
Indianapolis, IN 46204
317-264-5656

Indiana Business College
2 Executive Drive
Lafayette, IN 47905-4859
765-447-9550

Indiana Business College
830 North Miller Avenue
Marion, IN 46952
765-662-7497

Indiana Business College
8150 Brookville Road
Indianapolis, IN 46239
317-375-8000

Indiana Business College
411 West Riggin Road
Muncie, IN 47303-6413
765-288-8681

Indiana University Northwest
3400 Broadway
Gary, IN 46408-1197
219-980-6991

Indiana University-Purdue
University Indianapolis
355 North Lansing
Indianapolis, IN 46202-2896
317-274-4591

International Business
College
7205 Shadeland Station
Indianapolis, IN 46256
317-841-6400

International Business
College
3811 Illinois Road
Fort Wayne, IN 46804
219-459-4513

ITT Technical Institute
4919 Coldwater Road
Fort Wayne, IN 46825-5532
219-484-4107

ITT Technical Institute
9511 Angola Court
Indianapolis, IN 46268-1119
317-875-8640

ITT Technical Institute
10999 Stahl Road
Newburgh, IN 47630
812-858-1600

Ivy Tech State College-Central
Indiana
1 West 26th Street,
PO Box 1763
Indianapolis, IN 46206-1763
317-921-4612

Ivy Tech State College-
Columbus
4475 Central Avenue
Columbus, IN 47203-1868
812-372-9925 Ext. 129

Ivy Tech State College-
Eastcentral
4301 South Cowan Road,
PO Box 3100
Muncie, IN 47302-9448
765-289-2291

Ivy Tech State College-
Kokomo
1815 East Morgan St,
PO Box 1373
Kokomo, IN 46903-1373
765-459-0561 Ext. 318

Ivy Tech State College-
Northeast
3800 North Anthony Blvd
Fort Wayne, IN 46805-1430
219-482-9171

Ivy Tech State College-
Northwest
1440 East 35th Avenue
Gary, IN 46409-1499
219-981-1111 Ext. 420

Ivy Tech State College-
Southeast
590 Ivy Tech Drive,
PO Box 209
Madison, IN 47250-1883
812-265-2580 Ext. 4114

Ivy Tech State College-
Southwest
3501 First Avenue
Evansville, IN 47710-3398
812-426-2865

Ivy Tech State College-
Wabash Valley
7999 US Highway 41, South
Terre Haute, IN 47802
812-299-1121

Oakland City University
143 North Lucretia Street
Oakland City, IN 47660-1099
812-749-1222

Olympia College
707 East 80th Place, #200
Merrillville, IN 46410
562-437-0501

Professional Careers Institute
7302 Woodland Drive
Indianapolis, IN 46278-1736
317-299-6001

Sawyer College-Southlake
3803 East Lincoln Highway
Merrillville, IN 46410
219-736-0436

Vincennes University
1002 North First Street
Vincennes, IN 47591-5202
812-888-4313

Iowa

AIB College of Business
2500 Fleur Drive
Des Moines, IA 50321-1799

College of Hair Design
Squires Square, 722 Water
Street, Suite 201
Waterloo, IA 50703
319-232-9995

Hair Tech School of
Technology
402 West Montgomery Street
Creston, IA 50801
641-782 6537 Ext. 20

Hamilton Technical College
1011 East 53rd Street
Davenport, IA 52807-2653

Hawkeye Community
College
PO Box 8015
Waterloo, IA 50704-8015
319-296-2320 Ext. 4000

Iowa Western Community
College
2700 College Road, Box 4-C
Council Bluffs, IA 51502
712-325-3289

Kaplan College
1801 East Kimberly Road,
Suite 1
Davenport, IA 52807
563-355-3500 Ext. 40

La' James College of
Hairstyling
227 East Market Street
Iowa City, IA 52240
319-338-3926

La' James College of
Hairstyling
6336 Hickman Road
Des Moines, IA 50322
515-278-2208

La' James College of
Hairstyling
6322 University Avenue
Cedar Falls, IA 50613
319-277-2150

La' James College of
Hairstyling
211 West 53rd Street
Davenport, IA 52807
319-386-7700

Marshalltown Community
College
3700 South Center Street
Marshalltown, IA 50158-4760

Mercy College of Health
Sciences
928 Sixth Avenue
Des Moines, IA 50309-1239
515-643-6605

Muscatine Community
College
152 Colorado Street
Muscatine, IA 52761-5396
563-288-6012

North Iowa Area Community College
500 College Drive
Mason City, IA 50401-7299
515-422-4104

Professional Cosmetology Institute
627 Main Street
Ames, IA 50010
515-232-7250 Ext. 2

Vatterott College
6100 Thornton, Suite 290
Des Moines, IA 50321
515-309-9000

Kansas

American Institute of Baking
1213 Bakers Way
Manhattan, KS 66502

The Brown Mackie College
126 South Santa Fe
Salina, KS 67401-2810

Butler County Community College
901 South Haverhill Road
El Dorado, KS 67042-3280
316-322-3396

Colby Community College
1255 South Range
Colby, KS 67701-4099
913-462-4690 Ext. 200

Cowley County Community College and Area Vocational-Technical School
125 South Second,
PO Box 1147
Arkansas City, KS
67005-1147
800-593-2222 Ext. 5368

Garden City Community College
801 Campus Drive
Garden City, KS 67846-6399
316-276-9531

Labette Community College
200 South 14th Street
Parsons, KS 67357-4299

Lawrence Career College
3300 Clinton Parkway Court
Lawrence, KS 66047
785-841-9640 Ext. 21

North Central Kansas Technical College
Box 507 Highway 24
Beloit, KS 67420
785-738-2276

Pittsburg State University
1701 South Broadway
Pittsburg, KS 66762
800-854-PITT

Pratt Community College and Area Vocational School
348 NE State Route 61
Pratt, KS 67124-8317
620-672-5641 Ext. 217

Salina Area Technical School
2562 Scanlan Avenue
Salina, KS 67401
785-825-2261 Ext. 424

Seward County Community College
Box 1137
Liberal, KS 67905-1137
620-629-2714

Southwest Kansas Technical School
2215 North Kansas
Liberal, KS 67905-1599
620-626-3819

Vatterott College
6130 East Central Avenue
Wichita, KS 67208-9771
316-686-7355

Vernons Kansas School of Cosmetology-Central
501 E. Pawnee Ste. 525
Wichita, KS 67211

Washburn University of Topeka
1700 SW College Avenue
Topeka, KS 66621
785-231-1010 Ext. 1391

Kentucky

Cumberland Valley Technical College-Harlan
164 Ball Park Road
Harlan, KY 40831
606-573-1506 Ext. 2225

Cumberland Valley Technical College-Middlesboro
1300 Chichester St.
Middlesboro, KY 40965
606-242-2145 Ext. 2073

Daymar College
250 Sturgis Road
Marion, KY 42064
270-926-4040

Daymar College
3361 Buckland Square
Owensboro, KY 42301
270-926-4040

Decker College
981 South Third Street,
Suite 106
Louisville, KY 40203

Draughons Junior College
2424 Airway Court
Bowling Green, KY 42103
270-843-6750

The Hair Design School
3968 Park Drive
Louisville, KY 40216
502-459-8150

The Hair Design School
4160 Bardstown Road
Louisville, KY 40218
502-499-0070

The Hair Design School
7285 Turfway Road
Florence, KY 41042
859-283-2690

ITT Technical Institute
10509 Timberwood Circle,
Suite 100
Louisville, KY 40223-5392
502-327-7424 Ext. 21

Jenny Lea Academy of Cosmetology
114 North Cumberland Ave
Harlan, KY 40831
606-573-4276

Kaufman's Beauty School
701 East High Street
Lexington, KY 40502
859-266-2024

Louisville Technical Institute
3901 Atkinson Square Drive
Louisville, KY 40218-4528
502-456-6509

Meade County Area Technology Center
110 Greer Street
Brandenburg, KY 40108

National College of Business & Technology
139 South Killarney Lane
Richmond, KY 40475
859-623-8956

National College of Business & Technology
288 South Mayo Trail, Suite 2
Pikeville, KY 41501
606-432-5477

National College of Business & Technology
3950 Dixie Highway
Louisville, KY 40216
502-447-7634

National College of Business & Technology
407 Marquis Avenue
Lexington, KY 40502-2140
859-253-0621

National College of Business & Technology
7627 Ewing Boulevard
Florence, KY 41042
859-525-6510

Pat Wilsons Beauty College
326 North Main
Henderson, KY 42420

Rowan Technical College
100 Vo-Tech Drive
Morehead, KY 40351
606-783-1538 Ext. 314

Spencerian College
4627 Dixie Highway,
PO Box 16418
Louisville, KY 40256-0418
502-447-1000

Sullivan University
3101 Bardstown Road
Louisville, KY 40205
502-456-6505

Tri-State Beauty Academy, Inc.
219 West Main Street
Morehead, KY 40351
606-784-9335

Western Kentucky University
One Big Red Way
Bowling Green, KY
42101-3576
270-745-4241

Louisiana

Ayers Institute, Inc.
PO Box 3941
Shreveport, LA 71133-3941
318-635-0280

Baton Rouge School of
Computers
9255 Interline Avenue
Baton Rouge, LA 70809-1971
225-923-2525

Career Technical College
1611 Louisville Avenue
Monroe, LA 71201
318-323-2889

Cloyd's Beauty School #1
603 Natchitoches Street
West Monroe, LA
71291-3131
318-322-5465

Cloyd's Beauty School #2
1311 Winnsboro Road
Monroe, LA 71202
318-322-5314

Cloyd's Beauty School #3
2514 Ferrand Street
Monroe, LA 71201-3539
318-322-5465

Crescent City Bartending
School
209 N. Broad St.
New Orleans, LA 70119
504-822-3362

Delta School of Business &
Technology
517 Broad Street
Lake Charles, LA 70601
337-439-5765

Education America,
Remington College,
Baton Rouge Campus
1900 North Lobdell
Baton Rouge, LA 70806
225-922-3990

Education America,
Remington College, Lafayette
Campus
303 Rue Louis XIV
Lafayette, LA 70508
337-981-4010

Education America,
Southeast College of
Technology, New Orleans
Campus
321 Veterans Memorial Blvd
Metairie, LA 70005
504-831-8889

Elaine P. Nunez Community
College
3710 Paris Road
Chalmette, LA 70043-1249
504-680-2472

Guy's Shreveport Academy
of Cosmetology
3954 Youree Drive
Shreveport, LA 71105
318-865-5591 Ext. 26

Herzing College
2400 Veterans Boulevard,
Suite 410
Kenner, LA 70062
504-733-0074

ITT Technical College
13944 Airline Highway
Baton Rouge, LA 70817-5998
225-752-4230

ITT Technical Institute
140 James Drive, East
St. Rose, LA 70087
504-463-0338

Louisiana Technical College-
Natchitoches Campus
PO Box 657
Natchitoches, LA 71458-0657
318-357-7007

Louisiana Technical College-
Slidell Campus
1000 Canulette Road
Slidell, LA 70459-0827
504-646-6430 Ext. 116

Nick Randazzo Vocational
Training Institute
1415 Whitney Avenue
Gretna, LA 70053
504-366-5409

University of Phoenix-
New Orleans
1 Galleria Boulevard,
Suite 725
Metairie, LA 70001
504-461-8852

Maine

Central Maine Medical
Center School of Nursing
300 Main Street
Lewiston, ME 04240-0305
207-795-2843

Eastern Maine Technical
College
354 Hogan Road
Bangor, ME 04401-4206
207-941-4680

Headhunter II School of Hair
Design
1041 Brighton Avenue
Portland, ME 04102

Landing School of Boat
Building and Design
PO Box 1490
Kennebunkport, ME
04046-1490

Maine Medical Center School
of Surgical Technology
Smtc Fort Road
South Portland, ME 04106
207-767-9402

Mid-State College
88 East Hardscrabble Road
Auburn, ME 04210-8888
207-783-1478

Northern Maine Technical
College
33 Edgemont Drive
Presque Isle, ME 04769-2016
207-768-2786

Maryland

Aaron's Academy of Beauty
340 Post Office Road
Waldorf, MD 20602
301-645-3681

AccuTech Business Institute
5310 Spectrum Drive
Frederick, MD 21703
301-694-0211

Allegany College of
Maryland
12401 Willowbrook Road, SE
Cumberland, MD 21502-2596
301-784-5199

Anne Arundel Community
College
101 College Parkway
Arnold, MD 21012-1895
410-777-2827

Baltimore School of Massage
6401 Dogwood Road
Baltimore, MD 21207
410-944-8855

Bennett School of Travel
8659 Baltimore National Pike
Ellicott City, MD 21043
410-465-8555 Ext. 219

Broadcasting Institute of
Maryland
7200 Harford Road
Baltimore, MD 21234
410-254-2770

Carroll Community College
1601 Washington Road
Westminster, MD 21157
410-386-8405

Chesapeake College
PO Box 8
Wye Mills, MD 21679-0008

Fleet Business School
2530 Riva Road, Suite 201
Annapolis, MD 21401

Hagerstown Business
College
18618 Crestwood Drive
Hagerstown, MD 21742
800-422-2670

International Fabricare
Institute
12251 Tech Road
Silver Spring, MD 20904

L'Academie de Cuisine
16006 Industrial Drive
Gaithersburg, MD 20877
800-664-CHEF

Lincoln Technical Institute
9325 Snowden River Pkwy
Columbia, MD 21046
410-290-7100

Medix School
700 York Road
Towson, MD 21204-2511
410-337-5155

The Omega Studios' School of Applied Recording Arts and Sciences
5609 Fishers Lane
Rockville, MD 20852
301-230-9100

RETS Technical Training Center
1520 South Caton Avenue
Baltimore, MD 21227-1063
410-644-6400

Smart I.T. Training
1502 Woodlawn Drive
Baltimore, MD 21207
410-944-4444 Ext. 220

Strayer University at Anne Arundel Campus
1111 Benfield Boulevard, Suite 100
Millersville, MD 21108
410-923-4500

Strayer University at Montgomery Campus
20030 Century Boulevard, Suite 300
Germantown, MD 20874
301-540-8066

Strayer University at Prince George's County
4710 Auth Place, 1st Floor
Suitland, MD 20746
301-423-3600

TESST College of Technology
803 Glen Eagles Court
Towson, MD 21286
410-296-5350

Ultrasound Diagnostic School
8401 Corporate Drive, Suite 500
Landover, MD 20785
301-918-8221

University of Phoenix-Maryland Campus
8830 Stanford Blvd, #100
Columbia, MD 21045
410-872-9001

Massachusetts

Assabet Valley Regional Vocational-Technical
215 Fitchburg Street
Marlborough, MA 01752-1288
508-485-9430

Bancroft School of Massage Therapy
333 Shrewsbury Street
Worcester, MA 01604
508-757-7923

Bristol Community College
777 Elsbree Street
Fall River, MA 02720-7395
508-678-2811 Ext. 2177

Bryman Institute
1505 Commonwealth Avenue
Brighton, MA 02135
617-783-9955

The Cambridge School of Culinary Arts
2020 Massachusetts Avenue
Cambridge, MA 02140-2124
617-354-2020 Ext. 130

Cape Cod Community College
2240 Iyanough Road
West Barnstable, MA 02668-1599
508-362-2131 Ext. 4311

Catherine E. Hinds Institute of Esthetics
300 Wildwood Avenue
Woburn, MA 01801
781-935-3344 Ext. 247

Computer-Ed Institute
375 Westgate Drive
Brockton, MA 02301-1818

Computer-Ed Institute
5 Middlesex Avenue
Somerville, MA 02145
617-776-3500 Ext. 267

Computer-Ed Institute
100 Sylvan Road, G 500
Woburn, MA 01801
617-776-3500 Ext. 233

Computer-Ed Institute
211 Plain Street
Lowell, MA 01852
978-458-4800 Ext. 208

Computer-Ed Institute
477 Washington Street
Boston, MA 02111
617-348-9857

Elizabeth Grady School of Esthetics
55 North St.
Medford, MA 02155
781-391-9380 Ext. 14

Funeral Institute of the Northeast
77 University Avenue
Westwood, MA 02090
781-461-9080

Henri's School of Hair Design
276 Water Street
Fitchburg, MA 01420
978-342-6061

ITT Technical Institute
333 Providence Highway
Norwood, MA 02062
781-278-7200 Ext. 231

ITT Technical Institute
10 Forbes Road
Woburn, MA 01801
Phone: 781-937-8324

Katharine Gibbs School
126 Newbury Street
Boston, MA 02116
Phone: 617-578-7100

Learning Institute for Beauty Sciences
384 Main Street
Malden, MA 02148
781-324-3400

Massachusetts School of Barbering and Men's Hairstyling
152 Parkingway Street
Quincy, MA 02169-5058
617-770-4444

Mount Wachusett Community College
444 Green Street
Gardner, MA 01440-1000
978-632-6600 Ext. 238

Muscular Therapy Institute
122 Rindge Avenue
Cambridge, MA 02140
617-576.1300 Ext. 3021

New England Institute of Art & Communications
10 Brookline Place, West
Brookline, MA 02445
800-903-4425

North Shore Community College
1 Ferncroft Road
Danvers, MA 01923-4093

RETS Technical Center
965 Commonwealth Avenue
Boston, MA 02215
617-783-1197

Rittner's School of Floral Design
345 Marlborough Street
Boston, MA 02115

Rob Roy Academy, Inc.
150 Pleasant Street
Worcester, MA 01609
508-799-2111

Ultrasound Diagnostic School
365 Cadwell Drive, 1st Floor
Springfield, MA 01104-1739
413-739-4700

University of Phoenix-Boston Campus
150 Grossman Drive
Braintree, MA 02184
480-927-0099 Ext. 1216

Michigan

Alpena Community College
666 Johnson Street
Alpena, MI 49707-1495

Baker College of Cadillac
9600 East 13th Street
Cadillac, MI 49601
231-876-3100

Baker College of Clinton Township
34950 Little Mack Avenue
Clinton Township, MI 48035
810-791-6610

Baker College of Jackson
2800 Springport Road
Jackson, MI 49202
517-788-7800

Baker College of Muskegon
1903 Marquette Avenue
Muskegon, MI 49442
231-777-5200

Baker College of Owosso
1020 South Washington St
Owosso, MI 48867
989-729-3350

Baker College of Port Huron
3403 Lapeer Road
Port Huron, MI 48060
810-985-7000 Ext. 102

Bayshire Beauty Academy
917 Saginaw Street
Bay City, MI 48708
989-894-2431

Conlin Hallissey Travel
School, Inc.
3270 Washtenaw Avenue
Ann Arbor, MI 48104
734-677-1562

David Pressley Professional
School of Cosmetology
1127 South Washington St
Royal Oak, MI 48067
248-548-5090 Ext. 10

Detroit Business Institute-
Southfield
23077 Greenfield Road
Ste. Ll28
Southfield, MI 48075
248-552-6300 Ext. 16

Dorsey Schools
31542 Gratiot Avenue
Roseville, MI 48066
810-296-3225

Dorsey Schools
30821 Barrington Avenue
Madison Heights, MI 48071
248-588-9660

Dorsey Schools
34841 Veteran's Plaza
Wayne, MI 48184
734-595-1540

Dorsey Schools
15755 Northline Road
Southgate, MI 48195
734-285-5400

Flint Institute of Barbering
3214 Flushing Road
Flint, MI 48504-4395
810-232-4711

Gogebic Community College
E-4946 Jackson Road
Ironwood, MI 49938
906-932-4231 Ext. 306

ITT Technical Institute
1522 East Big Beaver Road
Troy, MI 48083-1905
248-524-1800

ITT Technical Institute
4020 Sparks Drive, SE
Grand Rapids, MI
49546-6197
616-956-1060

Lawton School
20755 Greenfield Road,
Suite 300
Southfield, MI 48075
248-569-7787

Michigan College of Beauty
15233 South Dixie Highway
Monroe, MI 48161
734-241-8877

Michigan School of Canine
Cosmetology
3022 South Cedar Street
Lansing, MI 48910

Mott Community College
1401 East Court Street
Flint, MI 48503-2089
810-762-0242

National Institute of
Technology-Dearborn
23400 Michigan Avenue,
Suite 200
Dearborn, MI 48124
248-799-9933

North Central Michigan
College
1515 Howard Street
Petoskey, MI 49770-8717
231-348-6605

Northwestern Michigan
College
1701 East Front Street
Traverse City, MI 49686-3061
231-995-1058

Olympia Career Training
Institute
2620-2630 Remico Street, SW
Wyoming, MI 49509-9990
616-364-8464

Olympia Career Training
Institute
1750 Woodworth Street, NE
Grand Rapids, MI 49525
616-364-8464 Ext. 34

Professional Drivers Institute
18266 W. US 12 W.
New Buffalo, MI 49117
800-222-1782

Specs Howard School of
Broadcast Arts Inc.
19900 West Nine Mile Road
Southfield, MI 48075-3953
248-358-9000

Travel Education Institute-
Warren Campus
30100 Van Dyke Avenue,
Suite 200
Warren, MI 48093
810-751-5634

University of Phoenix-Grand
Rapids Campus
318 River Ridge Drive,
Suite 200
Grand Rapids, MI 49544
888-345-9699

University of Phoenix-Metro
Detroit Campus
5480 Corporate Drive,
Suite 240
Troy, MI 48098
248-924-4100

Washtenaw Community
College
4800 E Huron River Dr,
PO Box D-1
Ann Arbor, MI 48106
313-973-3676

Minnesota

Academy College
3050 Metro Drive, Suite 200
Minneapolis, MN 55425
952-851-0066

The Art Institutes
International Minnesota
15 South 9th Street
Minneapolis, MN 55402
800-777-3643

Brown Institute
1440 Northland Drive
Mendota Heights, MN
55120-1004
651-905-3419

Capella University
222 South 9th Street,
20th Floor
Minneapolis, MN 55402
888-227-3552 Ext. 8

Cosmetology Careers
Unlimited-Duluth
121 West Superior Street
Duluth, MN 55802
218-722-7484

Cutting Edge Pet Grooming
School
4902 France Avenue N.
Minneapolis, MN 56429
763-537-3669

Dakota County Technical
College
1300 East 145th Street
Rosemount, MN 55068
651-423-8301

Duluth Business University
412 West Superior Street
Duluth, MN 55802
218-722-3361

Globe College
7166 North 10th Street
Oakdale, MN 55128
651-730-5100

Hazelden Foundation
Box 11
Center City, MN 55012
651-213-4175

Hennepin Technical College
9000 Brooklyn Boulevard
Brooklyn Park, MN 55445
763-550-2115

Herzing College, Minneapolis
Drafting School Campus
5700 West Broadway
Minneapolis, MN
55428-3548
763-535-3000

High-Tech Institute
5701 Shingle Creek Parkway
Brooklyn Center, MN 55430
612-560-9700

Itasca Community College
1851 Highway 169 East
Grand Rapids, MN 55744
218-327-4464 Ext. 4464

Lakeland Medical-Dental
Academy
1402 West Lake Street
Minneapolis, MN 55408
612-827-5656

McConnell School, Inc.
1201 Marquette Avenue,
Suite 100
Minneapolis, MN
55403-2456
612-332-4238

Minneapolis Business
College
1711 West County Road B
Roseville, MN 55113
651-636-7406

Minneapolis School of
Massage and Bodywork, Inc.
85 22nd Avenue, NE
Minneapolis, MN 55418
612-788-8907

Minnesota Cosmetology
Education Center, Inc.
704 Marie Avenue
South St. Paul, MN 55075

Minnesota School of
Business
1401 West 76th Street
Richfield, MN 55423
612-861-2000

NEI College of Technology
825 41st Avenue, NE
Columbia Heights, MN
55421-2974
763-782-7330

Normandale Community
College
9700 France Avenue South
Bloomington, MN
55431-4399
952-487-8200

NTI School of CAD
Technology
11995 Singletree Lane
Eden Prairie, MN 55344-5351
952-944-0080

Oliver Thein Beauty School
150 Cobblestone Lane
Burnsville, MN 55337

Rasmussen College Eagan
3500 Federal Drive
Eagan, MN 55122
651-687-9000

Rasmussen College Mankato
501 Holly Lane
Mankato, MN 56001-6803
507-625-6556

Rasmussen College
Minnetonka
12450 Wayzata Boulevard,
Suite 315
Minnetonka, MN 55305-1928
952-545-2000

Rasmussen College St. Cloud
226 Park Avenue, South
St. Cloud, MN 56303-3091
320-251-5600

Rochester Community and
Technical College
851 30th Avenue, SE
Rochester, MN 55904-4999
507-285-7219

St. Cloud Technical College
1540 Northway Drive
St. Cloud, MN 56303-1240
320-654-5089

Sister Rosalind Gefres
School of Professional
400 Selby Avenue Ste. G.
St. Paul, MN 55102
651-554-3010

Mississippi

Meridian Community College
910 Highway 19 North
Meridian, MS 39307
601-484-8895

Virginia College at Jackson
5360 I-55 North
Jackson, MS 39211
601-977-0960

Missouri

Allied Medical College
500 Northwest Plaza Tower,
Suite 400
St. Ann, MO 63074
314-739-4450

Bryan Career College
1700 South Campbell,
Suite L
Springfield, MO 65807
417-862-5700

Crowder College
601 Laclede
Neosho, MO 64850-9160
417-455-5466

East Central College
PO Box 529
Union, MO 63084-0529
636-583-5195 Ext. 2220

Hickey College
940 West Port Plaza
St. Louis, MO 63146
314-434-2212

ITT Technical Institute
13505 Lakefront Drive
Earth City, MO 63045-1416
314-298-7800

ITT Technical Institute
1930 Meyer Drury Drive
Arnold, MO 63010
636-464-6600

Kansas City College of Legal
Studies
402 East Bannister Road,
Suite A
Kansas City, MO 64131
816-444-2232

Metro Business College
1407 Southwest Boulevard
Jefferson City, MO 65109
573-635-6600

Metro Business College
1202 East Highway 72
Rolla, MO 65401
314-364-8464

Metro Business College
1732 North Kingshighway
Cape Girardeau, MO 63701
573-334-9181

Missouri Tech
1167 Corporate Lake Drive
St. Louis, MO 63132-2907
314-569-3600

Moberly Area Community
College
101 College Avenue
Moberly, MO 65270-1304
660-263-4110 Ext. 239

Neosho Beauty College
116 North Wood Street
Neosho, MO 64850
417-451-7216

Nevada Regional Technical
Center
900 West Ashland
Nevada, MO 64772
417-448-2090

Patricia Stevens College
330 North Fourth Street
St. Louis, MO 63102

Patsy and Rob's Academy of
Beauty
18 NW Plaza
St. Ann, MO 63074
314-298-8808

Research Medical Center
2316 East Meyer Boulevard
Kansas City, MO 64132
816-276-4068

Rhodes College
1010 West Sunshine
Springfield, MO 65807
417-864-7220

Rockhurst University
1100 Rockhurst Road
Kansas City, MO 64110-2561
816-501-4767

Rolla Technical Institute
1304 East Tenth Street
Rolla, MO 65401-3699

Saint Charles Community
College
4601 Mid Rivers Mall Drive
St. Peters, MO 63376-0975
636-922-8229

Sanford-Brown College
3555 Franks Drive
St. Charles, MO 63301
636-949-2620

Sanford-Brown College
520 East 19th Avenue
North Kansas City, MO
64116-3614
816-472-0275

Sanford-Brown College
75 Village Square
Hazelwood, MO 63042
314-731-1101

Sanford-Brown College
1203 Smizer Mill Road
Fenton, MO 63026
636-349-4900

University of Phoenix-Saint
Louis Campus
Riverport Executive Center II,
13801 Riverport Drive
St. Louis, MO 64043
314-298-9755

Vatterott College
12970 Maurer Industrial
Drive
St. Louis, MO 63127
314-843-4200

Vatterott College
3925 Industrial Drive
St. Ann, MO 63074-1807
314-428-5900 Ext. 205

Vatterott College
3131 Frederick Boulevard
St. Joseph, MO 64506
816-364-5399

Vatterott College
1258 East Trafficway
Springfield, MO 65802
417-831-8116

Vatterott College
8955 East 38th Terrace
Kansas City, MO 64129
816-861-1000

Vatterott College
5898 North Main
Joplin, MO 64801
417-781-5633

Montana

Jerry Malson's Montana
Guide Training Center
22 Swamp Creek Road
Trout Creek, MT 59874
406-847-5582

Miles Community College
2715 Dickinson
Miles City, MT 59301-4799
406-234-3518

Rocky Mountain College
1511 Poly Drive
Billings, MT 59102-1796
406-657-1148

Sage Technical Services
3044 Hesper Road
Billings, MT 59102
406-652-3030

Nebraska

Bahner College of Hairstyling
1660 North Grant
Fremont, NE 68025
402-721-6500

College of Hair Design
304 South 11th Street
Lincoln, NE 68508-2199
402-477-4040

ITT Technical Institute
9814 M Street
Omaha, NE 68127-2056
402-331-2900

Lincoln School of Commerce
1821 K Street
Lincoln, NE 68508
402-474-5315

Metropolitan Community
College
PO Box 3777
Omaha, NE 68103-0777
402-457-2418

Nebraska College of
Business
3350 North 90th Street
Omaha, NE 68134
402-572-8500

Nebraska Methodist College
8501 West Dodge Road
Omaha, NE 68114-3426
402-354-4879

Northeast Community
College
801 East Benjamin Ave,
PO Box 469
Norfolk, NE 68702-0469
402-844-7260

Vatterott College
5318 South 136th Street
Omaha, NE 68137
402-891-9411

Vatterott College
5141 F Street
Omaha, NE 68117
402-731-3636

Nevada

Computer-Ed Institute
2290 Corporate Circle Drive,
Suite 100
Henderson, NV 89074
702-269-7600 Ext. 201

ITT Technical Institute
168 North Gibson Road
Henderson, NV 89014
702-558-5404

Las Vegas College
4100 West Flamingo Road,
#2100
Las Vegas, NV 89103
702-368-6200

Nevada Career Institute
3025 East Desert Inn Road,
Suite 11
Las Vegas, NV 89121
702-893-3300

Prestige Travel School
6175 West Spring Mountain Rd
Las Vegas, NV 89146
702-251-5552

Southern Nevada School of
Real Estate
3441 West Sahara Avenue,
Suite C1
Las Vegas, NV 89102-6059

Truckee Meadows
Community College
7000 Dandini Boulevard
Reno, NV 89512-3901
775-673-7041

University of Phoenix-
Nevada Campus
333 North Rancho Drive, #300
Las Vegas, NV 89106
702-638-7868

New Hampshire

Continental Academie of Hair
Design
311 Lincoln Street
Manchester, NH 03101
603-222-5851

McIntosh College
23 Cataract Avenue
Dover, NH 03820-3990
Phone: 800-624-6867

Portsmouth Beauty School of
Hair Design
138 Congress Street
Portsmouth, NH 03801-4084

St. Joseph Hospital-School of
Health Occupations
5 Woodward Avenue
Nashua, NH 03060
603-594-2567 Ext. 63943

St. Joseph School of Practical
Nursing
5 Woodward Avenue
Nashua, NH 03060
603-594-2567 Ext. 63943

New Jersey

Berdan Institute
265 Route 46 West
Totowa, NJ 07512-1819
973-256-3444

Berkeley College
430 Rahway Avenue
Woodbridge, NJ 07095
732-750-1800

Berkeley College
100 West Prospect Street
Waldwick, NJ 07463
201-652-0388 Ext. 114

Brookdale Community
College
765 Newman Springs Road
Lincroft, NJ 07738-1597
732-224-2375

The Chubb Institute
8 Sylvan Way
Parsippany, NJ 07054-0342
973-682-4950

The Chubb Institute
651 US Route 1 South
North Brunswick, NJ 08902
732-448-2642

The Chubb Institute
40 Journal Square
Jersey City, NJ 07306-4009
201-876-3810

The Chubb Institute
2100 Route 38 and Mall Drive
Cherry Hill, NJ 08002
856-755-4825

The Cittone Institute
160 East Route 4
Paramus, NJ 07652
201-845-6868

The Cittone Institute
1000 Howard Blvd, 2nd Floor
Mt. Laurel, NJ 08054-3414
856-722-9333

Computer Insight Learning
Center
3301-C Route 66
Neptune, NJ 07753
732-922-2700

County College of Morris
214 Center Grove Road
Randolph, NJ 07869-2086
973-328-5100

Dover Business College
East 81 Route 4, W
Paramus, NJ 07652
201-843-8500

Engine City Technical Institute
2365 Route 22 West
Union, NJ 07083-8517
908-964-1450

Financial Supermarkets
100 North Sixth Street,
PO Box 3066
Paterson, NJ 07509-3066
973-427-0065

Gibbs College
50 Church Street
Montclair, NJ 07042
201-744-6962

Harrison Career Institute
1386 South Delsea Drive
Vineland, NJ 08360-6210
856-696-0500

Harrison Career Institute
2105 Highway 35
Oakhurst, NJ 07755
732-493-1660

Harrison Career Institute
2 Carnegie Road
Lawrenceville, NJ 08648
609-406-1505

Harrison Career Institute
4000 Route 130 North,
2nd Floor, Suite A
Delran, NJ 08075
856-764-8933

Harrison Career Institute
The Plaza at Deptford,
1450 Clements Bridge Road
Deptford, NJ 08096
856-384-2888

Harrison Career Institute
600 Pavonia Avenue
Jersey City, NJ 07306
201-222-1700

Harrison Career Institute
525 South Orange Avenue
South Orange, NJ 07079
973-763-9484

Harris School of Business
654 Longwood Avenue
Cherry Hill, NJ 08002
856-662-5300

HoHoKus School
10 South Franklin Turnpike
Ramsey, NJ 07446
201-327-8877

Joe Kubert School of Cartoon
and Graphic Art Inc.
37 Myrtle Avenue
Dover, NJ 07801-4054
973-361-1327

Katharine Gibbs School
180 Centennial Avenue
Piscataway, NJ 08854
732-885-1580

Gibbs College
50 Church Street
Montclair, NJ 07042
201-744-6962

Lincoln Technical Institute
70 McKee Drive
Mahwah, NJ 07430
201-529-1414

Lincoln Technical Institute
2299 Vauxhall Road
Union, NJ 07083-5032
908-964-7800

Medical Technology Institute
300 McGaw Drive
Edison, NJ 08837
732-346-1900

Natural Motion Institute of
Hair Design
2800 Kennedy Boulevard
Jersey City, NJ 7306
201-659-0303

Ocean County College
College Drive, PO Box 2001
Toms River, NJ 08754-2001
732-255-0304

Pennco Tech
99 Erial Road, PO Box 1427
Blackwood, NJ 08012-9961
856-232-0310

RETS Institute
103 Park Avenue
Nutley, NJ 07110-3505
973-661-0600

Technical Institute of Camden
County
343 Berlin-Cross Keys Road
Sicklerville, NJ 08081-4000
856-767-7002 Ext. 5267

Teterboro School of
Aeronautics, Inc.
Teterboro Airport,
80 Moonachie Avenue
Teterboro, NJ 07608-1083
201-288-6300

Ultrasound Diagnostic
School
675 US Route 1, 2nd Floor
Iselin, NJ 08830
732-634-1131

Worldwide Educational
Services
24 Commerce Street,
12th Floor
Newark, NJ 07102
973-242-1260

Worldwide Educational
Services, Inc.
121-125 Newark Avenue
Jersey City, NJ 07302
201-435-5111

Worldwide Educational
Services, Inc.-Passaic
1410 Main Avenue
Clifton, NJ 07011
973-772-9393

New Mexico

Clovis Community College
417 Schepps Boulevard
Clovis, NM 88101-8381
505-769-4021

ITT Technical Institute
5100 Masthead Street, NE
Albuquerque, NM
87109-4366
505-828-1114

Mesa Technical College
911 South Tenth Street
Tucumcari, NM 88401
505-461-4413 Ext. 103

Metropolitan College of
Court Reporting
1717 Louisiana, NE, Suite 207
Albuquerque, NM
87110-4129
505-888-3400

New Mexico State
University-Alamogordo
2400 North Scenic Drive
Alamogordo, NM
88311-0477

New Mexico State
University-Carlsbad
1500 University Drive
Carlsbad, NM 88220-3509
505-234-9220

Phoenix-New Mexico
Campus
7471 Pan American Fwy, NE
Albuquerque, NM 87109
505-821-4800

New York

Apex Technical School
635 Avenue of the Americas
New York, NY 10011
212-645-3300

Berkeley College
3 East 43rd Street
New York, NY 10017
212-986-4343

Briarcliffe College
1055 Stewart Avenue
Bethpage, NY 11714-3545
516-918-3600

The Chubb Institute
22 Cortlandt Street
New York, NY 10007
212-266-5007

The Chubb Institute
190 East Pond Road
White Plains, NY 10601
914-683-8306

The Chubb Institute
1400 Old Country Road
Westbury, NY 11590
516-997-1400

Clinton Community College
136 Clinton Point Drive
Plattsburgh, NY 12901-9573
518-562-4170

The Culinary Institute of
America
1946 Campus Drive
Hyde Park, NY 12538-1499
845-451-1327

Elmira Business Institute
303 North Main Street
Elmira, NY 14901

Erie 2 Chautauqua-
Cattaraugus BOCES
8685 Erie Road
Angola, NY 14006
716-549-4454 Ext. 4026

Finger Lakes Community
College
4355 Lakeshore Drive
Canandaigua, NY
14424-8395
716-394-3500 Ext. 7278

Five Towns College
305 North Service Road
Dix Hills, NY 11746-6055
631-424-7000 Ext. 110

The French Culinary Institute
462 Broadway
New York, NY 10013
212-219-8890

Gemological Institute of
America, Inc.
580 5th Avenue, Suite 300
New York, NY 10036-4794
212-944-5900

Institute of Audio Research
64 University Place
New York, NY 10003-4595
212-777-8550

ITT Technical Institute
13 Airline Drive
Albany, NY 12205
518-452-9300

ITT Technical Institute
2295 Millersport Highway,
PO Box 327
Getzville, NY 14068-0327
716-689-2200

ITT Technical Institute
235 Greenfield Parkway
Liverpool, NY 13088-6651
315-461-8000

Jamestown Business College
7 Fairmount Avenue,
PO Box 429
Jamestown, NY 14702-0429
716-664-5100

Jamestown Community
College
525 Falconer Street
Jamestown, NY 14701-1999
800-388-8557 Ext. 2239

Katharine Gibbs School
200 Park Avenue
New York, NY 10166
212-867-9300

Katharine Gibbs School
320 South Service Road
Melville, NY 11747
516-370-3300

Learning Institute for Beauty
Sciences
3272 Hempstead Turnpike
Levittown, NY 11756
516-731-8300

Long Island Business
Institute
6500 Jericho Turnpike
Commack, NY 11725
631-499-7100

Mandl School
254 West 54th Street
New York, NY 10019-5516
212-247-3434

Modern Welding School
1842 State Street
Schenectady, NY 12304
518-374-1216

Monroe College
434 Main Street
New Rochelle, NY
10801-6410
914-632-5400

Monroe College
Monroe College Way
Bronx, NY 10468
718-933-6700

Monroe Community College
1000 East Henrietta Road
Rochester, NY 14623-5780
716-292-2200

National Tractor Trailer
School, Inc.
PO Box 208
Liverpool, NY 13088-0208
315-451-2430

New School of Radio and
Television
50 Colvin Avenue
Albany, NY 12206
518-438-7682 Ext. 10

New York Career Institute
15 Park Row
New York, NY 10038
212-962-0002

New York Restaurant School
75 Varick Street, 16th Floor
New York, NY 10013
212-226-5500 Ext. 6005

New York School for
Medical/Dental Assistants
116-16 Queens Boulevard
Forest Hills, NY 11375-2330
718-793-2330

New York School of Interior
Design
170 East 70th Street
New York, NY 10021-5110
212-472-1500 Ext. 202

North Country Community
College
20 Winona Avenue,
PO Box 89
Saranac Lake, NY
12983-0089
518-891-2915 Ext. 285

Oswego County BOCES
Country Route 64
Mexico, NY 13114
315-963-4256

Paul Smith's College of Arts
and Sciences
Routes 86 and 30
PO Box 265
Paul Smiths, NY 12970-0265
518-327-6227

Plaza Business Institute
74-09 37th Avenue
Jackson Heights, NY 11372
718-779-1430

Ridley-Lowell Business and
Technical Institute
116 Front Street
Binghamton, NY 13905
607-724-2941

Rochester Business Institute
1630 Portland Avenue
Rochester, NY 14621
716-266-0430

Rochester Education
Opportunity Center SUNY
Brockport
305 Andrews
Rochester, NY 14604
716-232-2730 Ext. 235

Sessions.Edu
476 Broome Street
New York, NY 10013
800-258-4115 Ext. 21

State University of New York
College of Agriculture
and Technology at Cobleskill
Cobleskill, NY 12043
800-255-8588

State University of New York
College of Agriculture
and Technology at Morrisville
PO Box 901
315-684-6046

TCI-The College for
Technology
320 West 31st Street
New York, NY 10001
212-594-4000 Ext. 437

Ultrasound Diagnostic
School
120 East 16th Street, 2nd Fl
New York, NY 10003
212-460-8567

Ultrasound Diagnostic
School
1 Old Country Road, LL1
Carle Place, NY 11514
516-248-6060

Ultrasound Diagnostic
School
2269 Saw Mill River Road
Elmsford, NY 10523
914-347-6817

Westchester Business
Institute
325 Central Avenue
White Plains, NY 10606
914-948-4442

Wood Tobe-Coburn School
8 East 40th Street
New York, NY 10016-0190
212-686-9040

North Carolina

American Institute of Applied
Science
PO Box 639
Youngsville, NC 27596-0639
919-554-2500

Art Institute of Charlotte
Three LakePointe Plaza,
2110 Water Ridge Parkway
Charlotte, NC 28217-4536
800-872-4417 Ext. 5872

Brookstone College of
Business
7815 National Service Road,
Suite 600
Greensboro, NC 27409-9423
336-668-2627 Ext. 18

Carolina School of
Broadcasting
7003 Wallace Road, Suite 100
Charlotte, NC 28212

Carolinas College of Health
Sciences
PO Box 32861,
1200 Blythe Boulevard
Charlotte, NC 28232-2861
704-355-5043

Center For Employment
Training-Research Triangle Pk
4022 Stirrup Creek Dr.
Ste. 325
Research Triangle Pk, NC
27703-9000
919-686-4153

Coastal Carolina Community
College
444 Western Boulevard
Jacksonville, NC 28546-6899
910-938-6246

ECPI College of Technology
4800 Airport Center Parkway,
#100
Charlotte, NC 28208-5886
704-399-1010

ECPI College of Technology
7802 Airport Center Drive
Greensboro, NC 27409-9654
336-665-1400

ECPI Technical College
4509 Creedmoor Road
Raleigh, NC 27612
919-571-0057

Fayetteville Technical
Community College
PO Box 35236
Fayetteville, NC 28303-0236
910-678-8274

Gaston College
201 Highway 321 South
Dallas, NC 28034-1499
704-922-6214

Haywood Community
College
185 Freedlander Drive
Clyde, NC 28721-9453
704-627-4505

King's College
322 Lamar Avenue
Charlotte, NC 28204
704-372-0266 Ext. 5509

Martin Community College
1161 Kehukee Park Road
Williamston, NC 27892
252-792-1521 Ext. 268

Miller-Motte Business
College
606 South College Road
Wilmington, NC 28403
910-392-4660

.Rockingham Community
College
PO Box 38
Wentworth, NC 27375-0038

Rowan-Cabarrus Community
College
PO Box 1595
Salisbury, NC 28145-1595
704-637-0760 Ext. 212

Wilkes Community College
1328 Collegiate Drive,
PO Box 120
Wilkesboro, NC 28697
336-838-6141

Winston-Salem Barber
School
1531 Silas Creek Parkway
Winston-Salem, NC 27127-
3757
336-724-1459

North Dakota

Aakers Business College
4012 19th Avenue Southwest
Fargo, ND 58103
701-277-3889

Bismarck State College
PO Box 5587
Bismarck, ND 58506-5587
701-224-5766

Josef's School of Hair
Design, Inc.
627 North P. Avenue
Fargo, ND 58102
701-235-0011

Lake Region State College
1801 College Drive North
Devils Lake, ND 58301-1598
701-662-1600 Ext. 512

Minot State University-
Bottineau Campus
105 Simrall Boulevard
Bottineau, ND 58318-1198
701-228-5451

Ohio

American School of
Technology
2100 Morse Road,
Number 4599
Columbus, OH 43229
614-436-4820

Bradford School
2469 Stelzer Road
Columbus, OH 43219
614-416-6200

D-E3, Inc.
18234 South Miles Parkway
Cleveland, OH 44128-4232
216-663-1500

Education America,
Remington College,
Cleveland Campus
14445 Broadway Avenue
Cleveland, OH 44125
216-475-7520

Gallipolis Career College
1176 Jackson Pike, Suite 312
Gallipolis, OH 45631-2600
740-446-4367

Hamrick Truck Driving School,
Inc.
1156 Medina Road
Medina, OH 44256-9615
330-239-2229

Health Occupations Program-
Columbus Public School
100 Arcadia Avenue
Columbus, OH 43202
614-365-5241

Hobart Institute of Welding
Technology
400 Trade Square East
Troy, OH 45373
800-332-9448 Ext. 5215

International College of
Broadcasting
6 South Smithville Road
Dayton, OH 45431
937-258-8251 Ext. 202

ITT Technical Institute
1030 North Meridian Road
Youngstown, OH 44509-4098
330-270-1600 Ext. 14

ITT Technical Institute
14955 Sprague Road
Strongsville, OH 44136
440-234-9091

ITT Technical Institute
3325 Stop Eight Road
Dayton, OH 45414-3877
937-454-2267

ITT Technical Institute
4750 Wesley Avenue
Norwood, OH 45212
513-531-8300

Jefferson Community
College
4000 Sunset Boulevard
Steubenville, OH 43952-3598

Madison Local Schools-
Madison Adult Education
600 Esley Lane
Mansfield, OH 44905
419-589-6363

Marion Technical College
1467 Mount Vernon Avenue
Marion, OH 43302-5694
740-389-4636 Ext. 237

Marymount School of
Practical Nursing
12300 McCracken Road
Garfield Heights, OH 44125
216-587-8160

Northern Institute of
Cosmetology
667-669 Broadway
Lorain, OH 44052

Northwest State Community
College
22-600 State Route 34
Archbold, OH 43502-9542
419-267-5511 Ext. 318

Ohio Business College
4020 Milan Road
Sandusky, OH 44870-5894

Ohio Valley Business College
16808 St. Clair Avenue,
PO Box 7000
East Liverpool, OH 43920
330-385-1070

Practical Nurse Program of
Canton City Schools
1253 Third Street, SE
Canton, OH 44707-4798

RETS Tech Center
555 East Alex Bell Road
Centerville, OH 45459
937-433-3410

Sanford-Brown Institute
17535 Rosbough Drive,
Suite 100
Middleburg Heights, OH
44130
440-239-9640

Sinclair Community College
444 West Third Street
Dayton, OH 45402-1460
937-512-3060

Southeastern Business
College
3879 Rhodes Avenue
New Boston, OH 45662
740-456-4124

Southeastern Business
College
1855 Western Avenue
Chillicothe, OH 45601
740-774-6300

Southeastern Business
College
504 McCarty Lane
Jackson, OH 45640
740-286-1554

Stautzenberger College
5355 Southwyck Boulevard
Toledo, OH 43614
419-866-0261

TDDS, Inc.
1688 North Pricetown Road,
SR 534, , PO Box 506
Lake Milton , OH 44429
330-538-2216

Technology Education
College
288 South Hamilton Road
Columbus, OH 43213-2087
614-759-7700

Total Technical Institute
6500 Pearl Road
Parma Heights, OH 44130
216-485-0900

University of Phoenix-Ohio
Campus
5005 Rockside Road,
Suite 325
Independence, OH 44131
216-447-8807

Virginia Marti College of
Fashion and Art
11724 Detroit Road
Lakewood, OH 44107
216-221-8584

Oklahoma

Broken Arrow Beauty College
400 South Elm Place
Broken Arrow, OK 74012

City College, Inc.
2620 South Service Road
Moore, OK 73160
405-329-5627

Dickinson Business
School/Career Point Business
School
3138 South Garnett Road
Tulsa, OK 74146-1933

Metro Area Vocational
Technical School District 22
1900 Springlake Drive
Oklahoma City, OK 73111
405-605-4436

Metropolitan College
1900 NW Expressway, R302
Oklahoma City, OK 73118
405-843-1000

Metropolitan College
4528 South Sheridan Road,
Suite 105
Tulsa, OK 74145
918-627-9300

Northeastern Oklahoma
Agricultural and Mechanical
College
200 I Street, NE
Miami, OK 74354-6434

Northwest Technology Center
1801 South 11th Street
Alva, OK 73717
405-327-0344

Northwest Technology Center
801 Vo-Tech Drive
Fairview, OK 73737

Platt College
3801 South Sheridan Road
Tulsa, OK 74145-1132
918-663-9000

Rogers State University
1701 West Will Rogers Blvd
Claremore, OK 74017-3252
918-343-7565

Spartan School of
Aeronautics
8820 East Pine St,
PO Box 582833
Tulsa, OK 74158-2833
918-831-5208

State Barber and Hair Design
College Inc.
2514 South Agnew
Oklahoma City, OK
73108-6220
405-631-8621

Tulsa Welding School
2545 East 11th Street
Tulsa, OK 74104-3909
918-587-6789 Ext. 240

University of Phoenix-
Oklahoma City Campus
6501 North Broadway
Extension, Suite 100
Oklahoma City, OK 73116
405-842-8007

University of Phoenix-Tulsa
Campus
10810 East 45th Street, #103
Tulsa, OK 74146
918-622-4877

Vatterott College
4629 Northwest 23rd Street
Oklahoma City, OK 73127
405-945-0088

Vatterott College
555 South Memorial
Tulsa, OK 74112
918-835-8288

Western Technology Center
621 Sooner Drive,
PO Box 1469
Burns Flat, OK 73624
580-562-3181 Ext. 2213

Oregon

Apollo College
2600 Southeast 98th Avenue
Portland, OR 97266
503-761-6100

The Art Institute of Portland
2000 Southwest Fifth Avenue
Portland, OR 97201
888-228-6528

College of Hair Design
Careers
3322 Lancaster Drive, NE
Salem, OR 97305-1354

ITT Technical Institute
6035 Northeast 78th Court
Portland, OR 97218-2854
800-234-5488

Linn-Benton Community
College
6500 Southwest Pacific Blvd
Albany, OR 97321
541-917-4817

Northwest Nannies Institute,
Inc.
11830 SW Kerr Parkway,
Suite 100
Lake Oswego, OR 97035
503-245-5288

Oregon Institute of
Technology
3201 Campus Drive
Klamath Falls, OR
97601-8801
541-885-1000

Portland Community College
PO Box 19000
Portland, OR 97280-0990
503-977-4519

University of Phoenix-
Oregon Campus
13221 Southwest 68th
Parkway, Suite 500
Portland, OR 97223
503-670-0590

Western Business College
425 Southwest Washington St
Portland, OR 97204
503-222-3225

Western Culinary Institute
1201 Southwest 12th Avenue,
Suite 100
Portland, OR 97205
503-223-2245 Ext. 335

Pennsylvania

Allentown Business School
1501 Lehigh Street
Allentown, PA 18103
610-791-5100

Allentown School of
Cosmetology, Inc.
1921 Union Boulevard
Allentown, PA 18103-1629
610-437-4626

Antonelli Medical and
Professional Institute
1700 Industrial Highway
Pottstown, PA 19464-9250
610-323-7270

The Art Institute of
Philadelphia
1622 Chestnut Street
Philadelphia, PA 19103-5198
215-567-7080

Baltimore School of
Massage, York Campus
170 Red Rock Road
York, PA 17402
866-699-1881

Berks Technical Institute
2205 Ridgewood Road
Wyomissing, PA 19610-1168
610-372-1722

Bradley Academy for the
Visual Arts
1409 Williams Road
York, PA 17402-9012
717-755-2300

Bucks County Community
College
Swamp Road
Newtown, PA 18940-1525
215-968-8122

Bucks County School of
Beauty Culture, Inc.
1761 Bustleton Pike
Feasterville, PA 19647
215-322-0666

Business Institute of
Pennsylvania
335 Boyd Drive
Sharon, PA 16146
724-983-0700

Butler Beauty School
233 South Main Street
Butler, PA 16001

Cambria-Rowe Business
College
221 Central Avenue
Johnstown, PA 15902-2494

Cambria-Rowe Business
College
422 South 13th Street
Indiana, PA 15701
724-463-0222

Career Training Academy-
Monroeville Campus
105 Mall Boulevard, West,
Suite 300
Monroeville, PA 15146

CHI Institute
Lawrence Park Shopping
Center, 1991 Sproul Road,
Broomall, PA 19008
610-353-7630

CHI Institute
520 Street Road
Southampton, PA 18966
215-357-5100

Chubb Institute-Keystone
School
Marple Crossroads Mall,
400 South State Road
Springfield, PA 19064-3957
610-338-2419

The Cittone Institute
3600 Market Street
Philadelphia, PA 19104
215-382-1553 Ext. 204

The Cittone Institute
1 Plymouth Meeting,
Suite 300
Plymouth Meeting, PA 19462
610-941-0319 Ext. 129

The Cittone Institute
2180 Hornig Road, Building A
Philadelphia, PA 19116
215-969-0869 Ext. 210

Clarion University of
Pennsylvania
Clarion, PA 16214
814-393-2306

Computer Learning Network
1110 Fernwood Avenue
Camp Hill, PA 17011-6996
717-761-1481

Computer Learning Network
2900 Fairway Drive
Altoona, PA 16602-4457
814-944-5643

Computer Learning Network
401 East Winding Hill Road,
Suite 101
Mechanicsburg, PA 17055-
4989
717-761-1481

Consolidated School of
Business
1605 Clugston Road
York, PA 17404
717-764-9550

Consolidated School of
Business
2124 Ambassador Circle
Lancaster, PA 17603-2389
717-394-6211

Crawford County Area
Vocational Technology
School-Practical Nursing
Program
860 Thurston Road
Meadville, PA 16335
814-724-6028

Douglas School of Business
130 7th Street
Monessen, PA 15062-1097
724-684-3684

Duff's Business Institute
Kossman Building, 100
Forbes Avenue, Suite 1200
Pittsburgh, PA 15222
412-261-4520

Erie Business Center, Main
246 West 9th Street
Erie, PA 16501
814-456-7504 Ext. 12

Erie Business Center South
170 Cascade Galleria
New Castle, PA 16101-3950
800-722-6227

Great Lakes Institute of
Technology
5100 Peach Street
Erie, PA 16509
814-864-6666 Ext. 242

Hanover Public School
District-Practical Nursing
Program
403 Moul Avenue
Hanover, PA 17331

Harrison Career Institute
844 West Market Street
Kingston, PA 18704
717-331-2006

Harrison Career Institute
2101 Union Boulevard
Allentown, PA 18109-1633
610-434-9963

Harrison Career Institute
1619 Walnut Street, 3rd Floor
Philadelphia, PA 19103
215-640-0177

Hazleton Area Career Center
Practical Nursing Program
1451 West 23rd Street
Hazleton, PA 18201
570-459-3178

Hussian School of Art
1118 Market Street
Philadelphia, PA 19107-3679
215-981-0900

ICM School of Business &
Medical Careers
10 Wood Street
Pittsburgh, PA 15222
412-261-2647 Ext. 222

ICT School of Welding
100 Pennsylvania Avenue
Selinsgrove, PA 17870-9339
570-743-5500

Immaculata College
1145 King Road, Box 500
Immaculata, PA 19345-0500
610-647-4400 Ext. 3015

Information Computer
Systems Institute
2201 Hangar Place
Allentown, PA 18103-9504

International Academy of
Design & Technology
555 Grant Street,
Oliver Avenue Entrance
Pittsburgh, PA 15219
800-447-8324

ITT Technical Institute
8 Parkway Center
Pittsburgh, PA 15220
412-937-9150

ITT Technical Institute
105 Mall Boulevard,
Suite 200E
Monroeville, PA 15146
412-856-5920

ITT Technical Institute
3330 Tillman Drive
Bensalem, PA 19020
215-244-8871

ITT Technical Institute
5020 Louise Drive
Mechanicsburg, PA 17055
717-691-9263

JNA Institute of Culinary Arts
1212 South Broad Street
Philadelphia, PA 19146
215-468-8801

Katharine Gibbs School
2501 Monroe Boulevard
Norristown, PA 19403
866-724-4227

Keystone College
One College Green
La Plume, PA 18440
570-945-5141 Ext. 2403

Lansdale School of Business
201 Church Road
North Wales, PA 19454
215-699-5700 Ext. 112

Lebanon County Career
School
18 East Weidman Street
Lebanon, PA 17046
800-694-8804

Le Cordon Bleu at
International Culinary
Academy
555 Grant Street,
Oliver Avenue Entrance
Pittsburgh, PA 15219
412-471-9330

Lincoln Technical Institute
9191 Torresdale Avenue
Philadelphia, PA 19136
215-335-0800

Lincoln Technical Institute
5151 Tilghman Street
Allentown, PA 18104-3298
610-398-5300

Manor College
700 Fox Chase Road
Jenkintown, PA 19046
215-884-2216

Montgomery County
Community College
340 DeKalb Pike
Blue Bell, PA 19422-0796
215-641-6550

New Castle School of Trades
Route 422 Newcastle-
Youngstown Road
Pulaski, PA 16143
724-964-8811

Northampton County Area
Community College
3835 Green Pond Road
Bethlehem, PA 18020-7599
610-861-5500

Northern Tier Career Center-
Practical Nursing Program
RR 1, Box 157A
Towanda, PA 18848-9731
570-265-8113

Orleans Technical Institute
1330 Rhawn Street
Philadelphia, PA 19111-2899
215-728-4700

Orleans Technical Institute-
Center City Campus
1845 Walnut Street, 7th Floor
Philadelphia, PA 19103
215-854-1842

Penn Commercial Business
and Technical School
82 South Main Street
Washington, PA 15301-6822
724-222-5330 Ext. 1

Pennco Tech
3815 Otter Street
Bristol, PA 19007-3696
215-824-3200

Pennsylvania Academy of
Cosmetology and Sciences
2445 Bedford Street
Johnstown, PA 15904

Pittsburgh Beauty Academy
415 Smithfield Street
Pittsburgh, PA 15222

Pittsburgh Institute of
Mortuary Science,
Incorporated
5808 Baum Boulevard
Pittsburgh, PA 15206-3706
412-362-8500 Ext. 101

Pittsburgh Technical Institute
635 Smithfield Street
Pittsburgh, PA 15222
412-809-5100

Pittsburgh Technical Institute-
Boyd School Division
1111 McKee Road
Oakdale, PA 15071
412-809-5350

Pruonto's Hair Design
Institute
705 12th Street
Altoona, PA 16602

Randy Rick Beauty Academy
450 Penn Street
Reading, PA 19602
610-378-1005

The Restaurant School
4207 Walnut Street
Philadelphia, PA 19104-3518
215-222-4200

St. Josephs Medical Center
School of Radiation
Technology
12th and Walnut St.
Reading, PA 19603
610-378-2230 Ext. 2234

Schuylkill Institute of
Business and Technology
171 Red Horse Road
Pottsville, PA 17901
570-622-4835

Stroudsburg School of
Cosmetology
100 North Eighth Street
Stroudsburg, PA 18360-1720
570-421-3387

Thompson Institute
University City Science
Center, 3440 Market Street
Philadelphia, PA 19104
215-387-1530

Thompson Institute
5650 Derry Street
Harrisburg, PA 17111
717-564-4112 Ext. 846

Thompson Institute
2593 Philadelphia Avenue
Chambersburg, PA 17201
717-709-9400

Triangle Tech, Inc.-DuBois
School
PO Box 551
DuBois, PA 15801-0551
814-371-2090

Tri-State Business Institute
5757 West 26th Street
Erie, PA 16506
814-838-7673

Ultrasound Diagnostic
School
5830 Ellsworth Avenue,
Suite 102
Pittsburgh, PA 15232
412-362-9404

Ultrasound Diagnostic
School
3 Neshaminy Interplex,
Suite 117
Trevose, PA 19053
215-244-4906

University of Phoenix-
Philadelphia Campus
170 South Warner Road,
Suite 200
Wayne, PA 19087
610-989-0880

University of Phoenix-
Pittsburgh Campus
Penn Center West 4,
Suite 100
Pittsburgh, PA 15276
412-747-9000

University of Pittsburgh
4200 Fifth Avenue
Pittsburgh, PA 15260
412-624-7488

West Virginia Career Institute
PO Box 278
Mount Braddock, PA 15465
724-437-4600

Wilma Boyd Career Schools,
Inc.
1412 Beers School Road
Moon Township, PA
15108-2549
412-809-5316

Wyoming Technical Institute
135 West Market Street
Blairsville, PA 15717
877-523-5132

York County Area Vocational
Tech School-Practical Nursing
Program
2179 South Queen Street
York, PA 17402
717-741-0820 Ext. 2313

York Technical Institute
1405 Williams Road
York, PA 17402-9017
717-757-1100

Rhode Island

Computer-Ed Institute
622 George Washington
Highway
Lincoln, RI 02865

The International Yacht
Restoration School
449 Thames St.
Newport, RI 2840
401-848-5777

Johnson & Wales University
8 Abbott Park Place
Providence, RI 02903-3703
401-598-2310

Katharine Gibbs School
178 Butler Avenue
Providence, RI 02906
401-861-1420

New England Institute of
Technology
2500 Post Road
Warwick, RI 02886-2266
800-736-7744 Ext. 3308

South Carolina

Academy of Hair Technology
3715 East North Street,
Suite F
Greenville, SC 29615
864-322-0300

Bob Jones University
1700 Wade Hampton Blvd
Greenville, SC 29614
800-252-6363

Charleston Cosmetology
Institute
8484 Dorchester Road
Charleston, SC 29420
843-552-3670

Columbia Beauty School
1824 Airport Boulevard
Cayce, SC 29033
803-796-5252

Columbia Junior College
3810 North Main Street
Columbia, SC 29203
803-799-9082

ECPI College Of Technology
15 Brendan Way, #120
Greenville, SC 29615-3514
864-288-2828

Forrest Junior College
601 East River Street
Anderson, SC 29624
864-225-7653 Ext. 204

ITT Technical Institute
Patewood Business Center,
1 Marcus Drive, Building
Greenville, SC 29615
864-288-0777 Ext. 21

Johnson & Wales University
701 East Bay Street

Charleston, SC 29403
803-763-0200

Midlands Technical College
PO Box 2408
Columbia, SC 29202-2408
803-738-7764

Miller-Motte Technical College
8085 Rivers Avenue
Charleston, SC 29406
843-574-0101

North American Institute of
Aviation
Conway-Horry County
Airport, PO Box 680
Conway, SC 29528-0680
843-397-9111 Ext. 423

Northeastern Technical
College
PO Drawer 1007
Cheraw, SC 29520-1007
803-921-6933

Orangeburg-Calhoun
Technical College
3250 St Matthews Road, NE
Orangeburg, SC 29118-8299

Piedmont Technical College
Emerald Road, PO Box 1467
Greenwood, SC 29648-1467
864-941-8603

Southern Methodist College
541 Broughton Stret,
PO Box 1027
Orangeburg, SC 29116-1027
803-534-7826

Spartanburg Technical
College
PO Box 4386
Spartanburg, SC 29305-4386
864-591-3817

Trident Technical College
PO Box 118067
Charleston, SC 29423-8067
843-574-6383

South Dakota

Kilian Community College
224 North Phillips Avenue
Sioux Falls, SD 57104-6014
605-336-1711

Tennessee

Arnold's Beauty School
1179 South Second Street
Milan, TN 38358

Chattanooga Barber College
405 Market Street
Chattanooga, TN 37402-1204
423-266-7013

Chattanooga State Technical
Community College
4501 Amnicola Highway
Chattanooga, TN 37406-1097
423-697-2478

Cleveland State Community
College
PO Box 3570
Cleveland, TN 37320-3570
423-478-6212

Draughons Junior College
340 Plus Park Boulevard
Nashville, TN 37217
615-361-7555

Draughons Junior College
1860 Wilma Rudolph
Clarksville, TN 37040
931-552-7600

Education America,
Southeast College of
Technology, Memphis
Campus
2731 Nonconnah Boulevard,
Suite 160
Memphis, TN 38132-2199
901-345-1000

High-Tech Institute
2710 Old Lebanon Road,
Suite 12
Nashville, TN 37214
615-902-9705

ITT Technical Institute
10208 Technology Drive
Knoxville, TN 37932-3343
865-671-2800

ITT Technical Institute
1255 Lynnfield Road,
Suite 192
Memphis, TN 38119
901-762-0556

ITT Technical Institute
441 Donelson Pike
Nashville, TN 37214-8029
615-889-8700

Jackson State Community
College
2046 North Parkway
Jackson, TN 38301-3797
731-425-2601

Knoxville Business College
720 North 5th Avenue
Knoxville, TN 37917
865-524-3043

Massage Institute of
Memphis
3445 Poplar Avenue, Suite 4
Memphis, TN 38111
901-324-4411

Miller-Motte Technical College
1820 Business Park Drive
Clarksville, TN 37040-6023

Nashville Auto Diesel College
1524 Gallatin Road
Nashville, TN 37206-3298
615-226-3990

Nashville State Technical
Institute
120 White Bridge Road
Nashville, TN 37209-4515
615-353-3214

North Central Institute
168 Jack Miller Boulevard
Clarksville, TN 37042
931-431-9700

Tennessee Institute of
Electronics
3203 Tazewell Pike
Knoxville, TN 37918-2530
865-688-9422

Tennessee Technology Center
at Athens
1635 Vo-Tech Drive
Athens, TN 37303
423-744-2814 Ext. 204

Tennessee Technology Center
at Hartsville
716 McMurry Boulevard
Hartsville, TN 37074
615-374-2147 Ext. 15

Tennessee Technology Center
at Jacksboro
Elkins Road
Jacksboro, TN 37757
423-566-9629 Ext. 10

Tennessee Technology Center
at Livingston
740 Airport Road, PO Box 219
Livingston, TN 38570
931-823-5525 Ext. 136

Tennessee Technology Center
at Murfreesboro
1303 Old Fort Parkway
Murfreesboro, TN
37129-3312
615-898-8010 Ext. 114

Tennessee Technology Center
at Shelbyville
1405 Madison Street
Shelbyville, TN 37160
931-685-5013 Ext. 108

Vatterott College
6152 Macon Road
Memphis, TN 38134
901-761-5730

William R. Moore School of
Technology
1200 Poplar Avenue
Memphis, TN 38104

Texas

American Commercial
College
2007 34th Street
Lubbock, TX 79411
806-747-4339

American Commercial
College
2115 East 8th Street
Odessa, TX 79761
915-332-0768

American Commercial
College
3177 Executive Drive
San Angelo, TX 76904
915-942-6797

American Commercial
College
402 Butternut Street
Abilene, TX 79602
915-672-8495

American School of Business
4317 Barnett Road
Wichita Falls, TX 76310
940-691-0454

The Art Institute of Dallas
2 North Park East,
8080 Park Lane, Suite 100
Dallas, TX 75231-9959
800-275-4243 Ext. 620

The Art Institute of Houston
1900 Yorktown
Houston, TX 77056
800-275-4244

ATI-American Trades Institute
6627 Maple Avenue
Dallas, TX 75235-4623
214-352-2222

ATI-Career Training Center
10003 Technology Blvd, West
Dallas, TX 75220
214-902-8191

ATI-Career Training Center
235 Northeast Loop 820,
Suite 110
Hurst, TX 76053-7396
817-284-1141

Austin Business College
2101 South IH 35, Suite 300
Austin, TX 78741
512-447-9415

Border Institute of
Technology
9611 Acer Avenue
El Paso, TX 79925-6744
915-593-7328 Ext. 24

Career Centers of Texas
8360 Burnham Road,
Suite 100
El Paso, TX 79907
915-595-1935

Career Point Business School
485 Spencer Lane
San Antonio, TX 78201
210-732-3000 Ext. 252

Cisco Junior College
Box 3, Route 3
Cisco, TX 76437-9321
915-673-4567

Coastal Bend College
3800 Charco Road
Beeville, TX 78102-2197
361-354-2245

Collin County Community
College District
4800 Preston Park Boulevard
Plano, TX 75093-8309
972-881-5174

Commonwealth Institute of
Funeral Service
415 Barren Springs Drive
Houston, TX 77090
281-873-0262

Conlee College of
Cosmetology
402 Quinlan
Kerrville, TX 78028
830-896-2380

Court Reporting Institute of
Dallas
8585 North Stemmons
Freeway, Suite 200N
Dallas, TX 75247-3821
214-350-9722

Culinary Institute
7070 Allensby
Houston, TX 77022
713-692-0077

Dallas Institute of Funeral
Service
3909 South Buckner Blvd
Dallas, TX 75227
800-235-5444

Del Mar College
101 Baldwin Boulevard
Corpus Christi, TX
78404-3897
361-698-1248

Eastfield College
3737 Motley Drive
Mesquite, TX 75150-2099
972-860-7105

Education America, Dallas
Campus
1800 Eastgate Drive
Garland, TX 75041
972-686-7878

Education America, Fort
Worth Campus
300 East Loop 820
Fort Worth, TX 76112
817-451-0017

Education America, Houston
Campus
9421 West Sam Houston Pwy
Houston, TX 77099
713-773-2500 Ext. 203

Hallmark Institute of
Aeronautics
10401 IH-10 West
San Antonio, TX 78230
210-690-9000 Ext. 212

High-Tech Institute
4250 North Beltline Road
Irving, TX 75038
972-871-2824

Institute of Cosmetology
7011 Harwin Drive, Suite 100
Houston, TX 77036
713-783-9988

International Aviation and
Travel Academy
4846 South Collins Street
Arlington, TX 76018
817-784-7000

International Business
College
1155 North Zaragosa,
Suite 100
El Paso, TX 79907-1806
915-859-3986

International Business
College
4121 Montana Avenue
El Paso, TX 79903-4699
915-566-8643

ITT Technical Institute
15621 Blue Ash Drive,
Suite 160
Houston, TX 77090-5818
281-873-0512

ITT Technical Institute
2101 Waterview Parkway
Richardson, TX 75080
972-690-9100

ITT Technical Institute
2222 Bay Area Boulevard
Houston, TX 77058
281-486-2630

ITT Technical Institute
2950 South Gessner Road
Houston, TX 77063-3751
713-952-2294

ITT Technical Institute
551 Ryan Plaza Drive
Arlington, TX 76011
817-794-5100

ITT Technical Institute
5700 Northwest Parkway
San Antonio, TX 78249-3303
210-694-4612

ITT Technical Institute
6330 Highway 290 East,
Suite 150
Austin, TX 78723
512-467-6800

Jacksonville College
105 B J Albritton Drive
Jacksonville, TX 75766-4759
903-586-2518 Ext. 225

Joe G. Davis School of
Vocational Nursing-
Huntsville Memorial Hospital
485 Interstate Highway 45
South, PO Box 4001
Huntsville, TX 77340
409-291-4545

Lamar State College-Orange
410 Front Street
Orange, TX 77630-5899
409-882-3362

Lamar State College-Port
Arthur
PO Box 310
Port Arthur, TX 77641-0310
409-984-6165

Lamar University
4400 Martin Luther King Pwy
Beaumont, TX 77710
409-880-8321

Lincoln Technical Institute
2501 East Arkansas Lane
Grand Prairie, TX 75052
972-660-5701

MTI College of Business and
Technology
7277 Regency Square Blvd
Houston, TX 77036-3163
713-974-7181

National Education Center-
National Institute of
Technology
3622 Fredricksburg Road
San Antonio, TX 78201-3841
210-733-6000

National Institute of
Technology
4150 Westheimer Road,
Suite 200
Houston, TX 77027
713-629-1637 Ext. 102

National Institute of
Technology
3622 Fredericksburg Road
San Antonio, TX 78201
210-733-6000

National Institute of
Technology-Greenspoint
255 Northpoint, Suite 100
Houston, TX 77060
281-447-7037 Ext. 102

National Institute of
Technology-Hobby
7151 Office City Drive,
Suite 200
Houston, TX 77087
713-645-7404

Panola College
1109 West Panola Street
Carthage, TX 75633-2397
903-693-2055

PCI Health Training Center
8101 John W. Carpenter Fwy
Dallas, TX 75247-4720
214-630-0568 Ext. 305

San Antonio College of
Medical and Dental
4205 San Pedro Avenue
San Antonio, TX 78212
210-733-0777 Ext. 1543

San Jacinto College South
Campus
13735 Beamer Road
Houston, TX 77089-6099
281-484-1900 Ext. 3350

School of Automotive
Machinists
1911 Antoine Drive
Houston, TX 77055-1803
713-683-3817

Southeastern Paralegal
Institute
5440 Harvest Hill, #200
Dallas, TX 75230
972-385-1446

South Texas Community
College
3201 West Pecan
McAllen, TX 78501
956-668-6495

Texas Christian University
2800 South University Drive
Fort Worth, TX 76129-0002
817-257-7130

Texas Culinary Academy
6020 Dillard Circle
Austin, TX 78752
888-553-2433

Texas School of Business
711 East Airtex Drive
Houston, TX 77073
281-443-8900

Texas School of Business
Friendswood
17164 Blackhawk Boulevard
Friendswood, TX 77546
281-648-0880

Texas School of Business
Southwest
6363 Richmond, Suite 500
Houston, TX 77057
713-975-7527

Texas State Technical College
300 College Drive
Sweetwater, TX 79556-4108
915-235-7349

Texas State Technical
College-Waco
3801 Campus Drive
Waco, TX 76705-1695
254-867-2360

Trinity Valley Community
College
500 South Prairieville Street
Athens, TX 75751-2765
903-675-6306

Tyler Junior College
PO Box 9020
Tyler, TX 75711-9020
903-510-2398

Ultrasound Diagnostic
School
10500 Forum Place Drive,
Suite 200
Houston, TX 77036
713-779-1110

Ultrasound Diagnostic
School
2998 North Stemmons Blvd
Dallas, TX 75247
214-638-6400

Universal Technical Institute
721 Lockhaven Drive
Houston, TX 77073-5598
281-443-6262

Universal Technical Institute,
Inc.
721 Lockhaven Dr.
Houston, TX 77073
281-443-6262

University of Phoenix-
Dallas/Ft. Worth Campus
Churchill Tower,
12400 Coit Rd, Suite 100
Dallas, TX 75251
480-927-0099 Ext. 1216

University of Phoenix-
Houston Campus
11451 Katy Freeway,
Suite 200
Houston, TX 77079
480-927-0099 Ext. 1216

Vernon Regional Junior
College
4400 College Drive
Vernon, TX 76384-4092
940-552-6291 Ext. 2205

Virginia College at Austin
6301 East Highway 290
Austin, TX 78723
512-371-3500

Western Technical Institute
1000 Texas Avenue
El Paso, TX 79901-1536
915-532-3737

Western Technical Institute
4710 Alabama Street
El Paso, TX 79930
915-566-9621

Westwood College of
Aviation Technology-Houston
8880 Telephone Road
Houston, TX 77061
713-644-7777

Westwood Institute of
Technology-Ft. Worth
8721 Airport Freeway
North Richland Hills, TX
76180
817-605-8111

Utah

Bon Losee Academy of Hair
Artistry
2230 North University Pkwy,
Building 5
Provo, UT 84604
801-375-8000

Bridgerland Applied
Technology Center
1301 North 600 West
Logan, UT 84321
435-750-3250

Cameo College of Beauty
Skin and Electrolysis
1600 South State Street
Salt Lake City, UT 84115

Center for Travel Education
9489 South 700 East
Sandy, UT 84088

Certified Careers Institute
1455 West 2200 South,
Suite 103
Salt Lake City, UT
84119-7218
801-973-7008

Certified Careers Institute
775 South 2000 East
Clearfield, UT 84015
801-774-9900

ITT Technical Institute
920 West Levoy Drive
Murray, UT 84123-2500
801-263-3313

LDS Business College
411 East South Temple Street
Salt Lake City, UT 84111-1392
801-524-8144

Mountain West College
3280 West 3500 South
West Valley City, UT 84119
801-840-4800

Provo College
1450 West 820 North
Provo, UT 84601
801-375-1861

Stevens-Henager College
2168 Washington Boulevard
Ogden, UT 84401
800-977-5455

Stevens-Henager College of
Business-Provo
25 E. 1700 S.
Provo, UT 84606-6157
801-375-5455

Stevens-Henager College-
Provo
25 East 1700 South
Provo, UT 84606
800-977-5455

Stevens-Henager College-
Salt Lake City
635 West 5300 South
Salt Lake City, UT 84123
800-977-5455

Uintah Basin Applied
Technology Center
1100 East Lagoon 124-5
Roosevelt, UT 84066
435-722-4523

University of Phoenix-Utah
Campus
5251 Green Street
Salt Lake City, UT 84123
800-224-2844

Weber State University
1001 University Circle
Ogden, UT 84408-1001
801-626-6067

Western Governors
University
2040 East Murray Holladay,
Suite 106
Salt Lake City, UT 84117
801-274-3280 Ext. 15

Vermont

Distance Learning
International, Inc.
80 North Main Street,
PO Box 846
Saint Albans, VT 05478-0846
802-524-2223

New England Culinary
Institute
250 Main Street
Montpelier, VT 05602-9720
802-223-6324

New England Culinary
Institute at Essex
48 1/2 Park Street
Essex Junction, VT 05452
802-223-9295

Vermont Technical College
PO Box 500
Randolph Center, VT
05061-0500
802-728-1245

Virginia

Advanced Technology
Institute
5700 Southern Boulevard
Virginia Beach, VA 23462
757-490-1241

Applied Career Training
1100 Wilson Boulevard,
Mall Level
Arlington, VA 22209
703-527-6660

The Art Institute of
Washington
1820 North Fort Myer Drive
Arlington, VA 22209
877-303-3771

Beta Tech
7914 Midlothian Tpk
Richmond, VA 23235
804-330-0111

Blue Ridge Community
College
PO Box 80
Weyers Cave, VA 24486-0080
540-234-9261 Ext. 2329

Bryant and Stratton College,
Virginia Beach
301 Centre Pointe Drive
Virginia Beach, VA
23462-4417
757-499-7900

Central Virginia Community
College
3506 Wards Road
Lynchburg, VA 24502-2498

The Chubb Institute
1741 Business Center Drive
Reston, VA 20190-5300
703-438-2804

Community Hospital of
Roanoke Valley-College of
Health Sciences
PO Box 13186
Roanoke, VA 24031-3186
888-985-8483

Dabney S. Lancaster
Community College
100 Dabney Drive,
PO Box 1000
Clifton Forge, VA 24422
540-863-2819

Danville Community College
1008 South Main Street
Danville, VA 24541-4088
804-797-8420

ECPI College of Technology
1919 Commerce Drive, #200
Hampton, VA 23666-4246
757-838-9191

ECPI College of Technology
21010 Dulles Town Circle,
#200
Dulles, VA 20166
703-421-9191

ECPI College of Technology
5555 Greenwich Road,
Suite 300
Virginia Beach, VA
23462-6542
757-490-9090

ECPI Technical College
800 Moorefield Park Drive
Richmond, VA 23236
804-330-5533

ECPI Technical College
4305 Cox Road
Glen Allen, VA 23060
804-934-0100

ECPI Technical College
5234 Airport Road
Roanoke, VA 24012
540-563-8080

Gibbs School of Northern
Virginia
1980 Gallows Road
Vienna, VA 22182
703-556-8888 Ext. 145

Henrico County-Saint Marys
Hospital School of Practical
Nursing
201 E. Nine Mile Road
Highland Springs, VA 23075
804-328-4095

Hicks Academy of Beauty
Culture
436 Boush Street
Norfolk, VA 23510
757-399-2400 Ext. 202

ITT Technical Institute
300 Gateway Centre Parkway
Richmond, VA 23235
804-330-4992

ITT Technical Institute
863 Glenrock Road
Norfolk, VA 23502-3701
757-466-1260

J. Sargeant Reynolds
Community College
PO Box 85622
Richmond, VA 23285-5622
804-371-3029

Kee Business College
803 Diligence Drive
Newport News, VA 23606
757-873-1111

Kee Business College-
Chesapeake
825 Greenbrier Circle,
Suite 100
Chesapeake, VA 23320-2637
757-361-3900

Medical Careers Institute
5501 Greenwich Road,
Suite 100
Virginia Beach, VA 23462
757-497-8400

Medical Careers Institute
11790 Jefferson Avenue
Newport News, VA
23606-2571
757-873-2423

National College of Business
& Technology
PO Box 6400
Roanoke, VA 24017
540-986-1800

National College of Business
& Technology
1819 Emmet Street
Charlottesville, VA 22901
434-295-0136

National College of Business
& Technology
51 B Burgess Road
Harrisonburg, VA 22801
540-986-1800

National College of Business
& Technology
300A Piedmont Avenue
Bristol, VA 24201
540-669-5333

National College of Business
& Technology
100 Logan Street,
PO Box 629
Bluefield, VA 24605
540-326-3621

National College of Business
& Technology
734 Main Street
Danville, VA 24541
800-664-1886

National College of Business
& Technology
104 Candlewood Court
Lynchburg, VA 24502
804-239-3500

National College of Business
& Technology
10 Church Street
Martinsville, VA 24114
540-632-5621

New River Community
College
PO Box 1127
Dublin, VA 24084-1127
540-674-3603

Paul D. Camp Community
College
PO Box 737,
100 North College Drive
Franklin, VA 23851-0737
757-569-6725

Potomac Academy of Hair
Design
350 South Washington Street
Falls Church, VA 22046
703-532-5050 Ext. 110

Potomac Academy of Hair
Design
8255 Shopper's Square
Manassas, VA 20111
703-361-7775

Potomac College
1029 Herndon Parkway
Herndon, VA 20170
703-709-5875

Southwest Virginia
Community College
PO Box SVCC
Richlands, VA 24641-1510
540-964-7294

Stratford University
7777 Leesburg Pike,
100 South
Falls Church, VA 22043
703-821-8570

Stratford University
13576 Minneville Road
Woodbridge, VA 22192
703-821-8570

Strayer University at
Alexandria Campus
2730 Eisenhower Avenue
Alexandria, VA 22314
703-329-9100

Strayer University at
Arlington Campus
3045 Columbia Pike
Arlington, VA 22204
703-892-5100

Strayer University at
Chesterfield Campus
2820 Waterford Lake Drive,
Suite 100
Midlothian, VA 23112
804-763-6300

Strayer University at
Fredericksburg Campus
4500 Plank Road
Fredericksburg, VA 22407
540-785-8800

Strayer University at Henrico
Campus
11501 Nuckols Road
Glen Allen, VA 23059
804-527-1000

Strayer University at
Loudoun Campus
45150 Russell Branch
Parkway, Suite 200
Ashburn, VA 20147
703-729-8800

Strayer University at
Manassas Campus
9990 Battleview Parkway
Manassas, VA 20109
703-330-8400

Strayer University at
Woodbridge Campus
13385 Minnieville Road
Woodbridge, VA 22192
703-878-2800

TESST College of Technology
6315 Bren Mar Drive
Alexandria, VA 22312
703-548-4800

Virginia School of Technology
100 Constitution Drive,
Suite 101
Virginia Beach, VA 23462
757-499-5447

Washington County Adult
Skill Center
848 Thompson Drive
Abingdon, VA 24210

Washington

Apollo College
1101 North Fancher Avenue
Spokane, WA 99212
509-532-8888

The Art Institute of Seattle
2323 Elliott Avenue
Seattle, WA 98121
206-239-2242

Bellingham Beauty School
211 West Holly Street
Bellingham, WA 98225
360-739-1494

Big Bend Community
College
7662 Chanute Street
Moses Lake, WA 98837-3299
509-762-5351 Ext. 226

Bryman College
17900 Pacific Highway South,
Suite 400
Seatac, WA 98188
206-241-5825

Clover Park Technical College
4500 Steilacoom Blvd, SW
Lakewood, WA 98499
253-589-5541

Columbia Basin College
2600 North 20th Avenue
Pasco, WA 99301-3397
509-547-0511 Ext. 2761

Eton Technical Institute
209 East Casino Road
Everett, WA 98208
425-353-4888

Gene Juarez Academy of
Beauty
2222 South 314th Street
Federal Way, WA 98003
206-368-0210

Glen Dow Academy of Hair
Design
309 West Riverside Avenue
Spokane, WA 99201
509-624-3244

International Air Academy
2901 East Mill Plain Blvd
Vancouver, WA 98661-4899
360-695-2500 Ext. 319

ITT Technical Institute
Argonne Office Park, North
1050 Argonne Road
Spokane, WA 99212-2610
509-926-2900

ITT Technical Institute
Canyon Park East,
2525 223rd Street, SE
Bothell, WA 98021
425-485-0303

ITT Technical Institute
12720 Gateway Drive,
Suite 100
Seattle, WA 98168-3333
206-244-3300

North Seattle Community
College
9600 College Way North
Seattle, WA 98103-3599

Pierce College
9401 Farwest Drive, SW
Lakewood, WA 98498-1999
253-964-6501

Pierce College-Puyallup
1601 39th Avenue SE
Puyallup, WA 98374
253-840-8470

Pima Medical Institute
1627 Eastlake Avenue East
Seattle, WA 98102
206-324-6100 Ext. 28

Renton Technical College
3000 Fourth Street, NE
Renton, WA 98056
425-235-2463

Seattle Midwifery School
2524 16th Avenue S. Rm 300
Seattle, WA 98144
206-322-8834

Skagit Valley College
2405 College Way
Mount Vernon, WA
98273-5899
360-416-7620

Tacoma Community College
6501 South 19th Street
Tacoma, WA 98466
253-566-5120

University of Phoenix-
Washington Campus
7100 Fort Dent Way,
Suite 100
Seattle, WA 98188
877-877-4867

Western Business College
Stonemill Center,
120 Northeast 136th Avenue
Vancouver, WA 98684
360-254-3282

West Virginia

Computer Tech
2000 Green River Drive
Fairmont, WV 26554
304-534-5677

Huntington Junior College of
Business
900 5th Avenue
Huntington, WV 25701
304-697-7550

National Institute of
Technology
5514 Big Tyler Road
Cross Lanes, WV 25313
304-776-6290

Opportunities
Industrialization
Center-Tri-State
1448 Tenth Avenue,
PO Box 2105
Huntington, WV 25701
304-525-9178 Ext. 10

Real Estate Career Center
523 11th Street
Huntington, WV 25701
304-525-7765

Roane-Jackson Technical
Center
4800 Spencer Road
Leroy, WV 25252-9700

Valley College of Technology
330 Harper Park Drive
Beckley, WV 25801

Valley College of Technology
616 Harrison Street
Princeton, WV 24740

West Virginia Junior College
148 Willey Street
Morgantown, WV 26505
304-296-8282

West Virginia Junior College
176 Thompson Drive
Bridgeport, WV 26330
304-363-8824

West Virginia Junior College
1000 Virginia Street, East
Charleston, WV 25301
304-345-2820

West Virginia Junior College
148 Willey Street
Morgantown, WV 26505
304-296-8282

West Virginia Northern
Community College
1704 Market Street
Wheeling, WV 26003-3699

West Virginia University at
Parkersburg
300 Campus Drive
Parkersburg, WV 26101-9577
304-424-8218

Wisconsin

Diesel Truck Driver Training
School
7190 Elder Lane
Sun Prairie, WI 53590
608-837-7800

Gill-Tech Academy of Hair
Design
423 West College Avenue
Appleton, WI 54911

Herzing College
5218 East Terrace Drive
Madison, WI 53718
608-663-0846

ITT Technical Institute
6300 West Layton Avenue
Greenfield, WI 53220-4612
414-282-9494

ITT Technical Institute
470 Security Boulevard
Green Bay, WI 54313
920-662-9000

Lakeshore Technical College
1290 North Avenue
Cleveland, WI 53015-1414
920-693-1627

Lakeside School of Massage
Therapy
1726 North 1st Street
Milwaukee, WI 53212
414-372-4345

Lakeside School of Massage
Therapy
6121 Odana Road
Madison, WI 53719
608-274-2484

Madison Area Technical
College
3550 Anderson Street
Madison, WI 53704-2599
608-246-6262

State College of Beauty
Culture
5271/2 Washington Street
Wausau, WI 54403

Western Wisconsin Technical
College
304 6th Street North,
PO Box C-908
La Crosse, WI 54602-0908
608-785-9834

Wisconsin Indianhead
Technical College
1019 South Knowles Avenue
New Richmond, WI 54017
715-468-2815 Ext. 2280

Wisconsin School of
Professional Pet Grooming,
Inc.
PO Box 175, N51 W34917
Wisconsin Avenue
Okauchee, WI 53069
262-569-9492

Wyoming

Casper College
125 College Drive
Casper, WY 82601-4699
307-268-2213

Central Wyoming College
2660 Peck Avenue
Riverton, WY 82501-2273
307-855-2231

Laramie County Community
College
1400 East College Drive
Cheyenne, WY 82007-3299
307-778-1212

Northwest College
231 West 6th Street
Powell, WY 82435-1898

Sage Technical Services
2368 Oil Drive
Casper, WY 82604
307-234-0242

Wyoming Technical Institute
4373 North 3rd Street
Laramie, WY 82072-9519
307-742-3776

Bibliography

ADDITIONAL RESOURCES

BOOKS PUBLISHED BY PETERSON'S AND ARCO

100 Best Careers for the 21st Century, 2nd Edition, by Shelly Field. Arco

Careers without College (Building, Cars, Computers, Emergencies, Entertainment, Fashion, Fitness, Health Care, Kids, Money, Music, Office, Sports, and Travel) . Peterson's

Campus Life Exposed: Advice from the Inside, by Harlan Cohen. Peterson's

Christian Colleges & Universities, 8th Edition. Peterson's

College Applications & Essays, 4th Edition, by Susan D. Van Raalte. Arco

College Money Handbook 2003. Peterson's

Colleges for Students with Learning Disabilities and Attention Deficit Disorders, 6th Edition, Peterson's

College Survival, 6th Edition, by Greg Gottesman and Daniel Baer. Arco

Culinary Schools 2003. Peterson's

Game Plan for Getting into College, by K. Patricia Aviezer. Peterson's

Guide to Career Colleges 2003. Peterson's

Guide to College Visits 2002. Peterson's

Honors Programs & Colleges, 3rd Edition. Peterson's

The Insider's Guide to Writing the Perfect Resume, by Karl Weber and Rick Kaplan. Peterson's

The Insider's Guide to Paying for College, by Don Betterton. Peterson's

Nursing Programs 2003. Peterson's

Peterson's College and University Almanac 2001. Peterson's

Peterson's Competitive Colleges 2002–2003. Peterson's

Peterson's Complete Guide to Financial Aid 2003

Peterson's 2 Year Colleges–2003. Peterson's

Peterson's 4 Year Colleges–2003. Peterson's

Peterson's Sports Scholarships and Athletic Programs. Peterson's

Peterson's Vocational and Technical Schools 2003. Peterson's

Professional Degree Programs in the Visual & Performing Arts 2003. Peterson's

Reading Lists for College-Bound Students, 3rd Edition, by Doug Estell, Michele L. Satchwell, and Patricia S. Wright. Arco

Scholarships, Grants and Prizes 2003. Peterson's

Smart Parents Guide to College, 5th Edition, by Ernest L. Boyer and Paul Boyer. Peterson's

Study Abroad 2003. Peterson's

Summer Jobs in the USA 2003. Peterson's

Summer Opportunities for Kids and Teenagers 2003.
Peterson's

The Ultimate College Survival Guide, 2nd Edition,
by Janet Farrar Worthington and Ronald Farrar.
Peterson's

The Ultimate High School Survival Guide, by
Julianne Dueber. Peterson's

Winning Money for College, 4th Edition,
by Alan Deutschman. Peterson's

You're Hired! Secrets to a Successful Job Search,
by Sharon McDonnell. Arco

ORGANIZATIONS

ACT Assessment, P.O. Box 414, Iowa City,
Iowa 52243-0414 (telephone: 319-337-1270)

Air Force Recruiting Services, Air Force Opportunity
Center, P.O. Box 3505, Capitol Heights,
Maryland 20791-9988 (telephone: 800-423-USAF)

Alcoholics Anonymous, 475 Riverside Drive,
11th Floor, New York, New York 10115
(telephone: 212-870-3400)

American Association of Community Colleges,
One Dupont Circle, NW, #410, Washington, D.C.
22206-1176 (telephone: 202-728-0200)

American Cancer Society, 1599 Clifton Rd. NE,
Atlanta, Georgia 30329 (telephone: 800-ACS-2345)

Amer-I-Can Program, Inc., 1851 Sunset Plaza Drive,
Los Angeles, California 90069
(telephone: 310-652-7884).

Association on Higher Education and Disability,
P.O. Box 21192, Columbus, Ohio 43221-0192
(telephone: 614-488-4972)

Brighten Your Future, P.O. Box 991, Logan,
Ohio 43138 (telephone: 740-385-5058)

Career College Association, 10 G Street, NE,
Ste. 750, Washington, DC 20002
(telephone: 202-336-6800)

Cleveland Scholarship Programs, Inc., 850 Euclid
Avenue, Suite 1000, Cleveland, Ohio, 44114
(telephone: 216-241-5587)

Crime Prevention Association of Philadelphia, Suite
4E, 230 South Broad Street, Philadelphia, PA, 19102
(telephone: 215-545-5230)

Department of Veterans Affairs, 1120 Vermont Ave,
NW, Washington, DC 20421
(telephone: 202-691-3030)

Disabilities Organizational Development Services,
5984 Pinerock Place, Columbus, Ohio 43231-2334
(telephone: 614-895-0238)

Educational Testing Service, Rosedale Road,
Princeton, New Jersey 08541
(telephone: 609-921-9000)

Enlisted Association of the National Guard of the
United States, P.O. Box 261, Groveport, Ohio 43125
(telephone: 800-642-6642)

Federal Trade Commission, 600 Pennsylvania
Avenue NW, Washington, D.C. 20580
(telephone: 877-FTC-HELP)

Gender Issues Education, 5625 SE 38th Avenue,
Portland, Oregon 97202 (telephone: 503-775-6533)

Higher Education Council of Columbus, c/o Ohio
State University, Mount Hall, Room 204, 1050
Carmack Road, Columbus, Ohio 43210
(telephone: 614-688-4610)

Hispanic Scholarship Fund, 1 Sansome Street, Suite
1000, San Francisco, California 94104
(telephone: 877-HSF-INFO)

NAACP, National Offices, 4802 Mount Hope Drive,
Baltimore, Maryland 21215
(telephone: 877-622-2798)

Narcotics Anonymous, P.O. Box 9999, Van Nuys,
California 91409 (telephone: 818-773-9999)

National Association of Anorexia Nervosa and
Associated Disorders, P.O. Box 7, Highland Park
Illinois 60035 (telephone: 847-831-3438)

National Association of College Admission
Counselors, 1631 Prince Street, Alexandria, Virginia
22314-2818 (telephone: 703-836-2222)

National Association of Intercollegiate Athletics,
6120 South Yale Avenue, Suite 1450,
Tulsa, Oklahoma 74136 (telephone: 918-494-8828)

National College Access Network, 204 East Lombard Street, Fourth Floor, Baltimore, Maryland 21202 (telephone: 410-244-7218)

National Collegiate Athletic Association Clearinghouse, P.O. Box 4043 , Iowa City, Iowa 52243-4043 (telephone: 319-339-3003)

National Institute on Drug Abuse, Community Drug Alert Bulletin-Club Drugs. 6001 Executive Blvd., Bethesda, Maryland 20892 (telephone: 301-443-1124)

North-American Interfraternity Conference, 3901 West 86th Street, Suite 390, Indianapolis, Indiana 48268 (telephone: 317-872-1112)

Peterson's Education Services, 2000 Lenox Drive, P.O. Box 67005, Lawrenceville, New Jersey 08648 (telephone: 800-338-3282)

The College Fund/UNCF, 8260 Willow Oaks Corporate Drive, P.O. Box 10444, Fairfax, Virginia 22031 (telephone: 703-205-3400)

The Compelling Communications Group, 15 Sausalito Blvd., Sausalito, California (telephone: 415-331-6336)

The Education Resource Institute, 330 Stuart St., Ste. 500, Boston, Massachusetts 02116 (telephone: 800-255- 8374)

U.S. Department of Education, Federal Student Aid Information Center, P.O. Box 84, Washington, D.C. 20044 (telephone: 800-4-FEDAID)

Vocational Instructional Materials Laboratory, The Ohio State University, Columbus, Ohio